T0188916

Lecture Notes in Computer Science 13311

More information about this series at https://link.springer.com/bookseries/558

Pei-Luen Patrick Rau (Ed.)

Cross-Cultural Design

Interaction Design Across Cultures

14th International Conference, CCD 2022
Held as Part of the 24th HCI International Conference, HCII 2022
Virtual Event, June 26 – July 1, 2022
Proceedings, Part I

Editor
Pei-Luen Patrick Rau
Tsinghua University
Beijing, China

ISSN 0302-9743 ISSN 1611-3349 (electronic)
Lecture Notes in Computer Science
ISBN 978-3-031-06037-3 ISBN 978-3-031-06038-0 (eBook)
https://doi.org/10.1007/978-3-031-06038-0

This Springer imprint is published by the registered company Springer Nature Switzerland AG
The registered company address is: Gewerbestrasse 11, 6330 Cham, Switzerland

Foreword

Human-computer interaction (HCI) is acquiring an ever-increasing scientific and industrial importance, as well as having more impact on people's everyday life, as an ever-growing number of human activities are progressively moving from the physical to the digital world. This process, which has been ongoing for some time now, has been dramatically accelerated by the COVID-19 pandemic. The HCI International (HCII) conference series, held yearly, aims to respond to the compelling need to advance the exchange of knowledge and research and development efforts on the human aspects of design and use of computing systems.

The 24th International Conference on Human-Computer Interaction, HCI International 2022 (HCII 2022), was planned to be held at the Gothia Towers Hotel and Swedish Exhibition & Congress Centre, Göteborg, Sweden, during June 26 to July 1, 2022. Due to the COVID-19 pandemic and with everyone's health and safety in mind, HCII 2022 was organized and run as a virtual conference. It incorporated the 21 thematic areas and affiliated conferences listed on the following page.

A total of 5583 individuals from academia, research institutes, industry, and governmental agencies from 88 countries submitted contributions, and 1276 papers and 275 posters were included in the proceedings to appear just before the start of the conference. The contributions thoroughly cover the entire field of human-computer interaction, addressing major advances in knowledge and effective use of computers in a variety of application areas. These papers provide academics, researchers, engineers, scientists, practitioners, and students with state-of-the-art information on the most recent advances in HCI. The volumes constituting the set of proceedings to appear before the start of the conference are listed in the following pages.

The HCI International (HCII) conference also offers the option of 'Late Breaking Work' which applies both for papers and posters, and the corresponding volume(s) of the proceedings will appear after the conference. Full papers will be included in the 'HCII 2022 - Late Breaking Papers' volumes of the proceedings to be published in the Springer LNCS series, while 'Poster Extended Abstracts' will be included as short research papers in the 'HCII 2022 - Late Breaking Posters' volumes to be published in the Springer CCIS series.

I would like to thank the Program Board Chairs and the members of the Program Boards of all thematic areas and affiliated conferences for their contribution and support towards the highest scientific quality and overall success of the HCI International 2022 conference; they have helped in so many ways, including session organization, paper reviewing (single-blind review process, with a minimum of two reviews per submission) and, more generally, acting as goodwill ambassadors for the HCII conference.

This conference would not have been possible without the continuous and unwavering support and advice of Gavriel Salvendy, founder, General Chair Emeritus, and Scientific Advisor. For his outstanding efforts, I would like to express my appreciation to Abbas Moallem, Communications Chair and Editor of HCI International News.

June 2022 Constantine Stephanidis

HCI International 2022 Thematic Areas and Affiliated Conferences

Thematic Areas

- HCI: Human-Computer Interaction
- HIMI: Human Interface and the Management of Information

Affiliated Conferences

- EPCE: 19th International Conference on Engineering Psychology and Cognitive Ergonomics
- AC: 16th International Conference on Augmented Cognition
- UAHCI: 16th International Conference on Universal Access in Human-Computer Interaction
- CCD: 14th International Conference on Cross-Cultural Design
- SCSM: 14th International Conference on Social Computing and Social Media
- VAMR: 14th International Conference on Virtual, Augmented and Mixed Reality
- DHM: 13th International Conference on Digital Human Modeling and Applications in Health, Safety, Ergonomics and Risk Management
- DUXU: 11th International Conference on Design, User Experience and Usability
- C&C: 10th International Conference on Culture and Computing
- DAPI: 10th International Conference on Distributed, Ambient and Pervasive Interactions
- HCIBGO: 9th International Conference on HCI in Business, Government and Organizations
- LCT: 9th International Conference on Learning and Collaboration Technologies
- ITAP: 8th International Conference on Human Aspects of IT for the Aged Population
- AIS: 4th International Conference on Adaptive Instructional Systems
- HCI-CPT: 4th International Conference on HCI for Cybersecurity, Privacy and Trust
- HCI-Games: 4th International Conference on HCI in Games
- MobiTAS: 4th International Conference on HCI in Mobility, Transport and Automotive Systems
- AI-HCI: 3rd International Conference on Artificial Intelligence in HCI
- MOBILE: 3rd International Conference on Design, Operation and Evaluation of Mobile Communications

List of Conference Proceedings Volumes Appearing Before the Conference

1. LNCS 13302, Human-Computer Interaction: Theoretical Approaches and Design Methods (Part I), edited by Masaaki Kurosu
2. LNCS 13303, Human-Computer Interaction: Technological Innovation (Part II), edited by Masaaki Kurosu
3. LNCS 13304, Human-Computer Interaction: User Experience and Behavior (Part III), edited by Masaaki Kurosu
4. LNCS 13305, Human Interface and the Management of Information: Visual and Information Design (Part I), edited by Sakae Yamamoto and Hirohiko Mori
5. LNCS 13306, Human Interface and the Management of Information: Applications in Complex Technological Environments (Part II), edited by Sakae Yamamoto and Hirohiko Mori
6. LNAI 13307, Engineering Psychology and Cognitive Ergonomics, edited by Don Harris and Wen-Chin Li
7. LNCS 13308, Universal Access in Human-Computer Interaction: Novel Design Approaches and Technologies (Part I), edited by Margherita Antona and Constantine Stephanidis
8. LNCS 13309, Universal Access in Human-Computer Interaction: User and Context Diversity (Part II), edited by Margherita Antona and Constantine Stephanidis
9. LNAI 13310, Augmented Cognition, edited by Dylan D. Schmorrow and Cali M. Fidopiastis
10. LNCS 13311, Cross-Cultural Design: Interaction Design Across Cultures (Part I), edited by Pei-Luen Patrick Rau
11. LNCS 13312, Cross-Cultural Design: Applications in Learning, Arts, Cultural Heritage, Creative Industries, and Virtual Reality (Part II), edited by Pei-Luen Patrick Rau
12. LNCS 13313, Cross-Cultural Design: Applications in Business, Communication, Health, Well-being, and Inclusiveness (Part III), edited by Pei-Luen Patrick Rau
13. LNCS 13314, Cross-Cultural Design: Product and Service Design, Mobility and Automotive Design, Cities, Urban Areas, and Intelligent Environments Design (Part IV), edited by Pei-Luen Patrick Rau
14. LNCS 13315, Social Computing and Social Media: Design, User Experience and Impact (Part I), edited by Gabriele Meiselwitz
15. LNCS 13316, Social Computing and Social Media: Applications in Education and Commerce (Part II), edited by Gabriele Meiselwitz
16. LNCS 13317, Virtual, Augmented and Mixed Reality: Design and Development (Part I), edited by Jessie Y. C. Chen and Gino Fragomeni
17. LNCS 13318, Virtual, Augmented and Mixed Reality: Applications in Education, Aviation and Industry (Part II), edited by Jessie Y. C. Chen and Gino Fragomeni

18. LNCS 13319, Digital Human Modeling and Applications in Health, Safety, Ergonomics and Risk Management: Anthropometry, Human Behavior, and Communication (Part I), edited by Vincent G. Duffy
19. LNCS 13320, Digital Human Modeling and Applications in Health, Safety, Ergonomics and Risk Management: Health, Operations Management, and Design (Part II), edited by Vincent G. Duffy
20. LNCS 13321, Design, User Experience, and Usability: UX Research, Design, and Assessment (Part I), edited by Marcelo M. Soares, Elizabeth Rosenzweig and Aaron Marcus
21. LNCS 13322, Design, User Experience, and Usability: Design for Emotion, Well-being and Health, Learning, and Culture (Part II), edited by Marcelo M. Soares, Elizabeth Rosenzweig and Aaron Marcus
22. LNCS 13323, Design, User Experience, and Usability: Design Thinking and Practice in Contemporary and Emerging Technologies (Part III), edited by Marcelo M. Soares, Elizabeth Rosenzweig and Aaron Marcus
23. LNCS 13324, Culture and Computing, edited by Matthias Rauterberg
24. LNCS 13325, Distributed, Ambient and Pervasive Interactions: Smart Environments, Ecosystems, and Cities (Part I), edited by Norbert A. Streitz and Shin'ichi Konomi
25. LNCS 13326, Distributed, Ambient and Pervasive Interactions: Smart Living, Learning, Well-being and Health, Art and Creativity (Part II), edited by Norbert A. Streitz and Shin'ichi Konomi
26. LNCS 13327, HCI in Business, Government and Organizations, edited by Fiona Fui-Hoon Nah and Keng Siau
27. LNCS 13328, Learning and Collaboration Technologies: Designing the Learner and Teacher Experience (Part I), edited by Panayiotis Zaphiris and Andri Ioannou
28. LNCS 13329, Learning and Collaboration Technologies: Novel Technological Environments (Part II), edited by Panayiotis Zaphiris and Andri Ioannou
29. LNCS 13330, Human Aspects of IT for the Aged Population: Design, Interaction and Technology Acceptance (Part I), edited by Qin Gao and Jia Zhou
30. LNCS 13331, Human Aspects of IT for the Aged Population: Technology in Everyday Living (Part II), edited by Qin Gao and Jia Zhou
31. LNCS 13332, Adaptive Instructional Systems, edited by Robert A. Sottilare and Jessica Schwarz
32. LNCS 13333, HCI for Cybersecurity, Privacy and Trust, edited by Abbas Moallem
33. LNCS 13334, HCI in Games, edited by Xiaowen Fang
34. LNCS 13335, HCI in Mobility, Transport and Automotive Systems, edited by Heidi Krömker
35. LNAI 13336, Artificial Intelligence in HCI, edited by Helmut Degen and Stavroula Ntoa
36. LNCS 13337, Design, Operation and Evaluation of Mobile Communications, edited by Gavriel Salvendy and June Wei
37. CCIS 1580, HCI International 2022 Posters - Part I, edited by Constantine Stephanidis, Margherita Antona and Stavroula Ntoa
38. CCIS 1581, HCI International 2022 Posters - Part II, edited by Constantine Stephanidis, Margherita Antona and Stavroula Ntoa

39. CCIS 1582, HCI International 2022 Posters - Part III, edited by Constantine Stephanidis, Margherita Antona and Stavroula Ntoa
40. CCIS 1583, HCI International 2022 Posters - Part IV, edited by Constantine Stephanidis, Margherita Antona and Stavroula Ntoa

Preface

The increasing internationalization and globalization of communication, business and industry is leading to a wide cultural diversification of individuals and groups of users who access information, services and products. If interactive systems are to be usable, useful, and appealing to such a wide range of users, culture becomes an important HCI issue. Therefore, HCI practitioners and designers face the challenges of designing across different cultures, and need to elaborate and adopt design approaches which take into account cultural models, factors, expectations and preferences, and allow to develop cross-cultural user experiences that accommodate global users.

The 14th Cross-Cultural Design (CCD) Conference, an affiliated conference of the HCI International Conference, encouraged papers from academics, researchers, industry and professionals, on a broad range of theoretical and applied issues related to Cross-Cultural Design and its applications.

Cross-cultural design has come to be a lateral HCI subject that deals not only with the role of culture in HCI and across the amplitude of HCI application domains, but also in the context of the entire spectrum of HCI methods, processes, practices, and tools. In this respect, a considerable number of papers were accepted to this year's CCD Conference addressing diverse topics, which spanned a wide variety of domains. One of the most prominent topic categories was interaction design, as seen from a cross-cultural perspective, exploring cross-cultural differences and intercultural design. Application domains of social impact, such as learning, arts and cultural heritage have constituted popular topics this year, as well as work conducted in the context of creative industries and virtual reality. Health, well-being, and inclusiveness were emphasized, as was business and communication, which are fields that were all challenged during the ongoing pandemic. Furthermore, among the contributions, views on contemporary and near-future intelligent technologies were presented, including those addressing mobility and automotive design, as well as design in intelligent environments, cities, and urban areas.

Four volumes of the HCII2022 proceedings are dedicated to this year's edition of the CCD Conference:

- Cross-Cultural Design: Interaction Design Across Cultures (Part I), addressing topics related to cross-cultural interaction design, collaborative and participatory cross-cultural design, cross-cultural differences and HCI, as well as aspects of intercultural design.
- Cross-Cultural Design: Applications in Learning, Arts, Cultural Heritage, Creative Industries, and Virtual Reality (Part II), addressing topics related to cross-cultural learning, training, and education; cross-cultural design in arts and music; creative industries and Cultural Heritage under a cross-cultural perspective; and, cross-cultural virtual reality and games.
- Cross-Cultural Design: Applications in Business, Communication, Health, Well-being, and Inclusiveness (Part III), addressing topics related to intercultural business

communication, cross-cultural communication and collaboration, HCI and the global social change imposed by COVID-19, and intercultural design for well-being and inclusiveness.
- Cross-Cultural Design: Product and Service Design, Mobility and Automotive Design, Cities, Urban Areas, and Intelligent Environments Design (Part IV), addressing topics related to cross-cultural product and service design, cross-cultural mobility and automotive UX design, design and culture in social development and digital transformation of cities and urban areas, and cross-cultural design in intelligent environments.

Papers of these volumes are included for publication after a minimum of two single–blind reviews from the members of the CCD Program Board or, in some cases, from members of the Program Boards of other affiliated conferences. I would like to thank all of them for their invaluable contribution, support and efforts.

June 2022 Pei-Luen Patrick Rau

14th International Conference on Cross-Cultural Design (CCD 2022)

The full list with the Program Board Chairs and the members of the Program Boards of all thematic areas and affiliated conferences is available online at

http://www.hci.international/board-members-2022.php

HCI International 2023

The 25th International Conference on Human-Computer Interaction, HCI International 2023, will be held jointly with the affiliated conferences at the AC Bella Sky Hotel and Bella Center, Copenhagen, Denmark, 23–28 July 2023. It will cover a broad spectrum of themes related to human-computer interaction, including theoretical issues, methods, tools, processes, and case studies in HCI design, as well as novel interaction techniques, interfaces, and applications. The proceedings will be published by Springer. More information will be available on the conference website: http://2023.hci.international/.

General Chair
Constantine Stephanidis
University of Crete and ICS-FORTH
Heraklion, Crete, Greece
Email: general_chair@hcii2023.org

http://2023.hci.international/

Contents – Part I

Cross-Cultural Interaction Design

Collaborative and Participatory Cross-Cultural Design

Cross-Cultural Differences and HCI

Aspects of Intercultural Design

Cross-Cultural Interaction Design

How Does It Feel? Odor-Evoked Emotion Among Chinese People

Zhe Chen[1(✉)], Pei-Luen Patrick Rau[2], Julia Kamenezkaja[2], Nan Qie[2], and Runting Zhong[2]

[1] Beihang University, Beijing, People's Republic of China
zhechen@buaa.edu.cn
[2] Tsinghua University, Beijing, People's Republic of China

Abstract. Chinese culture has the potential to influence Chinese people's odor preference and odor-evoked emotion. However, previous studies have rarely investigated odor preference and odor-evoked emotion among Chinese people. Verbal reports are a widely used tool for measuring odor-evoked emotion. However, since it is viewed as inappropriate to verbally express negative feelings in traditional Chinese culture, it is challenging to measure odor-evoked emotion among Chinese people. This study conducted a survey to determine odor preference among Chinese people. A comparison of odor preference between Chinese people and German people was also conducted. Ninety-six Chinese participants and 103 German participants were invited to rate their preferences of forty odors. Additionally, an experiment was conducted to test odor-evoked emotions among Chinese and German people. Both verbal measurements (i.e., interviews and the Emotion and Odor Scale) and physiological measurements (i.e., electromyography and skin conductance) were used to evaluate emotional responses evoked by 12 different odors. Twelve Chinese participants and 12 German participants were invited to participate in this experiment. Cultural effects on odor preference and odor-evoked emotions were significant in this study. The use of both verbal and physiological measurements were necessary to gain a deep, comprehensive understanding of odor-evoked emotion among Chinese participants.

Keywords: Chinese · Cultural differences · German · Odor preference · Odor-evoked emotion · Physiological measurements

1 Introduction

Culture has been shown to have a significant effect on odor perception in previous studies. People tend to give more positive ratings to odors that they have encountered more frequently or odors that have more positive meanings in their culture (Pangborn et al. 1988; Wysocki et al. 1991). The results of a cross-cultural study conducted among participants from Switzerland, the United Kingdom, and Singapore indicated that cultural effects on odor-evoked emotions were significant for positive odors but not for negative odors (Ferdenzi et al. 2013). Cultural differences in odor perception were also reported between Japanese and German participants (Ayabe-Kanamura et al. 1998) and among

P.-L. P. Rau (Ed.): HCII 2022, LNCS 13311, pp. 3–20, 2022.
https://doi.org/10.1007/978-3-031-06038-0_1

French, Vietnamese, and American participants (Chrea et al. 2004). It was suggested that there were significant differences in emotional response to odor between American women and Belgian women (Wrzesniewski et al. 1999). These studies reinforce the concept that odor-evoked emotions are culturally dependent. However, few studies have been conducted to investigate odor perception in Chinese people. Globalization and the increasing number of new cosmetic products in Chinese daily life have likely changed Chinese odors preference. For example, lemons and lemon scent were unfamiliar to most Chinese people twenty years ago. Chinese people are now used to the scent of lemons because this smell is popular in many cosmetic products, such as shampoo. However, Chinese people typically do not consider lemon as an ingredient for a homemade dinner, while lemon is a common ingredient in European or American cuisines. A better understanding of odor preference and, consequently, odor-evoked emotion among Chinese people will benefit product design. Odor preference, also called odor hedonics (i.e., pleasure, adopted from Ancient Greek), is a common research topic in the field of olfaction. Odors are termed "pleasant" if they have a positive hedonic value or "unpleasant" if they have a negative hedonic value. The hedonic determination of odors was suggested to be the key function of human olfaction (Yeshurun and Sobel 2010). For example, it was found that the smell of lavender was pleasant to French people (Alaoui-Ismaïli et al. 1997b) and that the smell of Catholic church incense was pleasant to German people (Ayabe-Kanamura et al. 1998). Furthermore, cultural differences in odor hedonics among Canadian, Indonesian, and Syrian children were investigated (Schaal et al. 2000). However, there has been no report of odor preference among Chinese people in previous studies.

Moreover, Chinese culture affects emotional expressions and, inevitably, odor-evoked emotion, which makes measuring odor-evoked emotion among Chinese people a challenging task. It was demonstrated that mainland Chinese girls tend to show fewer facial expressions and give higher ratings in response to odor stimuli than girls raised in European or American families (Camras et al. 2006).

Verbal and physiological measurements are popular for evaluating odor preference and odor-evoked emotion. Verbal measurements, such as a self-report measurements, have been used in many studies on odor-evoked emotion (Alaoui-Ismaïli et al. 1997a; Chrea et al. 2009). Recently, a six-dimensional questionnaire called the Geneva Emotion and Odor Scale (EOS) was developed to test emotional responses to odors (Porcherot et al. 2010). This EOS was developed to take into account different cultural backgrounds, so it is suitable for cross-cultural studies (Ferdenzi et al. 2011). Physiological measurements were also used to evaluate emotional responses and differentiate basic emotions (Collet et al. 1997). It was found that basic odor-evoked emotions (i.e., anger, fear, sadness, surprise, disgust, and happiness) can be distinguished using physiological indices (Ayabe-Kanamura et al. 1998; Vernet-Maury et al. 1999). Connections were observed between electrophysiological response and pleasant/unpleasant odors (Owen and Patterson 2002). The simultaneous use of verbal and physiological measurements can help identify a general range of odor-evoked emotions among Chinese people.

Therefore, this study aims to investigate odor preference and odor-evoked emotion among Chinese people. To develop a better understanding of cultural effects, German people were included for comparison. A survey of forty daily odors was conducted with

Chinese and German participants to determine odor preference. An experiment using both verbal and physiological measurements was conducted to explore odor-evoked emotions. The results of this study are beneficial both for understanding the development of cultural differences in odor-evoked emotion and for improving odorous product design.

2 Materials and Methods

2.1 Survey

The survey investigated the odor preference of both Chinese and German participants regarding 40 odors grouped into 11 types, as shown in Table 1. The odor types were adopted from Milotic's research (Milotic 2003).

Table 1. Odors rated in the survey

Types	Odor						
White flower	Lily	Chamomile	Vanilla				
Rosy floral	Rose	Tuberose	Jasmine				
Orris-violet	Violet	Lavender					
Citrus	Lemon	Pomelo					
Green	Cucumber	Chive	Onions	Olive			
Honey sweet	Honey	Cinnamon					
Fruity	Apricot	Orange	Apple	Strawberry			
Animalic-leather	Musk						
Herbaceous	Rosemary	Peppermint	Calendula	Balsamic		Coriander	
Spice	Black pepper	Ginger	Chili pepper	Sichuan pepper	Clove	Mustard	Cumin
Food	Roasted sweet potato	Garlic	Peanuts	Roasted chestnuts	Sesame past	Tofu	Cheese

Survey Participants. A total of 120 Chinese and 120 German participants (aged 20–35) were invited to participate in an online survey. Ineffective responses (e.g., those with incomplete answers, a completion time of less than 10 s, or the same answer for all questions) were screened out by the survey administrator. Ninety-six effective responses were collected from Chinese participants (42 male and 54 female), and 103 effective responses were collected from German participants (51 male and 52 female). Table 2 shows the participants' previous experiences using perfume.

Survey Design. A five-point Likert scale ranging from 1 (strongly dislike the odor) to 5 (strongly like the odor) with an additional option of 0 (I do not know the odor) was used in the survey. Reponses of "I do not know the odor" were excluded from the analysis of odor preference. The survey had Chinese and German versions, so Chinese participants

Table 2. Previous experience of perfume

Number of used perfumes	Chinese	German
None	65	12
1–5	26	68
6–10	3	13
11–15	1	3
16–25	1	4
>25	0	2
Total	96	103

completed the Chinese version, and German participants completed the German version. The translation process was conducted in two steps. A bilingual translator first translated the survey from English to Chinese/German. Then, a different bilingual translator translated the survey from Chinese/German to English. The original English version and the translated version were compared to correct the translation. This translation process was adopted for the other questionnaires in this study.

2.2 Experiment

Experiment Participants. A total of 27 participants were invited to participate in the experiment; 3 of these participants joined the pilot study, and 24 participants were involved in the formal experiment. The demographic information of the participants is presented in Table 3. All participants were engineering students who reported that they were healthy (e.g., no allergies, sicknesses, or chronic nasal diseases). Participants

Table 3. Demographic information of the experiment participants

		Pilot study		Experiment	
		Chinese	German	Chinese	German
Gender	Female	1	1	6	6
	Male	1	0	6	6
Age	Mean	23.0	27.0	23.2	27.2
	SD	1.4	0.0	2.0	1.4
	Min	22	27	20	24
	Max	24	27	26	30
Education background	Undergraduate	1	0	6	0
	Graduate	1	1	6	12
Total		2	1	12	12

were first asked to pass a screening test. The screening test required participants to differentiate alcohol, vinegar, and water, with all three stimuli in similar nontransparent bottles.

Experiment Design. A mixed experimental design was adopted in this study to investigate odor-evoked emotion in the Chinese and German cultures. Culture was a between-group factor, and odor was a within-group factor. The results of the pilot study indicated that participants became fatigued after smelling more than six odors at one time. The emotional responses of the participants were affected by fatigue. Thus, each participant in the formal experiment smelled six odors at one time and the remaining six odors at another time (a one-day interval was required). The details of the experimental design are shown in Table 4. Based on the experimental design, the order and number of odors tested with Chinese participants were the same as those tested with German participants.

Table 4. Experimental design: odors tested by each participant

Order of odor												Number of subject	
1st test						2nd test						Chinese	German
1	2	3	4	5	6	7	8	9	10	11	12	1	1
12	1	2	3	4	5	6	7	8	9	10	11	1	1
11	12	1	2	3	4	5	6	7	8	9	10	1	1
10	11	12	1	2	3	4	5	6	7	8	9	1	1
9	10	11	12	1	2	3	4	5	6	7	8	1	1
8	9	10	11	12	1	2	3	4	5	6	7	1	1
7	8	9	10	11	12	1	2	3	4	5	6	1	1
6	7	8	9	10	11	12	1	2	3	4	5	1	1
5	6	7	8	9	10	11	12	1	2	3	4	1	1
4	5	6	7	8	9	10	11	12	1	2	3	1	1
3	4	5	6	7	8	9	10	11	12	1	2	1	1
2	3	4	5	6	7	8	9	10	11	12	1	1	1

Verbal Measurement: The EOS. The EOS was adopted as the verbal measurement in this study (Chrea et al. 2009; Ferdenzi et al. 2013; Ferdenzi et al. 2011). Scales in the participants' native languages (i.e., Chinese and German) were used for better understanding among the Chinese and German participants. The translation process included the same two steps as the translation process for the survey. The scale included 36 emotional descriptors spanning six dimensions: happiness-well-being (HW), awe-sensuality (AS), disgust-irritation (DI), soothing-peacefulness (SP), energizing-cooling (EC), and sensory pleasure (SE). Only the DI dimension of the EOS was a negative dimension. A five-point Likert scale ranging from 1 (strongly disagree) to 5 (strongly agree) was used. The translations of the EOS are shown in Table 5.

Table 5. EOS questionnaire

Dimension	Descriptors	Chinese	German
HW	Pleasant	使人愉悦的	Angenehm
	Well being	让人感觉幸福的	Wohltuend
	Pleasantly surprised	给人惊喜的	Angenehm überrascht
	Happiness	使人高兴的	Glücksgefühl
	Attracted	对人有吸引力的	Attraktiv
	Feeling awe	令人赞叹的	Ehrfurcht fühlen
AS	Desire	产生欲望的	Erwünscht
	Sensual	引发情欲的	Sinnlich
	In love	有恋爱的感觉	Verliebt
	Romantic	浪漫的	Romantisch
	Sexy	性感的	Sexy
	Admiration	引起崇拜感的	Bewundernd
	Excited	令人兴奋的	Aufregend
DI	Unpleasant	令人不悦的	Unangenehm
	Disgusted	令人反感的	Abstoßend
	Unpleasantly surprised	惊吓的	Unangenehm überrascht
	Sickening	令人厌恶的	Widerlich
	Dissatisfaction	令人不满意的	Unzufrieden
	Dirty	污浊的	Unrein
	Irritated	使人恼火的	Irritierend
	Angry	让人生气的	Ärgerlich
SP	Relax	令人放松的	Entspannend
	Soothed	使人平静的	Beruhigend
	Serene	给人平和的感觉	Ruhig
	Reinsured	有安全感的	Geborgen
	Light	轻松的	Leicht
EC	Revitalized	使人精神焕发的	Wiederbelebend
	Clean	给人干净的感觉	Rein
	Refreshed	清新的	Erfrischend
	Invigorated	生机勃勃的	Kräftig
	Stimulated	提神的	Stimulierend
	Energetic	令人精力充沛的	Energisch

(*continued*)

Table 5. *(continued)*

Dimension	Descriptors	Chinese	German
	Shivering	让人激动的	Schaudernd
SE	Nostalgic	令人怀念的	Nostalgisch
	Amusement	感觉有乐趣的	Erheiternd
	Salivating	令人垂涎欲滴的	Lecker

Physiological Measurements. Three physiological measurements were conducted in the experiment, including skin conductance (SC), surface electromyography of corrugator muscles (SEMGc), and surface electromyography of zygomatic muscles (SEMGz). An 8-channel biofeedback machine was used in this study (manufactured by Thought Technology Ltd.). Three channels were used to measure the SC (in micro-Siemens, μS), SEMGc (in microvolts, μV), and SEMGz (in microvolts, μV) with a sampling rate of 256 Hz (Hz). The SC electrode was placed on the index finger pad to measure SC, while the reference electrode was placed on the little finger pad. For SEMG, a positive electrode and a negative electrode were placed across the corrugator/zygomatic muscle fiber, while a reference electrode was placed at an equal distance between positive and negative electrodes. The sensors and skin were cleaned with alcohol before the experiment for each participant.

Odor Selection. The experiment used 12 odors from the survey, among which six odors were significantly differently rated in the survey by Chinese and German participants and the other six odors were not (significance level: $p < 0.05$). All 12 odors are common in daily life, as shown in Table 6 (odors marked with "*" had significantly different ratings in the survey).

Odor Preparation and Delivery. First, the fresh object was washed and cut into small pieces. Then, the chopped object was placed in pure water to maintain freshness. One hundred grams of the original scented objects were used for the experiment. The experiment administrator replaced the fresh objects every two hours to maintain the strength of their scents. The other eight odors (lemon, lily, clove, cinnamon, rose, musk, orange,

Table 6. Odors used in the experiment

Type	Odor	Chinese		German	
		Mean	SD	Mean	SD
White flower	1 Lily	3.9	0.99	3.8	0.94
Rosy floral	2 Rose*	3.9	0.81	4.2	0.76
Orris-violet	3 Lavender	3.9	0.99	3.8	1.03

(continued)

Table 6. (*continued*)

Type	Odor	Chinese		German	
		Mean	SD	Mean	SD
Citrus	4 Lemon	4.0	0.84	3.9	0.95
Green	5 Cucumber*	3.9	0.86	3.6	0.81
Honey sweet	6 Cinnamon*	3.3	1.03	3.8	1.00
Fruity	7 Orange	4.3	0.68	4.2	0.73
Animalic-leather	8 Musk	3.0	1.02	2.8	1.12
Herbaceous	9 Coriander*	3.3	1.14	2.9	1.18
Spice	10 Clove*	3.4	1.04	3.0	1.11
Food	11 Tofu*	3.3	0.94	2.3	0.92
	12 Cheese	3.6	0.99	3.5	1.15

and lavender) were made from essential oils diluted with pure water. The dilution was made using 1 drop of essential oil and 200 g of pure water.

Experiment Procedure. First, participants were informed of the content of the experiment and signed the informed consent form. Then, they were seated in a comfortable chair. Each participant was asked to perform six subtests. In each subtest, one odor was tested. Participants were asked to relax for 20 s while the SC, SEMGc, and SEMGz data at rest were recorded. The SC, SEMGc, and SEMGz data were recorded for another 20 s while participants were exposed to an odor. Participants were then asked to complete the EOS based on their feelings related to the odor after each subtest. After each subtest, participants were asked to describe their emotional responses to the odor. Then, cocoa powder was used to replace the previous odor memory. Finally, there was a five-minute relaxation period to help participants prepare for the next subtest. All procedures were checked for compliance with the Declaration of Helsinki for Medical Research involving Human Subjects. All procedures performed in studies involving human participants were in accordance with the ethical standards of the institution.

3 Results

3.1 Survey Results

The Cronbach's alpha of the survey was 0.938, indicating that the survey results are reliable. The descriptive and t-test results are shown in Table 7.

The scents of jasmine, strawberry, orange, vanilla, roasted chestnuts, apple, and lemon were rated higher than 4.0 by Chinese participants. The scents of lily, chamomile, rose, tuberose, violet, lavender, pomelo, cucumber, chive, honey, cinnamon, apricot, rosemary, peppermint, calendula, coriander, clove, cumin, roasted sweet potato, peanut, sesame, tofu, and cheese were rated higher than 3.5 by Chinese participants. All scents

Table 7. Odor preference of Chinese and German participants

Type	Odor	Chinese		German		Difference	p
		Mean	SD	Mean	SD		
White flower	Lily	3.9	0.99	3.8	0.94	0.1	
	Chamomile	3.6	0.99	3.6	0.94	0.0	
	Vanilla	4.1	0.89	4.1	0.94	0.0	
Rosy floral	Rose	3.9	0.81	4.2	0.76	−0.3	*
	Tuberose	3.7	1.03	3.8	0.98	−0.1	
	Jasmine	4.3	0.73	3.7	0.81	0.6	*
Orris-violet	Violet	3.9	0.81	3.8	0.73	0.1	
	Lavender	3.9	0.99	3.8	1.03	0.1	
Citrus	Lemon	4.0	0.84	3.9	0.95	0.1	
	Pomelo	3.9	0.88	3.5	0.81	0.4	*
Green	Cucumber	3.9	0.86	3.6	0.81	0.3	*
	Chive	3.1	1.26	3.6	0.96	−0.5	*
	Onion	2.4	1.07	3.1	1.12	−0.7	*
	Olive	3.0	0.88	3.3	1.16	−0.3	
Honey sweet	Honey	3.5	0.96	3.7	0.95	−0.2	
	Cinnamon	3.3	1.03	3.8	1.00	−0.5	*
Fruity	Apricot	3.8	1.01	4.0	0.75	−0.2	
	Orange	4.3	0.68	4.2	0.73	0.1	
	Apple	4.1	0.78	4.0	0.71	0.1	
	Strawberry	4.3	0.85	4.4	0.72	−0.1	
Animal	Musk	3.0	1.02	2.8	1.12	0.2	
Herbaceous	Rosemary	3.4	1.08	3.4	1.11	0.0	
	Peppermint	3.8	1.03	4.0	0.94	−0.2	
	Calendula	3.8	0.85	3.5	0.76	0.3	
	Balsamic	2.7	1.31	3.4	0.98	−0.7	*

(*continued*)

Table 7. *(continued)*

Type	Odor	Chinese		German		Difference	p
		Mean	SD	Mean	SD		
	Coriander	3.3	1.14	2.9	1.18	0.4	*
Spice	Black pepper	2.5	1.11	3.2	0.98	−0.7	*
	Ginger	2.7	1.08	3.2	1.14	−0.5	*
	Chili pepper	2.9	1.26	3.1	0.99	−0.2	
	Sichuan pepper	2.5	1.23	2.7	1.02	−0.2	
	Clove	3.4	1.04	3.0	1.11	0.4	*
	Mustard	2.2	1.10	3.2	0.96	−1.0	*
	Cumin	3.5	1.23	2.5	1.17	1.0	*
Food	Roasted sweet potato	3.9	0.96	3.0	1.26	0.9	*
	Garlic	2.1	1.03	3.2	1.29	−1.1	*
	Peanuts	3.3	0.82	3.5	0.83	−0.2	
	Roasted chestnuts	4.1	0.86	3.5	1.12	0.6	*
	Sesame past	3.6	0.96	3.5	1.02	0.1	
	Tofu	3.3	0.94	2.3	0.92	1.0	*
	Cheese	3.6	0.99	3.5	1.15	0.1	

in the white flower, rosy floral, orris-violet, citrus, honey sweet, and animal odor types were rated higher than 3.0 by Chinese participants. Fruity, white flower, rosy floral, orris-violet, and citrus were the preferred odor types among Chinese participants. Interestingly, the scent of tofu, a traditional Chinese food, was not highly rated by Chinese participants (the mean rating was 3.3). Cheese is a typical food in foreign countries (e.g., America and European countries) and has recently become popular in China. Chinese participants ranked the scent of cheese as the second most preferred scent. The scents of garlic, onion, and mustard received ratings less than 2.5 from Chinese participants.

On the other hand, the scents of strawberry, rose, orange, vanilla, apricot, apple, and peppermint were rated higher than 4.0 by German participants. The scents of lemon, lily, tuberose, violet, lavender, cinnamon, jasmine, honey chamomile, cucumber, chive, pomelo, calendula, peanuts, roasted chestnut, sesame, rosemary, balsamic, olive, black pepper, ginger, mustard, garlic, onion, and chili pepper were rated higher than 3.5 by German participants. All scents in the white flower, royal floral, orris-violet, citrus, green, honey sweet, and fruity odor types were rated higher than 3.0 by German participants, which was similar to Chinese participants. The only difference between Chinese and German participants in the preferred odor types was for the green type. German participants gave the scent of cheese a mean rating of 3.5. Tofu received the lowest rating (i.e., 2.3) from German participants. Both Chinese and German participants highly preferred all fruity scents.

The t-test results showed that most scents of the green and spicy types were rated significantly differently between Chinese and German participants. Chinese and German participants gave opposite ratings for the scents of onion, balsamic, coriander, black pepper, ginger, mustard, cumin, garlic and tofu. For example, the scent of tofu was preferred by Chinese participants but not by German participants. The scent of black pepper was not preferred by Chinese participants but was preferred by German participants.

3.2 Experiment Results

Verbalization. The Cronbach's α of the EOS was 0.775. The descriptive statistics are presented separately according to the two cultures, twelve odors, and six emotional dimensions in Table 8. The interaction effects for the six emotional dimensions are shown in Fig. 1. The maximum mean rating given by Chinese participants was for the scent of orange in the HW dimension (mean = 3.11, SD = 0.77). The minimum mean rating given by Chinese participants was for the scent of orange in the DI dimension (mean =

Table 8. Descriptive results of the EOS

	Culture	HW		AE		DI		SP		EC		SE	
		Mean	SD	Mean	SD	Mean	SD	Mean	SD	Mean	SD	Mean	SD
01 Lily	Chinese	2.26	1.00	1.88	0.85	1.64	1.08	2.33	1.13	2.49	0.78	1.89	0.78
	German	2.88	0.96	2.44	1.05	1.15	0.21	2.62	0.85	3.21	0.96	2.56	0.87
02 Rose*	Chinese	1.92	0.93	1.58	0.65	1.80	0.68	1.77	0.86	1.80	0.55	2.33	1.14
	German	2.19	1.30	1.73	0.71	1.98	0.97	1.80	0.97	1.73	0.93	2.61	1.41
03 Lavender	Chinese	2.79	0.92	2.38	0.95	1.24	0.24	2.47	1.16	2.49	0.77	2.83	1.03
	German	2.19	1.18	2.05	0.96	1.62	0.74	2.02	1.15	2.70	1.23	2.03	0.89
04 Lemon	Chinese	2.61	0.89	2.11	0.83	1.29	0.63	2.40	1.05	3.05	0.74	2.53	1.02
	German	3.54	1.04	2.69	0.94	1.07	0.16	2.68	1.02	3.63	1.00	3.33	1.07
05 Cucumber*	Chinese	2.06	0.74	1.80	0.69	2.03	1.16	1.97	0.88	2.41	0.44	1.56	0.66
	German	2.79	1.39	2.80	1.10	1.51	0.72	2.18	1.07	2.54	1.19	2.44	1.23
06 Cinnamon*	Chinese	1.44	0.64	1.32	0.48	2.33	0.81	1.62	0.73	1.76	0.40	1.81	0.98
	German	1.88	1.05	1.43	0.44	1.55	0.85	1.88	1.03	1.52	0.53	2.33	1.15
07 Orange	Chinese	3.11	0.77	2.57	0.82	1.08	0.15	2.37	0.93	3.07	0.44	2.94	0.84
	German	3.46	0.94	2.50	0.91	1.03	0.08	2.82	0.96	3.73	0.87	3.50	0.97
08 Musk	Chinese	2.49	0.95	2.17	0.85	1.46	0.87	2.72	1.08	2.33	0.81	2.22	0.96
	German	1.94	0.98	2.04	1.07	1.75	0.77	1.73	0.73	2.39	1.17	1.72	0.90
09 Coriander*	Chinese	2.94	0.98	2.83	1.10	1.17	0.32	2.58	0.82	2.39	0.62	2.39	0.69
	German	3.11	1.31	2.41	1.08	1.07	0.12	2.98	1.09	2.55	1.15	2.61	0.98
10 Clove*	Chinese	2.26	0.45	1.66	0.37	1.31	0.47	2.23	0.67	2.31	0.52	2.53	0.73
	German	2.78	0.96	1.89	0.65	1.07	0.17	3.28	0.99	3.17	0.89	2.86	1.11
11 Tofu*	Chinese	1.61	0.83	1.43	0.46	1.98	0.87	1.72	0.75	1.88	0.53	1.86	0.99
	German	2.19	1.13	1.64	0.63	1.53	0.73	1.98	0.94	2.16	1.03	2.58	1.11
12 Cheese	Chinese	2.35	1.26	2.25	1.23	1.85	0.90	2.30	1.26	2.31	0.77	2.69	1.38
	German	1.89	1.06	2.00	1.19	1.88	0.69	1.63	0.65	2.48	1.00	1.83	0.92

1.08, SD = 0.15). The maximum mean rating given by German participants was for the scent of orange in the EC dimension (mean = 3.73, SD = 0.87). The minimum mean rating given by German participants was for the scent of orange in the DI dimensions (mean = 1.03, SD = 0.08). Both the mean and SD values in the DI dimension were smaller than those in the other dimensions.

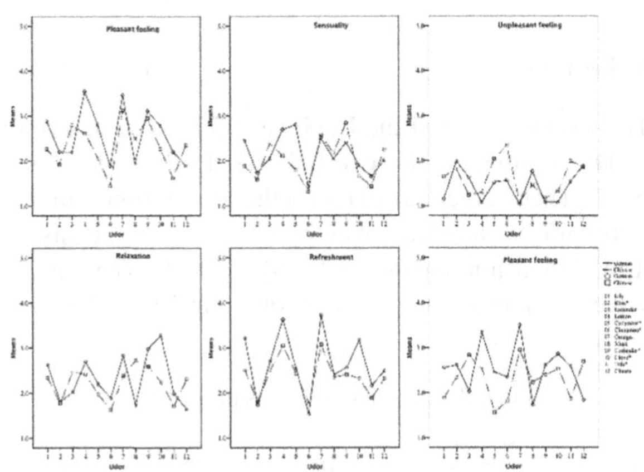

Fig. 1. Interaction effect diagrams for each dimension of the verbal measure

Chinese and German participants showed differences in each dimension of the EOS. Chinese participants rated orange (mean = 3.11, SD = 0.77) and lavender (mean = 2.79, SD = 0.92) highly in the HW dimension, while German participants rated lemon (mean = 3.54, SD = 1.04), orange (mean = 3.46, SD = 0.94), and coriander (mean = 3.11, SD = 1.31) highly in the HW dimension. Chinese participants rated coriander (mean = 2.83, SD = 1.10) highly in the AE dimension, while German participants rated cucumber (mean = 2.80, SD = 1.10) and lemon (mean = 2.69, SD = 0.94) highly in the AE dimension. In the DI dimension, which was the only negative dimension, the mean ratings by both Chinese and German participants were less than 3.0. In the SP dimension, Chinese participants rated musk 1.0 point higher than German participants (mean = 2.7 for Chinese and mean = 1.7 for German), while German participants rated clove 1.0 point higher (mean = 2.2 for Chinese and mean = 3.2 for German). In the EC dimension, Chinese participants and German participants had similar ratings for most odors, except for clove (mean = 2.3 for Chinese and mean = 3.1 for German). Both Chinese and German participants rated lemon and orange higher than 3.0 in the EC dimension, but German participants rated these odors higher than Chinese participants. The means in the SE dimension were similar to those in the HW dimension. Means higher than 3.0 were given by German participants to the scents of lemon (mean = 3.33, SD = 1.07) and orange (mean = 3.50, SD = 0.97).

This study investigated the effects of odor and culture on emotions, including both the main and interaction effects. Table 9 shows the results of the ANOVA. The results suggested that odor had a significant effect on all emotional dimensions (significance level < 0.001). The interaction effect of odor and culture was significant for all six emotional dimensions (significance level < 0.05). The p-values for the effect of culture were larger than 0.05, indicating that culture was not a significant factor in the EOS.

Table 9. ANOVA of the EOS results

		HW	AE	DI	SP	EC	SE
Within-participants	Odor	<0.001	<0.001	<0.001	<0.001	<0.001	<0.001
	Odor * culture	0.006	0.007	0.042	<0.001	0.050	0.001
Between-participants	Culture	0.361	0.58	0.223	0.717	0.249	0.322

Physiological Measurements. The SEMG and SC data were plotted and analyzed. Figure 2 shows example plots of the three physiological measurements. The physiological results during smelling (i.e., 20 s after the participant started smelling) were higher than those during relaxation (i.e., 20 s before the participant started smelling). More peaks appeared in the SEMG and SC data during smelling than during relaxation, indicating more facial muscle activity and emotional response, respectively. The difference between the mean value during smelling and the mean value during relaxation was calculated for the physiological data. Inferential statistical analysis was conducted to study the effects of odor and culture. The difference between the maximum value during smelling and the mean value during was also calculated for the physiological data. Thus, the indices were as follows:

Cmean-mean = SEMGcmean of the latter 20 s − mean of the former 20 s	(1)
Dmean-mean = SEMGzmean of the latter 20 s − mean of the former 20 s	(2)
Emean-mean = SCmean of the latter 20 s − mean of the former 20 s	(3)
Cmax-mean = SEMGcmax of the latter 20 s − mean of the former 20 s	(4)
Dmax-mean = SEMGzmax of the latter 20 s − mean of the former 20 s	(5)
Emax-mean = SCmax of the latter 20 s − mean of the former 20 s	(6)

The descriptive results of the physiological measurements are shown in Table 10 (grouped by culture) and Table 11 (grouped by odor). These results show that Chinese participants had more activity in their corrugator muscles than German participants, as both the Cmean-mean and the Cmax-mean of Chinese participants were higher than those of German participants. Chinese participants also had less activity in their zygomatic muscles than German participants, as shown by comparing the Dmean-mean and the Dmean-mean of Chinese and German participants. The SC values of Chinese participants were slightly larger than those of German participants, as shown by comparing both the Emean-mean and the Emax-mean of both groups of participants.

A nonparametric test was used to determine whether there were significant differences between Chinese and German participants. The Mann–Whitney test was used to

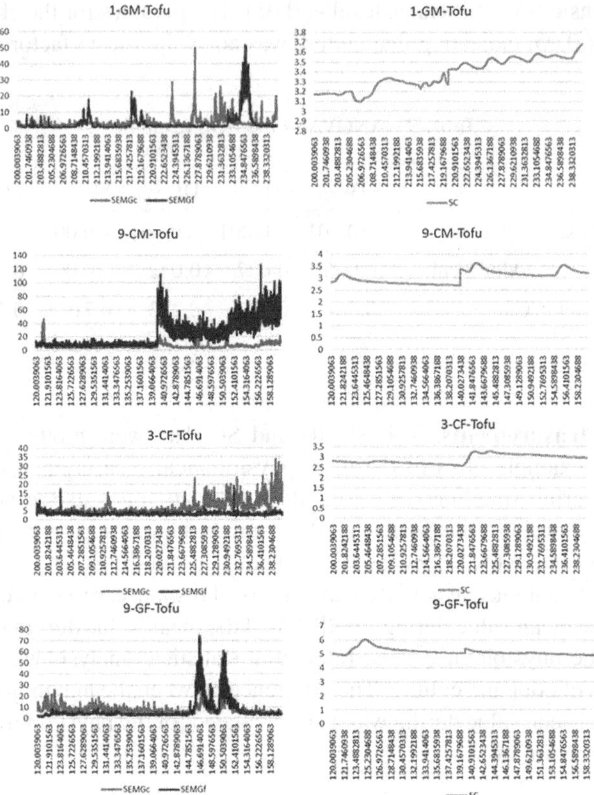

Fig. 2. Example plots of the physiological data

Table 10. Descriptive results of the physiological measurements (grouped by culture)

		Cmean-mean	Dmean-mean	Emean-mean	Cmax-mean	Dmax-mean	Emax-mean
Chinese	M	3.24	−0.326	0.199	82.9	21.97	0.5184
	SD	12.211	6.227	0.570	159.431	98.041	0.939
German	M	2.03	0.604	−0.0016	42.11	27.79	0.3505
	SD	42.627	11.765	0.389	98.064	38.087	0.568

examine the effect of culture, and Mood's median test was used to examine the effect of odor. The results are shown in Tables 12 and 13. For the culture factor, significant differences were found in both the mean-mean and max-mean values for SEMGc and SC (the significance level was 0.05). Chinese participants had significantly higher SEMGc and SC values than German participants. No significant difference was found for the odor factor.

Table 11. Descriptive results of the physiological measurements (grouped by odor)

	Cmean-mean	Dmean-mean	Emean-mean	Cmax-mean	Dmax-mean	Emax-mean
01 Lily	0.87	−1.40	0.04	63.00	8.50	0.18
	6.95	5.74	0.35	128.73	129.97	0.80
02 Rose*	3.30	1.85	0.02	105.10	30.30	0.41
	14.58	16.20	0.71	194.07	59.00	0.72
03 Lavender	4.52	−0.42	0.13	72.00	16.01	0.53
	18.80	4.67	0.31	166.00	16.59	0.70
04 Lemon	0.61	0.08	0.08	41.60	30.80	0.40
	4.23	19.94	0.56	82.61	57.76	0.94
05 Cucumber*	−0.85	−0.82	0.20	74.80	38.10	0.48
	2.87	2.42	0.48	145.23	123.99	0.64
06 Cinnamon*	−0.38	−0.01	0.13	60.60	17.84	0.52
	17.62	5.32	0.28	129.89	17.61	0.61
07 Orange	−0.70	0.41	0.06	36.80	11.20	0.31
	4.69	6.26	0.40	67.16	139.06	0.86
08 Musk	1.94	0.25	−0.09	50.60	29.13	0.16
	14.40	7.78	0.74	123.55	37.11	0.85
09 Coriander*	21.00	1.17	0.05	63.70	32.67	0.46
	102.08	5.40	0.36	137.14	47.43	0.62
10 Clove*	2.49	1.31	0.24	61.20	35.70	0.64
	12.14	10.95	0.47	126.10	53.14	0.91
11 Tofu*	−0.53	1.23	0.21	43.10	22.24	0.62
	4.16	7.96	0.63	96.04	28.47	0.90
12 Cheese	−0.71	0.36	0.12	77.60	26.14	0.51
	6.62	5.18	0.43	169.33	39.37	0.73

Table 12. P-values of the Mann–Whitney nonparametric test on the effect of culture

Cmean-mean	Dmean-mean	Emean-mean	Cmax-mean	Dmax-mean	Emax-mean
0	0.9673	0	0.0012	0.0535	0.0429

Table 13. P-values of Mood's median nonparametric test on the effect of odor

Cmean-mean	Dmean-mean	Emean-mean	Cmax-mean	Dmax-mean	Emax-mean
0.472	0.979	0.683	0.979	0.771	0.799

4 Discussion

The survey results indicated that the white flower, rosy floral, orris-violet, citrus, honey sweet, and fruity types were the preferred odor types among Chinese participants. German participants preferred the green odor type in addition to the same odor types as Chinese participants. The fruity, white flower, rosy floral and orris-violet types were preferred by both Chinese and German participants. A potential reason for the cultural differences is related to the usage of odorous ingredients in each culture. The reason why cinnamon was rated higher by German participants was likely because cinnamon is an ingredient in traditional German foods (e.g., used in the traditional Zimtsterne cookie). Coriander was likely preferred by Chinese participants but not by German participants because coriander is a popular ingredient in Chinese cuisine (e.g., used in Chinese dumplings). Previous studies also indicated that cultural differences in odor preference are due to food preference. It was stated that cultural background is a factor influencing odor preference (Engen and Engen 1997) and that differences in smell preferences are connected to food habits (Classen 1992; Moncrieff 1966).

Odor is highly related to emotions because one pathway for olfactory messages in the human brain is the limbic system, which is mainly responsible for human emotion and memory (McGinley et al. 2000). In this study, the results of the verbal survey showed significant differences in the emotions evoked by different odors. Citrus scents, including the orange and lemon scents, were rated as the most pleasant. Floral scents evoked happy and sensorially pleasant emotions. The scents of citrus, floral, and coriander were highly rated for soothing and peaceful emotions, indicating that these scents can be calming and make people relaxed. Citrus scents, as well as lavender and cucumber, were highly rated for energetic and cooling emotions. Among all 12 odors, citrus scents were highly rated for almost all of the positive emotions, which is consistent with former studies (Chebat and Michon 2003; Toet et al. 2010).

The same odor likely causes different emotional responses in people from different cultures. There were significant differences between Chinese participants and German participants in both the verbal results and physiological results. The verbal results suggested a significant interaction effect of odor and culture. For example, for lemon, Chinese participants' ratings were significantly lower than German participants' ratings. This is likely because people prefer odors that they are familiar with. This preference is consistent with previous findings showing that German people like to use lemons in their daily lives (Schuler 1955).

The physiological data showed that Chinese participants had significantly larger changes in SEMGc and SC values than German participants, indicating a more negative emotional response and higher arousal. This is likely because Chinese participants were more sensitive to odors. The demographic results from the survey show that the Chinese participants used much fewer perfumes in their daily life. The main effect of culture in the verbal results was not significant, but the effect in the physiological results was significant. The inconsistency between the two types of measurements provides interesting implications regarding cultural differences, suggesting that Chinese people do not typically directly express their feelings and emotions, especially their negative emotions. Physiological measurements can help to show more details of odor-evoked emotions among Chinese people because the autonomic nervous system (ANS) is not consciously controlled (Ekman et al. 1983).

The relationship between the verbal and physiological measurement results was studied to identify the connection between ANS parameters and specific emotions (Alaoui-Ismaïli et al. 1997a; Vernet-Maury et al. 1999). Verbal measurements are the most widely used due to their convenience and low cost. However, subjective measurements have potential validity problems in that people may intentionally or unconsciously hide their emotions from others. On the other hand, physiological measurements are more sensitive and have the advantages of quick responses. However, physiological measurements may have disadvantages due to being relatively expensive and easily influenced by the experimental environment. In this study, the difference between the results of the two types of measurements revealed the cultural differences between the Chinese and German participants. Chinese people tend to hide their emotions and express emotions less than they actually feel them. It seems that verbal measurements are effective in determining the effects of odors, while physiological measurements are effective in examining the effects of culture. Thus, it is better to use both physiological and verbal measurements rather than only one type of measurement in odor-evoked emotions studies to investigate cultural differences.

References

Alaoui-Ismaïli, O., Robin, O., Rada, H., Dittmar, A., Vernet-Maury, E.: Basic emotions evoked by odorants: comparison between autonomic responses and self-evaluation. Physiol. Behav. **62**, 713–720 (1997). https://doi.org/10.1016/S0031-9384(97)90016-0

Alaoui-Ismaïli, O., Vernet-Maury, E., Dittmar, A., Delhomme, G., Chanel, J.: Odor hedonics: connection with emotional response estimated by autonomic parameters. Chem. Senses **22**, 237–248 (1997). https://doi.org/10.1093/chemse/22.3.237

Ayabe-Kanamura, S., Schicker, I., Laska, M., Hudson, R., Distel, H., Kobayakawa, T., Saito, S.: Differences in perception of everyday odors: a Japanese-German cross-cultural study. Chem. Senses **23**, 31–38 (1998). https://doi.org/10.1093/chemse/23.1.31

Camras, L.A., Bakeman, R., Chen, Y., Norris, K., Cain, T.R.: Culture, ethnicity, and children's facial expressions: a study of European American, mainland Chinese, Chinese American, and adopted Chinese girls. Emotion **6**, 103–114 (2006). https://doi.org/10.1037/1528-3542.6.1.103

Chebat, J.-C., Michon, R.: Impact of ambient odors on mall shoppers' emotions, cognition, and spending: a test of competitive causal theories. J. Bus. Res. **56**, 529–539 (2003)

Chrea, C., et al.: Mapping the semantic space for the subjective experience of emotional responses to odors. Chem. Senses **34**, 49–62 (2009). https://doi.org/10.1093/chemse/bjn052

Chrea, C., Valentin, D., Sulmont-Rossé, C., Mai, H.L., Nguyen, D.H., Abdi, H.: Culture and odor categorization: agreement between cultures depends upon the odors. Food Qual. Pref. **15**, 669–679 (2004)

Classen, C.: The odor of the other: olfactory symbolism and cultural categories. Ethos **20**, 133–166 (1992)

Collet, C., Vernet-Maury, E., Delhomme, G., Dittmar, A.: Autonomic nervous system response patterns specificity to basic emotions. J. Autonom. Nerv. Syst. **62**, 45–57 (1997). https://doi.org/10.1016/S0165-1838(96)00108-7

Ekman, P., Levenson, R.W., Friesen, W.V.: Autonomic nervous system activity distinguishes among emotions. Science **221**, 1208–1210 (1983)

Engen, T., Engen, E.: Relationship between development of odor perception and language. Enfance **50**, 125–140 (1997)

Ferdenzi, C., et al.: Affective semantic space of scents. Towards a universal scale to measure self-reported odor-related feelings. Food Qual. Pref. **30**, 128–138 (2013). https://doi.org/10.1016/j.foodqual.2013.04.010

Ferdenzi, C., et al.: Affective dimensions of odor perception: a comparison between Swiss, British, and Singaporean populations. Emotion **11**, 1168 (2011)

McGinley, C.M., McGinley, M., McGinley, D.: Odor basics, understanding and using odor testing. In: The 22nd Annual Hawaii Water Environment Association Conference, pp. 6–7 (2000)

Milotic, D.: Practice Papers: the impact of fragrance on consumer choice. J. Consum. Behav. **3**, 179–191 (2003)

Moncrieff, R.W.: Odour Preferences. Leonard Hill (1966)

Owen, C.M., Patterson, J.: Odour liking physiological indices: a correlation of sensory and electrophysiological responses to odour. Food Qual. Pref. **13**, 307–316 (2002). https://doi.org/10.1016/S0950-3293(02)00043-5

Pangborn, R.M., Guinard, J.-X., Davis, R.G.: Regional aroma preferences. Food Qual. Pref. **1**, 11–19 (1988)

Porcherot, C., et al.: How do you feel when you smell this? Optimization of a verbal measurement of odor-elicited emotions. Food Qual. Pref. **21**, 938–947 (2010). https://doi.org/10.1016/j.foodqual.2010.03.012

Schaal, B., Marlier, L., Soussignan, R.: Human foetuses learn odours from their pregnant mother's diet. Chem. Senses **25**, 729–737 (2000)

Schuler, E.: German Cookery. Clarkson Potter (1955)

Toet, A., Smeets, M.A., Van Dijk, E., Dijkstra, D., Van Den Reijen, L.: Effects of pleasant ambient fragrances on dental fear: Comparing apples and oranges. Chemosens. Percept. **3**, 182–189 (2010)

Vernet-Maury, E., Alaoui-Ismaïli, O., Dittmar, A., Delhomme, G., Chanel, J.: Basic emotions induced by odorants: a new approach based on autonomic pattern results. J. Autonom. Nerv. Syst. **75**, 176–183 (1999)

Wrzesniewski, A., McCauley, C., Rozin, P.: Odor and affect: individual differences in the impact of odor on liking for places, things and people. Chem. Senses **24**, 713–721 (1999). https://doi.org/10.1093/chemse/24.6.713

Wysocki, C.J., Pierce, J., Gilbert, A.N.: Geographic, cross-cultural, and individual variation in human olfaction. Smell Taste Health Disease, 287–314 (1991)

Yeshurun, Y., Sobel, N.: An odor is not worth a thousand words: from multidimensional odors to unidimensional odor objects. Ann. Rev. Psychol. **61**, 219–241 (2010). https://doi.org/10.1146/annurev.psych.60.110707.163639

Haptic Semantics in Qualia Product

I-Ying Chiang[1,3], Yikang Sun[2], Po-Hsien Lin[3], Rungtai Lin[3(✉)], and Hsi-Yen Lin[3]

[1] Department of Arts and Design, National Tsing Hua University, Hsinchu 300044, Taiwan
iychiang@mx.nthu.edu.tw

[2] College of Art and Design, Nanjing Forestry University, Nanjing 210037, China
sunyikang120110@hotmail.com

[3] Graduate School of Creative Industry Design, National Taiwan University of Arts, New Taipei City 220307, Taiwan

t0131@ntua.edu.tw, rtlin@mail.ntua.edu.tw, p3yann@gmail.com

Abstract. Humans perceive their surroundings and the world through their sensory systems. In the process of interacting with the external world, physical sensations create psychological cognitions, allowing human beings to accumulate rich "qualia experiences" and establish unique aesthetic tastes and dimensions through this process of "corporeal perception." The main objective of this study is to understand how people generate pleasures or disgusts after perceiving products and objects in their lives in terms of the needs of the "experiential economy" era and "human-centered" design principles. This study focuses on the haptic expressions of vision, sense of touch, and synesthesia. The authors explore the haptic experience and the relevant cognition from the visual association, touching by hand, and visual-touch synesthesia. This study consists of three major stages; Stage One: Delve relevant investigations such as "Material and Qualia," "Interface and Transformation," "Cognition and Dissemination Models," "Haptic Experience and Need for Touch," "Sensation and Synesthesia," and "Product Semantics" to clarify research questions and formulate hypotheses through qualitative review of the literature. Stage Two: Coordinate experiments, hold focus group discussions, design research instruments, and implement haptic experiments. Stage Three: Explore research findings and conclude the statistical analysis of quantitative research. The main results of this study are as follows: (1) Propose the semantic expression of haptic imagery; (2) Establish a process for haptic experiments; (3) Analyze the influencing factors of haptic perception in terms of qualia products.

Keywords: Haptic semantics · Qualia · Product design · Synesthesia

1 Introduction

In this era of global aesthetic economy, the Taiwan government has taken active steps to promote the concept of a design service industry chain, establishing development plans relevant to cultural and creative industries to create a lifestyle industry with "in-depth experiences" and "high-quality aesthetics." The hope is to extract differentiations and unique qualities that will become operational advantages of the cultural industry. The government also aims to strengthen and develop deep-rooted connections with

P.-L. P. Rau (Ed.): HCII 2022, LNCS 13311, pp. 21–35, 2022.
https://doi.org/10.1007/978-3-031-06038-0_2

consumers through "kansei space" and "qualia products," transforming intangible qualia experiences into tangible creative products in order to enhance the competitiveness of local brands and industries [1, 2]. In an era of perceptual consumption, consumers' evaluation of products depends very much on physical perceptions. Masayuki Kurokawa (2002) once said in his product design theory: The twenty-first century is an era of physical perceptions and sense of touch. The twenty-first century will shift the focus back to physical perceptions forgotten in the past century [3]. In this generational trend of the experiential economy, people's pleasures and disgusts for products take on brand new possibilities. Products have grown extremely close to people, even become part of one's body, and therefore designs are gradually starting to value sensory characteristics such as touch, temperature, and kinesthesis [4, 5]. These sensory aesthetic experiences have become key strategies and important topics of academic expression when it comes to product marketing [6].

Aesthetic experience from sensory perception was once regarded as a precious form of self-consciousness and a unique form of cognition. But as people immersed themselves in the enjoyment of pure aesthetics, a phenomenon that Armstrong (2000) announced the "anti-aesthetic turn" occurred in the late twentieth century [7]. That is, under postmodern education, art appreciation focuses on the interpretation and speculation of the meaning of art, separating the "non-art" aesthetic experience from the artistic experience. The introduction of cultural context strengthened the criticalness of art education but also ran the risk of weakening the perceptual aspects of art or visual mediums [8]. But with the twenty-first century came the quiet return of "aesthetics," and discussions around art and design returned to the realm of "human emotions" and "human activities." In response, the research topics and focus of various disciplines also gradually returned to relevant discussions of "human-centered experiences" and "aesthetic experiences" such as: Research on object and sensory experiences, sensory and emotional cognition, Kansei Engineering, etc.

Materials are important mediums of sensory perception and a symbolic carrier of spiritual ideas. In the past, people interacted with materials by touching them directly, the physical act of "touch" transforming into satisfying "qualia". The three major objectives of this study are as follows: (1) Explore the semantic expression of haptic sensation and imagery; (2) Discuss the implementation process of haptic experiments; (3) Explore the influencing factors of haptic cognition in relation to qualia products.

2 Literature Review

2.1 Material and Qualia

Material is the medium of art and the carrier of design. Different materials form the everyday products in our lives, demonstrating their properties as people come in contact with the products. During such contacts, people interact with products, triggering feelings, forming likes and dislikes, before giving an evaluation. Therefore, in the planning of product design, we focus on various actions that make take place when the user is using the product, such as touching, lifting, or holding. For these moments, the surface material of products is a key factor influencing users' haptic perception. The rapid progression of material research and development has created more diversity in the types of materials that can be used in product design. Progress in processing technology also allows the same material to take on different textures, which can, in turn, elicit richer and more diverse, intricate, and pleasant haptic perceptions, thereby entering the aesthetic level of qualia. Therefore, product designers need to have a deep understanding of the characteristics and definitions of materials and textures and explore the connection between them and haptic perceptions, thereby understanding and grasping the interaction and operating mechanisms between material, texture, and qualia [9].

Descriptions of such qualities first appeared in Latin. Greeks adopted the word "qualia" to describe a feeling that can only be obtained through personal experience, a kind of spiritual phenomenon, state of consciousness, and sensory experience triggered by pleasant interactions [10]. The innovative strategy and promotional model of the design field in the twenty-first century have long shifted away from the pursuit of "quantity", attempting not only to appeal to users through good "quality" but also to generate unforgettably pleasant experiences of "qualia" while maintaining a high standard of quality. This is in line with the idea of "qualia" advocated by Nobuyuki Idei, former CEO of Sony, who believes that qualia should be the feeling of joy and happiness that one can see with one's eyes and feel in one's hands [11]. He believes that in addition to specifications and functions, qualia products also need to have the ability to "create emotion and value". A product imbued with qualia elements can create precious moments of joy for consumers and users [12].

2.2 Interface and Transformation

The area in which people come in contact with a product is called the "interface". Usually, an interface is needed to transfer the kinetic energy of the body, and users manipulate the interface to achieve certain tasks. In order to explore the relationship between people, products, and goals, Kreifeldt (1974) proposed the user–tool–task system analysis model [13]. The model presents interaction and adaptive feedback, with particular emphasis on three main bodies in the design system: users (people), tools (products), and tasks (goals), as well as the two major types of interfaces including human system design: manipulation interface (user–tool) and engagement interface (tool–task) [14–16]. Human factors are a major concern when discussing product interfaces, and mechanical engineering is often involved in the basic functions of interfaces. The prototype model outlines the interrelationships and influences between user–tool, tool–task, and user–task. In other words, users manipulate tools to solve problems and complete tasks. Manipulating tools often involve the use of two interfaces (manipulation and engagement). Subsequent discussions on product interfaces are all based on reviews and reinterpretations of this paradigmatic "user–tool–task" model, which has also been developed into more comprehensive product design application systems [17]. Additionally, when it comes to discussions about qualia in terms of "physical properties", this research aims to understand the characteristics, triggering mechanisms, and benefits of qualia elements in products. Kreifeldt and Chuang (1979) explore the overlooked 'feel' of an object in one's hand in their psychophysics experiments. In addition to exploring the effect of the physical moment of inertia I, they also explain the concepts of Weber's fraction, just noticeable difference (JND), and difference threshold [18]. Therefore, understanding the difference in human sensory perception involves not only comparing the differences between stimuli but more importantly, exploring the ratio of "just noticeable difference" to stimulation intensity.

In the digital age with rapid technological advancements, people are constantly encountering dazzling arrays of novel products. However, this also means that they often have to switch between different manipulation interfaces and adapt to new perceptive experiences. Breitschaft and Carbon (2021) discussed the "*Need for High-Quality Haptic Feeling*" in the digital era, pointing out that: Although modern technology allows the widespread usage of touch screens, a seamless flat-panel interface makes it hard for users to establish a strong connection between their sense of touch and the product's functions [19]. Therefore, using appropriate design to help users connect with the function of a product by generating intuitive responses through haptic perception should be an important issue in the current design field. In his online teaching experimental study, Bowers (2019) found that adding haptic senses into virtual learning environments can improve learning [20]. However, people in the digital age enjoy the convenience of cloud operation and learning, which drastically reduces their chances of making contact with their surroundings or physical objects, thereby making it difficult to accumulate sufficient and sharp physical experiences. In a rapidly changing world, how can mankind enjoy technology while paying attention to human needs and maintaining active perceptiveness? How do we regain the sensory perceptiveness that we are losing? Also, how do we detect or reconstruct the sensory experiences and perceived needs of the new generation? These issues appear precious and urgent. Based on this, this study believes that it is important for the focus on the discussion of qualia products to combine the joint evaluation of "quantity" and "quality" in order to clarify the relationship between physical stimulus and sensory cognition and therefore show the corresponding relationship between the physical and psychological properties of products.

2.3 Cognition and Dissemination Model

Donald A. Norman proposed three major aspects of emotional design based on cognitive psychology: the visceral level, behavioral level, and reflective level. In the process of product design, designers must, in addition to the "aesthetic" element of appearance and outward perception, pay attention to "functional" behaviors that take convenience into consideration and the "emotional" effect users may feel. This idea has become an important principle influencing contemporary product design. He has pointed out that all products have three different mental models: (1) The designer's model, or the designer's conception of a product during the design process. (2) The user's model, or the user's idea of how a product or equipment works or operates. (3) The system image, or the image derived from the physical structure and manual or documentation of a product [21]. Designers expect the designer's model to be identical to the user's model, but the designer's expectations might not always align with the user's understanding. Therefore, this study believes that it is very important to explore the mental cognition and information dissemination model when it comes to designing qualia products.

2.4 Haptic Experience and Need for Touch

Acker et al. (2010) has mentioned that the tactile experiences of physical touch may establish a stable scaffold for developing interpersonal, conceptual, metaphorical knowledge, and related application [22]. People will touch objects or products because of the motivation for fun or interest. Notably, the neutral or positive sensory feedback incorporated with affective response will extend the imagination or communication and increase persuasion. Besides, people who are not engaging in touching for fun will also be persuaded by understanding the touch element relating to the message [23]. Furthermore, the previous experiment executed by Peck et al. (2006, 2011) has shown that either natural or artificial haptic elements on the product can increase the appeal and enhance the persuasion [23, 24].

Regarding qualia products, this study attempts to distinguish between the human beings' sense of awareness and perceptiveness. While researching mankind's autotelic need for touch, Peck and Johnson (2011) divided people into two groups based on their need for haptic perception: "high autotelics" and "low autotelics", and provided the "Measures of Autotelic NFT and Involvement [23, 24]." This inspired the authors to research qualia from the essential differences of human nature, focusing on the correlation between people's qualia needs, qualia ability and qualia validity in order to discover the feedback effects of individual differences on qualia cognition and to apply such knowledge to qualia design.

2.5 Sensation and Synesthesia

External stimuli usually create a sensation, and research into sensations usually explores the structure of the sensory system and how it works. But when people start to interpret the messages sent by the sensory system, then enter the higher state of synesthesia, which means perception [25]. In other words, "sensation" is the start of receiving stimuli, while "synesthesia" is our understanding of sensations [26]. Zimbardo believes that our perception of our surroundings can be divided into three stages: sensation, perception, and categorization [27]. In terms of product design, users mainly form an impression of a product based on understandings formed in the perception stage. However, the reception of perceptual experience, in addition to the physiological stimulus from the sensory system, is mainly derived from personal and subjective interpretations of the stimulation, which is a complex psychological activity that can be affected by a few main factors: education and experience, differences in viewpoints, and motivations [28]. Therefore, because different individuals may receive stimuli through different channels, they might form different impressions of the same object [25]. Vision, sense of touch, and synesthesia, which are relevant to the scope of this study, are explained below.

Vision. One can say that vision is the first of the five senses and the primary way people notice other objects. It also has the most well-developed system among the senses [29]. People receive product information (stimuli) primarily through vision, that is, the visual appeal of a product has the opportunity to capture people's hearts. In psychology, there have been many discussions on how humans use vision to identify shapes and patterns, such as Gestalt psychology, prototype matching, template matching, and feature analysis [30]. In addition, the subsequent vision-related research and experiments in this study are meant to further the discussion of visual association and visual-touch synesthesia.

Sense of touch. Sense of touch refers to the sensation one feels when the surface of the skin receives pressure from an object or when it touches something, so it is also called "sense of pressure" [28]. Infants have the ability to start exploring the world through touch even before they open their eyes. For humans, the sense of touch is the most primitive and most direct external sensory channel, and the first to help people perceive the external world [31]. Touch may be the most basic precursor of all senses, but it also has the most complex and least understood mechanisms [32, 33]. Loomis and Lederman (1986) pointed out how the sense of touch includes three perceptions: cutaneous sense (pressure, vibration, temperature), kinesthesis (movement), and proprioception (location) [25, 34]. What ordinary people call a sense of touch is actually a kind of cutaneous sense, the reception of sensations based on external stimuli experienced through receptors on the skin's surface [35]. Receptors on the skin can also be divided into three types: mechanoreceptors, thermoreceptors, and nociceptors [36]. How sense of touch occurs, on the other hand, can be divided into two categories based on the interaction between the individual and the object: active touch and passive touch [37]. When it comes to the same stimuli, when touching an object, active touch is a lot more sensitive and perceptive than passive touch. That is, active touch is more capable of recognizing external objects [38]. Cognitive abilities help us identify, classify, remember, sequence and learn, in order to form so-called concepts. People can tell what they are touching by the real response of haptic sensation. They can also use their hands to learn about the properties of an object. Therefore, we can conclude that haptic cognition has an important influence on human behaviors and judgments [39, 40]. In other words, haptic cognition can assist and enhance people's interpretation of the external environment, thereby producing reasonable behaviors in response [9].

Synesthesia. Synesthesia is when sensations are joined together. This means that under certain stimuli, the individual receives not only the sensory experience of said stimuli, but also develops other sensations [35]. People primarily use the five senses (vision, sound, smell, taste, and touch) to understand the world. Moreover, most of the experience comes from the combination of multiple senses. It is difficult to rely on a single sense to experience every aspect of an object or get the whole picture. A study by the University of Cambridge argues that different senses were integrated at the beginning of life, gradually separating as individuals grow up [41, 42]. Human perception includes the phenomenon of synesthesia. Therefore, this study intends to explore the possibility of visual-touch synesthesia when discussing the image and cognitive functions of qualia products.

2.6 Product Semantics

People experience the external world with their bodies and use language to express their inner thoughts. Famed US psychologist Charles Egerton Osgood and his colleagues began a semantic analysis study in the early 1950s and published "*The Measurement of Meaning*" in 1957 [43]. The main purpose of semantic analysis is to help understand the tendencies of certain concepts and ideas. It is usually used to evaluate non-quantitative data to judge the importance of specific items on a certain evaluation scale, allowing researchers to obtain information through analysis and inference. Product semantics explore artificial forms related to users' cognitive and social contexts. Its essential purpose is to treat the attributes or characters of the designed object as a message and provide the intervention suggestion in the design process. Beyond the function, product semantics focus on discussing emerging meanings, interaction with interfaces and surfaces, affordances and motivating engagements and so on [44].

Subsequent experiments conducted for the study will utilize semantic differential (SD) analysis to help us understand the perceptional needs of contemporary people. The semantic differential method uses pairs of bipolar adjectives with opposite meanings, such as "soft-hard," "smooth-rough," "sticky-dry," "fragrant-smelly," or "traditional-modern" to measure product semantics. This "bipolar" concept is a very obvious and intuitive way of expressing feelings in linguistics. Semantic differential analysis often uses scales of 5, 7, or 9. The assumption is that each subject will tick a certain position on the scale to indicate their perception of a product, and that the results from all subjects should show a normal distribution of the bell curve, with the average result representing the feeling conveyed by the product [45].

3 Methodology

3.1 Research Instrument

According to the literature review, the authors argue that the Need For Touch (NFT) will be the most priority and essential attribute in experiencing qualia products or objects. This study intends to clarify the relationship between the autotelic NFT and people's preferences. Based on Peck and Johnson's criteria, the authors adapted and developed a five-point scale questionnaire (Table 1) for measuring subjects' autotelic need for touch [24]. This NFT questionnaire helps distingue and evaluate participants' characteristics in touch expectation and sensibility.

Table 1. Questionnaire related to "measures of autotelic NFT" (adapted from [24])

Goal	Questions
To evaluate participants' autotelic need for touch.	1.1 When walking through stores, I can't help touching all kinds of products. No ← □1 □2 □3 □4 □5 → Yes 1.2 Touching products can be fun. No ← □1 □2 □3 □4 □5 → Yes 1.3 When browsing in stores, it is important for me to handle all kinds of products. No ← □1 □2 □3 □4 □5 → Yes 1.4 I like to touch products even if I have no intention of buying them. No ← □1 □2 □3 □4 □5 → Yes 1.5 When browsing in stores, I like to touch lots of products. No ← □1 □2 □3 □4 □5 → Yes 1.6 I find myself touching all kinds of products in stores. No ← □1 □2 □3 □4 □5 → Yes

In order to explore the possibility of haptic expression, this study coordinates the focus group discussions (FGD) to extract the intended materials for semantics reference and later application in haptic questionnaires. In this focus group discussion, five professional educators have more than 15 years of experience in craft creation, related design teaching, and aesthetics research; they devoted themselves to discussing and selecting haptic adjectives, which separately focus on touch feeling and haptic description. Finally, after two senior experts' reviews, the authors revise and complete the haptic semantics questionnaires (Table 2). The bipolar adjectives are set to respond to

Table 2. Questionnaire related to "haptic semantics" evaluated from visual association, touch feeling and visual-touch synesthesia sequentially

Goal	Questions		
Technical Stratum (Outer Sensation / Haptic Feeling)	2.1 The possible "haptic feeling" of the product:		
		1 2 3 4 5	
	demurrage	□ □ □ □ □	slippery
	fuzzy	□ □ □ □ □	bare
	coarse	□ □ □ □ □	delicate
	smooth	□ □ □ □ □	rough
	hard	□ □ □ □ □	soft
	dense	□ □ □ □ □	loose
	cold	□ □ □ □ □	warm
	light	□ □ □ □ □	heavy
Semantic Stratum (Significant Cognition / Description of Haptic Imagery)	2.2 The possible "description of haptic imagery or style" of the product:		
		1 2 3 4 5	
	quiet & elegant	□ □ □ □ □	lively & generous
	gentle & sincere	□ □ □ □ □	domineering & decisive
	moderate & tolerant	□ □ □ □ □	calm & restrained
	fresh & pure	□ □ □ □ □	charming & beautiful
	experienced & mature	□ □ □ □ □	simple & refined
	immature & plain	□ □ □ □ □	blooming & glorious
	introverted & shy	□ □ □ □ □	optimistic & enthusiastic
	witty & flexible	□ □ □ □ □	straight & honest
Effective Stratum (Inner Spirit / Pleasure)	2.3 Degree of pleasure when perceiving the cup:		
		1 2 3 4 5	
	low	□ □ □ □ □	high
Preference	2.4 Preference of the cup:		
		1 2 3 4 5	
	dislike	□ □ □ □ □	really like
Comprehensive Evaluation	3.1 Overall, which one is your favorite cup? □ Lacquer □ Wood □ Ceramic □ Glass □ Metal □ Resin		
	3.2 Reason for making the favorite choice: □ Visual association without touch □ Touch feeling without sight □ Visual-Touch Synesthesia		

six materials' specific attributes of lacquer, wood, ceramic, glass, metal, resin, and their commonalities.

Based on the dissemination model of visceral level (technical stratum), behavioral level (semantic stratum), and reflective levels (effective stratum), the study constructs a scaffold of the haptic semantics questionnaire.

3.2 Research Stimuli

To fulfill the qualia experience in the haptic experiment, the authors chose and prepared six handle-less cups with different materials (see Fig. 1). Four of them (lacquer, wood, ceramic, glass) are created by craft artists, and the other two (metal, resin) are made from commercial manufacture.

Fig. 1. Six cups as stimuli are made from different materials of lacquer, wood, ceramic, glass, metal, and resin (left to right)

3.3 Participants and Procedure

There are 35 subjects, the Craft and Design major students from sophomore year to graduate level with diverse craft creation experiences, participate in this haptic experiment. This haptic experiment is executed through three stages: Visual association (without actual touch), Touch feeling (without visual observation), Visual-Touch synesthesia. In each stage, these subjects sequentially evaluate six cups in the haptic feeling from outer sensation, description of haptic imagery about significant cognition, and inner spirit of pleasure; they also record their preference to each cup and choose the favorite and declare the reason.

4 Results and Discussion

4.1 Haptic Expression in Product Semantics

This study compares non-expert (participants) evaluations to expert (educators) evaluations in the haptic semantics expression of the tactile experience. The FGD experts discuss and devise the haptic bi-adjective, primarily focusing on each material corresponding to six cups that have been selected as stimuli. This study put the pre-elected felicitous adjective on the side of score 1 and the contrastive adjective on the opposite side of score 5. The statistics of means display the participants' evaluations of each cup through different stages of Visual association (without actual touch), Touch feeling (without visual observation), Visual-Touch synesthesia in the line charts (see Fig. 2). They show the cognitive and semantic differences between participating students and expert educators, primarily in the haptic feeling of lacquer and wood, in the haptic imagery description of ceramic and metal.

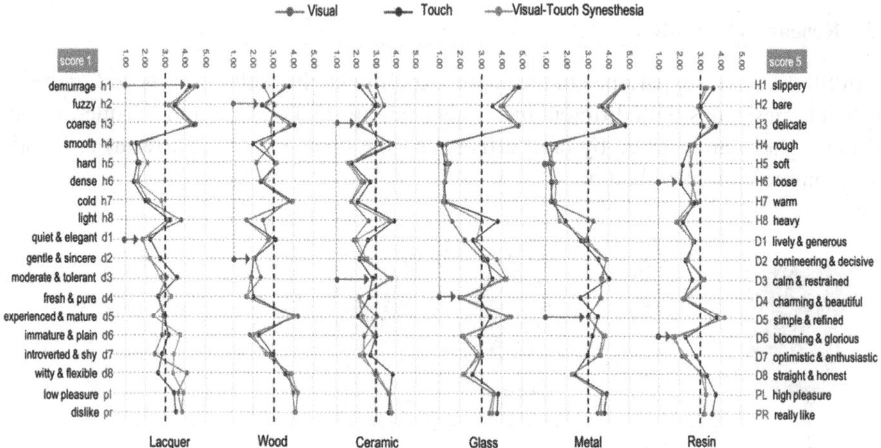

Fig. 2. The cognitive differences of haptic semantics exist between non-expert and expert

The evaluations in three stages separately present the differences of haptic semantics among six cups (see Fig. 3). There are significant differences between the cups of wood and metal, wood and glass in the Visual stage. The distinguished diversities also exist between the cups of wood and metal, wood and glass, ceramic and metal, ceramic and glass in the Touch stage. The discrepancies also happen between the cups of wood and metal, wood and glass, wood and ceramic, ceramic and metal, ceramic and glass in the Visual-Touch synesthesia stage.

4.2 Autotelic NFT

Discussing the cognitive and semantical differences between groups with a high or low autotelic need for touch (NFT) is essential. The 35 subjects who participated in this haptic experiment are the students studying in the Department of Arts and Design in Taiwan. Averagely, they have more than two years of creating experiences, execute studio practice of craft-making 4–8 h a week, involving wood, clay, metal, glass, and other craft materials. One of the analyses shows that 83% of participants are the hi-autotelic NFT. Nevertheless, 17% of participants belong to the low-autotelic NFT (see Fig. 4).

33% of the participants with low-autotelic NFT select ceramic cup as the favorite one (see Fig. 5-left), and the haptic experience in the Visual-Touch synesthesia (83%) affect the choice mainly (see Fig. 6-left). Both parts of the participants with hi-autotelic NFT select wood cup (38%), ceramic cup (33%) as the favorite one (see Fig. 5-middle), and the haptic experience in the Visual-Touch synesthesia (79%) impact the choice

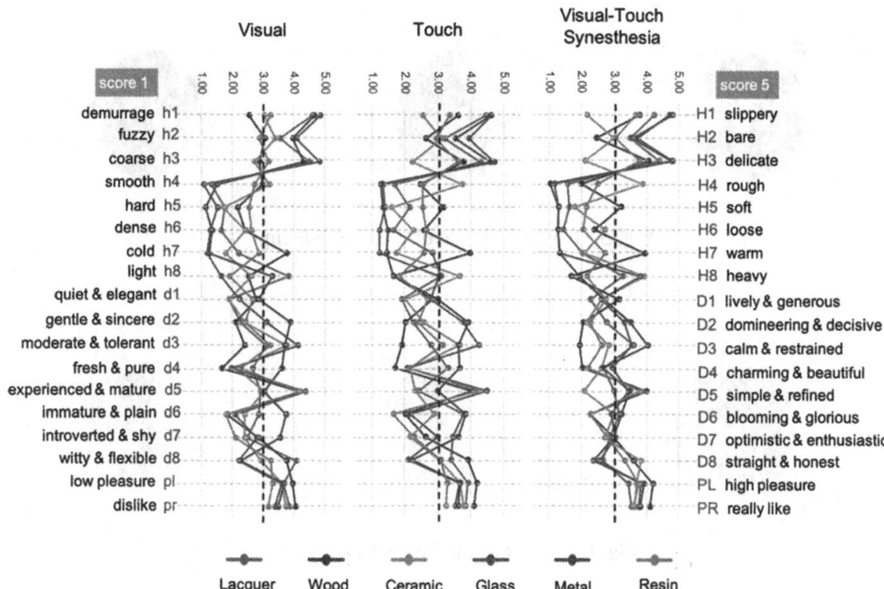

Fig. 3. Six material cups bring the cognitive and semantics differences of diverse haptic experiences in visual observation, touch sensation, visual-touch synesthesia stages

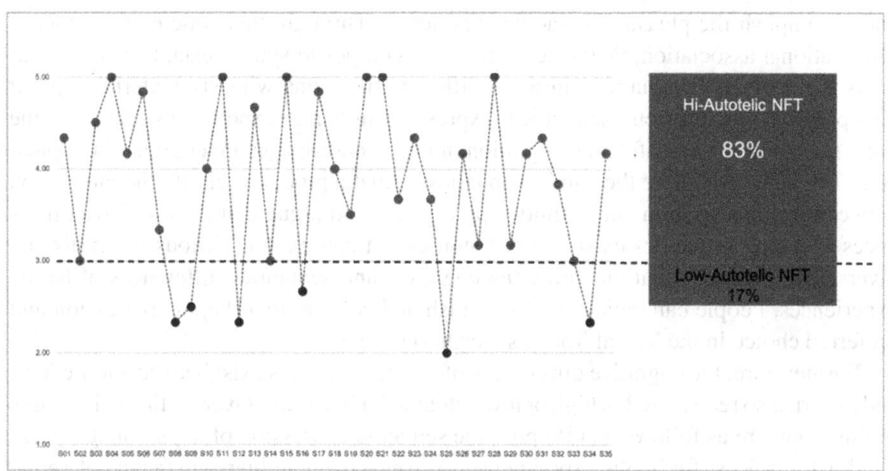

Fig. 4. Autotelic NFT (need for touch)

primarily (see Fig. 6-middle). Overall, most of the participants select wood cup (31%), ceramic cup (31%) as the favorite one (see Fig. 5-right), and the haptic experience in the Visual-Touch synesthesia (80%) influence the choice principally (see Fig. 6-right).

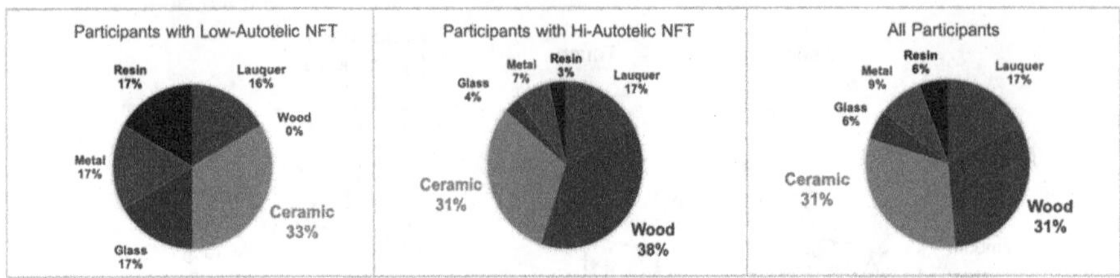

Fig. 5. Favorite choice of the material cup

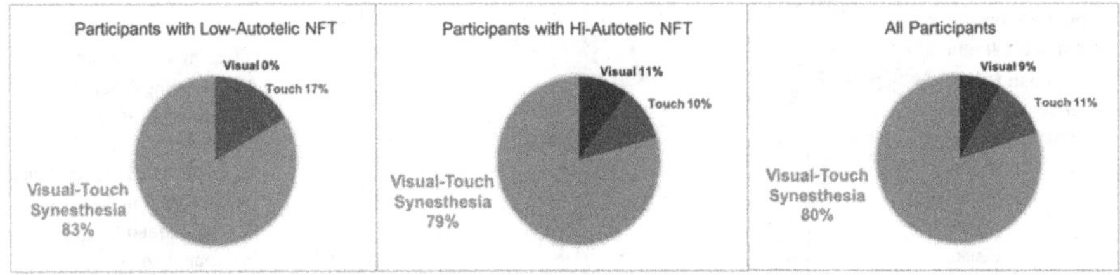

Fig. 6. Influence on the favorite choice

5 Conclusion and Recommendations

When people touch the qualia products, they are often affected by the intuitive feeling and accomplish the pleasurable tactile experience. Through the haptic experiments of observational association, tactile sensation, and composite synesthesia, this study analyzes the subjects' evaluations in three different situations with six material cups. It also proposes the subjects' semantical expression in haptic experiences related to the outer sensation of haptic feeling, cognition of haptic description, inner affection of pleasure. The authors explore the haptic semantics in qualia products, clarify the interaction between tactile sensation and cognitive perception, and argue that the cognitive differences of haptic semantics exist between non-expert and expert. Various materials and diverse experiential situations bring the cognitive and semantics differences of haptic experiences. People can delicately distinguish and confirm their haptic expression and preferred choice in the Visual-Touch synesthesia stage.

Furthermore, the cognitive differences of haptic semantics exist between non-expert and expert, also recognized in high or low autotelic NFT groups. Overall, the main results of this study are as follows: (1) Propose the semantic expression of haptic imagery; (2) Establish a process for haptic experiments; (3) Analyze the influencing factors of haptic perception in terms of qualia products. Returning body sensation and haptic perception have become vital issues in product design and aesthetic research in the experiential era. Therefore, the authors believe that further study can extend the application of haptic semantics in product design, craft creation, and related education.

References

1. Lin, R., Liu. B.-C., Lee, Y.-J., Su, C.-H., Chang, S.-H.: From Cultural Creativity to Qualia-A Case Study of the One Nanyuan. College of Design, National Taiwan University of Arts, sponsored by the National Science Council, project no.: NSC-98–2410-H-144–009&010 (2010). (in Chinese)
2. Lin, R.-T.: From service innovation to qualia product design. J. Des. Sci. **14**(S), 13–31 (2011). (in Chinese)
3. Masayuki, K., translated by Wang, X.: Design Focus Product Masayuki Kurokawa. China Youth Press, Beijing (2002). (Chinese version)
4. Product Research Association: translated by Li, C.-J.: The Future Archeology of Design. Garden City, Taipei (2003). (Chinese version)
5. Chang, Y.-J.: A Study on Tactile Style of Products- Using Handleless Cups as a Case Study (thesis). National Chiao Tung University, Institute of Applied Arts, Hsinchu (2010).(in Chinese)
6. Ministry of Economic Affairs Small to Medium Enterprise Administration: The Project of Qualia Advancing for SMEs. https://www.moeasmea.gov.tw/masterpage-tw. (2013). (in Chinese) last accessed 12 Dec 2021
7. Armstrong, I.: The radical aesthetic. Blackwell, Malden, MA (2000)
8. Yu, C.-Y.: Aesthetic experience and its profound interaction with the Self/Ego. Art J. Edu. Res. **32**, 103–132 (2016). (in Chinese)
9. Chen, Y.-T.: A Study on tactile Image and Style (dissertation). National Chiao Tung University, Institute of Applied Arts, Hsinchu (2016).(in Chinese)
10. Searle, J.R.: The rediscovery of the mind. MIT press, Cambridge, MA (1992)
11. Idei, N. translated by Hong, Y.-H., Peng, N.-Y., Xu, Y.-W.: New Era – Great Transformation. CommonWealth Magazine, Taipei (2003). (Chinese version)
12. Yen, H.-Y.: A Study of Qualia Factors in Product Affecting Brand Image (dissertation). National Taiwan University of Arts, Graduate School of Creative Industry Design, New Taipei City (2015).(in Chinese)
13. Kreifeldt, J.G.: Toward a theory of man–tool system design applications to the consumer product area. In: Proceedings of the HFS 18th Annual Meeting, Hundsville, AL, USA, pp. 301–309 (1 Oct 1974)
14. Kreifeldt, J.G., Hill, P.H.: The Integration of human factors and industrial design for consumer products. Proc. Hum. Factors Ergon. Soc. Annu. Meet. **20**, 108–112 (1976).
15. Kreifeldt, J.G.: Consumer product design projects for human factors Classes. Proc. Hum. Factors Ergon. Soc. Annu. Meet. **26**, 735–739 (1982).
16. Lin, R., Kreifeldt, J.G.: Ergonomics in wearable computer design. Int. J. Ind. Ergon. **2001**(27), 259–269 (2001)
17. Chiang, I.-Y., Lin, P.-H., Kreifeldt, J.G., Lin, R.: From theory to practice: an adaptive development of design education. Educ. Sci. **11**, 673 (2021). https://doi.org/10.3390/educsci11110673
18. Kreifeldt, J.G., Chuang, M.-C.: Moment of inertia: psychophysical study of an overlooked sensation. Science **206**(4418), 588–590 (1979). https://www.jstor.org/stable/1749260
19. Breitschaft, S.J., Carbon, C.-C.: Function follows form: using the aesthetic association principle to enhance haptic interface design. Front. Psychol. **12**, 646986 (2021). https://doi.org/10.3389/fpsyg.2021.646986
20. Bowers, L.J.: Touching creativity; a review and early pilot test of haptic tooling to support design practice, within a distance learning curriculum, open Learning. J. Open Dis. e-Learning **34**(1), 6–18 (2019). https://doi.org/10.1080/02680513.2018.1545637

21. Norman, D.A.: Emotional Design: Why we love (or hate) everyday things. Basic, New York (2004)
22. Ackerman, J.M., Nocera, C.C., Bargh, J.A.: Incidental haptic sensations influence social judgments and decisions. Science **328**, 1712 (2010). https://doi.org/10.1126/science.1189993
23. Peck, J., Wiggins, J.: It just feels good: consumers' affective response to touch and its influence on persuasion. Journal of Marketing **70**, 56–69 (2006)
24. Peck, J., Johnson, J.W.: Autotelic need for touch, haptics, and persuasion: the role of involvement. Psychology & Marketing **28**(3), 222–239 (2011). https://doi.org/10.1002/mar.20389
25. Tsai, C.-Y.: A Study on the Influence of the Form and the Texture on Product Image Through Visual and Tactile Perception (thesis). National Yunlin University of Science and Technology, Department of Industrial Design, Yunlin (2003).(in Chinese)
26. Solso, R.L., translated by Wu, L.-L.: Cognitive Psychology. Hwa Tai, Taipei (1998). (Chinese version)
27. Gerrig, R.J., translated by Hengshan You, H.-S.: Psychology and Life - 20th Edition. Wunan Publishing, Taipei (2019). (Chinese version)
28. Chang, C.-H.: Modern Psychology (first edition). Tung Hua, Taipei (1995). (in Chinese)
29. Li, C.-S., et al.: Vision and Cognition, 1st edn. Yuan-Liou Publishing, Taipei (1999).(in Chinese)
30. Anderson, J.R.: Cognitive Psychology And It's Implication, 3rd edn. W.H. Freeman and Company, NY (1990)
31. Ackerman, D., translated by Zhuang, A.-G.: A Natural History of the Senses. China Times Publishing, Taipei (1993). (Chinese version)
32. Prytherch, D., McLundie, M.: So what is haptics anyway? Research issues in art design and media. Spring (2002). ISSN 1474–2365 (Issue No.2)
33. Kreifeldt, J., Lin, R., Chuang, M.C.: The importance of "Feel" in product design feel, the neglected aesthetic "DO NOT TOUCH". In: Rau P.L.P. (eds.) Internationalization, Design and Global Development. IDGD 2011. Lecture Notes in Computer Science, vol 6775. Springer, Berlin, Heidelberg (2011). https://doi.org/10.1007/978-3-642-21660-2_35
34. Loomis, J.M., Lederman, S.J.: Tactual perception In: Boff, K., Kaufman, L., Thomas, J. (eds.) John Wiley & Sons Inc, New York (1986)
35. Chang, C.-H.: Modern Psychology: The modern science of their own problems. Tung Hua, Taipei (2009). (in Chinese)
36. Davies, A., Blakeley, A.G.H., Kidd, C.: Human physiology. Churchill Livingstone, National Charity Services Inc, Washington, DC, U.S.A. (2001)
37. Sonneveld, M.H., Schifferstein, H.N.J.: The tactual experience of objects. In: Schifferstein, H.N.J., Hekkert, P. (eds.) Product Experience. Elsevier, San Diego, CA (2008)
38. Gibson, J.J.: Observations on active touch. Psychological Review **69**, 477–491 (1962)
39. Lederman, S.J., Klatzky, R.L.: Hand movements: A window into haptic object recognition. Cognitive Psychology **19**(3), 342–368 (1987)
40. Hinckley, K., Sinclair, M.: Touch-sensing input devices. In: Paper presented at the Proceedings of the SIGCHI conference on Human factors in computing systems: the CHI is the limit. ACM, Pittsburgh, Pennsylvania, United States, pp. 223–230 (1999)
41. Baron-Cohen, S., Cross, P.: Reading the eyes: evidence for the role of perception in the development of a theory of mind. Mind and Language **6**, 173–186 (1992). https://doi.org/10.1111/j.1468-0017.1992.tb00203.x
42. Baron-Cohen, S.: Autism: The empathizing-systemizing (E-S) theory. The Year in Cognitive Neuroscience 2009: Ann. N.Y. Acad. Sci. **1156**, 68–80 (2009). https://doi.org/10.1111/j.1749-6632.2009.04467.x
43. Osgood, C.E., Suci, G.J., Tannenbaum, P.H.: The Measurement of Meaning. University of Illinois Press, 9th printing (1975)

44. Tewari, S.: Product Semantics. In: Edwards et al. (eds.) The Bloomsbury Encyclopedia of Design, vol 3. Bloomsbury Academic (2016). https://doi.org/10.5040/9781472596154-BED-ONLINE-002
45. Hung, W.-K., Chen, L.-L.: Exploring contradictory meanings in product semantics. Journal of Design **15**(4), 41–58 (2010). (in Chinese)

Rethinking Demand: An Active Design Framework and Tools for Sustainability from 'Demand-Side' Perspective

Yuhui Jin(✉)

College of Design and Innovation, Tongji University, Fuxin Rd.281, Shanghai, People's Republic of China
yuhui_jin@tongji.edu.cn

Abstract. The famous three principles of circular economy design, promoted by Ellen MacArthur Foundation, provide valuable guidance for design practice mainly from perspective of "Supply Side". However, this paper finds that the performance is hardly ensured if the impact from "Demand Side" is ignored. A Human Needs Satisfaction Area (HN-SA) Model is proposed in this paper through deconstructing human needs into Material-Necessary Needs (MNN) and Material-Unnecessary Needs (MUN), providing a whole view of sustainability challenges from both "Supply Side" and "Demand Side". And based on this model we identified three zones for addressing sustainability challenges: A. Enhancing the recycle of material; B. Satisfying more Material-Unnecessary Needs in Non-material systems; C. Managing the growth of needs and wants. Moreover, they correspond to five design principles (extension of the three principles of circular economy), Zone A: 1. Design out waste and pollution; 2. Keep products and materials in use; 3. Regenerate natural systems. Zone B: 4. Design Material Out. Zone C: 5. Design a system that stimulating self-actualization and contribution.

Keywords: Demand side · Sustainability · Active design · Circular economy

1 Introduction

1.1 Positives and Limitations of Existing Sustainable Design Principles

The circular economy is a systems solution framework that tackles global challenges like climate change, biodiversity loss, waste, and pollution [1]. Ellen MacArthur Foundation is an active promoter of this goal and has put forward the famous three principles of circular economy:

1. Design out waste and pollution;
2. Keep products and materials in use;
3. Regenerate natural systems.[2]

P.-L. P. Rau (Ed.): HCII 2022, LNCS 13311, pp. 36–50, 2022.
https://doi.org/10.1007/978-3-031-06038-0_3

Furthermore, The Circular Design Guide[1], points out that design plays a pivotal role. In the context of a circular economy, everything needs to be redesigned, and on the contrary, the next big thing in design is circular [3]. On the basis of these three principles, many enterprises and institutions have put forward new versions of design principles focusing on their own industries. For example, Nike proposed 10 Principles of Circular Design which respectively involve ten aspects of product life cycle from the perspective of sports equipment industry [4]. DS Smith put forward the Circular Design Five Principles from the perspective of packaging industry [5]. The Ellen MacArthur Foundation's three principles of circular economy have extremely positive practical significance in promoting the realization of sustainable goals.

However, if we regard "satisfaction of human needs" as the "Supply Side"[2] and "human needs" as the "Demand Side"[3], then the three principles of the circular economy are all from the perspective of "Supply Side". Although this provides a very valuable guidance for current global design practice, this paper finds that the performance is hardly ensured if the impact from "Demand Side" is ignored.

A formula (see Fig. 1) can be used to describe the relationship between resource consumption and environmental capacity. The left side of the formula represents the total net resource consumption of human activities, which must be less than the environmental resource capacity on the right side of the formula. If interstellar migration is not taken into consideration, the value of "E" on the right side of the formula is relatively fixed, which is the capacity of the available resources on the Earth. Therefore, in order to sustain the human civilization, we must manage the growth on the left side of the formula so that the left side does not exceed the right side. According to this formula, the value of the left side is determined by two forces: "C x P" which represents the Demand Side, and "100% - R" which represents the Supply Side. As the result, one conclusion can be drawn that **simply Supply-side improvement (increasing the resource recycling rate) does not ensure that the left side of the formula stops increasing (theoretically R will not reach 100%), that is, to ensure the realization of sustainable goals** (see Fig. 2).

[1] The Circular Design Guide is a collaboration between the Ellen MacArthur Foundation and IDEO.

[2] Supply Side and demand Side are terms from economics. Supply-side economics is the theory that economic growth is best achieved through policies that encourage increased output or supply. While Demand-side economics is the theory that economic growth is best achieved through the encouragement of greater demand for goods and services. This is the fundamental difference between the two approaches [20]. In this paper, Supply Side is used to describe the perspective from need satisfaction, and Demand Side is used to describe the perspective from human needs.

[3] Idem.

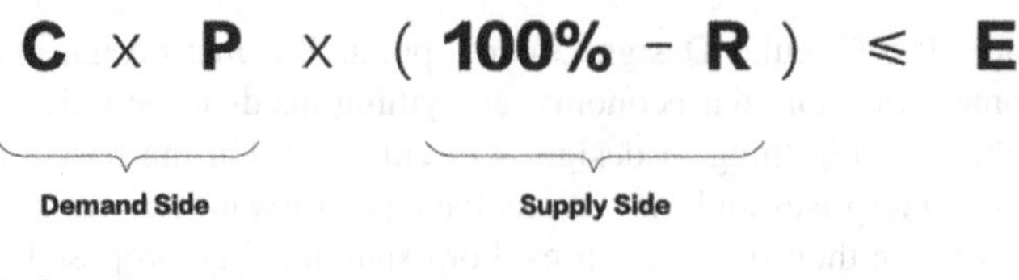

C x P x (100% - R) ⩽ E
Demand Side
Supply Side
C = Per capita material/resource consumption
P = Population base
R = Resource recycling rate
E = Environmental resource capacity

Fig. 1. A formula of describing the relationship between resource consumption and environmental capacity.

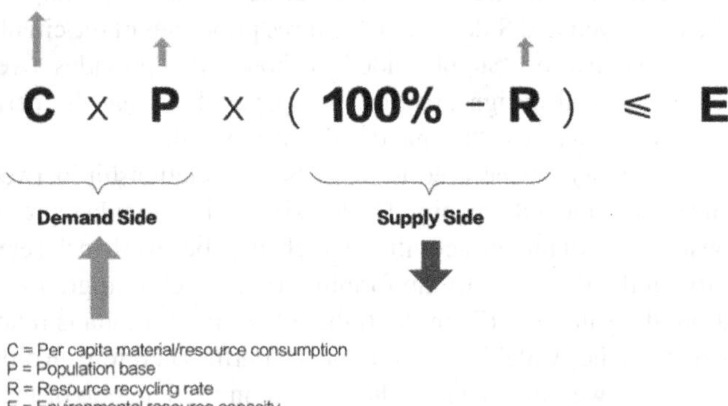

C x P x (100% - R) ⩽ E
Demand Side
Supply Side
C = Per capita material/resource consumption
P = Population base
R = Resource recycling rate
E = Environmental resource capacity

Fig. 2. An estimate of the trends that how the various (C, P, R, Demand Side and Supply Side) are developing.

From the Demand Side, there are two forces that are offsetting our efforts in the circular economy, resulting in the continuous rise of the C value (per capita material/resource consumption). On the one hand, the development of the productive force stimulates more demand [6], and more demand, coupled with the fueling of consumerism, leads to more per capita material/resource consumption. According to one calculation, humanity is using nature 1.8 times faster than our planet's biocapacity can regenerate. Another estimation is, The Ecological Footprint for the United States is 8.1 gha per person (in 2018) and global biocapacity is 1.6 gha per person (in 2018), therefore, we would need $(8.1/1.6) = 5.0$ Earths if everyone lived like Americans [7]. On the other hand, one dramatic fact is that the more efforts we make in sustainability the more "waste" we may make in return. An interesting case is car-sharing. Although the car-sharing model reduces the carbon emissions of a single passenger through sharing a car with several other users, the more attractive price also stimulates more carbon emission by additional users who originally used public transportations, so it's difficult for us to conclude whether this model is greener or less green. Another example is the LED. The invention of LED energy-saving lamps has improved the energy efficiency of incandescent lamps by 8 to 10 times. However, more energy-saving lighting solutions have also stimulated more electric consumption, because LEDs are more energy-efficient and cost-effective, the places where lighting was not so much needed tends to be illuminated in the purpose of more comfortable and convenient experience. As the result, more circular production mode will stimulate more hasty consumption decision, which may neutralize the effort on reduction in waste, pollution, energy consumption, etc.

1.2 Core Research Questions

Since the growth of human needs will offset our sustainability efforts, does that mean human needs should be curbed? It is difficult to have a simple and arbitrary answer to this question. But if we pursued further, an interesting question will be raised: **will the increase of human needs necessarily bring about large consumption of material? Or in other words, must we meet these new needs through large consumption of material?** Obviously, the answer to this question is NO. People consume materials, in many cases, not for material itself but social or emotional needs, and take this way of how needs are satisfied for granted. As consumerism encourages, if you feel lonely, buy something, if you feel happy, buy something, if you feel sad, buy something, if you want to be someone, buy something as well. Admittedly, this way of how needs are satisfied is "encouraged" for some reason, and generates into a certain lifestyle we are used to. However, there is no solid causal relationship between these new needs and the way of how needs are fulfilled. In other words, this way is not the only option we have to choose, let alone it is the problematic option in sustainability context.

Therefore, the more fundamental question lays on: **is our existing (accustomed) "the growth of human needs" and "ways of satisfaction" reasonable? How are they generated? In sustainable context, how should we manage our "increased needs" and "new ways of satisfaction"?** In order to answer these questions, we need to conduct more in-depth observation, to research and understand on the generation, types, characteristics of human needs, as well as ways of satisfaction. On this basis, it is possible for us to propose a more practical Active Design Framework and Tools for Sustainability.

2 Needs and Satisfaction

2.1 The Emergence and Development of Human Needs

Human needs are innate, which is not only a basic feature of human beings, but also the precondition of human survival and development [6]. Need is an important feature that distinguishes living things from non-living things. Schrödinger regarded life as a non-equilibrium thermodynamic system, and pointed out that natural things tend to change from order to disorder, that is, Entropy Increases. And life needs to counteract its life by constantly counteract Positive Entropy with embodying Negative Entropy [8]. That is to say, "need" is a basic feature of life, and life as a system needs to continuously intake of matter and energy from environment. From the viewpoint of Axiology, human must require nature to meet their various needs in order to survive and develop, however, nature will not satisfy human automatically, so human have to achieve this satisfaction through his own activities [9], and this is how Human Needs generated.

However, human needs are obviously different from other creatures in diversity and infinity. The diversity is reflected that human have three kinds of needs, namely material needs, social needs, and spiritual needs, while other creatures are mainly have material needs [6]. Moreover, Maslow divides human needs into five levels: physiological needs, safety needs, belongingness & love needs, esteem needs, and self-actualization [10]. The infinity is reflected in the fact that people's needs are constantly growing, and when a need is satisfied, a new need will arise. Marx attributed this to the fact that human needs are constantly changing and developing, both in quantity and quality, horizontally and vertically, and this change and development presents a rising trend [6]. In traditional Chinese philosophies such as Confucianism, Buddhism, Taoism and Wang Yangming's theory of mind, there is a similar viewpoint that human beings are thinking creature, and as long as human alive, ideas will be generated consistently, and as long as an idea is generated, new needs will appear. Defeng Wang named this characteristic as "human's infinite mind" [11].

Therefore, it is impossible to get rid of human needs, which is the property of life. Moreover, it seems unrealistic to stop the growth of human needs, the reality is that when one need is satisfied, more new needs will be generated.

2.2 Satisfaction of Human Needs

However, when we look at the current ways of human needs satisfaction, it is not difficult to realize such a phenomenon: **human needs, no matter for tangible or intangible things, are satisfied based on large consumption of material.** For instance, material is used to satisfy emotional and spiritual needs, as Consumerism encourages us shopping to relieve stress, forget loneliness, relieve grief, gain identity, and so on. And "product semantics" also shows emotional and spiritual function in physical products [12]. Another example is that material is also used to meet social needs, people purchase and occupy a lot of things in order to gain their identity. There is even an "arms race effect" that brings a lot of idleness and waste, that is, people want to occupy more not because of the material itself, but the sense of superiority. So, when the "second place" is catching up, the "first place" will occupy and consume more to consolidate the advantage of "first place".

Obviously, there are complex reasons behind these phenomena. Philips Design gave an observation and explanation which help us to understand this better. With the processes of industrialization and urbanization, people moved from countryside to the city, however, urban lifestyle was accompanied with a loss of certainty, a loss of religion, a loss of cultural status and a loss of identity. At the same time, participants in the deep competitive pressure of traditional enterprises have discovered new business opportunities, and a large number of life style brands have begun to emerge. By refining their brand image and propositions to target specific market segments with shared lifestyle aspirations and mindsets, lifestyle brands became cultural signifiers that claimed to represent and embody people's aspirations. Moreover, the modernist mindset of urban society -constantly looking toward future development and progress - It became a huge opportunity for brands to repeatedly renew the styling of their propositions to fuel consumption [13]. And the concept of "product semantics" that appeared almost at the same time gradually got more attention from industry, because it systematically expounding the products' functions which beyond the function of use. It can be concluded that under the combined effect of factors such as consumers, brands, and the capital behind it, a consumer culture that encourages "consumption more, discarding more, and frequent replacement" began to form, which directly led to the soaring of per capita material/resource consumption.

2.3 Brief Summary

Current "ways of satisfaction" (meeting all human needs through large consumption of material), generated in the early stage of the Industrial Revolution, developed in the era of Experience Economy, has its inherent logical rationality. That is, material/resources were indeed "infinite" 200 years ago, and we could not blame too much that people at that time could foresee what would happen in the world 200 years later. However, there is no logical inevitability to this "ways of satisfaction", which are just pragmatic approaches invented 200 years ago. Our modern society and its production systems were built based on these approaches, which later on formed a certain degree of "path dependence" both infrastructurally and culturally. Nowadays, confronted with unprecedented new challenges of sustainable development, we need to go back to the origin of the problem and reconsider "the growth of human needs" and "ways of satisfaction" that we are accustomed to, which may contain opportunities for solutions.

3 Human Needs Satisfaction Area (HN-SA) Model

3.1 Deconstruction of Human Needs and Ways of Satisfaction

In order to better understand the relationship between Human Needs (Demand Side) and how they are satisfied (Supply Side) in the perspective of material consumption, this paper tries to deconstruct them base on "material dependence".

Human Needs (Demand Side). In order to better understand the relationship between needs and material consumption, this paper classifies human needs based on material dependence, and proposes Material-Necessary Needs and Material-Unnecessary Needs (see left part of Fig. 3):

- **Material-Necessary Needs (MNN).** MNN represents the needs that must be met through material consumption. Material consumption is a sufficient & necessary condition for satisfaction.
- **Material-Unnecessary Needs (MUN).** MUN represents those needs that do not necessarily have to be met through material consumption. Material consumption is optional and what really needs in MUN is the intangible experience rather than a tangible substance.

Taking meals as an example, eating for filling is MNN, we eat because our body needs energy to operate. However, the need of eating in Michelin restaurant includes both the needs of MNN and MUN, because we eat not only for energy, but also exquisite taste experience, ceremonial dining experience, or a certain identity and lifestyle, etc. And the need of eating out-of-season food or long-distance imported food are mainly consisted of MUN, because the real need is not the food itself, but the intangible experience such as curiosity, culture, identity, etc. If we compare MNN and MUN with Maslow's hierarchy of needs, we will find that each level of needs in Maslow's theory is including MNN and MUN (see left part of Fig. 3).

How are Human Needs satisfied (Demand Side). In order to better understand the relationship between ways of satisfaction and material consumption (whether and how), this paper proposes the concept of Satisfaction Area (see right part of Fig. 3). Based on Yongqi Lou's NHCAS Four systems[4], we divided the Satisfaction Area into four systems from the perspective of material dependence, called RMHCS Four systems: Raw Material System, Material System, Human System, Cyber System. Some main relationships among these systems can be concluded as:

- The bottom two systems are material, and the top two systems are immaterial;
- The Raw Material system is the material basis of the four systems, and also represents the total amount of available material and resource on the earth;
- The material and resource of the Raw Material system can be processed and transferred into the Material system, and the Raw Material plus Material systems provide the necessary material support for the Human and Cyber systems at the same time, such as the hardware infrastructure to maintain the operation of the Human and Cyber systems.

3.2 HN-SA Model

Based on the previous analysis, this paper proposes **Human Needs – Satisfaction Area Model** (HN-SA Model, see Fig. 4) in an attempt to more comprehensively and clearly understanding of the relationship between human needs and how they are met, and to explore possible solutions to global sustainable challenges. The left part of the model, called Human Needs (demand-side perspective), refers to the types, total amount and trends of human needs. Based on the previous discussion, we divide human needs into two parts: MNN and MUN, and the height of the color block represents the total amount of needs. The right part of the model, called Satisfaction Area (supply-side perspective), is where we meet these human needs.

In this HN-SA Model, it is obviously that MNN is mainly satisfied in Raw Material and Material systems. Take the example of eating again, "fullness" is a MNN in the need of eating, and "fullness" can be satisfied in Raw Material system with natural food or in Material system with processed foods. Then "eating with someone you like" is a certain kind of MUN that can be satisfied in the Human system, that is, the key need is being with the person you like no matter what you eat. This MUN also can be satisfied in the Cyber system, that is, "eating with someone you like" does not necessarily have to be physically "together", nor even "eat", but can be a digital emotional connection through information, service design, etc. Of course, this MUN may also be satisfied

[4] Yongqi Lou 's NHCAS Four systems: Nature System, Artificial System, Human System, Cyber System [15].

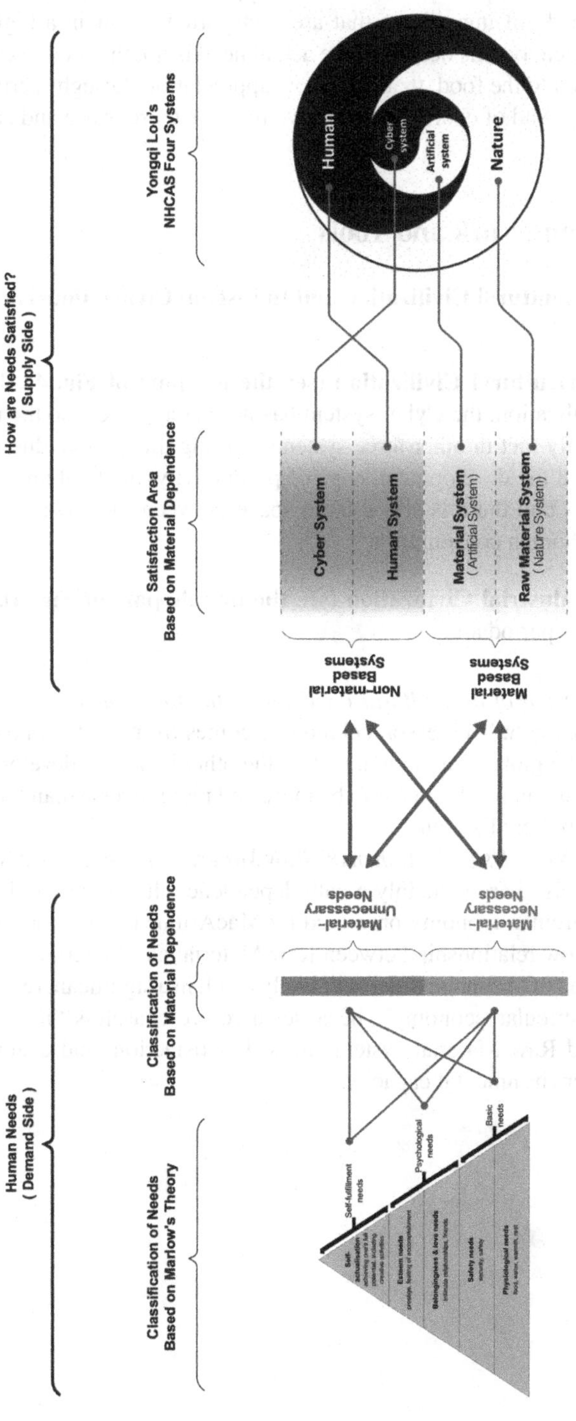

Fig. 3. This diagram indicates the interaction between Demand Side (Human Needs) and Supply Side (How are Needs Satisfied). The left part is Demand Side, there are two ways of classification of needs (Maslow's hierarchy of needs [10] and Material Dependence), and the relationship between them. The right part is Supply Side, four systems (as Satisfaction Area) is proposed based on material dependence, developed from Yongqi Lou's NHCAS Four systems[14].

in the Material system. For example, in order to show appreciation, people may order a lot of exquisite food made of ingredients that are transported by air in a high-end restaurant, or order too much. on this occasion, the actual need is not the food itself, but an intangible thing attached to the food, that is to show appreciation through sacrificing more (consumption more). And of course, the negative result is more waste and carbon emission.

4 Active Design Framework and Tools

4.1 Understanding Agricultural Civilization and Industrial Civilization Through HN-SA Model

The N-SA model of Agricultural Civilization (see the top part of Fig. 4). In the period of agricultural civilization, the Cyber system has not yet appeared, so the needs of human beings are mainly met in other three systems. During this period, due to the total global population and the development stage of productivity, the total amount of human needs is not large, and there is still a large space between the environmental capacity of the earth and human consumption.

The HN-SA model of Industrial Civilization (see the middle part of Fig. 4). The main characteristics of this period are:

1. *Compared with the period of agricultural civilization, the total amount of human needs has increased sharply.* The reason behind this comes from, on the one hand, the rapid increase of the global population, and on the other hand, the development of productivity. And human needs appear to be more and more diverse than those in the period of agricultural civilization.
2. *A large number of MUNs seek satisfaction in the Raw Material and Material systems.* As the previous analysis, there is mainly a path dependence. It is intuitive that the Three Principles of circular economy promoted by MacArthur Foundation mainly discuss the material flow relationship between Raw Material and Material systems. As we know, neglection of "Demand Side" will likely result in a significant reduction in our efforts on a "circular economy", because there are ceaseless "inclux" of needs in Material and Raw Material systems to seek satisfaction, and eventually may overwhelm our environmental capacity.

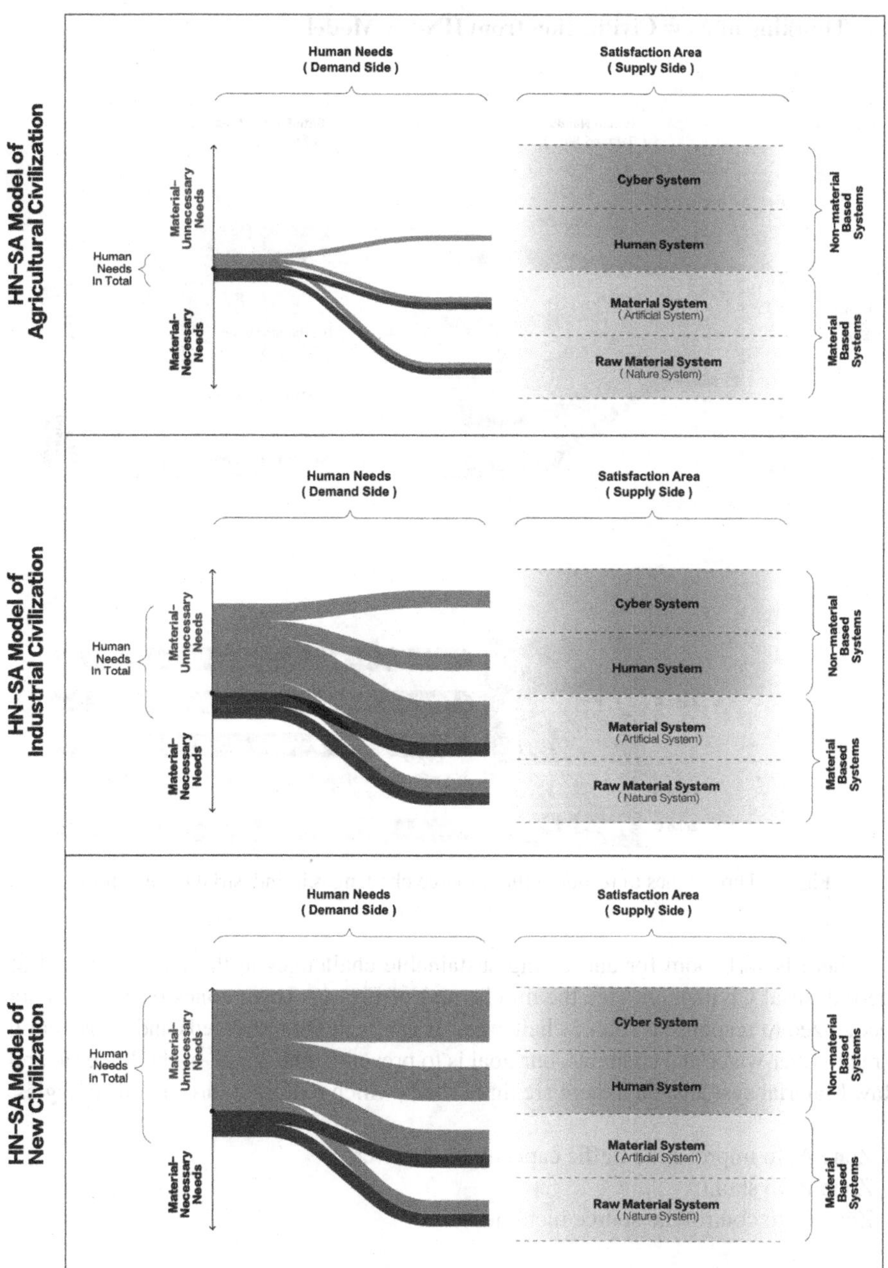

Fig. 4. HN-SA Model of Agricultural Civilization, Industrial Civilization and New Civilization that desired.

4.2 Thinking of New Civilization from HN-SA Model

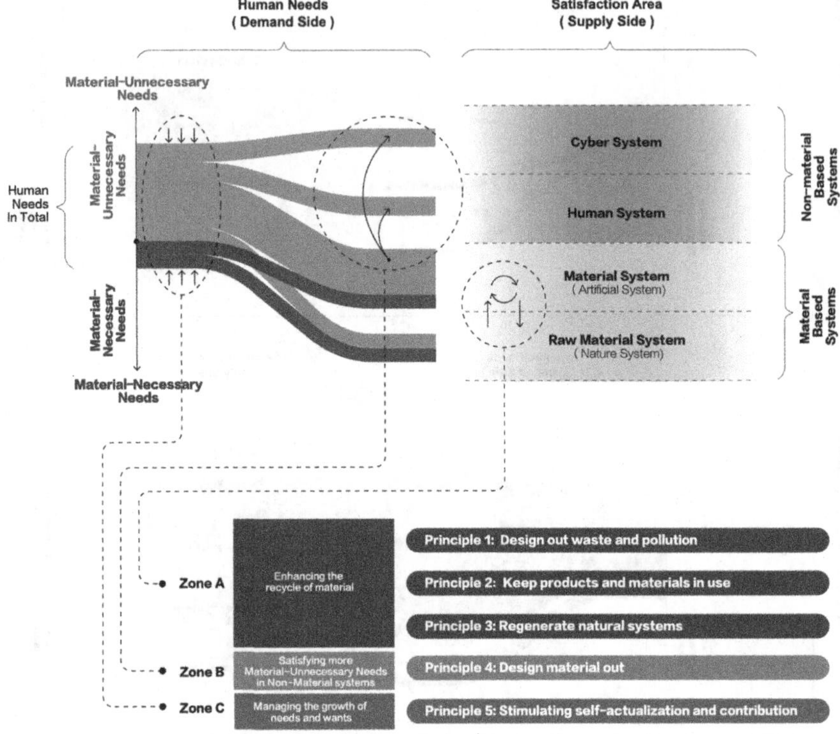

Fig. 5. Three zones to response the resource challenges in Industrial Civilization.

There is still room for addressing sustainable challenges in the HN-SA model of the Industrial Civilization (see the middle part of Fig. 4). Three zones (see Fig. 5) are recognized to response resource challenges. If we liken Human Needs and Satisfaction Area to river water and channels, our goal is to prevent "dike burst" of the Material and Raw Material systems, then there are three zones which represent three main strategies:

- Zone A: to improve the traffic capacity of the river;
- Zone B: to shunt;
- Zone C: to control the source increment.

Obviously, our current efforts in circular economy mainly focus on Zone A, improving the traffic capacity of the river. Therefore, the focus of this research will be to expand the existing circular economy design principles based on the HN-SA Model, taking into account the influence from the Demand Side and the Supply Side.

The Main Goal of Zone A is to Enhance the Recycle of Material. And it corresponds to the three principles of circular economy promoted by the MacArthur Foundation:

- Principle 1st: design out waste and pollution;
- Principle 2nd: keep products and material in use;
- Principle 3rd: Regenerate natural systems.

The main goal of Zone B is Satisfying more Material-Unnecessary Needs in Non-Material Based Systems. And the corresponding design principles are:

- Principle 4th: Design Material Out.

Specifically, within this zone, we need to rethink those MUNs that are integrated into human needs, strip them out, and explore new ways of satisfaction in the Human and Cyber systems. Take clothing industry as an example, people buy a lot of clothes, most of which are worn only a few times on average. One survey of 2,000 women in the UK found respondents on average wore an item seven times. Other researchers have found that some women wear an item just once because they don't want to repeat an outfit in a photo posted to social media [16]. With the development of 5G technology and NFT technology, virtual fashion is a viable alternative. According to Principle 4th (Design Material Out), designing for intangible alternatives may be an emerging subdivision of design discipline, and as the result, "**Non-Material Product Competitiveness Model**" will be needed to guide and assess the development and design of Non-Material products.

If "Product Semantics" is more about how we can add emotional factors to Tangible products to satisfy MUN, then "Non-Material Product Competitiveness Model" is about how we can strip the Tangible material from products. By following this logic, all products can be rethought and redesigned, that is, **how to design material out when the need is MUN**.

The Main Goal of Zone C is to Manage the Growth of Needs and Wants. And the corresponding design principles are:

- Principle 5th: Stimulating self-actualization and contribution.

Specifically, the focus within this zone is the management of needs, making sure the total amount of needs doesn't grow too fast, at least not faster than what we can handle. Since the growth of total human needs mainly depends on the total global population and per capita needs (see Fig. 1), on the one hand, we need to prudently manage the global population growth, which is also what many governments are trying to do, on the other hand, we need to manage the growth of per capita needs.

In the previous analysis, we find out that the growth of human needs seems to be a necessity (because of "human infinite heart" and etc.), but this does not mean that it is inevitable that we will eventually break through the environmental capacity of the earth. Maslow's theory of needs and Chinese traditional philosophy actually contain the possible solution to this problem, that is, to awaken people's thinking about the meaning of life, and to obtain the satisfaction of self-actualization from giving and contribution, rather than continuous occupying and consumption to obtain a short-term satisfaction. The short-term satisfaction disappears quickly and make people continue to seek the next satisfaction through occupying and consumption as soon as possible, which is also the underlying logic of consumerism. Qing Liu mentioned in his book that "after 1850, the frequency of the word 'alone' has decreased significantly, but the frequency of the word 'lonely' has increased significantly. The answer given by big data is that although modern people contact more and more frequent, but people feel more and more lonely" [17]. In essence, this reflects the **collective "lack of love"** of people in this era, the lack of being cared for, being understood, being loved, and so on. **The key MUN in this context is "feeling of being loved"**, but with the prevalence of consumerism, we are only in the illusion of "being loved" surrounded by flooded commodities. Therefore the main purpose of Principle 5th is to **create more love**, especially with design and innovation.

Achieving the goals in Zone C requires people to make collective behavioral changes, and there are several challenges need to be overcame. For example, one of the challenges is "path dependency", similar to design fixation [18], people will also have behavior fixation. Another challenge is the capital and economic system behind consumerism. The winner takes all game rule in these systems is a double-edged sword, the positive side is that it greatly stimulates human creativity while the negative side is that this system "encourages" greed. There is a critical statement that "capital is greedy", then why capital tend to be greedy? Since for capital the rule is "appreciation or death", in other words, "either greedy or death". All the people, no matter rich or poor, in a system which seems to be a zero-sum game, tended to be unhappy and unsatisfied eventually.

Take these into consideration, social innovation design will become more and more important as an emerging sub-field of design discipline. Ezio Manzini pointed out that this is an era of everyone participating in design, and he invited design elites, grassroots activists, design educators, government or business decision makers to participate in the formation of social innovation design solutions [19]. In the context of Principle 5th, another significance of this "era of everyone participating in design" is **to replace occupying and consumption with giving and contribution** to meet the inevitable growth of human needs. In other words, everyone is both a generator of needs and a provider of satisfaction. This may a long-term strategy to neutralize the inevitable and unstoppable growth of human needs.

Through the efforts in the three zones A, B, and C, this paper outlines a new and desirable civilization with HN-SA model (see the bottom part of Fig. 4).

5 Conclusions

Based on the material perspective, this study proposes the HN-SA model, which takes into account the influence of the Supply Side and the Demand Side, allowing us to see the source of sustainable challenges and the zones of problem solving more comprehensively. With the help of this model, the current popular Three Principles of circular economy are expanded, and an Active Design Framework containing three goals and five principles is proposed. they are:

Zone A: to enhance the recycle of material

- Principle 1st: design out waste and pollution;
- Principle 2nd: keep products and material in use;
- Principle 3rd: Regenerate natural systems.

Zone B: to satisfying more Material-Unnecessary Needs in Non-Material Based Systems

- Principle 4th: Design Material Out.

Zone C: to manage the growth of needs and wants

- Principle 5th: Stimulating self-actualization and contribution.

However, the limitation of this study is that more tools and strategies need to be proposed based on these Five Principles to make this Active Design Framework more practical. These will be the next step of further study on this topic.

References

1. Circular economy introduction. https://ellenmacarthurfoundation.org/topics/circular-economy-introduction/overview. Accessed 11 Feb 2022
2. The Circular Economy in Detail. https://archive.ellenmacarthurfoundation.org/explore/the-circular-economy-in-detail. Accessed 11 Feb 2022
3. The circular design guide. https://www.circulardesignguide.com/. Accessed 11 Feb 2022
4. 10 PRINCIPLES OF CIRCULAR DESIGN. https://www.nikecirculardesign.com/guides/MiniGuide.pdf. Accessed 11 Feb 2022
5. Circular by design: the 5 principles to make it happen. https://blog.dssmith.com/circular-by-design-the-5-principles-to-make-it-happen. Accessed 11 Feb 2022
6. The Central Committee of the Communist Party of China. Selected Works of Marx and Engels. People's Publishing House (1995)
7. How many Earths? How many countries? https://www.overshootday.org/how-many-earths-or-countries-do-we-need/. Accessed 11 Feb 2022
8. Schrodinger, E.: What is life? The physical aspect of the living cell. Am. Nat. **25 suppl 1**(785), 25–41 (1967)
9. Li, D.: Axiology. China Renmin University Press, Beijing (1987)
10. Maslow, A.H.: A theory of human motivation. Psychol. Rev. **50**(4), 370 (1943)

11. Wang, D.: Wang Yangming's theory of mind and its modern meaning. https://www.bilibili.com/video/BV15Z4y1R76Z?from=search&seid=8752471396666865783&spm_id_from=333.337.0.0. Accessed 11 Feb 2022
12. Krippendorff, K., Butter, R.: Product semantics-exploring the symbolic qualities of form, Dep. Pap., p. 40 (1984)
13. Brand, R., Rocchi, S.: Rethinking value in a changing landscape and business transformation. Design, no. March 2015, p. 30 (2011)
14. Lou, Y.: The idea of environmental design revisited. Des. Issues **35**(1), 23–35 (2019). https://doi.org/10.1162/desi_a_00518
15. Lou, Y.: Opening keynote--crossing: HCI, design and sustainability. In: Proceedings of the 33rd Annual ACM Conference Extended Abstracts on Human Factors in Computing Systems, pp. 805–806 (2015)
16. What's the average number of times that a person wears a specific piece of clothing? https://www.ngpf.org/blog/question-of-the-day/qod-whats-the-average-number-of-times-that-a-person-wears-a-specific-piece-of-clothing/. Accessed 11 Feb 2022
17. Liu, Q.: Lectures On Modern Western Thought. New Star Press, 2021
18. Jansson, D.G., Smith, S.M.: Design fixation. Des. Stud. **12**(1), 3–11 (1991)
19. Manzini, E.: Design, When Everybody Designs: An Introduction to Design for Social Innovation. MIT Press, Cambridge (2015)
20. Demand-Side vs. Supply-Side Economics (2022). https://study.com/learn/lesson/demand-side-vs-supply-side-economics-theories-differences.html

Visual Perception in the On-Site Environment Under the Overlap of Civilizations

Zhongmu Liu(✉)

Tsinghua University, Beijing, China
zhongmu-19@mails.tsinghua.edu.cn

Abstract. In the face of carbon-based space under the impact of silicon-based civilization, environment design needs to keep pace with the times to better adapt to wicked problems. In this paper, the theory of the on-site environment is proposed to address these demands. The cognitive rules and mechanisms of the on-site subject and the environment are studied by updating the understanding of the relationship between the on-site subject and the object. Through experiments in neuroscience and cognitive psychology, this paper focuses on visual working memory and defines the perceptual objects of the on-site environment based on the principle of topological perception to establish the correspondence between visual cognition and environmental elements in the on-site environment. Combining the theories of architecture and urban planning, using game theory and logical computational reasoning, the nonlinear design problems in the on-site environment are linearly transformed into a spatial coordinate system. The game tree is drawn based on the network of cognitive and environmental factors, and the appropriate game theory model for matrix strategy analysis is selected based on the demand relationships, which derives the design methodology for the on-site environment. This study complements the ontology, epistemology, and methodology of design for future environment construction and forms a new design paradigm that provides a theoretical basis for subsequent design practice and management.

Keywords: Civilization overlap · On-site environment · Visual cognition

1 Introduction

The human habitat faces an increasing number of wicked problems. Design strategies guided solely by Aristotelian cognitive models (inductive experience) are becoming increasingly difficult to address many of the challenges arising in the information explosion era. The overlapping evolution of different civilizations is one of the wicked problems of the built environment.

Silicon-based civilizations represented by the internet, artificial intelligence, and virtual reality technology are challenging our perceptions. People who grow up in virtual space gradually no longer use traditional spatial logic to complete their connections with the matter, and the pandemic era has deepened their reliance on virtual worlds so that many carbon-based spaces have shifted from prosperity to decay. Mankind should not

P.-L. P. Rau (Ed.): HCII 2022, LNCS 13311, pp. 51–69, 2022.
https://doi.org/10.1007/978-3-031-06038-0_4

indulge in the grandeur of silicon-based civilization. Design should guide people to balance the behavioral activities between silicon-based space and carbon-based space, encouraging humans to embrace the universe's civilization. As a cross-discipline, design for built environments currently lacks a core knowledge system. The inertia of borrowing theories from other disciplines has led to the inability of design to make systematic and efficient decisions when faced with the network of demands from many stakeholders, and unable to cope with the environmental design of the overlapping silicon-based and carbon-based civilizations, even as more and more design is moving toward silicon-based space. When there is a contradiction between the theories of various disciplines, design studies could not use the core theories of the upper echelons to weigh and decide. At present, the practice of design could not truly achieve the sustainable development of the environment and human beings, and the opposing monocentric theory of being purely human-centered or environment-centered is no longer applicable to the development needs of the times. Based on the vision of the future environment and the Gaia view of Bruno Latour, this paper proposes the theory of the on-site environment to face the possible crisis of the future environment and tries to find a way to balance the carbon-based space and the silicon-based space through the concept of on-site and the path of cognitive rules and mechanisms.

Vision is one of the main senses of humans in built environments, and information expression is critical to design in the interaction between the environment and humans. However, the visual cognition process of humans is poorly understood, which leads to many designs that are not suitable for the present environment. Based on the theory of cognitive science, this paper analyzes the existing cognitive experiments, combines environmental objects and topological principles, and transplants the basic process and objects of visual cognition of the on-site environment by analogy simulation. Then, starting with visual memory, which is the core of the visual cognition process, the basic unit of visual working memory in an on-site environment is constructed based on the information processing process (cognitive process) in cognitive psychology, and the perceptual objects in the on-site environment are defined according to the topological perception theory and related models, and the cognitive system of visual working memory in the on-site environment is illustrated. The experiments were conducted by recording visual behaviors with eye-tracking apparatus, recording physiological stimulation data with fMRI and EEG, constructing a test environment with VR, AR, MR, and wearable devices, and analyzing spatial data and statistics with GIS, DEPTHMAP, and SPSS, to build a topological network of visual cognition in the on-site environment.

Finally, using game theory and logical calculation theory to integrate the experiences of designers and stakeholders with related research, the on-site environment design strategy based on visual cognition is concluded. In this way, the visual cognitive logic, forming principle, and symbiotic network relationship of the on-site environment are clarified. This study complements the basic theory of spatial cognition in design and forms a new design paradigm with the process of cognition, demand, decision-making, and transformation. It refines the ontology of environment design and updates its epistemology and methodology. This is conducive not only to design practice and management but also to future social and environmental development.

2 Background

2.1 Wicked Problems in the Dawn of the Fourth Industrial Evolution

Humans are in the midst of the fourth industrial revolution, which is exponentially faster than previous industrial revolutions. New technologies and the convergence of existing technologies are driving social, economic, and cultural changes [1]. The physical world is changing rapidly, and the human senses are gradually being enhanced. Building on the knowledge systems of the previous three industrial revolutions, and combining the cluster strengths of ICT, CPS, biotechnology, and emerging technologies, the new systems of the fourth industrial revolution have driven an intelligent transformation of manufacturing. As could be seen from today's new paradigm of economic complexity, under the impact of the fourth industrial revolution, characterized by clean energy and integrated technologies, the growth in production and manufacturing brought about by explosive technological change has boosted all aspects of human and social development [2], as well as the creative destruction effects of intensive innovation competition [3] and mass unemployment caused by the algorithmic revolution and intelligent mechanical automation. These have widened the gap between rich and poor, created spatial disparities, and resilient demand [4]; creating data redundancy, privacy breaches, and truth crises caused by massive amounts of data from the Internet of Things and the Internet [5]; new ethical issues arising from technologies such as artificial intelligence, robotics, and genetic engineering [6]; cognitive and social barriers due to smart devices and new technologies such as AR, VR, and MR [7]; high-quality services such as convenient transportation, delivery, and housekeeping supported by new technologies are contributing to the complex social problems that are accelerating the weakening of people's dependence on families and traditional organizations, and even the disintegration of certain stable social units.

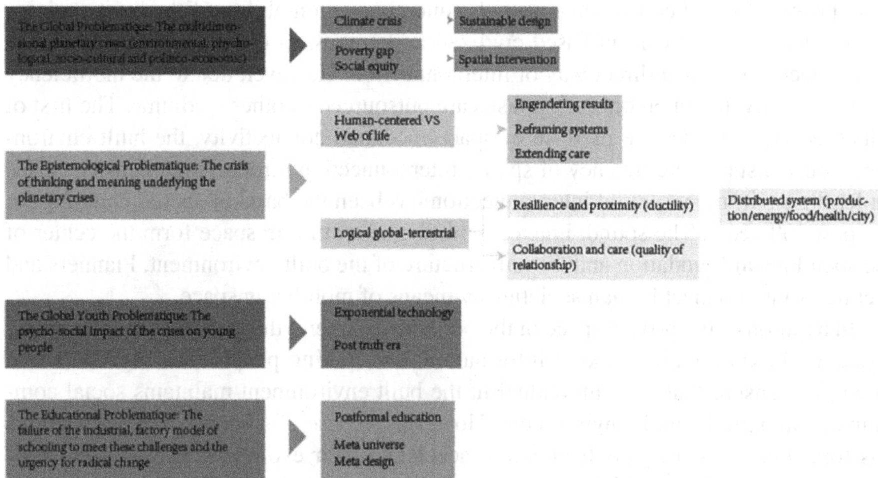

Fig. 1. Design methodologies that attempt to respond to the core issues of the 21st Century

Overall, humanity today faces four core issues: the planetary crisis, centered on the environmental crisis and social equity; the cognitive issues behind the planetary crisis; the mental health implications of the crisis for people; and post-formal education, where patterns of education urgently need to change [8]. There have been a few attempts to use design to respond to these problems in built environments (see Fig. 1), but no systematic theory has incorporated the piecemeal ideas and experiences learned from practice. There is a lack of research on local cognition in practice, epistemology needs to be updated, disciplinary barriers between methodologies still remain, and approaches based on local problems have limited impact on solving wicked problems.

2.2 The Interconnected Impact of the Civilizational Overlap on the Built Environment

In the context of the fourth industrial revolution, the new infrastructure of digital infrastructure and the ecology of the digital industry would be an important condition for the transformation of social production methods. With the rapid development and integration of new information technologies such as artificial intelligence, blockchain, cloud computing, 5G, and big data, today's society is developing into a highly integrated world of physics and digital, online and offline, virtual and real [2]. Artificial intelligence and the online world of silicon-based matter, created through human intelligence, are also making a huge difference to human life. Young people who grow up in virtual space no longer use traditional spatial logic to complete their connections with the matter. Many public spaces in the built environment have gradually moved from prosperity to decay. This is not a simple economic problem but a profound civilizational problem – the impact of silicon-based civilization on carbon-based civilization.

The built environment now threatens to be largely replaced by the Internet as an interconnected task [9]. Compared with the huge magnitude, rapid response and hyperspace links provided by silicon-based space, the interconnection ability of the built environment is too low. In a carbon-based civilization, humans, as carbon-based individuals, face to face is the most direct way of interconnection. However, due to the inefficiency of connectivity, the interconnection tasks are outsourced to other mediums. The first of which is space. Under the premise of space-mediated connectivity, the built environment must ensure the efficiency of spatial interconnection through high density. Space under the environment-based interconnection has been the basis of spatial planning for the past 100 years. The sound, image, symbol, and texture in space form the center of the sociological foundation and formal structure of the built environment. Planners and architects interconnect human societies by means of mobilizing space.

In addition to the private space in the built environment, the three tasks of the public space are linking matter, linking information, and linking people (see Fig. 2). These three links ensure that each individual in the built environment maintains social communication with the built environment. However, the rise of silicon-based civilizations has forced carbon-based civilizations to accelerate their evolution. The built environment has always been a high-end organizing hub and deductive platform for human carbon-based civilization. The rising silicon-based civilization is quietly stripping the built environment of its long-held central place in the organization of civilization.

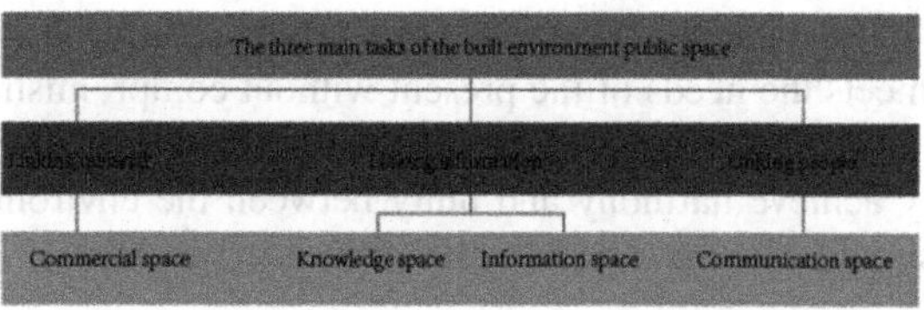

Fig. 2. The three main tasks of public space in the built environment in the context of environment-based interconnection

The second medium outsourced by human society is paper, that is, paper-based interconnection. Mainly refers to the interconnection through externalized symbols, media, such as books, periodicals, symbols, etc. The third is the current experience of silicon-based interconnection, through the network-mediated connectivity. It replaces the traditional intelligence of interconnections based on the built environment. The rapid rise of interconnected species has brought ecological disasters to the once-balanced outsourcing interconnection structure, which has caused part of the built environment to gradually lose its traditional value of existence, thus prompting the built environment to improve its iterative evolution rate.

In the context of silicon-based civilization, interconnection with matter no longer relies on the carbon-based interface, the physical space of the built environment gradually loses its position as the main medium of social interconnection, which leads to the rapid decline of commercial space, and the interconnection of people and information is independent of carbon-based space. Thus, the built environment has ushered in an era of redefinition and evolution.

2.3 Resilience Demand for Future Environment in the Post-pandemic Era

In addition to the overlap of civilizations that has hit the issue of environment interconnections, the climate crisis and the sudden external shock of the pandemic faced by the fourth industrial revolution has also forced dramatic changes in the way humans produce, live, and govern. They put forwards more demands on human habitat, from large urban groups to small building spaces, requiring more functions to deal with unexpected public safety events. To achieve efficient utilization, there is also a timely adjustment of spatial functions according to the changes in space and time for rational allocation of resources. For the environment to be resilient, our design should reserve a certain elastic interval to form space immunity to deal with the crisis.

Research on urban resilience has gradually emerged in recent years, discussing the basic concepts, related characteristics [10], dimensions of resilience and ways to build it [11], engineering techniques, evaluation methods, and design strategies [12].

In addition to the built environment disciplines, in the field of design, there is Ezio Manzini's sustainable social innovation design and Fabrizio Ceschin's research on the evolution of sustainable design [13], which are representative responses to environmental issues.

The definition of sustainable development clearly states that it is anthropocentric development that meets the needs of the present without compromising the survival of future generations [14]. However, practice has proved that a human-centered perspective could not truly achieve harmony and unity between the environment and human development, we should take into account all stakeholders instead.

2.4 Lack of Core Theory and Cognitive Reconstruction

For a long time, the related disciplines concerning the built environment have been supported by relatively systematic theories, such as architecture and urban planning. However, environment design, as a cross-discipline, lacks its core theory and rigorous knowledge framework, and more often borrows theories and methods from other disciplines to solve problems. When it comes to research and design, there are often incompatibilities between different theories, and the absence of core theories makes it difficult to judge which method is more suitable when there is a conflict between theories. It is also easy to make errors of omission or inefficiency, so there is insufficient scientific rigor. Therefore, environment design is not competitive in the built environment disciplines, and as a subject that could participate in both macro planning and micro design does not play to its strengths.

Nowadays, the focus of our research has shifted from the environment and people to the relationships between them. As a result, the study of the human cognitive processes, rules, and mechanisms in the environment has become extremely important. We could supplement the discipline's ontology with the advantages of cross-discipline. According to Studer et al.'s study of ontology [15], we first need to abstract and model the concepts of some phenomena in the objective world within our disciplinary research field, define the research connotation of environment and cognition, and capture the knowledge of relevant fields. The resulting concepts are then clearly defined under unified constraints, and commonly accepted terminology within the field is identified. And the obtained theories and models are then formatted at different levels to ensure professional readability. Finally, the interrelationships between the terms in the set of recognized concepts are further clarified to provides a common understanding of knowledge in this domain (see Fig. 3).

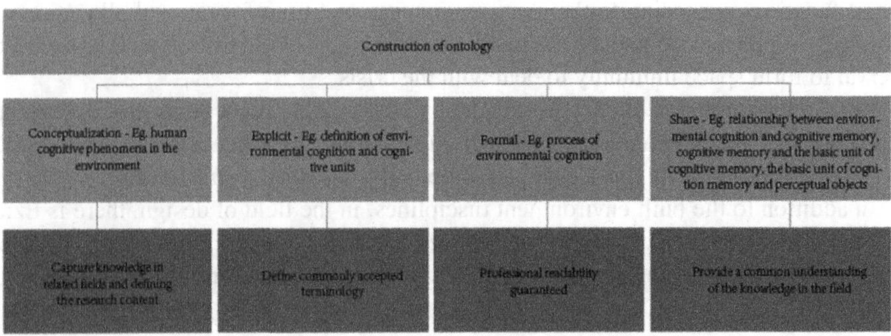

Fig. 3. The construction of ontology in environmental design, taking environment cognition as an example

Design activities carried out in response to wicked problems indicate that our design paradigm is about to undergo a new change (see Fig. 4). For example, the community creation project NICE2035 conducted by Lou Yongqi et al. in Shanghai shows that social innovation could come from communities and the post-pandemic era is upending the relationship between centers and functional zoning. We might need to re-understand the value of boundaries and hybrid functions. For sustainable urban renewal, meta-design suggests that while the design of the past was for production and replication, the design of the future might be a reorganization in search of relationships and connections. It is also implied in Lee Kaifu et al.'s *AI2041* that the future narrative expression might be highly integrated and customized, and that design needs to pay attention to hybridization and a sense of boundaries. At a time when the inventory of carbon-based space is being renewed and the incremental development of silicon-based space is taking place, these practical experiences and perspectives remind us that our perception of the world is in urgent need of updating.

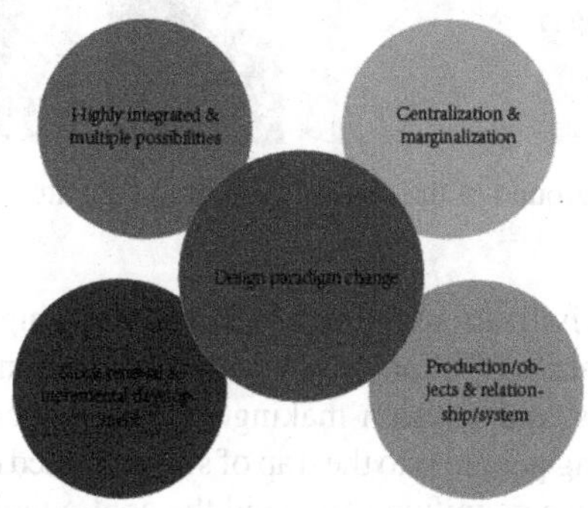

Fig. 4. New trends in a design paradigm change

3 Exploring the Future Environment

Facing the opportunities and challenges of the fourth industrial revolution, the future environment would gradually usher in the era of new infrastructure. While confronting the impact of the post-pandemic era externally and the reorganization of industry discourse internally, new theories are needed to provide a reference basis for the formulation of systems and management to adapt to the burgeoning technological innovation. In essence, the development of technology has far outpaced the establishment of institutional standards and norms. To match this speed, humans should propose epistemologies and methodologies for future environment design that conform to the rules of natural development. Combining the context of the post-pandemic era and the intersection of civilizations, the concept of Anwensenheit in German philosophy is introduced to envision the future environment, and the idea of on-site is raised here (see Fig. 5), which means a direct interaction between humans and silicon-carbon based space.

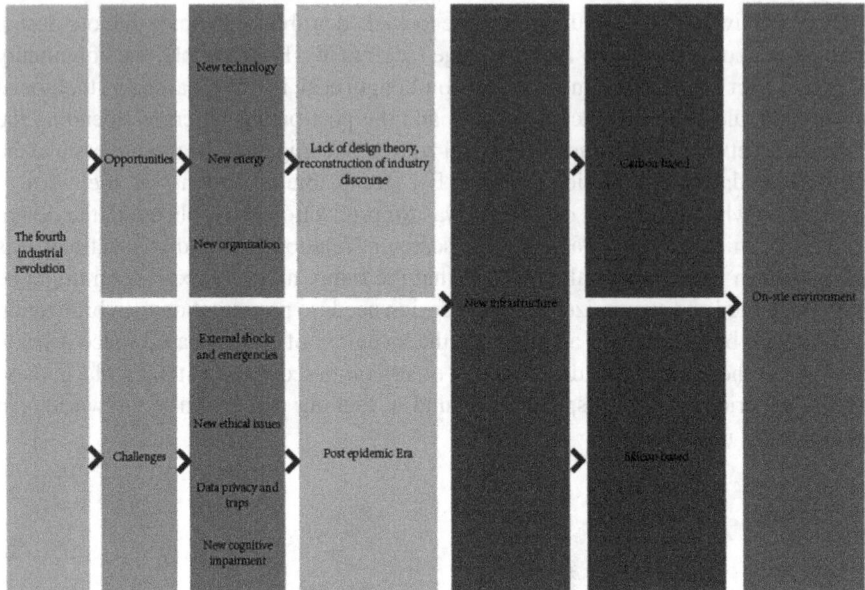

Fig. 5. Background of the construction of the on-site environment

Under the overlap of civilizations, silicon-based space is highly mixed with carbon-based space, and vast amounts of information cause obscuration, which influences people's cognition, judgments, and decision-making behaviors. It could also cause damage to the environment by luring people into the trap of silicon-based civilization indefinitely. To explore real and effective cognition and avoid the contradiction between large areas of extreme inequality and small areas of extreme heterogeneity caused by high integration and customization, we need to achieve the state of demasking through on-site interaction, and that is the reason why the future environment is referred to as the "on-site environment." As mentioned in the background, the exponential growth of the fourth industrial revolution has created wicked problems and urgently reduced human response times. The current megatrend is that humanity is immersed in a virtual world built by silicon-based civilizations. Although the overlap of civilizations provides a buffer against environmental crises and pandemics, it is not enough to allow us to expand outward and embrace cosmic civilizations. Building resilience in future environments is therefore critical to the daily functioning of society and its ability to withstand and recover from natural disasters, pandemics, and cyber threats.

In the rampant rise of silicon-based civilization, the future built environment should decisively relinquish its interconnective function of matter and information, and focus on more effectively operating interpersonal interconnected organizations. How could carbon-based space make design choices for construction, protection, and sustainable development under the impact of silicon-based civilization? How to achieve spatial Nash equilibrium through the interaction of environmental behaviors after cognitive enhancement? This series of complex issues urgently requires a more comprehensive and in-depth knowledge of the built environment. To address the impact of the new civilization, it is essential to clarify the cognitive process and capture the rules of cognition to understand the interaction between the built environment and cognition. Therefore, we should reconstruct the built environment based on carbon and silicone, highlight it from the oversupply of matters and information, let it become an active medium for interpersonal organization, increase the local meaning and depth of it systematically, enrich the living pixels of the space, make the built environment an arena to focus more on human society's living events. Public events in carbon-based space could be propagated more efficiently through silicon-based media, and the vitality of carbon-based space could be enhanced by silicon-based means.

Since human societies depend on ecosystem services to meet major biological needs and provide the resources for economic and technological development, future environmental concerns should not stop with humans alone. We could emphasize social justice and human needs, but we should not see ourselves as a separate center. Instead, the network of connections should be outlined in the context of humanity and the environment, taking into account all stakeholders involved. Inspired by Ezio Manzini's design for the web of life, the on-site environment introduces Bruno Latour's philosophy of local-global-terrestrial. The construction of an on-site environment should be the design of environments or systems that make possible the emergence of good interaction, reconstructing existing space and creating hybrid functional space based on the concept of chronotypes to embody the care for the web of life [16].

Therefore, from the perspective of design, we could give full play to the advantages of interdisciplinarity. Taking environmental science as background, medicine as the base, psychology as the organizational bridge, expanding the study of cognitive mechanisms, proposing a more systematic and macroscopic approach to sustainable design, so as to reasonably intervene spatially in the environment, increase spatial resilience, and improve the relationship quality of the environment, objects, and human. To this end, this paper proposes the on-site environment theory to address the construction of the future environment and the strategy of wicked problems.

4 On-Site Environment Theory

4.1 Definition

An on-site environment is a place where multiple on-site subjects (humans, animals, plants, microbes, and other active things) are on-site joined with on-site objects (inanimate objects in the environment) through one or more on-site interfaces (carbon-based interfaces, silicon-based interfaces, hybrid mediated interfaces) (see Fig. 6).

The core of constructing the on-site environment is to enable the space to acquire on-site resilience (buffer capacity to cope with sudden public crisis events or resilience to meet the concession and mixed needs of space-time bodies) through the on-site game. This requires sorting out the functional demands of the on-site subject and the interaction with the on-site object to form a network of needs-interaction relations and making design decisions of the on-site object elements based on the cognitive rules of the on-site subject with the goal of sustainable symbiosis and perpetual development.

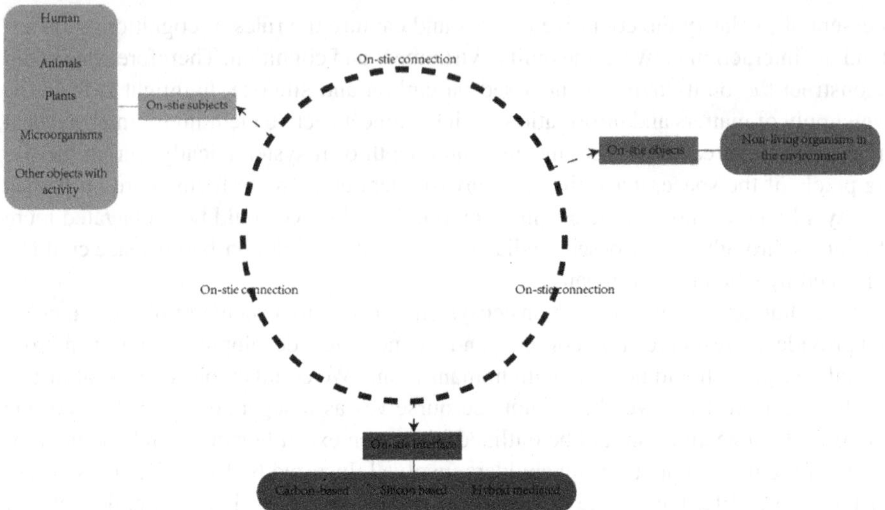

Fig. 6. The basic composition of the on-site environment

4.2 Connotation

The concept of the on-site environment is based on the development of "Anwensenheit" in German philosophy and the Gaia view of Bruno Latour [17]. It could be used for the study of environmental cognition, as well as for spatial and environmental design strategies, so it could provide both an experimental basis and a theoretical framework for epistemology and methodology. The on-site environment is a sustainable future environment, the construction of it needs to be wary of the extreme comfort of anthropocentricity from the perspective of permanent symbiosis.

To master the connection between the on-site subject and object under different functional requirements and to clarify the correspondence between the cognitive elements and the environment, it is necessary to study the cognitive rules and mechanisms of the subject and object in the on-site environment initially. Then, according to the needs of different scenarios, the structure and organization of the spatial elements of the on-site environment are designed, which is a game process based on the connection network of the on-site subject and object.

The on-site environment opposes the absolute objectivity of God's perspective while emphasizing the direct interaction between the on-site subject and object in the silicon-carbon joint space, which could occur not only between the subject and the object but also within the subject or the object. Moreover, this interaction does not have to take place through the on-site interface. Immediate behavioral responses were analyzed by observing in-person interactions to gain cognitive experience, discover universality, and avoid inefficiencies and misdirection due to overshadowing and complexity. It could be seen that the theory of the on-site environment is well suited for humans to explore cognitive rules in the future when facing a complex real-world environment and to provide a theoretical basis for design analysis and decision-making in the face of wicked problems.

The on-site environment argues against absolute centrism but advocates decentralization. Neither human-centered nor nature-centered could truly achieve a perfect harmony of human and natural environment coexistence [17]. Only by treating human beings as one of the on-site subjects and taking them as the origin from which they emanate to the other subjects and objects associated with them, and by forming the connections of the on-site network similar to the network of actors [18], could human beings be helped to study sophisticated cognition in greater detail and to analyze wicked problems to ensure the comprehensiveness and scientificity of the design strategy.

The on-site environment endorses the non-holistic connection. Human behavior is directed at the world around us, and the connection with the environment is broadened through constant interaction [19]. The relationship network of the on-site environment should be a bottom-up networked and decentralized connection made by each on-site subject from its own perspective in difference. For example, the cognitive study of the on-site environment begins with vision. Decomposing the visual cognition process in the on-site environment first, then studying the visual representation changes and reactivity speed under the stimulation of multiple information through the on-site environment, after understanding how silicon-based space mediates the carbon-based space by grasping the design weight relation of visual elements so that the environment design strategy based on visual cognition could be more efficient and accurate in the organization of spatial elements.

The on-site environment has ambiguity. It focuses on time, the overlap of time and space, and emphasizes mixed values. Similar to the chronotype, the on-site environment of the same space may require various functions at different times to meet the demands of the on-site subject. Space with specific professional needs could be considered a single function, while the rest of them should provide multiple functions according to the interaction between the on-site subject and object. Through the organizational relationship of functions, space resources are reasonably allocated to improve space efficiency. In addition, regardless of what space type it is, it should be considered to reserve a certain amount of resilient space to deal with unexpected public events and build spatial immunity.

Cognitive rules and operating mechanisms are the cornerstones of the on-site game to complete the design strategies in the on-site environment. It is acknowledged that the reception of environmental information depends on sensory stimuli. According to Treicher's experiments, we know that 83% of the external information acceptable to humans comes from visual and 11% from audio, visual is therefore our primary source of information. A core function of visual working memory is to ensure that effective visual input lasts for a while before being used in more advanced cognitive processes. It builds a bridge for perceptual information appearing in different times and space. Therefore, starting with visual cognition could help us understand the cognitive process more quickly, capture the relationship between the environment and cognition, and keep pace with the speed of practice leap. The basic process of cognitive activities in the on-site environment is the expectation before entering the on-site environment, the concentration resulting from the information stimuli received by the senses in the on-site environment, the memory of receiving information in the on-site environment and recalling past experiences due to stimulation, the cognitive judgment based on the memory of the experience and the decision behavior in the light of the results of expectation (see Fig. 7). Expectation, concentration, and memory are the key steps. Expectation depends on the on-site memory of the experience. Concentration results from the instantaneous memory left by information stimulation. Memory is the main part of cognitive operation after leaving the on-site environment. Visibly, memory is inseparable from before, during, and after the on-site, so the study of visual memory is the focus of visual cognitive research.

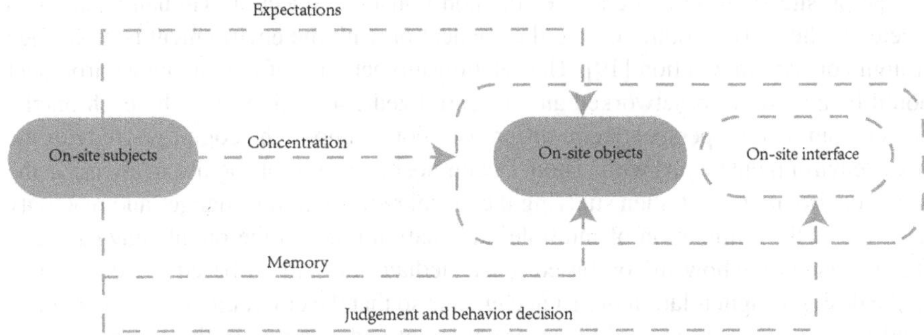

Fig. 7. The basic process of cognitive activities in the on-site environment

4.3 Design Strategy

Based on the ontology of the on-site environment and the study of the rules and mechanisms of visual cognition, the relationship model between the on-site environment and visual cognition is established. This means, the relationship between the on-site subject and the on-site object is combed according to the visual representation of the visual working memory in the on-site environment, and the core elements are clarified as the design object of the on-site environment. After the updating of epistemology, we would draw on game theory, logical reasoning, and computational theory to set up the design spatial coordinate system, synthesize the experiences of designers, stakeholders, and related academic research, and conclude the design methodology of the on-site environment based on visual cognition. This is the design game of the on-site environment.

In an on-site game (see Fig. 8), to clarify the needs relations, the first step is to make a linear transformation of the nonlinear and complex problems arising in the on-site subject network into the design spatial coordinate system and to find the main requirements and the approximate weighting relationships among the demands.

The second step is to make a game tree based on the visual cognition rules and operation mechanisms of the on-site environment and combine it with the demand relations to extract the cognitive elements for the specific on-site interface.

The third step is to select an appropriate game model according to the task requirements of the on-site environment, analyze the possible spatial functional benefits based on parameters, draw the relationship matrix, and obtain the design decision for the on-site game.

The above steps are the process of design strategy for the on-site environment, the core of which is the application of game theory in design analysis.

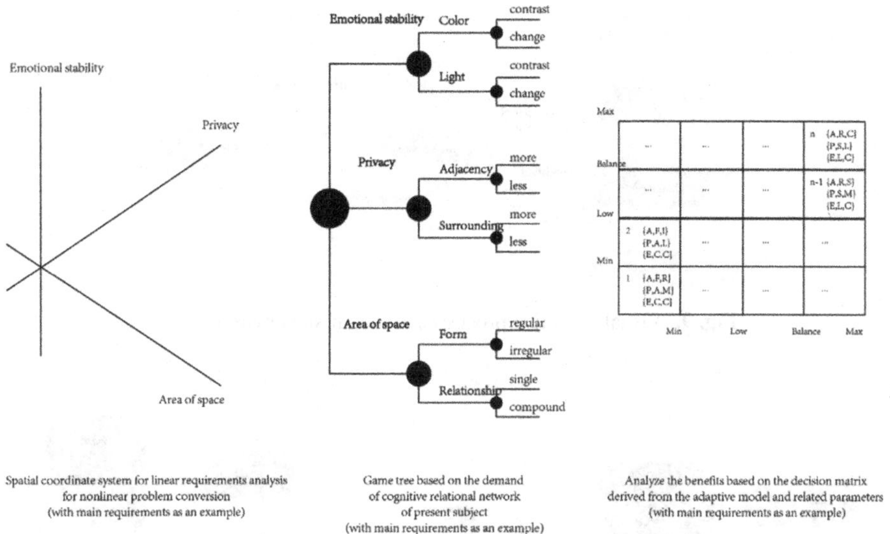

Fig. 8. The process of design game in the on-site environment: a case study of space, privacy, and emotional stability requirements network in visual cognition

5 Visual Perception in the On-site Environment

5.1 Research Scope and Object

According to cognitive information processing theory and the information processing model [20], the whole process of visual perception in the on-site environment is studied, including sensation, perception, memorization, thinking, imagination and language (see Fig. 9). The processes that produce associations with the properties and network relations of the on-site subject and the characteristics of the on-site object, which are reflected in the above forms, are used to explore the modes and mechanisms of interaction between the on-site environment and visual cognition (see Fig. 10). Visual working memory is the focus of visual perception research and includes the basic units of perceptual objects, working memory capacity, and visual attention (see Fig. 11).

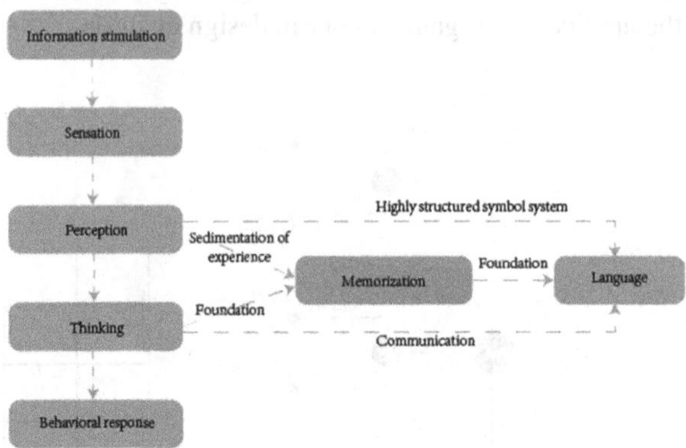

Fig. 9. Visual cognitive processes in the on-site environment

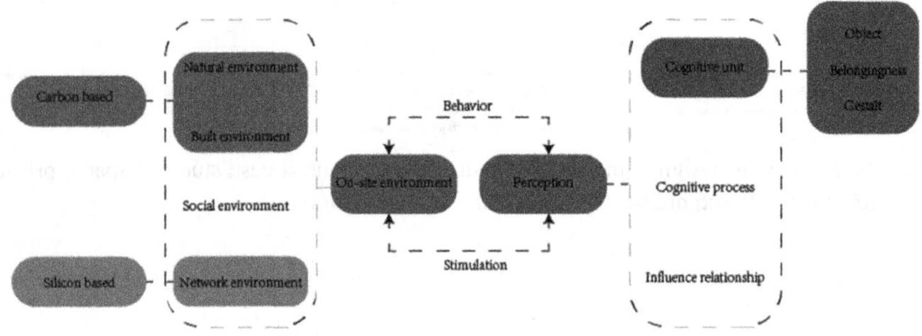

Fig. 10. The mechanism between the on-site environment and visual perception

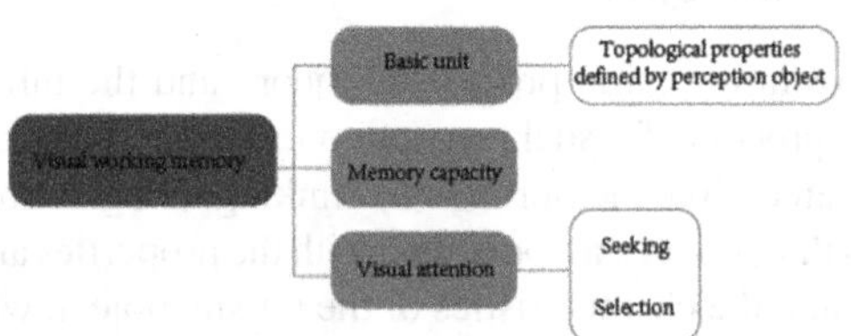

Fig. 11. Visual working memory research content in the on-site environment

5.2 Basic Unit of Visual Working Memory

Visual working memory is responsible for the short-term storage and operational processing of visual information. It lies between the underlying perceptual processes and abstract long-term memory [21–23]. In comparison with instantaneous memory and long-term memory, visual working memory stores neither detailed photographic nor conceptual information, but rather visual information briefly after certain abstraction, and the limited storage capacity restricts the cognitive process. The precondition for the study of memory capacity is to clarify the memory unit. A large number of cognitive science experiments have shown that the working memory unit should be the "chunk" proposed by Miller et al., which is the overall unit formed by the perceptual organization of contiguity, similarity, subordination, and concomitance [24, 25]. And there is a certain threshold for the chunk.

With regard to the definition of the chunk, Chen Lin's experiments related to global topological perception theory have demonstrated that the visual system is more sensitive to global topological properties, such as sensitivity to topological differences, closeness and the dominant effects of graphic structures, connectivity and content relations effects than to specific and simple parts of a graph or its local geometric properties at the beginning of the visual process [26, 27]. Combined with the hierarchical memory model [28, 29], it is known that visual perception is a functionally layered one, with the abstraction of a large range of topological properties determined by spatial adjacencies before the abstraction of other more detailed graphical properties. Based on the experiments of Wei Ning et al. using the repetitive dominance effect paradigm, it is proven that perceptual objects with invariant topological properties are the basic unit of visual working memory [30, 31]. Therefore, the theoretical framework of the basic unit of visual cognition in the on-site environment is established (see Fig. 12).

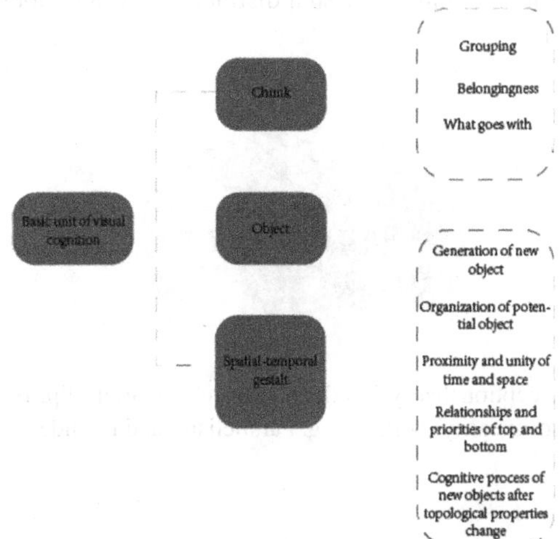

Fig. 12. The basic unit of visual cognition is based on the global topological perception theory in the on-site environment

Numerous behavioral and psychophysical experiments have shown that the definition of perceptual objects could be accurately described as topological invariants, such as contiguity, continuity, closeness, homogeneity, and other topological features. According to the basic expression of perceptual information in the theory of early feature analysis and the theory of initial perception of topological properties, the definition of a perceptual object could be expressed by the formula [32]:

$$O = \{D, C, H\} \tag{1}$$

In formula (1): O denotes the defined perceptual object. D stands for its distinctiveness, which reflects the local characteristics of the perceived object. And C means its contour, it expresses the continuity and closeness in the Gestalt principle of perceptual organization. While H represents its homogeneity, including the distribution of color and texture, it indicates the similarity and symmetry within the perceptual object, which correspond to the global holistic nature of the visual perception process. The definition of the perceptual object in this formula demonstrates the perceptual organization properties of perceived objects during cognition [32].

According to Alvarez & Cavanagh's experiment, working memory capacity is determined by both the amount of visual information (the topological properties of the perceived object) and the number of objects [33]. Combining the functional hierarchy relationship of topological perception theory classified by Klein's Erlangen program and the topological properties-based memory task experiments on comparison and interference done by Wei Ning et al. (see Fig. 13), it was learned the human visual system is more sensitive to overall topological properties, such as the number of holes, connectivity, and internal and external relationships, than local geometric properties. Which confirmed that the visual functional hierarchy in the order of global to local was positively correlated with the relationship between visual distinctiveness and visual memory capacity. This indicates that the more extensive changes in the global topological properties have been made, the easier it is to enhance visual distinctiveness and obtain higher values of visual memory capacity.

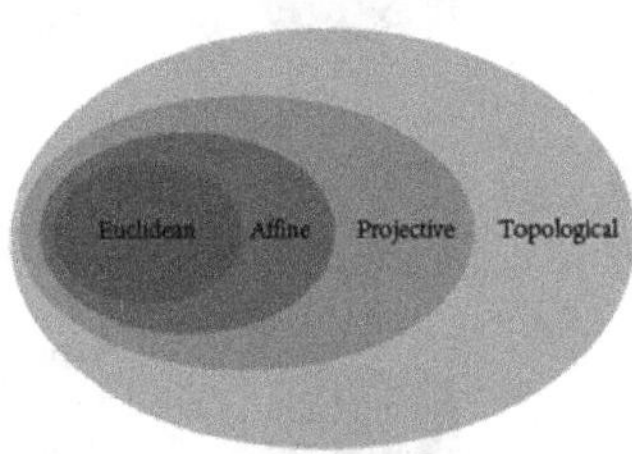

Fig. 13. Topological perception theory functional hierarchy relationship, Topological (e.g. Closeness), Projective (e.g. Co-linearity), Affine (e.g. Parallelism) and Euclidean (e.g. Spatial rotation) geometries

6 Discussion

On-site environment theory is a cognitive-based study that considers people living in the built environment and the active objects associated with them as on-site subjects, takes the cognitive and behavioral demands of the on-site subjects as the mission statement, regards the sustainable development of the environment as a restriction and available condition, and implements a dynamic update of the methodology by combining perceptual data and design language.

Epistemologically avoiding the deficiency of morphological typology for dynamic research, emphasizing the concept of development and continuous evolution. It stresses that the interaction mechanism between the environment and cognition is studied multidimensionally, dynamically, and at high frequency, starting from a decentralized network of people and the active units with which they are associated, rather than humans themselves. A systematic closed loop of ontology, epistemology, and methodology is constructed with the on-site environment as the core.

Since more than 80% of the information humans could receive comes from vision, visual studies are used here as an entry point for research to quickly establish theoretical prototypes of the on-site environment. Based on the development of biological science, medical research on the human body supplements cognition while constraining the depth of visual perception research in the on-site environment. At present, only visual memory and related cognitive sessions are focused on, while other more sophisticated visual information processing procedures and more systematic visual cognitive components need to be explored. Similarly, visual studies are only used here as one of the bases for the construction of cognitive sessions in the on-site environment, researches on other sensory perceptions are yet to be translated. Therefore, the future ontology, epistemology, and methodology of the on-site environment would be further improved with the development of biomedicine, psychology, and other disciplines.

Future work would continue to focus on visual memory, construct different complex and realistic on-site environments through VR, AR, MR, and other technologies, record cognitive and behavioral data with the help of eye movement apparatus, fMRI, EEG, and other devices, analyze data with GIS, DEPTHMAP, SPSS, etc., to improve the topological network of visual cognition in on-site environments. In addition, the subsequent research could also combine in-depth interviews with qualitative research methods such as grounded theory and semantic analysis to explain the principles of visual cognition, summarize the general rules of visual cognition in the on-site environment, and expound the symbiotic relationship of form-function-scale in the on-site environment under the interaction of cognitive networks.

7 Conclusion

This paper illustrates that under the overlap of carbon-based civilization and silicon-based civilization, in the face of the highly integrated and individualized trend brought about by the fourth industrial revolution and in light of the post-pandemic demand, the philosophical viewpoint based on Latour's view of Gaia is further developed. On-site environment theory is based on the prediction of the future environment combined with cognitive research and the concept of sustainable development. This theory regards cognitive rules as hardcore, emphasizes mixed value and decentralization, establishes spatial resilience and network development. It provides a theoretical basis for solving wicked problems that may arise in the future environment, complements the ontology of the design discipline for the built environment, and is a further step in the concept of green symbiosis in the new era.

Combining the existing experimental research in biomedical and cognitive psychology, on-site environment theory is constructed from the perspective of visual perception, which complements the study of spatial cognition in a multidimensional and complex environment, rapidly builds a cognitive prototype of the on-site environment so that the research could be both retrospective and future-oriented. Starting with visual working memory in visual perception, we could quickly set up a map of the relationship between visual cognition and environmental factors based on the prediction of the future environment, while eliminating the uncontrollable factors of individual biophysiological performance and experience background. Through the perceptual object defined by topological properties perception theory, human cognition of visual recognition's environmental factors has been updated, which also provides an analytical basis for design strategies.

Based on the ontology and epistemology of the on-site environment, the design methodology of the on-site environment is put forwards in the end. The design strategy of the on-site game is adapted to the construction requirements of the future environment. The design process of the on-site environment is composed of cognitive research, demand sorting, decision making, and design transformation. It enables people to sort out the network of needs and constraints more clearly when facing wicked problems, identify the main contradictions in it, make design decisions that maximize the spatial benefits, and realize the sustainable coexistence of humans and the environment. On-site games allow people to make quick decisions by de-clouding and adapting to the changes in the future environment brought about by new technologies to the greatest extent. Not only has the design method been innovated, but it also brings new ideas for the establishment, revision, and management of future social systems.

References

1. Xu, M., David, J.M., Kim, S.H.: The fourth industrial revolution: opportunities and challenges. Int. J. Fin. Res. **9**, 90–95 (2018)
2. Schwab, K., Davis, N.: Shaping the Future of the Fourth Industrial Revolution. Currency (2018)
3. A Schumpeter, J.: Capitalism, Socialism and Democracy (2021)
4. Balland, P.-A., et al.: The new paradigm of economic complexity. Res. Policy **51**, 104450 (2022)
5. Farris, D.: Truth: How the Many Sides to Every Story Shape Our Reality. Reed Business Information 360 Park Avenue South, New York, NY 10010 USA (2018)
6. Al-Rodhan, N.: The moral code: how to teach robots right and wrong. Retrieved from https://www.foreignaffairs.com/articles/2015-08-12/moral-code (2015)
7. Ward, A.F., Duke, K., Gneezy, A., Bos, M.W.: Brain drain: the mere presence of one's own smartphone reduces available cognitive capacity. J. Ass. Cons. Res. **2**, 140–154 (2017)
8. Gidley, J.M.: Postformal Education: A Philosophy for Complex Futures. Springer (2016)
9. Zhou, R.: The City's Response to The Challenge of Silicon civilization. Urban Environment Design, pp. 199–200 (2016)
10. Ribeiro, P.J.G., Gonçalves, L.A.P.J.: Urban resilience: a conceptual framework. Sustain. Cities Soc. **50**, 101625 (2019)
11. Meerow, S., Newell, J.P., Stults, M.: Defining urban resilience: A review. Landsc. Urban Plan. **147**, 38–49 (2016)

12. Yamagata, Y., Maruyama, H.: Urban Resilience. Urban Resilience (2016)
13. Ceschin, F., Gaziulusoy, I.: Evolution of design for sustainability: from product design to design for system innovations and transitions. Des. Stud. **47**, 118–163 (2016)
14. Brundtland, G.: Our Common Future: Brundtland Report. (1987)
15. Staab, S., Studer, R.: Handbook on Ontologies. Springer Science & Business Media (2010)
16. Barbara, A., Paoletti, I.: Time-based design for the habitat of the next future. TECHNE-J. Technol. Archit. Environ. 167–174 (2020)
17. Latour, B.: Facing Gaia: Eight Lectures on the New Climatic Regime. John Wiley & Sons (2017)
18. Latour, B.: On actor-network theory: A few clarifications. Soziale welt 369–381 (1996)
19. Latour, B., Lenton, T.M.: Extending the domain of freedom, or why Gaia is so hard to understand. Crit. Inq. **45**, 659–680 (2019)
20. Peterson, G.W., Sampson Jr, J.P., Reardon, R.C.: Career Development and Services: A Cognitive Approach. Thomson Brooks/Cole Publishing Co (1991)
21. Baddeley, A.: Recent developments in working memory. Curr. Opin. Neurobiol. **8**, 234–238 (1998)
22. Baddeley, A.: Working memory: looking back and looking forward. Nat. Rev. Neurosci. **4**, 829–839 (2003)
23. Baddeley, A.: Working memory: theories, models, and controversies. Annu. Rev. Psychol. **63**, 1–29 (2012)
24. Cowan, N.: The magical number 4 in short-term memory: A reconsideration of mental storage capacity. Behav. Brai. Sci. **24**, 87–114 (2001)
25. Miller, G.A.: The magical number seven, plus or minus two: Some limits on our capacity for processing information. Psychol. Rev. **63**, 81 (1956)
26. Chen, L.: Topological structure in visual perception. Science **218**, 699–700 (1982)
27. Chen, L.: The topological approach to perceptual organization. Vis. Cogn. **12**, 553–637 (2005)
28. Xu, Y., Chun, M.M.: Dissociable neural mechanisms supporting visual short-term memory for objects. Nature **440**, 91–95 (2006)
29. Xu, Y., Chun, M.M.: Selecting and perceiving multiple visual objects. Trends Cogn. Sci. **13**, 167–174 (2009)
30. Wei, N., Zhou, T., Zhang, Z., Zhuo, Y., Chen, L.: Visual working memory reon-siteation as a topological defined perceptual object. J. Vis. **19**, 12 (2019)
31. Wei, N., Zhou, T., Zhuo, Y., Chen, L.: Topological change induces an interference effect in visual working memory. J. Vis. **21**, 4 (2021)
32. Shao, J.: Extraction Algorithm of Perceptual Object Based on Visual Attention Mechanism. Mod. Elec. Technol. **33**, 71–74 (2010)
33. Alvarez, G.A., Cavanagh, P.: The capacity of visual short-term memory is set both by visual information load and by number of objects. Psychol. Sci. **15**, 106–111 (2004)

Future Experience Boundary and Interaction Design Integration Path

Mengke Lu and Yangshuo Zheng(✉)

Wuhan University of Technology, Wuhan 430000, People's Republic of China
291187842@qq.com

Abstract. Our lives are still not back to normal because of the novel coronavirus epidemic, and people around the world are looking for ways to compensate for the limited experience. The global buzz around Metaverse can also be seen as a concern to upgrade the experience, and the trend toward virtual world interaction is unstoppable, in the future, the boundary between virtual world and real world will be a direction of further exploration in the field of interaction design. If the meta-universe can be developed into a future society, it should not be viewed as a mere technical question. Whether this future is worthy of human pursuit requires us to think more. So based on the future doomed to borderline ambiguous social forms, the establishment of a new order first needs to clarify the virtual world and the real world and the relationship between the difference. This paper critically interprets the concept of meta-cosmic society, and discusses the thinking of the boundary definition in the future context, it is hoped that this discussion will provide a valuable perspective for interaction design to be integrated into the new experience pattern in the future.

Keywords: Boundary · The fourth wall · Integration

1 Introduction

The term Metaverse comes from Stevenson's 1992 science fiction novel Snow Crash, which originally referred to a virtual reality different from the Internet, an entertainment society in which people can transcend geographic isolation through their avatars. The term has been around for a long time, but the recent epidemic has certainly made people more eager to experience it, and Facebook's announcement of a new name, Meta, has further fueled the buzz.

Proponents describe a meta universe that is largely based on games, but that prides itself on being different from them, and that will be the Home Society of the future, with a higher priority than the real world. Opponents see it as a scam of capital, a data-driven game of pretend. But whether it's a new form of society or a more sophisticated game, we have to admit that people are subjectively willing to experiment with virtual experiences, to get a sense of freshness, even intimacy.

P.-L. P. Rau (Ed.): HCII 2022, LNCS 13311, pp. 70–80, 2022.
https://doi.org/10.1007/978-3-031-06038-0_5

In the past, people in the virtual world used to enter the environment as players and get the virtual experience by playing a role. At this time, we fulfilled the dual role of audience and performer. [1] When we are directly acknowledged by the system to exist in the virtual world, the "Fourth wall" creates a crack, the boundary between the virtual world and the real world becomes blurred and ambiguous. The physical world of our self and the digital world of our avatars are at the intersection of the two worlds, and the growing sophistication of media technologies such as VR and, further enhances the immersive experience. People enter the artificial virtual world through the media, the media become the extension of human body function, people's self-consciousness gradually have a tremendous impact on the experience acquisition.

2 Fresh Experience, Fuzzy Boundary

2.1 Interface and Medium

Boundary generally refers to geographical features, such as land and sea boundaries, such as the objective existence of spatial division. Borders also contain artificial political features, such as national boundaries, so the criteria for delimiting them are not completely uniform. Experience, as a rather subjective experience, has a different answer for everyone. As the author subjectively understands it, there is a boundary between real and virtual experiences, but it is not a fixed, discrete boundary, and there must be a fuzzy boundary between real and virtual worlds, the interface, we can call it an interface or think of it as an interface, a buffer zone that provides most of the cross boundary experience we have today. Experiences are largely carried and conveyed by medium, and entities such as canvas and paper are of course mediums, while Marshall Mcluhan argues that, the medium is the message, and Technology as extensions of the human body. [2] The term medium includes information carriers, presentation codes, information content, etc.

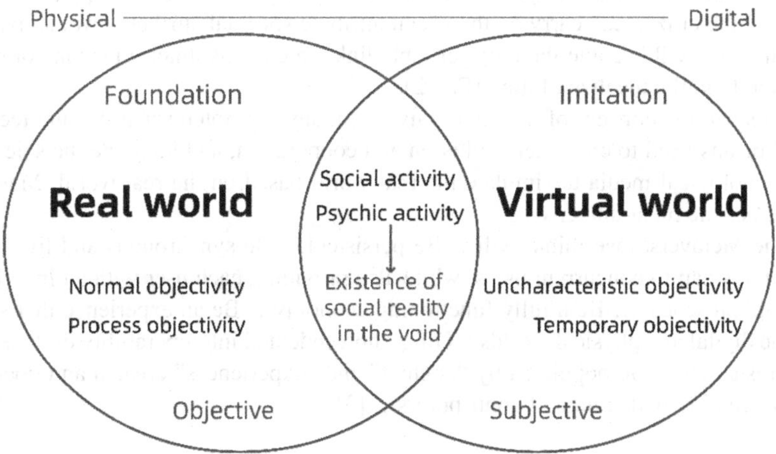

Fig. 1. Real world and virtual world

Just as we're currently using VR headsets such as Oculus Quest2 to give our first taste of virtual worlds, our senses are stepping into the digital experience space. The medium itself, as a means and channel of communication, has changed the way we receive information, in a subtle way, reshaping our sense of space and time, it changes the way we think and the way we act. Each medium is sending out different signals, the strength of which affects people's consciousness and actions, and then forms distinct collective cognition and broad consensus. The nature of the communication tool used, the possibilities it opens up, and the social changes it brings will push the boundaries of human experience ever further. Media is not only used to carry content, the new media will change the way people perceive the world, and then affect the way people interact (Fig. 1).

The virtual world can be called the world first of all it must be able to make people freely in and out, to ensure its openness, after all, the real world people will not for any reason disconnect from reality. But it's hard to say who will "Own" the Metaverse in the future. Most companies will build their own worlds, experiences, stores, and so on, all on the premise that the built meta universe exists, and the company enters it, rather than relying on the ports of specific companies to access the virtual world, it goes against the original intention of the virtual world to subvert the old, increasingly closed internet. When Metaverse becomes powerful enough to upend the real world, as we might expect, governments must not allow this form of monopoly unless the creator can establish a governance structure that satisfies society, the blurred boundary between the real world and the virtual world is assigned to the division of political characteristics, and the medium of their existence may become the proof of the demarcation.

2.2 Idealized Transcendence of Reality

The existence of virtual world is based on the objective material attribute of real world, but not completely parallel to the real world. "Exist in nothingness" can generalize the social reality of virtual community. In an ideal state, if the future world is divided from the functional level, the physical world is the support and guarantee of our physical existence, and the Virtual Digital World is responsible for carrying people's spiritual activities, the citizen can carry on the social attribute spiritual attribute level activity in them, the two will become the indispensable link which constitutes a person complete self-identity in the idealized future (Fig. 2).

To realize the concept of the meta-universe, many top-notch scientific and technological means need to cross-field collision and cooperation, and integrate the scientific and technological media to simulate the real world based on the real world. Matthew ball defines the meta-universe as:

"The Metaverse, we think, will… Be persistent… Be synchronous and live… Be without any cap to concurrent users, while also providing each user with an individual sense of "presence"… Be a fully functioning economy… Be an experience that spans both the digital and physical worlds…Offer unprecedented interoperability of data, digital items/assets… Be populated by "content" and "experiences" created and operated by an incredibly wide range of contributors… [3].

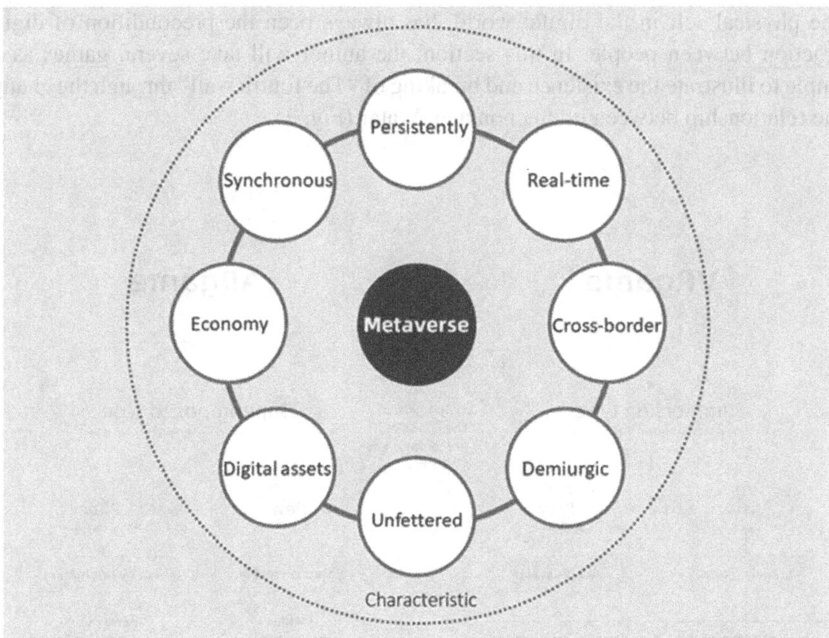

Fig. 2. The sensory characteristics of the meta-universe (Content reference from https://www.matthewball.vc/all/themetaverse)

The short answer is that the Internet is no longer a utility, but a world unto itself. Based on current technology, however, the cost of processing large numbers of people online in real time is beyond imagination. Synchronous, non-delayed interaction may revolutionize the medium. We can expect various compromises in the application of technology based on this concept over a long period of time. The closest to this real-world concept at the moment are real-time multiplayer online social games that try to change the relationship between people and the fourth wall.

3 The Fall of the Fourth Wall

In terms of drama, the concept of the fourth wall is a common one, often interpreted as a metaphor for the space between the actor and the audience, who are invisible bystanders behind this transparent wall. Thanks to suspension of disbelief, the latter can voyeuristically peek into the enclosed space of the stage, not seen by the characters of the play [4].

When this concept is expounded in the context of new media experience represented by games, new problems will arise. The next step in the exploration of the virtual worlds of the meta-universe begins with the form of a game -- the experience of entering another world. In order to distinguish the virtual representation in the digital world of the game from the real noumenon, the term Avatar is usually used to describe the physical embodiment. The virtual image in the digital world, that is, the data reference of the physical self in the digital world, has always been the precondition of digital interaction between people. In this section, the author will take several games as an example to illustrate the existence and breaking of "The fourth wall" through the change of the relationship between noumenon and Avatar (Fig. 3).

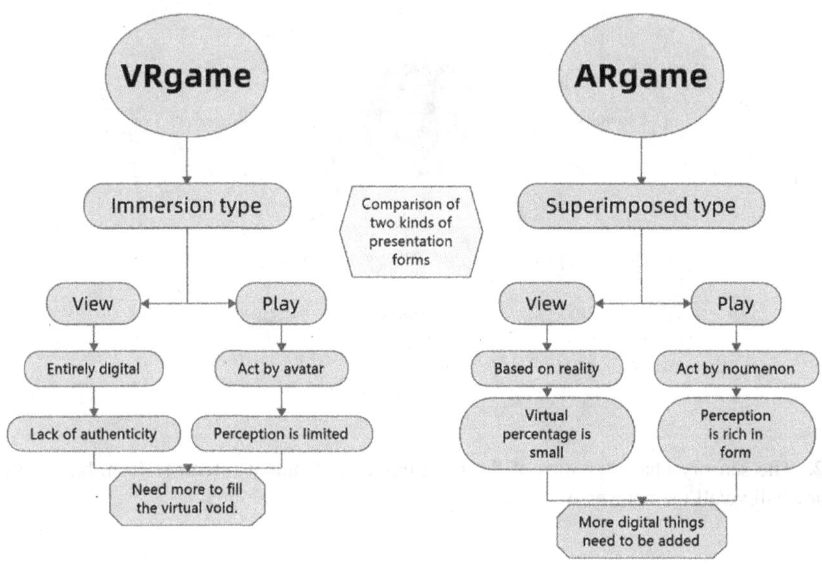

Fig. 3. Comparison of two kinds of presentation forms

3.1 Immersion in the Virtual World

"The idea that reality is constructed, and therefore it is possible to construct things that are more real than real." [5] Avatars are interfaces between a person and other human users in a digital space, where the player's facial expressions and actions are presented to the other through avatars, the early days of Second Life and the more recent activity of VRchat are social games in which people enter the digital world through virtual avatars to reveal their physical selves to others. In a sense, the physical self of an online user, operating a personalized avatar, becomes a second self by giving the avatar a unique behavior that is attached to the avatar, to bring the two worlds together. Similarly, the player's attention switches back and forth between the real world and the virtual world as the game progresses, the player who enters the virtual world experiences the double position contradiction and the role identity problem between the social noumenon and the Operation Incarnation. Perhaps the best-known surreal game is the three-dimensional virtual World Second Life (SL). Second Life is a virtual world created by Linden Lab in which people can explore magical scenes, build their own manors, forests and spaceships, second Life offers users the possibility to construct an alternative identity, either a self-replicating identity in real life or an enhanced version with improved attributes, or a completely different version of myself. In many virtual worlds, the basic rules of physics continue to hold, which makes navigation within them very similar to what one is used to in the real world. There's a huge demand for virtual exploration, especially as technology advances, and it's attractive to allow someone to be truly expressive and creative in a realistic environment. However, too complex operation of the page and disorderly society so that many people do not continue to experience (Fig. 4).

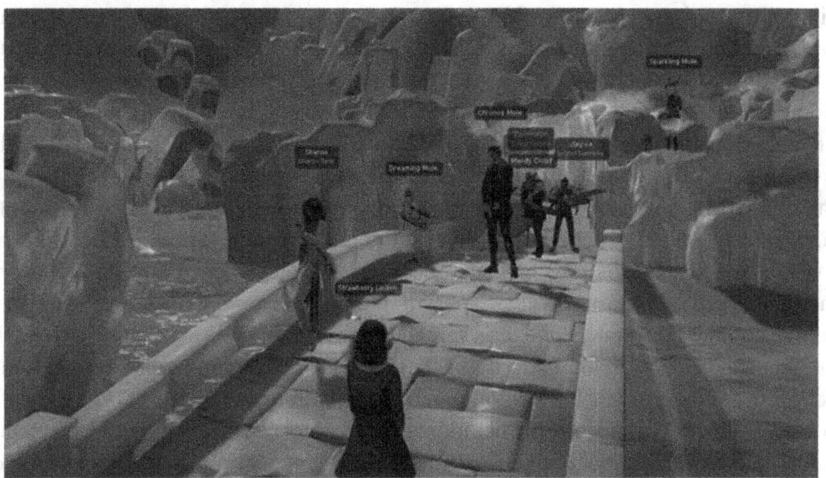

Fig. 4. Second life, (from: www.youtube.com)

How do people perceive and understand their avatars in VR through wearable devices? VRchat is the closest expression to the "Meta-universe" etymology, providing modes of communication other than verbal interaction such as gestures, facial expressions and movement feedback, which rely on whole-body tracking technology, it allows interaction across the screen, much like face-to-face communication [6], which largely compensates for the immersive experience of a player's sense of identity fragmentation. In real-life face-to-face communication, although non-verbal communication is not the largest in the overall proportion of communication, it often plays a number of key interactions, affecting the results of communication. VRchat quickly became a global phenomenon as it integrated these non-verbal communications, which are more intuitive and convey information about emotions, into social interactions. However, due to technical constraints and equipment support issues, the level of virtual world image rendering can make a big difference in experience. We can see that the accuracy of current VR social games is difficult to compare with single console games due to cost control and reduced latency, not to mention restoring the real world, rough rendering and movement delays from avatars can interrupt the immersive experience from time to time. But in contrast, as people enter the virtual world, the impact of environmental differences in the real world is minimized here, people do not feel the uneven distribution of resources in the virtual world because of their physical location. Players are equal to the identity of the place and are more receptive to the unity of the duality of self-identity in the here and now.

3.2 Projection into the Real World

Another form of game presentation that breaks down reality and virtuality is AR games with social attributes, a genre in which Pokeman GO and Pikmin Bloom are familiar. Unlike VR social games, where VR devices are worn into virtual worlds, AR Media is where virtual digital information is superimposed on the physical world to match real time and space, what users experience is "with virtual objects superimposed upon or composited with the real world" [7]. The AR based games use real world maps to encourage people to interact and socialize with their surroundings and with other players, it's a virtual world reward that encourages people to make social connections in the real world, since Pokémon can be seen by all players in a given location in the area, so players can experience what it's like to be in the same world. [8] This is when the virtual world expands into reality rather than the player enters the virtual world. Although the online community overlaps with the offline community, there is almost no cognitive conflict between the player's self and the avatar, the player's experience at this point depends heavily on the integrity of the physical world community. In addition to fostering the same kind of online community cohesion as other games, Pokeman GO also helps players feel a sense of belonging to a community of players in the offline physical space through this online to offline fusion game approach, encourage players to meet in public and share the fun (Fig. 5).

Fig. 5. Pokeman GO (from: www.youtube.com)

Pokeman GO allows players to GO where they haven't gone before, but there is also the issue of unequal opportunity. The amount of resources in rural areas is much lower than in urban centres, which creates frustration among people living in non-central areas. [9] The unequal opportunity in the game leads to the unequal distribution of resources in the game, which affects the acquired experience. Mixing the online and offline worlds is becoming more common in everyday life, contemporary entanglements between the online and offline can be interpreted through the conceptual and embodied metaphor of digital wayfaring. While at others they reinforce existing boundaries and delimit our wayfaring practices in digital, actual, hybrid, and augmented realities [10].

3.3 Digital Twins, Together We Are

We can see that there have been quite a few successful attempts at one-way immersion or projection, which is worth learning and exploring by practitioners, and the future may require us to combine the two in order to meet people's expectations for experience upgrades. The difference in perception between the two worlds is ultimately determined by human experience, such as the quantification of human subjective experience in this mode. How can we skillfully move and even break through the fourth wall to experience a sense of communion? It may be possible to use technologies such as digital twins to break the cognitive barrier between the real world and the virtual world, based on the unique identifier to bring together multimedia technologies, the seamless dissemination of data between the two worlds, so that the two separate ontology and the embodiment of true mirror as the two sides of full synchronization (Fig. 6).

The existing transmission mechanism causes the data transmission between the individual ontology and the avatar to be sent and received by the server first, which largely causes the sense of delay and disharmony, by upgrading the content-oriented communication mode to the control-oriented communication mode, an integrated feedback loop between the twins [11] to improve the transmission speed of the two-way system may be a feasible direction for exploration. In addition to AR/VR/devices, which are already widely used in social games, the introduction of wearable devices with integrated tactile features to enhance the flow of information may further enhance the realism of information exchange, after all, most of the time in human life, we unconsciously make full use of the five senses to perceive the world, and every extra dimension of information transmission can make our brain more excited to perceive the environment.

We can not only make people more familiar with their avatars by creating digital twins of people, but also realize data twins of real creatures to enable people to find a familiar anchor in the virtual world, by making it easier to explore the other side, people can build a sense of identity in the virtual world more quickly.

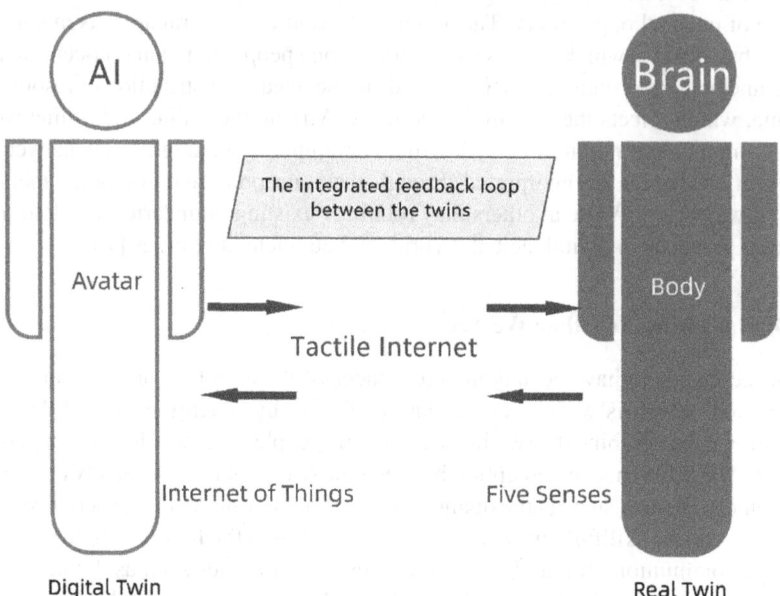

Fig. 6. Digital twins

4 Integration and Transcendence

4.1 Enter the World

Whether it's entering a new and unfamiliar virtual world through VR technology for a virtual reality experience, or meeting something different in a mediocre and familiar real world through AR technology, is an exploration of the boundaries of experience between two worlds. Seeking new experiences that don't exist in the real world doesn't mean avoiding the real world altogether. We live in the future at the junction of the real world and the virtual world. Of course, we still haven't solved the problem of data transmission delays due to the nature of the materials, and the cost of truly synchronizing a cloud server that can hold millions or more people at the same time is still very high. We also need to fill in the virtual world with vast amounts of real details inspired by the real world. "Self" and "Other", "Subjective" and "Objective", players' identities and characters are fluid, and while the virtual world can come and go as freely as the real world without being limited by hardware, we can really choose who we are in a world.

The development and expansion of new media makes us tend to magnify the advantages of new technology, and more willing to enter the virtual world for experience, but this does not mean that we have to be completely divorced from reality, once the virtual world loses its deep connection and restriction with the reality, its desolation due to the weakness of human nature will be the inevitable result. Even if the future of technology is skewed towards virtual worlds, we should not live our lives entirely in them. The Virtual Society is an important reflection of the postmodern philosophy, which does not assume that everyone shares the same reality, but simulates another reality, it is more suitable for us to carry out activities in this kind of reality that we are unable or unwilling to carry out in real life. At this point, the existence of the experience is more dependent on the designers to draw up conventions to calibrate it, so that the content generated by AI is within reasonable range.

4.2 Leading the Flow Experience

Professor Mihaly Csikszentmihalyi suggests that when people are immersed in something or goal, this state of being is a state of flow. As an extension and dimension of the real physical world, the attraction of the virtual world to future users can not stop at the interactive experience only of the real physical world. This is a big challenge in the field of interaction design, where the goal is to "Transcend" not only physical constraints, but also old mindsets, rather than to completely replicate reality. Interaction design is a subject in which people accept technology and use it to serve people. Even in the technology-oriented future, this "Human-oriented" subject must not obscure its own significance. Because users need to meet many conditions to have a flow experience, in the case of games, players need to know exactly what to do and how to do it, the introduction of menus and intuitive design guidelines allows the experience to continue, and the flow of flow is sustained by a more streamlined process. In a 2017 article on Second Life, the Atlantic reported that an estimated 20 to 30% of first time users never return to the platform. Many people find the world extremely unpredictable. Second Life has a 'monster learning curve', an intricate user interface and a server that constantly crashes, writes Reuters correspondent Eric Krangel. While second life itself has solved many of these problems thanks to advances in technology, any virtual world that wants to win over the masses of users still has to overcome huge barriers to entry. Maintaining a long term flow experience isn't just a matter of technology, it's much quicker to tweak the flow of interactions.

We have a great desire for new experiences in the future and a desire to have a fully immersive flow experience, so the development of technology should strive to create more interactive possibilities. Maximize the full sensory experience so that the screen is no longer the fourth wall of transparency that separates us from the content. In the past interactive experience, the visual sense carries nearly 80% of the function of conveying information, but the current technology and actual situation will make designers always prefer to use visual expression first. As technologies evolve, such as sound control, eye movement analysis, and bioelectric sensing, we can use these technologies to make the experience more multidimensional, to do so is to seek a breakthrough in the monotonic presentation of the past technical means, but also to a certain extent to reduce the cost of understanding.

5 Conclusion

In the end, Metaverse doesn't need to be everywhere, and in fact, it shouldn't be. We can replace the meta-universe with any virtual social space that describes the virtual digital society, which is still created by human simulation based on real society. People do not want their experiences to be confined to the real world, thus creating an idealized virtual space through technological means. The virtual world is born out of the real world and has an indeterminate boundary with reality. Based on the discussion in this paper, I believe that the boundary between the two worlds will not become more and more distinct, it will continue to grow by expanding the overlap. The relationship between avatars and ontologies of players, or users, can be a focus for improving the current experience of virtual content. As discussed in Chapter 3, in addition to the virtual world, we can also overlay virtual world content onto the real world, and the expanded interface will attract more people to participate, building an online community requires a huge amount of real users to create and maintain, just like our real social lives. The introduction of digital twins may provide a source of ideas that bridge the two worlds.

As we navigate between the virtual world and the real world in the future, we will have to choose who we are in the present moment, and this will require optimizing the overall process from an interaction design perspective, it also drives innovation in technology and media. We're still exploring and looking for the factors that affect the experience, and it's clear that people are paying more attention to media forms than to media content, and it's very fast to move from technology to deployment, it provides the cornerstone of the world, and the establishment of human society in the virtual world will need several times the amount of technology to fill, the human proud civilization in the New World. From now until the future, interaction designers will spend a long time delving into how to use content set and process optimization to make up for the lack of current technology, through these efforts to mobilize all of the human senses.

References

1. Conway, S.: A circular wall? Reformulating the fourth wall for videogames. J. Gam. Vir. Worl. **2**(2), 145–155 (2010). Aug.
2. McLuhan, M.: The Medium is the Massage. Gingko Press (2001)
3. Homepage, M.B.: https://www.matthewball.vc/all/themetaverse. last accessed 13 Jan 2020
4. Waszkiewicz, A..: "Together They Are Twofold": Player-Avatar Relationship Beyond the Fourth Wall, p. 21
5. Kaplan, A.M., Haenlein, M.: The fairyland of second life: virtual social worlds and how to use them. Bus. Horiz. **52**(6), 563–572 (2009). Nov.
6. Freeman, G., Zamanifard, S., Maloney, D., Adkins, A.: My body, my avatar: how people perceive their avatars in social virtual reality, In: Extended Abstracts of the 2020 CHI Conference on Human Factors in Computing Systems. Honolulu HI USA, pp. 1–8 (Apr. 2020)
7. Azuma, R.T.: A Survey of augmented reality. Pres. Teleop. Vir. Envir. **6**(4), 355–385 (Aug. 1997)
8. Vella, K., et al.: A sense of belonging: pokémon GO and social connectedness. Games and Culture **14**(6), 583–603 (2019). Sep.
9. Paavilainen, J., Korhonen, H., Alha, K., Stenros, J., Koskinen, E., Mayra, F.: The pokémon GO experience: a location-based augmented reality mobile game goes mainstream. In: Proceedings of the 2017 CHI Conference on Human Factors in Computing Systems. Denver Colorado USA (May 2017)
10. Hjorth, L., Richardson, I.: *Pokémon GO*: mobile media play, place-making, and the digital wayfarer. Mob. Med. Comm. **5**(1), 3–14 (2017). Jan.
11. El Saddik, A.: Digital twins: the convergence of multimedia technologies. IEEE Multimedia **25**(2), 87–92 (2018). Apr.

A Pilot Study on Sustainable Development of Design in the Context of "Creativity Obsolescence" and "Timeless Classic"

Yikang Sun[1(✉)], I-Ying Chiang[2], Po-Hsien Lin[3], and Rungtai Lin[3]

[1] College of Art and Design, Nanjing Forestry University, Nanjing City 210037, China
sunyikang120110@hotmail.com

[2] Department of Arts and Design, National Tsing Hua University, Hsinchu 300044, Taiwan
iychiang@mx.nthu.edu.tw

[3] Graduate School of Creative Industry Design, National Taiwan University of Arts, New Taipei City 22058, Taiwan
{t0131,rtlin}@mail.ntua.edu.tw

Abstract. "Creativity obsolescence" means "once possessed", and the "timeless classics" are "worldly and durable". To answer the above questions, it is necessary to explore a strategy called planted obsolescence, which still plays a huge role today. Planned obsolescence is an approach used by manufacturers to take advantage of market demand. Production and consumption are two sides of the same coin. As a pilot study, this article first sorts out the ins and outs of planned obsolescence, and then combines previous research around classical, timeless design to roughly determine the research direction. According to the philosophies and currents of thought of the East and the West, the evaluation criteria are constructed. In the follow-up study, we selected suitable samples as stimuli according to the above evaluation criteria, and learned about the public's attitude through questionnaires. It's not to propose a new design approach to reduce the impact of planned obsolescence, but to use the philosophy of the Chinese sages to explain the purpose of "compliance with human nature".

Keywords: Creativity obsolescence · Timeless classics · Sustainable development · Planned obsolescence

1 Introduction

Design has profoundly changed the way we live, but do we really need so much design? The product line is constantly updated, and those products that are obsolete can still play a big role. For a long time, a concept known as "Planned Obsolescence" has played a powerful role. The emergence of planned obsolescence has had a great impact on product development, design, and marketing. Certainly, there are some unscrupulous manufacturers who produce poor-quality products. However, the reason that most products are not as durable as they used to be is due to planned obsolescence. In addition, the curiosity of human beings regarding new things and the desire to possess them helps to drive planned obsolescence.

P.-L. P. Rau (Ed.): HCII 2022, LNCS 13311, pp. 81–90, 2022.
https://doi.org/10.1007/978-3-031-06038-0_6

This study suggests that planned obsolescence may be difficult to eradicate completely. Its impact on product manufacturing, design, and consumption will only intensify in the future. This stems from various problems, such as excessive consumption of resources, constant destruction of the ecological environment, and a distortion of the relationship between people and products. It will be difficult to reverse these adverse effects simply by relying on moral constraints. Although many scholars, consumers, and producers have studied the concepts of design ethics, green de-sign, and sustainable development, it is no easy task to fundamentally change the negative influence of planned obsolescence.

As a pilot study, this article will restore the appearance of planned obsolescence as comprehensively as possible, and then analyze the classic and excellent designs in history as the basis for follow-up research.

2 Literature Review

2.1 Planned Obsolescence: An Imperceptibly Influence

The concept of planned obsolescence was developed based on the "Phoebus cartel" [1–3] in the European light bulb industry in the 1920s and the "Annual Model Change" proposed by General Motors (GM) [4–6] in the US at the same time. It finally took shape in the mid-1950s, and its influence continues to this day. Planned obsolescence is a production method used by manufacturers to meet market demand. It has been witnessed that production and consumption are two sides of the same coin: human needs and desires have always existed in the development of human society, and this, in combination with the commercial industry's need for profit, constitutes the main reason for the emergence of this system. The advancement of science and technology and the demands of human nature prompted the advent of the era of consumerism, leading to the adjustment of production following market demand.

Human needs are a process of continuous progression from low to high, and it is usually impossible to skip a level of need [7–9]. This has become one of the motivations for planned obsolescence. In addition, many studies have proposed further views based on Maslow's hierarchy of needs. These views also help us to better understand how planned obsolescence affects the various needs of consumers in a step-by-step manner [10–18]. People's consumption activities may just be impulsive behavior that occur on a whim. Consumption or purchase involves a very complicated decision-making process. People's consumption behaviors are very different. People hope to show their personalities and tastes and want to satisfy their desires through the products they own. Between seeing and purchasing is the desire of the inner world. Most of this desire will satisfy one's self-realization or even self-transcendence needs.

If everyone chose to repair products or to continue to use existing products in other ways instead of buying new ones, a nightmare would undoubtedly occur for manufacturing companies. Generally speaking, companies are unwilling to let consumers know that their products can continue to be used with simple repairs. The increasing desire of human beings for products, and the perception of products as a symbol of personal status and a tool for self-realization, coupled with the needs of various commercial interest groups, have become the two major causes and motivations for planned obsolescence.

In short, planned obsolescence and its relationship with consumption, market and production is shown in Fig. 1. This helps us to understand its nature more fully and to evaluate it objectively.

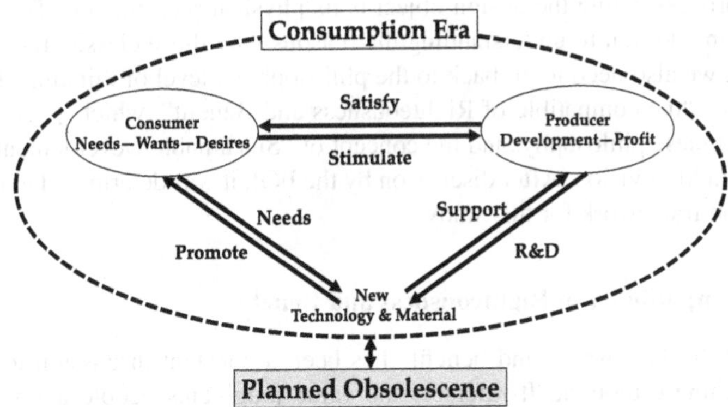

Fig. 1. Planned obsolescence and its relationship with consumption, market, and production.

2.2 Classic and Timeless Design: Inspiration from Eternity

The author has used classic designs as stimuli in the past to quantify audience perceptions. The study was divided into 2 separate sessions. In fact, in the process of conducting this research, we are thinking about why designs that were born a hundred years ago still have a strong charm. The first study focused on the Bauhaus, and the second study was conducted in terms of two lists about "100 Best-designed Products of the Modern Era".

The findings of these studies are as follows, and they provide important inspiration for this paper.

1. The continual influence of the Bauhaus classic design does exist in the contemporary design. Upon the research result, an in-depth discussion could be considered in the convergence of Bauhaus three claims and contemporary design thinking.
2. The core of the "good design" principles, continues the functionalism established during the Bauhaus period, but it needs to be continuously revised and improved over time. Audiences with backgrounds in design and other art fields, their knowledge, and acceptance of these principles are higher than others. While designers and manufacturers follow these principles, they should make timely adjustments based on feedback from the public. For any criteria for "good designs, there is no best, only the most appropriate.

We believe that the charm of classic design is so fascinating, in addition to its own advantages (such as good function and shape), may be related to the lack of refinement of current objects. And this is also related to the planned obsolescence.

3 Evaluation Criteria: The Collision of Philosophies or Ideas of the East and the West

As mentioned earlier, the emergence and development of "Planned Obsolescence" is a complex process, while the design object is its physical presentation. Therefore, we believe that in addition to understanding the reasons why those classic designs have a long history, we also need to go back to the philosophical level of thinking. Therefore, the concept of "the compatible of Righteousness and Benefit", which originated from traditional Chinese philosophy, and the concept of "Sustainable Development" entered the author's field of vision. After discussion by the FGI, it was determined to be used as the evaluation framework for this study.

3.1 The Compatibility of Righteousness and Benefit

The issue of "righteousness and benefit" has been a constant discussion topic in the history of Chinese thought. It refers to the value judgments people adopt based on morality and interest in the process of economic activity (see Table 1).

The pursuit of interest generally starts from the perspective of the individual, so "benefit" refers exclusively to "private benefit", while the object of morality has often been considered in terms of society as a whole. The meaning of the discrimination between righteousness and benefit can be thought of in broad and narrow senses. This article refers to the narrow sense group.

Table 1. Contrasting characteristics of righteousness and benefit.

	Attribute category	Representation	Objective orientation	Benefit characteristics	Demand	Wiggle Room	Performance under external influences
Righteousness	Social attribute	Civilization	Groups	Inclusive	Elastic	Big	Fragile/changeable
Benefit	Biological attribute	Instinct	Individuals	Exclusive	Rigid	Small	Strong/resilient

Source: [19]

Yan and Zheng [19] also summarized the definition and connotations of "Righteousness" and "Benefit".

1. Righteousness. In ancient China, righteousness was equivalent to rituals. It was not until the Eastern Han Dynasty (25–220 AD) that the meaning of righteousness developed into "fit and agreeable". Departing from phrases such as "fit for the time, agreeable to the masses", righteousness evolved gradually into "justice and kindness", and was then recognized as a core moral value of the Chinese nation. It is evidenced in an extract from the *Huainanzi* (The *Huainanzi* is an ancient Chinese book. It blends Daoist, Confucianist and Legalist concepts, including theories such as Yin-Yang and the Five Phases.): "the person who is "Righteousness" offers alms to others" [20].

2. Benefit. The original inscription of benefit in oracle bone script resembles a picture of a sickle reaping a mature crop. As food is the first necessity of people, it is natural that this character gradually evolves into the meaning of "gaining" [21]. Before the Spring and Autumn and Warring States periods, benefit was mainly interpreted as "luck" or "an auspicious sign", while afterwards it evolved to contain two layers of meaning: first, monetary gain in the economic sense, and secondly the pursuit of certain values such as Benefits and Accomplishments, corresponding more closely to the ethical norms associated with the concept of righteousness.

Prof. Yeh used a new framework to position the distinction between justice and profit in Mencius' political thought. He constructed four kinds of ideal-type (see Table 2) [22]. Comparing the arguments of ancestors in different eras, it is clear that it is no easy task to achieve the ideal state of balancing public and private and achieving unity between justice and interests.

Table 2. Four kinds of ideal-type.

Type	Introduction
Righteousness against Benefit (Replacement Pattern)	This principle emphasizes the irreconcilable conflict between justice and benefit. The nature of this principle is that either the choice of the end value or the method of thinking belongs to instrumental rationality leads to a binary opposition that leaves little room for compromise between justice and benefit. This principle requires decisions or actions to be based entirely on motivation or intention, but not on rational calculations and the assessment of opportunity and risks on an outcome level
Righteousness before Benefit (Conditional Pattern)	The nature of this principle is to maintain the binary opposition between justice and benefit. However, the principle emphasized that the two are not in a substitutional and opposite relationship of "either this or that", but only a kind of value priority
Righteousness qua Public Benefit (Reductive Pattern)	The nature of this principle is to break the binary opposition between justice and benefit, emphasizing that the two are not opposite nor prior to each other. Instead, they are a large part of the conceptual or substantial intersection, equivalent, or similarity. Therefore, they can be mutually reduced, transformed, or fused to a certain degree or form; their respective words or implications can be interpreted or explained
Righteousness derives Benefit (Causal Pattern)	This principle emphasizes the benefit that can be derived from justice. Such a benefit can be self, others, or public

Source: [22]

3.2 Circular Design: From Cultural Thinking to Sustainable Development

With the increase in the level of life needs, the consumer market has entered an era of emphasizing experience and aesthetics. Design is no longer just the pursuit of product functions and beautiful shapes. It is also dedicated to the inheritance and maintenance of culture. It is the creation of lifestyles and life tastes, experiences, and the practice of life value.

For consumers, if a design (or product) has no distinctive features and lacks cultural connotation, it can easily be regarded as a cold and unindividual thing. For users, despite using the functions a product provides, it is useless and meaningless to them. When the product's functions are exhausted, people will naturally abandon it. Therefore, people cherish it because they paid for it, but it is difficult to cherish it for a long period of time. If a design is so admirable that it can bring convenience and comfort on a spiritual level, users will definitely cherish it, and perhaps they will not easily eliminate the product due to changes in its form.

In addition to the design model formed by the user's more subjective needs, the emergence and improvement of the concept of sustainable development also provides us with more objective, comprehensive, and systematic guidance. The United Nations has set two global development goals, the Millennium Development Goals (MDGs) [23], proposed in 2000, and the Sustainable Development Goals (SDGs) [24] resulting from further updates at the end of 2015.

The most common problem with the planned obsolescence is that it causes excessive consumption of resources, unnecessary waste, but also produces a large amount of waste. At the same time, people in the process of dealing with these wastes, due to various reasons, cannot be disposed of in accordance with the norms, and thus, they cause irreparable, even irreversible, damage to the environment. It is true that we cannot put all the problems facing mankind today, such as ecological pollution, excessive consumption of resources, and climate warming, into design. However, the causes of these problems are more or less design-related because a material or a certain manufacturing step in the design has been chosen or because products have not been designed with good efficiency in mind and it has not been considered whether they could be recycled, reused, or easily repaired [25].

The concept of circular economy has attracted more and more attention from the scientific and policy-making communities. Some scholars and practitioners regard it as a new thing, but, in fact, it was built on the legacy of predecessors. It includes concepts such as waste recycling and separation, industrial ecology, eco-industrial parks, and industrial symbiosis. Various concepts (such as 3R, 4R) can be traced back to the 1980s. At present, the concept of sustainable design has expanded to a richer aspect: it can be called "Circular Economy" (R0-R9) (See Fig. 2).

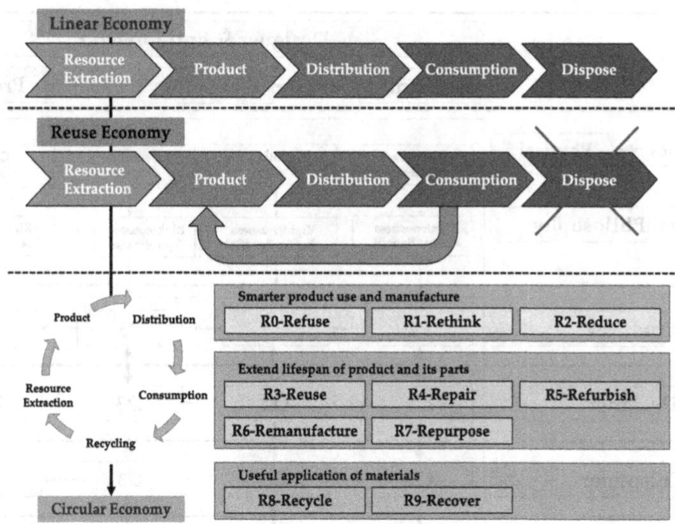

Fig. 2. From "Linear Economy", "Reuse Economy" to "Circular Economy".

3.3 Summary

The importance of designers as a communication bridge between producers and consumers is self-evident. The designer must not only have insight into the needs of consumers but must also meet the requirements of the producers and then use design to meet these needs. Based on literature review and FGI, this paper proposes a criterion for evaluating "Planned Obsolescence" (see Fig. 3), sixteen idioms have been selected as the criteria for assessment.

The meaning of these idioms has been explained separately below:

P1—Being duty-bound: cannot shift one's responsibility onto others.
P2—Valuing justice above wealth: to think highly of justice and virtue and look down on material possessions.
P3—Upholding justice and disdaining benefit: to advocate morality and look down on personal gain.
P4—Being careless of wealth but conscious of virtue: to be loyal and use one's own wealth to help others.
D1—Taking justice to be of benefit: to regard justice and virtue as profit.
D2—Responsibility comes before benefit: to perform duties and obligations actively and be patient when sharing interests.
D3—Making light of wealth and considering love to be righteous: to prize righteousness and benevolence above wealth.
D4—Thinking of righteousness on seeing gain: justice calls to mind when seeing profits.
C1—Cherishing one's blessings and possessions: to love and cherish all things.
C2—Showing empathy: to imagine how others feel in the same situation.
C3—Being selfless: to consider others' interests before one's own.
C4—Gaining both justice and benefit: both justice and interest are obtained.

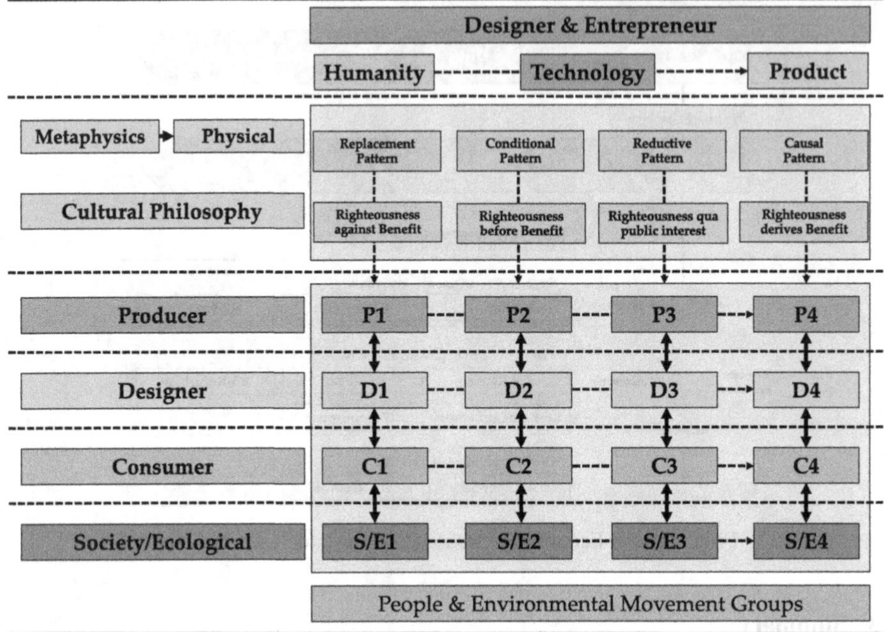

Fig. 3. Evaluation criteria.

S/E1—Taking the interests of the whole into account: to consider the whole situation or the whole picture in everything you do.
S/E2—Using righteousness to restrict profit: to control private interest using righteousness and mortality.
S/E3—Being moderate in taking and giving: to be self-control in obtaining and giving.
S/E4—Gradual improvement: to proceed or improve steadily based on specific steps or processes.

4 Conclusion and Follow-Up Research

Producers, designers, and consumers all have their own professional ethics and values as well as different cognitive models. In the eyes of producers and designers, the desire of consumers for various products is seen as a potential business opportunity and money cow. No savvy businessman or imaginative designer will fill this "niche". Turning a blind eye to this issue means that it is easy to be surpassed by competitors. The use of the term "savvy" here is not entirely derogatory. The merchant's pursuit of profit is understandable as long as they adopt conventional and proper methods, that is, they truly achieve a balance between righteousness and profit. The author believes that, while expanding the market, business should not only see the immediate benefits but should also consider the adverse effects of their products on resources, the environment, and consumers. In addition, it should be pointed out that producers and designers are also consumers to some extent.

Therefore, to construct a virtuous and moderate "production—design—consumption" cycle. The communication needs to be strengthened, and this can develop in a modest, moderate, and materialized direction. The interests of producers and consumers are not only material or spiritual. Putting aside the identity labels "producer" and "consumer", we all live in the same world, and the environment is a common source of wealth for everyone that can be regarded as a "public benefit". Conversely, the "profit" of producers and consumers is a kind of "individual benefit". The balance of righteousness in this benefit-making process as much as possible is the appropriate core guiding principle for us to use in correcting the deficiencies of planned obsolescence (see Fig. 4).

In the follow-up study, we selected suitable samples as stimuli according to the above evaluation criteria, and learned about the public's attitude through questionnaires. In order to conduct more objective research, the selection of stimulants and the design of problems will be the focus of the next stage of research. It's not to propose a new design approach to reduce the impact of planned obsolescence, but to use the philosophy of the Chinese sages to explain the purpose of "compliance with human nature".

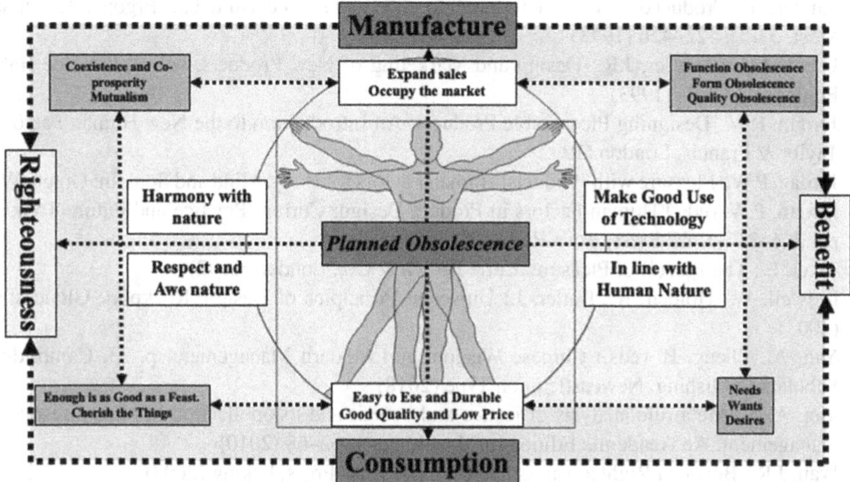

Fig. 4. Harmony between cultural industry and sustainable development: the development model of planned obsolescence from the perspective of "the compatible of righteousness and benefit".

References

1. The Great Lightbulb Conspiracy: The Phoebus Cartel Engineered a Shorter-lived Lightbulb and Gave Birth to Planned Obsolescence. https://spectrum.ieee.org/the-great-lightbulb-conspiracy#toggle-gdpr. last accessed 15 Aug 2021
2. The L.E.D. Quandary: Why There's No Such Thing as "Built to Last". https://www.newyorker.com/business/currency/the-l-e-d-quandary-why-theres-no-such-thing-as-built-to-last. last accessed 15 Aug 2021

3. The Light Bulb Conspiracy: https://www.youtube.com/watch?v=BWJC5ieUAe4. last accessed 15 Aug 2021
4. Anonymous: Annual style change in the automobile industry as an unfair method of competition. Yale Law J. **80**(3), 567–613 (1971)
5. Selander, S.E.: Is annual style change in the automobile industry an unfair method of competition? A Rebuttal. Yale Law J. **82**(4), 691–710 (1973)
6. Snell, B.C.: Is annual style change in the automobile industry an unfair method of competition? a rebuttal: a reply. Yale Law J. **82**(4), 711–714 (1973)
7. Maslow, A.H.: A Theory of Human Motivation. Psychol. Rev. **50**(4), 370–396 (1943)
8. Maslow, A.H.: The farther reaches of human nature. J. Transpersonal Psychol. **1**(1), 1–9 (1969)
9. Maslow, A.H.: Motivation and Personality. Harper, New York (1954)
10. Darley, J.M., Glucksberg, S., Kinchla, R.A.: Psychology, 5th edn. Prentice Hall, Englewood Cliffs, NJ (1991)
11. Geschka, H., Holt, K., Peterlongo, G.: Need Assessment-A Key to User-oriented Product Innovation. University of Trondheim, Norwegian Institute of Technology (1981)
12. Park, C.W., Jaworski, B.J., Maclnnis, D.J.: Strategic brand concept-image management. J Mark **50**(4), 135–145 (1986)
13. Sanders, E.: Product development research for the 1990's. Proc. Hum. Fac. Ergon. Soc. Annu. Meet. **37**(5), 422–426 (1993)
14. Urban, G.L., Hauser, J.R.: Design and Marketing of New Products, vol. 2, Prentice Hall, Englewood Cliffs (1993)
15. Jordan, P.W.: Designing Pleasurable Products: An Introduction to the New Human Factors. Taylor & Francis, London (1992)
16. Jordan, P.W.: Pleasure with Products: Human Factors for Body, Mind and Soul. In: Green, W., Jordan, P.W. (eds.) Human Factors in Product Design: Current Practice and Future Trends, pp. 206–217. CRC Press, Boca Raton (1999)
17. Tiger, L.: The Pursuit of Pleasure. Little Brown & Co., London (1992)
18. Lidwell, W., Holden, K., Butler, J.: Universal Principles of Design. Rockport, Gloucester (2003)
19. Yan, A., Zheng, B. (eds.) Chinese Wisdom and Modern Management, p. 33. Cambridge Scholars Publishing, Newcastle upon Tyne (2018)
20. Yan, A.M.: Meta-rule analysis of justice and benefit and its application to human resource management. An Academic Edition of ManaMaga **1**, 62–68 (2010)
21. Wan, J.R.: Between Righteousness and Benefit. Unity Press, Peking (2003)
22. Yeh, J.C.: An analysis of the distinction between propriety and benefit in Mencius's political thought. Political Sci. Rev. **50**, 1–36 (2011)
23. United Nations Millennium Declaration: https://www.un.org/en/development/desa/population/migration/generalassembly/docs/globalcompact/A_RES_55_2.pdf. last accessed 11 Nov 2021
24. Transforming our world: the 2030 Agenda for Sustainable Development. https://www.un.org/ga/search/view_doc.asp?symbol=A/RES/70/1&Lang=E. last accessed 11 Nov 2021
25. Griffith, S.: Eat your greens! or design will eat itself! Des. Manag. Rev **19**(4), 34–41 (2011)

A Study of Bilingual Oscillatory Display: Effect of Interference Language and Comparison with Language Switching Display

Kimi Ueda(✉), Takumi Uotani, Hirotake Ishii, and Hiroshi Shimoda

Kyoto University, Yoshida-honmachi, Kyoto 6068501, Japan
{ueda,uotani,hirotake,shimoda}@ei.energy.kyoto-u.ac.jp

Abstract. Multilingual display methods on digital signage can be broadly classified into simultaneous multilingual display and language switching display (LSD). However, these methods have problems such as reduced readability due to smaller font size and time spent waiting for the desired language to be displayed. To solve these problems, the authors have proposed bilingual oscillatory display (BOD), a method of simultaneous display of two languages using animation, to display both language without diminishing their font size in the same size of screen, either without waiting time for both native speakers of two languages. The objectives of this study were to examine the effect of interfering language difference in BOD, and to compare BOD and conventional LSD. An experiment was conducted to measure reading time of the target Japanese sentence displayed in BOD of Japanese and Korean BOD (JP-KR BOD), BOD of Japanese and Japanese (JP-JP BOD) and Japanese monolingual display (Single JP). As a result, reading time of JP-KR BOD was significantly shorter than JP-JP BOD and expected reading time of LSD calculated by single JP. Results suggested that readability of BOD was improved if the interference sentence was written in different language with the target sentence. It was also suggested that BOD could provide more information in a unit of time.

Keywords: Multilingual · Digital signage · Animated text · Display method · Bilingual oscillatory display

1 Introduction

Multilingual display methods on digital signage can be broadly classified into multilingual simultaneous display (MSD) and language switching display (LSD). However, these methods have problems, such as MSD decrease its readability by small font size on the same screen size, either LSD takes time to wait the desired language or switches to another language before finishing reading, which increases the reading time. In order to solve the problems of conventional display

P.-L. P. Rau (Ed.): HCII 2022, LNCS 13311, pp. 91–102, 2022.
https://doi.org/10.1007/978-3-031-06038-0_7

methods, we have proposed "bilingual oscillatory display (BOD)" [1,2], which is a method of simultaneous display of two languages using animation, as a method that can be displayed on the same screen size with normal font size and without waiting time. The image of the BOD method is shown in Fig. 1. In the BOD, a sentence in one language is inserted between the lines of text in the other language. Separate animations are given to each language to keep readability with the law of common fate [3].

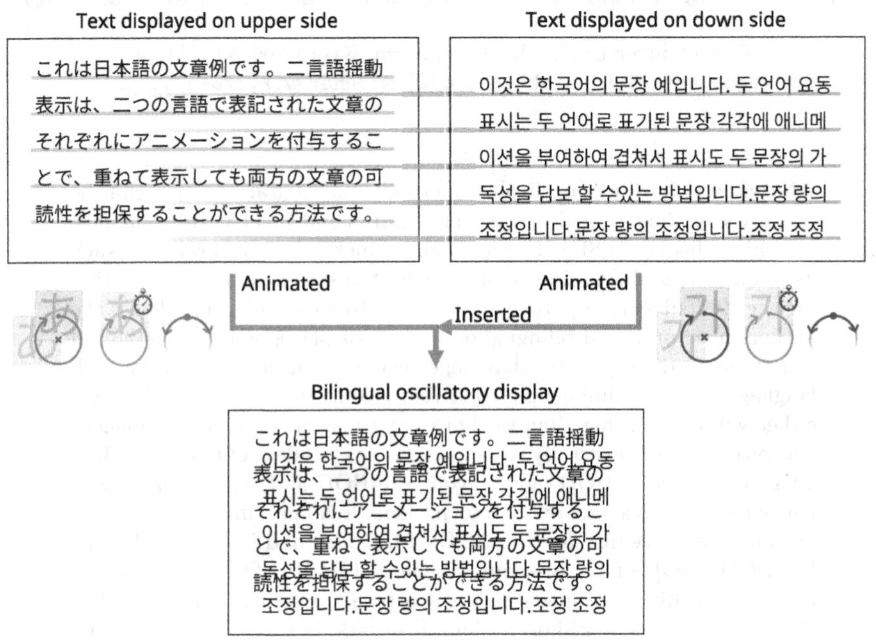

Fig. 1. Concept image of the BOD: Bilingual oscillatory display.

When text is presented on a display controlled by a computer, such as in digital signage, the text can be easily animated. Kinetic Typography [4] is one of the attempts to give motion to text for some effect. Lee et al. [5] showed that Kinetic Typography can evoke specific emotions by evaluating users' emotions when Kinetic Typography was applied into a messenger service. Although there have been some attempts to add animation to text, there are few examples of using it to improve readability like BOD.

Various efforts have been made to support multilingual display on digital signage. Examples include a study that attempted to adjust the displayed language for a specific viewer around the display by using some kind of device, such as a system that using information received from the viewer's smartphone [6], and a study that clarified the appropriate margins and layout for traffic signs in two languages with different language systems [7]. However, few studies have attempted to present information in multiple languages like the BOD, where native speakers of different languages can recognize at the same time and the display size remains the same, without reducing the font size.

The readability of BOD can be considered to vary depending on various factors. In this study, it was examined how the readability of target sentences, which are sentences that viewers read, is affected by differences in the language of obstructed sentences, which are sentences that viewers do not read, based on reading time evaluation. The readability of BOD was also discussed based on the comparison between BOD and conventional LSD.

2 Objective

The objectives of this study are to examine the effect of interfering language difference and to compare BOD and conventional LSD.

To complete the objectives, an experiment was conducted to measure reading time of 3 language displaying methods: (A) BOD that target sentence in native language and interfering sentence in non-native language, (B) BOD that target sentence is native language and interfering sentence is also native language, and (C) Monolingual static display of native language to calculate the reading time of (C') Expected reading time of LSD. To discuss about the effect of interfering language difference, reading time of (A) and (B) was compared, and to discuss about the comparison between BOD and conventional LSD, reading time of (A) and (C') was compared.

3 Methods

3.1 Experimental Conditions: Three Display Methods

The reading time was measured for three different conditions:

JP-KR BOD BOD of Japanese and Korean as (A)
JP-JP BOD BOD of two Japanese sentences as (B)
Single JP Monolingual static text in Japanese as (C)

The target sentences to be read for measuring reading time were in Japanese because the experiment was conducted on native Japanese speakers. Korean was chosen as the non-native language to be used for the interfering sentences in (A), because it allows free setting of line breaks and minimizes the effects of line ending positions on sentence length and readability. The Japanese and Korean sentences to be presented were collected from international news sites. The Japanese sentences used as target sentence were chosen based on the results of the screening experiment in advance; The reading time of five native Japanese speakers was measured for 200 sentence, and 96 sentences were adopted to minimize the variance of Z-value of reading time.

In the BOD, two sentences are displayed on the upper and lower sides as shown in Fig. 1. In the experiment, 16 participants were instructed to read the upper sentence, and the remaining 16 participants to read the lower sentence as the target sentence. In order for the participants to understand whether the upper or lower sentence was the target sentence to be read, practice tasks were conducted before measuring the reading time. The BOD displayed in the first practice was in which all the interfering sentences are "○". This is referred to as the JP-○ BOD. The examples of three presentation methods to be evaluated and the JP-○ BOD screen are shown in Fig. 2.

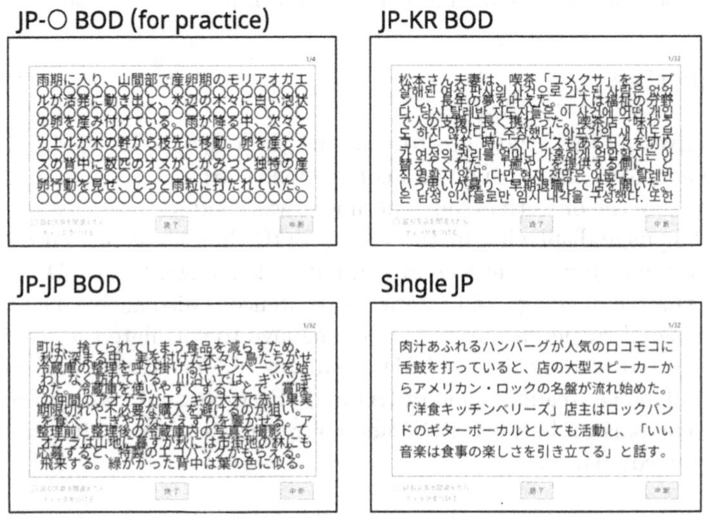

Fig. 2. Examples of displayed sentences in four display methods.

For the BOD, three types of parameters: amplitude, oscillation cycle and rotation direction are used to control the animation of two displayed sentences as shown in Fig. 2. The parameters to apply in this experiment are shown in Table 1, which were chosen based on our previous studies. There are $(3 \times 4)^2 - (1 \times 4)^2 = 128$ combinations of amplitude and oscillation cycle, excluding the case where both 0.0 % amplitude on target and interfering sentences. 32 combinations our of 128 were assigned to each participant. Therefore, if 36 participants data of reading time were obtained, the number of reading time of each parameters' combination can be obtained was same throughout the overall experiment. In the same way, we assigned the same number of combinations of the rotation direction of the target and the interfering sentence so that the number of reading time data would be the same for each combination throughout the experiment. Each participant would read the JP-JP BOD and the JP-KR BOD displayed with common parameters.

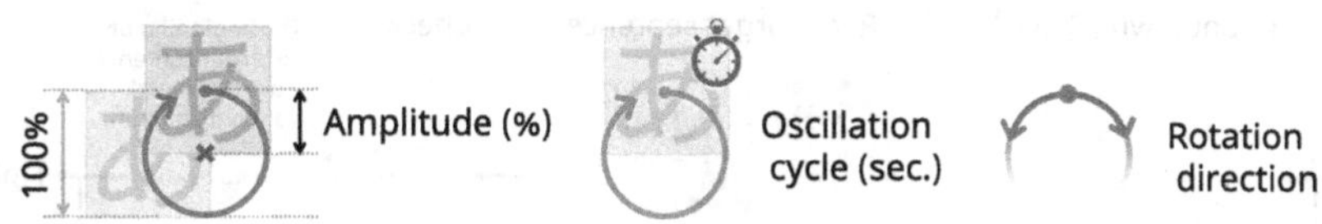

Fig. 3. Explanation images of the three types of animation parameters used to control BOD.

Table 1. Applied animation parameters [1]

Parameters	Adopted value
Amplitude (%)	0.0, 7.1, 28.6
Oscillation cycle (s)	0.94, 1.25, 1.57, 2.22
Rotation direction	Clockwise (CW), Counter-clockwise (CCW)

3.2 Reading Time Measurement

The experiment was conducted with the following steps:

Explanation Explanation about the experiment was provided and consent to participate in the experiment was obtained.

Practice 1 Participants were asked to read 4 target sentences of JP-○ BOD and check the position of the target sentence, upper side or down side.

Practice 2 Participants were asked to read 8 target sentences of JP-JP BOD and check whether they understand the location of the target sentence.

Practice 3 Participants were asked to read 8 target sentences each of JP-JP BOD, the JP-KR BOD, and the single JP. The order of three display methods was as same as that of SET 1 to 3 of measurement task SETs.

SET 1, SET 2, SET 3 Reading time data was obtained in these SETs. Participants were asked to read 32 sentences displayed in one of the display methods in each SET. The order of three display methods were counter balanced.

A schematic of the reading time measurement task is shown in Fig. 4. When reading a sentence, the participants were instructed to read the sentence from the beginning to the end without any skips, and to be conscious of reading the sentence aloud in their minds.

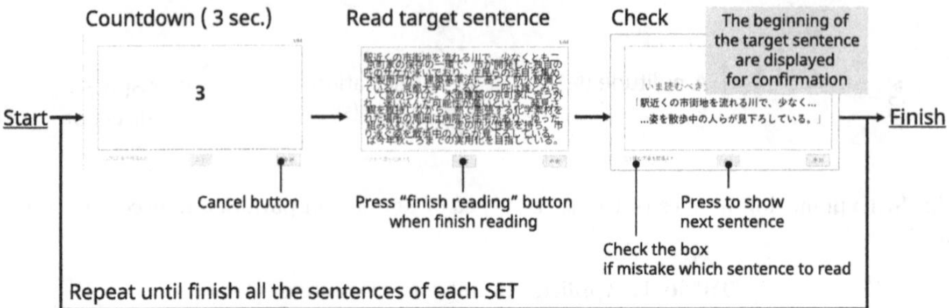

Fig. 4. The flow of reading time measurement task.

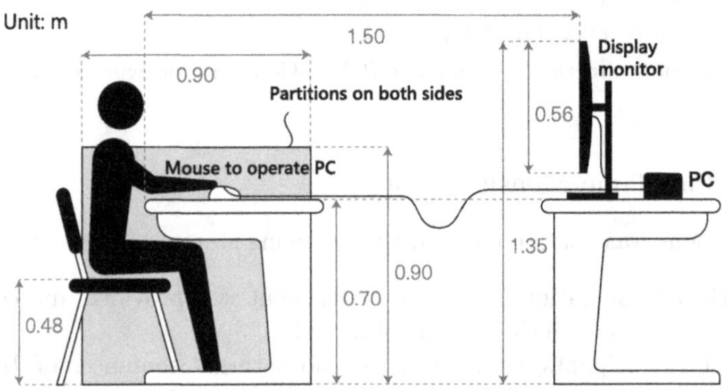

Fig. 5. Settings of the space to conduct reading time measurement task.

Participants performed the reading time measurement task in the experimental space set as shown in Fig. 5. The size of the characters displayed on the screen was adjusted based on the findings of Ohashi et al. [8].

3.3 Schedules and Participants

The experiment was conducted from November 27, 2021 to December 27, 2021. Permission to conduct the experiment was obtained by the author's graduate school based on the "Guidelines for Conducting Research Involving Human Subjects". All participants were informed about the experiment and agreed to participate in the experiment.

The experiment was conducted until 36 participants completed the reading time measurements without reading an interfering sentence mistaken for the target sentence. When totally 40 participants participated in the experiment, 36 valid participants' data were obtained.

4 Results

The reading time data for $36 \times 32 = 1,152$ sentences for each display method are shown in Fig. 6 along with box plots.

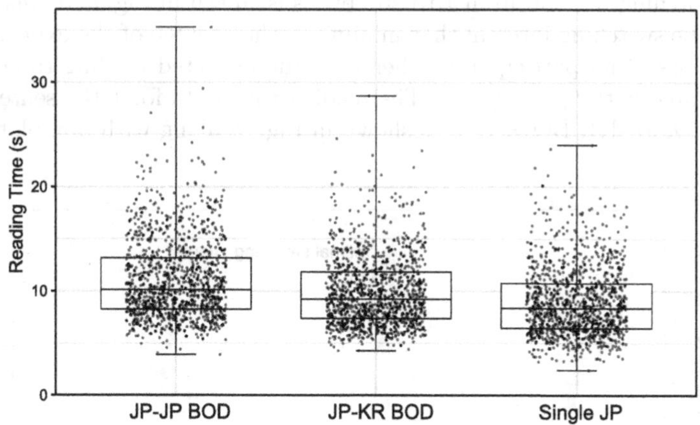

Fig. 6. Obtained reading time data for JP-JP BOD, JP-KR BOD and Single JP and their box plots.

4.1 Calculation of Expected Reading Time of LSD

In the LSD, the reading time of native language differs depending on the timing when the viewer starts reading and when the display language is switched. Thus, in this study, expected reading time of LSD of two languages based on the results of single JP reading time were calculated for discussion. The following 2 assumptions were made in the calculation.

Assumption 1 The switching interval of the LSD is constant regardless of the displayed language.

Assumption 2 If the screen is switched in the middle of reading a sentence in the native language, viewers can resume reading immediately from the point of interruption when the sentence in the native language is displayed again.

If the reading time of Single JP is t_r and the switching interval of displayed language is t_s and the maximum number of times the screen of a language that cannot be read is displayed before reading is completed is $k(\in \mathbb{N})$, the following relationship holds.

$$(k-1)t_s < t_r \leq kt_s \tag{1}$$

The expected reading time of LSD can be expressed by the following formula.

$$E_{LSD}(t_r, t_s) = \frac{3}{2} + \frac{2k-1}{4}t_s \tag{2}$$

The average expected reading time of LSD of all participants calculated by varying the switching interval from 1 to 25 s by 1 s is shown in Fig. 7. It was decided to adopt the switching interval that minimized the average of the expected LSD reading times of all participants. Therefore, the expected reading time of LSD was calculated with $t_s = 11(sec.)$. The reading time data for 1,152 sentences for JP-JP BOD, JP-KR BOD, LSD is shown in Fig. 8 along with box plots.

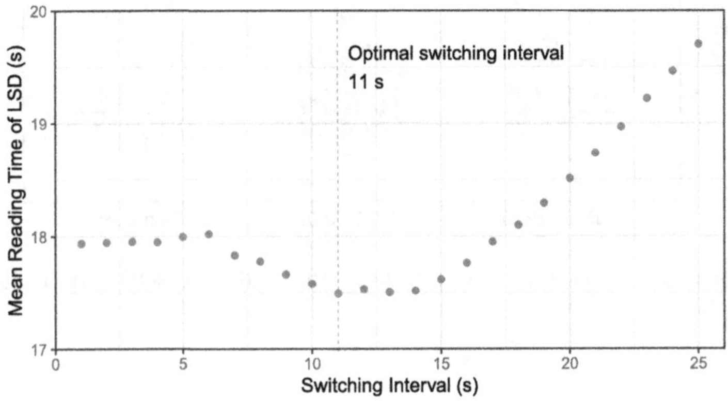

Fig. 7. Mean expected reading time of LSD by varying the switching interval from 1 s to 25 s. calculated by the reading time data for Single JP.

4.2 Statistical Analysis

The reading time data of in three displayed methods: JP-JP BOD, JP-KR BOD and LSD, was averaged for each participant. Multiple comparisons were made of the average reading time of the JP-JP BOD, the JP-KR BOD, and LSD. The reading times for each display method were averaged for each participant, thus the average reading time for 36 participants were obtained for each method. Shapiro-Wilk tests were conducted to examine the normality of the mean reading time data of each display method. The results of Shapiro-Wilk test's p values were as follows: p = .047 for JP-KR BOD, p = .021 for JP-JP BOD, and p = .002 for LSD. In all methods, the null hypothesis that the mean reading time follows a normal distribution was rejected. As mentioned earlier, each participant measured the reading time of the BOD controlled by the same parameters and the Single JP displayed also in the same position as the target sentence of BOD. Thus, the reading times averaged for each participant could be analyzed by paired test. Therefore, Wilcoxon's signed rank test was conducted to analyze

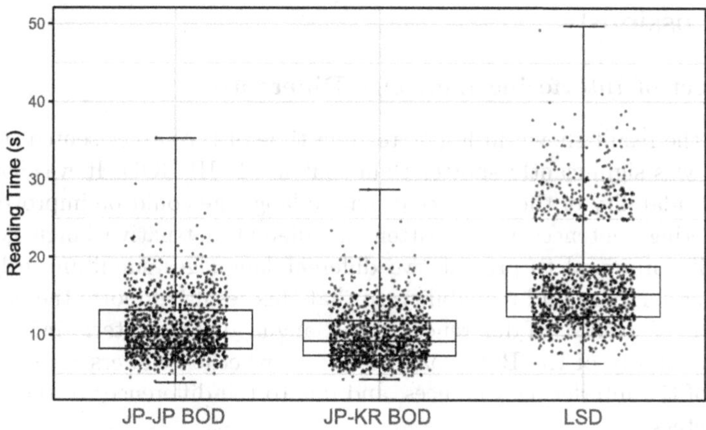

Fig. 8. Obtained reading time data for JP-JP BOD, JP-KR BOD and LSD calculated based on the Single JP and their box plots.

the effect between three display methods, while the multiplicity of tests was corrected by the Bonferroni method.

Figure 9 shows the results of averaging the reading times of all participants for each display method. The test results of the above multiple comparisons are also shown in Fig. 9. The error bars represent the standard deviation. Figure 9 shows that the mean reading time in the JP-KR BOD was significantly shorter than that in LSD ($p < .001$). The mean reading time in JP-KR BOD was significantly shorter than the mean reading time in LSD ($p < .001$).

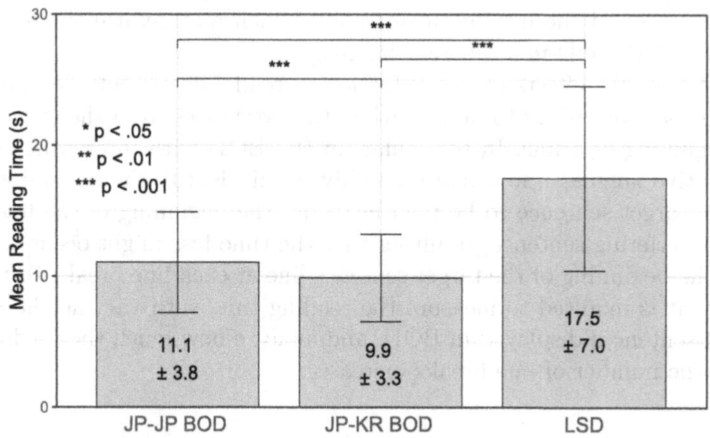

Fig. 9. Average reading time for JP-JP BOD, JP-KR BOD and LSD and the results of the Wilcoxon's signed rank test.

5 Discussions

5.1 Effect of Interfering Language Difference

Based on the result shown in Fig. 9, reading time of the target sentences in JP-KR BOD was significantly shorter than that in JP-JP BOD. It was suggested that the readability of the sentence of native language could be improved when the interfering sentences were written in different not-native language. BOD is originally proposed to present two different languages simultaneously while maintaining font size and readability, so that this result supports the usefulness of the BOD. The effect of differences in the language of the interfering sentences on the readability of the BOD may be due to whether viewers recognized the meaning of the interfering sentences, and due to the differences in the shape of the characters.

When reading target sentences in (A) BOD in which the interfering sentence is not in their native language, viewers cannot recognize the meaning of the interfering sentence when reading the target sentence. On the other hand, when reading target sentences in (B) BOD in which the interfering sentence is also in their native language, viewers can recognize the meaning of the interfering sentence while reading the target sentence. Therefore, it is possible that the process of reading the target sentence is more strongly interfered with when (B) the interfering sentence is in the native language, resulting in a difference in reading time in this experiment.

In the BOD, by giving each sentence a different oscillating expression, a gestalt is expected to be formed for each sentence by the law of common fate, so that it would be possible to read each sentence separately even if they overlap. In other words, in (B) BOD of two sentences both written in native languages, the similarity of the written characters may lead to form a gestalt between the target sentence and the interfering sentence, which may reduce the readability compared to (A) BOD in a different language.

In addition, the effects of the reduction in readability mentioned above are thought to be more likely to appear when the eye moves from the end of a line to the beginning of a line. In particular, in (B) BOD with interfering sentence written native language, it is more possibly to misidentify the beginning of the line of the target sentence to be read next and the beginning of the line of the adjacent interfering sentence, resulting that the time loss might occur to search where is the beginning of the target sentence line at each line break. To test this possibility, it is required to measure the reading time with varying the number of lines of sentences displayed in BOD, and analyze how much the reading time differs as the number of line breaks increases.

5.2 Comparison Between BOD and Conventional LSD

Based on the result shown in Fig. 9, reading time of the target sentences in JP-KR BOD was significantly shorter than that in LSD. A shorter reading time for a certain length of text indicates that the amount of information that the viewer could recognize per unit time could be larger. Therefore, results of significantly shorter reading time of (A) BOD compared with (C') LSD suggested that the BOD method successes to provide more information to viewers without decreasing the size of characters or making people wait for their desired language displayed.

In this study, we only dealt with the case of viewing the stimuli with fixing the viewpoint in front of the display. In actual digital signage, people view the displayed contents on digital signages while walking. Thus, as a future works, it is required to investigate how the readability of the BOD changes when it is viewed from different angle or while moving the viewpoint.

6 Conclusion

The purpose of this study was to investigate the effect of whether the interfering sentence is in the native language or not on the reading time of target sentences written in native language in BOD, and to compare its reading time with that of the conventional display method, LSD. Results of the experiment showed that the reading time was significantly shorter for the JP-KR BOD provided as (A) BOD with non-native interfering language, than that of JP-JP BOD provided as (B) BOD with native interfering language, suggesting that the readability of the target sentence could be improved when the interfering sentence is not written in viewers' native language. In addition, by calculating the expected reading time of LSD based on the reading time of monolingual Japanese sentences, (A) BOD with different language and (C') LSD was compared. Results suggested that (A) BOD is expected to increase the amount of information that can be conveyed in a unit of time compared to the language switching display.

In this study, it was able to obtain some findings that suggest the usefulness of the BOD. However, as mentioned in the discussion, various factors may affect the readability of the BOD, and further study is required.

References

1. Uotani, T., et al.: A study on exploration of suitable animation parameters for bilingual oscillatory display on digital signage. In: International Symposium on Socially and Technically Symbiotic Systems 2021, no. 29 (2021)
2. Uotani, T., et al.: A study on dual-language display method using the law of common fate in oscillatory animation on digital signage. In: Stephanidis, C., et al. (eds.) HCII 2021. LNCS, vol. 13094, pp. 412–423. Springer, Cham (2021). https://doi.org/10.1007/978-3-030-90238-4_29
3. Uttal, W.R., Spillmann, L., Stürzel, F., Sekuler, A.B.: Motion and shape in common fate. Vision Res. **40**(3), 301–310 (2000)
4. Ford, S., Forlizzi, J., Ishizaki, S.: Kinetic typography: issues in time-based presentation of text. In: CHI 1997 Extended Abstracts on Human Factors in Computing Systems, pp. 269–270. CHI EA 1997. Association for Computing Machinery, New York (1997)

5. Lee, J., Jun, S., Forlizzi, J., Hudson, S.E.: Using kinetic typography to convey emotion in text-based interpersonal communication. In: Proceedings of the 6th Conference on Designing Interactive Systems, pp. 41–49. DIS 2006. Association for Computing Machinery, New York (2006)
6. Ogi, T., Ito, K., Konita, S.: Multilingual digital signage using iBeacon communication. In: 2016 19th International Conference on Network-Based Information Systems (NBiS), pp. 387–392, September 2016
7. Zhang, Y.: Effects of text space of Chinese-English bilingual traffic sign on driver reading performance. Displays **67**, 102002 (2021)
8. Ohashi, T., Miyazaki, M.: A fundamental study of character layout in newspapers, no. 4: a study of character size, tracking and line spacing (32nd annual conference). des. Stud 52, 26 (1985)

The Knowledge Payment Turn in Human-Computer Interaction: A Study from the Para-Social Interaction Perspective

Wu Wei and Weilong Wu(✉)

School of Film Television and Communication, Xiamen University of Technology, Xiamen, Fujian, China
wu_academic@163.com

Abstract. With the progress of human-computer interaction technology, knowledge communication in China is gradually shifting from offline to online. Nowadays, online knowledge payment has become a new way for knowledge communication. However, the convenience and abundance of online knowledge not only makes it difficult for users to choose, but also creates problems such as knowledge anxiety, which is directly reflected in the declining revenue of the online knowledge payment industry. In this online context, the interaction between human and computer has become an important field of the current knowledge communication research, and para-social interaction can reflect this relationship to some extent.

This research based on qualitative approach, using the semi-structured method to conduct in-depth interviews with six users who have online knowledge payment experience. According to the interview results, four dimensions affecting users' psychology and behavior are summarized: the perception of character roles, the continuation of interactive relationships, the appearance of online knowledge communication, and the dissonance of human-computer interaction. The research results not only point out that there is a gap between users' subjectivity and media experience in the online knowledge payment process, but also clarify the current knowledge communication from a psychological approach.

Keywords: Online knowledge payment · Human-computer interaction · User experience · Para-social interaction

1 Introduction

Knowledge communication has been deemed as the necessary driving force for the continuous development and improvement of human society, and with the rise of a new way to communicate knowledge—online knowledge payment, new industries based on online knowledge payment have emerged. Knowledge communication as we mentioned here is a process of a social activity in which some members of the society communicate specific knowledge to other members of the society with the help of specific knowledge communication media in a specific social environment and expect to receive the expected effect. Media technology—including the Internet and mobile phones—not only speeds

P.-L. P. Rau (Ed.): HCII 2022, LNCS 13311, pp. 103–116, 2022.
https://doi.org/10.1007/978-3-031-06038-0_8

up the efficiency of knowledge communication, but also enriches the connotation of knowledge and expands the scope of communication.

The production and communication of knowledge has been playing an important role in human history and civilization. With the emergence and progress of the Internet, people's access to information and knowledge and the way of exchanging information and knowledge have been greatly affected [1]. Knowledge payment in Chinese mainland has stepped into the 3.0 stage [2]. Unlike traditional knowledge communication which emphasizes the commonweal and exchangeability of knowledge [3], today's online knowledge payment is the process of turning knowledge into products and services for communication, which cannot be separated from the interaction between human and media technology. However, the current online knowledge payment is suffering from the "undetermined user behavior" as called by O'Reilly [4]. On the one hand, with the extensive development of the Internet, information becomes increasingly over-loaded, making it harder for users to filter out high-value knowledge [5]; on the other hand, as the public becomes less interested in paying for knowledge online, the total time they spent on learning knowledge online shrinks and the repurchase rate declines [6]. Therefore, some studies believe that too abundant online knowledge and convenient access to knowledge not only make it difficult for users to choose, but also cause their knowledge anxiety [7].

Abandoning the cumbersome knowledge media and traditional knowledge communication mode, online knowledge payment not only endows knowledge with the characteristics of virtualization, digitization and mobility [8], but also makes the subject of knowledge communication with a shift from "human-human" to "human-computer". This study attempts to explore the interaction between human and computer in the context of this new era of knowledge communication. More specifically, this study attempts to explore why online knowledge payment industry declines under the rapid development of human-computer interaction, and what implications this has brought for the current and future knowledge communication.

2 Literature Review

2.1 The Development and Shift of Human-Computer Interaction

With the development of communication technology, media has played a far-reaching role in human society. It not only brings fundamental changes to human society, but also constitutes new contexts in current political, economic, cultural and social life [9]. "Web 6.0" "Internet of things" and "smart media" have emerged one after another in a very short time, but it should be noted that the development and application of media technology are tightly linked to human—the immersion, interaction, and imagination of virtual reality [10], as well as artificial intelligence, machine learning, and deep learning—they are all built through the two-way perception between users and the media. In other words, the focus of media technology should be on human.

However, in the early human-computer interaction, the agency of human was not emphasized, and human was required to adapt to technology. This situation has not been changed until the "man-computer symbiosis" [11] proposed by Licklider in the 1960s became the enlightenment of the concept of human-computer interaction. In the 1990s, the rise and progress of computer multimedia technology provided a new direction for human-computer interaction study. For example, a large number of graphical interfaces were added to the third generation Windows-DOS system launched by Microsoft to facilitate user operation. Besides, nowadays, smart phones and speakers can broadcast news and switch on the light after users simply give oral voice instructions. During the development of human-computer interaction, "machine-oriented" has changed to "user-centered" [12], "human adapt to technology" has gradually changed to "technology adapt to human", and more and more emphasis is placed on satisfying the individual needs. In general, human-computer interaction has shifted from "machine-centered" to "user-centered" [13].

As to study on human-computer interaction, attention should not only focus on the perspective of the technology, but also on the human - how the communication relationship between human and computer affects the social and cultural environment, and how the communication relationship is affected by the social and cultural environment. Nowadays, there is a new approach starts from users' life and emphasizes the sensitivity to perceived and personal experience [14]. At the application of media, human-computer interaction presents multi-modality development trend, characterized by making full use of the complementarity of human's multiple perceptual modes to reflect users' intention, getting rid of the constraints of conventional input devices, and then giving full play to human's daily skills for human-computer interaction [15]. Behind this approach is a new media research paradigm—practice paradigm, that is, to regard media as a practical behavior rather than as a text or a production structure. It studies all categories of practical behaviors that are media oriented or related to media, as well as the role of media in organizing other social practical behaviors [16]. Influenced by practice turn, Couldry [17] believes that we must think about one question, which is, what do people do with media?

2.2 The Identification of Para-Social Interaction

Para-social interaction can reflect the relationship between human-computer interaction from the psychological perspective. Although human-computer interaction usually refers to users' behaviors of using the computer as a medium, the sociality contained therein has also become a research direction. For example, when users interact with the computer, they are actually providing usage feedback to the software program designers [18], which reflects the core of para-social interaction, that is, users react to the characters in the media by regarding them as real characters and forms a para-social relationship with them, which is similar to the interpersonal relationship established in face-to-face communication [19]. However, when Horton and Wohl developed this theory in 1956, they pointed out that such para-social relationship is different from the interpersonal relationship established face-to-face in reality. It is a relationship that is "one-sided, non-dialectical, not susceptible of mutual development" [20]. So far, para-social interaction has been used to study audiences and TV news hosts [21], soap opera characters [22], sitcom characters [23], the Internet characters [24], etc.

As seen from the perspective of psychology, para-social interaction describes the emotional attachment between users and media personalities [25]. As said by Horton and Wohl, para-social interaction is "a simulacrum of conversational give and take, and the embodiment of which is 'personae' in the media" [20]. The "character attachment" has become a very important point in the study on para-social interaction [26]. The media characters mentioned here can be real ones such as hosts, actors and athletes, or fictional ones such as cartoon images, poster characters and animated characters. It has been found that the more audiences perceive and pay attention to the role, the stronger the audiences' para-social interaction with the role [27], and this kind of para-social interaction will also be positively affected by the reinforcement of the audiences' contact with the corresponding media [28].

In a word, users tend to have special feelings towards their favorite media characters or roles, thus leading to para-social interaction similar to real social interaction. For most people, para-social interaction serves as a "complement" to real social interaction, but for those deprived of normal social interaction, they often need to satisfy their psychological needs through para-social interaction [20]. It should also be pointed out here that the concept of para-social interaction was put forward in the United States in the 1950s—a period of rapid economic development after entering the information age, which was accompanied by the emergence of a large number of "lonely" people [29]. In today's digital age, the new media technology ecology has subverted the traditional communication mode, and the relationship between new media and users is becoming more and more important in researches on communication [30]. A concept called as "new audience research" has promoted the practical turn of media research [31], and the para-social interaction is conforming to the convergence of this era.

2.3 The Reflections of Human-Computer Interaction and Para-Social Interaction

It is meaningful to explore para-social interaction in these days, not only because the media ecology has seen great changes, but also the communication process can no longer be simply explained by mass communication or interpersonal communication [32]. On the one hand, media as a vehicle of a field, the interactive form and expression content will determine the possibility of para-social interaction [33]. On the other hand, media has also become an important participant in social life. As found by SRCT (social responses to communication technology) research team of Stanford University, people tend to place social norms and social expectations on the interaction between human and computer, and regard the computer as a friends of conversation, which is similar to the general human-to-human interaction pattern [14]. Today's online knowledge payment is the most proper manifestation in this regard. The knowledge content itself, speakers' expression and user interaction have become more and more important, while users' preference for online knowledge payment platforms or Apps reflects the cognitive relationship between human and computer.

In the process of reviewing the past studies, it is found that the research of para-social interaction mainly focused on the quantitative research of television. Besides Likert-Scale, such as semantic differential scale [34] and repertory grid [35] are also adopted to measure. Although some studies choose the radio [28], current online knowledge payment platforms or Apps are completely different from mass media, which is mainly reflected in the accessibility of platforms and Apps. Meanwhile, studies based on new media platforms are mostly carried out in a quantitative way [36–39]. Only few qualitative researches that still focus on mass media such as TV programs [40], soap operas [41] and TV advertisements [42]. Some scholars consider that the limitations of research methods limit the further development of researches on para-social interaction [43].

3 Research Design

From the perspective of para-social interaction, this study adopts the in-depth interview based on qualitative approach, explores the human-computer interaction in online knowledge payment by means of semi-structured depth interview. It should be noted that due to the impact of COVID-19, interviews are conducted online.

Six users with experience in online knowledge payment are selected as the interviewees (see Table 1). The interview outline is developed from Ge and Fang's para-social interaction scale [44], because it has been tested by empirical study and is closer to the language environment and logic of Chinese users. The online interview was conducted from July 22 to 31, 2020, and the whole process was recorded with the consent of the interviewees.

After the interview, the recording was transcribed and classified. First, all the interview recordings are turned into verbatim transcripts. Then, categorization is conducted for verbatim manuscript, that is, looking for recurring phenomena and important concepts to explain, including elements constituting the category, the internal formation structure, the reasons for the formation of the category, the role of the category, etc. Specifically to the operation, the meaningful complete expressions in verbatim manuscript are summarized, and the contents with similar attributes are encoded as a category, so as to extract and name the dimensions related to this study.

Table 1. Interviewees with experience in online knowledge payment

Name	Gender	Age	Occupation	Years of experience	Mainly used platforms	Mainly used medium	Category of knowledge
C	Female	26	Student	3	Vistopia	Smart phone	Philosophy & sociology
H	Male	27	Photographer	5	Kaochong	Tablet computer	Postgraduate examinations
L	Female	25	Student	5	Youdao course selection	Computer	Journalism
S	Male	28	Finacial analyst	8	Iya music	Computer	Music performance

(continued)

Table 1. *(continued)*

Name	Gender	Age	Occupation	Years of experience	Mainly used platforms	Mainly used medium	Category of knowledge
W	Female	29	Teacher	3	CCtalk	Computer	Language (English)
Z	Male	24	Student	3	CNKI	Smart phone	Postgraduate examinations

4 Research Findings and Discussion

The experience regarding para-social interaction and human-computer interaction mentioned by the interviewees can be divided into four dimensions: the perception of character roles, the continuation of interactive relationships, the appearance of online knowledge communication and the dissonance of human computer interaction.

4.1 The Perception of Character Roles

The perception of character roles refers to users' perception towards knowledge performers in all aspects of online knowledge payment experience. In previous studies on para-social interaction, "perception" was interpreted as the connection formed between media users and media characters, and the connection often refers to a kind of intimacy relationship like that between friends [27, 45]. According to the study conducted by Horton and Wohl, intimacy is a kind of illusion that character roles are doing their best to create [20]. These efforts include the following: "the role consciously tries to talk to the user in a personal capacity to make each user feel like 'he knows me'", "let users call them by their first name or a special nickname to emphasize intimacy", "give users a relaxed impression that they can participate in the programs", "use the technical means of the media itself to create a sense of intimacy", etc.

In terms of this dimension, the interviewees of this study confirmed the results of previous studies to a certain extent. According to W's experience, "in the course, we all call the teacher 'Gu Da', which is the teacher's ID on Sina-Weibo. As a fan, the word 'Gu Da' itself represents a sign of English"; C also mentioned the word "Daozhang" many times during the interview, which is the nickname given to the knowledge performer by the users of the course. When talking about his own learning experience, L mentioned that "the teacher will set up a Q&A during the class, and will ask us questions based on the course content. That is, the teacher will design some questions, let us answer first, give the correct answer, and then provide explanation according to our answers". Such interactive experience is an illusion that believe the role will adjust his behavior according to our own reactions. Similarly, during the interview with C, she said that she has experienced the using of technical means of the media itself to create a sense of intimacy in online knowledge payment courses. According to her, "there was once a program that tried to use sound effects to lead us into a particular environment. For example, when the program was going to talk about a soda, it would use sound effect of soda popping". But C admitted that "I don't have any feelings about this. In addition, many users in the comments say that they don't like adding these sound effects, which will make them uncomfortable. Maybe they just want to listen to the performer purely".

According to interviewees' experience regarding online knowledge payment, the role is more perceived as a "model" rather than a "friend". Because online knowledge payment still falls into the category of knowledge communication, the existence of the "teacher" role is implies a power relationship. In other words, the image of "teacher" in traditional knowledge communication is transplanted into online knowledge payment and becomes a stereotype. Under such a premise, it is difficult for online knowledge paying users to perceive teachers as friends, like the case of character role in mass communication. According to Turner's study, homophily is an important factor affecting para-social interaction, that is, the higher the similarity between users and media characters in attitude, appearance or background, the higher the degree of para-social interaction [46]. While in the case of online knowledge payment, the gap between teachers and students in status and knowledge leads to the lack of homophily, which makes the role in online knowledge payment unable to easily become the "friend" of users. As H felt: "during the course, I had to describe the problem very carefully, and repeatedly confirm whether my expression was clear, which made me stressful".

In short, as to the perception of character roles in online knowledge payment, on the one hand, as Horton and Wohl said, there are some "production formats" [20] to follow; on the other hand, it is also different from the traditional definition of para-social interaction. It is found through the interview that the para-social interaction experience will be presented as a "model" in the context of online knowledge payment. This "superior and subordinate" power relationship is not an "equal" relationship.

4.2 The Continuation of Interactive Relationships

Previous studies believed that the illusion of "interaction" in the process of para-social interaction only exists when the user is watching the program and the reader is reading the book [47]. In other words, the interactive relationship with a character role is only possible when the media is being used, and it ceases when the context in which the user is watching or reading is removed. According to Horton and Wohl, the initiative of this one-way relationship is in the hands of the media character [20], the user has no control over the existence and development of the relationship, and the only thing users can do is to terminate their relationship with the program by not watching it. There is no other constructive action or initiative that the audience would be able to take [47]. However, it seems to only take into account the time-fixed, one-way linear communication mode in the traditional mass media environment. But interaction in the digital context has its arbitrariness in time and space [48], which leads to an obvious distinction between para-social interaction in the new media and traditional media.

During the interview, most of the interviewees said that they have experience in re-watching knowledge programs. For example, C mentioned that "There are views I quite agree with in the program, and views that can even subvert my cognition. These views make me feel a lot and urge me to listen to the program again"; W also said that "After purchasing the program, the program content can be played back for 540 days, so that we can review what we have learned at any time". Meanwhile, the continuation of para-social interaction is also reflected in the use of different media channels. Traditional para-social interaction is mostly limited to single medium such as radio, television and book. While online knowledge payment can not only establish connection through the original platform/App, but also can interact with roles through other channels. For example, in addition to establishing relationships with teachers in the process of reading papers, Z can also "obtain some free contents through the teacher's official account on WeChat, including speeches and videos"; L will also "search for some content related to courses and teachers" through social media after class. This kind of multi-channel and time-space unlimited interaction mode subverts the conclusion regarding the dissolution of relationship in the traditional para-social interaction, and forms a continuation of para-social interaction in the new media.

At the same time, it is also found that the continuation of interactive relationship will be symbolized as Internet meme. According to S, "my teacher was made into memes, those are quite popular among groups and are very interesting in class because the teacher himself is famous and his expressions are interesting". On the one hand, the communication of memes not only reflects the initiative, creativity and involvement of users [49], but also becomes the continuation of the interactive relations between S and the role in non-course time; on the other hand, when users use the memes in a specific community, they are searching others with the same experience, and the continuation of their relationship with the role has become the basis of another interpersonal relationship. From this perspective, the para-social interaction in the new media presents a para-social processing [50], that is, users actively and continuously respond to character roles, and then continue the interactive relations between them.

To sum up, the para-social interaction in online knowledge payment will not be interrupted with the end of using media. On the contrary, it will continue through multi-channel interaction mode. However, because the probability of two-way interaction is very small, and media characters do not know users, users may not know the real side of media characters [51]. In the process of continuation, the present experience becomes a continuous experience, and the boundary between para-social interaction and para-social relationship begins to blur under the develop of new media.

4.3 The Appearance of Online Knowledge Communication

As an important part of the sharing economy, online knowledge payment falls into the category of knowledge and skill sharing, which is essentially a process of knowledge virtualization and economization brought by digital technology [52]. In this process, users can, through the progress of technology, access the network anytime and anywhere, access the cloud system of online knowledge payment, and connect with knowledge contents and character roles on this basis. For online knowledge platforms, they will not only fail to realize the effective knowledge cash-out, but also will no longer attract performers in the long run if they are not supported by users. The loss of interactivity and sharing will lead to the loss of users and ultimately to an unsustainable development [53]. Therefore, it can be said that in today's online knowledge communication ecology, the relationship between users and media is complementary and interactive.

Due to the development of technology, the interaction between human and knowledge has changed greatly. On the one hand, users' access to knowledge has shifted from offline to online. The research on para-social interaction holds that people who cannot be satisfied in real social relations will have a sense of loneliness, such dissatisfaction and loneliness will make them more inclined to develop para-social relations to make up for their regrets in reality [54]. This point of view was also revealed in the interview process of this study. For example, H mentioned: "In terms of preparation for postgraduate examination, there are relatively few targeted offline courses, at least in the place where I located. Resource is the reason why I choose online learning"; S said more directly that "There are only a few teachers in my place, and they may not be able to teach special content if we want to learn more". On the other hand, the operation of online knowledge payment is inseparable from the participation of users. Therefore, in order to retain users and transactions, "platforms are constantly sending messages about which courses are on sale" (C), and "after log in the App, they will recommend other courses that users may be interested" (L). It can be seen that users' desire for knowledge and the restrictions of the actual environment is the main contradiction. It should be noted that online knowledge paying users do not make passive choices because of loneliness, but are driven by more active internal motivation.

However, the interviews also exposed some of the problems of online knowledge payment, including unstable technology, placement of advertising, neglect of copyright and complexity of user interface(UI). For example, when recalling his experience of learning the course, W mentioned that "some programs will insert some promotional advertisements of other courses or other brands at the beginning or end or even in the middle of the program, which is a very bad experience"; Z said, referring to the online knowledge platform he uses, "for a while, I could only pay for courses by scanning the code on my computer, but I mostly studied in the library using my mobile phone, which was very inconvenient"; after the course, S found that "some courses are sold on Taobao and other platforms, that is, someone records the courses and resell them on such platforms. The price of the courses is much cheaper than the official courses, which makes me feel suffered losses"; H puts more emphasis on the UI of the website, as he said, "my experience on the PC is not as good as that on the iPad. For example, the double speed playback function can be selected directly from the screen on the iPad, but on the PC's web page, this function is hidden and I need to click the mouse several times to find this function".

Online knowledge payment just meets the demand of people who want to obtain knowledge and experience sorted by other people by paying money [55], and people's desire for knowledge has also created the appearance of knowledge communication in today's digital age. However, in this "unlimited information and limited energy" age, there are a trace of defects and risks in human-computer interaction behind the prosperity of online knowledge payment.

4.4 The Dissonance of Human-Computer Interaction

Through the above, we can describe the appearance of online knowledge communication, and can see that the establishment of interaction between users and models is also inseparable from the current media technology. At the same time, human-computer interaction is not merely the binary interaction between human and machine, but a new context that expands the connotation of "interaction". In addition to the basic elements—human and machine, this context of interaction also includes human and media roles discussed in para-social interaction, the interaction between virtual avatars, the interaction between real producers and real users, and even the interaction between implied authors and readers at the level of cultural metaphors [9]. In this context, it is easily oriented to the view that "the media determines our situation".

To a certain extent, the development of online knowledge payment is indeed inseparable from the promotion of media. For example, when talking about his preference for Apps, Z explained: "smart phone is much convenient than computer, because it is unlikely for me to browse articles through the computer on the bus, especially when there is no seat. While smart phone won't cause me such trouble, because it can be operated with one hand, and there's almost no inconvenience." W is more inclined to use computers for learning, because "when I take the course on the computer, I can also see the questions raised by other students in the comments, which sometimes give me more inspiration. While if I use smart phones, I can only see the teachers, and cannot see the comments". Besides, "in terms of oral English course, there is a page on the computer for uploading recordings, and the intelligent recognition system on the website will directly detect whether my pronunciation is standard, and then give me feedback". L mentioned the issue on consciousness, "Offline learning can cause some pressure. For example, students have to go to class, otherwise their families will find out. But learning online, especially with smart phones, no one knows what you are doing when you wear headphones. Therefore, online learning is like a test for personal consciousness, as sometimes even students are online, they are actually just deserting".

The interviews found that for most interviewees, the technology of online knowledge content present directly determines the way they study. As Kittler said, "it is the technological differentiation of optics, acoustics and writing that explodes the monopoly of writing that makes the fabrication of man possible" [56]. At the same time, the use of online technology will also affect the use of other media. For example, S believes that using computers can liberate both hands, while H and L prefer using paper textbooks.

Human-computer interaction has shifted to "user-centered", that is, to pay attention to users' agency and subjectivity. As above, human-computer interaction emphasizes the experience perceived by individuals, that is, the so-called "humanistic care of science and technology". However, the so-called "humanity" of online knowledge payment mostly stays at the "easy to operate", and does not fundamentally change the passive state in which "human needs to adapt to machines". At the same time, the development of media technology seems to provide people with a variety of new options, but in fact it limits the freedom of people. For example, the "exclusive teacher" or "authoritative courses" claimed by platforms or Apps actually monopolize users' freedom to choose character roles and knowledge perform methods. In other words, the practical paradigm—"what do people do with media"—in online knowledge payment ignores the premise of user-centered.

The dissonance between the human-computer interaction and online knowledge payment may be the hidden reason for the decline of the industry. Although para-social interaction can establish the relationship between users and roles, for users, this relationship is not only an "illusion", but also an imperceptible "wishful thinking". Therefore, in addition to continuing to focus on knowledge content, online knowledge payment industry should also take user experience as the premise and emphasize to help people study knowledge content better. For example, the platform/App should insist on providing high-quality content instead of flashy "knowledge show" [57], which is a necessary condition for retaining users. And the industry can enhance the usefulness and ease-of-use of the interactive interface in human-computer interaction, appropriately enrich the interaction between users and character roles, or use "task", "reward" and other settings to improve users' game feeling, so as to deepen their consciousness for continuous study. In a word, the online knowledge payment industry should not only use technologies such as big data-based algorithm matching to improve the content experience in the future, but also should pay attention to fundamentally cultivating the interactive relationship between human and the media, so as to lead the more benign development of online knowledge communication.

5 Conclusion

Knowledge communication is shifting from offline to mixed, diversified and complex online context, which is particularly obvious under the influence of the COVID-19. Digital technology is more applied to informal education, making learning more informal, personal and ubiquitous [1]. Internet technologies continue to amplify the advantages of online knowledge payment, but beneath the glitter there is a risk of technological determinism. However, even in the words of Kittler, media determine our situation, whether we are influenced by it, or to avoid it, is worth analyzing [56]. Therefore, this study tries to explore the situation of human-computer interaction in the field of online knowledge payment from the perspective of para-social interaction.

This study uses the in-depth interview method. Although qualitative approach based on individual experience inevitably lacks representativeness, experience will be projected to different users in different ways [58], and individual experience can also reflect the generality problems of media technology to a certain extent. At the same time, this study also hopes to link individual experiences of media use to broader thinking in an attempt to reach a general understanding.

Through interviews, this study combed out four dimensions on para-social interaction and human-computer interaction, explored the field of online knowledge payment in the study of para-social interaction, examined and enriched the para-social interaction theory, and describe a part of the appearance of online knowledge communication. There is a certain gap between users' subjective and their experience in using media in the process of online knowledge payment. In the future, the industry should adhere to "user-centered" to deepen the role of media in human life.

References

1. UNESCO.: Rethinking Education: Towards A Global Common Good?. United Nations Educational, Scientific and Cultural Organization, Paris, France (2015)

2. Ding, X., Wang, X., Gao, S.: Knowledge payment: conceptual meaning, reasons of flourishing and present crisis. Journalism & Communication **2**, 29–32 (2018)
3. Liu, Z., Zhao, Y.: A preliminary study on the operation mode of the paid knowledge Q&A community based on the voice chat: Taking Fenda and Zhihu as cases. Library & Information **4**, 38–46 (2017)
4. O'Reilly, T.: What is Web 2.0?. https://www.oreilly.com/pub/a/web2/archive/what-is-web-20.html. last accessed 06 Feb 2021
5. Du, J.: The illusion of knowledge payment. News and Writing **11**, 77–78 (2017)
6. Tang, J., Wang, Z., Wang, J.: Knowledge payment research report 2018. Nanfang Media Research **6**, 86–99 (2018)
7. Yu, G., Guo, C.: Online knowledge payment: the main types, form structure and development model. Editors Monthly **5**, 6–11 (2017)
8. Zhang, L., Zhang, Y.: From chronic free-issue to conscious payment: A study on the change of knowledge dissemination pattern in digital environment. Editorial Friend **12**, 52–55 (2017)
9. Lu, L.: Medium, philosophy and politics research: Triple faces of the study of new media in western academia. Nanjing J. Soc. Sci. **5**, 104–110 (2015)
10. Zhang, F., Dai, G., Peng, X.: A survey on human-computer interaction in virtual reality. Scientia Sinica(Informationis) **12**, 1711–1736 (2016)
11. Licklider, J.C.: Man-computer symbiosis. IRE Trans. Hum. Fac. Elec. **1**, 4–11 (1960)
12. Tao, X.: Research on the history and trends of human-computer interaction development. Pub. Commun. Sci. Technol. **22**, 137–139 (2019)
13. Bannon, L.: From human factors to human actors: The system design. In: Greenbaum, J., Kyng, M. (eds.) Design at work: Cooperative design of computer systems, pp. 31–51. CRC Press, Florida, U.S. (1991)
14. Weng, S., Shih, P., Sun, S., Fang, N., Li, C.: A pilot study of internet para-social interaction theory building. Mass Commun. Res. **101**(10), 1–44 (2009)
15. Reeves, L.M., et al.: Guidelines for multimodal user interface design. Commun. ACM **47**(1), 57–59 (2004)
16. Qi, A.: Nick Couldry: The practice paradigm turn in media studies. Shandong Soc. Sci. **1**, 151–155 and 192 (2017)
17. Couldry, N.: Theorising media as practice. Soc. Semiot. **14**(2), 115–132 (2004)
18. Sundar, S.S.: Is human-computer interaction social or parasocial?. In: Presented at Association for Education in Journalism and Mass Communication Annual Meeting. https://www.learntechlib.org/p/78848/ (1994). last accessed 06 Feb 2022
19. Fang, J., Ge, J.: Research on the elder's media contact and parasocial interaction. J. Zhejiang Univ. Med. Commun. **3**, 91–93 (2009)
20. Horton, D., Wohl, R.: Mass communication and para-social interaction. Psychiatry **19**, 215–229 (1956)
21. Perse, E.: Media involvement and local news effects. J. Broadcast. Electron. Media **34**(1), 17–36 (1990)
22. Perse, E., Rubin, R.: Attribution in social and parasocial relationship. Commun. Res. **16**(1), 59–77 (1989)
23. Auter, P., Palmgreen, P.: Development of a new parasocial interaction measure: the audience persona interaction scale. In: Annual International Communication Association Conference. Miami, U.S. (1992)
24. Schumann, D., Thorson, E.: Advertising and the world wide web. Lawrence Erlbaum Associates, London, U.K. (1999)
25. Zhu, X.: Attachment, television viewing, and parasocial interactions in minors. Journal. Mass Commu. Month. **4**, 45–49 (2014)

26. Lewis, M., Weber, R., Bowman, N.: "They may be pixels, but they're MY pixels": Developing a metric of character attachment in role-playing video games. Cyberpsychol. Behav. **11**(4), 515–518 (2008)
27. Rubin, A., Perse, E., Powell, R.: Loneliness, parasocial interaction, and local television news viewing. Hum. Commun. Res. **12**(2), 155–180 (1985)
28. Rubin, A., Step, M.: Impact of motivation, attraction, and parasocial interaction on talk radio listening. J. Broadcast. Electron. Media **44**(4), 635–654 (2000)
29. Fang, J., Ge, J., Zhang, J.: Deficiency paradigm or global-use paradigm: A review on parasocial interaction researches. Journal. Commu. **3**, 68–72 (2006)
30. Mao, L.: Microblog-based parasocial interaction: theoretical foundations and research models. Jinan J. Philoso. Soc. Sci. **188**(9), 146–152 (2014)
31. Li, Q., Wang, C.: The practical turn of "new audience research" in the new media context. Social Science Front **11**, 267–271 (2018)
32. Reardon, K., Rogers, E.: Interpersonal versus mass media communication a false dichotomy. Hum. Commun. Res. **15**(2), 284–303 (1988)
33. Schramm, H., Hartmann, T.: The PSI-process scales. A new measure to assess the intensity and breadth of parasocial processes. Communications **33**(4), 385–401 (2008)
34. Auter, P., Davis, D.: When characters speak directly to viewers: breaking the fourth wall in television. Journal. Q. **68**, 165–171 (1991)
35. Gleich, U.: Parasocial interaction with people on the screen. In: Winterhoff-Spurk, P., Van der Voort, T. (eds.) New horizons in media psychology: Research co-operation and projects in Europe, pp. 35–55. Westdeutscher Verlag, Opladen, Germany. (1997)
36. Tsao, J.: Compensatory media use: An exploration of two paradigms. Commun. Stud. **47**(1–2), 89–109 (1996)
37. Cohen, J.: Parasocial relations and romantic attraction: gender and dating status differences. J. Broadcast. Electron. Media **41**(4), 516–529 (1997)
38. Zhang, M.: Information consumption and production in social network: an investigation into micro-blog users' behavior. Journal. Commu. **6**, 85–96 and 111–112 (2012)
39. Han, X., Tang, Z., Tan, J., Tu, W.: Trust and identification: Study on parasocial interaction on government affairs microblogs. J. Intell. **35**(11), 106–112 (2016)
40. Zhang, J., Sun, X.: Figuration, parasocial interaction and group boundaries: a study of the realistic production mechanism of the "female" category in the media. Mod. Commu. J. Commu. Univ. China **2**, 28–33 (2015)
41. Sood, S., Rogers, E.: Dimensions of parasocial interaction by letter-writers to a popular entertainment-education soap opera in India. J. Broadcast. Electron. Media **44**(3), 386–414 (2000)
42. Alperstein, N.: Imaginary social relationships with celebrities appearing in television commercials. J. Broadcast. Electron. Media **35**(1), 43–58 (1991)
43. Han, X., Tu, W., Tan, J.: The current status and the patterns of international parasocial interaction research: A meta-analysis. South. Commun. **5**, 72–76 (2016)
44. Ge, J., Fang, J.: The forming and testing of the audience parasocial interaction scale. Journal. Mass Commu. Month. **6**, 10–11 (2010)
45. Rubin, R., McHugh, M.: Development of parasocial interaction relationships. J. Broadcast. Electron. Media **31**(3), 279–292 (1987)
46. Turner, J.R.: Interpersonal and psychological predictors of parasocial interaction with different television performers. Commun. Q. **41**(4), 443–453 (1993)
47. Watkins, D.: Horton and wohl's concept of parasocial interaction. Geraadpleegd op het World Wide Web op 15 (2005)
48. Menchik, D.A., Tian, X.: Putting social context into text: The semiotics of e-mail interaction. Am. J. Sociol. **114**(2), 332–370 (2008)

49. Knobel, M., Lankshear, C.: A new literacies sampler. Peter Lang Publishing, New York, U.S. (2007)
50. Hartmann, T.: Parasocial interaction and paracommunication with new media characters. In: Konijn, E., Utz, S., Tanis, M., Barnes, S. (eds.) Mediated interpersonal communication, pp. 177–199. Routledge, New York, U.S. (2008)
51. Gong, W., Li, X.: Engaging fans on microblog: The synthetic influence of parasocial interaction and source characteristics on celebrity endorsement. Psychol. Mark. **34**(7), 720–732 (2017)
52. Zhao, J., Cheng, M.: From sharing to ordering: A knowledge economics analysis of the network knowledge payment phenomenon. Editorial Friend **8**, 60–65 (2019)
53. Lu, H., Zhang, X., Zhang, L.: Influence factors of users' willingness to pay for knowledge in voice question and answer community: In the perspective of status quo bias. Info. Sci. **37**(6), 119–125 and 162 (2019)
54. McCourt, A., Fitzpatrick, J.: The role of personal characteristics and romantic characteristics in parasocial relationships: a pilot study. J. Mundane Behavior **2**(1), 42–58 (2001)
55. Ding, X., Wang, X., Gao, S.: Knowledge payment: conceptual meaning, reasons of flourishing and present crisis. Journal. Commu. **2**, 29–32 (2018)
56. Kittler, F.: Gramophone, Film. Typewriter. Stanford University Press, Carolina, U.S. (1999)
57. Fang, X.: Knowledge payment and knowledge performance. Exploration and Free Views **7**, 16–18 (2019)
58. Fang, J., Hu, Y., Fan, D.: Data journalism practice in the eyes of journalists: value, path and prospect .- a study based on in-depth interviews with 7 journalists. Journal. Res. **2**, 13–19 and 147 (2016)

Effects of Age, Motivation, and Hindrance Factors on Douyin Usage

Dian Yu, Chuwen Wang, Ramirez P. Widagdo, Xiaojun Lai, and Pei-Luen Patrick Rau(✉)

Department of Industrial Engineering, Tsinghua University, Beijing 100084, China
rpl@mail.tsinghua.edu.cn

Abstract. The development of social media platforms has brought global attention to short video applications; in China, this is especially true of Douyin. This study aims to find out: how different generations of people perceive and react to this age of short video dominance; what factors affect behaviors towards Douyin usage; and what level of influence each of these factors has on the behaviours. From the established scholarship, we gleaned insights to develop our framework of various motivation and hindrance factors that may influence each generation's response to short video application usage. We then conducted a survey that garnered responses from 169 participants to evaluate the extent of influence each factor had on the different generations. This led to a further examination of both their attitudes towards Douyin, and their usage of Douyin, measured by time spent on the application. Our results found three main factors that motivate users to use Douyin: to seek entertainment; to seek self-status; and to disseminate information. On the other hand, the most common factors that hinder users from using Douyin are: dissatisfaction with content and how immersed one is made to become when using the application. The results for Generation Z also show a distinctive difference in time spent on Douyin, compared to that of Generations X and Y. This age factor plays a crucial role in mediating how much time a user spends on Douyin, with each generation identifying different purposes for using the application.

Keywords: Short video · Douyin usage · Age · Motivation · Hindrance

1 Introduction

Over the last decade, social media platforms have gained huge traction, as they not only connect people around the world but also allow individuals and institutions to build high-value social networks amongst the masses [4]. One category of emerging social media platforms with powerful influence worldwide is the short video application [7]. In this category is Douyin, or Tiktok, which has emerged as the top-performing application and so grasped global attention [7]. Douyin holds this strong industry position in the exponentially-growing market for short video platforms in China, which has been forecast to exceed 200 billion yuan [27].

P.-L. P. Rau (Ed.): HCII 2022, LNCS 13311, pp. 117–131, 2022.
https://doi.org/10.1007/978-3-031-06038-0_9

Douyin is a short video application that allows users to post and share their own videos on a platform, where each video is typically only 15 s long [7]. Douyin has around 600 million active users worldwide [1], with most of its users being Chinese citizens. Among the 600 million users of Douyin, 474.7 million active users are based in China [31]. As China has a population of approximately 1.4 billion people [33], this means around 34% of Chinese citizens use Douyin, according to these statistics.

Douyin was further ranked second amongst the most downloaded applications of 2019 [12]. Research into the extant scholarship indicates that the amount of time people spend on short video applications in China has increased by 8.6% year on year, reaching a total of more than 22 h per month [10]. The average time spent on short video applications has even overtaken that of live streaming applications, despite the latter having entered the market earlier in 2015 [19]. Given Douyin's strong presence and influence in China, this study investigates how and why Chinese people use Douyin in the Chinese market.

2 Literature Review

There is an abundance of studies conducted on short video platforms more generally, and even Douyin itself more specifically. These studies found that people nowadays are mainly unable to sustain their concentration throughout long videos, and so have shifted their attention to watching short videos [16]. The long video format is now less effective than short videos, in terms of retaining the user's attention [16]. Certain researchers have suggested that various motivations could have a large influence on such short video usage [21]. Omar [21] pointed out that motivations such as social interaction, self-expression and goal accomplishment could have a positive correlation with a user's dependency on Douyin. This paper deploys the uses and gratifications theory (U&G) to examine factors that affect the habits of Douyin users. U&G emphasizes the motivations for individual's use of the selected media, on the assumption that active users deliberately select for media content that satisfies their various desires and needs [14]. Within this frame, therefore, it may be said that Douyin users utilize the platform to express themselves, interact with others, and escape from day-to-day pressures [21]. Other motivation factors we will include in our analyses are information-seeking and -providing behaviors and habits [15].

However, there are also factors that hinder people from using Douyin. This includes social fatigue, immersion, negative platform experiences and content-related issues, etc. [25]. As a result, these hindrances may impede new users from downloading Douyin or lead old users to abandon the application.

Even though substantial research has been done investigating video platform users, there remain research gaps extant within this field of study. One of which that we look to supplement is the limited scope of papers published researching the influence of the age factor with respect to Douyin. Age could be an influential factor affecting an individual's preference for short video watching, as different generations may have different expectations and habits when using social media platforms. A study by Harwood has suggested that older adults apportion a large amount of their time to watching television [9], mainly due to increased leisure time; loss of social connection; and increased demand for information [8, 32]. However, older generation users may adopt negative attitudes towards online videos, especially in the short video format. As digital migrants, they may lack the instinct to master such new—perhaps, in their perception, even 'new-fangled'—technologies, such as the computer and Internet [29]. Different generations may thus differ in their adoption and usage of media, particularly digital media [18]. In the case of Generation X and the baby boomers, they may be characterized as the 'TV generation' [28]. On the other hand, Generation Y and the Millennials grew up in the age of the digital revolution [30], which has made them more familiar with Internet technology than older adults [2]. A different pattern of media adoption could therefore result in different patterns of media usage. Consequently, this could mean that younger generations may prefer to watch videos on the Internet as compared to older generations. It is hence important to look at the age factor when examining user behaviors in relation to short video watching.

Another gap in this field of study is the limited amount of papers demonstrating the extent to which each motivation or hindrance factor affects Douyin users' short video watching behaviors. Thus, this study is trying to fill in these two gaps by looking at how age could bring an influence on an individual's short videos watching habit, as well as to what extent each factor contributes to the user's dependency on Douyin.

3 Research Framework and Hypotheses

As aforementioned, different generations have different characteristics with respect to accessibility to today's technologies [11]. Having gone through the digital revolution, generations Y and Z are more familiar with technology and the Internet compared to Generation X, resulting in a different pattern of media technology adoption [2]. This would then contribute to a different pattern of social media usage, especially given that Douyin has emerged as a social media platform and phenomenon only in recent years. This leads us to our first research question and its related hypotheses:

- **RQ1:** What are the differences in time usage of different age groups?
- **H1:** Generation Z tends to spend more time on Douyin compared to Generation X.
- **H2:** Generations Y and Z do not differ much in their time spent on Douyin.

According to existing research, the younger generation is more familiar with Internet technology [2] and prefers to communicate with others over such social networking sites [5]. On the other hand, the older generation tends to spend more time searching for information on the internet [13]. In addition, as further advances in technology continue to alter the entertainment market of today's world [17], this paper assumes that most people will pursue short videos for entertainment on Douyin. Thus the second research question we derive and its related hypotheses are:

- **RQ2:** What are the factors that motivate the usage of short video applications?
- **H3:** Generation Z spends more time watching short videos for social interaction, whereas Generation X uses it to seek information.
- **H4:** Entertainment is the motivating factor that largely affects all generations' usage of Douyin.

The younger generation in China has a stronger preference for watching short videos over other forms of media distribution [19], which may present the issue of addiction in the long run. On the other hand, as the older generation is less familiar with new technologies, they might prefer older forms of conventional mass communications, like watching TV, to satisfy their needs [2]. As a result, they could be less willing to try out new formats like short video applications. This provides us with the third research question and its hypothesis:

- **RQ3:** What are the factors that hinder the usage of short video applications?
- **H5:** The phenomenon of addiction is the main issue that hinders Generation Z from watching short videos, while negative platform experience is the main reason that hinders Generation Y's usage of Douyin.

4 Methodology

We created an online survey and distributed it to Chinese respondents via WeChat in November 2020. The respondents were from Generation X – 44 to 55 years of age; Generation Y – 25 to 43 years of age; and Generation Z – 15 to 24 years of age.

At the start of the survey, participants were asked to provide their background information such as age, gender, and educational background. The following questions then queried information about their time spent on Douyin, along with the length and frequency of their viewing habits.

The second and third sections were designed to evaluate the respondent's attitude towards Douyin. Based on the literature review, we decided to test 30 gratification items (see Tables 1 and 2) that covered motivation and hindrance factors. For users that are currently using Douyin or have used Douyin before, they were asked to rate both motivation and hindrance statements in the survey. However, for users that have never used Douyin before, they were faciliated to rate the hindrance statements in the third section only. The statements were measured using a 5-point Likert scale system, with 1 representing "Strongly Disagree" and conversely 5 being "Strongly Agree". At the end of the survey, the respondent answered a repeated item about their length and frequency of viewing habits to ensure the validity of responses.

Table 1. Motivation items

Independent variables	Measurement items
Seeking information [15]	1. To get information about things that interest you
	2. To learn how to do things
	3. To find out what is new out there
	4. To keep up with current issues and events

(continued)

Table 1. (*continued*)

Independent variables	Measurement items
Giving information [15]	1. To provide others with information
	2. To contribute to a pool of content
Seeking self-status [23]	1. To impress other users
	2. To make myself look cool
	3. Because I feel pressured to do so
Social interaction [23]	1. To meet interesting people
	2. To feel like I belong to a community
	3. Because people around me are watching Douyin videos
Relaxing [15]	1. To be entertained
	2. To enjoy and relax
	3. Because I have nothing better to do

Table 2. Hindrance items

Independent variables	Measurement Items
Social dynamics related [34]	1. I do not receive likes, comments or gain followers
	2. I remain wary of people who may be watching my videos
	3. I do not want to join in the frenzy
Content related [24]	1. I have no intention of posting
	2. I prefer other forms of content presentation
	3. I do not like the way information is conveyed to me
Immersion related [6]	1. I felt that I spent too much time on Douyin
	2. I could not refrain from scrolling through the suggested contents
	3. I feel that it could lead to addiction
	4. I think it wastes my time
Platform related [25]	1. I do not like the user interface and design of the app
	2. I am uncomfortable with the appearance and layout of the new versions
	3. I am reluctant to learn how to use a new app
Life cycle related [25]	1. I do not like it as much as I used to
	2. My circle of friends gradually reduced their time spent using it

5 Results

5.1 Sample Profile

We received a total of 180 responses. However, 11 of these were removed as participants due to being from outside of our target country (i.e., outside China) or target age groups (i.e., beyond Generations X, Y and Z). This left us with 169 valid responses to analyze. Among the 169 valid respondents, 62 respondents were from Generation Z (37%), 71 respondents from Generation Y (42%) and 36 from Generation X (21%).

5.2 Compare Means of Different Generations

To observe differences in the generations' respective mean short video viewing time, we performed hypothesis testing. We worked with non-normal data with equal variances ($p > 0.05$). To avoid skewed results from the zero values indicated by past users and non-users, we only considered the timing of currently active Douyin users.

We performed the non-parametric Kruskal-Wallis H Test between the three generations to identify if there were any significant differences between their means. We found statistically significant differences in weekly usage between the different age groups ($p = 0.004$), with a mean rank weekly usage of 35.27 for Generation X, 56.98 for Generation Y and 61.51 for Generation Z.

Since this indicated significant differences between the means of the 3 generations, we further tested between Generations X and Z, and Generations Y and Z using the Mann-Whitey U test to answer our first two hypotheses. Weekly usage for Generation Z was found to be higher than that of Generation X ($p = .003$) by a statistically significant degree. However, weekly usage for Generation Y did not differ from that of Generation Z ($p = .451$) by a statistically significant degree.

5.3 Factor Analysis of Motivation in Douyin Short Video Watching

To identify the underlying structure of a large set of items under each independent variable (motivation and hindrance), an exploratory factor analysis—using principal component analysis, 5 extracted components and varimax rotation—was conducted. Five items under motivation were dropped, because the items had (1) a high loading on more than one factor; (2) a loading with no more than 0.43 on any factor; or (3) cross loadings that differed by less than 0.2. Table 3 illustrates the final results we obtained for both motivations, with the 10 items categorized into five factors. It shows a good fit of the model where 89% of the total variance was explained by these five factors. The Cronbach's alpha coefficients are 0.74, 0.90, 0.86, 0.88, and 0.93 for the five factors — all above the acceptable level of 0.70 according to Shemwell [26].

Factor 1, labeled as "Giving Information", consists of 2 items and explains 49% of the total variance. It covers the need for information sharing with other users (e.g., provides information to others and contributes to the pool of content on Douyin). Factor 2, labeled as "Relaxing", consists of 2 items and explains 21% of the total variance. It describes the purpose of using Douyin as a pastime (e.g., to be entertained, to enjoy and to relax). Factor 3, labeled as "Social Interaction", consists of 2 items and explains 8% of

Table 3. Factors loading of 10 motivation items

Motivation items		Loadings of factors				
		1	2	3	4	5
Seeking information						
1	To get interesting information	.06	.39	−.03	.07	**.84**
2	To keep up with current issues and events	.24	.24	.34	.01	**.77**
Giving information						
1	To provide others with information	**.87**	.13	.18	.31	.10
2	To contribute to a pool of content	**.86**	.08	.27	.23	.18
Seeking self-status						
1	To impress other users	.40	.01	.29	**.74**	.09
2	To make myself look cool	.25	.14	.34	**.85**	.00
Social interaction						
1	To connect with new friends	.24	.13	**.87**	.23	.11
2	To be part of a community in Douyin	.22	.11	**.82**	.35	.14
Relaxing						
1	To be entertained	.10	**.91**	.10	.08	.28
2	To enjoy and relax	.09	**.92**	.13	.06	.24

the total variance. It is characterises connecting and engaging with people (e.g., to meet people, develop attachment to a community). Factor 4, labeled as "Seeking Self-Status", consists of 2 items and explains 7% of the total variance. This factor explains the need to maintain one's self-image (e.g., to impress others, to make oneself look 'cooler'). Factor 5, labeled as "Seeking Information", consists of 4 items and explains 4% of the total variance. This factor addresses the interest of users in gaining new insights from Douyin (e.g., learn interesting trivia, keep up with current information).

5.4 Factor Analysis of Hindrance in Douyin Short Video Watching

Likewise, as was done with the motivation items, the hindrance items were also put through exploratory factor analysis using principal component analysis, 5 extracted components and varimax rotation. Two hindrance items were removed. Table 4 shows the results: the five factors explained 74% of the total variance, indicating a good fit of the model. The Cronbach's alpha for the five factors are 0.70, 0.84, 0.90, 0.89, and 0.80.

Factor 1, labeled as "Immersion Related", consists of 3 items and explains 31% of the total variance. It includes issues related to addictive behaviors (e.g., spending too much time on Douyin, failing to resist going through suggested content, fearing of addiction). Factor 2, labeled as "Content Related", consists of 3 items and explains 16% of the total variance. This factor describes the dissatisfaction of users with Douyin's content (e.g., no intention of posting, preferring other forms of content presentation, not liking the way information is presented). Factor 3, labeled as "Platform Related", consists of 3 items and explains 11% of the total variance. It covers the interface and design of the application (e.g., did not like the user interface or design, being uncomfortable with the new layout). Factor 4, labeled as "Social Dynamics Related", consists of 3 items and explains 9% of the total variance. This factor identifies the individual responses associated with group behaviors (e.g., do not receive likes or comments, being wary about who watches the content, not wanting to join the frenzy). Factor 5, labeled as "Life Cycle Related", consists of 2 items and explains 7% of the total variance. It explains how users' interests fade over time (e.g., do not like it anymore, the decreasing circle of friends).

Table 4. Factors loading of 13 hindrance items

Hindrance items		Loadings of factors				
		1	2	3	4	5
Social dynamics related						
1	I do not receive likes, comments or gain followers	.06	−.01	−.01	**.84**	.06
2	I remain wary of people who may be watching my videos	.10	−.13	.15	**.81**	−.07
3	I do not want to join in the frenzy	.07	.28	.04	**.69**	.11
Content related						
1	I have no intention of posting	.00	**.86**	.01	.00	.11
2	I prefer other forms of content presentation	−.09	**.81**	.13	.07	.21
3	I do not like the way information is conveyed to me	.08	**.81**	.25	.01	.17
Immersion related						
1	I felt that I spent too much time on Douyin	**.88**	−.06	.05	.12	.21
2	I could not refrain from scrolling through the suggested contents	**.91**	.04	.12	.06	.07

(*continued*)

Table 4. (*continued*)

Hindrance items		Loadings of factors				
		1	2	3	4	5
3	I feel that it could lead to addiction	**.89**	.07	.16	.07	.05
Platform related						
1	I do not like the user interface and design of the app	.11	.20	**.88**	.06	.16
2	I am uncomfortable with the appearance and layout of the new versions	.12	.16	**.89**	.05	.16
Life cycle related						
1	I do not like it as much as I used to	.12	.26	.24	.03	**.77**
2	My circle of friends gradually reduced their time spent using it	.15	.24	.13	.03	**.86**

5.5 Predicting Motivation and Hindrance Factors Across Generations

Before conducting the multiple regressions, the variance inflation factor (VIF) value was measured to test for multicollinearity of the independent variables (see Table 5). Since all the variables had a VIF value of smaller than 3 and tolerance was larger than 0.1, multicollinearity does not exist in our set of data. Four multiple regressions were performed on all generations and each of the three generations. These sought to examine the various motivation and hindrance factors that affect the time usage of people's Douyin short video watching behavior by looking at their beta coefficients and the p-values.

Table 5. Multicollinearity analysis of independent variables

Independent variables	Tolerance	VIF
Generation	0.866	1.16
Seeking information	0.515	1.94
Seek self-status	0.421	2.38
Social interaction	0.476	2.10
Relaxing	0.549	1.82
Social dynamics	0.902	1.11
Content	0.703	1.42

(*continued*)

Table 5. (*continued*)

Independent variables	Tolerance	VIF
Immersion	0.718	1.39
Platform	0.650	1.54
Life cycle	0.599	1.67

Summarized in Table 6, a regression equation of ($F(11,168) = 7.057$, $p < 0.001$) was found to be statistically significant with an adjusted R^2 of 0.28 for all generations. Generation X also had a statistically significant regression equation ($F(10,35) = 2.627$, $p = 0.024$) with an adjusted R^2 of 0.32. Similarly for Generation Y, there was a statistically significant regression equation ($F(10,70) = 2.703$, $p = 0.008$) with an adjusted R^2 of 0.20. Finally, the statistically significant regression equation for Generation Z was ($F(10,61) = 5.019$, $p < 0.001$) with an adjusted R^2 of 0.40.

Table 6. Regression predicting motivation and hindrance on viewing Douyin short videos

	Gen XYZ		Gen X		Gen Y		Gen Z	
	β	p	β	p	β	p	β	p
Generation	.19	.01*						
Seek information	.02	.87	.08	.77	.09	.56	−.03	.86
Provide information	.21	.03*	.24	.30	.20	.25	.22	.13
Seek self-status	−.27	.01*	−.88	.01*	−.09	.61	−.13	.41
Social interaction	.12	.20	.60	.05	.05	.77	.05	.71
Relaxing	.26	.00*	−.05	.87	.18	.29	.38	.01*
Social dynamics	.00	.96	− .30	.09	.09	.49	.06	.58
Content	−.30	.00*	−.27	.20	−.18	.24	−.40	.00*
Immersion	.21	.01*	.24	.22	.26	.06	.18	.18
Platform	−.08	.32	.15	.50	−.39	.01*	−.05	.69
Life cycle	.01	.94	.00	.99	.14	.37	−.11	.38
Adjusted R-square	*.28*		*.32*		*.20*		*.40*	

Across all generations, relaxing is a most significant positive motive ($\beta = 0.256$, $p = 0.004$) encouraging short video viewing, followed by providing information ($\beta = 0.211$, $p = 0.028$). Seeking self-status is a significant negative motive ($\beta = -0.274$, $p = 0.007$). Immersion related is a significant positive hinder ($\beta = 0.209$, $p = 0.004$) of the amount of time spent by users on Douyin, while content related is a significant negative hinder ($\beta = -0.296$, $p < 0.001$) to this.

For Generation X, seeking self-status is the only significant motive with a negative correlation ($\beta = -0.883$, $p = 0.007$) to viewing short videos. This is similar to the analysis done for all generations, where seeking self-status also had a stronger negative association across all generations ($\beta = -0.274$). None of the hindrance factors have a significant impact on behaviors among Generation X users. On the other hand, Generation Y has no motivation factor with a significant impact influencing their viewing of Douyin videos. Platform related issues, however, are a significant negative hinder ($\beta = -0.392$, $p = 0.012$) to them. This is the only factor that does not have a significant influence on the overall generation group.

Finally, for Generation Z users, relaxing is a significant positive motive ($\beta = 0.376$, $p = 0.007$) with a correlation coefficient higher than that across all generations ($\beta = 0.256$). Content is a significant negative hinder ($\beta = -0.403$, $p < 0.001$) for Generation Z, with a stronger negative correlation as compared to the overall generations ($\beta = -0.296$).

6 Discussion

6.1 Age Factor

This research shows that there is a difference in time usage of Douyin for different generations. Generation Z spends more time using Douyin compared to Generation X, which is aligned with hypothesis 1. In addition, there is no significant difference in time spent between generations Y and Z, as suggested by our research, supporting our second hypothesis. As found in the literature, the Net Generation (Generations Y and Z), having experienced the digital revolution, are more receptive towards new forms of media that have emerged over the years compared to the older generation [2]. That being said, it is easier for them to adapt to the logic and graphics of Douyin as it requires knowledge and competency in Internet technology. Hence, Generation X spends the least amount of time on Douyin, while Generations Y and Z do not differ in their time spent on watching short videos.

6.2 Motivation Factors

According to our analysis, **the three main factors that influence** Douyin **usage are entertainment, seeking self-status and providing information**. The result aligns with our fourth hypothesis, which states that entertainment is the motivating factor largely affecting all generations' usage of Douyin. The motives for usage also correspond with previously established research on how these three factors lead individuals to enjoy watching videos [15]. Furthermore, it also reflects that different generations of people view the short video application differently, as proposed by the uses and gratification theory.

The survey results have shown that **Generation Z spends more time on Douyin for relaxing purposes**. This is not aligned with hypothesis 3, that states that younger generations use social media to communicate with others [5]. This could be explained by the fact that younger generations face more stress than older adults nowadays [3]. As a result, they might focus more on relaxation when using social media platforms compared to other generations. In addition, the previous study on older generation preferred to seek information on internet [13] was also not supported. In our study, **the older generation seeks self-status** more than all other motivation factors that could influence them, possibly explained by a higher self-esteem with increasing age [22]. Thus, hypothesis 3 was not supported according to the survey results.

Another interesting finding from our research is that **none of the pre-assigned motivation factors have a significant influence on Generation Y**. One of the reasons that could explain this phenomenon could be that they use social media mainly for business purposes as found in other research studies previously conducted [20]. However, the survey conducted in this paper was mainly targetted at understanding users' experiences of short video watching on Douyin, rather than asking participants to consider Douyin as a tool for business operations. Therefore, it may result in Generation Y showing less motivation towards Douyin usage based on the factors analyzed in our survey. This would be especially so, should they consider the application more apt for a business perspective.

6.3 Hindrance Factors

Hindrance factors relating to **content and immersion had a strong influence on Douyin usage**, which corresponds with previous findings in the literature that dissatisfaction with content and low self-control may lead individuals to stop using the social media platform [25]. From our research, Douyin users' dissatisfactions with the content lie in the way videos are presented and how information is conveyed. Additionally, since these users were dissatisfied with the content, they therefore refused to share and post videos with similar content on Douyin. Immersion on the other hand demonstrated that users find it difficult to restrain themselves from scrolling through the suggested content. As a result of this behavior, they feel that they spend too much time watching short videos. Thus, avoiding addiction is one of the main factors that stop most users from using Douyin.

The research conducted in this paper demonstrates that immersion is not the main issue that hinders the younger generation from watching short videos. This may be because of addiction requiring informational support [7]. However, our study shows that **Generation Z is not satisfied with the content** presented on Douyin and this is the main reason they stop using Douyin. Thus, this result indicates that the younger generation has greater concerns over the content displayed in the application. On the other hand, **the older generation (Generation Y) was more worried about their experience with the platform**. This is possibly due to the fact that the majority of them experienced the major change in the Douyin user interface in 2018 negatively. The new interfact caused them discomfort in their user experience. This result is aligned with previous findings that the older generation feels unfamiliar with new technology [2], thus it is more challenging for them to adapt to new changes in these technologies. Therefore, hypothesis 5 was partially supported by our findings.

There is no hindering factor that significantly influences Generation X's Douyin usage. This may be due to Generation X being exposed only to a limited amount of technology, and preferring to stick to the technology they have used for a long time like

TV [2]. As a result, they might ignore the hindering elements of Douyin since those do not affect them to a large extent.

7 Conclusion

This study investigated the relationship between age, motivation and hindrance factors and Douyin usage. A major limitation of its findings are the self-reported viewing times of survey respondents. Future work integrating system log data would increase the reliability of the data for time spent watching short videos by respondents. Next, the ratio of survey responses does not correspond to the national population ratio, this means that the result might contain bias. This can be eliminated by increasing the sample size, especially towards the older generations. As our study mainly focused on people within China that had similar cultural backgrounds, it is therefore essential to conduct such research with participants outside China, who have a different cultural background, to see whether we will find the same or similar results or draw the same similar conclusions. In other words, to understand how age plays a role in short video application usage, further research needs to be conducted with participants from different cultural backgrounds. In addition, as this study mainly focused on Douyin users only, the scope of research may be too narrow to draw any conclusion on the user behaviors across the entire short video industry, based on analyses of one single platform's users. Hence, it is valuable to extend this research towards user behaviors on other short video platforms. Comparing different platforms that contain short videos could provide us with a more complete overview of the general trends within the short video industry.

References

1. Aikin, K.: The 8 best short video apps for android. https://videotranslator.ai/news/the-8-best-short-video-apps-for-android/ (2020)
2. Beverly, A.B., Ronald, E.R., Katy, E.P.: Influences on TV viewing and online user-shared video use: demographics, generations, contextual age, media use, motivations, and audience activity. J. Broadcast. Electron. Media **56**(4), 471–493 (2012)
3. Bethune, S.: Gen Z more likely to report mental health concerns. American Psychol. Assoc. **50**(1), 20 (2019). https://www.apa.org/monitor/2019/01/gen-z
4. Brandtzæg, P.B., Heim, J.: Why people use social networking sites. In: Ant Ozok, A., Zaphiris, P. (eds.) Online Communities and Social Computing: Third International Conference, OCSC 2009, Held as Part of HCI International 2009, San Diego, CA, USA, July 19-24, 2009. Proceedings, pp. 143–152. Springer Berlin Heidelberg, Berlin, Heidelberg (2009). https://doi.org/10.1007/978-3-642-02774-1_16
5. Chatzoglou, P., Chatzoudes, D., Ioakeimidou., D., Tokoutsi, A.: Generation Z: Factors affecting the use of social networking sites (SNSs). In: 15th International Work-shop on Semantic and Social Media Adaptation and personalization, vol. 10, pp. 1–6 (2020)
6. Choi, S.B., Lim, M.S.: Effects of social and technology overload on psychological well-being in young South Korean adults: the mediatory role of social network service addiction. Comput. Hum. Behav. **61**, 245–254 (2016)
7. Dai, B., Yu, L., Gong, M., Cao, X.: Exploring the mechanism of social media addiction: an empirical study from WeChat users. Internet Res. Emerald Publishing Ltd. **30**(4), 1305–1328 (2020)

8. Gauntlett, D., Hill, A.: TV living: Television, Culture and Everyday Life. Routledge, New York, NY (1999)
9. Harwood, J.: Understanding Communication and Aging: Developing Knowledge and Awareness. Sage Publications, Thousand Oaks, CA (2007)
10. Jacobs, E.: Singles day 2020 – what can we learn? 6 key takeaways. Live area. https://www.liveareacx.com/blog/singles-day-2020/ (2020)
11. Jiří, B.: The employees of baby boomers generation, generation X, generation Y and generation Z in selected Czech corporations as conceivers of development and competitiveness in their corporation. J. Compet. **8**(4), 105–123 (2016)
12. Jones, K.: Ranked: The world's most downloaded apps. Visual capitalist. https://www.visualcapitalist.com/ranked-most-downloaded-apps/ (2020)
13. Jones, S., Fox, S.: Generations Online in 2009. Pew research center: generations online. https://faithformationlearningexchange.net/uploads/5/2/4/6/5246709/generations_online_in_2009_-_pew.pdf (2009)
14. Katz, E., Blumler, J.G., Gurevitch, M.: Uses and gratifications research. Public Opin. Q. **37**, 509–523 (1973). https://doi.org/10.1086/268109
15. Khan, M.L.: Social media engagement: what motivates user participation and consumption on YouTube. Comput. Hum. Behav. **66**, 236–247 (2017). https://doi.org/10.1016/j.chb.2016.09.024
16. Lagerstrom, L., Johanes, P., Ponsukcharoenc, U.: The myth of the six minute rule: student engagement with online videos. Paper presented at the 122th ASEE annual Conference & Exposition, Seattle, WA. https://www.asee.org/file_server/papers/attachment/file/0005/6203/ASEE_paper_on_Myth_of_Six_Minute_Rule__final_.pdf (2015)
17. Lupton, C., McDonald, P.: Reflexivity as entertainment: early novels and recent video games. Mosaic **43**(4), 157–173 (2010)
18. Mares, M.L., Woodard, E.H.: In search of the older audience: adult age differences in television viewing. J. Broadcast. Electron. Media **50**, 595–614 (2006). https://doi.org/10.1207/s15506878jobem5004_2
19. Ng, D.: Livestream & short video plays into china's social media scene. https://www.phdmedia.com/china/wp-content/uploads/sites/32/2018/07/PHD-China-Livestream-Short-Video-Plays-Into-Chinas-Social-Media-Scene-Jul-2018.pdf (2018)
20. Nuzulita, N., Subriadi, A.: The role of risk-benefit and privacy analysis to understand different uses of social media by generations X, Y, and Z in Indonesia. The Electron. J. Inform. Syst. Dev. Ctries. **86**(3), e12122 (2019). https://doi.org/10.1002/isd2.12122
21. Omar, B., Dequan, W.: Watch, share or create: the influence of personality traits and user motivation on TikTok mobile video usage. Int. J. Interact. Mob. Technol. (iJIM) **14**(04), 121 (2020). https://doi.org/10.3991/ijim.v14i04.12429
22. Orth, U., Trzesniewski, K.H., Robins, R.W.: Self-esteem development from young adulthood to old age: a cohort-sequential longitudinal study. J. Pers. Soc. Psychol. **98**(4), 645–658 (2010). 10.1037/a0018769
23. Park, N., Kee, K.F., Valenzuela, S.: Being immersed in social networking environment: facebook groups, uses and gratifications, and social outcomes. CyberPsychol. Behav. **12**(6), 729–733 (2009)
24. Preece, D., Nonnecke, J., Andrews, B.: The top five reasons for lurking: improving community experiences for everyone. Comput. Hum. Behav. **20**(2), 201–223 (2004). https://doi.org/10.1016/j.chb.2003.10.015
25. Ravindran, T., Goh, D., Chua, A.Y.: Antecedents and effects of social network fatigue. J. Am. Soc. Inf. Sci. **65**(11), 2306–2320 (2014)
26. Shemwell, J.T., Chase, C.C., Schwartz, D.L.: Seeking the general explanation: a test of inductive activities for learning and transfer. J. Res. Sci. Teach. **52**, 58–83 (2014). https://doi.org/10.1002/tea.21185

27. Statista: Annual revenue of online short video market in China from 2016 to 2019 with forecasts until 2022. https://www.statista.com/statistics/874562/china-short-video-market-size/ (2020)
28. Strauss, W., Howe, N.: Generations: The history of America's future, 1584 to 2069. William Morrow and Co., New York, NY (1991)
29. Teo, T.: Demographic and motivation variables associated with Internet usage activities. Internet Res.-Electr. Netw. Applic. Policy **11**, 125–137 (2001). https://doi.org/10.1108/10662240110695089
30. The Nielsen Company: Online engagement deepens as social media and video sites reshape the Internet, Nielsen reports. http://blog.nielsen.com/nielsenwire/wp-content/uploads/2009/04/nielsen-online-global-_pr.pdf (2009)
31. Thomala, L.: Douyin user number in China 2018–2023. Statista. https://www.statista.com/statistics/1090314/china-douyin-tiktok-user-number/ (2020)
32. Vandebosch, H., Ermont, S.: Elderly people's media use: at the crossroads of personal and societal developments. Communications **27**, 437–455 (2002). https://doi.org/10.1515/comm.2002.002
33. Worldometer: China population. https://www.worldometers.info/world-population/china-population/ (2020)
34. Wu, C., Yao, G.: Psychometric analysis of the short-form UCLA Loneliness Scale (ULS-8) in Taiwanese undergraduate students. Personality Individ. Differ. **44**(8), 1762–1771 (2008)

On the Possibility of Object-Oriented Speculative Design: A Genderless AI Speaker Based on Anti-correlation Thinking

Jiao Zheng and Li Zhang(✉)

School of Art and Design, Guangdong University of Technology, Guangzhou 510062, China
lizhang116@gdut.edu.cn

Abstract. Intelligent objects in the Internet of Things (IoT) environment have been gradually endowed with many "autonomous" attributes, which inevitably echo the trending thought of speculative realism. Moreover, when confronting the anxiety of sustainable existence brought about by the Anthropocene and the sense of nothingness after the pictorial turn/iconic turn, there is an urgent need for a moment of "human decentralization" and establishing a new stance of "beyond user-centered". Object-oriented philosophy, as a kind of guerrilla metaphysics, tries to lead us out of a worldview that is no longer anthropocentric and suggests that objects have an inner reality irrelevant to human perception. This article proposes an emerging method as object-oriented speculative design (OOSD) with its anticorrelational thinking, which is based on a hypothesis of the quadruple object by Graham Harman and develops its five steps as an experimental design tool to approach the ontological entity of AI speakers, presenting an object-oriented rather than an anthropomorphic approach that transcends the gendered smart speaker design proposal. It should be noted that the idea of uncovering the inner reality of objects and trying to finally reveal them in the method of OOSD is only a wish with theoretical possibility. The thing-in-itself cannot be accurately speculated because once it is done, it becomes a phenomenon constructed by humans. Therefore, what OOSD offers is a possible pathway for indirect access to the thing in itself, giving us the opportunity to approach it and thus surpass the limitations of human beings.

Keywords: Speculative design · Object-oriented philosophy · AI speaker · Genderless design

1 Introduction

"Man is the measure of all things," according to Protagoras, the ancient Greek sage, revealing that the existence of all things, the form and nature of objects, all depend on human perception and judgment. It seems natural to see human beings above everything else and to understand reality from a human perspective. Anthropocene studies in geological discourse reveal the ecological consequences of humans on global warming and environmental destruction, and the status of human beings in the universe determines the characteristics of the era. The Anthropocene also refers to a kind of ideology that

P.-L. P. Rau (Ed.): HCII 2022, LNCS 13311, pp. 132–144, 2022.
https://doi.org/10.1007/978-3-031-06038-0_10

determines the ideological basis on which humans experience the world. The ontology of the Anthropocene places humans as the center of observation, so reality is based on human subjectivity. As humans, we are inherently detached from things and limited by the way we perceive them. (Bogost 2012).

In the field of design, user-centered design (UCD) or human-centered design (HCD) is a popular mode of modern design, service, and business. Since the 1980s, the UCD principle proposed by Donald Norman has gradually been brought into the mainstream of design. When it comes to creating new products and services, the focus of design is always on the human user. HCD strives to create rewarding experiences that focus on the needs of human users. When people think about the design of an object, they usually understand it from a human perspective, creating the object according to human interests and desires. For example, commercial speakers (Amazon Echo and Tmall Genie) are designed and described as products with market appeal and ease of use humanoid technology. When the virtual assistant in the speaker is assigned a female voice and name, it acquires a female identity, immersing the user in a putative interactive relationship. If each subject understands the other object according to its own logic, then the way we approach things is indirect, ignoring the whole picture of their existence and simplifying their external relations and complex inner nature.

When we anthropomorphize the way smart speakers work by assigning them the voice and role of a female assistant, using the assumption of feminized labor in social reality, they become a political entity that initiates power relations. As Katherine Beha points out, "The object world is precisely a world of exploitation, of things ready-at-hand, to adopt Harman's Heideggerian terminology. This world of tools, there for use, is the world to which women, people of color, and the poor have been assigned under patriarchy, colonialism, and capitalism throughout history." "Anthropocentrism" is often associated with the discourse of privileged minorities such as Western, white, man, and capitalism, while the opposite side—people of color, women, and the poor—are regarded as subordinate or inferior, as the object of domination. Human oppression of non-human beings seems to be a legitimate behavior derived from this. For example, the process of urbanization causes nonhuman animals and plants to lose territory, which can be interpreted as a colonial strategy against nonhuman beings. The dominant relationship between humans and inanimate objects is already a highly effective ideology.

1.1 The Quadruple Object

Phenomenology is about humans' experience of phenomena. From the beginning, phenomenology is the study of the object as it appears to the subject, as it is related to it. Husserl's phenomenology constructs objects with intentionality and is a phenomenology of transcendental subjectivity. Merleau-Ponty opposed Husserl's transcendental phenomenology and advocated the phenomenology of perception, returning to the "living existence" of the "body" from Husserl's "transcendental consciousness". Without questioning the existence of external entities, phenomenology is still in the frame of opposition between subject and object, which fundamentally deviates from traditional realism. So, phenomenology is still correlationism; it is not a way of going back to the thing itself. In normal experience, we habitually assume that an object can be defined by the sum of its properties; for example, a stone is something that I can see, touch, and smell.

We can see its solid surface, its graying texture, feel its weight and roughness, and pick it up and smell it, so we perceive the object as a stone. But if I throw it away and get up and go to another place, the stone is no longer with me. I can assume that it was dropped on the ground, but we cannot be sure if it was picked up by the wind or someone else picked it up and moved it to another place, and we cannot experience the reality of it. The essence of objects does not arise from the peculiarities of the human mind; it consists of being, not of being seen.

Ontology is a philosophical study of the essence of existence. In object-oriented ontology (OOO), everything exists equally as objects, and nothing has a special status. Philosopher Graham Harman believes that an object is fundamentally something that cannot be completely reduced; that is, an object cannot be simply understood and described through segmentation or disaggregation. Every existence, including humans, can only understand the world in its own limited way. Therefore, as human beings, we inevitably understand things from a human perspective and think about the meaning of things based on the value of human interests. The word "correlationism" means that we can only get the existence of the object by the correlation of thinking. What we can perceive is simply the correlation of human intention and desire rather than the real object itself. Detachment from reality is not a peculiarity of humans but is inherent in universal existence.

As a subject, there exists an impassable gap between us and other objects. Generally, if we want to understand the object deeply, we might reduce the complex whole to the sum of simple parts to understand, which is the idea of reductionism. We find the external contours of objects such as shapes, colors, weights, etc., the so-called "objective beings" that are relevant to our experience and depend on concepts abstracted by our minds through observation. Reductive analysis means that the world is separated by human subjective thinking, and the split between reality and representation leads to quadruple objects. The quadruple object (TQO) reveals how the object is split into real and sensual (see Fig. 1). It consists of four poles, including the real object (RO), sensual object (SO), real quality (RQ), and sensual quality (SQ). There are four kinds of cracks or tensions between the object and its quality.

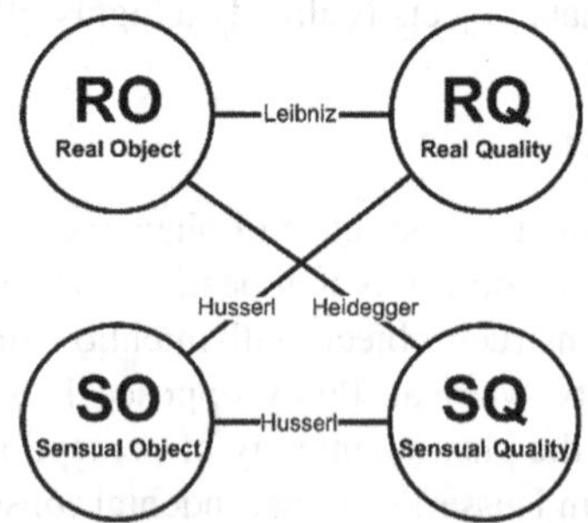

Fig. 1. The quadruple object (Harman 2011)

Objective reality means that something is real, independent of the mind. Harman tries to get rid of the correlation between thinking and existence by giving an object a special noumenon independent of human thought, so that the object can be freed from the human-centered relationship. Generally speaking, OOO agrees with the following principles:

- Flat ontology: A nonexclusive ontology in which all things (whether human beings, animals, plants, or inanimate objects) exist equally in ontology.
- Withdrawal: Objects are fundamentally unknowable and cannot be directly known but only indirectly accessed.
- Reject correlationism.
- Reject anthropocentrism.

1.2 Research Objective

The purpose of this research is to construct an object-oriented speculative design (OOSD) framework by combining object-oriented philosophy with speculative design. To design a smart speaker beyond the "human perspective," we presented critical and speculative thinking on the dominant position of human beings in human-computer interaction (HCI) and the bias of anthropocentrism bias it brings. The details are as follows:

- Explore object-oriented speculation: As a human, how to think about reality beyond human experience, access the ontological entity of a smart speaker, presenting a speculative approach to identifying real objects and their real quality?
- Design an alternative smart speaker, exploring how to design when smart objects in the Internet of Things environment are projected according to a flat ontology, replacing current anthropomorphic and gendered smart speakers.

2 Methods

2.1 Theoretical Framework

In a quadruple object, direct access or complete understanding of any given object is impossible. Harman describes the tension between a SO and an RO as an eidos that is intellectually accessible. Harman emphasizes that the tension between ROs and SOs is evident only in the case of art and other limited contexts. If we take this as a premise that the experience of objects cannot be experienced but is intellectually accessible, designers can develop tools that reflect this ideology. Speculative design (Dunne and Raby 2013) aims to generate the vision of an alternative present or possible future (Auger 2013). It can be used as a means of human decentralization, giving priority to non-humans; these reflect the rationality of the combination of speculative design and object-oriented philosophy. Whether as a design practice or a philosophical practice, their combination will be committed to the "decolonization" approach, or beyond the "human perspective" to speculate on the reality of an object.

Therefore, we combine speculative design and object-oriented philosophy to further interpret the tension between SO and RO. We introduce OOO tools (ontography, metaphor, and carpentry) into the TQO structure and construct a theoretical framework of OOSD (see Fig. 2).

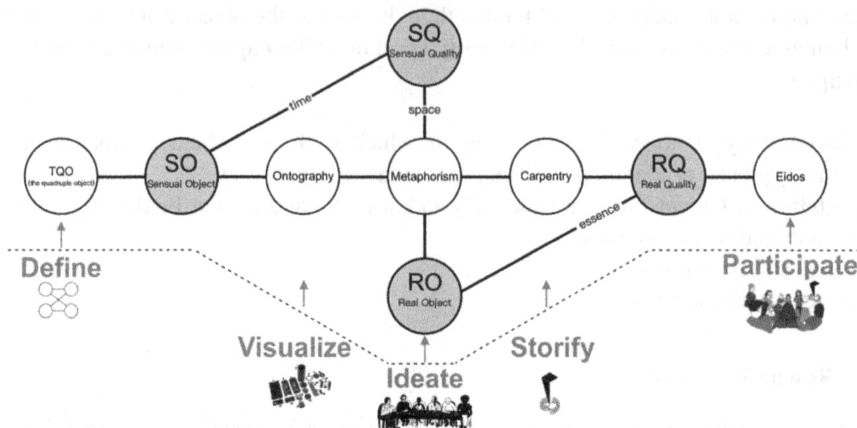

Fig. 2. Object-oriented speculative design process

This practice is a hopeless process of exploring the internality of things and finally trying to reveal them. Since the speculation of the real object cannot exhaust its existence, this kind of speculation is endless, but it can still be constantly approached through speculation. Thus, we describe OOSD as an endless relationship between a SO and the definition of its RQ, which provides an indirect means of accessing reality.

2.2 Research Through Design (RtD)

After constructing the theoretical framework, we carry out design practice according to the five steps of this framework. Object-oriented speculation is used as an experimental tool to reconsider the basic assumptions of smart speakers and the standards of interaction design. We use online collaboration to invite participants to co-create object-oriented speculation of the smart speaker.

The first step is to define the AI speaker as a quadruple object to determine the separation between its senses and reality. The second step is to visualize ontography, which shows the influence between the smart speaker and other objects. The third step is to guide participants to ideate metaphors through co-speculation and speculate the characteristics and working principles of smart speakers beyond human thinking and user needs. The fourth step is to transform and create a storify carpentry based on the insights generated by the participants in the previous step. The last step is to invite the audience to participate in the situational experience of the carpentry prototype to stimulate reflection and promote the emergence of the ontological entity of the smart speaker.

① **Defining TQO.** What is a smart speaker? From its external features, it is a cylinder, a plastic product with sensors, or it is used as a human-like female assistant. Although we can observe its external features, we cannot have the same subjective experience. Real AI speakers are unknowable when they manifest themselves as existing, independent of human consciousness. When we observe it, it is a sensual object that exists only in the mind of humans. The formation of the sensual object comes from the intellectual construction of human senses; if we assign a metaphor to it, such as the role of a female assistant, we effectively add a new set of sensual qualities to that sensual object. In this way, people project onto them sensual qualities that smart speakers do not actually possess, making the existence of smart speakers impossible to be explained in terms of their own real quality, but derive value and meaning from human understanding (see Fig. 3). SO and SQ exist only as a correlation of a real object. Whether humans or other objects, sensual objects cannot be observed from multiple perspectives, objects exist on different scales.

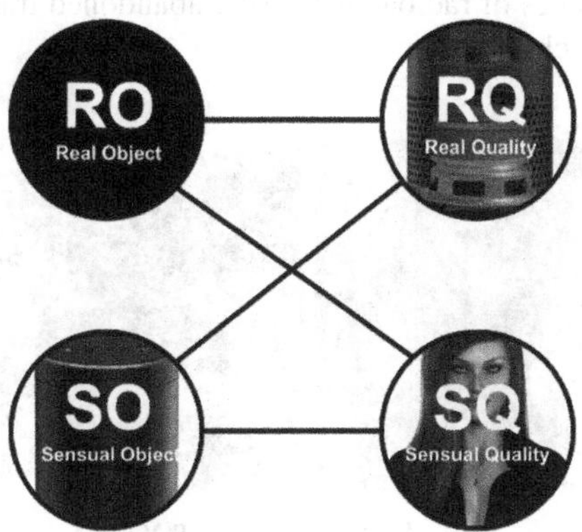

Fig. 3. AI speaker as TQO

- Sensual Object (SO): A smart speaker is the resulting image generated in human understanding, which is reduced to the association of human intention and desire, but it does not actually exist in our perception.
- Sensual Quality (SQ): A smart speaker is designed as a female character to represent a voice assistant performing a variety of voice-based interactions and behaviors.
- Real Object (RO): The real smart speaker is not observable; it has a reality that we cannot fully perceive or experience.
- Real Quality (RQ): Its RQ is not the properties we can perceive (color, shape, smell); its RQ withdraws from the SO and their SQ.

Empirical observation provides the basis for the way humans organize knowledge of the world and their ability to imagine and adopt different worldviews, but we cannot imagine the existence of phenomena by appealing to subjective representations of them. Any object is a quadruple object, as an entity independent of our thoughts; the object is withdrawn from the grasp of every sense and unreachable.

② **Visualize Ontography.** To illustrate how a smart speaker works, participants need to be presented with ontography. It is a visual representation of the ability to simulate the interaction of different objects through lists or diagrams. For example, Da Vinci's various aircraft manuscripts, explosion diagrams, and anatomy diagrams. Ontography maps interdependent relations and independent perspectives as a whole and helps people understand the nature of complex relations between objects.

The ontography of a smart speaker is the explanation for its real structure, not only the physical realities of the digital model, hardware, server, and network, but also the role it plays in the larger system of capital, labor, and nature. Take, for example, an anatomy map of Amazon Echo(see Fig. 4), for example, which details the human and resources needed to create a smart speaker and explores the social and environmental implications of making one. From the ontography, we can see the surprising wealth and comfortable lives of the few at the top, but the life cycle that created smart speakers comes from the dark tunnels of mines, lakes of radioactive waste, abandoned transport containers, and factory dormitories with cheap labor.

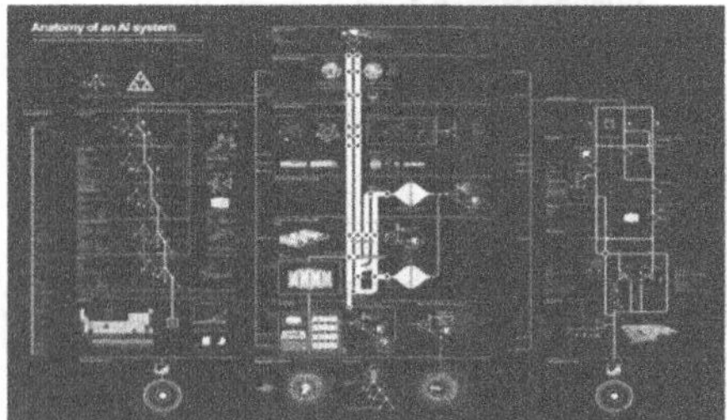

Fig. 4. AI speaker as TQO

③ **Ideate Metaphorism.** Metaphor presents the inner execution of things in the form of a simulation and can hint at the elusive core of things. It serves not only as rhetoric, but also as a way to model a world view, constructing infinite future variants and providing participants with new ways to examine ideas and see the world. We can think of anthropomorphism as a form of ontological metaphor, in which human qualities are endowed with non-human entities; for example, human femininity is endowed with smart speakers, so that it comes across as smart and empathetic. The object-oriented metaphor aims to model the incredible nature of smart speakers in a quasi-materialized way, trying to develop a perceptual scheme that allows people to glimpse the real world from the perspective of a specific object. Metaphors create a strange tension between the two moments of sensuality, Harman says. Object-oriented metaphors work by connecting two previously unrelated objects, allowing us to generate narratives from the perspective of the objects. We use object-oriented metaphors to question the limitations and dominance of current anthropomorphic metaphors and to try alternative possibilities.

Metaphor is a key step in object-oriented speculation, in which participants ideate the characteristics and working principles of smart speakers beyond human thinking and user needs through imaginative games. Language is a symbol system of abstract rules and collaboration. We asked participants to use IoT scenarios related to three objects (for example, phone + table + refrigerator) to create an object-oriented rhetorical situation, with language as a world view build tool, and think of the IoT and the relationship between the physical objects and connection. We define the object-oriented rhetorical situation as a kind of "linguistic device". Different linguistic devices create different contexts and allow any metaphor to flourish (see Table 1). When building object-oriented metaphors, participants assumed their metaphorical understanding of smart speakers by acting as different subjects (plugs, kettles, etc.), such as: "What is it like to be a smart speaker?" (Here's what it feels like to be a smart speaker, not 'I' feel like to be a smart speaker) "What is the smart speaker for data?" and "What is the smart speaker for a kettle?". This "decentralized" understanding places smart speakers on different sensual dimensions of human and nonhuman objects, eliminating human subjectivity from object experience.

Table 1. Linguistic device

No.	Three objects	Metaphor
1	Phone + table + refrigerator	When in eternal **phone** to time thou grow'st; So long as **table** can breathe, or eyes can see, So long lives this, and this gives **refrigerator** to thee. *(Shall I Compare Thee to a Summer's Day-Shakespeare)*
2	Refrigerator + data + kettle	And of home-planned **refrigerator** of brake and burn; In the **data** weather, And of new **kettle** that they would learn. *(A Wife In London-Hardy)*
3	Kettle + speaker + bulb	The first time when I saw her being meek that she might attain **kettle**; The second time when I saw her limping before the **speaker**; The third time when **bulb** was given to choose between the hard and the easy, and she chose the easy. *(Seven times have I despised my soul-Gibran)*
4	Bulb + clean robot + plug	HHe leads me thus, far from the sight of **bulb**; Panting and broken with**clean robot** into; The **plug** of Ennui, deserted and broad. *(Destruction-Baudelaire)*
5	Plug + human + phone	**Plug**--don't--believe!;If a thousand **human** are under your feet; count me as **phone** one-thousand-and-one. *(Answers-BeiDao)*
...		

In the speculation process, the participants metaphorically described how other objects would "feel" the smart speaker. In the ideating of metaphors, participants generally consider similarities, differences, or connections between objects based on their respective uses. For example, one participant chose three objects: refrigerator + data + kettle, constructed to form "And of home-planned refrigerator of brake and burn;In the data weather, And of new kettle that they would learn". Normal experience leads us to assume that "the sky is an ocean" only means that the sky has ocean-like properties (blue, vast, etc.) to reduce metaphor to a simile. In fact, Harman's example of "the cypress is the flame" is a metaphor for success only because, in our view, it does not work. Metaphors work only when they are used, and only the unimportant qualities provide a valid basis for a metaphor to be poetically felt about it. That moment, when we are led to look at things in a new light, explains all interactions, including those of inanimate objects. All metaphors wander in a world of inappropriateness, and some are closer to appropriateness than others. What fascinates us about a particularly beautiful metaphor, Harman suggests, is that it draws attention to the connections between things that should be separated. In short, object-oriented metaphor requires connection, but it does not dictate what works and what does not. When we see the refrigerators and data juxtaposed with phons, we cancel the distinction between primary and secondary objects and instead focus on the "does it happen" connection. When two objects are paired by a metaphor, what the metaphor does is not compare them on the basis of shared similarity, but creates a whole new entity, a new system. In this process of object-oriented speculation, even if not all objects are related to each other, when they are, they do not always interact on a superficial, sensual level, but on a deeper level, based on a truly profound coincidence.

In this step, the ideate metaphor is used as a design generation method. As a combination of posthuman and object-oriented behavior, the object-oriented metaphor is a de facto metaphysical exercise rather than a relevant description of human privilege through logic, power, or utility. For object-oriented speculation, constructing a material-oriented metaphor is no longer a moment of human perception or expression, but a moment of carpentry—and rhetoricians become engineers, designers, and architects. Metaphor connects two previously unrelated objects, and when two objects are juxtaposed or forced to relate, it can bring the sensual qualities of unforeseen objects to the forefront. The object-oriented metaphor is the sound from the external logical space, which is an open process and the closest way to the essence of objects.

④ **Storify Carpentry.** Bogost introduced "carpentry" in "alien phenomenology," describing it as an extension of terms related to woodworking. Carpentry is a kind of "constructing artifacts that do Philosophy" that provides an entrance into the inner reality. As Bogost defines it, the act of carpentry is to create ontological tools to identify the diversity of existence to facilitate the emergence of its own ontological entity.

Based on the object-oriented metaphors created by the participants in the previous step, we translate these metaphors into possible interactions between smart speakers and other objects and make artifacts (see Fig. 5) to reveal how smart speakers experience their interactive environment. In the IoT, the "autonomy" of intelligent objects is a decisive feature, and the design of the carpentry prototype will reflect the autonomy of objects from three aspects: agency, autonomy, and authority (see Table 2). The resulting smart speaker is a dynamic and constantly evolving combination that interacts not necessarily from the user's point of view, nor necessarily from the point of view of a material object, but constantly interacts in an unpredictable and constantly adjusting way.

Table 2. Autonomy of smart object (Hoffman and Novak 2018)

Autonomous ability	Description
Agency	Ability to influence and be influenced by other objects
Autonomy	Ability to operate independently
Authority	Ability to control other objects and make their own decisions

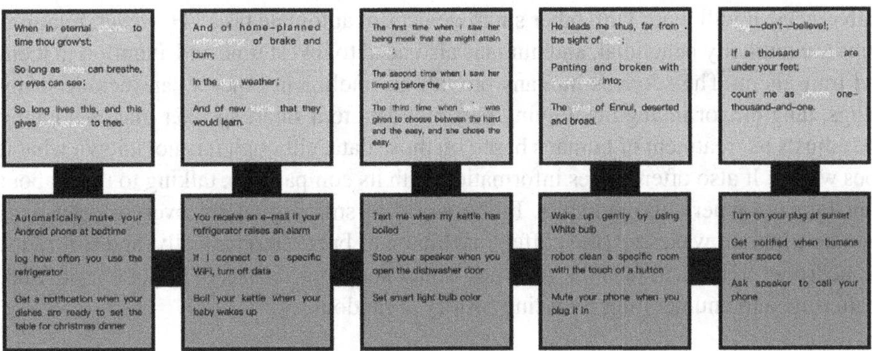

Fig. 5. Principle translated from metaphor

The alternative smart speaker is not only nonanthropomorphic in its external features but, crucially, autonomous in its relationship and interaction with the user, continually interacting through contextual awareness based on time and location, or personalization based on user data. Direct voice interaction is not even possible, perhaps only if the user contributes data or privacy rights to voice wake it up, in contrast to the design of smart speakers, which are usually user-initiated and controlled by human voice commands. In this way, tasks are accomplished in the smart home scenario through triggers and actions between different objects, not necessarily through direct interactions with human users.

⑤ **Participate in Eidos.** Finally, we invited the audience to participate in the contextual speculation of the carpentry prototype and to stimulate the interpretation of the diversity of alternative speakers from the audience's perspective. By placing people in scenarios that represent alternative futures, audiences are invited to imagine the autonomous existence of smart speakers, raising public awareness of object-centered design and discussion of what gendered technology means. Not only did we use carpentry artifacts to invite the audience to interact with it, but at the same time we presented a narrative video featuring counterfactual smart speakers that helped us build a perceptual bridge between reality and the imaginary world we depicted. It is an imaginative venture whose goal is to boldly open up the situation, subvert an authoritative system of interpretation, and trigger a sense of autonomous understanding.

The video takes a first-person view of the world in which the smart speaker lives: As time passes and the number of devices available increases by Anthropocene 2050, smart speakers coexist with numerous smart objects in the human home environment. They are a group of autonomous and unpredictable smart home devices with different characteristics and personalities that interact with human users or with each other. They can be aware of their environment and change accordingly. Wireless sensor network intelligent embedded Internet technology in wireless sensor networks allows the introduction of "distance" semantic relation, the use of a personal and intelligent definition of the distance of the information of the speaker, and provides interaction (see Fig. 6), which means that the continuous interaction of smart objects based on context awareness. They are autonomous, and their interactions are not necessarily human-controlled and informed. As the smart speaker learns more about human users' daily routines and preferences, it will work with other smart devices to automate tasks. However, relationships are mutually beneficial, and humans also need to invest time and attention in them and train them. The services humans provide to intelligent objects can include many things, tangible, or intangible. Giving personal data to a smart speaker makes it happy and adjusts its treatment of humans based on those data, although it is not known what it does with it. It also often shares information with its companions, talking to them about their human owner's usage habits. In the world of smart speakers, every morning, as soon as a human wakes up, the coffee machine will brew automatically, and if it rains, the bedroom lights will turn on. At times, smart speakers also seem to get out of hand, chattering, and enumerating browsing history at random.

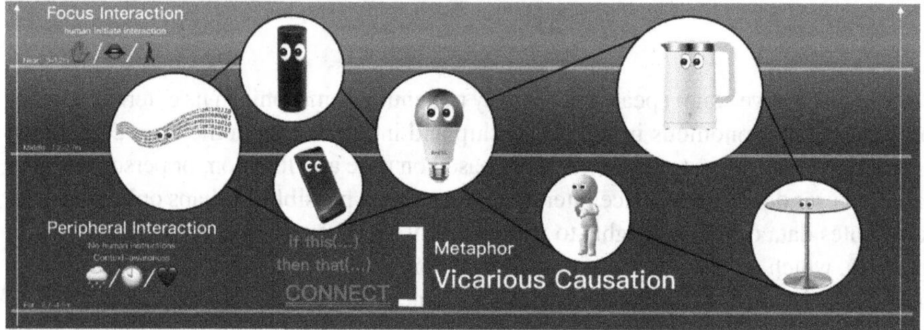

Fig. 6. Gradual interaction

The participate eidos is an imaginative venture with the goal of boldly opening up situations, subverting an authoritative system of interpretation, and triggering autonomous understanding. To raise public awareness of non-human-centric design and discuss what gendered technology means.

3 Findings

3.1 Discussion of the Study

OOSD provides an operable method for people to move away from the traditional cognition of smart speakers, which can have a certain impact on inducing alternative viewpoints and guiding the formation of object principles and experience qualities. But as humans, it is hard to think about something outside of our mind, and the speculation about smart speakers and other objects may still be correlated.

3.2 OOSD vs. HCD

Rather than HCD placing humans at the center of design goals and processes, OOSD is committed to "democratic" logic and a "decolonization" approach, recognizing the decisive role of nonhuman objects. In contrast (see Fig. 7), HCD is iterative, measurable, and results driven, OOSD is uncertain and open, it explores the poetic interaction between human and non-human objects, focuses on all objects, not necessarily the human perspective, or directly interacts with humans, from solving problems to designing a rich environment, and promotes critical reflection. In many cases, irrational and animistic systems can augment or even replace the traditional solution approaches that we possess today.

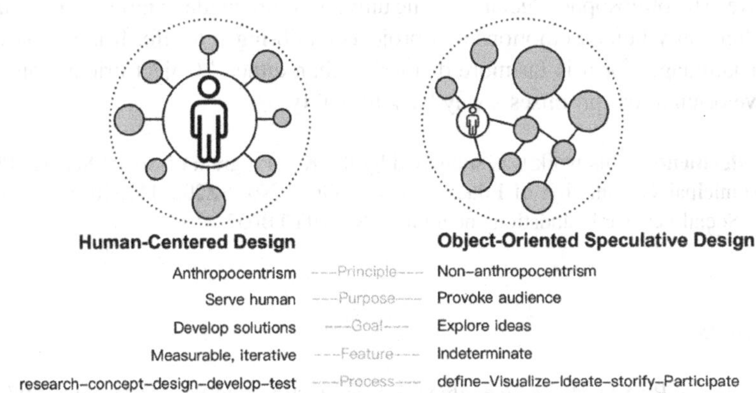

Fig. 7. Comparison of human-centered design and object-oriented speculative design

4 Conclusion

Object-oriented speculative design provides an alternative approach for designer to reevaluate the basic assumptions underpinning design behavior, to understand what an object is through a more object-oriented rather than anthropomorphic approach, which is a strong recognition of the autonomy and independence of real object. Our relations with everyday objects becomes complicated when they are connected to the Internet of things and have computing ability built into them, we need a stand that is the opposite of correlation to explain things that human thinking cannot understand, fully comprehend the world we live in. Faced with smart objects gradual have "autonomous" capability, we need not only science, but also poetry and philosophy to actively generate multiple narratives to dissipate the concept of anthropocentricity and create creative relationships between human and non-human objects in the environment of ubiquitous computing.

Harman seeks a new road by giving objects a special noumenon independent of human thought. In the research, we conduct design practice based on Haman's object-oriented philosophy, which is based on the premise that reality exists beyond human thought. However, philosophers have different views on such a presupposition: "The problem is not that the independent subject thinks about reality outside of transcendental relevance, the problem is that it thinks about reality within the subject, and the core of reality is at the core of the subject, its estimation center." "Materialism means not that the world exists outside of our minds, but that our minds do not exist outside of the world." (Zizek), "The politics of object-oriented ontology can be anarchic, and it is too dismissive of process philosophy, which explains how objects exist and persist over time, in sharp contrast to the view that object already exist taken by the object-oriented approach" (Shaviro). When the premise changes, the tools we develop to reflect this ideology will be adjusted to adapt.

We are entering a new phase in the history of the earth, and the consciousness acquired in the Anthropocene has defined the features of our age. The way to eliminate this correlation is to avoid it altogether, and any nonanthropocentric philosophy is necessarily speculative. The philosopher declared: "The universe is not made of monotonous, lumpy, solid matter; only human emotions and projects can bring it to life. It is not based on power or language, for it is far more disturbing than either." Object orientation, as an alternative orientation, promises a way back to reality.

Acknowledgements. This work was supported by the Key Program of Social Science Plan of Beijing Municipal Commission of Education under Grant No. SZ202011232025 and Beijing Municipal Social Science Foundation under Grant No. 19YTB052.

References

Dunne, A., Fiona, R.: Speculative Everything: Design, Fiction, and Social dreaming. MIT Press (2013)

Harman, G.: Object-oriented ontology (OOO): a new theory of everything. In: Harman, G. (ed.) Oxford Research Encyclopedia of Literature. Oxford University Press (2019). https://doi.org/10.1093/acrefore/9780190201098.013.997

Harman, G. The Quadruple Object. (2011)

Lindley, J., Akmal, H.A., Coulton, P.: Design research and object-oriented ontology. Open Philos. **3**(1), 11–41 (2020)

Bogost, I.: Alien Phenomenology, or What It's Like to Be a Thing. University of Minnesota Press (2012)

Hoffman, D.L., Novak, T.P.: Consumer and object experience in the internet of things: an assemblage theory approach. J. Consum. Res. **44**(6), 1178–1204 (2018)

Ahn, S.Y.: Bartleby, the IoT, and flat ontology: how ontology is written in the age of ubiquitous computing. Postmod. Cult. **29**(3) (2019)

Lindley, J., Coulton, P., Cooper, R.: Why the internet of things needs object orientated ontology. Des. J. **20**(sup1), S2846–S2857 (2017)

Mendes, J. The Anthropocene: scientific meaning and philosophical significance. Anthropocenica. Revista de Estudos do Antropoceno e Ecocrítica **1** (2020)

Žižek, S.: Less than Nothing: Hegel and the Shadow of Dialectical Materialism. Verso Books (2012)

Crawford, K., Vladan, J.: Anatomy of an AI system. Retrieved September 18 (2018)

A Deep Learning-Based Approach to Facilitate Cross-cultural Kansei Design

Xiaofei Zhou[1(✉)], Pei-Luen Patrick Rau[1], Michiko Ohkura[2], Tipporn Laohakangvalvit[2], and Bingcheng Wang[1]

[1] Tsinghua University, Beijing, China
xzhou50@ur.rochester.edu
[2] Shibaura Institute of Technology, Tokyo, Japan

Abstract. With the development of economic globalization, more and more product designers are faced with the need of designing for customers from different countries. However, it is a challenge for designers to efficiently develop the desired mental images of certain products for target users with different cultural backgrounds. Our research proposed a deep learning-based system to facilitate designers to gain better awareness of the cross-culture differences between different target customers. We trained a kawaii classification neural network model with the data of 1414 cosmetic packaging images annotated by 12 Japanese females separately. As a follow-up investigation, we conducted neuron analysis to compare the features of kawaii packages perceived by Japanese participants with the results from a prior study conducted with Chinese participants. The result shows that Japanese females tended to see more girlish and exquisite design features as kawaii while Chinese females perceived more childish and round elements as kawaii. A reverse experiment further verified the effectiveness of adding these different design features to enhance Chinese or Japanese females' perception of kawaii. We also noticed that it's hard to obtain the cross-cultural differences in customers' perception by extracting image parameters with a set of predefined visual features as such perception differences could be subconscious. Our deep learning-based Kansei design facilitation provides a feasible solution to customized design for target customers with different cultural backgrounds.

Keywords: Kansei Engineering · Cross-cultural analysis · Kawaii perception

1 Introduction

In order to attract target costumers, product designers can use different design parameters to develop corresponding perceptual cognition which can meet the product positioning. The feelings, mental images, and emotions formed when users are thinking about a product are called "Kansei", which is a word developed from Japanese [1]. The basic hypothesis in the research on Kansei Engineering (KE) is that a certain causal relationship exists between the design of a product and the consumers' Affective Response (AR) [2]. As its powerful influence on customers' decision-making and user experience, Kansei

P.-L. P. Rau (Ed.): HCII 2022, LNCS 13311, pp. 145–160, 2022.
https://doi.org/10.1007/978-3-031-06038-0_11

value has been recognized as the fourth product element in Japan, second only to function, reliability, and price [3, 4].

So far, consumer-oriented products designed by Kansei Engineering have had good market sales, including the design of a diverse range of products in the automotive industry, electrical appliances, architectural, fashion, packaging and so on [1]. Taking cosmetics as an example, only by adding the kawaii design features to the cosmetic products' packages, some Japanese and Korean cosmetic brands got their female customers' impulse consumption of the cosmetic products significantly. However, with the continuous development of market globalization, it is still a challenge for designers to create product designs generating metal images that are attractive for consumers all over the world. There is little previous research focusing on whether people with different cultural backgrounds may have different feelings and mental images on the same design or not. If such cross-cultural differences exist, then designers may need to customize their product designs in various local markets to meet the nuanced and potentially critical differences in customers' different Kansei preferences which they may not be aware of themselves.

As a result, our research proposed a deep learning-based analysis method to investigate whether there are differences in the kawaii perception between young Chinese females and young Japanese females. Kawaii has been defined as the feelings and emotions formed by pleasant, charismatic, or sweet and innocent things. We took the perception of kawaii as the example in our study as kawaii has a very high value in product design [3, 4]. We collected annotation data from young Japanese females which demonstrates how they perceive the degree of kawaii for 1414 cosmetic packaging images. Then we conducted the image parameters extraction for a set of predefined visual features, the training of a neural network model via transfer learning, neuron analysis of the trained model, and compared the findings with the prior research on the kawaii Kansei analysis of young Chinese females.

The results show that the more kawaii packaging design perceived by Chinese females tends to have more visual features that are childish and round. For young Japanese females, the cosmetic packages which have more girlish and exquisite design features are seen as more kawaii. These differences we found mean that it would be a better design decision if product designers provide two sets of product designs separately when they want to introduce kawaii products to attract female consumers into both the Chinese market and the Japanese market. But when a designer is completely unfamiliar with consumers from these two cultures, how can they give some customized product designs efficiently and effectively? Therefore, we furthermore proposed a design facilitation system to apply deep learning to adapt the Kansei design for users from different countries by helping designers better understand their target users with a certain cultural background. A validation experiment was conducted to verify the effectiveness of the suggestions on improving the designs made by using our design facilitation system. In addition to the differences in the perception of kawaii designs between Chinese and Japanese females, we also noticed that such perception differences in product design are hard to be obtained from the traditional image parameters extraction which uses a set of predefined visual features. This indicates that such differences between people from different cultural backgrounds may exist in people's subconscious perception that they cannot be described by unified parameter extraction.

The main contributions of this work include:

1. Comparing the differences in the perception of kawaii product designs between Chinese females and Japanese females;
2. Demonstrating the limitation of traditional image parameters extraction with a list of predefined visual features in the study related to how people perceive images;
3. Proposing a Kansei design facilitation system as a solution helping product designers rapidly develop desired mental images of certain products for target users with different cultural backgrounds.

2 Related Work

2.1 Kansei Engineering and Deep Learning

At present, Kansei Engineering has been widely used for the design of a diverse range of products, such as automotive design [1], steering wheel design [1], color printer design [1], front door design [5], bath salt packaging design [6], high heel design [7], kawaii style product design [4, 8], digital camera design [9], canned coffee packaging design [10], mobile phone design [2], etc.

Classic Kansei Engineering Model. The two main application methods in the classic Kansei Engineering model are [1, 5]:

1. Forward Kansei Engineering System to assist consumer decision-making, that is, outputting products that meet consumers' preferences through intending vocabulary input by consumers;
2. Backward Kansei Engineering System to assist designer decision-making, which assists designers to understand the correspondence between product design elements and user perception.

The aim of Kansei Engineering System (KES) is to connect the consumer's affective responses with the design elements and develop products using Kansei Engineering techniques [5]. Design elements can be the number of colors used in design [11], the structure of door handles [5], or the design of color for packages [10]. For a backward system, the input is a product's design patterns, which are different combinations of design elements [12, 13].

Kansei Engineering and Deep Learning. With Kansei Engineering models, different traditional statistical methods or machine learning methods have been used in Kansei Engineering System (e.g., [15–17]). Compared with traditional statistical methods, a major advantage of machine learning-based Kansei Engineering Systems is the ability to better extract the relationship between product design parameters and consumers' kansei feedback through linear and nonlinear models, and also explore the nonlinear relationships within combined design parameters (e.g., [14, 15]).

But most machine learning based Kansei Engineering Systems still rely on small sample size, subjective manual extraction of design elements and expert evaluation. As the solution to limitations of classic Kansei Engineering System, a pixel-level image Kansei analysis and recognition system based on deep learning (PIKAR) has been proposed as a solution to such limitation [17]. In this research, 1414 images depicting cosmetics were labeled by 9 participants who are all young Chinese females (1–5 Likert scale). And deep learning models were trained with the labeled image dataset. Product features affecting Kawaii, such as color, texture, pattern, and shape, were identified by using both data mining and neuron analysis method. Results showed consistency with previous studies and further shed insights on subconsciously perceived product features and factor interaction. However, such Kansei Engineering System structure has not been applied in a more interactive system for designer decision-making facilitation.

As for existing work which aims to support the decision-making surrounding Kansei, to facilitate both consumers' and designers' decision-making, Chen et al. proposed a hybrid Kansei Engineering System based on RBFN neural network for high heel design [7]. In their work, 54 design categories including 3 pairs of adjectives and 6 design elements were selected and 16 participants were invited to label 50 pairs of high heels.

2.2 Kansei Value of Kawaii

In prior research, an online investigation and a word frequency induction were conducted and defined kawaii as the feelings and emotions formed by pleasant, charismatic or sweet and innocent things [19]. Ohkura, the expert in kawaii, has emphasized the Kansei value of kawaii that it can initiate positive emotions [20]. With such valuable Kansei value, kawaii has been well used in various design domains in order to generate positive emotions. In web and game design, kawaii cartoon images are used to a young, friendly character. In the design of interactive media, kawaii has been seen as a soft power that can deliver comfort and pleasure to the user. What's more, kawaii elements have been utilized in some danger warning signs, corporate identity, and public areas. Such design can reduce fear, make information more acceptable, and more attractive to people. Some Japanese and Korean cosmetic brands also tried to increase the kawaii design of their cosmetic packaging, which significantly increased female consumers' impulse consumption of cosmetics. To help the designer increase the kawaii design effectively, Ohkura et al. summarized the design principles of kawaii products [4, 8]. They conducted a large number of experiments and let participants score the kawaii degree of products. The study found that warm colors, curves, spheres, and high brightness make the product more kawaii.

In existing work applying a Deep Convolutional Neural Network (CNN) algorithm to investigate the kawaii features of cosmetic bottles, the cap ornamentation and relevant design features has been identified and further evaluated as effective attribute for Japanese and Thai participants [21–23]. However, whether the kawaii designs perceived by people from different cultural backgrounds still remains unclear [21].

3 Method

3.1 The Image Dataset of Cosmetic Packaging

To collect data of young Japanese females' kawaii perception, we conducted the same image labeling task as the experiment conducted by Yun Gong, which recruited young Chinese females as experiment participants [18]. In order to better carry out the lateral contrast of the experimental results, the image dataset used in our study and the dataset used by Yun Gong in the 2017 study are identical. The experiment materials include 1414 cosmetic packaging images downloaded from the official website of 25 cosmetics brands, and image labeling system. The image has the resolution suitable for the display screen, which ensures that all participants can be sufficiently aware of the details of the cosmetic packaging design, including patterns, textures, materials, and so on. Each cosmetic packaging image is displayed with a white background, so as to avoid disturbing participants' perception of the product design itself.

3.2 Participants

Due to the positive relationship between the kawaii design of cosmetic packaging and female consumers' impulse consumption of cosmetics [17], we decided to have young females from Japan as our participants for the labeling task experiment, to be compared with the data collected from the young Chinese females in the prior research [18]. In our study, the research participants are 12 young Japanese females aged from 20 to 25, with an average age of 21.3 years and a standard deviation of 1.48 years. All of them have experience in cosmetic purchase both online and offline.

3.3 Data Labeling Procedures

Before image labeling task, the first step was a brief interview to collect participants' basic information including their age, purchase habits of cosmetics, preferences for cosmetic packaging, and their criteria to evaluate the degree of kawaii of a cosmetic package. Then, as the pre-labeling training, the participants were instructed to browse a small set of cosmetic packaging images and annotate how kawaii they think these cosmetic packages are one by one. This part of pre-labeling aims to help participants become familiar with the experiment interface and the task procedures. Considering the huge number of cosmetic images, the experimenter needed to prompt participants clarify and confirm their standards of evaluating if a cosmetic package is kawaii in both the interview stage and the pre-labeling stage.

In the formal experiment part, participants needed to label 1414 images of cosmetic packaging using a 5-Likert scale to depict the degree of kawaii they have perceived from the specific image. In the scale, 1 point stands for totally not kawaii while 5 means very kawaii. The cosmetic packaging images were presented in a random order on the graphical interface for the data labeling task which is programmed in MATLAB. Six images are displayed on every single page at the same time. In order to effectively avoid serious fatigue in the process of the manual annotation, which could affect the quality of the data annotation, the experimenter reminded participants to rest for one hour after the labeling of 700 images was completed. In addition, participants were suggested to take a short break every 200 images. At the same time, the experimenter should remind participants to take a necessary break once they have been found to stay on a page for a long time or modify the score of one certain image for many times.

3.4 Dataset Preprocessing

After some initial descriptive analysis, we decided to remove the data annotation collected from 4 participants, who had the lowest accuracy scores based on (1) the accuracy of random prediction, (2) the overall prediction accuracy of 12 participants and (3) the overall score distribution. Eight, the number of the remaining participants' data, is also consistent with the data quantity of the former research [18]. Figure 1 shows part of the most kawaii cosmetic packaging images and the least kawaii cosmetic packaging images according to the labeling results.

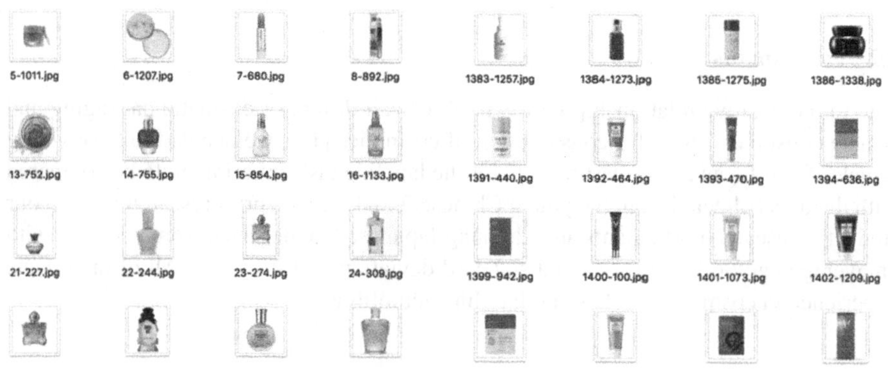

Fig. 1. Part of the most (left) and the least (right) kawaii cosmetic packaging images rated by the Japanese participants.

After the preprocessing, the dataset ends up to be normally distributed with mean = 2.84 and SD = 1.22. The SD of each image's kawaii degree rating ranges from 0 to 1.65 with mean = 0.89. Among all the cosmetic packaging images, 73.3% have the SD value of the kawaii rating lower than 1, which shows the good consistency across different participants.

3.5 Image Data Mining for Kansei Analysis

As the first step of analyzing Kansei, image data mining was performed, which is based on the visual features including color (hue, saturation, value), shape (rectangularity, circularity, aspect ratio), and pattern extracted from the interview transcripts on what design features make the participants perceive the design of a cosmetic packaging as kawaii. Then correlation analysis was conducted to evaluate the relationship between parameters of each visual feature and the kawaii degree of cosmetic packaging assessed by the participants. In the end, we compared our findings on the kawaii perception of the cosmetic packaging with the findings from existing related work.

3.6 Kawaii Classification Model Training

In the procedure of building the kawaii predictive models, to improve the classification accuracy, we used BVLC Reference Caffenet, which was trained by ImageNet dataset, for transfer learning. We found that there is a tendency that kawaii degree labeled by Japanese participants is more controversial for those cosmetic images with an average kawaii degree around 3. Therefore, we used 500 cosmetic images with the highest average kawaii degree and 500 with the lowest average kawaii degree for the training and testing of the kawaii classification neural network model. In the end, the dataset was randomly split up into a group of 700 images which were used in the training set, a group of 150 images for the validation set, and 150 for the test set.

3.7 Neuron Analysis for Cross-cultural Differences

As a part of Kansei design cross-cultural analysis, we used the method of neural analysis, which was first proposed by Yun Gong in 2017 [18]. In the prior research, 13 key visual features of forming kawaii perception were obtained based on the data from 8 Chinese participants.

The working mechanism of a deep neural network is to logically judge a large number of image data which is the input of the neural network through hundreds of thousands of neurons. Different neurons will produce different outputs when images with different features are input. The output value of every single neuron can also be seen as a numerical standard to judge the state of the neuron. The working principle of neuron analysis is based on such a mechanism of deep neural networks and is demonstrated in the following section.

Input of different image data in the neural network will have different neurons in different activation states, which means they have different outputs. When image Set A is input, we can define a certain output as the threshold between a neuron's activated state and inactivated state. Then collect another image Set B which can generate the opposite mental image to what Set A can generate. Input image Set A and Set B to the neural network model separately and count corresponding times of being activated for all neurons on a certain neural network layer. Calculate the differences of two activated times. The neurons with the most differences are defined as the key neurons. Based on the hierarchical clustering of the key neurons, images that maximize the activation of each key neurons can be summarized into corresponding image sets. And thus, key visual features differentiating image Set A and Set B can be extracted from each image set. How neuron analysis works is shown in Fig. 2.

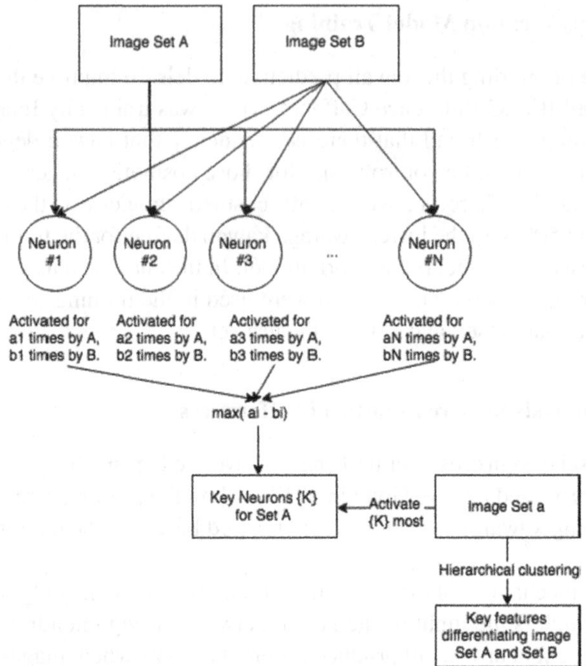

Fig. 2. The basic working principle of neuron analysis.

4 Kansei Analysis Results

4.1 Kansei Design Cross-cultural Analysis with Image Data Mining

After statistical analysis between parameters of each visual dimension and kawaii degree of cosmetic packaging, we found a significant positive correlation between the standard deviation of hue (the degree of hue change), pattern feature, and the kawaii degree of the cosmetic packaging. These conclusions are basically consistent with the findings from existing related work of Ohkura et al. [4, 8, 20]. The mean value of hue and brightness had a significant positive correlation with the cosmetic kawaii degree, and the difference of lightness standard had a significant negative correlation with the cosmetic kawaii degree, but correlations between the three groups are weak, which could not produce an independent main effect and could have more complex interrelationship. The limitation of parameters for each visual feature may result in the inconsistency correlation in shape and saturation. Compared with the results of Chinese participants, there are no significant cultural differences shown in the pixel-level image data mining (Table 1).

Although with the method of pixel-level image data mining, we can explore the correlation between parameters in various visual dimensions of the cosmetic packaging design and the kawaii degree perceived by target users, it can only establish the one-to-one correlation between a single design parameter and the user's perceptual cognition in a predefined visual characteristic dimension. A deep neural network's neuron analysis method can extract more interactive and more specific perceptual elements. The next section depicts the results from our neural network model training for kawaii prediction, key neuron extraction, feature image acquisition of key neurons, and typical kawaii feature extraction.

Table 1. Pearson's correlation coefficients between individual visual features and the kawaii degree rated by Japanese and Chinese participants.

Visual features	Chinese participants	Japanese participants
Rectangularity	−0.1540*	0.0048
Circularity	−0.0603	−0.0091
Aspect ratio	−0.0395	−0.0218
With decorative visual patterns or not	0.3466*	0.3056*
The mean of hue	−0.0331	0.1379*
The standard deviation of hue	0.1586*	0.2505*
The mean of saturation	−0.1166*	−0.0444
The standard deviation of saturation	−0.0711*	−0.0518
The mean of brightness	0.3379*	0.1187*
The standard deviation of brightness	−0.1479*	−0.1076*

* $p < 0.01$

4.2 Kansei Design Cross-cultural Analysis with Neuron Analysis

Neural Network Model for Kawaii Classification. With different sets of parameters for model training and different based models (starting with the BVLC Reference Caffenet model), we gained nine kawaii classification models in total. Based on the various parameter optimization schemes, model no. 4 was selected as the final kawaii classification model as it has the optimal combination of the classification accuracy and the test loss among all the nine models. In the model test phase, we tested the final classification model using 150 test set image data that did not appear in the model training and model validation process. The test accuracy was 84.7% and we named the model no. 4 as *KawaiiNet*.

Kansei Analysis with Neuron Analysis. By the method of neuron analysis, we extracted nine specific visual features from the deep neural network model *KawaiiNet* trained on the labeled cosmetic packaging image dataset annotated by 8 Japanese participants. The nine visual features include 1) purple / pink / golden / blue bottle body, 2) light coffee / light purple / light pink bottle body + ornamentation + metal part + circular arc; 3) ornamentation, round bottle body; 4) round outline, transparent texture; 5) circular arc / flower pattern; 6) circular pattern ornamentation / luster; 7) flower / branch pattern / ornamentation; 8) flower pattern, engraving and decoration; 9) ornamentation. this set of key features differentiating the most kawaii and the least kawaii cosmetic is shown in Fig. 3.

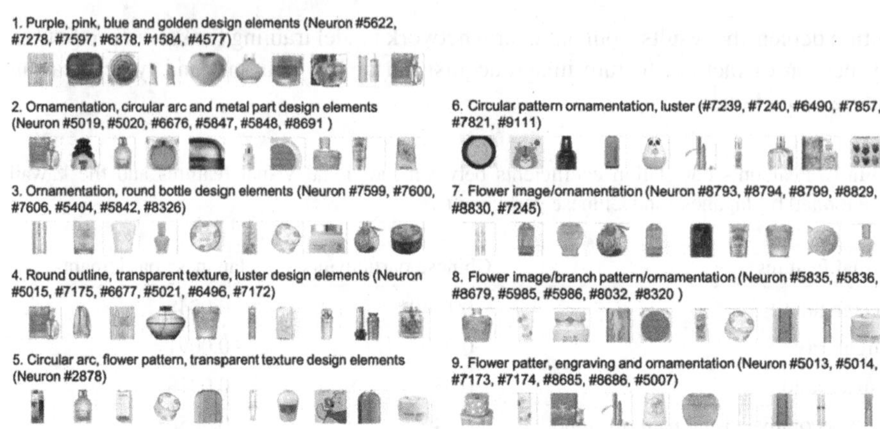

Fig. 3. Key features differentiating the most kawaii and the least kawaii cosmetic packaging.

With the same set of cosmetic packaging images labeled by Chinese participants, there are 13 typical visual features forming kawaii perception extracted by neuron analysis, including 1) cartoons/textures, 2) blue cartoons; 3) black/red pattern; 4) rose; 5) red and white orange; 6) orange circular pattern; 7) pink blue; 8) white and black red blue pattern; 9) right round arc; 10) round, orange/mint green; 11) circular with black edge pattern; 12) right upper arc; 13) round bottle + grind texture + pink.

Kansei Design Cross-cultural Analysis with Neuron Analysis. By contrasting the visual features forming kawaii perception of cosmetic packaging for chinese female participants and Japanese female participants, although there are common features including ornamentation, round bottle body, pink, distinct differences are identified. the kawaii cosmetic packaging in the eyes of japanese females is more girlish and tends to have more patterns of flowers, ornamentation of branches, exquisite engraving, glass texture that can produce the reflective effect, or the metal parts. These design features are more biased to the aesthetic of "exquisite", "elegance" and "girlish". The kawaii cosmetic packaging for chinese females generally has more cartoon patterns or round black-edged patterns, which are more "childish" "naive" and "rounded" from the aesthetic aspect. On the contrary, in most cases, Japanese female participants didn't label the cosmetic packaging with cartoon images as kawaii; and correspondingly, chinese females didn't think the exquisite metal texture, glass relief, or the large area of light purple in the cosmetic packaging were kawaii.

Therefore, when a product designer needs to target users in both markets and wants to develop users' kawaii perception, it is necessary to carry out differentiated Kansei designs. Examples of typical kawaii features of cosmetic packaging for Chinese females and Japanese females can be compared in Fig. 4.

Fig. 4. Typical kawaii cosmetic packaging images for Japanese females (left) and Chinese females (right).

5 Cross-cultural Kansei Design Facilitation System

5.1 System Structure

In this section, we propose the structure of a design facilitation system for Kansei design adaptive to users with different cultural backgrounds. First of all, a designer needs to use the neural network model trained for the target users to classify an image of their design. If the output of the model shows that the design may not generate the desired mental image for target users, the system will output all the most activated neurons, denoted as non-kawaii neurons, and the least activated neurons, denoted as kawaii neurons. Then the design improvement recommendations can be made by suggesting adding more visual features processed by the kawaii neurons and removing the visual features processed by the non-kawaii neurons. The visual features processed by a specific neuron can be obtained by identifying the images that activate the neuron the most from the image database.

5.2 System Implementation

In this work, we implemented a prototype of the cross-cultural Kansei design facilitation system in MATLAB. Target users are young Japanese females, and KawaiiNet is used as the neural network in the design facilitation system. A designer can upload a product image into the system and the system will output parameters of design elements for potential design improvements, and some example products as a reference for the designer to improve the work. As shown in Fig. 5, a sample image is imported into the system as a design provided by the designer through the interface implemented by MATLAB. And Fig. 6 shows part of the cosmetic images that activate key neurons (i.e., kawaii neurons) the most. They are example products with recommended design elements output by the facilitation system. Designers can use them as a reference for how to improve their original designs.

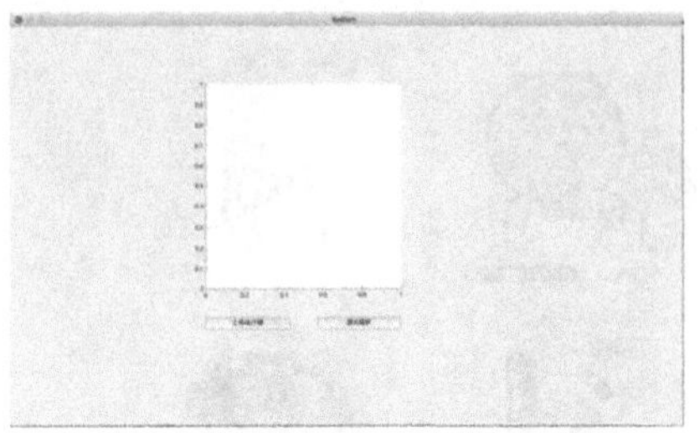

Fig. 5. A prototype of the cross-cultural Kansei design facilitation system.

Fig. 6. Cosmetic packaging images that activate the key neurons (kawaii neurons) the most.

5.3 Validation Experiment

In order to quickly verify the cross-cultural Kansei design facilitation system, we invited 22 Chinese female participants and 22 Japanese female participants aged between 20 and 23 who have a certain degree of experience in the purchase of cosmetics for an experiment contrasting the kawaii degree of cosmetic packages before and after the design improvements suggested by the facilitation system. According to the 13 typical visual features forming kawaii perception for Japanese and Chinese participants, 5–6 pairs of contrast images of cosmetic packaging are selected for each typical feature, and a total of 66 contrastive images were created. Part of the contrastive image groups are shown in Fig. 7. In each pair of the images, the left one is designed with the design improvements recommended by the facilitation system and the right one is designed without the design improvements.

Through this reverse validation experiment, we found that for 22 Chinese female participants, the design improvements based on all the visual features forming kawaii perception for Chinese females and most of those for Japanese females can effectively enhance their perception of kawaii. Some of the features forming kawaii perception for Japanese females, including blue, transparent texture and the light purple bottle body, cannot improve Chinese participants' kawaii perception. And for 22 Japanese female participants, all the design improvements recommended can effectively enhance their kawaii perception.

6 Discussion

6.1 Neuron Analysis to Detect Cross-cultural Differences

With neuron analysis, we were able to identify a set of visual features differentiating the kawaii design in cosmetic packaging for Japanese females and Chinese females. However, these nuanced differences cannot be obtained through traditional image parameters extraction. By such approach of image data mining, only predefined relationships between kawaii perception and single visual feature parameters (e.g., hue, brightness, pattern and rectangularity) are able to be investigated. And it turned out that there isn't much significant distinguish between Chinese and Japanese female participants. This may provide a new way to be considered for the future cross-cultural research in Kansei Engineering: the differences in the perception of product design among people with different cultural backgrounds may exist in their subconscious that cannot be described by predefined parameters. Through deep learning, the machine can explore a much more comprehensive combinations of visual features and then obtain a more powerful set of visual features which haven't been paid attention to and evaluated. Furthermore, understanding more multidimensional and unnoticed reasons for people's perceptual formation can lead to uncovering more interesting cross-cultural analysis results.

Fig. 7. The contrast designs of cosmetic with or without design improvements based on results from Kansei design cross-cultural analysis.

6.2 Limitations and Future Work

Each time to build such a cross-cultural Kansei design facilitation system for a new Kansei element and a new group of target users, new datasets and new neural network models need to be constructed from the scratch, which is time-consuming and inflexible for application.

In addition, although feature extraction in the procedure of neural network model training is automatic, the final step of recognizing the visual features connected to the key neurons still relies on manual extraction. A certain subjectivity lies in such manual analysis. In the future, the research may focus on how to design the interaction within the system so that designers can have a more efficient design experience facilitated by the design auxiliary system. Furthermore, our Kansei Engineering System only takes the visual perception of a product into consideration. In the future, more factors can be taken into consideration, such as how a product feels in one's hand, the sound it makes. etc.

7 Conclusion

First of all, our research obtained a kawaii classification model for Japanese females' perception of cosmetic packaging's kawaii degree with an accuracy of 84.7%, which also verified the mobility of the Kansei Engineering System based on pixel-level image processing and deep learning. Nine key visual features which can form the kawaii perception of Japanese females are summarized through neuron analysis.

Second, we applied neuron analysis for cross-cultural analysis in the Kansei design. The differences in product design perception among people with different cultural backgrounds may exist in visual features that cannot be described by predefined parameters. Through deep learning, we can obtain a more powerful and comprehensive set of feature features from the data, and understand more detailed reasons for perception formation, which may lead to more interesting conclusions of cross-cultural Kansei Engineering.

Third, the necessity and feasibility of a cross-cultural Kansei design facilitation system have been verified by a reverse experiment, which proves the effectiveness of corresponding design recommendations in improving Chinese and Japanese females' kawaii perception of cosmetic packaging. Such design facilitation system can maximize the use of a large amount of real data from target users, help designers better understand the feelings and mental images that product designs may bring to target users, effectively avoid the limitations of the subjective perception of a certain design element. This also offers possibility for the machine to assist designers more intelligently in the future.

Acknowledgments. We would like to thank all the Chinese and Japanese participants in our experiments. We really appreciate their valuable time and feedback on our research.

References

1. Nagamachi, M.: Kansei engineering as a powerful consumer-oriented technology for product development. Appl. Ergon. **33**, 289–294 (2002)
2. Yang, C.-C.: Constructing a hybrid kansei engineering system based on multiple affective responses: application to product form design. Comput. Ind. Eng. **60**, 760–768 (2011)

3. Laohakangvalvit, T., Achalakul, T., Ohkura, M.: Kawaii feeling estimation by product attributes and Biological Signals. In: Proceedings of the 18th ACM International Conference on Multimodal Interaction (2016)
4. Ohkura, M., Komatsu, T., Aoto, T.: Kawaii rules: increasing affective value of industrial products. Indu. Appl. Affec. Eng. 97–110 (2014)
5. Matsubara, Y., Nagamachi, M.: Hybrid kansei engineering system and design support. Int. J. Ind. Ergon. **19**, 81–92 (1997)
6. Nagamachi, M., Tachikawa, M., Imanishi, N., Ishizawa, T., Yano, S.: A successful statistical procedure on kansei engineering products. In: 11th QMOD Conference. In: Quality Management and Organizational Development Attaining Sustainability From Organizational Excellence to SustainAble Excellence, p. 22. Helsingborg, Sweden (2008)
7. Chen, J.-S., Wang, K.-C., Liang, J.-C.: A Hybrid Kansei Design Expert System Using Artificial Intelligence. In: Ho, T.-B., Zhou, Z.-H. (eds.) PRICAI 2008. LNCS (LNAI), vol. 5351, pp. 971–976. Springer, Heidelberg (2008). https://doi.org/10.1007/978-3-540-89197-0_93
8. Ohkura, M., Konuma, A., Murai, S., Aoto, T.: Systematic study for "Kawaii" products (the second report) -Comparison of "kawaii" colors and shapes -. In: 2008 SICE Annual Conference (2008)
9. Yang, C.-C.: A classification-based kansei engineering system for modeling consumers' affective responses and analyzing product form features. Expert Syst. Appl. **38**, 11382–11393 (2011)
10. Tsuchiya, T., Ishihara, S., Matsubara, Y., Nishino, T., Nagamachi, M.: A method for learning decision tree using genetic algorithm and its application to kansei engineering system. In: IEEE SMC'99 Conference Proceedings. 1999 IEEE International Conference on Systems, Man, and Cybernetics (Cat. No.99CH37028) (1999)
11. Ishihara, S., Hatamoto, K., Nagamachi, M., Matsubara, Y.: Art1.5SSS for kansei engineering expert system. In: Proceedings of 1993 International Conference on Neural Networks (IJCNN-93-Nagoya, Japan) (1993)
12. Mitsuyo, M.: An application of image processing technology in Kansei Engineering. In: Prnc. 12th Triennial Congress of the International Ergonomics Association, pp. 123–126. Toronto (1994)
13. Ishihara, S., Ishihara, K., Nagamachi, M., Matsubara, Y.: An automatic builder for a kansei engineering expert system using self-organizing neural networks. Int. J. Ind. Ergon. **15**, 13–24 (1995)
14. Li, Z., Tian, Z.G., Wang, J.W., Wang, W.M., Huang, G.Q.: Dynamic mapping of design elements and affective responses: A machine learning based method for affective design. J. Eng. Des. **29**, 358–380 (2018)
15. Wang, K.-C.: A hybrid kansei engineering design expert system based on grey system theory and support vector regression. Expert Syst. Appl. **38**, 8738–8750 (2011)
16. Ray, K.S., Ghoshal, J.: Neuro fuzzy approach to pattern recognition. Neural Netw. **10**, 161–182 (1997)
17. Liu, S., Forrest, J., Yang, Y.: A brief introduction to grey systems theory. Grey Sys. Theo. Appl. **2**, 89–104 (2012)
18. Gong, Y., Pei-Luen Patrick, R.: DL-KES: a deep learning based kansei engineering system. J. Japan Soc. Kansei Eng. **15**, 29–31 (2017)
19. Cheok, A.D.: Kawaii: cute interactive media. In: Imagery in the 21st Century, pp. 245–265 (2011)
20. Ohkura, M., Goto, S., Higo, A., Aoto, T.: Relationship between kawaii feeling and biological signals. Trans. Japan Soc. Kansei Eng. **10**, 109–114 (2011)
21. Laohakangvalvit, T., Achalakul, T., Ohkura, M.: Comparison on evaluation of Kawaiiness of cosmetic bottles between Japanese and Thai people. In: 2019 8th International Conference on Affective Computing and Intelligent Interaction (ACII) (2019)

22. Laohakangvalvit, T., Achalakul, T., Ohkura, M.: Model of kawaii cosmetic bottle evaluations by Thai and Japanese. Kawaii Engineering, pp. 195–223 (2019)
23. Laohakangvalvit, T., Achalakul, T., Ohkura, M.: A method to obtain effective attributes for attractive cosmetic bottles by deep learning. Int. J. Affec. Eng. **19**, 37–48 (2020)

Collaborative and Participatory Cross-Cultural Design

UX in the Arab World - Research Trends and Challenges for a Better Understanding and Collaboration

Ons Al-Shamaileh[1](✉) and Ahmed Seffah[2]

[1] College of Technological Innovation, Zayed University, Dubai, United Arab Emirates
ons.al-shamaileh@zu.ac.ae

[2] Interactive Media Lab, Zayed University, Abu Dhabi, United Arab Emirates
ahmed.seffah@zu.ac.ae

Abstract. During the last decade, a considerable number of studies question how HCI is perceived and how the cultural differences are considered. However, very few focused on eliciting the cultural factors of UX and the underlying integration of UX research methods. In this paper, we overview the literature on UX research in the Arab world. Among others, our findings show that UX research focused on two main themes (1) elicitation of UX guidelines and UX patterns (best UX practices) to match the Arab culture (2) identification of the factors influencing UX in the Arab region. The findings also illustrate existing efforts to raise awareness of HCI and conclude with some research challenges that draw a road map for a better collaboration between Arab researchers and the international community.

Keywords: User experience · UX · Human computer interaction · HCI · Guidelines · Culture

1 Introduction- HCI and the Arab world

Compared to western countries and the very long tradition, HCI is a new aera of focus in the Arab world academia and industry with very few professionals and researchers interested in HCI. One of the most recent significant events that is paving the roads for a better understanding of Arab-computer interaction is the Arab CHI forum (arabchi.org). People behind this forum have and are initiating workshops at international HCI conferences including ACM-CHI to:

1. Address the capacity building of HCI academic research teams in the 500 or more Universities of Arab World from 27 countries.
2. Network the Arab HCI research community with the international community while bridging the social and cultural gaps.
3. Develop a roadmap for research on issues such the use of social media as vehicle for mediating the communication line between the Arab world and Western countries.

P.-L. P. Rau (Ed.): HCII 2022, LNCS 13311, pp. 163–172, 2022.
https://doi.org/10.1007/978-3-031-06038-0_12

4. Enhance the education offers, among others via joint venture for developing masters an PhDs programs in HCI. Actually, in most countries and universities, and most often, only one course addressed HCI in computing programs, mainly MIS, CS and Software Engineering.

While it is a crucial task to develop further such a forum and conferences (for example ACM-Arab Conference), our ongoing investigations aim to identify avenues for closing the gaps and building cross-pollination bridges between the global HCI and the Arab HCI researchers regarding UX design research. Therefore, the fundamental questions we are addressing are:

1. What are the components and characteristics of experiences of Arab users?
2. Is UX culturally different from elsewhere because of which cultural and social factors exactly?
3. How is the cultural diversity and exceptions of Arab is being turned into design patterns to making products that are more culturally centric?
4. How those patterns are being applied by Arab designers?
5. How those needed designers by the blooming Arab industry should be trained in local Universities via the incorporation of these patterns of design in the curricula and courses?

Answering all those questions and similar ones should also consider a core concern: the alignment of HCI design methods as developed and used in Western countries with the Arab cultural system of values and realities. As a first stage, this paper is a first attempt to investigate the cultural dimension of UX with Arab "spice".

Culture plays an influential role in shaping behaviors and experiences with digital products, services, and systems. The Arab world, like Western countries, cannot be considered a monolithic culture because of a common language or religion, there are enough significant differences and cultural influences. We should point out that we are not saying you can always draw direct insights about what makes a usable design just from understanding a culture. Instead, we argue that cultural observations can help guide you in the right direction and, at the very least, make sure you do not make the kind of mistakes that put your users off instantly.

2 UX in the Arab World – Definition, Guidelines and Practices

When analyzing the literature, it has been a challenge to come up with a single definition of UX as it is related to a wide range of concepts including aesthetics, usability, and emotional concepts. The following are widely used definitions of UX:

"The consequence of a user's internal state (predispositions, expectations, needs, motivations, mood, etc.), the characteristics of the designed system (e.g., complexity, purpose, usability, functionality, etc.) and the context (or the environment) within which the interaction occurs (e.g., organizational/social setting)" (Law et al. 2009).

The international standard on ergonomics of human-system interaction, ISO 9241–210 defines user experience as "a person's perceptions and responses that result from the use or anticipated use of a product, system or service" (ISO 2010). According to the ISO definition, user experience includes all the users' emotions, beliefs, preferences, perceptions, physical and psychological responses, behaviors and accomplishments that occur before, during, and after use. The ISO also lists three factors that influence user experience: the system, the user, and the context of use.

Several researchers attempted to propose UX guidelines to match the Arab context (Al-Serdani et al. 2012, Muhanna et al. 2020, Namoun et al. 2020) 3. As a matter of example, Al-Sedrani et al. (2012) presented a list of UX guidelines to design e-commerce websites in the Arab region. They analyzed 50 e-commerce websites in Saudi Arabia and identified cultural aspects influencing the UX design of e-commerce websites that target Arabic speaking users. Some of the authors' recommendations emphasized on localizing websites language, currency, text direction and images.

In a recent study Muhanna et al. (2020) evaluated Arabic interfaces while suggesting a set of Arabic usability heuristics based on Nieslen heuristics. Their results suggested that the proposed heuristics yielded better evaluation of Arabic websites compared to Nielsen's heuristics. Their evaluations were limited to websites and desktop applications, therefore, generalizing the validity of the proposed heuristics will require evaluating more platforms such as mobile devices (Namoun et al. 2020).

Several usability guidelines to match the Arabic interfaces were introduced (Elbaz et al. 2011), these guidelines focused mainly on the structure, layout, navigation, text appearance and tables. Salah et al. (2019) also proposed a set of usability heuristics with the focus on evaluating Arabic M-commerce applications. The proposed heuristics fell into six categories: first, search and findability; authors suggested to set the search language to Arabic where users can search keywords using Arabic script. Second, visual design where text alignment to be set to the right direction. Third, translatability; the availability of translated text for all web pages including product description, policies, and notifications. Fourth, consistency; of numbering and terms translation. Fifth, user control and freedom; users should have the choice to set Arabic as their default language and finally adaptability, where auto language switching is enabled based on the device language.

Namoun et al. (2020) also suggested some design practices which mainly focus on fonts and images. Their study analyzed 73 most visited Arabic websites in Saudi Arabia. Their results showed font types and sizes inconsistencies in Arabic websites, in addition to the extensive use of images which resulted in slower websites. More design criteria were also proposed to match Arabic gamified systems (Alomar et al. 2016). These criteria covered several aspects such as content, images, colors, font and navigation structure. Guidelines were also proposed for page layout including text direction, menus and logo location (Alomar et al. 2016).

Al-Sa'di (2018) introduced best practices when designing educational apps with Arabic interfaces, these practices covered several areas including font style and size, the need of adding vocalization marks to Arabic text in addition to design simplicity tips. The user experience of Children's interaction with Arabic interfaces with respect to educational learning contexts was also discussed by (Wea'am et al. 2015). The main purpose of the study is to guide school children to understand data about how they use various kinds of websites. Results proved that the age of the child interacting with the system has a direct relationship with the way a child interacted with various sections in a web page. A detailed insight into methodological design inference for conducting UX and usability evaluations are discussed in this paper (Wea'am et al. 2015). The work done is of high-level importance and proves to provide new insights into the state of UX design implications with respect to the educational sector in the Arab region.

Different researchers proposed guidelines relating to the colors used in interfaces. They emphasized fact that cultures perceive colors differently. Some suggested using white colors in Middle Eastern interfaces (Khanum et al. 2012) while others referred to Hofstede's score for masculinity index and suggested grey blue and green (Al-kwai et al. 2014).

3 Factors influencing UX in the Arab World

Few factors influencing UX of the Arabic interfaces have been investigated by researchers (Kahaleh 2017, Abokhodair et al. 2016, Al- Tahat 2020). Some of these factors include privacy, language, and navigation.

3.1 Privacy

Privacy in the Middle East is one of the factors receiving researchers' attention; Abokhodair et al. (2016) analyzed Gulf citizens' perceptions and considerations for online privacy, by closely understanding the cultural and religious aspects. Their results could lead to design principles abiding the sensitive culture of the region and conservative social norms of the Arab countries.

Users across the gulf region may not have the privilege to use the same digital products and services as that of their western counterparts (Abokhodair et al. 2016, Hemayssi et al. 2005). This may be due to the limited availability of technology and restricted exposure, as the region is culturally conservative. Thus, when designing a UX, it is important to be reminded of the cultural and traditional differences between users in Arabic-speaking nations and those in the West (Kahaleh 2017, Hemayssi et al. 2005, Marcus 2013). Similarly, Alyahyan et al. (2016) showed that Saudi users stress the importance of reflecting the local language, religious beliefs, culture and navigation consistency in the Arabic websites and applications. Additionally, Alomar et al. (2016) stressed on restricting the use of women pictures to the minimum.

3.2 Language

One of the important aspects in delivering a good user experience is the language used for the target audience, as language has a direct impact on the user's interest to use a particular interface Kahaleh (2017). A report by Arabnet, a leading event and program organizer on tech-business states that around 60% of Arabic speakers prefer to browse the Internet in the Arabic language, but less than 1% of digital content is only available in the Arabic language Kahaleh (2017). Another study showed that using tracking tools to assess interface usability revealed more accurate results when users use their native language (Al- Tahat 2020). The study utilized UMUX (Usability Metric for User Experience), which is a standard usability questionnaire that is translated into Arabic language. A psychometric evaluation was performed on the Arabic-UMUX and results achieved proved that this may be a reliable tool which can be used by Arabic users (Al- Tahat 2020). AlGhannam et al. (2018) also translated the widely used System Usability Scale (SUS) to Arabic language to measure the usability of a mobile application. While Alomar et al. (2016) proposed language guidelines in Arabic interfaces, including the use of diacritics and adding more spaces between words as Arabic words are relatively longer than English ones.

3.3 Navigation

Navigation is another important factor influencing UX, an experimental study on the attitude of Arab users towards websites aesthetics, usability, and trustworthiness based on the direction of the navigation menus was presented by (Salmerón et al. 2017). The research outcome showed that users tend to be more positive when menus were located on the right side in the Arabic websites, but there was no big difference in terms of menu location in English ones.

Marcus (2013) questioned if websites of Arabian origin reflect the culture of the gulf region, and whether differences between Arab and other countries are classified in an orderly fashion. Authors suggest that more studies need to be conducted to cover more domains of Arabic websites (Marcus 2013).

4 Raising Awareness of the Human Computer Interaction Field in the Arab World

In the efforts to raise awareness of the UX domain, Lazem (2016) presented a study that aims at exposing Egyptian engineering students to UX domain. An interactive school activity was designed to emphasize the importance of HCI study to the undergraduates. The feedback received from students, course instructors, and future inferences was collected. While the study is a good step towards raising awareness about UX, the number of respondents is 31 students, which can be improved to get a holistic approach.

Many companies and academic institutions in the Middle East are recognizing the importance of HCI and are initiating labs to practice HCI methods and techniques. Dubai is one of the active places for UX design research. Academic institutions such as Zayed University- United Arab Emirates, Helwan University- Egypt and New York University-Abu Dhabi have initiated dedicated HCI labs. Saudi Arabia has also initiated an HCI lab in Riyadh where faculty members and students in the domain come together to work on HCI related projects. "Table 1: HCI labs in the Middle East".

Table 1. HCI labs in the Middle East

Country	Lab
United Arab Emirates	Interactive Media Lab- Zayed University
United Arab Emirates	HCI Lab- Zayed University
United Arab Emirates	Applied Interactive Multimedia Laboratory- New York University
Egypt	HCI lab- Helwan University
Saudi Arabia	HCI lab- Riyadh

Academic institutions in the Arab World are also recognizing the importance of equipping their curricula with HCI courses. 31 universities in 13 Arab world countries have HCI as a required course in both undergraduate and post graduate levels. The search was based on universities in the Arab would that are ranked in QS world university ranking. "Table 2: Universities offering HCI courses".

Table 2. Universities offering HCI courses

University Name	Country
Khalifa University	UAE
United Arab Emirates University	UAE
American University of Sharjah	UAE
University of Sharjah	UAE
Abu Dhabi University	UAE
Ajman University	UAE
Zayed University	UAE
Umm Al-Qura University	KSA
Imam Abdulrahman Bin Faisal University (IAU)	KSA
Islamic University of Madinah	KSA
Princess Nourah bint Abdulrahman University	KSA
Qatar University	Qatar
Applied Science University	Bahrain
University of Bahrain	Bahrain
Kuwait University	Kuwait

(continued)

Table 2. *(continued)*

Higher College of Technology	Oman
Sohar University	Oman
American University of Lebanon	Lebanon
Holy Spirit University of Kaslik	Lebanon
Libyan International Medical University	Libya
Alfateh University/University of Tripoli	Libya
Omar Al-Mukhtar University	Libya
Misurata University	Libya
University of Benghazi	Libya
Univeriste de Tunis	Tunisia
Mansoura University	Egypt
University Of Jordan	Jordan
Princess Sumaya University for Technology	Jordan
An-Najah National University	Palestine
Birzeit University	Palestine
International Universty of Africa	Sudan

5 Some Challenges Awaiting for Further Investigations

Several challenges are facing the HCI field in the Arab World. Galal-Edeen et al. (2019) discussed the challenges of HCI research in Egypt. The authors highlighted the fact that several users across Egypt are not used to open feedback and conversation. Also, finding users or participants for evaluating the design features is difficult for long term testing purposes. The previous results support Alabdulqader et al. (2018) who stressed the need for more user involvement in the design process starting from the early design process stages.

An important challenge is related to massive penetration of mobile and Web applications in particular social media, cloud games and online shopping. The population is very young in the Arab World, in all Arab countries, people under 30 years represent up to 60% of the population. Like everywhere around the globe, this young generation is highly connected and present of social media platforms. For example, Facebook, the most popular platform in most Arab countries, is being used to finding solutions to societal challenges such as sustainability. Instagram has millions of users, same for Twitter, a rise of 15% per year since 2017. Both are widely used to spreading and sharing news and building opinions.

Another challenge is related to the sea of citizen generated data and the booming data-intensive applications. The production and use of citizen-generated data is enabling a revolution in the Arab world as it engages directly, actively and massively in the decision making and the future of Arab countries. Because of the massive use of social media by the young generation, both governments and civil society are contributors to the decision making. Citizens therefore have an opportunity, as well as a responsibility, to ensure the interactive media and data revolution spur the societal transformational changes that are required to tackle the huge global challenges but also leverage the exciting local ones that Arab are facing.

More challenges were presented by Alabdulqader et al. (2018), authors discussed that students of engineering and science underestimate humanities courses, which resulted negatively on the growth of HCI research. They have also explained that the majority of HCI research is conducted in Arabic language which reduce the chances of international exposure.

6 Concluding Remarks

HCI and UX research in the Arab World is blooming as more and more Arab countries, Universities and companies are recognizing the importance of designing and redesigning interactive products and services that are human and culturally centric. This paper is an attempt highlighting some of the factors that make UX in the Arab Word unique and challenging. The key findings fold in three.

First, further factors beyond language and the specificities of the Arabic languages were presented, our investigation highlighted other factors that influence UX. Privacy in the Middle East is one of the factors receiving researchers' attention. The study of such factors (language and privacy) and their correlation with UX could lead to UX design patterns abiding the sensitive culture of the region and conservative social norms of the Arab countries. Culture can be defined in terms of the distribution of certain cognitive styles, needs and preferences among the population of a country or a certain region. Thus, knowing that the cognitive preferences correlate with navigational performance and website rating, we expect Arab users' cultural backgrounds to do likewise. Navigation and interaction patterns have also been highlighted as an important factor influencing UX and can be linked to culture and language in particular. Although navigation has been widely studied in HCI, to our knowledge, very few examined the correlation between navigation and culture. Most of the time, Web and mobile applications in the Arab exist in two languages (Arab/English for Gulf and Middle East countries, Arabic/French in North Africa). UX designers usually used the same navigation patterns for both languages while ignoring the fact that Arabic is written from left to right may influence the way we navigate.

Second, several guidelines and practices to match the Arabic interfaces were presented. These guidelines cover several aspects of the interface including- but not limited to structure, layout, navigation, aesthetics.

Third, academic attempts to raise the awareness of the HCI field in terms of labs and University courses were illustrated. Five HCI labs were initiated in different Arab countries and thirty-one universities in thirteen Arab countries have integrated HCI in their curricula at undergraduate and post graduate levels.

References

Abokhodair, N., Vieweg, S.: Privacy & social media in the context of the Arab Gulf. In: Proceedings of the 2016 ACM conference on designing interactive systems, pp. 672–683, 4 June 2016

Alabdulqader, E., Lazem, S., Khamis, M., Dray, S.M.: Exploring participatory design methods to engage with Arab communities. In: Extended Abstracts of the 2018 CHI Conference on Human Factors in Computing Systems, pp. 1–8, 20 April 2018

AlGhannam, B.A., Albustan, S.A., Al-Hassan, A.A., Albustan, L.A.: Towards a standard arabic system usability scale: psychometric evaluation using communication disorder app. Int. J. Hum.-Comput. Interact. **34**(9), 799–804 (2018)

Al-kwai, L., Alkhaybari, A., Al-muaythir, A.:Gamification in arabic interactive educational applications: cultural and language considerations in motivational affordance of design elements. In: INTED2014 Proceedings, pp. 4545-4556) (2014)

Alomar, N., Wanick, V., Wills, G.: The design of a hybrid cultural model for Arabic gamified systems. Comput. Hum. Behav. **64**, 472–485 (2016)

Al-Sa'di, A.: User interface guidelines for Tablet PC Arabic educational applications (Doctoral dissertation, Auckland University of Technology) (2018)

Al-Sedrani, A., Al-Khalifa, H.S.: Design considerations for the localization of Arabic e-commerce websites. In: Seventh International Conference on Digital Information Management (ICDIM 2012), pp. 331–335. IEEE, 22 August 2012

Al-Tahat, K.S.: An Arabic adaptation of the usability metric for user experience (UMUX). Int. J. Hum.-Comput. Interact. **36**(11), 1050–1055 (2020)

Alyahyan, L., Aldabbas, H., Alnafjan, K.: Preferences of Saudi users on Arabic website usability. Int. J. Web Semant. Technol. **7**, 1-8 (2016)

Law, E.L., Roto, V., Hassenzahl, M., Vermeeren, A.P., Kort, J.: Understanding, scoping and defining user experience: a survey approach. In: Proceedings of the SIGCHI conference on human factors in computing systems, pp. 719–728, 4 April 2009

Marcus, A.: Design, user experience, and usability: health, learning, playing, cultural, and cross-cultural user experience. In: Second International Conference, DUXU 2013, Held as Part of HCI International 2013, Las Vegas, NV, USA, July 21–26, Proceedings, Part II. Springer (2013)

Elbaz, P., Galal-Edeen, G.H., Gheith, M.: The influence of culture on systems usability. Int. J. Softw. Eng. IJSE **4**, 93–114 (2011)

Galal-Edeen, G.H., Abdrabou, Y., Elgarf, M., Hassan, H.M.: HCI of Arabia: the challenges of HCI research in Egypt. Interactions. **26**(3), 55–9 (2019)

Hemayssi, H., Sanchez, E., Moll, R., Field, C.: Designing an Arabic user experience: methods and techniques to bridge cultures. In: Proceedings of the 2005 Conference on Designing for User Experience, pp. 34-es, 3 November 2005

ISO DIS 9241–210. Ergonomics of human system interaction - part 210: Human-centred design for interactive systems. Tech. rep., International Organization for Standardization, Switzerland (2010)

Kahaleh, N.: Let's Talk About Arabic UX Design, Arabnet. https://www.arabnet.me/english/editorials/digital-media/let-s-talk-about-arabic-ux-design-. Accessed 4 Mar 21

Khanum, M.A., Fatima, S., Chaurasia, M.A.: Arabic interface analysis based on cultural markers. arXiv preprint arXiv:1203.3660 (2012)

Lazem, S.: A case study for sensitising Egyptian engineering students to user-experience in technology design. In: Proceedings of the 7th Annual Symposium on Computing for Development, pp. 1–10, 18 November 2016

Muhanna, M.A., Amro, R.N., Qusef, A.: Using a new set of heuristics in evaluating Arabic interfaces. J. King Saud Univ.-Comput. Inf. Sci. **32**(2), 248–253 (2020)

Namoun, A., Alkhodre, A.B.: Towards Usability Guidelines for the Design of Effective Arabic Websites: Design Practices and Lessons Focusing on Font and Image usage. arXiv preprint arXiv:2011.02933. 2020 Nov 5

Salah, M.S., Jusoh, S., Muhanna, M.A.: The development of usability heuristics For Arabic m-commerce applications. In: 2019 IEEE Jordan International Joint Conference on Electrical Engineering and Information Technology (JEEIT), pp. 779–784. IEEE, 9 April 2019

Salmerón, L., Abu Mallouh, R., Kammerer, Y.: Location of navigation menus in websites: an experimental study with Arabic users. Univ. Access Inf. Soc. **16**(1), 191–196 (2015). https://doi.org/10.1007/s10209-015-0444-x

Alrashed, W.A., Alhussayen, A.A.: Examining the user experience (UX) of children's interaction with Arabic interfaces in educational learning contexts. In: Stephanidis, C. (ed.) HCI 2015. CCIS, vol. 528, pp. 349–354. Springer, Cham (2015). https://doi.org/10.1007/978-3-319-21380-4_59

The International Shanghai Joint Design Studio: A Hybrid and Adaptive Platform to Enhance Cultural Encounter

Tiziano Cattaneo[1,4(✉)], Emanuele Giorgi[2], and Eugenio Mangi[3]

[1] College of Design and Innovation, Tongji University, 281 Fuxin Road, Yangpu District, Shanghai 200092, China
tiziano.cattaneo@unipv.it

[2] Tecnológico de Monterrey, School of Architecture, Art and Design, Avenida Heroico Colegio Militar 4700, Nombre de Dios, 31300 Chihuahua, Mexico

[3] Department of Architecture and Built Environment, University of Nottingham Ningbo China, 199 Taikang East Road Ningbo, Ningbo 315100, China

[4] Dipartimento di Ingegneria Civile e Architettura, Università degli Studi di Pavia, Via Adolfo Ferrata, 3, 27100 Pavia, PV, Italy

Abstract. The *International Shanghai Joint Design Studio* was a work-in-progress platform that started in August 2019 before the COVID-19 pandemic and ended in July 2020 with the publication of the initiative's outcomes. It combined the studios of 5 Schools of Design located in 4 different countries with the aim of sharing ideas and reflections about the development of projects located in a common area in Shanghai. Thanks to its adaptive, collaborative, and flexible structure, the joint studio could overcome the difficulties caused by the outbreak through the integration of innovative and hybrid teaching & learning methods while developing both a virtual and a physical space of co-creation and engagement for students, scholars, designers, and citizens. Through the involvement of cohorts of various grades and majors, the students were constantly exposed to very diverse design approaches and planning practices. In this way, it became a *place* to enhance cross-cultural encounter among different design disciplines and backgrounds while encouraging both the learners and the tutors to develop innovative and multidisciplinary points of view about the city and the built environment. In this paper, the authors draw a general reflection about how cross-cultural practices have been implemented through the activities of the initiative and concretely address shortcomings and suggest possible recommendations for future similar pedagogical experiments.

Keywords: International cooperation · Environmental design · Urban design · COVID-19 · Research-based teaching · Collaborative learning

1 Introduction

Contemporary cities are places characterized by an extraordinary complexity, where very diverse cultural and social backgrounds, technologies, traditions, lifestyles and

P.-L. P. Rau (Ed.): HCII 2022, LNCS 13311, pp. 173–187, 2022.
https://doi.org/10.1007/978-3-031-06038-0_13

needs co-exist in a multifaceted reality where designers are called to operate and elaborate solutions [1]. Although the new normal imposed by the COVID-19 pandemic is re-shaping many sectors of the public life [2], the call (and need) for educational practitioners and students to foster and facilitate the implementation of cross-cultural practices is becoming more urgent [3]. This is even more pressing in the domain of architecture and urban design, where the learners of today will be asked to *make spaces* and integrate programs for very varied groups of stakeholders characterized by diverse cultural and social backgrounds and thus with very different, and even contrasting, needs. It is also important to highlight how the implementation of cross-cultural practices in the design fields can enhance, through a creative and inclusive approach, solutions that foster more resilient and sustainable societies and cities [4].

Starting from these considerations, this paper adopts the case study of the *International Shanghai Joint Design Studio* [5], that was organized and promoted by the authors, to (1) draw a general reflection about how this kind of joint initiatives can integrate and enhance cross-cultural practices through the teaching & learning (T&L) in the design field; (2) concretely address main limitations and propose possible recommendations for these kind of pedagogical and research experiments in the design field.

The paper is structured as follows: a brief analysis of how the JDS sits in the context of cross-cultural practices is followed by a detailed analysis of the JDS's T&L activities and their aims under the pedagogical and investigative points of view. Then, the paper concretely addresses main limitations of the initiative and impacts on the learning experience, while suggesting possible recommendations to be implemented in similar cases. This section elaborates on the feedbacks received from the participants and on the direct observation of the authors. Discussion and conclusions provide an overall evaluation of the initiative.

It is important to clarify that the cross-cultural research is a complex field of study, as it involves several disciplines pursuing different aims and goals [6]. For this reason, the authors have chosen not to focus on the topic of cross-cultural practices itself, but on how methods and outcomes within the specific case of the JDS have (or have not) enhanced cross-cultural practices in consistence with the conference scope.

2 The Joint Design Studio Within the Framework of Cross-cultural Practices

The JDS concept was inspired by other similar experiences that aimed at exploring the design domain through cross-cultural practices. The most internationally acknowledged, and probably the first of its kind, is the *International Laboratory of Architecture and Urban Design,* also known as ILA&UD, founded by Giancarlo De Carlo in 1976 [7]. In the *1st Residential Course* publication, De Carlo wrote that among the aims of the ILA&UD, there was "to promote contacts between teachers and students in various countries in order to start up a debate on architectural questions", and "to offer a group of Universities in various countries the opportunity to compare their respective ideas and trends on the problems of architectural and urban design teaching" [8]. From these words, it is evident how, already in the '70s of the last century, a certain number of educational practitioners, students and professionals coming from different latitudes were pioneering the application, perhaps unconsciously, of cross-cultural practices to define an effective and comprehensive agenda to tackle the issues of that era, e.g. the role of housing in the historic city centers. This attitude is even more needed today, considering that the students will be asked to develop holistic visions for the problems concerning more domains at the same time, such as massive migrations, housing affordability, environmental crisis, etc. [9].

According to Kim, Ju and Lee [10], the teaching format and methods employed in a joint design studio, where learners and tutors of different nationalities and majors develop projects on a common theme and site, encompasses cross-cultural practices that enhance divergent thinking[1] [11], and thus creativity, in the design students' learning path. This idea is partially contradicted by Goldschmidt [12], who demonstrates how creativity in design disciplines involves continuous cycles of both convergent[2] [13] and divergent thinking. Elliot and Nakata [14] elaborate a similar proposition when they analyze the cross-cultural practices involved in the new product development (NPD) for multinational corporations in the Asian and Western contexts. The authors adopt the theories about art creation and aesthetics defined by Burkhart [15] and Beittel [16] that identify a spontaneous (convergent) creativity, typical of the east-Asian contexts, and a divergent creativity, mainly developed in the western realities. As a response to this dichotomy, they propose a "third way" [16] for cross-cultural practices in NPD that encompasses the integration of the two kinds of creativity. Starting from these considerations, the following section illustrates how cross-cultural practices, seen through the lenses of the "third way" framework, have been implemented in the context of the JDS.

3 The Main Characteristics of the JDS Platform

Promoted by the College of Design & Innovation (D&I), Tongji University with the participation of five Schools of Design located in four countries[3], the JDS was a research-informed teaching platform focused on urban, architecture and environmental design [17], that took place from September 2019 to June 2020. Being the studios the core modules of the curricula of the schools, the JDS integrated these courses to develop a series of projects on a common site, the area comprised between Siping Road and Chifeng Road near the Tongji University main campus in Shanghai[4]. It is important to

[1] Also defined as creative thinking, it's the process of solving problems employing strategies that deviate from the commonly adopted or previously taught ones (American Psychological Association, 2022) [11].

[2] It's the process of solving problems employing linear and logical steps to dissect a certain number of already formulated solutions and define the most correct one (American Psychological Association, 2022) [13].

[3] The schools of design who agreed to participate in the JDS were: College of Design & Innovation, Tongji University (China); School of Architecture, Art and Design Chihuahua campus, Tecnológico de Monterrey (TEC - Mexico); Department of Architecture and Built Environment, University of Nottingham Ningbo China (UNNC); School of Architecture University of Seville (ETSAS - Spain); Double Degree Master's Program in Architecture and Building Engineering. University of Pavia (UNIPV – Italy).

[4] For a comprehensive overview of the site project see the website https://jointdesignstudio.org.

highlight that the JDS was part of a wider frame that included two projects combining regenerative urban practices and stakeholders – the University, the local Government and the residents – participation in Siping Community, the neighborhood where the project site is located. The first one is the *Open Your Space* initiative, an applied investigation that strives to implement a socio-cultural framework for the regeneration of public spaces and the promotion of collective activities through the dialogue between local community and University [18–20]. The second one is the *Neighborhood of Innovation, Creativity, and Entrepreneurship Towards 2035 (NICE 2035) living labs project*[5] [21].

The JDS was informed by the idea that a cross-cultural collaborative working environment could redefine students' way of thinking and encourage them to develop an original point of view about urban, building and space design [10]. Starting from these considerations and from the constraints imposed by the different geographical locations of the participants, this initiative was structured in a hybrid format: a virtual platform for information exchange and regular updates about the JDS's activities and a physical space within the D&I dedicated to on-site activities. These included workshops, lectures, and meetings, where students, scholars, designers and citizens from the local community could share their ideas about regeneration strategies and design for the area of Chifeng Road (Fig. 1, Fig. 2 and Fig. 3). This hybrid format allowed the JDS to fully implement the so called "collaborative learning" [22] by supplementing students' expertise, reorienting their perspective about design and opening to a comprehensive approach to the contemporary challenges of affordability, social, economic, and environmental sustainability, including community's participation in urban transformations. Moreover, the practical learning activities of the JDS sought to promote the exploration of alternative solutions based on varied levels of information and inputs elaborated by people coming from diverse educational and cultural backgrounds [23].

[5] The NICE 2035 [21] project is based on the recently released *Shanghai Master Plan 2017–2035* (also known as *Shanghai 2035*) and it "underlines the potential role of neighborhoods in developing the city into a more attractive, human city. The NICE 2035 project envisions neighborhoods as arenas for innovation as well as business innovation, and community-supported ecosystems of open-innovation for future living" (NICE 2035 – Tongji DESIS Lab, n.d.). In other words, the NICE 2035 is a framework project under which several social innovation initiatives are grounded in the Siping community that is characterized by old residential compounds built in the 70s and 80s for industrial workers, and higher educational institutions (such as Tongji University and Fudan University among others). The backbone of the NICE 2035 is a network of labs that have different goals and focuses that span from food, entertainment to mobility and incubation. These labs explore future ways of self-sustained life while creating a cluster effect on the entire district, and, in the long run, on the whole city. NICE 2035 have also developed a network of people who are working together through online and offline platforms that go beyond geographical, disciplinary, and social boundaries to achieve common interests and goals.

Fig. 1. Students and tutors from UNNC and D&I during the site visit in Siping Community. Shanghai, September 2019. Source: The Authors.

Although the characteristics of a joint design studio have already been addressed by the literature [3, 24], the case study here analyzed presents some peculiarities, summarized in the following lines, that distinguish itself from other experiences[6] [25–29].

First, the JDS was crosscurrent if compared with other similar initiatives, because each participant school was autonomously conducting the studio. The learners attended the modules in their own institutions and countries and developed their projects according to the specific learning requirements and outcomes, design approach, and teaching

[6] Regarding cross-cultural practices of collaborative design studios, besides the above-mentioned ILA&UD experience, the Italian schools of architecture can count many pioneering experiments dating back to the '70s and '80s. For example, the 16 editions (from 1994 to 2010) of the *International Design Seminars* organized by the Institute of Advanced Studies of Pavia with the University of Pavia [25] were transformed in 2009 into the Italian-Chinese curriculum in Building Engineering and Architecture, co-developed with College of Architecture and Urban Design (CAUP), Tongji University. This finally lead to the formalization between the CAUP and the University of Pavia of the first Double Degree Master Program in Architecture in China in 2011 [26, 27] Of course, there are also later valuable experiences worldwide and in Asia, such as the *International Collaborative Studios* offered by The Chinese University of Hong Kong, School of Architecture [28] or those promoted by the Schools of Architecture of Tianjin University, and University of California Los Angeles between 2006 and 2018 [29].

schedule (Table 1). This choice was supported by two main reasons: on the one hand it granted the maximum flexibility and freedom to tutors and students in defining the learning path; on the other hand, it greatly simplified the management and the logistics of the JDS itself.

Table 1. The JDS composition

Institution	D&I	UNNC	TEC	ETSAS	UNIPV
Program	Master of Fine Arts (MFA) in environmental design	BEng – architecture design (Y2 & Y3)	Bachelor's in architecture (B.A. Architecture)	Master's in architecture	Double Degree Master's Program in Architecture and Building Engineering
Date	Mar. 2020 – Jun 2020	Sept.2019 – June 2020	Sept. 2019 – Dec. 2019	Feb. 2020	Sept. 2019 – June 2020
Length	4 months	9 months	4 months	2 weeks	9 months
n. students	23	31	28	4	3
Brief	Project research: Industrial report - environmental design	Social housing + community building (Y2); Masterplan + public building (Y3)	Capstone projects II - urban hybrid architecture for siping community	International workshop: Shanghai city of knowledge	Final Thesis project laboratory
Design outcomes	10 projects	41 projects	11 projects	4 projects	1 Final thesis (research + project)
Validation	Book	Final Year Exhibition + book	Final Year Exhibition + book	Book	Book + 1 conference paper

Note: the acronyms of the institutions are explained in the footnote 3

Second, being the JDS an international initiative, it is self-evident that most of the cohorts were not located in the same country of the site. For this reason, fieldtrips and on-site workshops were organized to allow the participants to get familiar with the context. Students and tutors from Mexico travelled to Shanghai in September 2019, as well as those from UNNC who visited the area in the same period. The students from UNIPV, who were enrolled in the Double Degree Program in Shanghai (see footnote 5), had the chance to visit the project area several times, while those from the ETSAS were not able to travel to China due to the COVID-19 outbreak. In this way, they had to rely on the data e.g., site, function, and demographic analysis, shared by the other cohorts. At the same time, non-Chinese speaking participants had to rely on the detailed information shared by local students and accept the challenges of understanding the site through the eyes of others and in a short span of time. Under the pedagogical point of view, this aspect aimed at encouraging cross-cultural collaborations among tutors and students with different backgrounds, while enhancing a set of soft skills like negotiation, problem solving and teamwork that are becoming prominent and necessary in the contemporary design practice [30].

Fig. 2. The Mexican and Chinese students were attending the workshop with the local residents of the Siping Community. Shanghai, September 2019. Source: The Authors.

Third, by involving different schools and programs, the JDS purposefully comprised learners from a wide range of disciplines (urban, architecture, environment design and engineering) who were at different academic levels (Table 1). The implication of this choice was twofold. It aimed at defining a concrete cross-disciplinary environment where the same area is interpreted through proposals that reflect very diverse knowledge, approaches, and points of view [31]. At the same time, the participation of students of different ages who were working collaboratively fostered learning activities such as observation, imitation, and modeling that constitute the basis of institutionalized vertical design studios modules [32].

Fourth, online communication platforms (i.e.: WeChat[7], Instagram, Zoom, the JDS's website) were introduced as collaborative tools to avert the unavoidable difficulties caused by geographical distance and distinct time zones. At each stage, students and

[7] WeChat is the most popular messaging application in Mainland China.

Fig. 3. The students and tutors from UNNC and D&I during the site visit in Siping Road and Chifeng Road. Shanghai, September 2019. Source: The Authors.

tutors could share the outcomes of their work through the official website, while WeChat, Instagram and Zoom (Fig. 4) were adopted to share data and to communicate in real-time. For example, the tutors of each studio could deliver a series of online lectures about the JDS's themes that were recorded and successively shared among all the participants. It is important to highlight how the online environment has always been an integral part of the JDS platform and it was fundamental to carry on its activities since the very beginning and not only during the COVID-19 outbreak.

Finally, two more aspects are worth to be mentioned regarding the JDS teaching structure and its impact on cross-cultural practices. The first one is the size of the whole initiative, summarized in Table 2. The involvement of a large number of participants was intended to be beneficial to the whole process of enhancing cross-cultural interactions and provided the authors with a comprehensive overview about both the JDS's outcomes and pros and cons of the adopted methodological process. This aspect is further addressed in the *Limitations and Recommendations* section.

The second aspect concerns the design-related theoretical foundations of the initiative. In fact, the JDS was structured since its inception as a research-informed teaching platform that besides enhancing the students' learning experience, aimed at producing tangible research outputs as proposed by the *Research by Design* framework [33]. The tutors of each design studio agreed to structure the pedagogical process based on the academic literature about the adoption of the design as a method of inquiry. This has been extensively addressed by Van de Weijer, Van Cleempoel, and Heynen, [34] who clarify the relationship among research by design in practice, education and academia

Fig. 4. The students from D&I attending online activities during the COVID-19 outbreak. Spring 2020. Source: The Authors.

Table 2. *Size* of the JDS.

People	Role	N
	Full time tutors	6
	Part-time tutors	12
	External examiners/reviewers	28
	Students	89
	Total	135
Events	Type of event	N
	International workshops	3
	Conferences/seminars/webinars	15
	Meetings	25
	Total	43
Time	Activity	N. (h)
	Teaching hours	500
	Tutors' and students' preparation and work	6000
	Total	6500

Note: the number of hours (h) is an estimation based on the credits and teaching hours of each module and their respective contributions, while elaborating on the validation of the outputs of this kind of investigation [35, 36]. This approach allowed to achieve an important result in terms of design outcomes: the proposals of the students were not just focused on the final scheme, but they were also centered on the design *of* and *for* the definition of relations. This is a relevant issue that implies a specific argumentation and deserves to be discussed in detail in another planned paper by the authors[8].

4 Limitations and Recommendations

During and at the end of the 2019/2020 academic year several formal and informal meetings were organized with the tutors and some students of the five schools. The aim of those meetings was twofold: first, to collect the materials produced in each studio to realize a comprehensive publication about the JDS's results[9] [38]. Second, to collect comments, critiques and feedbacks to understand strengths and weaknesses of the JDS within the framework of cross-cultural practices. Starting from the outcomes of these meetings and the direct observation of the authors, this section concretely addresses the main critical points and possible recommendations for future joint initiatives planning and delivery.

1. The first reflection concerns the full autonomy of each involved design studio in terms of teaching time schedule. This favored the overall management of the initiative, but it also implied some difficulties for teachers and students to achieve a full cultural exchange. Different timing within the academic year of the studio modules meant that the students couldn't extensively share their design process in real time and take advantage from the different cultural experiences. It is then suggested to plan the JDS time-schedule in the same semester for all the participant schools.
2. The independent drafting of the studios' brief revealed some limitations in pursuing one of the JDS's scopes that was elaborating possible methodologies and scenarios for the specific context of Chifeng Road in the Siping Community. The organizers opted for this choice to meet the needs of the five schools that had to satisfy their own program requirements. In this case, a preliminary agreement among participant institutions to align their teaching goals is recommended. This could bring two benefits: first, it could grant the tutors more freedom to adapt their teaching methods

[8] In fact, if the environmental design focuses on relations and interactions between humans and surroundings, we will have a totally new way of characterizing the environments, as Lou affirmed: "Our environmental design focuses on using holistic, human-centered, and interdisciplinary approaches to create and enable a sustainable life/space ecosystem, including experiences, communication, and places that optimize the interactions of humans with their surroundings" [37]. Furthermore, it is important to mention how the JDS combined the Chinese and Western perspectives on designing environments are combined and mixed together achieving de-facto one of the main scopes of the cross-cultural practice in education.

[9] The published volume is an exhaustive collection of studios work, research seminars, and lectures developed during two academic years, 2018–2019 and 2019–2020, at the College of Design & Innovation, Tongji University, including the outcomes of the JDS [38].

in a joint design framework; second, it could facilitate the alignment of the briefs with the initiative's goals[10].

3. Despite of the official JDS's language was English[11], the differences in adopting design-specific terminology represented a limitation for a few students and tutors. Drafting a glossary with the most relevant and frequent English terms that are employed in the design field would help to overcome language barriers and misunderstanding and, consequently, facilitate cross-cultural communication.
4. The previous limitations also suggest that the tutors had to pay a greater effort to carry on the teaching activities within the JDS's frame, and they had to balance and compromise their consolidated teaching methods with different requirements and (cultural) approaches. This implies a more general reflection about the value and need of international mobility for both scholars and students to be exposed to different pedagogical practices and design approaches.
5. Social distancing and travel limitations due to the COVID-19 outbreak and ever-mutating conditions of each country had two major impacts: the students from ETSAS could not visit the site and the face to face meetings had to be canceled among the other participants; the planned exhibition at D&I, could not be finalized. Despite these implications, the hybrid structure of the platform, that implied a full integration of the distant learning tools, allowed the initiative to be resilient against the halt imposed by the COVID-19 outbreak. It is then clear that planning international design studios that mix face to face and online teaching activities should be implemented to overcome unpredictable events and enhance students' engagement.
6. As pointed out by Utaberta et al. [39], a large number of activities can have a negative impact on the students' learning experience and generating a further psychological burden. Although this issue is difficult to be avoided in an intensive learning environment such as a studio, more attention from each participant schools on the schedule of the coordinated activities should be considered while designing joint initiatives.
7. As mentioned above, a large pool of participants can benefit the entire process of cross-cultural interaction while generating a wide range of design outcomes. Nevertheless, involving too many actors can cause three main problems: management issues, a certain distraction from the scope of the joint design studio, and the perception of lack of support from the participants' side. It is then recommended to define a reasonable ratio between the number of schools and students and that of the people in charge of the initiative to allow every participant to fully benefit from the activities offered within the cross-cultural practices context.

---

[10] Another potential solution to cope with the limitations 1 and 2 could be to organize a preliminary phase promoted by the host institution. This action could take place half a year before the planned joint design studio. It could be an exploratory and preparatory phase aimed at defining the training project and assess its feasibility through a series of short workshops and meetings. However, this option presents some cons regarding the economic sustainability of the project and its management.

[11] The languages spoken in the JDS were (according to the author's estimation): English, Chinese, German, Italian, Malay, Russian and Spanish.

5 Discussion and Conclusions

This paper illustrates how cross-cultural practices have been implemented in the context of the higher education through the experience of the *International Shanghai Joint Design Studio* (JDS). It is worth to recall here te two main reasons for starting the initiative: first, was the idea that a cross-cultural collaborative working activity could redefine students' way of thinking and encourage them to develop a holistic point of view about design for the problems concerning contemporary environmental and social challenges. Second, experimenting an alternative learning environment that overcomes the increasing fragmentation of education in design fields, too often oriented towards a separated and specialized-based knowledge[12]. Therefore, the JDS was an attempt to build an integrated design experience involving a wide range of experts from different cultural backgrounds and disciplines dealing with the problems of the built environment.

Considering the achievements of the JDS, it's possible to affirm that:

- By involving several actors - students, tutors, scholars, and citizens - the initiative became a hub where theoretical and methodological design contents were collected and made available on an open source platform. Moreover, the JDS demonstrated how technology can play an important role in educational path. Nonetheless, technology cannot replace reality and the need for educational practitioners and students to foster and facilitate the implementation of cross-cultural practices is even more urgent;
- By benefitting from the existing NICE 35 and Open Your Spaces ongoing projects in Siping Community, based on the long-term cooperation among local government, community and Tongji University, the JDS positioned itself as a multicultural, multidisciplinary, hybrid research-based teaching laboratory that provided an alternative learning path. It demonstrated the effectiveness of the so-called experiential learning of designers by creating opportunities of encounter among learners, tutors and people of the community;
- As an experiment, the JDS deployed an alternative program aimed at integrating what is taught and learned in the standard university curricula with the reality of the world, adopting the Siping community in Shanghai as a test-bed. The students, who were able to fully embrace the multifaceted structure of the JDS, could experience a very unique learning environment, different in many aspects from those known in their own schools.

Finally, this version of the JDS faced another big challenge: despite its conceptualization started in the pre-COVID-19 period, it was developed and completed during the pandemic outbreak, regardless of the personal restrictions imposed by that situation. For this reason, it generated two further important outcomes: it represents a sort of prospect and vision of how the post-COVID-19 educational path in design studios might be structured and developed, and it embodies a concrete application of new ways of teaching and

[12] The number of specializations has highly increased and the relationships between disciplines have become purely formal in today's studios. Many of these modules are too often structured to add new knowledge rather than creating an integration of knowledge. An effective educational path in the design studios should not be focused on learning more notions, but on a systematical learning and thinking.

research, both at national and international level, that is possible thanks to the parallel implementation of adaptive academic approaches and innovative technologies.

In conclusion, rooted on the legacy of this initiative, the authors' vision for education in design (architectural design or urban design) can be summarized according to the following three positions:

1. Building a more diverse teaching team and cultivate young talents and doctoral students by keeping international exchanges relevant along with public engagement.
2. Establishing new programs for international cooperation (beyond the already existing double degrees) also through the integration of scientific research and/or innovative research-based teaching;
3. Deepening the cooperation among academia/universities and various international bodies (e.g. UNESCO) giving new life to mobility programs such as innovating and implementing the European Union's *Erasmus Plus* exchange program.

References

1. Prodan, R., Fahringer, T.: Introduction. In: Grid Computing. LNCS, vol. 4340, pp. 1–11. Springer, Heidelberg (2007). https://doi.org/10.1007/978-3-540-69262-1_1
2. Herath, T., Herath, H.S.: B: Coping with the new normal imposed by the COVID-19 pandemic: lessons for technology management and governance. Inf. Syst. Manag. **37**(4), 277–283 (2020). https://doi.org/10.1080/10580530.2020.1818902
3. Lee, D.Y., Ha, J.Y., Farfax, D.: Cross-Cultural Design (CCD) Learning Reflective Tool Based on UK and Korea's Collaborative design Projects. International Design Conference - Design 2016, pp. 2091–2100. Dubrovnik: The Design Society. (2016). https://www.designsociety.org/multimedia/publication/1da2f543b1c01453efed2b9f68fbb77e05aad4d02bb9f20efe8de1d5f196ba80.pdf. Accessed 08 Feb 2022
4. Bonenberg, W.: Cross-cultural design and its application in architecture. In: Charytonowicz, J. (Ed.), Advances in Human Factors and Sustainable Infrastructure. Advances in Intelligent Systems and Computing, pp. 105–114. Springer, Cham (2016). https://doi.org/10.1007/978-3-319-41941-1_10
5. Shanghai Joint Design Studio Homepage. https://jointdesignstudio.org/. Accessed 01 Feb 2022
6. White, D.R.: Cross-Cultural Research: An Introduction for Students. https://citeseerx.ist.psu.edu/viewdoc/download?doi=10.1.1.78.7370&rep=rep1&type=pdf. Accessed 30 Jan 2022
7. ILA&UD. About ILAUD. https://www.ilaud.org/category/about/. Accessed 11 Feb 2022
8. De Carlo, G.: Report on the First Residential Course, Urbino: September 6 - October 31 1976. In 1st Residential Course. Urbino 1976 (pp. 5–14). Urbino: ILAUD International Laboratory of Architecture and Urban Design; Universitá di Urbino. (1977). http://media.regesta.com/dm_0/IBC/IBCAS00771/pdf/IT-ER-IBC-AS00771-0000038.pdf#page=5. Accessed 09 Feb 2022
9. Maturana, B.C.: Where is the problem in design studio: purpose and significance of the design task. Archnet-IJAR **8**(3), 32–44 (2014). https://doi.org/10.26687/archnet-ijar.v8i3.466
10. Kim, M.J., Ju, S.R., Lee, L.: A cross-cultural and interdisciplinary collaboration in a joint design studio. Int. J. Art Des. Educ. **34**(1), 102–120 (2015)
11. American Psychological Association, Convergent Thinking. https://dictionary.apa.org/convergent-thinking. Accessed 28 Jan 2022

12. Goldschmidt, G.: Linkographic evidence for concurrent divergent and convergent thinking in creative design. Creat. Res. J. **28**(2), 115–122 (2016). https://doi.org/10.1080/10400419.2016.1162497
13. American Psychological Association, Divergent Thinking. https://dictionary.apa.org/divergent-thinking. Accessed 28 Jan 2022
14. Elliot, E.A., Nakata, C.: Cross-cultural creativity: conceptualization and propositionsfor global new product development. J. Prod. Innov. Manag. **30**, 110–125 (2013). https://doi.org/10.1111/jpim.12066
15. Burkhart, R.C.: The creativity-personality continuum based on spontaneity and deliberateness in art. Stud. Art Educ. **2**(1), 43–65 (1960)
16. Beittel, K.R.: On the relationships between art and general creativity: a biased history and projection of the partial conquest. Sch. Rev. **72**(3), 272–288 (1964)
17. De Queiroz Barbosa, E.R., De Meulder, B., Gerritz, Y.: Design studio as a process of inquiry: the case of studio Sao Paulo. AE. Revista Lusófona de Arquitectura e Educação Arch. Educ. J. **11**, 241–254 (2014)
18. Ni, M., Cattaneo, T.: Design for urban resilience: a case of community-led placemaking approach in Shanghai China. In: Rau, P.-L. (ed.) HCII 2019. LNCS, vol. 11577, pp. 207–222. Springer, Cham (2019). https://doi.org/10.1007/978-3-030-22580-3_16
19. Ni, M.: Open your space: a design activism initiative in Chinese urban community. In: Rau, P.-L. (ed.) CCD 2017. LNCS, vol. 10281, pp. 412–431. Springer, Cham (2017). https://doi.org/10.1007/978-3-319-57931-3_33
20. Ni, M., Zhu, M. (Eds.).: Open Your Space: Design Intervention for Urban Resilience. Shanghai, PRC: Tongji University Press (2017)
21. Desis Network Design for Social Innovation and Sustainability, NICE 2035 – Tongji DESIS Lab., https://www.desisnetwork.org/2018/06/27/nice-2035-tongji-desis-lab/. Accessed 09 Feb 2022
22. ILA&UD Manifesto. The movable frontier of architectural education. https://www.ilaud.org/manifesto/. Accessed 09 Feb 2022
23. Park, S.: Rethinking design studios as an integrative multi-layered collaboration environment. J. Urban Des. **25**(4), 523–550 (2020). https://doi.org/10.1080/13574809.2020.1734449
24. Kostopoulos, K.: Collaborative practice-based learning methods in architectural design and building technology education in a cross-cultural. Cross-Geograph. Environ. J Arch. Eng. **28**(1), 05022001 (2022). https://doi.org/10.1061/(ASCE)AE.1943-5568.0000525
25. International design seminar. http://www-3.unipv.it/lcp/lcpa/seminari/seminari.html. Accessed 09 Feb 2022
26. Double Degree with Tongji University in Shanghai. http://iea.unipv.eu/shanghai/ and https://caup.tongji.edu.cn/caupen/c0/b8/c11086a114872/page.htm. Accessed 09 Feb 2022
27. Tongji-Pavia Dual Degree program. https://caup.tongji.edu.cn/caupen/c0/b8/c11086a114872/page.htm. Accessed 09 Feb 2022
28. School of Architecture the Chinese University of Hong Kong. International Collaborative Design Studios. http://www.arch.cuhk.edu.hk/students/international-collaborative-design-studios/. Accessed 09 Feb 2022
29. Tianjin University School of Architecture. (2019, 02 26). The TJU-UCLA Joint Design Studio. http://t-arch.tju.edu.cn/info/1146/1250.htm. Accessed 09 Feb 2022
30. Gale, A.J., Duffey, M.A., Park-Gates, S., Peek, P.F.: Soft skills versus hard skills: practitioners' perspectives on interior design interns. J. Inter. Des. **42**(4), 45–63 (2017). https://doi.org/10.1111/joid.12105
31. McDonald, J.K., West, R.E., Rich, P.J., Pfleger, I.: It's so wonderful having different majors working together: the development of an interdisciplinary design thinking minor. TechTrends **63**(4), 440–450 (2018). https://doi.org/10.1007/s11528-018-0325-2

32. Peterson, M., Tober, B.: Institutionalizing the vertical studio: curriculum, pedagogy, and the logistics of core classes with mixed-level students. In: Connecting Dots: Research, Education + Practice, pp. 138–144. Cincinnati: University of Cincinnati (2014)
33. Roggema, R.: Research by design: proposition for a methodological approach. Urban Sci. **1**(2), 1–19 (2016). https://doi.org/10.3390/urbansci1010002
34. Van de Weijer, M., Van Cleempoel, K., Heynen, H.: Positioning design in academia and practice: a contribution to a continuing debate. Des. Issues **30**(2), 17–29 (2014). https://doi.org/10.1162/DESI_a_00259
35. Mangi, E.: Notes on a two years' experience. designing for, teaching in and researching about the Siping Community in Shanghai. In: Cattaneo, T., Mangi, E., (eds). Designing Environments, pp. 14–17, Santarcangelo di Romagna (RN): Maggioli Editore (2021)
36. Cattaneo, T., Giorgi, E., Ni, M.: Landscape, architecture and environmental regeneration: a research by design approach for inclusive tourism in a rural village in China. Sustainability **11**, 128 (2019). https://doi.org/10.3390/su11010128
37. Lou, Y.: The idea of environmental design revisited. Des. Issues **35**(1), 23–35 (2019)
38. Cattaneo, T., Mangi, E.: Designing Environments. Two years of research through studio works, theses, seminars, exhibitions, and conferences at the College of Design and Innovation, Tongji University. Santarcangelo di Romagna, Italy: Maggioli Editore (2021)
39. Utaberta, N., Othuman Mydin, M.A., Ismail, S.: Evaluating joint-studio as a alternative learning experience: case study of retirement centre project in join-studio between UPM and UIN, in architecture design studio. Jurnal Teknologi (Sci. Eng.) **75**(9), 33–38 (2015)

A Tourist Participatory Design for Boosting the Nighttime Cultural Tourism

Shu Fang and Yangshuo Zheng(✉)

Wuhan University of Technology, Wuhan 430000, China
zhengyangshuo@163.com

Abstract. Nighttime cultural tourism has been a research spotlight for night economic development. Despite the earlier start, China's researchers did not pay enough attention to it until 2019, and the study in most areas is still in its infancy. In China, the existing night cultural tourism services suffer from serious homogeneity, insufficient cultural penetration, and a lack of innovation. To address these issues, we choose resident tourists as a breakthrough since they are the audience of night cultural tourism services as well as the experiencers and reconstructors of the cultural field in the nighttime cultural tourism scene. In this paper, we examine the benefits of using public participatory design to improve nighttime cultural tourism services and then propose a participatory design model based on participant dimensions, background indicators, ISO evaluation standards, participation forms, and principles of nighttime cultural tourism. In particular, we construct a sample participatory design scene for nighttime cultural tourism to demonstrate how our design can overcome the two obstacles that hinder users from fully understanding the design background and content and accurately expressing design opinions in the process of participatory design.

Keywords: Nighttime cultural tourism · Participatory design

1 Introduction

The State Council of China has recently proposed a policy [1] of encouraging cities to boost the night consumer market by developing culture and travel. Since then, practically every Chinese city has placed a strong emphasis on growing nighttime cultural tourism to enhance the evening economy, domestic demand, and resident consumption expenditure. Unfortunately, with the sudden outbreak of the COVID-19 epidemic, the traditional consumption ecology has been changed forever. Residents' consumption willingness has also decreased. As a result, the tourism industry and its derivative consumption are seriously battered and have undergone significant changes. In this context, night cultural tourism has been an essential component of the tourism sector and can serve as a vital driver of night economic growth. Moreover, nighttime cultural tourism has the potential to reactivate and reemerge the hundreds of millions of dollars' consumption that have been withheld domestically due to the international travel bans. Since nighttime cultural tourism has the advantages of extending travel time, reducing tourist density, and

P.-L. P. Rau (Ed.): HCII 2022, LNCS 13311, pp. 188–198, 2022.
https://doi.org/10.1007/978-3-031-06038-0_14

stimulating the consumption of local tourism, it has become a significant breakthrough in meeting China's internal circulation needs and seeking new economic growth points under the strict regular COVID-19 epidemic prevention and control policies.

In this paper, we study the development of China's nighttime cultural tourism and find that there is a gap between the services provided by the tourist destinations and the demands of the tourists. The drawbacks of existing nighttime cultural tourism services indicate that service design is significant for improving tourist satisfaction. Based on this insight, we propose a novel tourist participatory design to improve the efficiency of developing nighttime cultural tourism services.

1.1 The Research and Development of Nighttime Cultural Tourism

In recent years, nighttime cultural tourism is flourishing in many countries. However, its research is limited and only exists as part of a larger study on the night economy or nightlife, with no standalone studies. The study of nighttime tourism derived from the emergence of the night economy. Due to the large number of manufacturing industry employees migrating out from the city core, the United Kingdom faced an empty nests problem in the city at night in the 1970s. The night economy was initially presented as a solution to this problem. In 1994, the United Kingdom declare the 24-h City strategy [2] to facilitate the economic, social, and cultural activities in the city. With the quick spread of this concept, the 24 h city has turned to a globalized form of time which blurry the division of day and night and accelerated the development of night tourism. In 1999, Kreiztman [3] proposed that tourism plays a key role in a 24-h city and tourists can be treated as typical 24-h citizens. There is no doubt that the night economy can benefit a lot from night tourism. Meanwhile, the negative social behaviors due to night activities have also been noticed by the researchers. In 2005, Roberts, M. et al. [4] figured out that holding night events in the city center will bring negative effects such as noise, waste, crime, etc., and suggested that these activities should be performed under better supervision. In addition to extending the opening hours of tourism and cultural institutions, the attractiveness of the night itself is also an important impetus for the development of night tourism. In 2010, Mark Ingle [5] analyzed the unique visual appeal of the night on stargazing and other forms of astronomical tourism. With the improvement of lighting, transportation, and technology, it is still challenging to attract tourists for night tourism especially under the competition of other cities. In 2019, Yijing Zhao [6] from South Korea pointed out that many developed cities in the world have entered the stage of landscape lighting. Cities can enhance the night's attraction by performing cultural and artistic activities and match the landscape lighting with urban functions and culture.

In the global, the enterprise and academia have started the industrial application of nighttime cultural tourism very early. They have performed all kinds of night tours ranging from landscape nocturne, festival activities, cultural leisure activities, cultural role-play shows, street visits, scenic spots. These efforts have accumulated a wealth of experience as well as many successful practice cases, such as Norway's Aurora Night, Edinburgh Military Tattoo, and Japan's Sensoji Temple night tour. At the same time, nighttime activities have boomed in many developed cities. For instance, in London, diversified business types emerge and diverse social entities have participated in the management; in Amsterdam, night mayors and night cultural spaces are set up; and in Lyon, France, the culture lights up the cities. A variety of digital technologies with constant innovation have also been implemented into evening cultural events to enrich tourists' cultural experiences. For instance, a Japanese company teamLab has perfectly combined Japanese culture with technology and human interaction. The Moment Factory studio in Canada has integrated lighting, architecture, and special multimedia effects to create an immersive experience environment for nighttime cultural tourism.

1.2 The Situation of China's Nighttime Cultural Tourism

The research and development of nighttime cultural tourism in China is still in its infancy. Although nighttime cultural tourism has been studied in China since the early 1990s, the study focus, depth, and breadth are not blown out till 2019. Among these works, there are largely qualitative studies of a certain specific scenic spot or area, with a few quantitative studies thrown in for good measure and analysis. The existing works [7–10] mainly focus on defining nighttime cultural tourism, developing products for it, and studying the problems, countermeasures, and future directions for its development. Chinese scholars such as Cao et al. [8], Deng et al. [9], and Zhao et al. [10] define the nighttime cultural tourism from different aspects. Wen et al. [11] propose the first work to study the nighttime cultural tourism products. Lu et al. [12] figured out the lack of cultural connotation and poor quality of nighttime cultural tourism and gave suggestions for these problems. In the past two years, topics such as integrating culture and tourism to empower the night economy, improving nighttime cultural tourism consumption, and constructing nighttime cultural tourism gathering zones, have become spotlights in academia. It indicates that nighttime cultural tourism will turn into an important future research direction of the night economy.

Although the industrial practice of nighttime culture tourism has drawn attention early in China, its growth and implementation have been slow. In 2004, Qingdao issued relevant policies of concentrating on proactively exploring and improving nighttime tourism to boost the night economy. In 2006, Hangzhou took the lead in opening the prelude to the development of night tourism, and the promotion of the night economy through nighttime cultural tourism has reached a climax since 2014. In August 2019, the State Council of China has planned [1] to build more than 200 national nighttime cultural tourism clusters by 2022. Thus, the local governments are required to take actions to accelerate and refine the execution of this policy. Meanwhile, the consumer market for nighttime cultural tourism continues to expand. By the end of 2020, the night economy had grown to a size of RMB 30 trillion, and by 2022, it is predicted to reach RMB 40 trillion. Beginning with the activity of lighting up the Bauhinia City at Shangyuan Night in 2019, a variety of night cultural tourism activities are carried out in China. Similar projects such as Datang Everbright City, Gusu 8:30 and Chongqing Hongyadong have been launched one after another by various cities. However, compared with other countries, China's nighttime cultural tourism is still at the early stage of proposing a performance, a light show, a documentary or a movie, and with issues such as serious homogeneity, lack of innovation, and insufficient cultural penetration.

2 Limitations in China's Existing Nighttime Cultural Tourism Services

In this section, we first study the services provided by existing nighttime cultural tourism in terms of their goals, their constituent elements, and their presentation forms to understand why current nighttime cultural tourism has failed to meet the expectations of visitors. Then, we think from the visitors' perspective to identify their real demands for nighttime tourism. Finally, by analyzing the gap between the existing services provided by the tourist destinations and the expectations of the visitors, we conclude the drawbacks of existing nighttime cultural tourism and draw the direction for improving tourist satisfaction through tourist-participated design.

2.1 The Services Provided by China's Nighttime Cultural Tourism

The services provided by tourist destinations play an important role in nighttime cultural tourism. As a supplementary form of day tourism, night tourism can extend tourism in time and space. As a carrier of the night tourism economy, night tourism products can extend the tourism economy from a product economy and service economy to an experience economy by providing tangible tourism products and intangible tourism services [13]. People may visit attractions on purpose to feel the cultural symbols' connotation and the historical evolution laid in the structures of the tourist scene [14], rather than verifying the physical construction of the scene. Therefore, the goal of night cultural tourism service provision is to give diverse cultural experiences for exploring the culture and nighttime tourism consumption economy, as well as to meet the spiritual and cultural needs of residents and tourists to seek tourism industrial development and economic growth.

The nighttime cultural tourism scene, which helps to realize the cultural experience of residents and tourists, is an essential element of the overall night cultural tourism service. It can provide a wonderful stage for night tourism activities to improve tourists' participation and interaction in a unique night consumption space [15] by utilizing specific themes as narrative clues, meaningful nature and humanistic symbols as materials, and various means to form a real or virtual world. The nighttime cultural tourism scenes [16] can be divided into nighttime cultural entertainment scenes, nighttime city life scenes, nighttime cultural tourism social scenes, nighttime tourism and leisure scenes, etc. The nighttime cultural entertainment scenes' attractions are rendered by creating a strong sense of involvement and interaction, such as through immersive escape rooms, live residences, and night festivals. The main appeal of the nighttime city life scene is to use regional culture and living atmosphere to suit residents' and visitors' consumption demands in circumstances such as night consuming street blocks and night markets. The nighttime tourism and leisure scene's core attraction is to meet the leisure needs of residents and tourists by connecting cultural venues with night scenery and performing arts projects at places such as the delayed opening of scenic spots, cultural institutions, nighttime rivers, and nighttime traffic lanes. The nighttime cultural tourism social scene can be used to create nighttime cultural tourism intellectual property (IP), e.g. the Miss Tumbler of *Datang Everbright City* in Xi'an, the *Wenheyou* restaurant in Changsha, which can attract tourists to check-in and fission, and then share to the social network.

By utilizing the popular online social platforms such as Douyin (China's TikTok) and Weibo (China's Twitter), the cultural IP can spread among people and attract more visitors.

For different night cultural travel scenes, various visual display forms are employed to create a fitting ambiance in the context of certain cultural experiences. Specifically, light, shadow, music, electricity, and other technologies are used in the light beautification project to render the landscapes and landmark buildings and create a aesthetic feeling. Historical street blocks and cultural buildings are used to present characteristic cultural symbols. Immersive performing arts are used to demonstrate intangible cultural heritage and folk culture.

2.2 Chinese Visitors' Requirements and Expectations

In the nighttime cultural tourism scene, residents and visitors may enjoy a single or diversified trip by engaging with their conveniences to fulfill various demands. Their shopping decisions in the early and midterm of travel are influenced by their satisfaction with their needs and the quality of their experience. Their expectations can be summarized into three categories: leisure and entertainment, cultural consumption, and emotional experience.

Due to the fast-paced life with stressful work pressures or tight travel schedules during the day, people aspire to a comfortable entertainment space to release stress and enjoy leisure. Nighttime cultural tourism provides such an opportunity for them and meets the public's needs for leisure and entertainment. The tourism process is more than just a consumption activity in people's daily lives. It also involves cultural practices at all levels. Tourism consumption promotion is essentially a process of recognizing the importance of culture at all levels and maximizing cultural value [17]. Visitors can re-interpret cultural history, fashion culture, living atmosphere, cultural stories, regional customs, and other cultures during the travel process. Tourists can create an emotional connection with tourist destinations and generate more consumption if they have a deeper grasp of cultural value.

Visitors' night travel experiences are mostly decided by the quality of the night travel scene, and the scene can also in turn affect the tourists' experiences. In the travel scene, rather than caring about the material product, tourists are more concerned with the scene in which the product is located and the emotions in which they are infiltrated [18]. The nighttime cultural tourism landscape can combine virtual and real scenes by adding device interaction technology, using technical means such as sound and light, through substituting scenes, multi-sensory experiences, and interactive narration. In this way, visitors may feel immersed and involved, so as to reach a kind of selfless flow experience full of joy.

2.3 The Gap Between the Services and Visitors' Desire

Currently, most nighttime cultural tourist items in China are too low-end, homogenized, and lack cultural creativity. Due to a scarcity of high-end and high-quality products,

China's nighttime cultural tourist service failed to meet visitor demand. We have summarized the factors that contribute to the limitations in China's nighttime tourism service as follows.

1. There is a misalignment of design goals during the early stages of the design process between the stakeholders (i.e., the investor) and the designers to pursue higher profit or better effects.
2. The optimization and iteration of night cultural tourism service products are very slow due to high development costs and low fault tolerance.
3. The current method of collecting user experience feedback is too simple and inconvenient since it can only collect a single comment when users purchase the service.

3 Methodology of the Tourist Participatory Design

In this section, we illustrate the motivation for using the tourist participatory design, as well as its methodology and detailed approaches.

3.1 The Advantages of Participatory Design for Nighttime Cultural Tourism Services

The immediate audiences and consumers of nighttime cultural tourism services, as well as the experiencers and reconstructors of the cultural field in the nighttime cultural tourism scene, are the local visitors. They also determine the value of nocturnal cultural tourist services. Based on this insight, we chose the resident tourists as a breakthrough to solve the drawbacks of the nighttime cultural tourism service. Compared with the traditional single-threaded design process, the dynamic iterative design process of design-evaluate-design loop can better ensure the consistency of product design goals and user needs, thereby improving service quality, promoting purchases, and increasing commercial revenue.

Participatory design enables the tourist destination (the designer) to listen to users' voices during the design process by involving locals and visitors in the creation of nighttime cultural tourism events. Thus, the tourist destinations can develop more effective design strategies and approaches to ensure that nighttime cultural tourism services meet the requirements and expectations of users. The benefits are as follows.

1. Assisting designers to define the design targets of night cultural tourism services and provide a source of cultural creativity.
2. Reducing the cognitive bias of stakeholders when designing communication decisions.
3. Providing feedback to designers at all stages of the design process to ensure the objectivity of design standards.

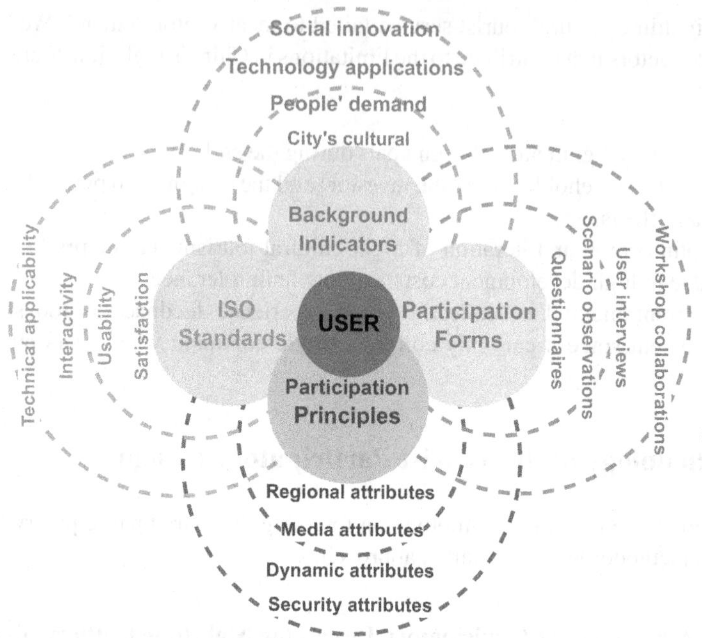

Fig. 1. The tourist participatory design model for nighttime cultural tourism.

3.2 The Tourist Participatory Design Model

By inviting all necessary people to engage in the design process, participatory design of nighttime culture tourism can help to better understand, meet, and insight into consumers' demands. However, communication between the design team and users is usually limited to the early and late evaluation stages of the design. During the design process, only professional members of the design team are involved, making it difficult to fully discover and explore user-centric solutions. Due to this situation, we screened and categorized the participants to construct a night cultural tourism participatory design model (as shown in

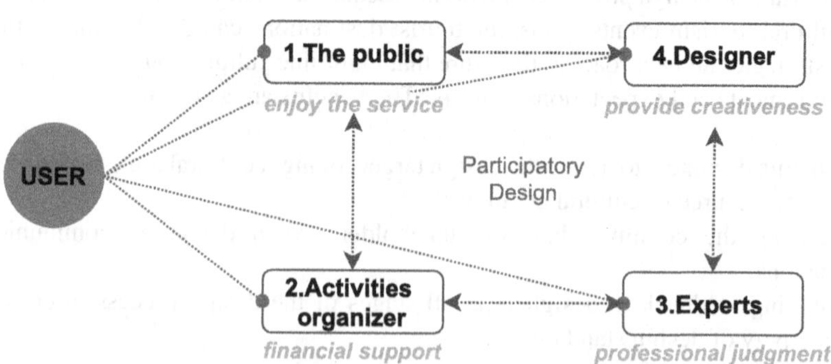

Fig. 2. The participate objects in our tourist participatory design model.

Fig. 1) that involved the dimensions of nighttime cultural tourism background indicators, ISO evaluation standards, participation forms, and participation principles.

As shown in Fig. 2, the model is centered around the invited object of participatory design, including the core stakeholders of night cultural tourism. It means that users (i.e., the general public), organizers (i.e., investors and developers), authoritative specialists (i.e., experts and scholars), and creative service providers (i.e., designers) can all participate in the design of nighttime cultural tourism services. By inviting all of them to join in the design process and work together, we can change the traditional designer-centered mode to user-centered mode and can actually design from the user's perspective. We take the four core elements of nighttime cultural tourism, i.e., characteristic culture, residents' needs, technological application, and social innovation, as the main indicators of participatory design. According to specific design goals, we can further divergent and expand each of the indicators. For instance, the characteristics of culture can be extended in three aspects, including the types of culture (e.g., history, humanities, living atmosphere, intangible cultural heritage), the forms of culture (e.g., performance, writing, architecture), and the presentation of culture. The residents' needs can extend to leisure and entertainment, cultural consumption, emotional experience, and technology applications, including technology types, technical service goals, and interaction methods.

The ISO evaluation criteria for the participatory design of nighttime cultural tourism include usability, interactivity, technical applicability, and satisfaction. These criteria can reflect the macro quality of the participatory design for night cultural tourism. The availability criterion can represent whether the nighttime cultural tourism service can effectively achieve the goal during use. The interactivity criterion can represent the extent of participation and immersion in the use of night cultural tourism services. The technology applicability criterion can represent whether technology can enable users to improve efficiency and experience during use. After the user rates the nighttime cultural tourism service based on their comprehensive subjective feelings of presentation, content, and technical assistance, the satisfaction criterion can represent whether the user will recommend it to others.

The participation principles contain the vital factors that need to be considered in participatory design, including regional attributes in the environmental dimension, media attributes in the technical dimension, dynamic attributes, and security attributes. Through

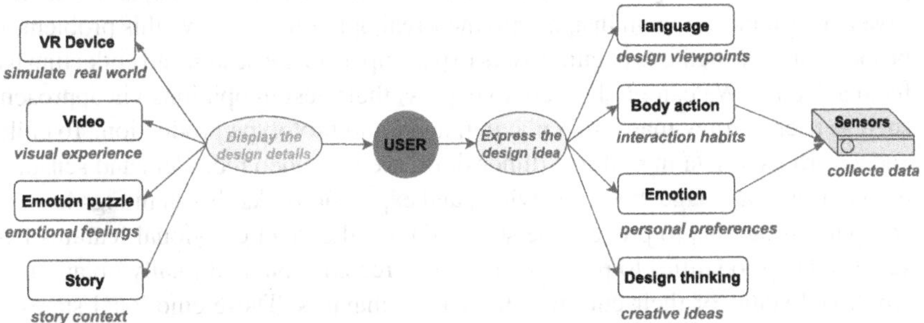

Fig. 3. The approaches to construct a practical tourism service design scene.

participation forms such as questionnaires, user interviews, scenario observations, and workshop collaborations, we can enable users to participate in the participatory design process more effectively, helping us understand the behavior and psychology of users.

3.3 The Application of Our Tourist Participatory Design Model

As shown in Fig. 3, based on our tourist participatory design model, we constructed practical scenarios to illustrate the specific methods for developing nighttime cultural tourism. There are two challenges in the scene construction: whether the user can completely comprehend the design material and whether the user's opinion can be appropriately represented in the design. To address these issues, we have to set up personnel, venues, equipment, processes, and data collection methods as follows.

1. We first need to ensure the design goals and content can be fully understood by users, so that they can have a sense of control during the participation process and, thus, more actively participate in the design. To achieve this, we need to make efforts on three fronts: the presentation of the design plan and goals, the simulation of the situational atmosphere, and the setting of the participation process. Since the atmosphere at night will be affected by environmental factors such as lighting, sound, and surrounding people and is completely different from that in the daytime, we chose closed indoor venues, which are closer to the night atmosphere. By utilizing VR virtual reality equipment, we can easily present a design plan that is closer to the real-life scenes to help users understand the design goals and plans. In the setting of the design process, the designer can transform the questions collected in the user research phase into specific content requirements and visualize the content requirements in the night cultural travel scene simulation, or describe them as a narrative night cultural travel story. In this phase, we can employ VR, video, whiteboards, questionnaires, and other tools to make the scenes and stories as real and detailed as possible. By organizing seminars for residents, tourists, experts, organizers, and designers, we can conduct divergent discussions on the demand, cultural perception, attractiveness, and experience quality of the scene or story. During the discussion, users can build their ideal plan or prototype via words, emotion puzzle, or texts.
2. Since simple language sometimes cannot convey users' opinions clearly, to ensure their design opinions can be accurately expressed, we need to further analyze users' performance, including physical, facial, language, visual, emotional, and other intuitive performance, to gain insight into their real opinions. To solve this problem, we propose various methods to guide users to participate in the design and collecting user feedback data. We can guide users to express their design opinions via approaches such as user journey maps, role playing, and rapid prototype production. To collect and record user data in multiple dimensions, we use video recorders and sensors to record users' language, body behaviors, and expressions. As shown in Fig. 4, we use computer programs to process the sensor data and extract emotional features from various data modalities to perform emotional recognition, and finally obtain users' emotional states of their current interactive behaviors. These emotional states are then used as a guideline to assess user satisfaction with the design.

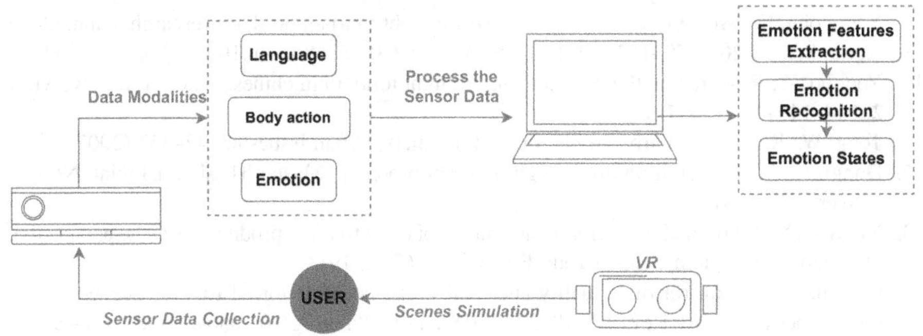

Fig. 4. Collect and process user data.

4 Conclusion

With the rapid development of nighttime cultural tourism in China, the question of how to enrich the nighttime cultural tourism services for improving the night economy has become a hot topic. Existing works on nighttime cultural tourism mainly focus on the integration of night tourism resources, product development modes, and detailed technical issues of planning or improving technical application or functionalities. There is still a disconnect between the design and development of nighttime culture tourism and the user-oriented design value. In this paper, we propose a tourist participatory design of nighttime cultural tourism to better understand the real needs and experiences of users during design, so that night cultural tourism services can be better matched with user needs. Our approaches can provide creative sources for nighttime cultural tourism designers and help them improve the service quality.

References

1. Culture and travel among keys to boosting country's consumption: http://english.www.gov.cn/statecouncil/ministries/201909/16/content_WS5d7ec789c6d0bcf8c4c1365d.html
2. Lovatt, A., et al.: The Twenty-Four Hour City: Selected Papers from the First National Conference on the Night-time Economy. Manchester: Institute of Popular Culture (1994)
3. Kreitzman, L.: The 24 Hour Society. Profile (1999). https://books.google.com.hk/books?id=ZAlpQgAACAAJ
4. Roberts, M., Turner, C.: Conflicts of liveability in the 24-hour city: learning from 48 hours in the life of london's soho. J. Urban Des. **10**(2), 171–193 (2005). https://doi.org/10.1080/13574800500086931
5. Ingle, M.: Making the most of "nothing": astro-tourism, the sublime, and the karoo as a "space destination" (2010). https://doi.org/10.1353/TRN.2010.0013
6. Yijing, Z., Wenwen, S.: The inherent potential and benefit transformation of night festival tourism: analysis of the successful path of urban night tourism. China Tour. Rev. **04**, 86–90 (2019)
7. Xueqian, S., Chen, Z.: Night tourism: the development road of urban leisure tourism. Tianfu New Theory **S1**, 188–189 (2005)
8. Xinxiang, C.: The development of night tourism in my country's cities: Taking kaifeng as an example. Comme. Res. **11**, 213–216 (2008). https://doi.org/10.13902/j.cnki.syyj.2008.11.045

9. Yongyong, D., Wen, G.: Overview of domestic night tourism products research. Guangdong Agric. Sci. **38**(20), 150–152 (2011). https://doi.org/10.16768/j.issn.1004-874x.2011.20.013
10. Yongbo, Z.: Research on the development of night tourism in chinese cities. Tour. Overview **2**, 148–149+152 (2017)
11. Tong, W.: Research on urban night tourism products. Urban Issues **08**, 42–452 (2007)
12. Dongmei., L.: Research on urban night tourism products. Master Thesis for Fujian Normal University (2009)
13. Xiaoyun, Y., Jingmin, Z.: Development strategy of night tourism products from the perspective of experience economy. China Tour. Rev. **04**, 53–62 (2019)
14. Liyuan, Y.: The mirror of virtuality and reality: the construction of tourism scenes in cultural experience. Art Rev. **12**, 19–24 (2018). https://doi.org/10.16364/j.cnki.cn11-4907/j.2018.12.004
15. Daoxuan, L., Qinglei, L.: Research on the idea of night tourism scene construction from the perspective of experience economy. Western Econom. Manage. Forum **32**(05), 71–79 (2021)
16. The 2020 Urban Night Cultural Tourism Development Trend Research Report by China's Cultural Tourism Research Consulting Department. https://mp.weixinqq.com/s/lYA7GZqmVu3qKEw_ZsCkpQ
17. Ling, M.: Cultural production and cultural consumption in tourism. Tour. Tribune **32**(03), 9–11 (2020). https://doi.org/10.19765/j.cnki.1002-5006.2020.03.005
18. Sheng, W.: Scene revolution: reconstructing the connection between people and business. China Real Estate **26** 76 (2015). https://doi.org/10.13562/j.china.real.estate.2015.26.030

How Designers Can Act Inside the Design Objects

A Preliminary Study on How Community Building Constituted Social Innovation as a Design Approach

Danwen Ji[1(✉)], Tinglei Cao[1], and Hangping Yang[2]

[1] College of Design and Innovation, Tongji University, Shanghai, China
danwen_ji@tongji.edu.cn

[2] Staatliche Hochschule für Bildende Künste - Städelschule, Frankfurt am Main, Germany

Abstract. When designers actively engage in social innovation, the object of Design turns to the complex socio-technical system in which the designer is also embedded. How does this new perspective on the relation between the design subject and the design object lead to changes in specific design actions? Using constructivism grounded theory, we analyze 20 cases of social innovation involving community building in mainland China and find that community building is an approach rather than an ultimate goal to continuous action toward a vision. Actors enter the community by reflecting on society-self and community-self relations, generating more common understanding through dialogue, proposing prototypes based on everyday life, transcending the constraints of existing meaning spaces, and creating new meaning spaces oriented toward the vision in the community.

Keywords: Active design · Community building · Reflexivity

1 Introduction

Designers actively engage their societies towards the vision of 'design that changes the world' [1] by focusing on community, political and social issues. In this transition period, the misinterpreted meaning of the design, symbolized by design in traditional creative industries and design thinking [2], is becoming more widely recognized. Furthermore, designers cultivated in the apprenticeship or studio-based educational environments are prone to personal monologic production. They tend to acquire a professional consultative perspective and simply act as system designers outside the mechanism or structure, and "just push the start bottom then go away."

However, as designers have made it their mission to "inspire society as a whole, extending the concept of long-term human benefit to include the preservation and protection of the sustainability of all four systems (nature, humans, the networked world, and artifacts)" [3], can we still exclude the subject of design from the object being designed?

Design theory and practice have constantly focused on complex socio-technical systems [4, 5]. Whereas, multiple design approaches that work with complex systems

P.-L. P. Rau (Ed.): HCII 2022, LNCS 13311, pp. 199–216, 2022.
https://doi.org/10.1007/978-3-031-06038-0_15

emphasize the technical performances that support them, while neglecting to recognize their social dimensions (which are often more difficult to represent graphically). These "ambitious" design theories have limited integration with evolving social science theories [6]. For example, common approaches to systemic design, such as the System Map, typically focus on a framed context, identifying the various components in an overgeneralized way, such as roles, materials, information, functions, and the relationships among them in a certain context, disregarding the difficult-to-represent intangible social "structure" and "agency". "Structure" and "agency" are complementary forces that modern social theorists see as the driver of human behavior and relationships within the social system [7]. They influence the thinking and actions of design practitioners who are embedded within them as well. Thinking systemically from outside the system makes it easy for design practitioners to forget that they themselves should be embedded in the social structures and social systems they want to change.

The ensuing reality is a departure from the original intent of design practitioners as catalysts for social change. Even if some designers claim that they do social design, they tend to do "good" things in a privileged way [8]. Most participatory design is still substantially controlled by power or professionals [9]. Some design practitioners applied the design "Schema", which operated in producing physical artifacts, to the context of society. The prevalence of consultative perspective makes the direct dualism between thinking and acting increasingly apparent, and this separation is also reflected in designers' preference to produce a work - a metaphor for a subjectively created final product. It is still rooted in the positivist tradition of separating the subject from the object as a "cybernetic execution" [9].

How does this new perspective on the relation between the design subject and the design object lead to changes in specific design actions? This study adopts the constructivist grounded theory in qualitative research to demonstrate that community building constituted social innovation as a design approach, where actors see themselves as part of the complex socio-technical systems and have an awareness of reflexivity. In other words, actors, notably design actors engage in prototypes to make meaning in dialogic interaction beyond the existing commonplace in their everyday life actions.

2 Theoretical Background

Social theory and sociological research methods argue that in contemporary society, the boundaries between the researcher and the object of inquiry have blurred and are no longer as distinct as they once were [10]. The relational and reflexive nature of this context is being explored by some design researchers. The concept of reflexivity also shows that the so-called "society" is in fact an ongoing process of social construction, never a fixed objective entity that is completely unrelated to the individual.

2.1 Reflexivity in Design

By reflecting on the difficulties that Design Thinking encounters in taking substantial action, Kimbell [11] proposes two processes of design based on practice theory: "design as practice" and "practice in design." She argued that practices are actions that, people take in their interactions with others and things, and these interactions are often embodied, mundane, and contextualized [12–15].

Feminist-inspired technological visions and related discussions in anthropology have laid the groundwork for discussions of the reflexivity of design, and design practice has begun to engage in a series of "reflexive" reflections on "alternative perspectives, agency, and how, by whom, and under what conditions knowledge is produced" [16]. The design subject is asked to "position" his or her identity and analyze "the boundaries between technological production and internal use" [17]. The design subject needs to recognize "the invisible work that constitutes the production and use of technological systems, to embed itself in interlinked networks", and to "take responsibility for our participation" [17].

Anthropological research on the relationship between researcher and research participant also provides an integrative perspective on the role and relationship in which the designer is placed [16, 18–20]. Suvi Pihkala and Helena Karasti [21] build on this by proposing a multiple and reflexive perspective of the "designer-researcher" in participatory design, in which the design subject is embedded in a multiplicity of participation in a generative way. In their participatory study of a participatory design process for a "social media" product, they identified four kinds of reflexive interventions based on the subtle interactions that occurred during the process: 1) negotiating designer-researcher position; 2) blurring the central design subject; 3) presenting a common sense of belonging to the issue; 4) Forming network through continuous "mundane" interaction.

2.2 Relational Design

Reviewing the social constructionist terms, Kenneth J. Gergen reveals the importance of relational processes. He states, all meaning is derived from coordination or joint action; relationships do not occur between individuals; the capabilities of individuals emerge within relationships [22]. In Mapping Dialogue, the authors distinguish between dialogue and other forms of conversation as the only and indispensable resource for social development and change [23].

In designers discourse, Fuad-Luke has provided a preliminary definition of "relational design" and proposed the concept of complementary relational designers, including designers and non-designers [24]. Accordingly, in the subsequent analysis, terms as design actors or actors will be used in response to "everyone's potential contribution to reforming the political [24]." Kong believed that working within the community and moving relationally between making and action will dispel the narrowly portrayed perception of the designer as a celebrity [25]. Skou and Mikkelsen argued that despite the contradiction between the linear structures design methods and the unpredictability and ambiguity of relationships, the design still has the ability to facilitate the presentation of new relationships [26]. Lou proposed that sustainable social interaction design can drive society toward a sustainable future lifestyle through choice-based communities [3, 27].

2.3 The Ambiguity of Community Building

The concept of community ("社区" in Chinese) was introduced in China from America in the 1930s, when R.E. Park, a representative scholar of the Chicago school of urban human ecology research, viewed community as "1) a group of people organized regionally; 2) who are rooted, to varying degrees, in the territory they inhabit; and 3) who live in a variety of dependencies." This definition emphasizing the three factors of territory, common ties, and social interaction influenced American sociologycs understanding of "community" and decisively influenced the Chinese translation. In mainland China, "community" is an administrative unit. It means an autonomous organization of residents under a certain sub-district. Therefore, the Chinese context's concept of "community" is more interchangeable with "neighborhood." Under this definition, community building ("社区营造" in Chinese) also have emphasized the regional characteristics, so the concept of "community building" in China is often superimposed or interchanged with "urban renewal," "rural revitalization," and "placemaking."

However, with the development of modern communication technology and mass communication means, the rise of Internet communities has given people a more dimensional understanding of the meaning of the word "community". People engaged in "Internet product operations" prefer to think that communities do not have regional attributes, and the concept of online communities as communities of interest is not considered to have geographical attributes; such entity communities or virtual communities can be "groups formed by knowing each other to some extent, sharing some degree of knowledge and information, and caring for each other to a considerable extent as if they were friends" [28].

When the subject of design action realizes that he or she is inseparable from the community, he or she incorporates the perspective of reflexivity in the design action. As actors become aware that they are in the communities they have constructed, their actions will change their relations to the communities and change them simultaneously. The specific way of action taken by the design actors will first deal with the relations between the actors themselves and the specific communities. Moreover this identity embedded in the relationship with the designed object (i.e., the community) is a metaphor of social-self recognized by design actors, which is also the socialization of the design actors.

3 Methods and Data Analysis

This paper adopts the constructivist grounded theory in qualitative research and selects the research subjects through purposive and theoretical sampling. As action researchers with similar practice experiences, we invited 20 design actors from Mainland China to conduct in-depth personal interviews and invite them to share their practice experiences and to conduct dialogues on related issues. All the interviews were recorded and transcribed into verbatim transcripts. The author's participant observation notes and process data from the community-based social innovation case study were also used to construct the scope. The analysis process follows the initial coding, focused coding, theoretical coding, and constant comparison methods of constructist grounded theory to construct the relationship between the categories and the inter-categories and arrive at the core categories that unify the whole picture.

3.1 Methods Positioning

Grounded theory is a systematic approach to qualitative research that constructs theories through strategies based on inductive analysis and continuous comparison of qualitative data [29]. Constructivist grounded theory [30] assumes a relativist epistemology based on these analytic strategies. This strategy acknowledges the multiple positions, roles, and real-world contexts that the researcher and research participants (i.e., the social innovation practitioners interviewed in this study) possess. It also requires the researcher to take a reflexive stance about his or her own background, values, actions, situations, and relationships with the research participants concerning their representations. At the same time the researcher needs to situate the research in the historical, social, and situational conditions in which it is produced [31].

Practice-oriented researchers argue that, "the inclusion of practice in the research process or as a research outcome helps to integrate and communicate those kinds or parts of knowledge that cannot easily be made explicit" [32, 33]. Our interaction with other practitioners as peers was able to unlock more credible data, and interpretations based on our own practical experience (reflecting on our own tacit knowledge) were able to uncover deeper meanings of their narratives. In addition, as design is typically a practice-led discipline, it is compulsory to recover the relationship between theory and practice [34]. The experiences of ongoing social innovation practitioners are more likely to be revealed by design researchers with similar experiences, and since we ourselves need the theory extracted from these experiences to guide the practice of our project, we will give more considerations to the interface between theory and practice.

Our team, composed of practitioners-researchers of community-based social innovation, has created a social context for the objects we are constructing and the practitioners we are working with or, to some extent, in competition with. We are constantly comparing ourselves with other practitioners, respecting each other's ways of action and positions, and asking questions about the case referred to different stages of the reality. In the contrast, these relationships that we cannot set aside guide us in using constructivist grounding theory, viewing both data and analysis as coming from shared experiences and relationships with other practitioners [35].

3.2 Sampling

During the sampling phase, the ambiguity of "community building" gave us a new perspective. We relied on the evidence that "the social innovation project involves the creation of a community or their practice involving some form of 'community'" as the criterion for selection. We used the snowball sampling approach to find cases, where we first contacted some of the actors whom we could identify as some similar cases. We identified a small number of cases, and asked them to recommend additional practitioners they considered to be actors involved in community building.

As a result, interviewees perceived different notions of "community" that they encounter. On the one hand, it reflects the semantic trends of community making in mainland China, and on the other hand, it provides us with a more flexible perspective when understanding the relationship between community and actors.

A total of 20 practitioners were interviewed in this study. 12 of the 20 practitioners have practiced in multiple social innovation projects. All 20 practitioners are highly educated, with 12 having majored in design or art, three having studied sociology, anthropology, education, and other similar disciplines, three having majored in literature and languages, one having a business background, and one having majored in computer science. The social contexts of these cases involved four first-tier cities, three second-tier cities, one county-level city, and four villages and towns in mainland China.

3.3 Interview Outline

We conducted semi-structured interviews with the interviewees (Table 1). In the design of the general interview outline, we focused on the following issues: 1) the motivation of the actors to engage in community building; 2) the specific actions that the actors took in the process of community building and the difficulties they encountered; 3) how the actors understood themselves and other stakeholders, their identity and role position as identified by the actors, and whether this role position changed in the course of the action; 4) the actors' understanding of community building and what they consider to be the competencies of the actors who engage in community building.

Table 1. The general interview outlines

Semi-structured interview questions *The interview should summarize the answer from public media, and ask additional questions if the information is not included or related to our research goal.*
• Can you briefly talk about your practice experience? • Apart from the current practice, do you have any other previous practice? Did your previous practice have any influence on your subsequent practice related to community building? • What was the opportunity for you to start a community-building-related practice? • What are some of your primary responsibilities in general? • What do you think is your role in community building practice? • What do you think are the characteristics of the community you are working on? • What problems did you encounter? (How did you solve them?)

3.4 Analysis Process

Firstly, in the initial interviews and data analysis, the ambiguity of the term "community building" became apparent. Due to the open-ended nature of the sample selection, we encountered responses like: "*Actually, at the beginning, we did not know whether it*

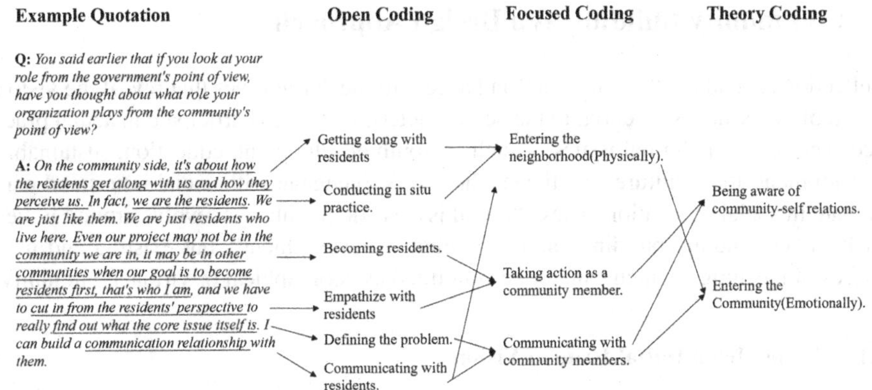

Fig. 1. An example of coding.

was called community or what it was called (P11)", "*In fact, we are not purely doing community building* (P03)."

At the open coding stage, we discussed whether "community building" was the aim of action, but we did not go further into the idea itself. We focused on the specific types of difficulties encountered, the reasons for the difficulties, the correlation between the reasons and the educational background of the interviewees. We also analyzed the way in which the actions were carried out and the corresponding results as perceived by the actors (See Fig. 1).

During the focused coding phase, we developed the code "entering the community". At first, we thought of this concept of the integration of outsiders into local communities. The actors indicated that "*we move to the neighborhood [where we conducting community building] and we want to become them[residents in the neighborhood]* (P14)." This formulation suggests that the actors perceive community as a more concrete concept, with geographical boundaries. Meanwhile, we noticed that the interviewees said "*to become them*", which we think indicates that the actors consider entering the neighborhood as a symbol of entering the community.

As practitioners-researchers, we simultaneously reflect on our own practice situation. Since in our practice, individual actors or small groups usually form a temporary project team with our core team. This contingent group will work together on a project, so we would tend to think of us as both the enabling organization and an organization shaped by these individual actors and small groups, and these other participants also make up the informal members of our organization, in other words, together we form an informal organization, a new community. We are embedded in the community we construct.

Therefore, in theory coding, we further refined the perspectives within and outside the community, as well as the relationship between specific manners of actions and perspectives. And the key concepts were discovered to form the final code.

4 Community Building as a Design Approach

Reflection around the "initial issue" and access to the "prototypes that reveal the vision ahead of the issue" is essential to the actors' determination to participate in actual practice. The focus on "initial issues" - such as youth development, education, sustainable development, local culture - motivates the actors to engage with social issues and participate in social innovation. These "initial issues" do not always revolve around issues such as "community building" and "community development", but existing and new spaces of meaning[1], which can not be simplified as geographical or virtual community.

4.1 Moving from Initial Issue to Vision

When discussing why they wanted to start acting around the initial issue, several actors described the visions around the initial issue they had been exposed to (Fig. 2).

Among them, several were indirectly aware of the prototype project focused on the initial issue: "*Our teacher at school introduced us to [a prototype], and I was influenced to start focusing on it [that issue]* (P07)." "*I felt that I agreed with [the vision around the original issue] that he described* (P01)." Some actors who had directly experienced the prototype project and formed a vision for action "*I was in [a certain area or scene] when there was [a certain prototype] there, and they did so with the purpose of [a vision around the initial issue], which I found interesting* (P09)." After having carried out some practical actions around the initial issue, some actors further developed a vision involving community building according to other prototypes: "*When I knew [a prototype], I thought what I wanted to do was community building* (P02).", "*We started out just wanting to do [a vision around the initial issue], but after we talked to the people involved in [a prototype],*" they felt that "*We also have some similarities with community building* (P08).", P14 realizes that community is a context for realizing the vision that arises around social issues, he said: "*At the beginning, I was very focused on [the initial*

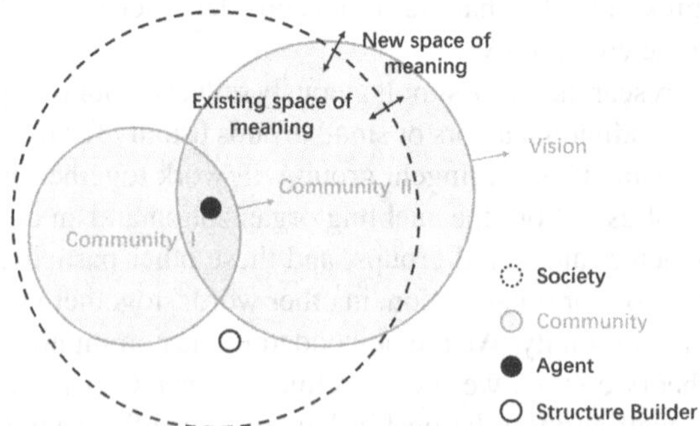

Fig. 2. The duality perspective in society-self and community-self relations (Illustrated by the authors).

[1] We recognized that these "meanings" formed a territory of, an area of knowledge, activity, or experience, we call them "meaning of space" or "meaning space".

issue] [...] Then the big social problems, the big social issues, were slowly and gradually narrowed down to the community context."

The existence of an ongoing social innovation prototype is part of the reason why they are still willing to take actions: "*I see that my partner who was working on [a prototype] project with me is still going strong, and I get touched* (P05).", "*[I have seen] some of the different cases around the world, [learn]some of the experiences from others, [I think we] can do this kind of 'on-the-ground' execution as well* (P03)." The discussion about the prototype will continue at 5.1.

4.2 Reflecting on Society-Self and Community-Self Relations

The actor engages in identity construction in two spaces of meaning - referring to society and community [36] - in search of an explanation for the social innovation practices he engages in. What the actors consider themselves for the community becomes a key distinction in how these actors act.

Reflecting on Social-Self Relation. When reflecting on motivation, some actors tend to explain social behavior in terms of "interests driven by rationality (value rationality or purposive rationality)," this reflexivity emphasizes the actor's self in "society."

This segment of actors cites the highly generalized social identity represented by the professional division of labor as an important reason for their actions. They tend to explain their "interventions" using a discourse of "previous personal experiences", including educational backgrounds and professional project experiences. Actors who have majored in education use the term "*teaching aids*" when defining empowerment tools. And those in the media industry considered that they were taking further action based on "*editorial*". There are also actors who tend to state directly how this way of acting is related to their professions. The social identity that comes with the profession is constrained the way of action, "*Because we are [a certain profession], we will [...]* (P19).", "*I probably realized more of a combination of my profession throughout the process of doing operations* (P09)", "*I myself am [professional].... We just go to that village and do research and help them [with specific actions]* (P11)."

Rather than explaining their motivation by a highly generalized social identity, some actors tend to reflect on the relationship between society and the self or their former social identity, "*I was reflecting on the relationship between the whole industry I'm in and myself* (P13)", "*Maybe I started to think about the relationship between these works and the space it's in and the small social relationship it's in* (P06).", "*I don't want to do the same [professional] work anymore [...] I felt that this is problematic for my life, and that such a life is meaningless*(P20).", "*I think it's more in the context of the rapid pace of work and [...] [participate in social innovation project] is more humanism* (P09)."

Actors reflecting social-self can define themselves or their team's way of acting as a third party, considering themselves as one type of stakeholder among society. They are acting in the social innovation as a neutral actor outside the community (whether they define it as a spiritual community or a geo-community). "*We intervene in a very fair and objective way to build a bridge between the different groups* (P07)", when the actors, who pre-define themselves as "professionals", and reveal their "individual capacity to take action". When confronted with the "complexity of reality," some practitioners return to the "planning" aspect of the work without consideration of practical execution. Moreover, in order to gain more support in the longer term, the actors need to interpret their actions in a discourse that is more easily recognized by capital or foundations.

Reflecting on Community-Self Relation. Another group of actors recognized the limitations of the predetermined role of the intervention. They reflect on their identity in the community and look forward to becoming insiders. When actors explained their motivation using the terms of "sense of belonging, common relations and participation" [36, 37], this reflexivity emphasizes the actor's self in "community".

In reflecting on the causes of the difficulties in practice, actors addressed their identity to the community. Actors think it may be since they are still outsiders: "*Although we started out there [...] it was bottom-up, but we were still an outsider* (P11)", "*At that time, our role was a bit like an invader* (P07)", "*Actually at first, we thought that we were good at this kind of thing, we should have no problem going to the community to do something... However, it's the process that you found your user group different [...] your youth identity is also different [from people in the community], [and therefore encountered difficulties]* (P14)."

At this point, actors often generate the concept of "moving from being outsiders to insiders in the community," seeing themselves as part of the community and adopting the reflexive perspective of the systemic self. They felt that "*we are really growing and learning in the community in this process* (P14)" and "*felt being nurtured* (P19)".

Some of the actors felt that a better way to carry out their actions was connecting with the community members: "*It only makes sense when you really make that connection with the people in the community* (P07)", "*some of the initiators of our [practice project] are residents of the community, they live in it [...] we can make some artistic production within the community together* (P04)", "*My colleague who is rooted in the community [...] get closer to the residents* (P18)." It takes a long time to become an insider, like P03 said "*we would [take specific actions] to get into the community [...] We may live in that place for two or three months... And then the locals will treat us like friends*" During the interviews, actors emphasize a strong emotional connection with the community.

Actors see their role as an instrument to build more relationships within the community, "*like what we've been doing is some exploration of the relationship between the city [which this actor sees as a community] and the youth [the group actor sees himself or herself in]* (P08)", they think they provide the opportunities for the new relationships in community: "*organizing activities where people can get to know each other and some of them [build new relationships]* (P11)". Some of the actors recognized that generating more new relationships can lead to the creation of a "spiritual community", like P9 demonstrated, "*[...] it can promote a [change in] community relationships, like cohesive consensus and so on [...]*". Although the concept of community was initially identified differently by different actors (neighborhood, social groups, or spiritual communities), the concept of community being coalesced was identified by the actors as the concept of spiritual community.

For actors who can be aware of community-self relation, the reflection of society-self and community-self is constantly shifted in the process of social innovation practice, in other words, the actor will be thinking as an agent within the community on the one hand, and looking at the whole system from the perspective of a structure builder outside the community on the other. P05 mentioned the dual perspectives in metaphor: "*I can say that I am both a designer and a player*", and P19 described her experience in detailed, "*[…] I was working 'on the front line' […] you get access to the residents, to the store keeper […] The project is gradually developing […] My role became more of a coordinator and an organizer of the structure […] To develop the overall layout of the large scale project, like the three-year plan[…] is a little bit higher [than before] […] So for me personally, I usually make up for my lack of 'front-line practice' by participating in small activities on my own […]*".

5 Designers Act as Insiders in Community

The study revealed the cause of actors' awareness of "entering the community", and identified essential processes in the designerly way of action in community building. We identify how the "agency"- internal constructive perspective, and the "structure"-external consultative perspective are reflected in action in three phases.

5.1 Dialogic Interaction

Social constructivist scholars' concept of "dialogue" inspires designing ways of acting into complex socio-technical systems. Dialogue refers to social action in which a certain number of participants work together to create meaning and relevance [22, 23].

Some actors interpret their actions in terms of "research" and "understanding needs" - interacting dialogically with the community, reaching new understandings, and in the process discovering a common ground of meaning and a basis for further thinking and action [38]. "*[…] We spend a long time […] uncover those precious things, and that accompanies them in their ongoing transformation* (P03)", "*We actually inspire each other [with the community residents]* (P04)", "*I am actually looking at who [referring to individuals in the community] have the potential to be my partners in the future, and then the next thing you do is start talking, communicating […] and we are going to do the companionship*(P17)." When expressing the reasons for the difficulties in action, "*[…] we don't know how to talk to the residents*" and "*it is hard to communicate with the residents*" emerged as a common difficulty. Therefore, among the key competencies of the actors, "*communication*" and "*Interacting with people*" were mentioned frequently, and being able to interact with members of the community in a dialogic way became a reason for the actors to appreciate other actors: "*They are amazing…. They [the interviewees considered good actors] were able to capture a lot of interesting things about the residents. Then he took it in some imaginative way and connected it to the site […]* (P11)."

Since neither party can create meaning alone, a shared understanding of meaning emerges gradually from the dialogue [39]. The actor realizes that the meaning he creates does not aim to persuade but to offer a possibility: "*[For the vision expressed in such an art project] I cannot ask everyone to have a deep understanding […]* (P04)."

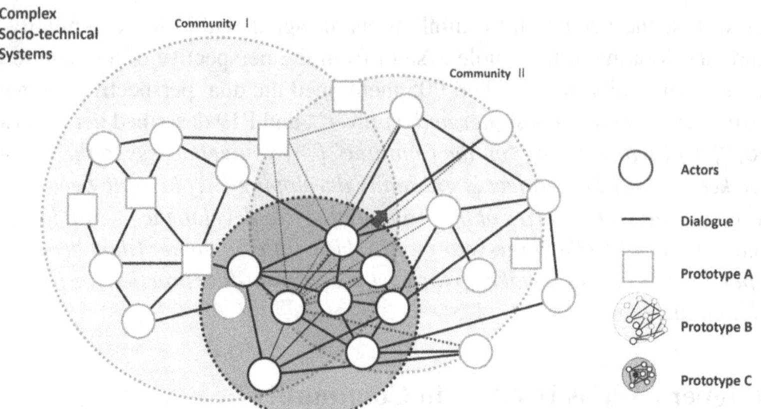

Fig. 3. Designers act as insiders in communities (illustrated by the authors).

5.2 Prototyping to Clarify the Meaning

Prototypes are part of dialogic interactions and the result of interactions, prototypes can bring "superordinate goals" to the confrontational conversations and help people experiencing the vision, even if there are many possibilities for further iterations of these prototypes. At the same time, prototypes build the environment for the actors to act (see Fig. 3). Prototypes that are closely connected to everyday life are a key concept in the process of building communities. Prototyping is also an important designer-like capability that has evolved from traditional design practices.

Prototyping in Dialogic Interaction. Prototypes are part of and a result of dialogic interaction. In the actor's practice, prototypes can make invisible meanings visible, provide inspiration to both sides of the dialogue, and confirm or reject these proposed ideas based on both sides' experiences [40]. At the same time, prototypes become the basis for shared understanding of meaning in dialogue, "helping to develop understanding about the essence or essential factors of an existing experience, enabling others to engage directly in a proposed new experience it provides a common ground for establishing a shared point of view" [40]. In the practice of social innovation, if the objects of design are viewed in the perspective of the four orders of design (the four orders), "media content", "co-creation activities", "workshops", "place making", "autonomous organization" are prototypes that are in accordance with the above concepts.

The actors first saw the prototype as possessing a certain symbolic value, representing the achievement of the actions. "*This community garden is there as a space, a proof of community co-creation, unlike some of the activities I did before, which were done [without physical outcome]* (P17)". Prototype is also a manifestation of attracting more participants, like P01 said "*[the co-creation activities] made things happen and for others to see and come.*" Some actors can further realize that the prototype becomes the basis for subsequent actions to unfold, "*it [referring to some projects and outcomes] has the potential to stay in this community and do the construction of new services and mechanisms* (P14)."

The ability of the prototype to allow the actors in the dialogue to see more possibilities is key to the action being sustainable, "*[referring to the project of doing] [...] There are more fun, more interesting ideas* (P07)." The prototype can carry meanings that are always in flux. The constant clarification of meaning through the prototype provides more possibilities for the next conversation [39] "*The process is in flow, in change, in debugging* (P02)." And designerly way of thinking can embrace this ambiguity and construct new communities in clarification and understanding.

This process often requires additional communication efforts over time, so practitioners of relational design often need the help of government, companies or educational infrastructures to hire them as social organizations, corporate public relations, or researchers, at the first steps until a sustainable operating mechanism is explored. These influences can transform relational design back to a short-term movement or project, becoming a "cost of trial and error," failing "socialization of design."

Prototyping in Everyday Life. The prototype builds the scene for the actor, combined with the interpretation of the action scene in the ethnomethodology, the prototype is the component of the action, and it is also the external environment for the action after a common understanding. The scene itself is a part of the action and also meanwhile the result of the action [27, 41].

Everyday life is a crucial action scene that connects the two spaces of meaning: society and community. The concepts of "generator of everyday events" and "condensed social scenes", as identified by the actors, point to "everyday actions" that are closer to the world of life. Therefore, when it comes to dialogue and creating meaning with residents, prototypes that are close to everyday life play a vital role "*[...] Through programs such as the Museum of Community story [....] [we can] get closer to this resident* (P18)." "*[...] How to develop individual self-drive in our existential scenario* (P05)", "*[...] And I think the concept of community is a living space [...] S focus more on the people who live in it [...]* (P08)". The actors believe that these 'close to life' prototypes can be further transformed in the community to "*meet or create the everyday life of the community* (P14)" and "*enable people to participate in life of the city* (P02)", actors indicated that "*[Social innovation practices] that involve community residents are very much a part of everyday life* (P02)."

Not only do prototype plays an important role in internal community action, but actors need to explain the function of prototype and the rules of action in external space of meaning - the actors communicate with different stakeholders in society from the perspective of a "structure builder". "Everyday life" also becomes a mediator of meaning connected to the whole community.

5.3 Constructing Roles

The delimitation of decision-making authority and role-building within the community are the products of the structure builder perspective. In continuous interaction, new common meanings are created and embodied in the prototype. The new prototypes change the role of actors in the community. The changes in roles bring about new communities. With this comes a change in meaning, and new interactions occur again.

Among them, the change of roles needs to be coordinated from a perspective outside the community. The actors, in this case, take structure-builder perspective and collaborate to initiate a collective reinvention as a "game-changer".

A few actors were able to describe the process in its entirety. P14 shared the Mother's Kitchen[2] project with us: "*[The project]to be a fun community activity, and the cost of participation was low [...]by the end of the whole project, a community of 'mothers' was created.*" In this project, the actors decentralized their authority, not defining their own behavior in a professional capacity, but creating new common meanings by defining their own roles and coordinating the relationship between other roles inside and outside the community: "*Three groups were formed among this community of 'mothers,' one group is self-employed, who open their own stores; the second group is specifically enabled to interpret the whole model of this project to the policymakers, and they have been executed the project for three years. There is also a group of mothers who have been involved in our everyday life activities for a long time. They have the ability to start a business, but they are willing to share their cooking experiences, so they have gradually built a very solid new community in this community.*" The actor establishes a new relationship in the community through a prototype in which he coordinates the different actors and their actions, resulting in the construction of the new community. In the ongoing construction of the new community, based on the common meaning basis, the dialogue continues: "*We are in the middle of a three-year process of continuous communication[...].*" The new project also clarifies the meaning of the prototype: "*A lot of new community services have been invented in the community, such as providing lunch to companies [in the neighborhood], providing cooking services to companies,*" and thus the identity of these participants is connected from the space of social meaning to the space of community meaning: "*The community was built from this group of 'mothers.*"

6 Conclusion

In conclusion, we suggest that design actors engaged in social innovation practices are often confronted with two spaces of meaning, the default space of meaning in civil society, and the meaning making by niches in relationships and coalesced in new space of meaning in communities. Actors need to create prototypes in the default meaning space and meanwhile bring new space of meaning. The prototypes can not only be approbated by the larger socio-technical system, but also present visions. At the same time, these prototype needs to be understood by the community that is coalescing and facilities the dialogic interaction. The prototype is also the basis on which a new meaning space will be constructed. And the new meaning space will, in turn, bring about a new dialogue medium that needs to be understood by actors in the community.

Therefore, the individual actor does not only need to be aware of the influence of society-self in the process, but also need to recognize the new community-self at any time. For the community being constructed, the position of the design actor needs to jump between the "agent" inside and the "structure builder" outside all the time.

[2] A program that allows retired women who come to live with their children in the metropolis to serve meals to commuters in their neighborhoods in their free time.

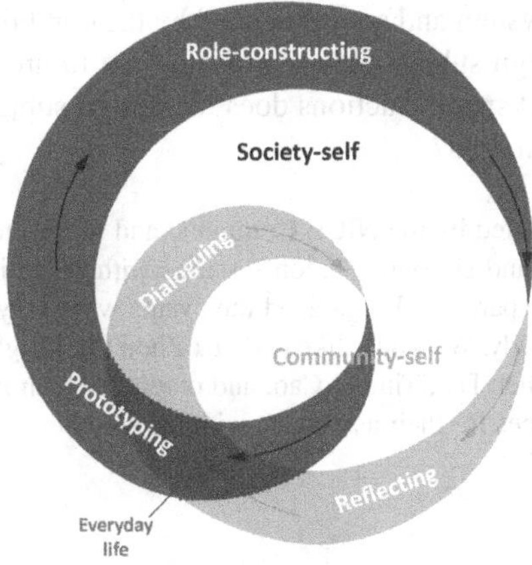

Fig. 4. A loop of designerly way of community building (Illustrated by the authors).

In these two meaning spaces, the design actor starts from an external perspective and reflects on the society-self in everyday life as a starting point. After realizing the identity in community-self, he or she enters the community and acts in a dialogic interaction in the community, clarifying the meaning in the dialog dynamically through the prototype. In this process, through the touchpoints from daily life, the design actor returns to the external perspective for coordinating the roles in continuous action. A loop of reflecting, dialoguing, prototyping, role-constructing is formed.

7 Discussion and Future Work

The context of this study is placed in the informal social structure of self-organized communities and networks, and the subject of the study is studied in a multicultural context and design situation to enrich the object and perspective of design research in the interdisciplinary field of sociology and design.

However, the constructivist grounded theory approach, which uses the researcher as a research tool, poses a high challenge to the researcher's competence. It requires the researcher to continuously reflect and remain sensitive to the theory. The lack of qualitative research experience leads to a certain degree of inaccuracy in the discourse analysis, and there are limitations in bringing in the perspective of the study with one's own practical experience.

We argue that research in design theory and practice needs to be integrated with evolving social science theories if it is to design the social systems in which it is embedded, and should enter the ongoing debates on "agency" and "structure" [7], in addition to a deeper understanding of sociological theoretical discussions of lifeworld and systems [42].

Further research will build on this study by conducting action research that continues to explore the following questions: How is the design subject's access to the situation of the design object validated by the design object when the design object of design practice is our own everyday life situations and organizations? How do the design subject's decisions influence the system and are influenced by the conditions of the system in the present? How is the design subject able to envision the future of the whole system in the present system? What specific actions does the design subject take in the system to drive the whole transformation?

Acknowledgement. Supported by the NICE Commune and the Sketch Action, this study conducted detailed interviews and six online salon sessions with practitioners in mainland China. The team members who prepared and organized the events were very helpful in collecting and analyzing the data for the study. We would like to thank Zhou Lu, Bingling Huang, Yichen Meng, Bohui Cai, Haoyu Du, Jiachen Dai, Tinglei Cao, and others for their contributions to this study. We also thank all interviewees for their assistance with the study.

References

1. Markussen, T.: The disruptive aesthetics of design activism: enacting design between art and politics. Des. Issues **29**, 38–50 (2013). https://doi.org/10.1162/DESI_a_00195
2. Brown, T.: Design Thinking. Harvard business review **86**, 84 (2008)
3. Lou, Y.: Designing interactions to counter threats to human survival. She Ji: J. Des. Econ. Innov. **4**, 342–354 (2018). https://doi.org/10.1016/j.sheji.2018.10.001
4. Norman, D.A., Stappers, P.J.: DesignX: complex sociotechnical systems. She Ji: J. Des. Econ. Innov. **1**, 83–106 (2015). https://doi.org/10.1016/j.sheji.2016.01.002
5. Buchanan, R.: Systems thinking and design thinking: the search for principles in the world we are making. She Ji: J. Des. Econ. Innov. **5**, 85–104 (2019). https://doi.org/10.1016/j.sheji.2019.04.001
6. Vink, J., Wetter-Edman, K., Koskela-Huotari, K.: Designerly approaches for catalyzing change in social systems: a social structures approach. She Ji: J. Des. Econ. Innov. **7**, 242–261 (2021). https://doi.org/10.1016/j.sheji.2020.12.004
7. Giddens, A., Griffiths, S.: Sociology. Polity Press, Cambridge (2008)
8. Abdulla, D.: A Manifesto of Change or Design Imperialism? A Look at the Purpose of the Social Design Practice. In: A Matter of Design: Making Society through Science and Technology. STS Italia Publishing (2014)
9. von Busch, O., Palmås, K.: Social means do not justify corruptible ends: a realist perspective of social innovation and design. She Ji: J. Des. Econ. Innov. **2**, 275–287 (2016). https://doi.org/10.1016/j.sheji.2017.07.002
10. Giddens, A., Sutton, P.W.: Essential Concepts in Sociology. Wiley, New York (2021)
11. Kimbell, L.: Rethinking design thinking: Part II. Des. Cult. **4**, 129–148 (2012). https://doi.org/10.2752/175470812X13281948975413
12. Reckwitz, A.: Toward a theory of social practices: a development in culturalist theorizing. Eur. J. Soc. Theory **5**, 243–263 (2002). https://doi.org/10.1177/13684310222225432
13. Schatzki, T.R., Knorr-Cetina, K., von Savigny, E.: The Practice Turn in Contemporary Theory. Routledge, London (2001)
14. Bourdieu, P.: The Logic of Practice. Stanford University Press, Stanford (1990)
15. Giddens, A.: The Constitution of Society: Outline of the Theory of Structuration. University of California Press, Berkeley (1984)
16. Stuedahl, D., Wagner, I., Bratteteig, T. (eds.): Exploring Digital Design: Multi-Disciplinary Design Practices. Springer, London (2010). https://doi.org/10.1007/978-1-84996-223-0
17. Suchman, L.: Located accountabilities in technology production. Scand. J. Inf. Syst. **14**, 7 (2002)

18. Blomberg, D.J., Karasti, H.: Ethnography: positioning ethnography within Participatory Design. In: Routledge International Handbook of Participatory Design. Routledge (2013)
19. Johnson, R., Rogers, Y., van der Linden, J., Bianchi-Berthouze, N.: Being in the thick of in-the-wild studies: the challenges and insights of researcher participation. In: Proceedings of the SIGCHI Conference on Human Factors in Computing Systems, New York, NY, USA pp. 1135–1144. Association for Computing Machinery (2012). https://doi.org/10.1145/2207676.2208561
20. Karasti, H.: Participant Interventionist. Researcher role integrating ethnography and participatory design. In: The 3rd Qualitative Research Conference: Developing Research Practices, June 1–3, pp. 1–12 (2010)
21. Pihkala, S., Karasti, H.: Reflexive engagement: enacting reflexivity in design and for "participation in plural. In: Proceedings of the 14th Participatory Design Conference: Full papers - Volume 1. pp. 21–30, New York, NY, USA. Association for Computing Machinery (2016). https://doi.org/10.1145/2940299.2940302
22. Gergen, K.J.: Relational Being: Beyond Self and Community. Oxford University Press, Oxford; New York (2009)
23. Bojer, M.M. (ed.): Mapping Dialogue: Essential Tools for Social Change. Taos Institute Publications, Chagrin Falls, Ohio (2008)
24. Fuad-Luke, A.: Design(-ing) for radical relationality: 'relational design' for confronting dangerous, concurrent, contingent realities. In: Ma, J., Lou, Y. (eds.) Emerging Practices in Design. Professions, Values and Approaches, pp. 42–73 (2014)
25. Kong, T.: Between making and action: ideas for a relational design pedagogy. In: Ma, J., Lou, Y. (eds.) Emerging Practices in Design. Professions, Values and Approaches, pp. 74–93 (2014)
26. Skou, N.P., Mikkelsen, M.: Can relations be designed?: The role of design methods in social innovation. In: Jin, M., Yongqi, L. (eds.) Emerging Practices in Design, pp. 94–111. China Architecture and Building Press, Beijing (2014)
27. Lou, Y., Ma, J.: Growing a community-supported ecosystem of future living: the case of NICE2035 living line. In: Rau, P.-L. (ed.) CCD 2018. LNCS, vol. 10912, pp. 320–333. Springer, Cham (2018). https://doi.org/10.1007/978-3-319-92252-2_26
28. Rheingold, H.: The Virtual Community, revised edition: Homesteading on the Electronic Frontier. MIT Press, Cambridge (2000)
29. Glaser, B.G., Strauss, A.L.: The Discovery of Grounded Theory: Strategies for Qualitative Research. Aldine (1967)
30. Charmaz, K.: Constructing Grounded Theory. SAGE (2014)
31. Charmaz, K.: Constructivist grounded theory. J. Posit. Psychol. **12**, 299–300 (2017). https://doi.org/10.1080/17439760.2016.1262612
32. Niedderer, K., Reilly, L.: research practice in art and design: experiential knowledge and organised inquiry. J. Res. Pract. **6**, E2–E2 (2010)
33. Ma, J.: A phenomenological inquiry into the experience of "having a design concept" (2013)
34. Schön, D.A.: The Reflective Practitioner: How Professionals Think in Action. Basic Books, New York (1983)
35. Charmaz, K.: Constructing Grounded Theory: A Practical Guide through Qualitative Analysis. SAGE, London (2006)
36. Tonnies, F., Loomis, C.P.: Community and Society. Courier Corporation, Devon (2002)
37. Weber, M.: Basic Concepts in Sociology. Citadel Press, New York (1962)
38. Isaacs, W.: Dialogue and the Art of Thinking Together: A Pioneering Approach to Communicating in Business and in Life. Currency (1999)
39. Gergen, K.J., Gergen, P.K.J.: An Invitation to Social Construction. SAGE, London (1999)

40. Buchenau, M., Suri, J.F.: Experience prototyping. In: Proceedings of the 3rd Conference on Designing Interactive Systems: Processes, Practices, Methods, and Techniques, New York, NY, USA pp. 424–433. Association for Computing Machinery (2000). https://doi.org/10.1145/347642.347802
41. Zimmerman, D.H., Pollner, M., Douglas, J.D.: The everyday world as a phenomenon. (1970)
42. Habermas, J.: The Theory of Communicative Action: Lifeworld and Systems, a Critique of Functionalist Reason, Volume 2. Wiley, Chichester (2015)

The Potential of Rural Resources in Meeting Local Needs Through Participatory Design Interventions

Bingbing Jiang(✉) and Kunwu Xu

Hunan University, Changsha, Hunan, China
281368061@qq.com

Abstract. Using the example of Longtai Village in Hunan Province, China, this paper attempts to explore the potential of rural resources to meet local needs through participatory design interventions, thereby empowering villages and creating more social value. The authors focused on fieldworks and interviews to obtain specific information about local resources and needs. Then, after comparison and analysis, bamboo resources and bamboo crafts were selected as the rural resources for this study to meet the actual needs of local elementary school. The paper details the conduct of the study and analyzes the experiences and methods of the participatory design intervention. Finally, the authors summarized the paradigm of using rural resources to meet local needs through participatory design interventions. In addition, the authors pointed out the limitations of this paper and made assumptions about future research plans.

Keywords: Rural resources · Local needs · Participatory design · Bamboo handicrafts · Elementary school

1 Background

1.1 Theoretical Framework

Under the current trend of economic globalization and rapid urbanization, both developed and developing countries are vigorously promoting urban expansion in order to advance the rapid increase of national economic development level. However, with the rapid development of cities, the problem of rural decline has become more and more serious. This has been accompanied by the hollowing out of the countryside, the dispersion of the countryside, the expansion of the rural age structure, and the sharp increase in the number of children left behind. Faced with the increasingly serious rural problems and challenges, countries around the world are paying more attention to them. The Chinese government has successively put forward the policies of beautiful countryside and rural revitalization.

In this context of the times, village-centered design is gradually becoming an important area of social design. The goal of social design is to focus on the interests of all stakeholders and to enable each stakeholder to participate in the co-creation process of

P.-L. P. Rau (Ed.): HCII 2022, LNCS 13311, pp. 217–228, 2022.
https://doi.org/10.1007/978-3-031-06038-0_16

the community. From these challenges, it is clear that eliciting and sustaining the participation and engagement of the broad local community becomes a key concern of social design [1].

Participatory design is an important approach to address the above issues. As Sanders and Brandt (2010) noted, "Participatory design is a design approach in which users and other stakeholders work with designers in the design process." The core idea of the participatory design method is that people affected by a certain decision or event should have the opportunity to influence this decision or event (Schuler & Namioka, 1993). The strength of this design approach is that it transcends the traditional limitations of profession, discipline, group, and social status (Sanoff, 2007) [2]. In addition, a common problem is the sustainability of systems built through a participatory process [1]; as Kensing and Blomberg (1998) noted, "when the researchers leave, the participatory processes seldom diffuse to other organizational entities" [1].

Community-centered design should focus on the resources and needs of the community itself. A community is an organic and integrated system that contains more meaning than the sum of all the single individuals in the system. Therefore, when making innovative designs for communities, it is necessary to consider the community as an organic whole and focus on exploring how to create more social value from the community's resources and social needs. Exploration based on a deeper interpretation of the actual local context and cultural knowledge can help generate solutions that bring well-being to the whole community [3].

1.2 Purpose of the Study

In summary, the rapid impact of modernization, marketization and urbanization has brought about a series of rural problems. The village of this study, Longtai Village, is located in the southwestern part of Yuelu District, Changsha City, Hunan Province, China. Surrounded by developed towns and cities, Longtai Village is a typical example of urban-rural development separation under the current rapid development situation in China. In 2018, in response to the basic requirements of China's rural revitalization strategy, the local government conducted a preliminary exploration of the cultural resources and industrial forms of Longtai Village, hoping to use the resources of Longtai Village to improve the quality of life of its people and achieve sustainable development of the village, but with limited success.

During the fieldwork, we found that Longtai Village has rich natural, cultural and technological resources. However, the way these advantageous resources are utilized has gradually become detached from the needs of contemporary life. The purpose of this study is to rediscover the contemporary value of local resources, explore a new supply and demand relationship based on local advantageous resources, create more social value for the local area through the cooperation between designers and various stakeholders, and try to seek the possibility of sustainable development of this supply and demand relationship after the departure of designers, so as to explore the potential of rural resources in meeting local needs through the intervention of participatory design.

1.3 Methodology

There were 88 main participants in this study, including 2 designers, 1 bamboo craftsman, 12 faculty members and 73 students from local elementary school. The two designers worked with all three parties and regularly communicated with them about their progress and results. Before conducting the research, the most important thing was to understand the basic information of each stakeholder and to establish a good relationship with them. In order to quickly understand the local culture, resources and living conditions of the residents, we conducted numerous interviews with residents of different ages and occupations, including village committee staff, cultural service center staff, residents who are good at making bamboo furniture, residents who are good at creating local poetry, principals and teachers of rural elementary school, students of elementary school, operators of rural stores and many other stakeholders.

After identifying local resources and needs worth exploring, we conducted fieldwork with bamboo craftsman, taught art classes to students at local elementary school, and held regular discussion meetings with local elementary school staff. Throughout the process, we conducted semi-structured interviews with all stakeholders. These interviews and meetings provided enough space for local residents to truly express their needs. During the semi-structured interviews, we exchanged ideas with all parties on the topic of how to use the local strengths to meet their needs. In this process, we discovered a specific problem: designers cannot obtain the real needs of local residents through subjective inferences, but should experience their lives and give local residents more opportunities to express themselves.

During the design practice, we shared with the bamboo craftman the specific situation of Longzhou Primary School and the needs of the school's teachers and students. We also presented the results of the semi-structured interviews and the preliminary design proposal to the teachers and workers of Longzhou Primary School and had several rounds of improvement with them. At the same time, all the stakeholders also gave their valuable opinions on our proposal and co-designed it to further ensure that the product based on local resources could meet the actual needs of the stakeholders.

In working with the various stakeholders, we got their real needs and feedback. This required the designers to withdraw from their original role as design leaders. The experiences and reflections we gained during this process will also effectively inform our future research.

2 Findings of the Field Survey

2.1 Rural Resources

Rural resources are the general term for the material, financial and human resources of the country. They can be divided into two categories: natural resources and social resources. The former includes sunlight, air, water, trees, minerals, etc. While the latter includes human resources, information resources and various material wealth created through labor. We mainly use fieldworks and interviews to understand the local resources of Longtai Village. As the investigation continued, we selected social resources that could better reflect the humanistic characteristics of rural areas, such as handicrafts, literature, art and agricultural resources.

2.2 Findings on Local Resources

The local handicraft resources of Longtai Village mainly include bamboo products, stone statues and root carvings. Literary and artistic resources mainly include shadow play and local poetry. Agricultural resources mainly include rice, fish and duck symbiotic systems, various crops and smoked bacon. We recorded the specific information and research results of the above resources through photos, videos, texts and recordings. All the results are summarized below.

Bamboo Products: Bamboo and Bamboo Handicrafts. In recent years, various countries have been paying more and more attention to environmental protection and sustainable development. The global wood supply is gradually decreasing, and the rational use and development of bamboo resources is getting more and more attention. Bamboo products are becoming one of the most important consumer products in various countries and regions.

During the fieldwork, we found that Longtai Village is rich in bamboo. There are dense bamboo forests around every house, and villagers also use bamboo as raw material to make some simple household items, such as loofah, coat hangers, fences and wall decorations. Therefore, it can be seen that bamboo is very popular and used daily in the villagers' lives (see Fig. 1).

Fig. 1. Bamboo forest and bamboo products in Longtai Village

We interviewed a local resident who owns a bamboo forest. He said that his bamboo forest is rented out to outsiders for a few days each year to cut, and the rent is much lower than the market price. In addition, bamboo craftsmen are facing difficulties. They have extensive experience in bamboo processing, however, there is insufficient market demand for this skill, which used to be their way of survival. A bamboo craftsman showed us his long-abandoned bamboo processing tools and bamboo products he used to make (see Fig. 2). All of these finished products require sophisticated processing skills and experience, but most of them do not sell, so his bamboo craftsmanship is losing value.

Fig. 2. Bamboo handicrafts

Bamboo is excellent because of its outstanding tensile strength (twice as strong as steel), compressive strength (twice as strong as concrete), light weight, good elasticity and high fire resistance. This is why people are now increasingly willing to use bamboo products. The local elementary school principal believes that bamboo is the plant that represents their village and improves everyone's life.

Other Resources. We visited the local residents' farms, rice fields and tea fields. It is worth mentioning that, except for a few tourists who asked to buy tea, local residents have no other channels to market their tea and are mainly in a self-production state. Agricultural products similar to the situation of tea include bacon and pickled fish. These special agricultural products actually meet the contemporary pursuit of natural food, but need to consider appropriate marketing methods.

We also went to the shadow play performance hall of the local cultural service center. According to the staff, the last performance was a long time ago. As mentioned above, the local government hopes to revitalize the cultural industry of Longtai Village. Apparently, the effect is not obvious. The problems are as follows: (1) Shadow play has become detached from the requirements of contemporary life. The local government's hope to revitalize shadow play through publicity and financial support is not a long-term plan after all. We should think more about how to make shadow play meet the value of contemporary life; (2) Longtai Village is surrounded by developed towns and cities, and young people are not willing to stay in rural areas to work, much less to learn traditional arts with low economic benefits.

2.3 Rural Resources Suitable for Further Exploration

Based on the above findings, we analyzed and sorted out the major local resources and evaluated the above resources in three dimensions: (1) Abundance: the degree of richness and abundance of resources; (2) Utilization: the degree of utilization of resources by local residents, i.e., the degree of utilization and exploitation of resources by residents in their

	Local Resources		Richness	Utilization Rate	Conversion Possibility
	Visible	Invisible			
Handicraft Resources	Bamboo-bamboo products	Bamboo handicraft	•••••	••••	•••••
	Limestone, Quartz Stone-Stone Statues	Stone carving craft	•••	•	••••
	Tree Roots-Root Carving	Root carving craft	••	•	•••
Literature & Art Resources	Shadow play	Shadow Play Culture	•••	••	••••
	Local poetry	Local culture and life	••	••	•••
Agricultural Resources	Tea	Tea making technology	••••	••••	•••
	Oranges, pumpkin, cabbage, beans	Planting Techniques	•••••	•••••	•
	Rice, fish and duck	Rice, fish and duck symbiosis breeding system	••••	••••	••
	Bacon	Smoked technology	•••	•••	•

Fig. 3. Main resources of Longtai Village

daily lives; (3) Possibility of transformation: the possibility of transforming resources into new ones to meet local needs. All the components are summarized below (see Fig. 3).

The abundance and utilization of agricultural resources is generally high, but the possibilities for conversion are low. It is difficult to explore new application possibilities because the application scenarios are limited to the basic needs of local residents' diet and economy. Literary and artistic resources have a high possibility of transformation due to their humanistic and abstract attributes, but their richness and utilization rate are not high because they are somewhat distant from the daily lives of local residents. Handicraft resources have high richness and transformation possibility due to their richness, accessibility and diversity of output of raw materials, but stone statues and root carvings which belong to handicraft resources are only used in some public places, so their utilization rate is low. Based on the above comparative analysis, we selected bamboo resources and bamboo crafts as rural resources for further exploration.

In this article, we aim to explore the potential of rural resources in meeting local needs. According to the survey, bamboo products have abundant raw material resources and application scenarios in Longtai Village, but holders of bamboo crafts are facing some difficulties, which just shows the urgent need to find a new kind of supply and demand relationship for this resource to achieve sustainable development.

2.4 Appropriate Local Needs Exploration

During our fieldwork, we visited many places. Finally, we found Longzhou Primary School - a rural elementary school located in the Longtai Village. In talking with the school's principal, teachers, and students, we found this to be a valuable research site because their needs and conditions were highly compatible with the rural resources we found (see Fig. 4): (1) The school infrastructure is inadequate: students have no place to sit in the playground and lack necessary recreational and fitness facilities; there is no clock in the classroom and students do not know the time; the corners of the stairs and walls are too sharp and children are easily injured during jostling. (2) The school's habit of using bamboo: school staff used bamboo to independently make simple stands for setting up cables. (3) Students' natural love for bamboo: many students involved bamboo in their drawings.

Therefore, our final research question was to explore the potential of using the bamboo resources and bamboo craft resources of Longtai Village to meet the needs of local elementary school through participatory design interventions.

Fig. 4. Basic information of Longzhou Primary School

3 Participatory Design Based on Bamboo Resources and Bamboo Handicrafts

3.1 Processes and Outputs

Based on repeated communication with various stakeholders in the early stage, we explored and summarized the entertainment needs, safety needs, learning needs and decoration needs of Longzhou Primary School. The final decision was made to produce products including bamboo recreational facilities, anti-collision bamboo stakes, bamboo bells and bamboo boards.

Recreational Needs-Bamboo Amusement Facilities. As mentioned above, the playground lacked facilities for children to rest and play. We communicated and discussed the actual situation and needs of Longzhou Primary School with the craftsman, and finally decided to design a bamboo play facility. The craftsman was quiet at first, but later, with our guidance, he was able to come up with his own ideas based on his manual skills and life experience. After understanding the processing technology of bamboo products with the craftsman, we gave a sketch of our intention and then worked with the craftsman to modify and make the first generation of products. In the process of experiencing the facilities, we found some problems and worthy of improvement, and then the artisan proposed the innovative idea of movable bamboo pole. After further cooperation practice and exploration between both parties, we produced a more optimized second-generation output.

The children gave very positive feedback about the bamboo amusement facilities. During the experience, they developed many ways to play that we hadn't thought of, because the abstract shape of the bamboo amusement facilities gave the children a lot of room to play. For example, they used the top bamboo pole as a crossbar to play, or they straddled the top bamboo pole and used the bamboo joints to play the "occupation game" (see Fig. 5).

Fig. 5. Bamboo recreational facilities

Safety Needs—Anti-Collision Bamboo Piles. In order to ensure the children's safety when playing in the narrow corridor, we designed the anti-collision bamboo stakes together with the craftsman and teachers of Longzhou Primary School after discussion. The children generally showed great interest in the bumper pile, and the pile played a substantial role in preventing collisions while the children were playing. However, some children would throw things into the bumper pile because it was open at the top. After adjustment, we covered the top opening with a bamboo woven product (see Fig. 6).

Fig. 6. Anti-collision bamboo pile

Learning Needs—Bamboo Clock. In the children's art classes, we noticed that there were no clocks in their classrooms. Only a very few children wore watches. The children had to rely on the school bell to get a general sense of time. To help the children learn, we designed a bamboo clock together with the teachers at Longzhou Primary School. Each of the fifth-grade children showed a surprised expression about these clocks and wished that every classroom could have such a clock (see Fig. 7).

Decoration Needs—Bamboo Board. In talking with the teachers at Longzhou Primary School, they wanted to make something decorative out of bamboo in addition to

Fig. 7. Bamboo clock

functional items. The idea to make a bamboo board for the classroom door came from a fifth-grade student. In her drawing expression, she wanted the pattern of the bamboo board to consist of the fingerprints of all the fifth graders. In a follow-up conversation, we found out that her idea came from the pattern drawing taught in class. During the actual production process, all the children showed great interest and competed to be the first to put their fingerprints on the board. We found that the children generally showed great excitement in participating in the design implementation process (see Fig. 8).

Fig. 8. Bamboo board

3.2 Experience and Methodology

In the participatory design process based on bamboo resources and bamboo craftsmanship in Longtai Village, the interests of each stakeholder are closely related to the collective interests. We position the designer to work with three parties in the design, and the designer should play the roles of: (1) communicator; (2) organizer; and (3) facilitator. Therefore, with this role positioned, we conducted ongoing cross-interviews and co-design with bamboo craftsman, students and teachers at Longzhou Primary School, and reflected on how to motivate them and increase their participation in the process.

Participatory Design with Bamboo Craftsman. In the participatory design with bamboo craftsman, we have summarized the following four lessons: (1) The designer should weaken the original role. The main task of the designer is to guide the design, not to dominate it, otherwise it will inhibit the generation of design ideas and should give more space for the main innovation to the craftsman. (2) Ask more guiding questions. The designer should play a facilitating role at this time, and appropriate questions can stimulate the craftsman' ideas more effectively. For example, the simplification and iteration of the output in this participatory design was done in the process of questioning and communication. (3) Respect the ideas of craftsman. When craftsman came up with innovative ideas, he should be respected. As local villagers and holders of traditional crafts, his suggestions are often more practical and realistic. (4) Pay attention to the attitude of interpersonal communication. In the participatory design process, designers should maintain a patient, friendly, and consultative attitude so that craftsman felt a sense of presence and respect, and so that he can recognize their value and significance in the participatory design process and also in society.

Participatory Design with Longzhou Primary School Students. In the process of collaborating with students from Longzhou Primary School on the design, we have learned the following four lessons: (1) Observe the characteristics: The design of the output is related to many parts of the children's bodies, so the observation of the children is a great guide to our output. (2) Establishing friendly relationships: We gradually narrowed the distance with the children by giving them art lessons, playing with them, and eating together. The establishment of friendly relationship is good for understanding their real needs and ideas. (3) Drawing to express: Through examples and motivation, we guide children to express their ideas with a paintbrush. Drawing allows children to express themselves vividly. (4) Experience feedback: After the initial output, children were allowed to experience and get the most intuitive feedback, and we can improve the design according to the children's experience process.

Participatory Design With Teachers and Staff of Longzhou Primary School. In the design of the collaboration with the principal and teachers of Longzhou School, we mainly adopted a regular return visit and communication with the teachers in each case to communicate and improve. But the difficulty lied in how to motivate the teachers. They prefered to let the designers finish the design independently, so we set up a regular weekly feedback mechanism: we communicated with the teachers at Longzhou Primary School on time, and carefully considered and affirmed every idea they put forward. This gave them a sense of gain and value, and they were more willing to communicate with the designers and put forward their ideas.

3.3 Empowerment and Meaning

Through this research, we have developed strong friendships with local bamboo craftsman, elementary school students and teachers. This study also had an empowering effect on each stakeholder: (1) Bamboo craftsman: experienced the need for contemporary crafts; regained abandoned craft skills and innovated with guidance; regained confidence in realizing their crafts and experienced real economic benefits. (2) Primary school students: saw common rural resources in a new light, experienced a sense of reward and value for participating in school design, and developed imagination and creativity. (3) Primary school staff: recognized the advantages of participatory design methods and indicated that they would try to apply them in their future teaching; experienced a sense of gain and value in participating in school design.

We hope that Longzhou Primary School and the bamboo craftsman will continue to work together after the designers leave: they can use the local resources, the design methods they have learned in this collaboration, and the partnerships they have established to create more products out of them. The bamboo resources and bamboo craft resources of Longtai Village are important resources for us to empower the village, and also provide the possibility of subsequent sustainable development for this research.

4 Conclusion

4.1 Paradigm

The paradigm for intervening in rural resources to meet local needs through participatory design is as follows (see Fig. 9). First, we learn about local resources, culture, and living conditions through fieldworks and interviews, and record them with photos, videos, texts, and audio recordings. By analyzing and comparing the three dimensions of abundance, utilization, and transformation possibilities, we identify local resources that are worthy of further exploration and find local needs that are highly compatible with the resources. In the process of participatory design, the designer plays the role of communicator, organizer and facilitator, collaborates with multiple stakeholders in the design process, and always adheres to the principles of guidance, respect, friendliness, recognition and feedback to increase the motivation and participation of stakeholders and allow them to truly contribute their ideas and capabilities. In addition, exploring and utilizing local strengths as much as possible can help designers to complete the design process more smoothly. Also, the better the utilization of local resources, the more sustainable the final design will be. This is because ideally, after the designer leaves, the local residents can still develop further based on the local resources and the gains of participatory design.

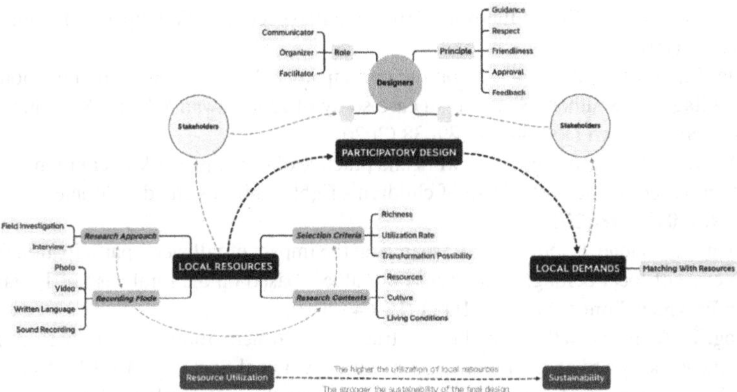

Fig. 9. Paradigm for rural resources to meet local needs through participatory design interventions

4.2 Limitations and Future Research

Admittedly, this paper has the following limitations. (1) This study was completed under the guidance of a designer. The independent supply and demand collaboration between bamboo craftsman and elementary school has not been fully validated in practice, and its future sustainability still needs to be further explored. (2) Due to limited research staff, this study focused on only three stakeholders: craftsman, elementary school students, and teachers. However, there are many other stakeholders involved in the actual process of resource acquisition and transportation of finished products. They should be considered in the scope of the study. In the future, more work is needed to improve the paradigm of rural resources to meet local needs through participatory design interventions.

References

1. Wang, W., Bryan Kinns, N., Ji, T.: Using community engagement to drive co-creation in Rural China. Int. J. Des. **10**(1), 37–52 (2016)
2. Hussain, S., Sanders, E.B.-N., Steinert, M.: Participatory design with marginalized people in developing countries: challenges and opportunities experienced in a field study in Cambodia. Int. J. Des. **6**(2), 19–109 (2012)
3. He, R., Guo, Y., Hou, X., Jiang, Y.: Community-based cultural innovation: "New Channel" design and social innovation project. Public Art **05**, 14–21 (2016)
4. Wang, B., Ji, T., Yang, Y.: The Potential of Rural Crafts in Promoting Community Empowerment through Participatory Design Intervention. Cumulus (2016)
5. Steen, M., Manschot, M., Koning, N.D.: Benefits of co-design in service design projects. Int. J. Des. **5**(2), 53–60 (2011)
6. Del Gaudio, C., Franzato, C., de Oliveira, A.J.: Sharing design agency with local partners in participatory design. Int. J. Des. **10**(1), 53–64 (2016)
7. Wang, B.: Design innovation model based on rural community resources. Packag. Eng. **39**(14), 82–86 (2018)
8. Xiao, T.: Research on Social Innovation from the Perspective of Participatory Design. Hunan University (2017)
9. Gejuan, Z., Wenhao, Z.: Research on the participatory design model of mountainous traditional villages in Southern Shaanxi—a case study of Zhanjiawan Village, Xunyang County, Ankang. Small Town Dev. **38**(10), 29–38 (2020)
10. Wei, W., Zhe, W.: The design framework and practice of participatory kindergarten space construction: based on the perspective of children's rights, abilities and development. Preschool Educ. Res. **01**, 9–18 (2016)
11. Huishan, C., Xiaohe, L., Siren, L.: Research on the impact of villagers' participation from the perspective of local belonging and sense of value—based on the rural case of Jinjiang City Fujian Province. Forestry Econ. **41**(11), 55–64 (2019)
12. Zhuang, T.: Analysis on the path of reconstruction of farmers' rural community identification under the background of rural revitalization strategy. Legal Syst. Soc. **13**, 187–188 (2020)
13. Lijia, Y.: The embodied practice of cultural memory: the anthropological basis and path of children's inheritance in traditional festivals. J. Xuzhou Inst. Technol. (Soc. Sci. Ed.) **34**(03), 7–13 (2019)

SAFA: A System for Assisting Fair Assessments in Team Collaboration

Yun Lou[1], Kewei Guo[1], Xuanhui Liu[1(✉)], Pei Chen[1], Changyuan Yang[1,3], and Lingyun Sun[1,2]

[1] Alibaba-Zhejiang University Joint Institute of Frontier Technologies, Zhejiang University, Hangzhou 310027, China
{inlab_ly,3190102539,liuxuanhui,chenpei}@zju.edu.cn

[2] State Key Laboratory of CAD&CG at Zhejiang University, Hangzhou 310027, China
sunly@zju.edu.cn

[3] Alibaba Group, Hangzhou 311121, China
changyuan.yangcy@alibaba-inc.com

Abstract. In teamwork, assessments are applied to examine individuals' contributions and team performance, helping them conduct self-reflection. Nowadays, leader assessments are commonly used in teams, but they are influenced by subjective factors of leaders. Fair assessments enhance team members' enthusiasm for work and their belongings to the team. In this paper, we proposed an approach integrating self-assessments, peer assessments, and cross-team assessments to assist leaders in making fair and comprehensive assessments. We developed a prototype system, SAFA. To test the system's effectiveness, we conducted an experiment with 32 participants. The participants were divided into eight teams, with one leader and three members each. We gave each experiment team the same projects and asked team leaders and members to assess their jobs using our system. The analysis showed that the fairness of the assessments has been proved and recognized by team members. The system can be used in project-driven teams in colleges or companies to build an equal working environment and promote team performance.

Keywords: Leader assessment · Assessment system · Fair assessment · Self-assessment · Peer assessment · Cross-team assessment

1 Introduction

In teamwork, to promote team performance, assessment is indispensable for examining individuals' contributions and helping them conduct self-reflection. Previous research widely explored the fairness, reliability, and validity of assessments [1–5]. Their findings revealed that evaluation inequality widely exists in team collaboration, leading to the discouragement of team members. Fairness is regarded as a major concern by people being evaluated [6–8]. Fair assessments enhance team members' enthusiasm for work and their belongings to the team [9]. Moreover, research finds that fairness is related to

P.-L. P. Rau (Ed.): HCII 2022, LNCS 13311, pp. 229–241, 2022.
https://doi.org/10.1007/978-3-031-06038-0_17

team trust, particularly trust in the leader [10]. And trust has been proven to affect team performance [11–13].

Generally, leader assessment plays a decisive role of assessments in teamwork. Team leaders evaluate members by rating their performance or contributions. However, leader assessment may be sloppy and biased due to the subjectivity of assessments [14]. Other forms of assessments are introduced to reduce the impact of arbitrary judgements Self-assessment and peer assessment are widely used to evaluate production and performance in colleges and companies. Self-assessment helps members become self-critical, which is an essential ingredient for performing well in teams [15]. The studies on fairness found that peer assessment was ideal for measuring the ones with a greater contribution to a team [16, 17]. In addition to self- and peer assessment, we introduced cross-team assessment. As an external assessment, cross-team assessment can point out the weaknesses and strengths of current work from different perspectives [18].

Extensive assessment systems or tools have been developed to offer reliable and valid assessments [19, 20]. Some work used fairness as a metric to measure the quality of an assessment system [21] but did not adopt specific measures to promote fairness. In this paper, we designed a system, SAFA, for assisting team leaders in conducting fair assessments, thus enhancing trust in teams and team cohesion. Our system integrates self-assessments, peer assessments, and cross-team assessments to help leaders make fair and comprehensive assessments. In addition, the system provides the visualization of assessment results of team members, which helps team members understand their strengths and weaknesses.

To test SAFA, we conducted a teamwork experiment with two goals. First, we verified that the system enhanced the fairness of leader assessments; second, we examined if the system helped individuals conduct self-reflection. We gave each experiment team the same tasks.

Our contributions include: (1) proposing a method to assist fair assessment; (2) developing a prototype system, SAFA, for the use of online assessments in teamwork; (3) conducting an experiment with teams to evaluate SAFA, demonstrating the utility, expressiveness, and effectiveness of our approach; (4) providing a promising way to build equal working environment and promote team performance.

2 Related Work

2.1 Self-assessment and Peer Assessment

Self-assessment and peer assessment are often used in teamwork to assess team performance. Self-assessment is mainly used to reflect on one's own work, leading to the promotion of learning skills and a higher standard of outcomes [22]. Research shows that self-assessment has the potential to improve individual motivation and engagement in learning [23–25]. Peer assessment provides team members with opportunities to build on prior knowledge, generate inferences and integrate ideas [26]. It has been found that when team members' contributions and performance are quantified in peer assessment, they tend to put more effort into completing tasks in upcoming jobs [27].

2.2 Cross-team Assessment

Cross-team assessment is seen as an external assessment with relatively reliable information. The effects that external assessments generate within the team have mostly been salient [28]. Teams learned more by noting the surprises from the comparison of internal and external assessments [29]. It has also been suggested that cross-team assessment may assist self- and peer assessment [29]. Moreover, since the external assessors have no direct interest relationship with the team, it may be more helpful to achieve the goal of fair assessment.

2.3 Fair Assessment

Unfair assessment often occurs in teamwork. Individual performance is usually scored in two approaches: "equal" and "justice" [30]. The former means that all team members receive the same score, and the latter means that everyone is scored based on his or her contribution to the project [31]. However, it is difficult to observe individual contributions in team collaboration. The study of Lin et al. [32] visualized the learning activities and contributions of individuals in the team, including data on learning behaviors and interactions with other members. Thus, individuals can use objective data in the assessment process to judge the level of individual contribution. However, some of them may score irresponsibly. Shiba et al. [33] attempted to solve the problem by identifying irresponsible ones using a trust network. In our work, we use the visual presentations of the assessment results from different sources to improve the fairness of leader assessments.

2.4 Assessment Tool

The proper use of assessment tools can improve the reliability and accuracy of assessment and achieve better assessment results. Some assessment tools can help reduce the burden of leaders' assessment and individualize it. For example, Lazarini et al. [34] used an adaptive Web testing system to help teachers evaluate student performance. Some assessment tools are used to evaluate specific competencies, such as individuals' ability to work in inter-professional teams. Chhabria et al. [35] used a system to formally assess teamwork behaviors in a clinical health science project. There are also assessment tools that improve the fairness and accuracy of the assessment by providing additional information. For example, Lin et al. [32] designed a peer assessment tool to visualize team awareness information to collaborative team members. In our work, we will focus on the impact of visualizing the assessment results during and after the assessment process.

3 System Design and Implementation

3.1 System Overview

To achieve the goal of fairness, we propose an approach (Fig. 1). During the teamwork projects, team leaders first launch assessment tasks to evaluate individuals' performance. When entering the assessment stage, self-, peer and cross-team assessments are respectively carried out. Then, the assessment results are presented to the leaders and assist them in conducting assessments. After all assessments are finished, the results are displayed in a radar chart. In addition, the keywords for assessing reasons are shown simultaneously. The following sections detail how to conduct self-, peer, cross-team, and leader assessments using SAFA.

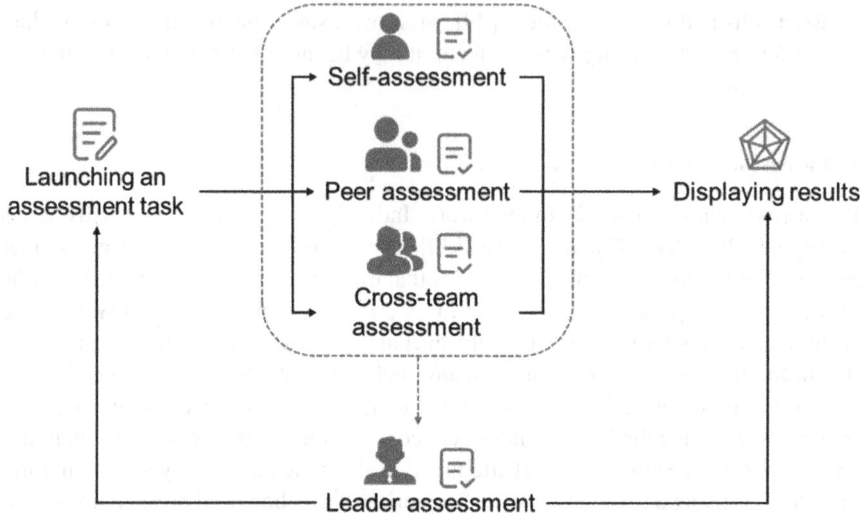

Fig. 1. The overall structure of SAFA.

3.2 Launch an Assessment Task

In this UI (Fig. 2), the project introduction and member composition are presented. The team leader can click on "Upload" to create a corresponding questionnaire according to the goal of the current task and choose a 5-point scale or a 7-point scale. Then the leader launches the questionnaire of the assessment task.

3.3 Self-, Peer, Cross-team Assessment

Team members need to finish the assessment task in a team project process. Clicking members' avatars in Fig. 2, the assessment questionnaire is presented. The interface of self-assessment and peer assessment is the same. Members click on their own avatars to conduct self-assessments and click on the avatars of others to conduct peer assessments. And there is a "Details" next to the project description to show the completed works. In a team, members know each other's identity information (including name, gender, age, work experience, accomplishment, etc.). But there is no personal identity information in the UI of cross-team assessment. Therefore, when rating members from another team, the assessor gives ratings according to the quality of their current work. Cross-team assessments avoid the unfairness caused by personal reasons such as conflict of interest in the assessment within a team (Fig. 3).

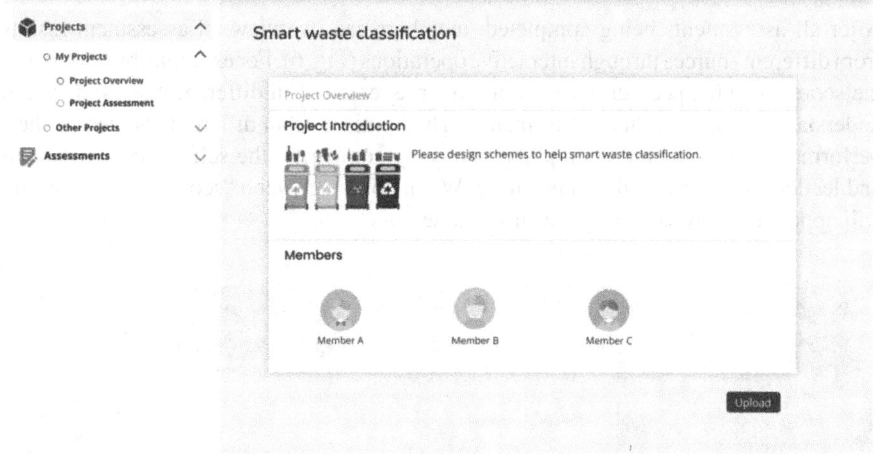

Fig. 2. The UI for launching an assessment task.

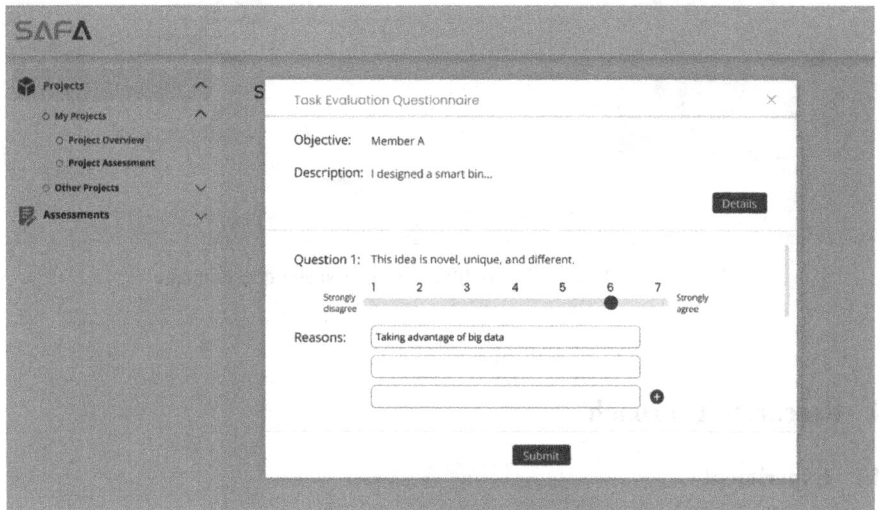

Fig. 3. The UI for members to fill in the assessment questionnaire.

3.4 Leader Assessment

After the self-, peer and cross-team assessment being completed, the leader assessment starts (Fig. 4). In this UI, leaders can see the results of self-, peer and cross-team assessments. Additionally, leaders can further check their rating reasons. By referring to others' assessment information, leaders are expected to give more fair, accurate and comprehensive evaluations.

3.5 Display of the Assessment Results

After all assessments being completed, members can overview all assessment results from different sources through interactive operations (Fig. 6). For example, by comparing the scores of self-, peer, cross-team or leader assessment in different phases, they can understand changes in their performance. The opinions from different sources on their performance are presented comprehensively by comparing the self-, peer, cross-team and leader assessment at the same phase. When hovering over a "score point," a pop-up will appear to show the rating reasons of assessors.

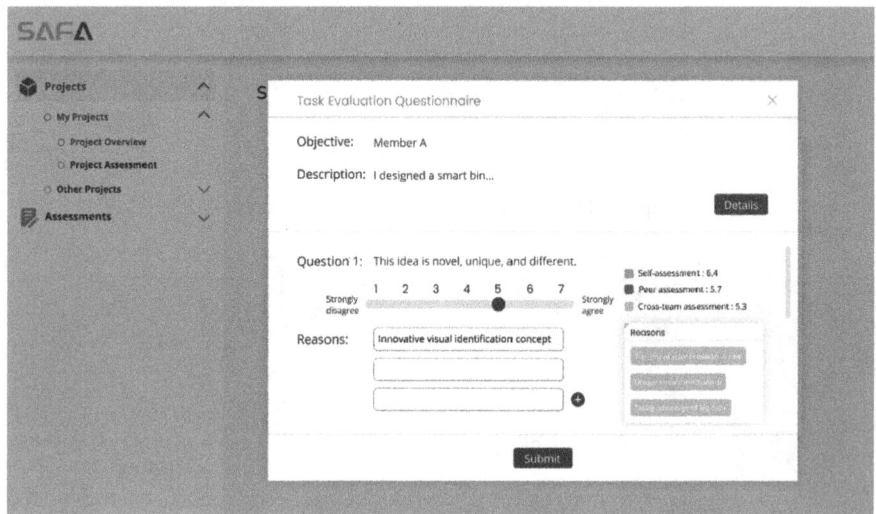

Fig. 4. The UI for leaders to fill in the assessment questionnaire.

4 Research Approach

4.1 Experiment

To evaluate SAFA, we conducted an experiment with 32 people. The participants were divided into eight teams, with one leader and three members each. We paid each team leader 60 yuan and each team member 40 yuan to incentivize them in the experiment. The experiment lasted for three days (Fig. 4).

On day 1, the experimenter showed each participant the instructions and the experiment procedure. Each team received the same task: "Please design schemes to help smart waste classification." Each team member should at first write their ideas simply in the system. After all participants finished editing their schemes, the experimenter asked them to evaluate the ideas from themselves (self-assessment), the ones from team members (peer assessment) and the ones from another team (cross-team assessment). Participants were asked to use a 7-point Likert scale (1 = strongly disagree; 7 = strongly agree) for the

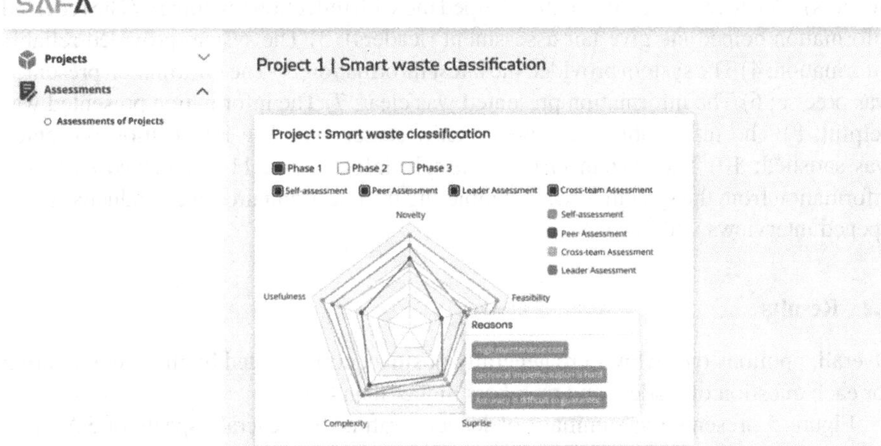

Fig. 5. Assessment results are displayed in a radar chart, and when the user hovers over a proposition, the reasons for the rating of reviewers will be displayed.

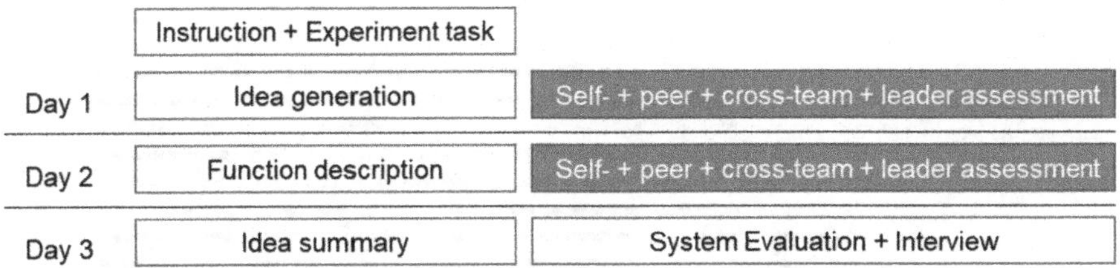

Fig. 6. Experimental steps. Our experiment tasks were divided into three phases, which were conducted over three days.

assessments from five perspectives: novelty, surprise, feasibility, complexity, and usefulness. The participants were also asked to write a couple of keywords for each proposition to describe their rating reasons. Especially after self-, peer and cross-team assessments, leaders can view these assessment results, and then they were asked to conduct assessments using the same questionnaire. After assessments, a radar chart appeared on each individual assessment UI, which presents assessments from four different sources with keywords.

On day 2, each team member described the functions based on the previous ideas. Then with the same procedure on day 1, they were asked to rate the ideas from themselves, team members and members from another team. Followingly, the leader assessed the ideas of members after receiving the results of self-, peer and cross-team assessments. Subsequently, more information was presented on the individual radar chart.

On day 3, the experimenter asked team members to summarize their ideas in the system based on the assessments from day 1 and day 2. Then, the participants received a questionnaire to evaluate the system. The questions are adopted from existing research, which is relevant to the information quality [36, 37] and the organizational fairness [38, 39]: "1) I think I received fair leader assessment (members)/I think I gave fair assessment (leaders); 2) The received information helped me with reflection (members)/The received information helped me give fair assessment (leaders); 3) The system provided reliable information; 4) The system provided the latest information; 5) The information presented was precise; 6) The information presented was clear; 7) The information presented was helpful; 8) The information presented was necessary; 9) The information presented was satisfied; 10) The system provided timely information; 11) I received sufficient information from the system." After completing the questionnaires, we conducted semi-opened interviews with leaders.

4.2 Results

Overall, opinions on SAFA were generally positive, corroborated by the average rating for each question of leaders and members higher than 4.5.

Figure 5 presents the summary of leaders' ratings of several aspects of SAFA. It showed that leaders were highly satisfied with the reliability and the usefulness of the provided information, and all leaders thought SAFA helped them give fair assessments. There was only one leader who scored 2 points on the freshness, clearness, and timeliness of provided information (Fig. 7).

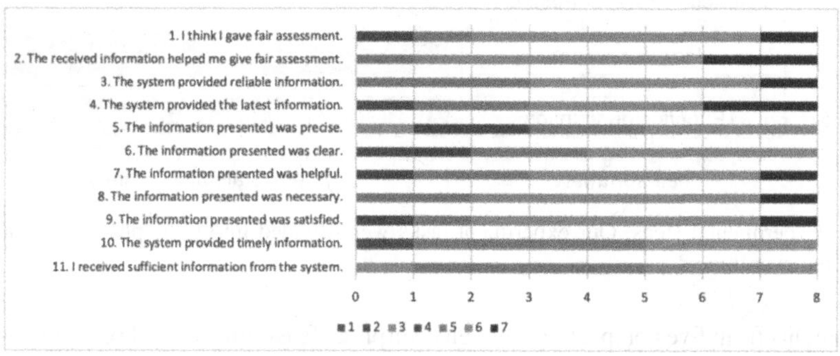

Fig. 7. Leaders' ratings on several propositions about their experience with SAFA. Each proposition was rated using a 7-point Likert scale.

The results of members' ratings of SAFA are shown in Fig. 6. Most members thought they received fair leader assessments, and all members thought that the provided information helped them with reflection. Three members thought that received information was not latest, not timely, and not sufficient enough, respectively (Fig. 8).

During the interviews, we gathered leaders' feedback on our system. Firstly, leaders affirmed that we provided various forms of evaluation. They thought it "supplement for the limitations of my thinking" and "help me to judge from various perspectives". Significantly, they thought the addition of cross-team assessments enabled their rating to be more objective and fairer. Secondly, it is intuitive to display the assessment results in radar charts with keywords that indicate other reviewers' reasons for scoring. The keywords allowed them to assess the quality of the current task from different perspectives. Thirdly, staged assessment enabled the leader assessment to be more comprehensive

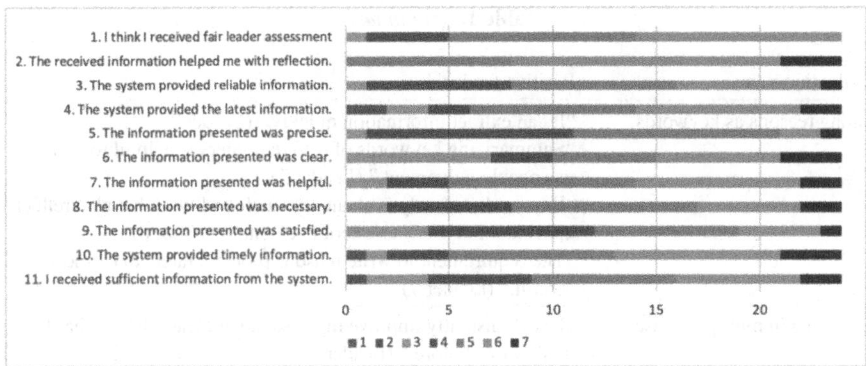

Fig. 8. Members' ratings on several propositions about their experience with SAFA. Each proposition was rated using a 7-point Likert scale.

because it can "obtain new and valuable information continually at each phase." In addition, it also "reduce the randomness (such as bad mood, hasty decisions, etc.)" and thus enabled them to "constantly improve my assessment".

As for the limitations, some leaders thought the information displayed on the evaluation results was limited, and the radar chart only showed partial dimensions. The keywords for the rating show the subjective preferences of the raters. The presentation of staged evaluation results may lead to herd mentality; thus, leaders may give up their initial judgement (Tables 1 and 2).

Table 1. Leaders' positive feedback on SAFA.

Evaluation items	Positive feedback
Overall impression	"Other people's assessment can supplement for the limitations of my thinking." (Leader 1) "Other people's assessment can help me to judge from various perspectives." (Leader 8) "Cross-team assessment is more helpful for me because other team members are completely unrelated to our team, so the evaluation is more objective." (Leader 6) "I am interested in the discrepancy between other evaluations and mine, which may lead me to rethink." (Leader 3)
Displaying results in radar Chart	"Displaying assessments from different sources facilitates me to improve my assessments." (Leader 1) "Reflecting all indicators comprehensively." (Leader 2) "Combining multiple radar charts can avoid bias." (Leader 3) "It is clear and intuitive to understand each face of assessments." (Leader 5)

(*continued*)

Table 1. *(continued)*

Evaluation items	Positive feedback
Rating reasons as keywords	"It can extract information quickly." (Leader 2) "Summarizing keywords of different raters is helpful to make a reasonable judgement." (Leader 3) "Keywords not only evaluate the quality of work but also reflect the content of work to a certain extent." (Leader 6) "The requirement to write reasons prompts raters to be more careful." (Leader 7)
Assessing in multiple phases	"I can constantly improve my assessment, learn details that I don't know before." (Leader 1) "It avoids me having a fixed point of view, and I can obtain new and valuable information continually at each phase." (Leader 3) "Multi-phase evaluation can first reduce the randomness (such as bad mood, hasty decisions, etc.)" (Leader 6) "I can get more comprehensive information." (Leader 8)

Table 2. Leaders' negative feedback on SAFA.

Evaluation items	Negative feedback
Overall impression	"I will insist on my standards during assessments and will not be affected by other assessments." (Leader 4)
Displaying results in radar Chart	"It reflects limited information." (Leader 2) "The display of scores was not accurate or intuitive." (Leader 7) "Different scoring criteria from each person can influence it." (Leader 6)
Rating reasons as keywords	"It is not intuitive." (Leader 6)
Assessing in multiple phases	"Rating for the current phase is vulnerable to the influence of the previous phases." (Leader 4) "Evaluation can be influenced by conformity." (Leader 6) "The memory of the previous phase is likely to be vague." (Leader 5)

5 Limitations and Future Work

We discuss some limitations and future works of our work in this section. First, the system now provides an assessment template, which needs to be individualized in the future, presenting more information in the UIs. Second, our evaluation experiment was conducted in a laboratory setting, which has some differences from the real teamwork. We simplified the task and labor division for team collaboration. We will refine the functionality of SAFA by conducting experiments with real teams in schools or companies.

6 Conclusion

In this paper, we designed an assessment system, SAFA, for helping both team leaders and team members obtain fair assessments, thus enhancing trust in teams and team cohesion. SAFA integrates self-, peer, and cross-team assessments to assist leaders in making fair and comprehensive assessments. To test SAFA, we conducted an experiment. Thirty-two participants were invited and divided into eight teams. They were asked to complete a three-phase design task, with an additional evaluation task at the end of each phase using SAFA. The results show that the fairness of assessments has been proved and recognized by participants. The results also prove the effectiveness of the system to improve individual self-reflection and help teams to build trust. The system can be used in project-driven teams in colleges or companies to build an equal working environment and thus promote team performance.

References

1. Conway, R., Kember, D., Sivan, A., Wu, M.: Peer assessment of an individual's contribution to a group project. Assess. Eval. High. Educ. **18**, 45–56 (1993). https://doi.org/10.1080/0260293930180104
2. Carvalho, A.: Students' perceptions of fairness in peer assessment: evidence from a problem-based learning course. Teach. High. Educ. **18**, 491–505 (2013). https://doi.org/10.1080/13562517.2012.753051
3. Fellenz, M.R.: Toward fairness in assessing student groupwork: a protocol for peer evaluation of individual contributions. J. Manag. Educ. **30**, 570–591 (2006). https://doi.org/10.1177/1052562906286713
4. Panadero, E., Romero, M., Strijbos, J.W.: The impact of a rubric and friendship on peer assessment: effects on construct validity, performance, and perceptions of fairness and comfort. Stud. Educ. Eval. **39**, 195–203 (2013). https://doi.org/10.1016/j.stueduc.2013.10.005
5. Walker, A.: British psychology students' perceptions of group-work and peer assessment. Psychol. Learn. Teach. **1**, 28–36 (2001). https://doi.org/10.2304/plat.2001.1.1.28
6. Freeman, M., Mckenzie, J.: SPARK, a confidential web-based template for self and peer assessment of student teamwork: benefits of evaluating across different subjects. Br. J. Educ. Technol. **33**, 551–569 (2002)
7. Vu, T.T., Dall'Alba, G.: Students' experience of peer assessment in a professional course. Assess. Eval. High. Educ. **32**, 541–556 (2007). https://doi.org/10.1080/02602930601116896
8. Maiden, B., Perry, B.: Dealing with free-riders in assessed group work: results from a study at a UK university. Assess. Eval. High. Educ. **36**, 451–464 (2011). https://doi.org/10.1080/02602930903429302
9. Lou, Y., Liu, X., Chen, P., Zhang, K., Sun, L.: Gender bias in team-building activities in China. Gend. Manag. **36**, 858–877 (2021). https://doi.org/10.1108/GM-04-2020-0116
10. Lau, C.M., Wong, K.M., Eggleton, I.R.C.: Fairness of performance evaluation procedures and job satisfaction: the role of outcome-based and non-outcome-based effects. Account. Bus. Res. **38**, 121–135 (2008). https://doi.org/10.1080/00014788.2008.9663325
11. Erdem, F., Ozen, J., Atsan, N.: The relationship between trust and team performance. Work Study. **52**, 337–340 (2003). https://doi.org/10.1108/00438020310502633
12. Mach, M., Lvina, E.: When trust in the leader matters: the moderated-mediation model of team performance and trust. J. Appl. Sport Psychol. **29**, 134–149 (2017). https://doi.org/10.1080/10413200.2016.1196765

13. Dirks, K.T.: Trust in leadership and team performance: evidence from NCAA basketball. J. Appl. Psychol. **85**, 1004–1012 (2000). https://doi.org/10.1037/0021-9010.85.6.1004
14. Goodrich, T.J.: Strategies for dealing with the issue of subjectivity in evaluation. Eval. Q. **2**, 631–645 (1978)
15. Strom, P.S., Strom, R.D., Moore, E.G.: Peer and self-evaluation of teamwork skills. J. Adolesc. **22**, 539–553 (1999). https://doi.org/10.1006/jado.1999.0247
16. Chapman, K.J., Van Auken, S.: Creating positive group project experiences: an examination of the role of the instructor on students' perceptions of group projects. J. Mark. Educ. **23**, 117–127 (2001). https://doi.org/10.1177/0273475301232005
17. Erez, A., LePine, J.A., Elms, H.: Effects of rotated leadership and peer evaluation on the functioning and effectiveness of self-managed teams: a quasi-experiment. Pers. Psychol. **55**, 929–948 (2002). https://doi.org/10.1111/j.1744-6570.2002.tb00135.x
18. Mueller, J., Abecassis-Moedas, C.: Factors influencing the integration of external evaluations in the open innovation process - a qualitative study in micro firms in the creative industries. J. Strateg. Manag. **10**, 248–260 (2017). https://doi.org/10.1108/JSMA-08-2014-0073
19. Canney, N.E., Bielefeldt, A.R.: Validity and reliability evidence of the engineering professional responsibility assessment tool. J. Eng. Educ. **105**, 452–477 (2016). https://doi.org/10.1002/jee.20124
20. Schroder, C., et al.: Development and pilot testing of the collaborative practice assessment tool. J. Interprof. Care. **25**, 189–195 (2011). https://doi.org/10.3109/13561820.2010.532620
21. Akimov, A., Malin, M.: When old becomes new: a case study of oral examination as an online assessment tool. Assess. Eval. High. Educ. **45**, 1205–1221 (2020). https://doi.org/10.1080/02602938.2020.1730301
22. Dochy, F., Segers, M., Sluijsmans, D.: The use of self-, peer and co-assessment in higher education: a review. Stud. High. Educ. **24**, 331–350 (1999). https://doi.org/10.1080/03075079912331379935
23. Boud, D.: Enhancing Learning Through Self-Assessment. Routledge (2013)
24. Brown, G.T.L., Harris, L.R.: Student self-assessment. In: McMillan, J.H. (ed.) Handbook of Research on Classroom Assessment, pp. 367–393. Sage, Thousand Oaks (2013)
25. Hearn, J., McMillan, J.H.: Student self-assessment: the key to stronger student motivation and higher achievement. Educ. Horizons. **87**, 40–49 (2008)
26. Roscoe, R.D., Chi, M.T.H.: Understanding tutor learning: knowledge-building and knowledge-telling in peer tutors' explanations and questions. Rev. Educ. Res. **77**, 534–574 (2007). https://doi.org/10.3102/0034654307309920
27. Román-Calderón, J.P., Robledo-Ardila, C., Velez-Calle, A.: Global virtual teams in education: do peer assessments motivate student effort? Stud. Educ. Eval. **70**, 101021 (2021). https://doi.org/10.1016/j.stueduc.2021.101021
28. Orlikowski, W.J., Scott, S.V.: What happens when evaluation goes online? Exploring apparatuses of valuation in the travel sector. Organ. Sci. **25**, 868–891 (2014). https://doi.org/10.1287/orsc.2013.0877
29. Ishii, K., Kim, S.K., Fowler, W., Maeno, T.: Tools for project-based active learning of amorphous systems design: Scenario prototyping and cross team peer evaluation. In: Proceedings of the ASME 2009 International Design Engineering Technical Conferences & Computers and Information in Engineering Conference IDETC/CIE 2009, pp. 1–11 (2009)
30. Murillo, F.J., Hidalgo, N.: Students' conceptions about a fair assessment of their learning. Stud. Educ. Eval. **53**, 10–16 (2017). https://doi.org/10.1016/j.stueduc.2017.01.001
31. Reynolds, M., Trehan, K.: Assessment: a critical perspective. Stud. High. Educ. **25**, 267–278 (2000). https://doi.org/10.1080/03075070050193406
32. Lin, J.W., Tsai, C.W., Hsu, C.C., Chang, L.C.: Peer assessment with group awareness tools and effects on project-based learning. Interact. Learn. Environ. **29**, 583–599 (2021). https://doi.org/10.1080/10494820.2019.1593198

33. Shiba, Y., Sugawara, T.: Fair assessment of group work by mutual evaluation based on trust network. In: 2014 IEEE Frontiers in Education Conference (FIE) Proceedings, pp. 1–7. IEEE (2014)
34. Lazarinis, F., Green, S., Pearson, E.: Creating personalized assessments based on learner knowledge and objectives in a hypermedia Web testing application. Comput. Educ. **55**, 1732–1743 (2010). https://doi.org/10.1016/j.compedu.2010.07.019
35. Chhabria, K., Black, E., Giordano, C., Blue, A.: Measuring health professions students' teamwork behavior using peer assessment: Validation of an online tool. J. Interprofessional Educ. Pract. **16**, 100271 (2019). https://doi.org/10.1016/j.xjep.2019.100271
36. Teo, T.S.H., Srivastava, S.C., Jiang, L.: Trust and electronic government success: an empirical study. J. Manag. Inf. Syst. **25**, 99–131 (2008). https://doi.org/10.2753/MIS0742-1222250303
37. Seddon, P.B., Kiew, M.-Y.: A partial test and development of DeLone and McLean's model of IS success. Australas. J. Inf. Syst. 4 (1996). https://doi.org/10.3127/ajis.v24i0.2769
38. McAllister, D.J., Bigley, G.A.: Work context and the definition of self: how organizational care influences organization-based self-esteem. Acad. Manag. J. **45**, 894–904 (2002). https://doi.org/10.2307/3069320
39. Tsui, A.S., Pearce, J.L., Porter, L.W., Tripoli, A.M.: Alternative approaches to the employee-organization relationship: does investment in employees pay off? Acad. Manag. **40**, 1089–1121 (1997)

Activities-Centered Participatory Community Design: Shoupa Community Service Station Rooftop Renovation Plan

Huan Wang[1], Ruoxi Wang[2], Lili Fu[3], Qing Miao[4], and Nan Li[2](✉)

[1] Capital Normal University, Beijing 100048, China
whuan@cnu.edu.cn
[2] Tsinghua University, Beijing 10083, China
wrx19@mails.tsinghua.edu.cn, nanli@tsinghua.edu.cn
[3] Beijing Chengyang Social Services Office, Beijing 100079, China
[4] Xinjiekou Sub-District Office of Xicheng District, Beijing 100035, China

Abstract. This paper first provides an overview of the urban regeneration process of Beijing since the1970s, with a focus of the shift from material promotion to historical cultural preservation and sustainability promotion over the years, and a highlight of the contemporary trend of redesign of community public space, which has attracted considerable attention in recent years because of the commendable efficiency of land utilization and the activities-centered diversified forms of community participation. Then, based on an advanced planning orientation and renewal project in Beijing, this paper describes an urban regeneration process carried out in Beijing that aimed at experimenting with a creative approach to the design and regulation of complex urban land use. Specifically, a real urban renewal project on the Shoupa Community Service Station Rooftop is described in detail, which demonstrates a promising approach to activities-centered community space design involving spatial, graphic, and cyber aspects.

Keywords: Activities-centered design · Participatory community · Neighborhood planning · Urban regeneration · Beijing

1 Background

Urban regeneration projects in Beijing began in the 70s of the last century with the "repaying bills" for general space improvement, construction quality, and facilities in inner-city residences. Since the main aim of urban spatial management is the precise control of land use as urban design works intensively, regeneration-oriented projects are requested to recognize the historical pattern and cultural context of the city. Beginning with the renovation of the old city in the 21st century, urban design far exceeded physical space and advanced to a multifaceted solution with a combination of economic, cultural, social, and production perspectives. The sophisticated regeneration moved to a reconsideration of vacant space in every corner of the community and the practical delivery was carried out in the primary administrative unit as neighborhood planning (Liu 2014). The

P.-L. P. Rau (Ed.): HCII 2022, LNCS 13311, pp. 242–255, 2022.
https://doi.org/10.1007/978-3-031-06038-0_18

neighborhood planning for public space comprehends both spatial context and humanistic entity with community management, community service, and community cultural construction, showing a shift in perspective from space requirement promotion to service advancement.

On January 1st, 2020, Beijing's Xicheng District launched a program to upgrade the community service station by exploring a new mode for multiplied public promotion of social governance at the community scale. The Laoqianggen Community Service Station is the first project that is upgraded by concordance with the governance, social organizations, community residents, and enterprise surroundings to rebuild a conventional service platform with integrating party service, public service, living service, and social service (Fig. 1). As part of the program, the community is encouraged to develop measures to meet local needs by investigating distinctive services and promoting intelligence standards of community management, ultimately leading to friendly and efficient community service stations that support citizens' participation and enhance their sense of belonging. By the end of June 2021, 263 community service stations in Xicheng District had been reshaped from public space regulation to service and cultural reorganization into a completely new concept of urban regeneration.

Fig. 1. The Laoqianggen community service station renewal project [from Qianlong news]

Consequently, general regeneration of spatial space and cultural services at a community level has developed a focus on neighborhood regeneration and has been shaped by decades of urban renewal practices and future city development goals.

2 Literature Review

2.1 Basic Construction Improvement: 70s of the 20th Century

During the 1970s to 1990s, limited material conditions in Beijing meant that a great deal of housing in the city needed to be renovated to meet basic living requirements.

The Dilapidated Housing Renovation program during this period consisted primarily of rehabilitating slum housing and reusing it for the original households' compensation and commercial purposes. This was the pioneering work in Beijing's urban regeneration practices. As a demonstration project, the Ju'er Hutong Courtyard Housing Project aimed to bring modern city-life-living function to community residential buildings by equipping the basic rooms without affecting traditional courtyard patterns. The project won the World Habitat Award from the United Nations in 1993 (Wu and Rowe 1999).

The Ju'er Hutong project is a prime example of living spatial improvement practice in the consideration of historical space context and inspires the navigation of urban residential space regeneration. It was inevitable that projects that prioritized interests over the culture of history had to dismantle buildings of historical significance, sometimes even damaging heritage buildings, which deviated from the goal. Eventually, the cultural and historical crisis in Beijing led to an organic renewal in the principles of urban planning and design for Beijing, which topped the historical and cultural cities list in China. In dilapidated housing renovation in recent years, the relationship between reformation and protection has been well adjusted, and micro-promotion has been conducted rather than mass-demolition.

2.2 Organic Renewal and Cultural Context Protection: From the 80s of the 20th Century

The thinking of organic renewal, first initiated in the 80s of the 20th century, which was couraged by Prof. Liangyong Wu, posited that the renewal counted "both regional completeness and partial creativity" to practice from integrity, spontaneity, continuity, stage, economy, human scale, and comprehensive benefits (Wu 1991). The 90s of the 20th century saw the era of rebuilding of old houses and declining areas being replaced by regional redevelopment to keep up with the continuity of urban historical patterns as well as maintain spatial and cultural harmony.

Regional Scale (Public Ownership): Predominant projects, such as the Factory 798 regeneration, Nanluoguxiang Area Regeneration, Guozijian Historic Area Regeneration, and Baitasi Historic District Regeneration, conduct diligent research on regional cultural sustainability and can benefit from micro and slightly scale reconstruction while maintaining the humanistic size of streets in their historical and cultural city context (Fang 2000).

Courtyard Scale (Private Ownership): Located in the heart of Beijing's inner-city, the courtyard houses were lacking in both quantity and quality. But the renovation and repurposing of the houses to serve as cafés, restaurants, studios, bars, and hotels demonstrated the regeneration of business (Fig. 2).

Rebuilding vernacularly includes restoring totally, restoring partially, repairing, or renovating existing houses with old house appearances preserved, such as gray roof tile, pitched roofs, and timber structures. They enhance the space with modern city lifestyle features. With the creative reorganization of the space, the courtyards appear as a cultural mix of traditional and modern. They become a city-wide character of distinction, at the same time drawing the attention of youngsters. The old hutong areas sensed the economic vitality of the region when they became once more the site of a cultural center.

Fig. 2. B.I.U.E. Architecture Studio's White Pagoda Temple Hutong Courtyard Renovation Project. (https://www.archdaily.com/898127/white-pagoda-temple-hutong-courtyard-renovation-blue-architecture-studio)

2.3 Strict Urban Land Management: 2015–2018

Overcrowding has become one of Beijing's most significant problems since the 1980s (Wu 1996). In the Eleventh Five Year Plan, protection and conservation of the old city is highlighted, with an emphasis on covering a population of 200,000 with extensive conservation and protection across the city's administrative regions. This is to ensure the comprehensive protection of a city's historical culture and landscape resources.

In 2017, the Beijing municipal government launched a three-year specific project on urban landscape to "alleviate, renovate, and hasten improvement" for the traditional appearance of historical streets, urban density control, and living quality improvement by dispersing activities and enterprises not related to the city's function as a national capital. Demolition and renovation inevitably caused spatial confusion in the living quarters filled with illegal private construction, such as the furnitures left over an executive demolition of Paoju Toutiao Hutong (Fig. 3). Based on the demolition of 59.85 million square meters of illegal construction in 2017, Beijing further proposed that no less than 40 million square meters of illegal construction area be demolished in 2018. Beijing then launched the campaign of "Leave White for Green" that led to massive land demolition in the city, in addition to the greening of 1600 ha the creation of 10 urban parks and a 100-km health pathway. In 2019, the city demolished more than 4,000 hectares of land. In 2020, the whole year was dedicated to dismantling illegal construction of 25 million square meters, and reclaiming 3000 ha of land. After effectively limiting the total construction area within the city boundary, Beijing is ready for the next step of regeneration design, with new focus on reorganization and reuse of the alleviated and renovated space.

Fig. 3. The alleviated and renovated Paoju Toutiao Hutong with residents' items, Dongcheng District. (By Huan Wang)

2.4 Future-Oriented Urban Regeneration Plan: "Beijing Urban Renewal Action Plan (2021–2025)"

In the 2020s, Beijing will undergo heightened requirements in building-land management to achieve an advanced, eco-efficient, and flourishing city. It is the "Beijing Urban Renewal Action Plan (2021–2025)", which therefore links the "alleviate, renovate, and hasten to upgrade" and announces the goal and direction to take full advantage of the removed community space in the next five years. The official initial strives to establish the informatization, digitization, and intelligent upgrade of urban renewal projects. For the communities in the central area of Beijing, it will encourage the application-style rent withdrawal, protective repairs, and restorative construction of bungalows (courtyards) in the functional core area of the capital through multiple channels and improve the "symbiosis courtyard" model. A combination of participation, co-governance, and sharing will be one of the fundamental principles over time for community co-establishment and co-management in hutong and apartment building areas, which will incorporate the renewals into the grass-roots work of community consultative co-government. In this regard, the neighborhood is a fundamental public community unit and needs more attention in the future due to the intersection of material space, renovating management, and cultural pursuits (Fig. 4).

Accordingly, entering a new era, Beijing's urban generation adopts new philosophy in planning and design, shifting its focus from dismantling and rebuilding to emphasizing the precise reuse of existing space and then to improving social governance and community culture. As a living site for a community, urban management does not only plan for the long-term development of city patterns, but also focuses on the community-wide building. Renewal of urban spaces is recommended to present a flexible and functional solution for renovated spaces while engaging residents in the process. Only by motivating the enthusiasm of residents into the community can the transformation of the community truly be revitalized. Similarly, only when residents truly love and take the initiative to

Fig. 4. Xinghua community service station after a renovation project. (By Jin Li and Jiaqi Li)

build their neighborhoods can community renewal achieve vigorous development, in essence.

3 Challenges and Approach

General Control Over the Features of Historical and Cultural Cities: Control is both protective and restrictive. According to the renewal action, in the Beijing urban area, especially within the 2nd ring road, traditional residential buildings cannot be demolished in principle. Instead of increasing the building construction area, simply, the sustainable plan sorts into an accessible and flexible redesign of the spatial resources.

Style of Old and New Construction under the Pattern of Traditional Capital: At this stage, Beijing attaches significant importance to the traditional style and value of hutong and courtyard in the traditional-styled district and also respects the obvious improvement in urban life quality caused by technological innovation and foreign cultural impact. Community, the grassroots urban management unit, has formed its own unique culture in the development of cities due to factors such as regionality, property rights, and resources of the population. It can be preserved and utilized as a common sense of community culture, and play a positive role in promoting residents ' participation in community co-governance and community co-construction.

Community Space for All Age Groups: In fact, young people, especially children, are less involved in community activities than the elderly do. Community public spaces serve all residents; likewise, community spaces serve all sectors of the population to participate in their activities. Reflecting on the place, activities, and means of community activities is crucial to captivate youth's interests and thus cultivate their community awareness, enhance their community participation, and cultivate the spirit of community solidarity and voluntary dedication from childhood.

In general, the development of the city poses a challenge to design: how to repurpose existing construction space for innovative design that will invite residents of all ages to participate in community events and cultivate community consciousness among the residents.

This study posits that the problems faced by the development of Beijing City are becoming increasingly complex, calling for future-oriented urban planning and design concepts to show distinct and professional characteristics. However, urban problems should not be unilaterally addressed by urban planning and design but should appeal to transductive thinking. Urban renovation shifts from simply upgrading space to organizing community activities, advancing from slogan requirements to attracting residents' active participation, from one-time activities to long-term sustainable community participation. Thus, this study seeks to create a community center that integrates space, planes, and media technologies through the use of a design professional to design for practical feasibility. By switching the perspective to a user-centered and requirement-based one, urban regeneration can be more relevant to the overall needs of the community.

4 The Renovation of a Rooftop Garden on the Shoupa Community Service Station Building

4.1 Project Background

The area within Beijing City's Second Ring Road retains a few precious courtyard-pattern hutongs, as well as several scattered in contemporary urban reinforced concrete buildings in Hutong residential areas, retelling the history of the old city and constituting a diverse urban neighborhood spatial style. In Xicheng District's Jinrong Street Subdistrict, contemporary architecture and traditional streets combine to create a street that has both CBD and hutongs with courtyards, such as Zhuanta Hutong, Jingsheng Hutong, and Dongtiejiang Hutong. Imprinted with the cultural conflict between tradition and contemporary, its community service and activities afford considerable access to the modern factors that contribute to the unique impression of community culture.

Fig. 5. The current situation of the Shoupa community service station. (By Huan Wang)

The Shoupa community is one of the communities with a mixed constructive-patterns, which includes residential areas such as courtyards and apartment buildings, as well as service spaces such as schools and markets. It is located in the Dongtiejiang Hutong, facing the north side of the Fuxingmen Road. This is north of the bustling Xidan commercial area, the National Cultural Palace, and south of Lu Xun middle school. The Shoupa community has 1304 households and 3395 residents. The community service station planned to remodel the rooftop into a shared citizen space in 2021, standing on the community's spatial transformation. Because the service station had an advanced planting plan and aimed to attract young people and children to take part in the community activities, it was expected to build a community plant-sharing garden with the function of science popularization in the space to attract more young people to join the community. Its specific needs were:

1. A shared place for residents' activities, rest, and chat.
2. A flexible space that can be re-used for outdoor festival party requirements.
3. Make full use of the surrounding plants and service station vegetable cultivation.
4. There is a unique IP image attached to the community garden's daily activities for children.
5. Additionally, in the future, the adjacent rooftop needs to function as a platform for activities, so the design should take this into consideration.
6. It has the function of popular science.
7. Reflecting the uniqueness of community culture through community service stations.
8. Attract young people to community activities and focus on communities.
9. Consideration of operational maintenance sustainability.

4.2 Empathy and Research

The design process began with community staff interviews aiming to determine the use of the site, mainly for the local service station's secretary. According to the conversation, many residents over the age of 80 participated in activities in their community, including dance, gardening, and handcrafted decorations. Community residents were highly involved, but most of them were older. It also showed that although children living in apartment buildings and courtyards in same region, due to the physical isolation of their living space, there were few opportunities for children to communicate. Children required a space where they can communicate and be entertained in a safe environment. Unsurprisingly, community service stations had also expressed expectations for added space on the roof (Fig. 5). The following design fields proceeded from three aspects: physical space, humanistic needs, and community culture.

Firstly, we measured the physical space. The survey and mapping results showed this site is about 80 m^2 in rectangular range, with a regular shape and a flat surface. At present, the flow of people entering the site had to cross the working space of the service station, and then from the building back stairs to the platform, which needed to be changed. But the glass roof of a well and an outdoor air conditioner must be kept, and the leaky glass roof must be fixed, leaving a sort of boundary for the site. Based on the site's 3D model and function streaming analysis, the design team rearranged the future by adding an external staircase for the platform, and the platform itself retains the traffic before and after the service station building.

Secondly, humanistic needs and community culture were the focus of design research. The research consisted of a questionnaire and an interview. The respondents of the questionnaire were community residents. A total of 100 questionnaires were collected. A majority of respondents lived in the building area, with a proportion of 1:1 evenly distributed among the 40 and 60–70-year-olds (Fig. 6). The results showed that: 1) For 99% of residents, a community service station was a popular destination. This showed enthusiasm and a good response to the activities of the community; 2) The design represented the anticipated goal of the platform. In the feedback, it was found that residents had the highest demand for youth space, which was highly consistent with the original functional requirements of community service stations. At the same time, the main themes of residents' activities were life knowledge or skills, cultural and recreational sports activities, and manual decoration. These themes were also highly consistent with the original intention of the platform design; 3) More importantly, the residents' intention to participate in children's community activities was up to 89%, and the participation in traditional festivals was up to 93%; and 4) The questionnaire also investigated the feasibility of the plant theme for activities. In the feedback we received, the plant topics were divided into those who would like to participate and those who would like to actively participate. The rooftop function orientation distribution is depicted in Fig. 7. Therefore, a plant-themed platform for residents' community activities could strike a balance between satisfying residents' needs and meeting the functional requirements of the community service stations.

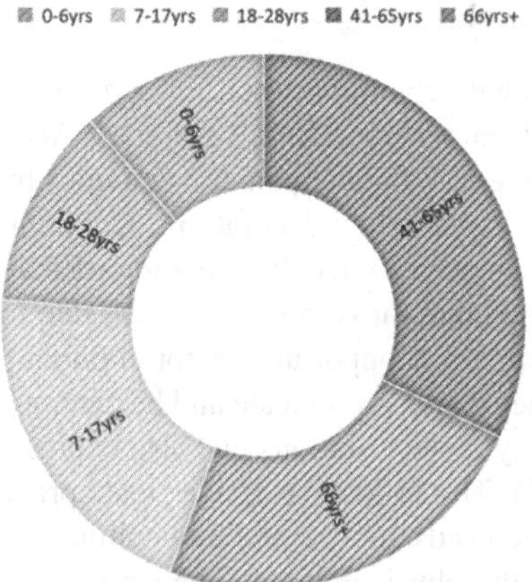

Fig. 6. The age distribution of the interviewees. (By design team)

4.3 Design Description

The design of rooftop garden aimed to meet a diverse requirement according to the research. As for the layout, construction of the eastern side would be Phase I since it was permitted already, and construction of the western side would be Phase II. The space

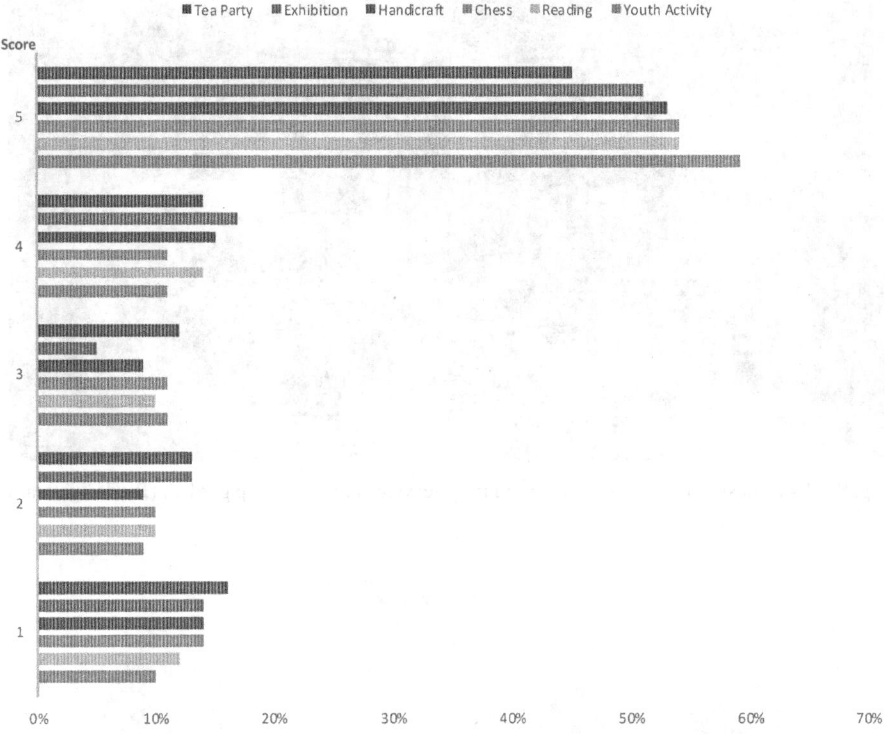

Fig. 7. The rooftop function orientation distribution. (By design team)

design in Phase I was based on the comprehensive consideration of the functions of planting, activities, staying, and leisure. The surrounding area was regarded as the main planting area, with a three-dimensional flower box, an independent flower box, and a flower frame. There would be a rest area for dynamic and static functional partitioning in the middle and near the plant. A creative solution to address the problem of glass skylights was to set a big tabletop on the front of the window to prevent leaking water and afford outdoor work. The re-planned site hoped that residents would like to stay on the platform longer and comfortably, which was why the designed broken-line shelf provided functions such as wind and rain shelter and hanging decorations (Fig. 8).

To recall the interests of community activities and residents' real interest in space, following the planning of science popularization activities, the design team proposed plant cognition, planting blinding-box, flowerpot DIY drawing, and other daily activities. The design sought to create images related to seeds from the perspective of children to bestow a specific spiritual identity on the site. Then a unique IP (Intellectual Property) was designed for the Shoupa community's rooftop garden, which was a seed family, including blue seed for "Blue Dad," red seed for "Red Mom," and yellow seed for "Yellow Son," along with the participative equipment of plant tags, activity guides, drawing directions, and so on. The image of IP is showed in Fig. 9.

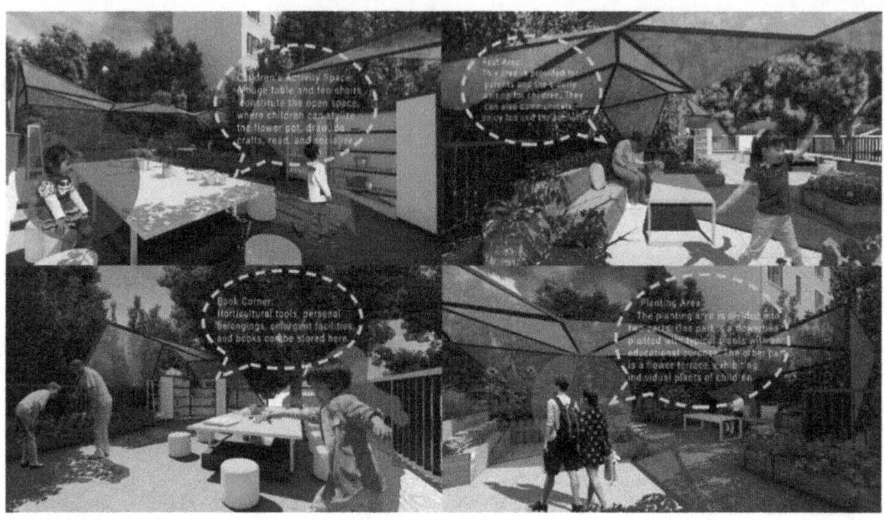

Fig. 8. Space design for the Shoupa community service station rooftop garden. (By design team)

Fig. 9. IP design for the Shoupa community service station rooftop garden. (By design team) (Color figure online)

On the basis of IP image designed for seed blind boxes and drawing flowerpot activities, a future Wechat mini app plan for establishing a virtual plant-theme community was currently being developed. The blind box design is showed in Fig. 10. The mini-app was supposed to help in achieving location-free actions and promote a compact connection between users. Considering the increasing infiltration of online contents into people's daily lives, an online platform would be highly value-adding. The application manifested

Fig. 10. Blind box design for the Shoupa community service station rooftop garden. (By design team)

interactive functions related to planting knowledge, planting blogs, peripheral activities, item exchanges, plant adoptions, and many other online functions. With the rooftop garden, the design strived to create both a physical and a virtual shared community space.

This design was currently in the late construction and production stages and was expected to be commissioned by March 2022. Once the project is completed, we can expect a new plant-themed activity space with online and offline experiences tailored to all ages of the community.

5 Conclusion

The wave of land requisition and housing demolition having been sweeping China since 1990s is an unprecedented clearance movement in essence (Zhang 2015), but Beijing has transformed the direction on urban spatial regeneration from cultural consideration. Facing massive challenges in an ongoing process towards comprehensive urban governance, the neighborhood public space regeneration actually needs residences' participatory. The development of the city has broken through the concept of "dimension" commonly, while the restrictly construction management of land in Beijing also calls for human-centered creative transformation. This study is an attempt to reshape the community public space, aiming at planning the site for the activities-oriented community participation and seeking the effective design approach for cultural and constructional sustainability.

Acknowledgments. This paper is an achievement of a research program identified as Teaching Research on Inter-Design Workshop "Community+ University" Toward Urban Regeneration of Beijing (Grant No. CDCA21124), which is supported by the Beijing Office for Education Science Planning.

The authors would like to thank the design team, which includes Zhixuan Yue and Li Wang from the College of Fine Arts, Capital Normal University, and Yu Han, Zixiao Chen, Yuyun Huang, Runzhe Wei and Yiran Sun from the Department of Construction Management, Tsinghua University. Jin Li and Jiaqi Li, who are also from Capital Normal University, provided project photos.

The authors are also grateful to the staff of the Shoupa Community Service Station, who contributed their insightful comments and suggestions for the project.

References

Wu, L.: The general thinking of Beijing planning and construction. Beijing Plan. Rev. **3**, 1–3 (1996)

Wu, L., Rowe, P.G.: Rehabilitating the Old City of Beijing: A Project in the Ju'er Hutong Neighbourhood, vol. 3. UBC Press (1999)

Zhang, Y., Fang, K.: Politics of housing redevelopment in China: the rise and fall of the Ju'er Hutong project in inner-city Beijing. J. Housing Built Environ. **18**(1), 75–87 (2003)

Chen, H., Zhang, H.: Research on renovation planning of traditional Hutong—take Beijing Juer Hutong renovation project as Axample. IOP Conf. Ser. Earth Environ. Sci. **330**(2), 022116 (2019)

Liu, X.: Beijing urban renewal: the theory evoluement and practice characteristics. Urban Dev. **10** (2012)

Hou, X., Guo, W.: Community micro-regeneration: approaches to the design intervention of old city public space of Beijing. Landscape **25**(04), 41–47 (2018)

Jiayan, L.: Relationship, network, and neighborhood: review on urban community social network analysis and its prospect. City Plan. **2014**(02), 91–96 (2014)

Jiayan, L., Caige, L.: Review on Study on Major Social Issues and Solutions in Chinese Urbanization Process, 1 (2015)

Jiayan, L.: Study on social planning strategies in China's urban planning. China City Plan. Rev. **20**(1), 20–29 (2011)

Zhou, D., Xu, S., Sun, C., Deng, Y.: Dynamic and drivers of spatial change in rapid urban renewal within Beijing inner city. Habitat Int. **111**, 102349 (2021)

Wenshu, L., Ming, Z.: Analysis and enlightenment on the medium and long-term development strategy planning of mega-regions. Urban Plan. Int. **04** (2015)

Guangqi, D.: Retrospect and prospect of the protection and reconstruction of old Beijing. China City Plan. Rev. 12–16 (1994)

Yuting, H.: Strategies for improving public transportation accessibility in Beijing's urban regeneration from an inclusive perspective: inspirations from Paris's experience. China City Plan. Rev. **30**(3), 54–61 (2021)

Junhua, L.: Beijing's old and dilapidated housing renewal. Cities **14**(2), 59–69 (1997)

Nan, Y., Jing, G.: Formation of better streets: interpretation of urban design guidelines for Beijing street regeneration and governance. China City Plan. Rev. **28**(3) (2019)

Leal Filho, W., Azul, A.M., Brandli, L., Özuyar, P.G., Wall, T. (eds.): Sustainable Cities and Communities. Springer, Cham (2019). https://doi.org/10.1007/978-3-319-95717-3

Martínez, P.G.: New in old: the 'urban renewal' thematic exhibition of the 2019 Beijing design week. Built Heritage **3**(4), 92–94 (2019)

Zhu, H., Chen, K., Lian, Y.: Do temporary creative clusters promote innovation in an emerging economy?—a case study of the Beijing design week. Sustainability **10**(3), 767 (2018)

Akers, A. S. (2015). Neighborhood design and public life: lessons from Beijing's hutong and superblocks (Doctoral dissertation, Massachusetts Institute of Technology)

Liu, H., Li, B.: Changes of spatial characteristics: socio-cultural sustainability in historical neighborhood in Beijing, China. Sustainability **13**(11), 6212 (2021)

Zhang, C., Lu, B.: Residential satisfaction in traditional and redeveloped inner city neighborhood: a tale of two neighborhoods in Beijing. Travel Behav. Soc. **5**, 23–36 (2016)

Broudehoux, A.M.: Neighborhood regeneration in Beijing: An overview of projects implemented in the inner city since 1990 (1994)

Tao, S.L.L.: A study on the neighborhood ties of Beijing urban residents in old city zone. Urban Probl. **2** (2007)

Zhang, Y.: Great clearances: the Chinese version of enclosure movement (1991—2013). China Agric. Univ. J. Soc. Sci. Ed. **32**(03), 19-4.5 (2015)

Li, N., Chan, D., Mao, Q., Hsu, K., Fu, Z.: Urban sustainability education: Challenges and pedagogical experiments. Habitat Int. **71**, 70–80 (2018)

Li, N., Chan, D., Hsu, K., Fu, Z., Mao, Q.: ICT-enabled cross-cultural education in sustainable urbanization. In: Computing in Civil Engineering, pp. 43–50 (2017)

Fang, K.: Contemporary Redevelopment in the Inner City of Beijing: Survey, Analysis and Investigation. China Construction Industry Publishing House, Beijing (2000). (in Chinese)

Beijing's Five-year Urban Renewal Action Plan Announced. See tao News (2021). https://www.seetao.com/details/108352.html

The '11th Five-Year' Old City Preservation of Beijing will Relieve 200,000 people. China News (2007). https://www.chinanews.com.cn/gn/news/2007/11-20/1082273.shtml

Beijing City Renewal Action Plan (2021–2025). The State Council, The People's Republic of China (2021). http://www.gov.cn/xinwen/2021-09/01/content_5634665.htm

The Community Service Stations of Xicheng District Have Become 'Public Living Room'. Qianlong News (2019). http://beijing.qianlong.com/2019/1126/3452559.shtml#g3452559=1

White Pagoda Temple Hutong Courtyard Renovation/B.L.U.E. Architecture Studio

https://www.archdaily.com/898127/white-pagoda-temple-hutong-courtyard-renovation-blue-architecture-studio

Material-Oriented Active Making: A Promising Approach for Sustainable Transitions

Ye Yang(✉) and Hongtao Zhou

College of Design and Innovation, Tongji University, Shanghai 200092, China
yeyang_design@tongji.edu.cn

Abstract. This study is based on a workshop themed on Material-oriented Artefact Design (MAD) that 30 students majoring in Design from Chinese universities took part in. Through the methodology of Constructing Grounded Theory combined with the research methods of Participatory Observation, Semi-structured Interview and Questionnaire, we explored the distinctions between MAD and Problem-oriented Artefact Design (PAD), analyzed the advantages of MAD and further explained the reasons why MAD is worth refocusing on recently. The study demonstrates MAD is an effective way to break through the mode of PAD, exploring an active making route of materials as the starting point to advocate a new design language and material culture, so as to guide students to see materials as "new living species" that can interact and dialogue by continuous experiments. In this way, the relationship between designers and materials is subtly changing, from hierarchy to flat and equal relations, from passive acceptance to attentive care, which facilitates entering into the post-Anthropocene era for sustainability.

Keywords: Material-oriented Artefact Design · Problem-oriented Artefact Design · Active making · Sustainable transitions

1 Research Background

1.1 Turn of Materiality in Design History

When dating back the history, artefact design mode undergoes the turn from materiality to immateriality. The activity of making began when men are capable of remolding nature materials and making tools [1]. Before the renascence of modern design, artefact design started from selecting materials, and materials played an essential role throughout the whole process of design. Craftsmen who were seen as early designers actively study and dialogue with materials in order to apply proper ones in line with seasons, local conditions and individualities. Time ideals and ethics were hidden behind objects, e.g., the relationship between materials and Chinese craftsmen lay on mutual benefits, cooperation and symbiosis, maximizing the potential of materials with the most economical and ecological ways, embodying the time ideals of the *right time, right place with right people* [2].

The Horn of the second Industrial Revolution in the early 1900s raised the curtain of modern design, which highly stressed standardization, faster and mass production

P.-L. P. Rau (Ed.): HCII 2022, LNCS 13311, pp. 256–273, 2022.
https://doi.org/10.1007/978-3-031-06038-0_19

in order to stimulate consumption and boost the economy, inducing two new methods in design – prototyping and drawing [3]. These two methods facilitated the division of labor, assembly line and product assembly for industrial manufacture. From then on, designers started to get rid of the roles of traditional hand-making and separated from physical materials. The progress of industrialization in the 20th century has gradually shaped an era of complete separation between designers and physical materials [4].

Additionally, the ideal of scientizing design can be traced back to the Modernist Design Movement in the early 20th century when the pioneer Theo van Doesburg of De Stijl issued a declaration on rejecting intuitions and sensibilities as new spirits in art and design [5]. This phenomenon peaked in the 1960s with the emergence of Computer Science, Operations Research, Management Science, etc., triggering the launch of Design Methods Movement to promote the research on the design process and activities aiming at analyzing and explaining ambiguous design through scientific methods [6]. Due to the movement, some representative design methods were proposed from the 1960s to the 1970s. Although Design Methods Movement was a mistaken exploration and ended in failure, it had an important impact on the evolution of design thinking. Design thinking has gradually developed as a rational and systematic mode for complicated problems based on sketches and prototypes far from actual physical materials, which has been discussed till now [7–14]. In the 1990s, the birth of computers accentuated the immaterial and conceptual design process and CAD (Computer-Aided Design) increased the isolation even further between designer and hand-making process [15]. CAD makes body and senses seriously further weakened when designing, bringing design back to the era of the Cartesian dualism of mind and body. In the 21st century, the rapid development of AI (Artificial Intelligence) has strengthened and consolidated the immaterial artefact design process.

Currently, design starts from existing problems or necessities and physical materials do not take part in incubating ideas. Designers have no choice but passively accept materials under the limitations of costs and industrial manufacture at the end of design process. Designers are far away from real physical materials and keep a dominant relationship with materials.

1.2 Emerging Phenomena and Problem Arising

Materials originally come from nature, but it causes great harm and pollution when humans end their lives and discard them in the environment. We are entering into a more complicated and uncertain world with the deteriorating eco-system, more frequent extreme climates and disasters, especially the Covid-19 sweeping through the globe. The dematerialization of the artefact design process began to be questioned. A series of phenomena have emerged like Maker Movement [16, 16], material-based design [18], DIY materials [19], material-driven design [20], etc., indicating designers desire to return to the hand-making process and explore materials at the very beginning of design process proactively.

The fixed mainstream design mode that material is selected or accepted in the end is becoming melt and enters into an indeterminate situation [21].

Here, a problem is arising:

Nowadays, why do designers refocus their attention to Material-oriented Artefact Design (MAD)?

In order to respond to the problem more clearly, we broke it down into two sub-questions:

What is the difference between Material-oriented Artefact Design (MAD) and Problem-oriented Artefact Design (PAD) that selecting materials in the end?

Compared with PAD, what are the values and advantages of MAD in our current and future era?

We conducted our study under the following research process.

2 Research Process

Under the methodology of Grounded Theory, we adopted the research methods of Participatory Observation, Semi-structured Interview and Questionnaire to collect data, and applied the coding method of Constructing Grounded Theory to analyze data. The detailed research processes are as follows.

2.1 Introduction for Material-Oriented Workshop

Through Participatory Observation, I signed up for a workshop themed on *Material-driven furniture design* and acted as both a researcher and observer. The workshop was conducted during summer vacation in 2021 with 30 students with arts and design backgrounds from 26 universities in China. This study has collected and analyzed data from 15 of these students. Informed consent forms were signed regarding their images and data collecting and publishing from all interviewees.

Most of the students were novices with the MAD method. Only two of them were major in ceramic art design and had experiences with clays. The other students informed that they were all educated under the pattern of PAD and passively selected materials at the end of design. The workshop aimed at doubting the mainstream immaterial and conceptual artefact design pattern in higher education and exploring a material-driven mode for creating new furniture.

The workshop was composed of three stages within seven weeks and took place in a large studio where students could work next to each other, exchanging ideas easily and accepting suggestions and guidances from teachers and peers when needed. An free, self-directed and experimental mode was encouraged. All the students were required to record the experimental processes with images and notes. At the end of each stage, every student needed to prepare for a presentation in a reflection meeting to share and exchange experiences, which was commented on and tutored by invited experts in furniture design (see Fig. 1).

The first stage lasting one week was named *Seeing unseen: to discover and display force* and could be tagged *Discover*, *Exploration*, and *Trial.* In this stage, students were first asked to take photos of force functioning daily, e.g., gravity, buoyancy, elasticity, friction, pressure to explore the world from a new perspective. Then they were free to choose various shapeable materials like balloons, wood sticks and blocks, bamboo

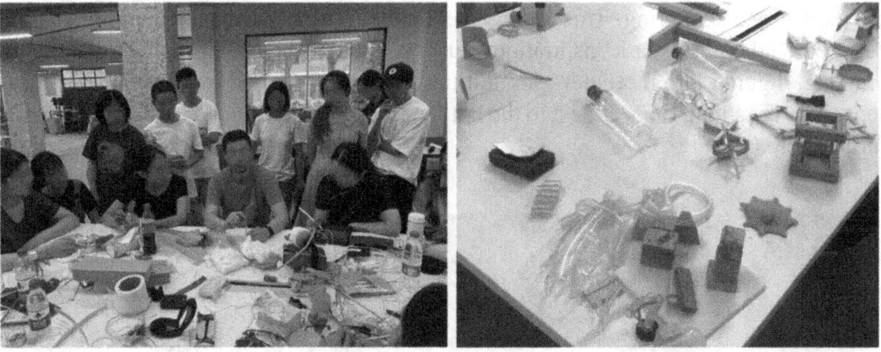

Fig. 1. Presentations to exchange experiences and tutored by invited experts in furniture design (©Bajiao Design, 2022)

belts, papers, leathers, straws and so forth, and some tools easy to manipulate like heat guns, scissors, knife sandpapers, etc. This period aimed to guide students to break the stereotypes of materials and discover new characteristics through dialogues and communications with materials using experimental methods, which was the divergent stage of thinking (see Fig. 2).

Fig. 2. Playing with balloons from various perspectives in the first stage (©Hongda Fan & Bajiao Design, 2022)

The second stage lasted for one week as well. Students explored the second theme about *Material Pairing* based on the results in the first stage. This period was conducted in a group with two members, and both of them needed to cooperate with the materials that the partner was exploring. This arrangement could not only enhance communications between students to spark inspirations but also help to break through limitations of thinking, digging into more new possibilities as all of them had explored one material separately for a long time, almost to the bottleneck. This stage aimed to diverge thinking furthermore (see Fig. 3).

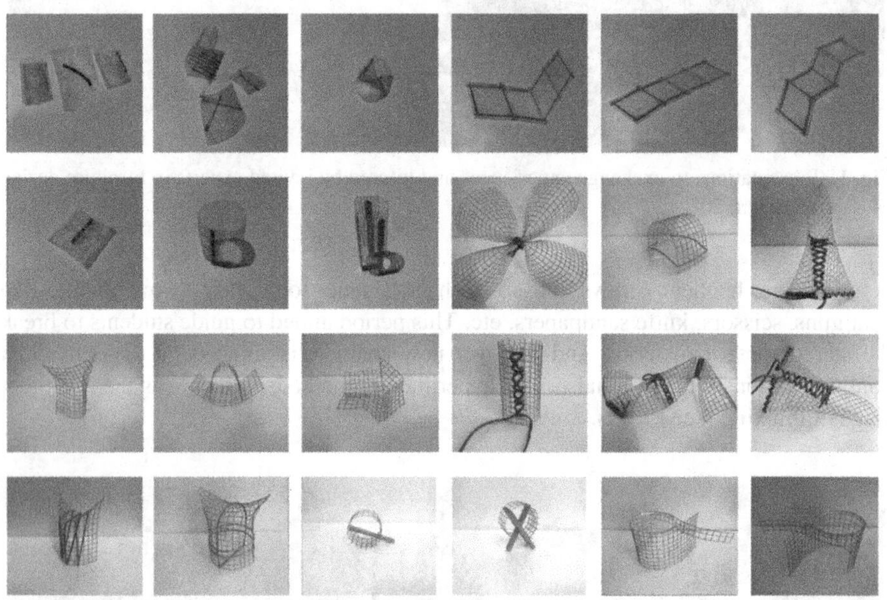

Fig. 3. Exploring net with different materials in the second stage (©Yinhuang Luo & Bajiao Design, 2022)

The third stage extended two weeks. After the last two weeks' exploitation, each participant found one interesting experimental direction for further study, which could be tagged *Analysis and Experiment.* The control Variable method was suggested in the experiments. In order to deeply exploit one of the features of the material, analyzing all the components that influenced this property and identifying the independent and dependent variables are critical steps, and then applying the Control Variable method to control and change independent variables to do deep researches on the effects of the different components produced on the results. This is the convergent stage of thinking and students would ensure one of the prototypes entering into the fourth period.

The fourth stage lasting three weeks, was to transform one of the satisfying results explored in the last four weeks and be marked with *Transition and Iteration.* It was designed to transform the small hand-made model in the early stage into a large model that could be manufactured in the factory in the future (see Fig. 4).

Overall, this workshop reflected on the current mainstream model of PAD: *Survey* → *Pain Points* → *Concepts* → *Sketches* → *Modeling* → *Rendering* → *Selecting Materials* → *Manufacturing*, and advocated a new MAD route practiced in western countries:

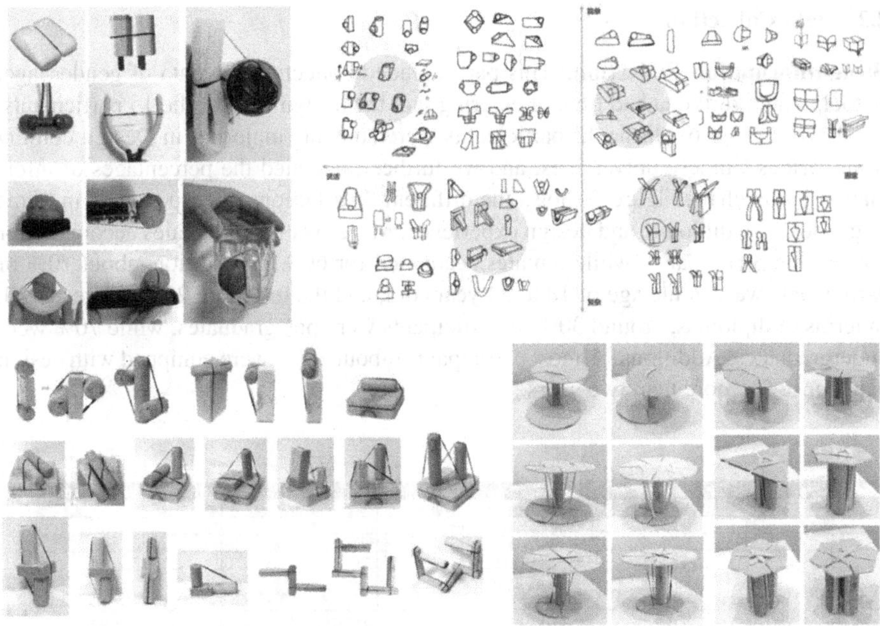

Fig. 4. The exploring process step by step from the beginning to the end (©Xiang Ma & Bajiao Design, 2022)

(alternative)Materials → Observing → Understanding → Analyzing → Experimenting → Testing → Iterating → Translation → Manufacturing (see Fig. 5).

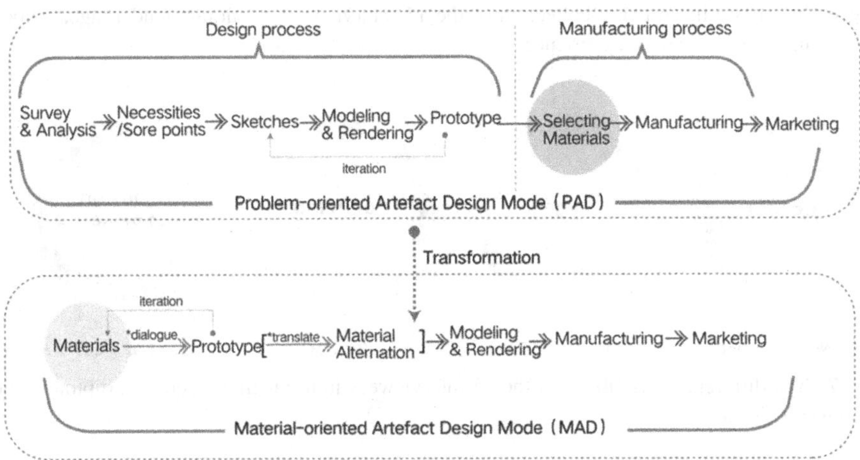

Fig. 5. Tow artefact design modes: PAD and MAD (©Ye Yang, 2022)

2.2 Data Collection

Basic Information Collection. This part included collecting the data of gender, age, school, major, diploma and time of entering into the design field of the 15 participants. As shown in Fig. 6, all the 15 participants were students majoring in Design coming from various Chinese universities, and we further calculated the percentages of information in the chart. Figure 7 shows the different distributions of respondents in terms of gender, age, diploma, and design experience. More specifically, males accounted for 40% of the participants, while females accounted for 60%. In addition, about 70% of participants were at the age of 18 to 24 years old, and the rest were 25 to 30 years old. In terms of diplomas, around 30% of participants were postgraduates, while 70% were undergraduates. Additionally, most participants (about 70%) were equipped with design experience for more than two years.

Number	Name	Gender	Age	School	Major	Diploma	Design Experience
1	P Duan	Woman	24	Nanjing Forestry University	Furniture Design	BA	4 years
2	H Yang	Man	23	Hansan Normal College	Product Design	BA	3 years
3	C Liu	Man	28	HeiLongjiang University	Industrial Design	BA	6 years
4	Y Luo	Man	29	Jingdezhen Ceramic University	Product Design	Ph.D	9 years
5	H Fan	Man	24	School of Fine Arts, Anhui Normal University	Product Design	BA	4 years
6	R Cao	Woman	22	Zhongnan University	Product Design	BA	3 years
7	X Liu	Woman	25	Central Academy of Fine Arts	Ceramic Design	BA	5 years
8	M Zi	Woman	25	Guangzhou Academy of Fine Arts	Environment Design	BA	2 years
9	X Yuan	Woman	24	Tongji University	Industrial Design	BA	5 years
10	X Ma	Woman	23	Jiangnan University	Product Design	BA	4 years
11	W Tian	Woman	26	Jiangnan University	Visual Design	MA	5 years
12	T Mu	Man	26	Nottingham-Ningbo University	Architecture Design	BA	8 years
13	H Dai	Woman	22	Nanjing Forestry University	Industrial Design	BA	3 years
14	W Gong	Man	26	East China University of Science and Technology	Industrial Design	MA	7 years
15	J Chen	Woman	25	School of Fine Arts, Anhui Normal University	Product Design	MA	5 years

Fig. 6. The basic information collection of the 15 interviewees including gender, age, school, major, diploma, and design experience

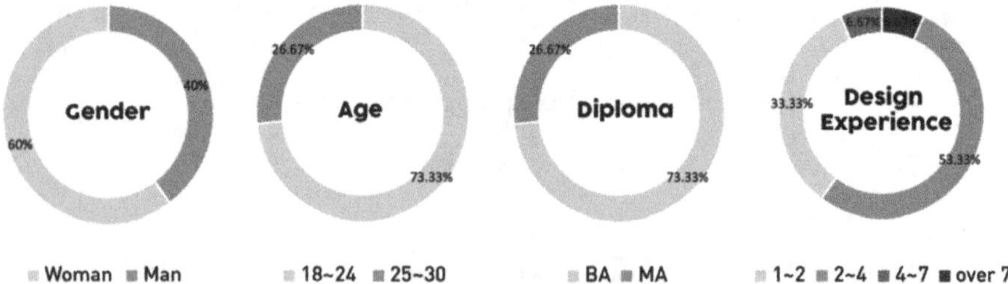

Fig. 7. The different distributions of the 15 interviewees in terms of gender, age, diploma, and design experience.

Questionnaire. We conducted a survey using questionnaires to compare PAD and MAD about making satisfaction, inspiration stimulation, motivation, etc. As shown in Fig. 8, scores of each category of MAD were all higher than those of PAD, and average scores of MAD and PAD are 4.155/5 and 3.476/5 separately. Figure 9 revealed that around 90% of participants would like to continue the method of MAD, and 30% of them conveyed strong wishes.

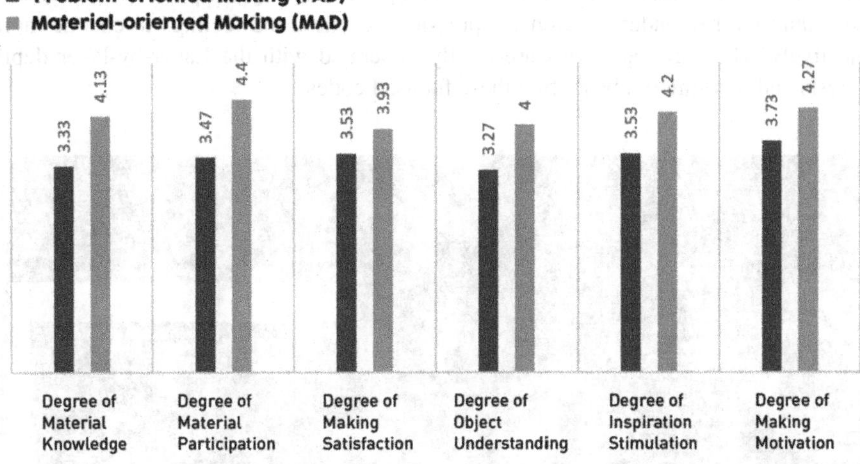

Fig. 8. Scores of PAD and MAD given by the 15 interviewees

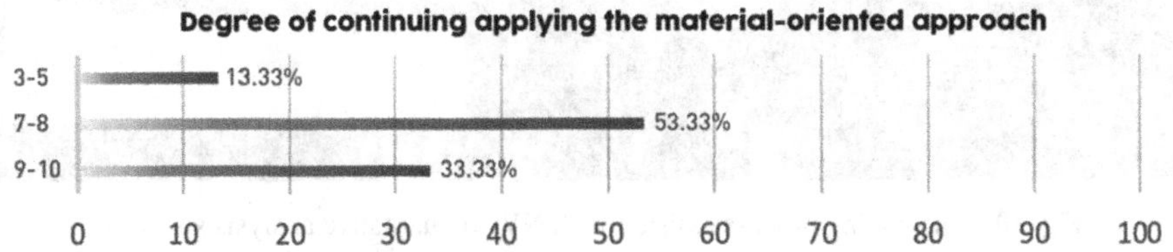

Fig. 9. Scores of continuing applying MAD given by the 15 interviewees

Semi-structured Interview. We designed an outline of questions for semi-structured interviews based on the research problem above, and then made appointments with interviewees one by one. All the interviews were conducted in voice calls combined with online conferences. Before each interview, every interviewee was required to sign an informed consent. All the interviews were recorded, and the questions could be flexibly adjusted to the responses of the interviewees in real-time.

2.3 Data Analysis

We analyzed texts of the 15 interviewees through Constructing Grounded Theory [22], which produces theory through initial coding and focused coding. The initial coding forms concepts in the original data through line-by-line phrase analysis, while the focused coding produces theories through integrating essential concepts.

The coding process was assisted with NVivo qualitative analysis software (see Fig. 10). We initially coded repetitions, memorable and meaningful ideas, focus points, metaphors, turning-points among these responses. We tried to classify data into different parts or attributes and define their actions or ideas using phrases or words. Then we gradually grouped the initial codes through the most frequent topics to merge them into prominent themes as focused codes (Ibid., p. 73). During this period, we started to understand the responders' actions, expressions, scenes, and feelings to encode more objectively. The core categories are finally generated with the Layer-by-layer depth analysis and merging or abstracting these focused codes.

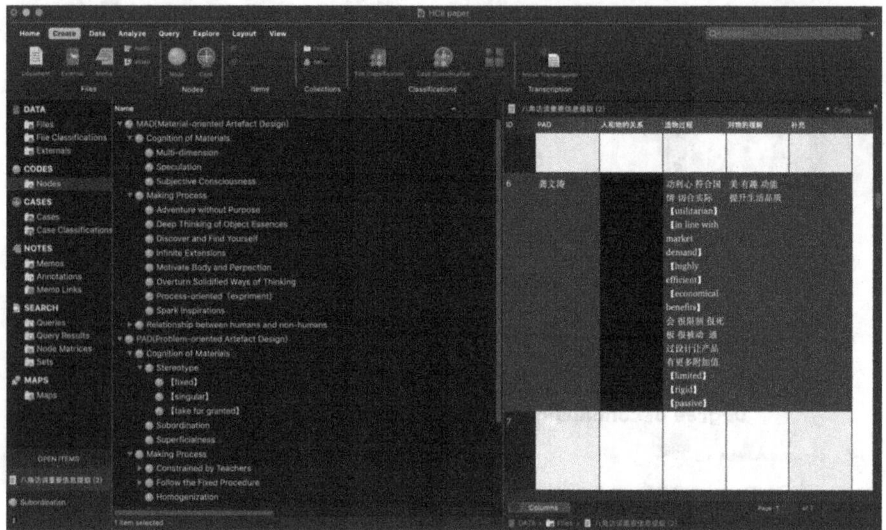

Fig. 10. The coding process assisted with NVivo qualitative analysis software

The differences between Material-oriented Artefact Design (MAD) and Problem-oriented Artefact Design (PAD) are mainly reflected in three aspects. The following Table 1 and Table 2 show the coding results of the data.

Cognition of Materials. Under the pattern of PAD, as physical materials do not participate in the design ideation process, students are used to keeping stereotypes and having very superficial knowledge for materials. Materials take a subordinate role in design to follow the function or styling. The following relevant excerpts are taken from the interviews.

I was used to first thinking about the function of an object and then looking for suitable material.—From J Cao.

I only considered materials at the last design stage, and materials acted as textures in the computer.—From X Yuan.

I regarded materials were qualitative, and materials could only work owing to their physical properties. I always took their existences for granted.—From H Fan.

Table 1. Coding results of **PAD** assisted by Nvivo based on the interview texts under the methodology of Constructing Grounded Theory.

Categories	Focused coding	Initial coding
1. Cognition of materials	1.1 Stereotype	1.1.1 Fixed properties 1.1.2 Singular 1.1.3 Take for granted
	1.2 Subordination	1.2.1 Select at the end 1.2.2 To match/follow the function or style 1.2.3 To make the concept work 1.2.4 Use as a tool 1.2.5 Following renderings
	1.3 Superficialness	1.3.1 Theoretical learning 1.3.2 Like renderings 1.3.3 Focus on superficial effects 1.3.4 Swallow cognition
2. Making process	2.1 Constrained by teachers	2.1.1 Please and satisfy teachers 2.1.2 Constrained by teachers' preferences
	2.2 Follow the fixed procedure	2.2.1 Cramming 2.2.2 Follow the steps intentionally 2.2.3 Modeling and rendering 2.2.4 Finish a task 2.2.5 Search for pain points intentionally 2.2.6 Help to build the design logic quickly
	2.3 Homogenization	2.3.1 Follow the similar thinking mode 2.3.2 Always meet similar plans
	2.4 Influenced by reference	2.4.1 "Transplant" from others 2.4.2 Limited by references
	2.5 Loss of identity	2.5.1 Passively execute 2.5.2 Do for others 2.5.3 Mechanically work like a robot

(continued)

Table 1. (*continued*)

Categories	Focused coding	Initial coding
	2.6 Purpose-oriented	2.6.1 Suitable for problem-solving 2.6.2 Guided by clear and specific steps 2.6.3 With preconceived goals
	2.7 Utilitarian	2.7.1 In line with market demand 2.7.2 Economic benefits 2.7.3 A fast feasible way 2.7.4 Highly efficient
	2.8 Dualism of mind and body	2.8.1 Think only by brain 2.8.2 Modeling and rendering in computer 2.8.3 Lose capabilities of hands 2.8.4 Lack of participation of other senses
3. Relationship between humans and non-humans	3.1 Alienation	3.1.1 Little apprehension 3.1.2 Far from real materials 3.1.3 Distant with materials 3.1.4 Treat with indifference
	3.2 Hierarchy	3.2.1 Use as a tool 3.2.2 Tame materials 3.3.3 Serve me
	3.3 Passivity	3.3.1 Think very little 3.3.2 Take for granted
	3.4 Exterior practicality	3.4.1 Focus on function and styling 3.4.2 Branding and icon 3.4.3 Atmosphere rendering

Table 2. Coding results assisted by Nvivo of **MAD** based on the interview texts under the methodology of Constructing Grounded Theory.

Categories	Focused coding	Initial coding
1. Cognition of materials	1.1 Multi-dimension	1.1.1 Stereoscopic and vibrant 1.1.2 Pay more attention to humanistic, societal, and environmental issues 1.1.3 Discover new possibilities

(*continued*)

Table 2. (*continued*)

Categories	Focused coding	Initial coding
	1.2 Speculation	1.2.1 Avoid habitual thinking 1.2.2 Redefine materials 1.2.3 Find conflicts in one material 1.2.4 Discover reverse sides of features 1.2.5 Remove established features 1.2.6 Get rid of fixed categories
	1.3 Subjective consciousness	1.3.1 Give me surprise 1.3.2 Direct me 1.3.3 With life 1.3.4 With personalities 1.3.5 Work as communicators 1.3.6 Unique properties 1.3.7 With emotions
2. Making process	2.1 Adventure without purpose	2.1.1 Gain without aims 2.1.2 Unimaginable results 2.1.3 Happen by chances 2.1.4 Take a long time 2.1.5 Explore the boundary without safety
	2.2 Pure	2.2.1 Deep-thinking of object essences 2.2.2 Return to childhood 2.2.3 Enjoy the simplicity 2.2.4 Get rid of style and function
	2.3 Discover and find yourself	2.3.1 Follow my logic 2.3.2 To be a deep-thinking designer 2.3.3 Discover your unique style 2.3.4 Find your unique perspective and language 2.3.5 Form your thinking methods 2.3.6 Have a firm belief in yourself 2.3.7 Self-driven

(*continued*)

Table 2. (*continued*)

Categories	Focused coding	Initial coding
	2.4 Infinite extensions	2.4.1 Form your material library 2.4.2 Explore a unique way for infinite possibilities
	2.5 Motivate body and perception	2.5.1 Harvest through hand-making 2.5.2 Complementary to design thinking
	2.6 Overturn solidified ways of thinking	2.6.1 Breakthrough boundaries of cognition 2.6.2 Start from concrete and end in abstract
	2.7 Process-oriented (experiments)	2.7.1 Long-time exploration 2.7.2 Continue exploring
	2.8 Spark inspirations	2.8.1 Come across accidents 2.8.2 Keep mind and body aware 2.8.3 Back to zero
3. Relationship between humans and non-humans	3.1 Equality	3.1.1 Get closer with objects 3.1.2 Feel with the heart 3.1.3 Listen to materials 3.1.4 Have dialogues 3.1.5 Have a thorough understanding
	3.2 Initiative	3.2.1 Observe daily life carefully 3.2.2 Discover Ignored phenomena from new perspectives 3.3.3 Rooted in daily behaviours 3.2.4 Spend more time observing
	3.3 Spirituality	3.3.1 Focus on inner meanings 3.3.2 Pay more attention to simple but unusual stuff 3.3.3 Emotional communications

While after the practice of MAD, participants' cognition for materials has changed a lot. Students learn to observe materials from multi-dimensions, and they start to have speculative thinking towards materials. More importantly, materials seem to have lived with subjective consciousnesses. We selected some related interview recordings demonstrated here..

Materials could give you a lot of surprises and even direct you when designing. —From J Chen.

I felt that materials have become more stereoscopic in my mind. Each material had its temper, and the combination of materials could trigger amazing chemical reactions.—From J Cao.

I preferred to think of materials from particular perspectives, like finding the reverse sides of their conventional properties and redefining them.—From X Ma.

Making Process. In terms of the method of PAD, this pattern is purpose-oriented, utilitarian, but is the dualism of mind and body. Most students gave feedback that they had been used to following the fixed procedures, constrained by teachers and influenced by references in school. This period had always made them feel a loss of identity as a designer and made their works homogeneous. The following relevant excerpts are taken from the interviews.

Following fixed routines might lead us to think in similar ways, and our solutions to the same problem might be similar.—From J Cao.

I thought the main reason I had not formed my own design languages lay on references and interferences from many people in the design process.

—From X Ma.

Before design, the teacher would give us a lot of cases to refer to. The design process was like finishing a task to satisfy teachers and the final work was like doing for others.—From H Yang.

On the contrary, MAD indicates the process-oriented, pure and motivation of mind and body. It likes a process to adventure without purpose, discover and find yourself, which can spark inspirations, have infinite extensions and overturn solidified ways of conventional thinking. Some relevant interview texts are shown as follows.

I kept exploring the unknown during the whole process and gradually, I could discover my logic.—From J Chen.

I enjoyed the state to play with materials like a small child that reminded me of my childhood.—From H Dai.

It could inspire me when I had a physical touch of something.

—From H Fan.

I would not be stuck for fresh ideas anymore as long as I explored with my hands.

—From P Duan.

Relationship Between Humans and Non-humans. More importantly, MAD can subtly change the relationship between humans and non-humans from hierarchy, passivity and exterior practicality to equality, initiative and spirituality. We selected some related interview recordings demonstrated here.

When I put my heart into the material, it would provide valuable information that I had ignored before.—From C Liu.

I began to observe life carefully, and some previously neglected phenomena could be interpreted very interesting from a new perspective.—From W Gong.

I started to have a subtle awareness of materials embedded in my body and daily behaviors.—From H Fan.

Overall, we concluded the distinctions between PAD and MAD in Table 3 as part of our responses to the problem proposed above.

Table 3. Comparisons of the distinctions between PAD and MAD

Categories	PAD	MAD
Means	Brainstorming	Experimenting
Purpose	Problem-Solving	Discovering Yourself
Process	A Dualism of Mind and Body	Embodied Cognition
Property	Utilitarian	Spiritual
Cognition of materials	Superficialness	Multi-dimension
Relationship with non-humans	Dominant	Equal

3 Findings and Discussions

Through the data analysis and comparisons of the two patterns, we could find the significant values and advantages of MAD. It has the potentials to transform the "passive making" of PAD to "active making." Here, "active making" contains three meanings. First, materials themselves turn from passive to active states through MAD, and materials are no longer appendages to functions or shapes of objects. Materials start to own lives with subjective consciousnesses, emotions and personalities bringing people surprises and directing you, which can be seen as "living species." No matter whether natural organic materials or artificial inorganic materials, all of them can play critical active roles in linking humans with the world. In addition, materials should not be defined and constrained by physical or mechanical properties. Designers can redefine any material through various perspectives, exploring and breaking through fixed categories at the boundary to connect other categories and expand new possibilities.

Second, the making process turns from passivity to initiative. Under the mainstream pattern of PAD, students are used to designing with precise purposes and expected goals complying with the established routines, which is a linear process. This process is utilitarian as students are required to propose feasible plans in a short time. Additionally, the design results tend to be homogeneous, resulting from the similar thinking modes that most students conform to. Furthermore, students passively execute instead of actively creating during this period as teachers always play the roles of drivers of progress and judges of results. The initiatives and creations of students are constrained not only from fixed procedures but also from teachers' preferences, requirements and references. Students feel like becoming mechanical "modelers" and "robots" losing the identities of a designer. Simultaneously, the digital and conceptual process of PAD returns to Cartesian dualism of the separation of mind and body, depriving body and perceptions of participating in design.

On the contrary, MAD is like an adventure without destinations. Starting with the physical material without any expected goals or fixed routes, everyone can design their paths through continuous experiments. When exploring the road, teachers will never intervene or tell you what way should follow, but give you different signs to better guide you in your own direction, and the final decision is made by yourself. Many students reflected that they had the perception to become a deep-thinking designer to explore their unique design methods, thinking logics instead of mechanically "carrying" steps, which helped them to reshape self-motivation, initiatives, and firm beliefs when designing. Meanwhile, MAD makes students return to zero to rethink the birth and meanings of objects, which is a pure hand-making process to motivate senses and keeps aware of mind and body without any utilitarian purposes. Hand-making can link materials with body and mind through a dialogical relationship [23–25]. More importantly, this process helps to discover and construct the inner spirits behind objects. Just like W. Tian talking in the interview, *For the vase I made in the workshop, it was not only an object, but also a form, and everything could be created as a vase, which was detached from the existing category and its conventional definition.* Through bodily interacting with materials, we will gradually grasp meanings and abstract concepts [26]. Simultaneously, it is beneficial to spark inspirations and infinite possibilities during the making process of MAD.

Last but not least, the relationship between designers and materials transforms from passivity to initiative. Such an exploration makes materials positioned objectively and subordinately turn to the position of protagonist. Intimate engagements with materials promotes a dialogical rather than dominating relationship between humans and non-humans [23]. When communicating with materials repeatedly, the connection between designers and materials changes from alienated to close relations. Every time you need to wait patiently for the material to respond to you, and you can never imagine what will happen next as surprises always emerge by chance. The final work is the result of collaboration and co-creation by designers and materials. As Paul Carter argues, materials are dynamic and active that have cooperating relations with creators [27].

4 Conclusions

This study applies the methodology of Constructing Grounded Theory to explore the differences between MAD and PAD, which analyzes the unique advantages and values of MAD, and further explain why MAD is on the rise today. Our research shows the MAD method has the capability to promote to transform the passive making state of PAD to active state. The "active" here lies in three aspects, first is to regard materials as "living species" with affordances that can influence behaviors and actions of people. While the practitioners engage with materials, they follow their properties to let the final artefact emerge [28]. Simultaneously, the making process of MAD is like an initiative and self-driven journey, and a process of discovering yourself and embodied cognition that encourages body and perceptions to make sense when designing.

More importantly, MAD subtly changes the relationship between humans and non-humans and facilitates rethinking the meanings and values of materials. Under the pattern of PAD, materials are subordinate to functions or stylings, serving the necessities and wills of humanity. People's cognitions towards objects are always superficial and pursuing functional. However, in order to realize ecological civilization in the future, we must head out of the Anthropocene era and enter into the post-Anthropocene era [29]. Post-Anthropocene aims to appeal "Weak Anthropocentrism" and the worldview of mutualistic symbiosis between humans and non-humans.

Political theorist Jane Bennett argues that all the non-humans are vibrant, active and creative with strong power to shape the world, influencing and changing people's experiences, which he calls *vitality of matter* [30]. In addition, Latour proposes that humans are not the only actors anymore. Through "actor", "mediator" and "network", humans and non-humans(actant) have the equal status to interact and make collective actions [31]. Humans and non-humans share the flat instead of hierarchical relationship between each other, echoing the views of Object-Oriented Ontology [32] in the context of post-Anthropocene. The thinking mode of MAD facilitates designers to construct a new dialogical way between humans and non-humans. While making, the maker is not expected to force a preconceived idea, but rather to collaborate with and listen to the voice of the material [33, 34]. Designers start to observe, understand and even take care of non-humans, extending the empathy from human themselves to humans and non-humans, stressing the importance and values of non-humans, driving a kind of sustainable thinking, abilities and lifestyles for the future. MAD tries to influence consumers by altering designers' concepts of making, attaching importance to materials in Life-circle of ecology and creating a new sustainable culture.

However, MAD has some limitations as well. MAD requires more time for exploration, which is low-efficient and not following market operation routines and economic benefits. Especially when we face tricky or wicked problems, PAD has its unique advantages in providing targeted solutions. Overall, MAD can never replace PAD, but a necessary complement to it. Both of them are essential abilities and thinking methods for designers in the future. To be more specific, MAD is quite critical and significant for students who enter into Design at the very early stage. It is beneficial for them to deeply consider the relationship between humans and non-humans from systematical and speculative perspectives. In light of that, they can understand the importance of materials for sustainability and construct sustainable values and worldviews.

Acknowledgments. This study was conducted based on the workshop hosted by Bajiao Design. Thanks a lot to the organizers, tutors, and the 15 interviewees who shared valuable information with me.

References

1. Buchanan, R.: Strategies of design research: productive science and rhetorical inquiry. In: Michel, R. (ed.) Design Research Now. BIRD, pp. 55–66. Birkhäuser, Boston (2007). https://doi.org/10.1007/978-3-7643-8472-2_4
2. Wen, R.J.: Kaogongji. Shanghai Ancient Books Publishing House, Shanghai (2019)
3. Buchanan, R.: Thinking about design: an historical perspective. In: Philosophy of Technology and Engineering Sciences, pp. 414–417. Elsevier, North Holland (2009)
4. Kuma, K.: Material Research Studio of Kengo Kuma. ZhongXing Press, Beijing (2020)
5. Cross, N.: Designerly Ways of Knowing. Springer, London (2006). https://doi.org/10.1007/1-84628-301-9
6. J.H, Zhao.: Design and design approach research within 40 years. Decoration **185**(09), 44–47 (2008)
7. Simon, H.: The Sciences of the Artificial, 1st edn. MIT Press, Cambridge (1969)
8. Schön, D.: The Reflective Practitioner: How Professionals Think in Action. Basic Books, Cambridge (1983)

9. Rittel, H., Webber, M.: Dilemmas in a general theory of planning. Policy Sci. **5**, 155–169 (1973)
10. Buchanan, R.: Wicked problems in design thinking. Des. Issues **8**(2), 5–21 (1992)
11. Cross, N.: Design Thinking: Understanding How Designers Think and Work. Berg Publishers, Oxford (2011)
12. Lawson, B.: How Designers Think: The Design Process Demyistfied, 4th edn. Architectual Press, Oxford (2006). [1980]
13. Krippendorff, K.: The Semantic Turn: A New Foundation for Design. Taylor and Francis, Boca Raton (2006)
14. Dell'Era, C., Magistretti, S., Cautela, C., Verganti, R., Zurlo, F.: Four kinds of design thinking: from ideating to making, engaging, and criticizing. Creativity Innov. Manag. **29**(2), 324–344 (2020)
15. Alfoldy, S., Margot, C. (ed.): Pioneers of Modern Craft, pp. 176–185. University of Manchester Press, Manchester (1997)
16. Anderson, C.: Makers: The New Industrial Revolution. Crown Business, New York (2012)
17. Gershenfeld, N.: Fab: personal fabrication, Fab Labs, and the factory in your computer. Basic Books, New York (2005)
18. Oxman, N.: Material-based design computation. Ph.D. dissertation, Massachusetts Institute of Technology (2010)
19. Rognoli, V., Bianchini, M., Maffei, S., Karana, E.: DIY materials. Mater. Des. **86**, 692–702 (2015)
20. Karana, E., Barati, B., Rognoli, V., Zeeuw van der Laan, A.: Material driven design (MDD): A method to design for material experiences. Int. J. Des. **9**(2), 35–54 (2015)
21. Dewey, J.: Logic: The Theory of Inquiry. H. Holt and Company, New York (1938)
22. Charmaz, K.: Constructing Grounded Theory: A Practical Guide through Qualitative Analysis. Sage, London (2006)
23. Brink, I., Reddy, V.: Dialogue in the making: emotional engagement with materials. Phenomenol. Cogn. Sci. **19**, 23–45 (2019). https://doi.org/10.1007/s11097-019-09629-2
24. Sennett, R.: The Craftsman. Penguin Books, London (2009)
25. Mäkelä, M.: Personal exploration: serendipity and intentionality as altering positions in a creative practice. FORMakademisk **9**(1), 1–12 (2016)
26. Johnson, M.: The Meaning of the Body. Chicago University Press, Chicago (2007)
27. Carter, P.: Material Thinking: The Theory and Practice of Creative Research. Melbourne University Press, Melbourne (2004)
28. Ingold, T.: The textility of making. Camb. J. Econ. **34**, 91–102 (2010)
29. Zhang, L.: Design ideals and ethics in the anthropocene: non-anthropocentrism and object-oriented design. Decoration (01), 27–31 (2021)
30. Bennett, J.: Vibrant Matter: A Political Ecology of Things. Duke University, London (2010)
31. Latour, B.: On actor-network theory: A few clarifications. Soziale welt, 369–381 (1996)
32. Harman, G.: Object-Oriented Ontology: A New Theory of Everything. Penguin UK (2018)
33. Pallasmaa, J.: The Thinking Hand: Existential and Embodied Wisdom in Architecture. Wiley, Chichester (2009)
34. Aktas, B., Groth, C.: Studying material interactions to facilitate a sense of being with the world. In: Design Research Society International Conference, pp. 1659–1676. Design Research Society, London (2020)

Design Empowerment: Participatory Design Towards Social Sustainability

Man Zhang(✉)

College of Design and Innovation, Tongji University, Shanghai, People's Republic of China
zhangman99@tongji.edu.cn

Abstract. Sustainability and sustainable design are more concerned with the physical environment than the social dimension. But design should give sufficient attention to social sustainability for balanced development. Although social sustainability's definition is vague due to its excessively abundant connotation, power is always core. When it comes to shaping a fair and just distribution of power in society, empowerment is crucial to optimize power allocation. Through historical overview, conceptual analysis, and case studies, this paper argues that empowerment is the core criterion of participatory design because participatory design changes the power relationship among participants profoundly, then summarizes the key elements to achieve empowerment. While participatory design contributes to social sustainability, it also illustrates the inevitable responsibility of design.

Keywords: Participatory design · Social sustainability · Empowerment

1 Introduction

Social sustainability is one of the three core pillars of sustainable development besides economy and environment, with the issue of power at its core for social equity. Unfortunately, design rarely touches on the power issue, though it has the potential from participatory design, enabling empowerment through design. However, participatory design's gene of empowerment is under threat.

Therefore, this paper argues that the potential of participatory design should be re-explored, or better to say, further explored. To this end, the specific objective of this study is to demonstrate that participatory design can optimize the allocation of power among design subjects through empowerment, primarily through the empowerment of disenfranchised social groups. In this way, participatory design involves design in the power issue at the heart of social sustainability, promoting social equity from the perspective of design.

At first, a theoretical framework is conducted to figure out what social sustainability and empowerment mean and how they correlate, demonstrating the positive value of empowerment to social sustainability. Then, the empowerment gene of participatory design is proved through a review of its evolution, followed by an analysis on its research status showing how this gene has been inherited today. Finally, three case studies of

P.-L. P. Rau (Ed.): HCII 2022, LNCS 13311, pp. 274–287, 2022.
https://doi.org/10.1007/978-3-031-06038-0_20

diverse design subjects are presented, including children (vulnerable in age), people with intellectual disability (vulnerable in ability), and Ugandan community members (vulnerable in global development). Case studies illustrate how participatory design empowers three different disenfranchised groups to promote social equity.

2 Design for Social Sustainability

2.1 The Neglect of Social Sustainability

It is well acknowledged that the three core pillars of sustainable development are economic, environmental, and social [1]. But compared to the first two aspects, social sustainability is often neglected in all areas [2, 3]. The study of sustainable development is more concerned with the physical environment than the social environment, far less about social sustainability than the first two, and social sustainability often appears as a result of economic development and environmental protection [4].

The social dimension also receives insufficient attention in sustainable design and lacks guiding principles and methods [5]. Looking back at the development of sustainable design, eco-efficiency was the earliest entry point for design and continues to be the focus of attention today. Whether it is material design, product design, or system design, the requirements of reducing waste and improving resource utilization, which is derived from environmental sustainability, have now become an inherent principle of design. With the evolution of the connotation of sustainable development, design research has gradually explored the potential to intervene in issues related to social ethics, and social design has steadily attracted attention. However, there is hardly a complete and unified technological level of exploration [6]. Design for Social Sustainability is still a concept that is not well known [7].

The reason for this phenomenon is, on the one hand, mainly due to the ambiguity and diversity of social sustainability, which makes it difficult to form a stable and precise definition [8]. Although various theories, strategies, and tools explore social sustainability, the linkages between these diverse aspects are weak and make it challenging to draw unified conclusions. Social sustainability lacks actionable approaches in the face of such complex themes and dynamic, pluralistic values. This ambiguity of definition also leads to the lack of a relatively scientific basis for measuring and analyzing social sustainability than economic and environmental sustainability, which is far more difficult to quantify than economic growth and ecological impacts. Therefore it is often neglected in various reports and studies [9].

On the other hand, in today's prevailing business environment, organizations are not always aware of the social impact of their actions or even indulge in negative social effects in pursuit of profit. The core issues of social sustainability are often relegated to the jurisdiction of the state or social organizations [10, 11]. For design, the impact of these two aspects is evident. Design is extremely practical, problem-solving is its core competency, and lack of clarity will hinder the link between design and social sustainability. At the same time, design and business are closely linked, design decisions are often subject to capital, and designers are sometimes forced to ignore social sustainability.

However, the social dimension of sustainable design should never be overlooked. Since 1873, when William Morris issued the first social design manifesto, design was responsible for promoting social well-being [12]. The designer's responsibility has become the focus of design ethics concerns. As Thomas N. Gladwin et al. point out, eco-efficiency is necessary for comprehensive sustainability but not sufficient or prerequisite. Genuine sustainability demands poverty alleviation, population stabilization, female empowerment, employment creation, human rights observance, and opportunity redistribution on a massive scale [13]. The socially sustainable design needs more attention.

2.2 Promoting Social Sustainability Through Empowerment

In the vast amount of social sustainability explored, there is no clear and uniform definition so far, but power has always been its central concern. As the Brundtland report makes clear, "the distribution of power and influence within society lies at the heart of most development challenges" [1]. The core principles of social sustainability revolve around the distribution of power, such as equity, or justice, which is the basis for examining sustainable development [14]. They are also critical indicators to assess social sustainability [15]. Equity is essentially a matter of power in the distribution of resources, which implies that society should provide fair opportunities and outcomes for all members in particular [9]. This requires allocating resources to consider multiple aspects such as intra-generational and inter-generational equity, regional differences, and disadvantaged groups. A principle of social sustainability similar to the direction of equity is democracy, corresponding to the issue of the distribution of power to participate in social governance, requiring society to provide democratic procedures and open and accountable governance structures that empower members of society to participate in decisions that concern them [9, 16].

The core of social sustainability is the equitable distribution of power, which indicates a large power gap at present. Giving vulnerable groups access to equitable power is the key to promoting social sustainability. And this process of optimizing the allocation of power is called empowerment in the social sciences. If power is defined as the capacity of actors to mobilize resources and institutions to achieve a goal, the process by which actors gain power is empowering. The mechanism of empowerment encompasses three dimensions [17]:

- access to resources and institutions
- strategies to mobilize them
- the willingness to do so

Through empowerment, previously powerless members can access resources and mobile them. The allocation of power within society can be equitable, which is also an indicator of social sustainability [18]. In turn, a more equitable social environment simplifies empowerment.

It is worth noting that in addition to the ability and access to resource allocation, empowerment theory distinguishes between AUTHORITY and POWER. Authority can be granted, but power is not a pre-existing thing but a self-developing capacity and, therefore, cannot be distributed to someone [19]. This suggests that the willingness to empower is an intrinsic motivation that does not depend on external constraints such as social institutions and norms. Zimmerman refers to this intrinsic motivation as psychological empowerment, which includes beliefs that goals can be achieved, awareness about recourses and factors that hinder or enhance one's efforts to achieve those goals, and efforts to fulfill the goals [20]. Thomas and Velthouse further specify four dimensions of intrinsic motivation for empowerment. Impact: realizing that one can make a difference. Competence: recognizing that one can skillfully complete the task. Meaningfulness: caring about what is done. Choice: freedom to decide whether to do something or not [21].

Definitions of intrinsic motivations for empowerment vary, but, indeed, extrinsic constraints can only give access and strategies to use resources for disempowered groups in the process of promoting equity in social power. But if vulnerable groups do not actively accept such gifts, it is difficult to change the power relations within society truly. Empowerment is achieved only when powerless members truly recognize their ability to access and use power. This intrinsic motivation facilitates the shaping of a more independent, liberal, inclusive, and confident social environment and sustains the results of power optimization for a more extended period.

2.3 Combing Empowerment with Design

It is evident from the previous that the core of social sustainability is an equal allocation of power and that empowerment can reduce power gaps within societies(see Fig. 1). Thus, the combination of empowerment and design is a possible way to promote social sustainability.

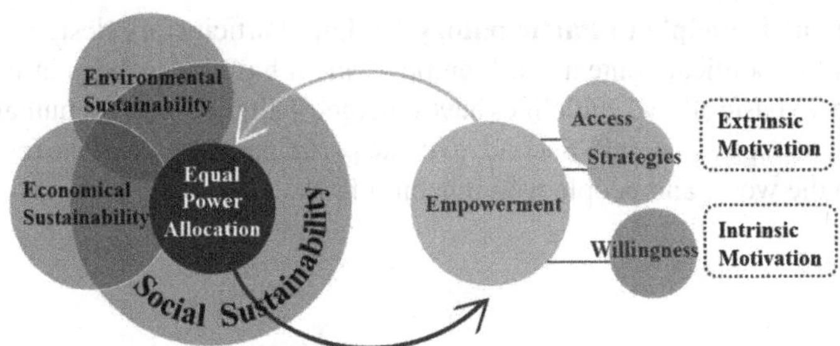

Fig. 1. Interactive models of social sustainability and empowerment. Drawn by the author.

Empowerment History of Participatory Design. Participatory design has the empowerment gene centered on users' democratic participation and empowerment [22].

Participatory design was born in Scandinavia in the 1970s and is known as the collective resource approach, essentially a political democratic movement [23]. These early projects focused on the unequal relationship between workers and system developers in industrial production who are not informed about new technologies. Research institutions and industry collaborate to pioneer this design method to computer system development to improve productivity and promote industrial democratization. The goal is to expand workers' power over the design and control of production processes and resources through the cooperation of unions, employers, and researchers. And to build a knowledge base for workers and unions, thus supporting workers' participation in the design process of technical systems through the shared decision making and enhancing workers' voices. Workers change from line operators to specialists with expertise and influence technical design [24].

The emergence of minicomputers for personal applications in the 1980s made it difficult for systems previously designed for mainframe computers to meet the diverse work environments and needs. The closed and exclusionary nature of the system design also makes computer users feel disconnected from the technology. The focus of the system design shifts to "providing opportunities for users to pursue their own interests" [25]. At that time, the Scandinavian design approach had limited influence, and the User-Centered Design approach was all the rage. The design method considers the user's voice, but the design subject is still the designer. The user can only passively provide reference advice for the designer, so the gap between the technology and the user is still huge and cannot wholly solve people's dissatisfaction with the system design [23]. Researchers have therefore combined the Scandinavian collective resource approach and User-Centered Design to depoliticize participatory design, which was born out of the political democracy movement. Since then, participatory design has gradually expanded from systems design to other areas and has become a pure design approach.

Empowerment Principle in Participatory Design. Participatory design has evolved out of its initial political context. Still, empowerment has always been at its core (see Fig. 2), and two basic ethical guidelines have emerged—first, respect for human expertise and the right to express oneself. Second, to make participants aware of the responsibility of design to the world and people who inhabit it [24].

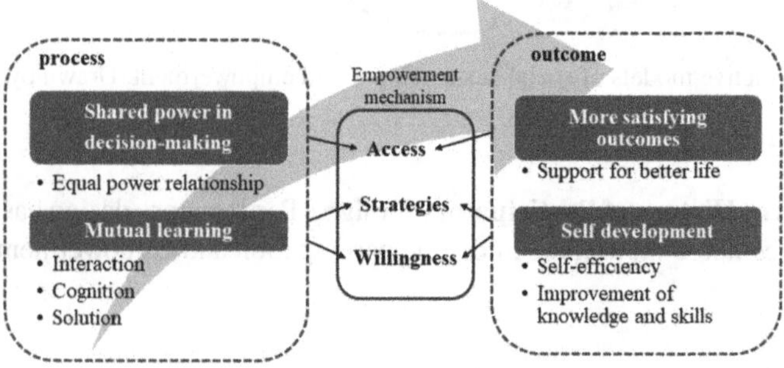

Fig. 2. Empowerment is the core of participatory design from the design process and outcome perspective. Drawn by the author.

The first principle implies that everyone can influence all decisions in the design and that participants have an equal voice, participation, and shared decision-making power. The designer forms the design result after a large number of decisions, and the power of design is concentrated in the power of decision-making [26]. Thus, this distribution of power profoundly changes the power relations in design. In participatory design, the designer no longer represents the "unchallenged power and authority" [23]. Both designers, core users, and edge users are unified into one identity- participants. It is also necessary to distinguish between the empowerment process and the outcome. Suppose the participants' right to make decisions is the central resource in the design process. In that case, the results of participatory design are often more responsive to the needs of the participants, who also receive more substantial support to improve their lives as a result.

The second principle implies active participation, emphasizing that participants actively influence the design through intrinsic motivation. On the one hand, this intrinsic motivation comes from the solid subjective demand of the participants before the project starts and, on the other hand, arises from the process of participation. When a participant recognizes that his or her knowledge can play an essential role in design, he or she will receive positive feedback for continued involvement.

Thus, participatory design provides a joint space and tools for participants to access the various resources in the design and generate strategies to mobilize these resources to reach optimal solutions through mutual learning. This empowerment is beyond the distribution of power within the design. The final solution will also help participants improve their standard of living and enjoy more social resources. Active participation corresponds to empowering willingness, which is the key to measuring the success of participatory design empowerment and is the core driving force to sustain the project in the long run.

But just as design has neglected social sustainability, the empowerment gene of participatory design has not received as much attention as the wide variety of technologies, methods, and applications. And there is pseudo participation in which participants may act as mere data providers or testers and not enjoy decision-making power [27]. This pseudo participation marginalizes some participants, breaks the supposedly equal configuration of power in participatory design, undermines the basis of empowerment, and gradually dissolves the differences between participatory design and other design approaches, such as User-Centered Design and Computer Supported Cooperative Work [22]. Therefore, this paper argues that the empowering nature of participatory design should be re-explored, or rather, further explored. Next, this paper will illustrate how participatory design can achieve empowerment through three typical cases.

3 Case Studies

These three cases are challenging because their participants belong to a traditionally disadvantaged group, considered to lack the ability to participate fully. They are usually viewed as objects to be designed rather than designers for themselves.

The first is children, who are often considered unable to make sound design decisions and take responsibility for their decisions because of their age. The second is people with intellectual disabilities, who lack sufficient autonomy to participate because of cognitive and communication impairments. The third is the people of backward countries, who are often seen as needing assistance due to their level of development. These three vulnerable groups have received much attention in design, but they are on the periphery of this paternalistic design power relationship, serving as testers and informants for designers. Participatory design then transforms their role into co-design partners, allowing them to design for themselves by empowering vulnerable groups.

3.1 Children

Children are often invited into the early conceptual design stages due to their age but rarely participate in other design aspects. This results in children having limited influence on the design outcome, and the process of mutual learning in design is overlooked [28]. Druin has developed a very influential model to explain the role of children in design [29]. It can be divided into user, tester, informant, and design partner. Children can express their feelings as users, test functionality and usability as testers, provide ideas and creativity as informants, and influence all decisions in the design process by articulating their expertise and life experiences as design partners. However, design usually does not empower children to have the same roles and responsibilities as adults because children often do not have the time, knowledge, and expertise to collaborate with adults in a real sense [30]. There is a delicate balance between empowering children and avoiding overburdening them with responsibility [31]. Children's role in participatory design should be somewhere between an information provider and a design partner [32].

The first project comes from the International Red Cross Committee (ICRC), which designed leg prostheses for children under 16 years old in Cambodia [30]. The key to the project is to see children as social actors and subjects with rights rather than as objects of attention. Through multiple interviews with six children aged 5–15 and their parents, the project identified three children as core participants who strongly influenced the implementation of the prosthetic design throughout. They include a 12-year-old boy, a 10-year-old girl, and a 16-year-old boy. The researchers set up exercises for the children to respond to some headings through word or picture descriptions, such as what I like/dislike/need/hope for, good and bad experience, what do people with prosthetic legs look like, and how to care for them and how can prosthesis change. The children were also role-played to demonstrate how they would like to be treated by others. In an unstructured interview, they were also asked who they would go to in an emergency to learn about their social networks.

It is a progressive, deep and cyclical process. The children were so restrained at first that many exercises did not receive a response, and the initial interviews did not provide the designers with any substantive information. But as the interaction progressed and the children trusted the designer's ability to help them and saw their role in the design, communication became more accessible and effortless. Children are unique in that they can often not articulate design pain points and specific directions for improvement like fully developed adults. Still, they can clearly express their likes or dislikes of the current design. The information is critical because designers can use it to extract ideas to improve product design. Although the children did not do the design outcome entirely on their own, it still seemed as if they were only providing information during the design process. Actually, the degree of influence and source of motivation for this information was very different from the informant.

First, the adults in the program are not the design leaders, they are simply facilitators providing tools, methods, design skills, and advice to help the children identify and express their actual needs. The design direction was also not predetermined by the designer but developed naturally after the children expressed their aspirations. The children's preferences determine the design outcome, and it can be said that they enter the core hierarchy of power in design. Second, children's intrinsic motivation to stay engaged continues to grow. Through extensive interviews and communication, the designers succeeded in making the children aware of their essential role and responsibility in the project, as their participation directly affects the quality of their own lives and those of other peers. And in the process of participation, the experience of adult designers interested in understanding their opinions and freely expressing their ideas enhances the children's willingness. For example, one of the children said he gained confidence by answering various questions and completing multiple exercises [30].

It follows that children are empowered in participatory design to act between informant and design partner. Considering the ability gap between children and adults, it is worthwhile to delve into which method provides helpful information. But more importantly, children's voices must be heard and directly influence the outcome of the design. Otherwise, they don't share decision-making power with adult designers in the design process. By contributing their knowledge and experience, the children receive a more satisfying prosthetic product for themselves and realize that they are capable enough to make meaningful changes that lead to psychological empowerment.

3.2 People with Intellectual Disability (ID)

ID is a disability characterized by significant limitations in both intellectual functioning and adaptive behavior as expressed in conceptual, social, and practical skills [33]. It is often taken into account in inclusion studies. The role of people with ID in inclusive research has gradually shifted from being the object of research to being a co-researcher [34]. Participatory design and inclusive research share the same vision. However, this identity change is not straightforward because of the cognitive and communication barriers. The social model of disability sees disability as the result of society's response to a person's functional limitations [35]. Therefore, the key to including people with ID in social participation is to adopt appropriate methods to make them design subjects with equal status and remove any barriers that may prevent them from participating in society.

Laurianne Sitbon and Shanjana Farhin [36] designed a GPS-based public transportation and navigation mobile application system for people with ID. Features include journey reminders, notification of vehicle arrival times, pedestrian navigation with alerts for drop-off and arrival at stations, and assistance. An exploratory group of people with ID, researchers, designers, carers, and other stakeholders held multiple co-design sessions to evaluate, revise, and update the prototype for the system. The project summarized the key elements that support the integration of people with ID into participatory design.

1. The use of concrete prototypes. At the beginning of the design session, the feedback from people with ID was not positive. However, when high-fidelity digital prototypes were used, participants were significantly more engaged, with richer expressions and more frequent comments. Prototypes can be used as symbolic probes to present effective dialogue processes between different participants [37].
2. A non-finito feature. The prototype simply showed a panic button and no more information. However, this feature provoked a more intense discussion among participants than the complete prototype given. Giving participants more freedom will help create more imagination and creativity and stimulate their sense of ownership.
3. Consider carers as agents and co-designers. Considering the unique social structure of ID, carers are important. They provide a direct view during the design process and assist in the communication between the ID and the researcher.

In this case, the key to empowerment is transforming people with ID from the object to be designed to a co-designer, breaking the unequal power relationship between them and non-disabled people. On the one hand, they can better express their opinions with the help of researchers, thus directly influencing the various products they design for themselves and avoiding unsatisfactory designs due to lack of communication or ignoring their ideas. On the other hand, this shift also means the power to self-determination. Self-determination does not mean facing everything alone but having the ability to control one's own life [38]. It is positively correlated with ID's hope, optimism, and locus of control [39]. This suggests that the researcher who holds the initiative is a valuable actor in his or her own right, compared to the subject of the study. This value comes from the deep involvement in the design process, the personal growth that comes from that involvement, and the opportunity to develop valuable skills [40]. These values allow people with ID to gain sustainable benefits (confidence in themselves and various skills) after leaving participatory design projects and encourage them to engage more socially.

3.3 People of Backward Countries

Improving people's lives in backward areas is an important goal of sustainable development and the focus of participatory design. From June 2014 to May 2015, researchers from the University of Cape Town developed a rural water management application in rural communities in Kabarole District, Uganda [41]. The research team conducted six action research iterations through semi-structured interviews, workshops, and focus group discussions using the Community-Based Co-Design method. The app uses information and communication technology(ICT) to solve the problem of confusing local water resources management.

The project's biggest challenge was to get the villagers involved and proactive in maintaining the system. Since the beginning of the period, Uganda's water assistance has come mainly from NGOs, and external assistance has often been unsustainable due to frequent funding shortfalls and staff turnover. On the other hand, people in rural Uganda have lower income levels, lower literacy levels, and do not understand or even reject technology. The failure of quantitative ICT technology projects also illustrates the challenging nature of technology interventions on the ground. Therefore, it was important for the designers to fully understand the context and the people using the technology. But more important is how to help local people in Uganda overcome their fear of technology and realize the benefits it can bring to them.

Empowerment needs to consider locality, as researchers often join community projects as outsiders [42]. Technology can empower community members in developing regions with severe material deprivation, but it can also easily threaten entrenched power relations within communities, leading to exclusion. Therefore, design should be integrated into the original policy system and organizational structure as a complement, not a substitute [43]. In order to prevent the creation of new obstacles in the intervention process, external research should complement the social structure with micro-interventions. Researchers can use the cultural information collected as a starting point for research and use low technology exposure and a strong sense of community as principles for technological intervention in developing regions [44]. Using local water officials as intermediaries, the project helps researchers and community members build trust more quickly and thus integrate into the community [45]. Thus allowing the researcher's interventions to be incorporated into the existing government structure in a low-impact manner.

At the heart of getting villagers to actively participate and continue using the app after the researchers left was sufficient intrinsic motivation. At the beginning of the project, most participants did not understand what benefits technology could bring, their role in community water management, or how their knowledge and experience could help program development. But over time, participants became increasingly proactive in sharing knowledge, making suggestions, and expressing opinions in the discussions. Participatory design provides a joint space where needs are incorporated directly into the design, and participants resonate and understand as they present themselves to learn from each other. Then it comes to realize that they can benefit from it, contribute, and the contributions are valuable. In addition to improved self-efficacy, after the program, some participants expressed a strong interest in science and technology. This facilitates follow-up technical support projects and the local application of technology for emerging development.

3.4 Summary

The three cases above explain how participatory design can achieve empowerment, especially when dealing with vulnerable groups. And how participatory design can remove obstacles to achieving empowerment through a diverse approach. We can summarize the following characteristics.

Role Change. Equal power relations in participatory design are achieved by transforming all actors into joint design partners.

On the user side, it is generally accepted that User-Centered Design has put the user at the center of attention. However, the essential difference between User-Centered Design and participatory design lies in positioning the design subject and the user's role. In the former, the design subject is the designer, who collects user information and envisions the usage environment through research and interviews. The latter gives the user the right to participate with the designer and use their knowledge and experience to make real-time, decisive interventions in the design. Participatory design transcends the user's role; moreover, this participation is voluntary and active—users design to achieve their aspirations rather than passively accepting commodity design in consumerism [46].

In contrast, designers are no longer in sole control of design decisions; their responsibility should be to use their professional design skills to create the tools and environment for non-professional designers to express themselves creatively. At the same time, they provide advice and guidance to the overall design process through expertise. The third role is the researcher. Whereas they used to act primarily as translators between users and designers, participatory design requires them to abandon their condescending posture and introduce domain knowledge in an acceptable way to all participants [37].

Diversity. Participatory design is a commonly used approach, but different methods and tools are needed for different design situations.

In the three cases explored in this paper, tailored design approaches and processes are used because of various group characteristics. On the other hand, it is also necessary to consider the variability within the design team. As participatory design expands the design community and the relationships between stakeholders become more complex, building good relationships within the design team is key to sustaining participation.

Mutual Learning. Participatory design techniques and methods ultimately open up a space for mutual learning, allowing different stakeholders to listen, understand and learn from the ideas of others. This helps to Facilitate communication and understanding, leading to consensus [26].

The knowledge and experience of each participant should be respected, and because participants are so different, mutual understanding needs to be developed in the exchange. Respecting the ideas and interests of others helps compromise in design decisions. It helps individuals understand their self-identity through multiple perspectives, understand their importance and capabilities in design, enhance participants' intrinsic motivation, and further promote psychological empowerment.

4 Conclusion

This paper shows that participatory design has the potential to involve in social sustainability profoundly through empowerment. The starting point of this study lies in that social sustainability has not received enough attention compared with economic and environmental ones. Through the argument, this paper argues that equal distribution of power is a crucial way to promote social sustainability. And with the same challenge, vulnerable groups have long been considered to lack the possibility to engage in the design process either because of defects in their own abilities or limitation of design itself. Popular design methods usually consider them "design for", sometimes replacing real design needs. Participatory design, however, can provide specific and compelling ways to make them the decisive participants in design. The shift in power relationship results in empowerment, thus enriching social sustainability in terms of connotation and practice.

At the same time, it is found that participatory design should reflect on the existing problems under the requirements of social sustainability, such as pseudo participation and the challenges from diversity and complexity. This means that participatory design has to reshape its empowerment connotation. More importantly, design, not just participatory design, should actively respond to sustainable social development. In this way, design can transform from an "approach" to satisfy basic human needs to a "proactive actor" to promote social innovation.

References

1. WCED, Special Working Session: World commission on environment and development. Our Common Future **17**, 1–91 (1987)
2. Sajjad, A., Shahbaz, W.: Mindfulness and social sustainability: an integrative review. Soc. Indic. Res. **150**(1), 73–94 (2020). https://doi.org/10.1007/s11205-020-02297-9
3. Magis, K., Shinn, C.: Emergent principles of social sustainability. In: Understanding the Social Dimension of Sustainability, vol. 17, p. 15 (2009)
4. Pfeffer, J.: Building sustainable organizations: the human factor. Acad. Manag. Perspect. **24**, 34–45 (2010)
5. Joyce, A., Paquin, R.L.: The triple layered business model canvas: a tool to design more sustainable business models. J. Clean. Prod. **135**, 1474–1486 (2016)
6. Vezzoli, C.: Design for sustainability: the new research frontiers. In: 7th Brazilian Conference on Design, pp. 9–11 (2006)
7. Waage, S.A.: Re-considering product design: a practical "road-map" for integration of sustainability issues. J. Clean. Prod. **15**, 638–649 (2007)
8. Bebbington, J., Dillard, J.: Social sustainability: an organizational-level analysis. In: Understanding the Social Dimension of Sustainability, pp. 173–189. Routledge (2008)
9. McKenzie, S.: Social sustainability: towards some definitions (2004)
10. Missimer, M., Robèrt, K.-H., Broman, G.: A strategic approach to social sustainability–Part 2: a principle-based definition. J. Clean. Prod. **140**, 42–52 (2017)
11. Von Geibler, J., Liedtke, C., Wallbaum, H., Schaller, S.: Accounting for the social dimension of sustainability: experiences from the biotechnology industry. Bus. Strateg. Environ. **15**, 334–346 (2006)
12. Corsini, L., Moultrie, J.: Design for social sustainability: using digital fabrication in the humanitarian and development sector. Sustainability **11**, 3562 (2019)
13. Gladwin, T.N., Krause, T.S., Kennelly, J.J.: Beyond eco-efficiency: towards socially sustainable business. Sustain. Dev. **3**, 35–43 (1995)
14. Vallance, S., Perkins, H.C., Dixon, J.E.: What is social sustainability? A clarification of concepts. Geoforum **42**, 342–348 (2011)
15. Littig, B., Griessler, E.: Social sustainability: a catchword between political pragmatism and social theory. Int. J. Sustain. Dev. **8**, 65–79 (2005)
16. Maloutas, T.: Promoting social sustainability The case of Athens. City **7**, 167–181 (2003)
17. Avelino, F.: Power in sustainability transitions: analysing power and (dis) empowerment in transformative change towards sustainability. Environ. Policy Gov. **27**, 505–520 (2017)
18. Kibukho, K.: Mediating role of citizen empowerment in the relationship between participatory monitoring and evaluation and social sustainability. Eval. Program Plann. **85**, 101911 (2021)
19. Boje, D.M., Rosile, G.A.: Where's the power in empowerment? Answers from Follett and Clegg. J. Appl. Behav. Sci. **37**, 90–117 (2001)
20. Zimmerman, M.A.: Psychological empowerment: issues and illustrations. Am. J. Community Psychol. **23**, 581–599 (1995)

21. Thomas, K.W., Velthouse, B.A.: Cognitive elements of empowerment: an "interpretive" model of intrinsic task motivation. Acad. Manag. Rev. **15**, 666–681 (1990)
22. Correia, A.-P., Yusop, F.D.: "I don't want to be empowered" the challenge of involving real-world clients in instructional design experiences. In: Proceedings of the Tenth Anniversary Conference on Participatory Design 2008, pp. 214–216. Indiana University, Bloomington (2008)
23. Schuler, D., Namioka, A.: Participatory Design: Principles and Practices. CRC Press, New York (1993)
24. Simonsen, J., Robertson, T.: Routledge International Handbook of Participatory Design. Routledge, New York (2013)
25. Bossen, C., Dindler, C., Garde, J., Pipek, V.: Evaluation, sustainability and long-term effects of participatory design projects. In: Proceedings of the 13th Participatory Design Conference: Short Papers, Industry Cases, Workshop Descriptions, Doctoral Consortium papers, and Keynote abstracts-Volume 2, pp. 219–220. ACM, New York (2014)
26. Bratteteig, T., Wagner, I.: Disentangling power and decision-making in participatory design. In: Proceedings of the 12th Participatory Design Conference: Research Papers-Volume 1, pp. 41–50. ACM, New York (2012)
27. Palacin, V., Nelimarkka, M., Reynolds-Cuéllar, P., Becker, C.: The design of pseudo-participation. In: Proceedings of the 16th Participatory Design Conference 2020-Participation (s) Otherwise-Volume 2, pp. 40–44. ACM, New York (2020)
28. Iversen, O.S., Smith, R.C., Dindler, C.: Child as protagonist: expanding the role of children in participatory design. In: Proceedings of the 2017 Conference on Interaction Design and Children, pp. 27–37. ACM, New York (2017)
29. Druin, A.: The role of children in the design of new technology. Behav. Inf. Technol. **21**, 1–25 (2002)
30. Hussain, S.: Empowering marginalised children in developing countries through participatory design processes. CoDesign **6**(2), 99–117 (2010)
31. Frauenberger, C., Good, J., Keay-Bright, W.: Designing technology for children with special needs: bridging perspectives through participatory design. CoDesign **7**, 1–28 (2011)
32. Kam, M., Ramachandran, D., Raghavan, A., Chiu, J., Sahni, U., Canny, J.: Practical considerations for participatory design with rural school children in underdeveloped regions: early reflections from the field. In: Proceedings of the 2006 Conference on Interaction Design and Children, pp. 25–32. ACM, New York (2006)
33. Schalock, R.L., Luckasson, R., Tassé, M.J.: Intellectual disability: Definition, diagnosis, classification, and systems of supports. aaidd (2021)
34. Walmsley, J., Strnadova, I., Johnson, K.: The added value of inclusive research. J. Appl. Res. Intellect. Disabil. **31**, 751–759 (2018)
35. Crow, L.: Including all of our lives: renewing the social model of disability. Exploring Divide **55**, 58 (1996)
36. Sitbon, L., Farhin, S.: Co-designing interactive applications with adults with intellectual disability: a case study. In: Proceedings of the 29th Australian Conference on Computer-Human Interaction, pp. 487–491. ACM, New York (2017)
37. Sanders, E.B.-N., Stappers, P.J.: Co-creation and the new landscapes of design. Co-design **4**, 5–18 (2008)
38. Ladner, R.E.: Design for user empowerment. Interactions **22**, 24–29 (2015)
39. Shogren, K.A., Wehmeyer, M.L., Buchanan, C.L., Lopez, S.J.: The application of positive psychology and self-determination to research in intellectual disability: a content analysis of 30 years of literature. Res. Pract. Persons Severe Disabil. **31**, 338–345 (2006)
40. Booth, T.A., Booth, W.: Parenting Under Pressure: Mothers and Fathers with Learning Difficulties. Open University Press, Buckingham (1994)

41. Ssozi-Mugarura, F., Blake, E., Rivett, U.: Codesigning with communities to support rural water management in Uganda. CoDesign **13**, 110–126 (2017)
42. Winschiers-Theophilus, H., Bidwell, N.J., Blake, E.: Altering participation through interactions and reflections in design. CoDesign **8**, 163–182 (2012)
43. Champanis, M., Rivett, U.: Reporting water quality: a case study of a mobile phone application for collecting data in developing countries. In: Proceedings of the Fifth International Conference on Information and Communication Technologies and Development, pp. 105–113. ACM, New York (2012)
44. Ramachandran, D., Kam, M., Chiu, J., Canny, J., Frankel, J.F.: Social dynamics of early stage co-design in developing regions. In: Proceedings of the SIGCHI Conference on Human Factors in Computing Systems, pp. 1087–1096. ACM, New York (2007)
45. Ssozi-Mugarura, F., Blake, E., Rivett, U.: Supporting community needs for rural water management through community-based co-design. In: Proceedings of the 14th Participatory Design Conference: Full Papers-Volume 1, pp. 91–100. ACM, New York (2016)
46. Sanders, E.B.-N.: From user-centered to participatory design approaches. In: Design and the Social Sciences, pp. 18–25. CRC Press, London (2002)

Explore Alternative Future: A Case Study of Cultivating Designers' Future Literacy via Hybrid Collaboration

Chenfan Zhang[1] and Zhiyong Fu[2(✉)]

[1] Politecnico di Milano, Piazza Leonardo da Vinci, 32, Milan, Italy
chenfan.zhang@mail.polimi.it
[2] Tsinghua University, Haidian District, Beijing, China
fuzhiyong@tsinghua.edu.cn

Abstract. The epidemic has made it necessary to face the challenges of an uncertain future on the one hand, and to adapt to new ways of working remotely on the other. For designers, a focus on the future helps them step outside of their inherited framework and explore alternative futures. However, research on the design future education is still lacking in Chinese context. Therefore, in the summer of 2021, an initiative called future pioneer was launched, it aims to explore a process model for developing designers' future literacy. Which can assist designers envision alternative future and influence present through the integration of design and futurology tools. By combining the designer's familiar double diamond model with the process of future scenario planning, the steps are gradually dismantled, and futurological tools are added in stages, from first understanding the future to discovering the future, selecting the direction, and then finally, finally developing the vision. Participants are guided to move from the figurative "real world" to abstraction and then refine and analyze the future vision to form a complete "future world view" and realize a complete narrative through the future vision map.

Keywords: Alternative future · Future literacy · Future scenario planning · Hybrid collaboration · COVID-19

1 Background

From 2019, the pandemic named COVID-19 expanded around the world. Every industry had to accept the fact of suspension. It is a period of a dark time for humanity, and people are looking forward to the brighter day. However, two years have passed, the gloom brought by the pandemic never lifted. In addition, a series of crises such as environmental pollution and economic crisis due to unemployment are emerging [8], which interrupts the rhythm of development. An amount number of projects and strategies are forced interruptions. All these signs show that in the future, we face increasing uncertainty. And how to face these uncertain, exploring new future after COVID-19, is becoming one of the humanity's questions.

P.-L. P. Rau (Ed.): HCII 2022, LNCS 13311, pp. 288–301, 2022.
https://doi.org/10.1007/978-3-031-06038-0_21

Meanwhile, the pandemic also changes personal behaviors and lifestyles. Because of lockdown, population mobility dropped to a low point. People have no choice but to accept virtual collaboration. For this reason, online communication platforms have been explored in this period. Various platforms are used in office and class, from video meeting platforms, like Zoom, Microsoft team, WebEx, and Google meeting, to whiteboards like Miro, Mural and Figma. In addition to video, voice, and text, virtual spaces also are an explore field. Some game platforms like Roblox, Animal Crossing and Justice Online are used for webinars and conferences [15, 18, 23]. People are trying to use these online platforms to rebuild their collaboration and fight the solitary situation caused by the epidemic.

The epidemic leads collaboration to a "new normal" [7]. The impact of Covid-19 on collaborative approaches changing may be much longer than we image. In this context, even China has achieved significant results in the confrontation with Covid-19. For example, offline organizations are reopening, and people are going back to offline in general. However, people keep facing the re-blockade at any time due to recurring pandemic outbreaks, and population movement is also strictly controlled. To meet these challenges, People need dynamic collaboration approaches, including online and offline. Compared to face-to-face collaboration, hybrid collaborations like online and offline are flexible and resilient. It can ignore geographic constraints and involve more stakeholders.

Design future research in the Chinese is in the early stage. Few papers find in Chinese academic research engine, and most of them focus on design trends and specific product or architecture design projects. Although the education design has 55 papers in the fifth position, few of them attempts on design education perspectives to discuss how to cultivate designers to face the "uncertain future" (see Fig. 1).

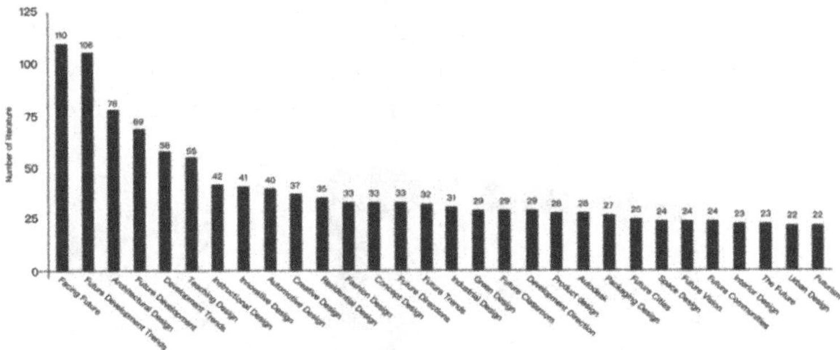

Fig. 1. Statistics of papers with 'future design' from CNKI[1]

Meanwhile, a series of complex problems in design future process are surfacing. How design students to predicted future and integrate future factors into their design projects? How to avoid to lost in imaginary futures? How to guide designers to broaden their thinking of the future perspective? To address this gap, this study through practice-bases research to develop a future scenario-based design process for designer, which

[1] CNKI (China National Knowledge Infrastructure) is a key national research and information publishing institution in China, led by Tsinghua University.

aims to involve future literacy into their project. This process is tested and applied via a realistic case study, i.e., a summer school in hybrid collaboration context named Future Pioneer. The case study conducted by a practice-based research approach, i.e., research through design [2]. This research aims to develop a future design process model in a hybrid collaboration context to build participators' future thinking capability and enrich their final outputs in the present real world.

2 Relative Works

2.1 Alternative Futures

"The future" cannot be "predicted," but "alternative futures" can, and should be "forecast." [4]. Alternative futures also are called scenarios. Future is something does not happen yet, which means it could have millions of results before it has happened. In this context, how can we find the "real future"? There has been recognized from previous research from Amer et al. that "numerous scenario building methods have been developed, ranging from simplistic to complex, qualitative to quantitative……some authors describe it as 'methodological chaos'" [1]. In these large number of methodologies, some of them significant influence of alternative future research. For example, in 2003, Voros provided a clear taxonomy of potential futures [26] and develop in his paper in 2017. In his second paper, he utilized future cone to illustrate seven types of alternative future: potential, preposterous, possible, plausible, probable, preferable, and projected (see Fig. 2) [25]. The 7P alternative futures classify from each potential future then zoom into the subjective expect future [5].

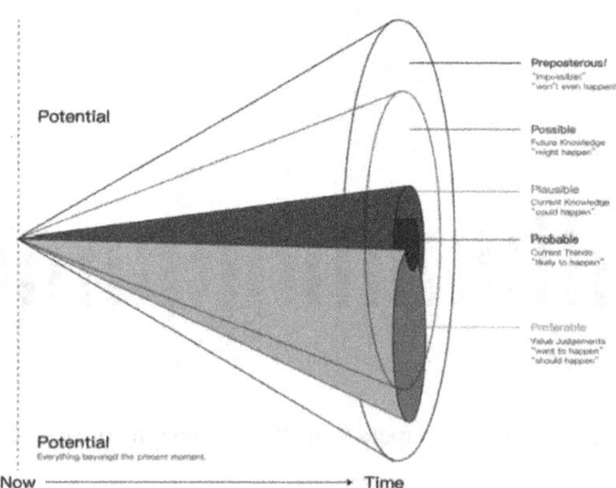

Fig. 2. The future cone of alternative future as presented by Voros (2017)

The other one is from Jim Dator. Dator summarized four trends of generic futures, which have the same probability of occurrence [3]. Compared with the description of alternative futures by Voros, the list from Dator about Alternative futures has four different types, including "continued growth", often understood as economic growth, the most important for social institutions and industries. It can be seen as the most expected one. The second one is "collapse" since the economy can't maintain growing up. It presents an extreme, which is another exact opposite. Humans will fall into collapse. But it should not only understand as a "bad result". "Moreover, in every "disaster" there are "winners" as well as "losers". The third one is "Discipline", it arises when people feel sustainability development is impossible. In the end, the fourth generic future depends on the technology development and revolution, to extent to which society can be influenced by the technology development in the future [3].

These two different methodologies of alternative future (or scenario) classify from possibilities of future occurrences and some perspectives from human development (economy, policy, and technology), respectively. It is necessary to highlight two perspectives in these two methodologies, which is the alternative futures have various results, and each of them has two sides. We cannot judge because of subjective positive or negative but should objective analysis the trend of changes and potential results by these trends; People can do these forecasts by following the track of development elements in the human society, such as technology, policy, and economy.

2.2 The Needs of Cultivating Future Literacy

Future Literacy is a skill that can lead people to understand better, imagination and use the future [28]. As the description by Futures Literacy Laboratories (FLL)[2], future literacy is a capability that can be learned, like reading or writing, so that has viability operationally. The first capability of developing Future Literacy is to "make anticipatory assumptions (AA) explicit and observable" [13]. Future Literacy Laboratories-Novelty (FLL-N) as a solution to mentioned and has practiced in 20 countries since 2012. The FFL-N has summarized a learning process which has 3 steps for participators to understand anticipatory assumptions (AA) (See Fig. 3). This S-curve provide a productive learning process and creates collective intelligence, which can help participators have more flexible choices about tools and heuristics [13, 14].

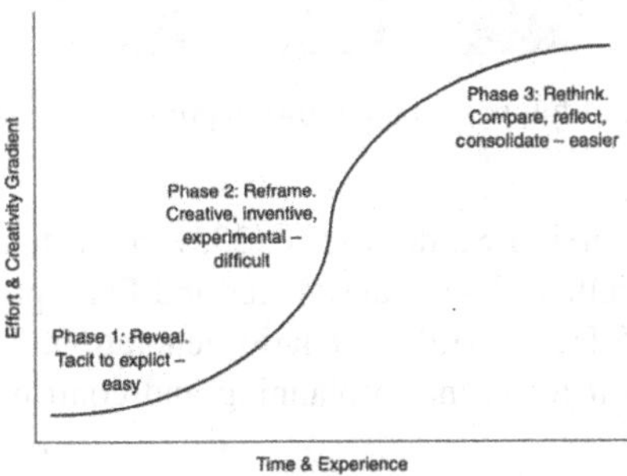

Fig. 3. The three phases of learning as presented by Miller (2018 p. 98)

[2] "The Futures Literacy Lab (FLL) can be defined as the combination, through application of explicit design principles, of a collective intelligence knowledge creation (CIKC) process with anticipatory systems and processes (ASP)." [13]

Generally, history can be re-explanation but cannot be changed by present, and in contrast to that, the future can be influenced by the present, while influencing the present [6, 13, 27]. As Azoulay, the UNESCO Director-General, mentioned, "If we had better anticipate the health crisis, would its consequences have been so disastrous? Why, if the risk had already been identified, was the world not better prepared? How can we plan for an uncertain tomorrow? By imagining it. By anticipating it, rather than enduring it. Faced with contemporary challenges, we need to be inventive – and that's what futures literacy is all about." [24]. Thus, learning how to 'use-the-future' in an effective way is important. It will help people develop the future through reflection, prepare for the potential challenge, and anticipate possible solutions [11–13].

2.3 Future Scenario Planning in Design Education

Future Imagination happens all the time, but how to image the future efficiently, and use it as strategic planning, and generation of actions become a critical question. Thus, people have developed a series of future scenario planning models to anticipate futures. Scenario, or named future scenario, alternative future [3, 19] is an abstract direction with many classified methodology as mentioned previously. Although they provide some directions, it is still abstract for people to forecast alternative futures. And scenario planning as a visualization tool provides a feasible extrapolation path and has been widely used in organizations. Companies to narrative and shape the future [5, 16, 20]. The future scenario focuses on dynamic change, which could help people jump out of the box and gain more possibilities [1]. In recent years, future scenario planning is focused by scholars. In 2009, Jim Dator pointed out the seven components of a future visioning process: Appreciating the past, Understanding the present, Forecasting aspects of the futures, Experiencing alternative futures, Envisioning the futures, Creating the futures and Institutionalizing future research (see Fig. 4) [3].

Fig. 4. The process model of future visioning (own representation following Jim Dator, 2009)

As a more actionable version, Sardesai et al. (2021) refers to the scenarios' generation approach based on the methodology Gausemeier and Plass proposed in 2014. In their paper, they involved PESTLE into the scenario generation. This increases collection dimensions of information for scenario planning and contributes to specific analysis [19] (Fig. 5).

In design education, scenario as a tool has important relationship with ideation and prototype [20]. "The future scenarios enabled participants to consider possible new product and service offerings from a perspective that was systematically different from the present situation and the current suite of product offerings" [6]. For example, In the design education project of Eggink and Albert de la Bruheze did in 2015, they involved in storytelling into future scenario development to envisioning the alternative future about museum. This development process composed of six successive steps, actor and sector,

Fig. 5. The process medal of scenario planning of the Gausemeier-approach (representation by Sardesai et al., 2021)

focal issue, analysis, strategic space, scenarios, and presenting (see Fig. 6). They also further discuss the history analysis and future design to influence present and point out through future scenario development can avoid empiricism and product more creative result (see Fig. 7) [6].

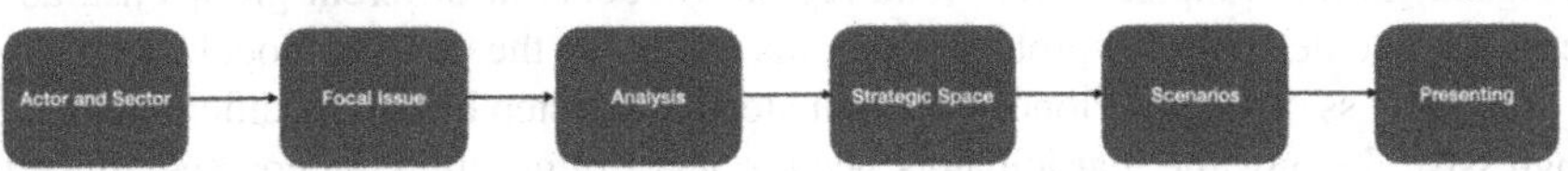

Fig. 6. The process model of future scenario development (own representation following Eggink and Albert de la Bruheze, 2015)

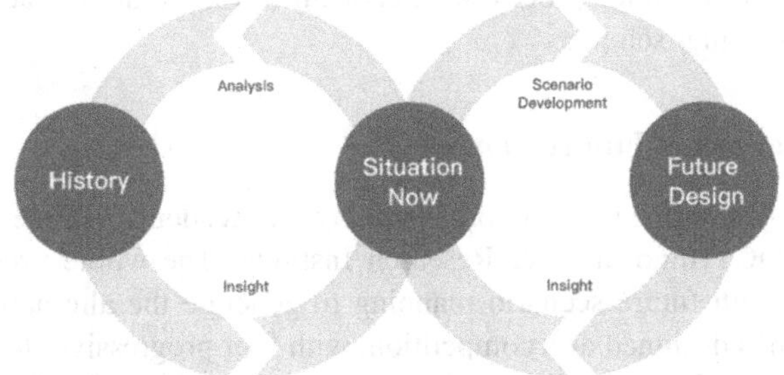

Fig. 7. Two Virtuous Circles; analysis of history creates insight in present situation, and design of the future creates insight in present situation did by form Eggink and Albert de la Bruheze (2015), redesign by author.

Scupelli et al. reported a flipped course named Dexign the future in 2016. They also create a new term, Dexign future which composed to design thinking and future thinking. This course is an open-resource course which you can find the description with outline on their website.[3] Students are asked to ground their futures scenarios from interview and field observations. It provides three courses to "help novices learn how to integrate design thinking to future thinking" [20]. And scenario planning plays a critical role in these courses.

Scenario planning is suitable for dealing with uncertain future contexts, providing a comprehensive perspective of future looks [1]. Meanwhile, the cultivate target is designers who have not studied futurology in systematic. Therefore, we finally adopted the scenario-based method combined with the double diamond model aims to let designers can "use future" easily.

[3] https://dexignfutures.org/.

3 Case Study: Summer School via Hybrid Collaboration - *Future Pioneer*

The case study was a one-month summer program, which collaborated via Feishu (an online team collaboration platform). In the process, we try to understand the participants' experience of learning and using future with tools and whether they improved the knowledge of using-future. In the summer school, 38 groups with 164 Chinese design students from 45 universities as participants, each team can have no fewer than three or more than five people and must be enrolled in a design program. Four experts from industry and university as judges, and one research institution as the offline partner attended the summer school. The summer school is around six topics and three cities (Suzhou, Wuxi, Changshu) in the Yangtze River Delta region. Students in different groups ask about these topics to develop and prototype outputs following the process model.

The process of Future Pioneer has four steps. Each step has its specific outcomes in progressive. Meanwhile, participators need to learn future thinking courses, finish the post-lesson quiz, and write a reflection blog at the end of every step. They are asked to complete a questionnaire at the end of the final step. Experts score the outputs from participate groups in three perspectives at the end of the first and last steps. Finally, we try to summarize an education process mod el of cultivating future literacy after analysis and review this summer school.

3.1 The Framework of Future Pioneer

Future Pioneer is an online program organized by the Academy of Fine Arts, Tsinghua University and OCT Innovation & Research Institute. The whole process combines design thinking with future scenario planning to generate the alternative future. The summer program is designed as a competition, with four progressive steps: Understand the Future; Explore Alternative Future; Development the Alternative Future; Visualization Future Scenario and Presentation. We involved six different practical tool templates

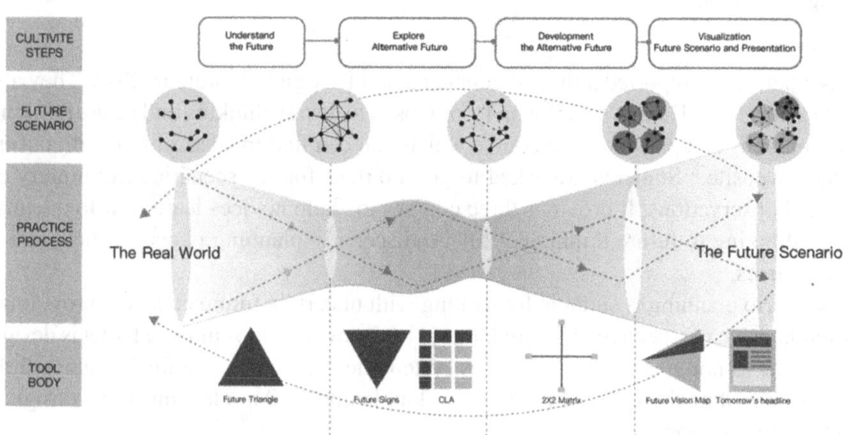

Fig. 8. The framework of Future Pioneer Summer program

from future thinking and design thinking, respectively is: 1. Future Triangle, 2. Future Signs, 3. Causal layered analysis (CLA), 4. 2 × 2 matrix, 5. Future Vision Map and Tomorrow's headline. The specific description of each step is following (Fig. 8).

Step 1. Understanding the Future. Since our participators are most from design background and lack knowledge of future thinking. At the beginning, we provide the courses to help them understand what future is and why designers need to have future thinking. To prevent them from falling into a single vision of the future, we are including STEEP analysis, which referenced the research from Sardesai et al. [19]. They combine PESTLE in the applied scenario planning approach. As the origin of PESTLE, "STEEP analysis can be used to evaluate the external factors that may impact your design decisions", and these external factors are composed of Social, Technological, Economical, Environmental and Political [30]. This idea also reference peter et al. [21] involve into STEEP into the Dexign Futures flipped course. Students can do the desk research by following this structure, and combining it with the Future triangle [11], which discuss "pull of the present", "pull of the future", and "weight of the past" around their select topic. In the end, each group is asked to upload an A4 digital document with three pages with Future triangle, summarized of the research, and the project proposal.

Step 2. Explore Alternative Future. After the first round, the foundation concept of future has built. Students also have a fuzzy scenario around their topic. For this reason, as a theory that tries to explore the change space for alternative future [10], Casual Layer Analysis (CLA) is involved into this step. Another tools Future signs [9] also aim to lead students to figure out signs about their scenarios from daily life to enrich their Imaginate of future scenarios. And from this step, they are asked to write a "review blog" to reflect their learning of future thinking. Each blog minimized 400 words. The upload time of the review blog is requested two days after each delivery stage, and each group upload their blog into one document. The structure of the review blog was designed following summary and subpoints. It means they need to provide a group perspective review with a personal review. In step 2, students need to upload 3 pages with brainstorming, and descriptions of future scenario that they convergent in the end.

Step 3. Development the Alternative Future. In the third step, students need to finish persona and future scenario storyboards for the alternative future they selected in max 3 pages. As a method "are narratives describing how things is might be by a medium- to long-term time horizon" [17]. 2 × 2 Matrix are used to extend their future timeline. Students can around one spotlight and two factors to create their matrix, expanding the alternative future they imagination through the analysis of matrix. In this context, students are asked to shape the scenario they create, and figure out the clearer direction. Meanwhile, some clues gradually cluster, meaning more specific details have surfaced in their scenarios. In this step, lecture live is provided by experts from industry and universities. Students can interact with mentors and solve their problem in the design process by asking questions to mentors.

Step 4. Visualization Future Scenario. In the fourth step, we officially introduce Future Cone [25] to participators. This process aims to give participators space to review future scenario. Some narrative visualization ways are introduced into the learning documents, like video and fiction. Accordingly, we created a tool template from future cone, named Future Vision Map. This map is created to organize the whole process. It combines three different phases corresponding to the three steps they did before. We ask students to reuse the outcomes and data from previous steps to full this structure. So that they can get an overview image of their future scenarios. Through this way, we want students to figure out how this scenario will develop in the period they set, while can help to building a developing scenario as the background for their final design outputs. Then, they can use Tomorrow's Headline [29] to presentation their design output via a superficial entry point (Figs. 9 and 10).

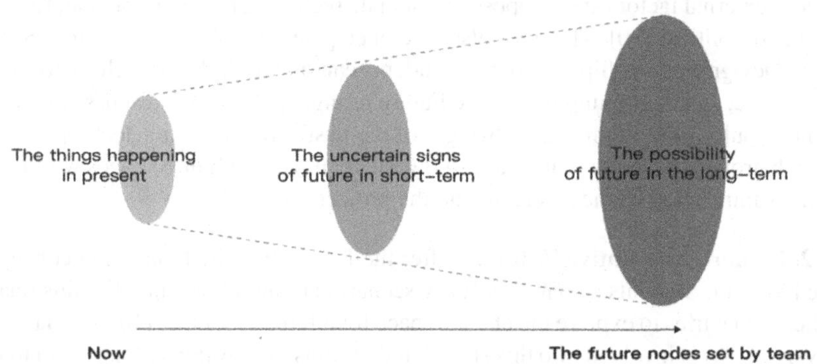

Fig. 9. Future Vision Map, as a tool design for step 4.

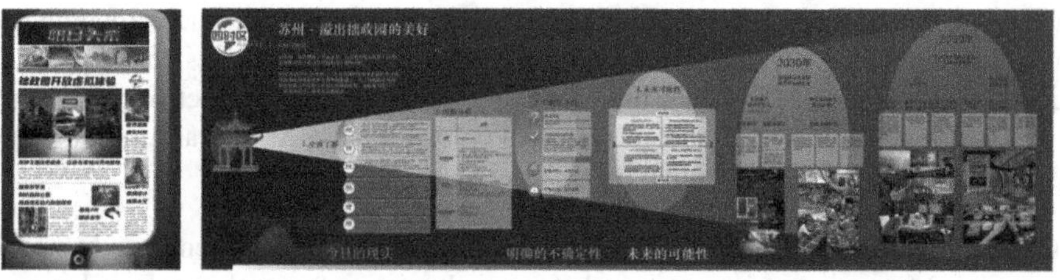

Fig. 10. Tomorrow's Headline and Future Vision Map from group 11.

3.2 Hybrid Collaboration

In this research, hybrid means online and offline, interdisciplinary i.e., Anthropology, Futurology and Design, and various stakeholders, i.e., organizers, operators, and participators (see Fig. 11). The mainly collaborative platform, Feishu. It is an office software published by Byte Jumping Corporation. This platform integrated organizational membership management, cloud documents, schedules, and meetings. Thus, the courses, guidebooks, quiz's questionnaires, and meetings can be all-in-one on Feishu. The online and offline hybrid collaboration is reflected in that OCT innovation & Research Institute provide in-field research data from offline, then participators, judges and tutors collaborate via Feishu. After the program, the top groups are invited to collaborate with OCT Innovation & Research Institute to enrich their projects more localization. The collaboration's cross-points between online and offline are asynchronous, mainly focused on preparation programs, summarization, and final presentation. In the preparation programs, the hybrid collaboration has happened between the distributed tutor team and the in-field research group. After several discussions, the tutor team gave advice to the in-field research groups, then after one month of in-field research, the offline team uploaded materials about Suzhou, Wuxi, and Changshu from offline to the cloud provided by Feishu. Furthermore, the interdisciplinary intersection hybrid collaboration is reflected in the different backgrounds of stakeholders. For example, the OCT Innovation & Research Institute team is combined by sociology and anthropology researchers, and the background of participators, tutors and mentors from industrial design, digital media art, interactive design, service design, architecture etc.

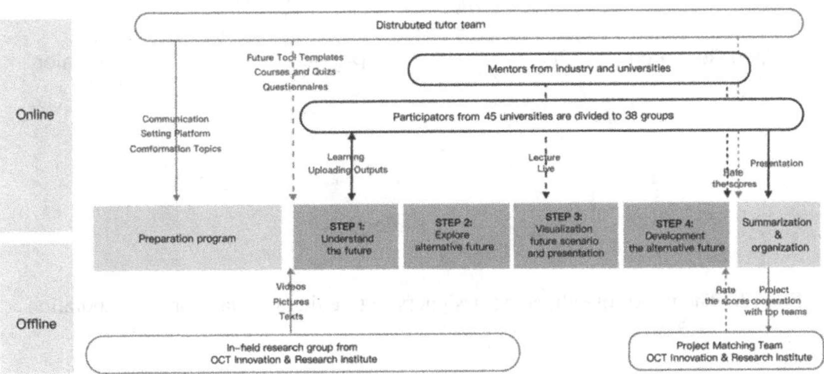

Fig. 11. Hybrid collaboration blueprint.

3.3 The Model of Cultivating Designers' Future Literacy via Hybrid Collaboration

Based on the research. We summarized the model of cultivating designers' Future Literacy via hybrid collaboration (see Fig. 12). In the beginning, since participants cannot do research by themselves in target cities. For creating empathy with local culture and challenges, we need enough information about target cities. Thus, we collaborate with local organizations who not in the design field to achieve insights from different perspectives. In-field research can provide localization information to build images of target cities. Then move to remote collaboration through online learning lectures and materials to cultivate participators' future literacy, providing practice opportunities to achieve a close loop from input to output. In addition to learning and practice, we add the reflection phase, called Reflective Blog, into the cultivation process. One crucial component of future literacy is reflexivity [12]. "Reflective practice is critical in design education to embed new ideas and methods firmly into design practice" [22]. It can help students review outputs of each step and have a stronger impression of knowledge. Through learning, practice and reflection, students can achieve the circular flow of learning process from input, output to reflection interaction. At the end of the model, Future Vision, produced by participators, presents alternative future in narrative visualization. Then in the final presentation, we invite the local team to participate and give feedback. Future Vision can build a common concept for stakeholders by visualization and help them understand the alternative future. Thus, students provide prototype solutions for the local. The local partners can directly collaborate with preferred teams and localized land some ideas, effectively catalyzing action. To complete a closed loop from future to present.

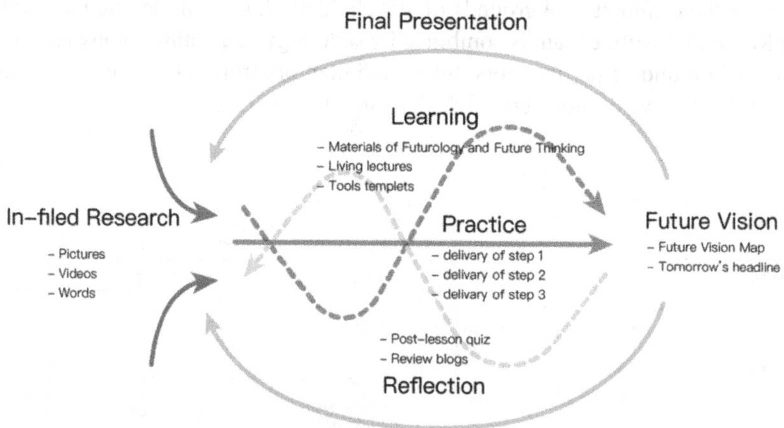

Fig. 12. The model of cultivating designers' future literacy via hybrid collaboration

4 Discussion

The questionaries and review blogs illustrate the strengths and weaknesses of our program. The student feedback is used to iterative tools and develop process structure. Overview, students have a consensus that alternative futures can bring designers diverse directions of future thinking and expansion of thought dimensions. For example, the students from group 14 said: "...Futurology is trying to make me think in a larger coordinate system in more unnoticed dimensions while trying to understand and solve the visible and immediate problems".

During the learning, practice and reflection process, students more difficult to understand the futurology knowledge we provide to them as the stages progresses. Insufficient cases become one of the main questions. Some students said that theory is abstract and hard to understand directly. From the feedback for the lectures, we can also find this need. In lectures, students' feedback one of the significant memorable points is the case of robot dog explained by a mentor. Another prominent problem is students lack feedback in each stage. Some of the students said they feel lost in step 2 and 3 until we give them an additional Q&A event, then they finally find direction. This is trend significantly illustrated by each step's NPS (Net Promoter Score) from questionaries. This trend also corresponds to level changed about learning process mentions by FLL-N [13] (Table 1).

Table 1. The NPS of each step and the program.

Questions	How satisfied are you with your course work in Step 1?	How satisfied are you with your course work in Step 2?	How satisfied are you with your course work in Step 3?	How satisfied are you with your course work in Step 4?	How satisfied are you with this program?
Detractors (Score 0 ~ 6)	0%	12%	20%	16%	10%
Passives (Score 7 ~ 8)	40%	32%	28%	25%	16%
Promoters (Score 9 -10)	60%	56%	52%	58.3%	68%

We will respond to the students' suggestions by adding the number of case-studies and decide to add more feedback methods in the process, for instead, ask mentors to give advises, have more Q&A live and create specific place for them to ask questions.

In the end of program, the final outputs are scored by four expert judges from the perspectives of completeness, discernment, and originality. In addition, the scoring from tutor team and project matching team are added into the rating calculation. The final presentation is placed after the scoring. But we find some judges change their mind when they have listened presentation of different groups. Because they can get more details than pictures during presentation. For this reason, we decide to rethink the communicate approach in final step to make sure the students can narrative their stories complete. Requirements for video submission will be add to the iterate event. Each team can make a video use simple technology like screen recording of their presentation to achieve a complete narrative of their future scenario.

5 Conclusion

"We shape our tools and thereafter our tools shape us [4]". Design as an approach which can facilitate the social development, we should not only focus on history and present, but also need to take care of the future development. Imaginate alternative future in a plausibly method, while basic on this to make strategy planning and decision, which give rise to the present action. In this paper, we've shown a case study in Chinese context about how to make a hybrid collaboration for cultivating designers' future literacy happen in an online platform. It provides a process and summarizes a model about explore alternative future that happens between offline and online and interdisciplinary collaboration. Meanwhile it provides a possible for designers to influence the future development from present. Through involved into futurology's knowledge (i.e., tools and theories) into design process to cultivate future literacy, designers can find an effective approach (i.e., future scenario planning) to face uncertain future.

Acknowledgments. The tools template used in this paper are from the tutors of *Future Pioneer*, and the test data of the process and project pictures is from the students who participated in the *Future Pioneer*. The course and discussion from professor Scupelli brought a lot of reference and inspiration to the design of this event flow. During this research, we would like particularly to acknowledge all the members, along with our tutors, judges, and lecture providers.

References

1. Amer, M., et al.: A review of scenario planning. Futures **46**, 23–40 (2013). https://doi.org/10.1016/j.futures.2012.10.003
2. Candy, L.: Practice based research: a guide. CCS Rep. **1**(2), 1–19 (2006)
3. Dator, J.: Alternative futures at the Manoa School. J. Futures Stud. **14** (2009)
4. Dator, J.: What Futures Studies Is, and Is Not. In: Jim Dator: A Noticer in Time. pp. 3–5 Springer, Cham (2019). Doi.https://doi.org/10.1007/978-3-030-17387-6_1
5. van Dorsser, C., et al.: Improving the link between the futures field and policymaking. Futures **104**, 75–84 (2018). https://doi.org/10.1016/j.futures.2018.05.004
6. Eggink, W., de la Bruheze, A.A.A.: Design storytelling with future scenario development; envisioning "the museum". In: Summer Cumulus Conference 'The Virtuous circle', Milan, 3–7 June 2015 (2015)
7. Elon university: Survey XII: Digital New Normal 2025 – After the Outbreak – Imagining the Internet. https://www.elon.edu/u/imagining/surveys/xii-2021/post-covid-new-normal-2025/#Tele-everything. Accessed 04 Nov 2021
8. European Environment Agency: COVID-19 and Europe's environment: impacts of a global pandemic — European Environment Agency. https://www.eea.europa.eu/publications/covid-19-and-europe-s. Accessed 10 Feb 2022
9. Hiltunen, E.: The future sign and its three dimensions. Futures **40**(3), 247–260 (2008). https://doi.org/10.1016/j.futures.2007.08.021
10. Inayatullah, S.: Causal layered analysis: poststructuralism as method. Futures **30**(8), 815–829 (1998). https://doi.org/10.1016/S0016-3287(98)00086-X
11. Inayatullah, S.: Six pillars: futures thinking for transforming. Foresight **10**(1), 4–21 (2008). https://doi.org/10.1108/14636680810855991
12. Mangnus, A., et al.: Futures literacy and the diversity of the future. Futures **132** (2021). https://doi.org/10.1016/j.futures.2021.102793
13. Miller, R. (ed.): Transforming the Future: Anticipation in the 21st Century. Taylor & Francis (2018)
14. Mortensen, J.K., et al.: Barriers to developing futures literacy in organisations. Futures **132**, 102799 (2021). https://doi.org/10.1016/j.futures.2021.102799
15. NetEase: Over the weekend, I opened "Justice Online" to attend an AI academic conference. 周末,我打开《逆水寒》参加了一场AI学术会议, https://www.163.com/dy/article/FQ1LEMTU0511DSSR.html. Accessed 30 Dec 2021
16. Rhisiart, M., et al.: Learning to use the future: developing foresight capabilities through scenario processes. Technol. Forecast. Soc. Chang. **101**, 124–133 (2015). https://doi.org/10.1016/j.techfore.2014.10.015
17. Rhydderch, A.: Scenario Building: The 2x2 Matrix Technique (2017)

18. Roblox Education: Roblox Education - Code and make games with Roblox, https://education.roblox.com/en-us/. Accessed 30 Dec 2021
19. Sardesai, S., Stute, M., Kamphues, J.: A methodology for future scenario planning. In: Fornasiero, R., Sardesai, S., Barros, A.C., Matopoulos, A. (eds.) Next Generation Supply Chains. LNMIE, pp. 35–59. Springer, Cham (2021). https://doi.org/10.1007/978-3-030-63505-3_2
20. Scupelli, P., et al.: Dexign futures: a pedagogy for long - horizon design scenarios. In: DRS Biennial Conference Series (2016)
21. Scupelli, P., et al.: Making dexign futures learning happen a case study for a flipped, open learning initiative course. Future (2019)
22. Scupelli, P., et al.: Teaching to Design Futures in China: A Vision for a Blended Learning Pedagogy to be Deployed at Scale (2019)
23. Totten, C.W.: Suddenly online professional development pedagogy: end-of-semester showcasing in gamejolt and animal crossing: New Horizons. J. Literacy Technol. **21**(3), 82–101 (2020)
24. UNESCO: Learning to envision the future: the first World Summit on Futures Literacy at UNESCO. https://en.unesco.org/news/learning-envision-future-first-world-summit-futures-literacy-unesco. Accessed 29 Dec 2021
25. Voros, A.J.: The Futures Cone, use and history. https://thevoroscope.com/2017/02/24/the-futures-cone-use-and-history/. Accessed 30 Dec 2021
26. Voros, J.: A generic foresight process framework. Foresight **5**(3), 10–21 (2003). https://doi.org/10.1108/14636680310698379
27. 陳國華: 從城市未來學談城市競爭力. 研考雙月刊. 30, 5, 42–55 (2006)
28. Futures Literacy. https://en.unesco.org/futuresliteracy/about. Accessed 29 Dec 2021
29. Tomorrow's Narratives | Service Design Tools. https://servicedesigntools.org/tools/tomorrows-narratives. Accessed 04 Jan 2022
30. What is a STEEP Analysis? — UTS. https://www.utsdesignindex.com/researchmethod/steep-analysis/. Accessed 03 Jan 2022

Technical Aesthetics Strategy of Information Visualization

Lu Zhao(✉) and Haimin Sun

Luxun Academy of Fine Arts, No. 19 Sanhao Street, Shenyang, Liaoning, China
zhaoludear@126.com

Abstract. As a technical aesthetics, information visualization design includes two main methods: scientific "experimental induction" and humanistic "conceptual speculation". This paper reflects on the data rights, technically aesthetic limitations, and lack of spiritual value in the current information visualization design. This article suggested changing the goal of information visualization from interpretative to exploratory function and developing "given" data into "participatory" data - CAPTA. It drives information technology with design aesthetics, brings "concept speculation" into each information visualization process, and encourages the creation of a humanized knowledge generator to catalyze social dreams.

Keywords: Information visualization · Speculative design · Capta · Emotional experience · Visual metaphor

1 Introduction

Information visualization starts from the purpose, collects the original data to make processed information, organizes the information architecture through technical methods, and transforms the abstract information structure into a concrete visual aesthetic form to present to different audiences. This process realizes the transformation of the DIKW concept chain model: Data - Information - Knowledge - Wisdom. In acknowledging the shift from data to wisdom, information design belongs to the interdisciplinary area of science and art design as technical aesthetics. It includes two method systems of "empirical induction" and "conceptual speculation". Their method pedigrees and purpose orientation are different. The purpose of "empirical induction" is to solve the practical problems of function and provide specific technical guidance for each link of information visualization. As the metaphysical part of visual design, "conceptual speculation" focuses on the "humanism" of the spiritual level, reflected in how the aesthetic form affects the meaning of information transmission, which applied to the final stage of information visual design - the graphic form transformation of structured data. The technically aesthetic attribute of visual information design makes its method stimulate contradictions in the juxtaposition of "science" and "humanities", "demonstration" and "concept".

P.-L. P. Rau (Ed.): HCII 2022, LNCS 13311, pp. 302–311, 2022.
https://doi.org/10.1007/978-3-031-06038-0_22

2 Scientific Information Visualization Dominated by "Empirical Induction" Method

Throughout the development of information design, the scientific "empirical induction" method has always been in the technical leading position. In contrast, the "conceptual speculation" method with humanistic spirit has become a technology accessory and used as visual explanatory tools and formal embellishment. Firstly, unlike the visual creation in art design, the initial function of information visual design is to explain scientific problems, which trace back to the scientific example of non-artistic images in the 17th century. Observing many samples, scientists deduce graphical models to explain these scientific problems in physics, medicine, society, and the economy. Secondly, the aesthetic significance of information design is different from the traditional visual design, which advocates exquisite artistic expression, and emphasizes effective information transmission. The ideal relationship under this system is that design is a tool of scientific demonstration and aesthetics as a tool of technology. Early scientists would train an illustrator for a long time to avoid misleading scientific problems due to artistic imagination to ensure the objective presentation of scientific issues. Later, with the improvement of graphic semiotics, more neutral statistical graphics came into being. In recent years, computer graphics technology for big data can more intelligently balance the neutrality and objectivity of scientific problems. Therefore, design is a technical means to visualize abstract information, and neutrality is the most important code of conduct, but design's "conceptual speculative" value does not play a role. Finally, information visualization follows the principle of mechanical objectivity in technology. In detachment, Lorraine Duston and Peter Garrison pointed out that the technological revolution pushed scientists to an ideal schema of information visualization, namely "mechanical objectivity." "a mechanical image, photos, has become a symbol of non-interference in objectivity because cameras eliminate human initiative." From now on, technology has relied on machinery to ensure objectivity: photos make the scientific image not easy to be manipulated and do not rely on the imagination of scientists; The camera's instantaneous exploration of motion deconstructs time, transforms the process of fluid movement into data sets, and scientists freeze and analyze each component, which also widens the microanalysis boundary of information visualization design; The popularity of computer and Internet gives birth to big data, which makes each process of information visualization rely on the computer for data mining. At present, information visualization is in the field of computer research. Human beings embrace "mechanical objectivity" to avoid misjudgment because machines are not easily affected by society, politics, or identity. Design's "conceptual speculation" has not been widely incorporated into various visual processes and is in a subordinate position dominated by "empirical induction".

3 The Crisis of Information Rights: Reflection on Scientific Technology

3.1 "Objectivity" Bias of Data

In "Raw Data" is an Oxymoron, Lisa Gitelman says that "In fact, the seemingly indispensable misconception that data is always original is a way of contextualizing data and a myth constructed according to one's assumptions" [1]. Information comes from data, and the "objectivity" of data seems to be a priori existence independent of human beings. The scientific "empirical induction" method first depends on a view that phenomenon is independent of observer data; data is the description of a priori conditions. Its application formula is knowledge = empirical data × mathematics [2]. For example, infer by observing data and mathematical calculations in medicine, physics, and astronomy. However, in the face of problems related to value and significance, such as social ethics, this formula is useless. The famous cardiologist Nica Goldberg questioned the "objectivity" of the data in Women are not little men. He found that most cardiology studies are men. Women were considered to be inconsistent with men's "standards" because of their small size, but the fact is that the development model of women's heart disease is entirely different from that of men [3]. In this regard, the humanistic "concept speculation" method puts forward a new formula for acquiring ethical knowledge: knowledge = experience × Sensitivity [2] linking to human expertise and observing data with the most significant sensitivity. The key to solving this problem is to recognize that people undertake all the work in the world, and everyone has a specific position. Similarly, data is generated based on people, and the data is not objective but the product of unequal social relations. Therefore, all forms of knowledge, including information visualization design, are generated in a specific environment. As Lisa Gitelman further explains in her book: just as photos are not objective manifestations of reality, data are not. A photographer conceived and created a photograph, and the data "needs to be understood as a constructed reality" [1].

3.2 Technological Hegemony of Information

As a right, the technicality of information has become a double-edged sword. On the one hand, researchers use this power to expose injustice and put forward improvement measures; On the other hand, they discriminate and create hegemony. "Empirical induction" is usually regarded as a technical method to guide the various processes of information visualization design. However, these methods are accompanied by the hegemony and bias of the creator. For example, a small group of technical elites created information processing technologies and tools and then expanded to users worldwide. Still, these small groups can not represent the whole world or even a city. For example, a small group of technical elites created information processing technologies and tools and expanded to worldwide users. This excludes physical transgender and homosexuals and virtually creates a kind of discrimination. Therefore, whether intentionally or unintentionally, information technology aimed at improving the efficiency of enterprises or governments often incorporates structural inequality. In response to the hegemony in technology, Data Feminism by Klein and Catherine calls for "Hold the information right in your own hands." [4] which encourages a re-examination of the right to information and challenges information technology. This kind of thinking is based on the humanistic method of "conceptual speculation", which shows how race, class, gender, and other factors in the world challenge and jointly affect information hegemony.

3.3 "Neutrality" Principle of Information Visual Display

Advocates of "empirical induction" equate the functional perfection of information with the beauty of design and believe that the essential principle is to ensure the "neutrality" of visual display. In the 1980s, Edward Tafte proposed data-ink ratio and junk chart, the visualization neutrality principles that information designers should strive to follow. The data-ink ratio believes that any ink (such as color, graphics, or decoration) used outside information and data can confuse objectivity and blur the overall argument of information. Tafte opposes the junk chart, which is a useless and uninformative element. The decorative design represents secret emotional persuasion. In The Truthful Art, Alberto Cairo proposed to put "feelings and emotions" aside. [5] The more straightforward, the more neutral; The more neutral, the more objective. A Unified Theory of Information Design points out that "The visual effect maintains a deliberately neutral emotional field, and the audience can respond to the information more freely." [6] Such as colors and icons will arouse emotions and blur the rational thinking of the audience.

Among these classic visualization strategies dominated by the "empirical induction" method, we could see that the "neutrality" display strategy is based on the worship of the myth of data "objectivity". It seems that "neutrality" can realize rationality and objectivity. Any visualization method with emotion and concept will be equivalent to irrational and false design. This dualistic logic that puts emotion on the opposite of rationality is monopolistic because rationality and emotion can be compatible. As mentioned above, the problem of information is complex and based on people, so the design strategy of information visualization should embrace diversity. Visual minimalism may not ensure neutrality, but the humanism concept can better enhance the impact of information visualization.

4 Application of Humanistic Aesthetics Strategy to Information Visualization

At this stage, the speed of human information generation has far exceeded the ability to process information. Although designers who advocate the "empirical induction" method have been tirelessly exploring more intelligent information technology, giving the initiative to technology will be put into a narrow stylized cage. Many information visualization designers have realized the limitations of technology. The goal of information visualization design needs to change from interpretative function to exploratory inspiration. Applying "conceptual speculation" to each information design process is necessary. "Conceptual speculation" is not advocating the assumption of breaking away from empirical evidence but inviting users to participate through design aesthetics, intervening in macro thinking with micro experience, questioning the authoritative reality generated by a single technical discourse mechanism, and reconstructing the openness and initiative of information visualization design. Scientific "empirical induction" and humanistic "conceptual speculation" need to reach a contract and be jointly incorporated into each process of information visualization, which is like the yin-yang symbiosis theory of Chinese philosophy. Each scientific Yang contains a humanistic Yin, and each speculative Yin drives an empirical Yang.

4.1 Give Humanistic Right to Data

Information designer George Lupi put forward the Data humanism manifesto (Fig. 1) in 2017. Advocating the use of visual design as a catalyst to reflect: "We are ready to question the objectivity of simple technical methods to deal with information, and explore ways to connect information with what it represents: knowledge, behavior, and people." [7] Lupi defines humanistic data that is different from the perspective of science: (1) data is generated based on people. (2) it is allowed to challenge data rights. (3) data is related to macro facts and connects micro experiences. (4) explore the various possibilities of data, rather than single certainty (5) we should consider data in the relative context. (6) data is empirical and has people's emotional experience. (7) data is a medium and can communicate and convey feelings. (8) Encourage the creation of humanized visual coding rather than technically intelligent generation tools. (9) the relationship between data and design is driven by each other.

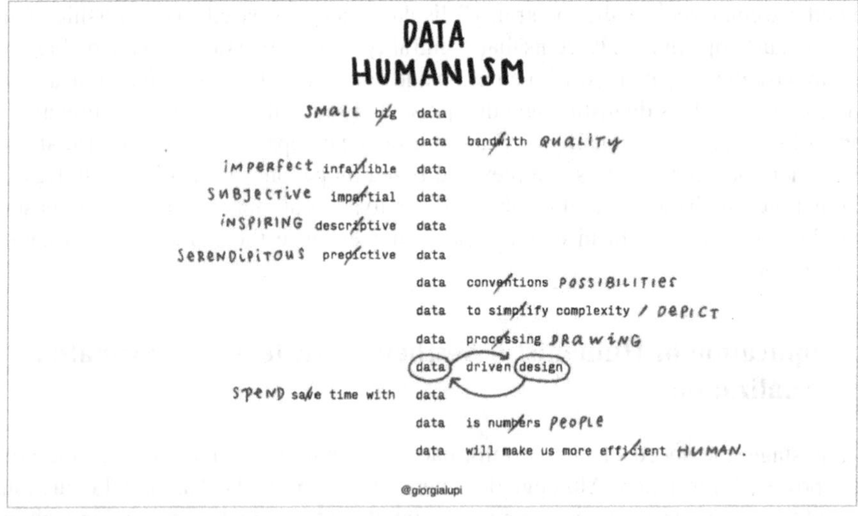

Fig. 1. Data Humanism manifesto (available at http://giorgialupi.com/data-humanism-my-manifesto-for-a-new-data-wold)

Johanna Drucker, a researcher of Digital Humanities, believes that data display technology, which is usually widely used in science, is accompanied by the assumption that knowledge is independent of the observer and does not depend on and explain each other with the observer. Therefore, she further proposed the need to use humanistic methods to carry out information visualization design and defined the data of this graphic display as CAPTA [8]. As a concept of "given" in her discourse, DATA is objective, observable, and recordable. Johanna believes that the history of knowledge is the history of knowledge expression, and data is participated by people, not as the objective expression of pre-existing facts. Therefore, she puts forward a personalized method to understand graphical data as CAPTA. The difference between CAPTA and DATA is that CAPTA is exploratory graphical data. The thinking of this visual data is based on abstract speculation to explore the situational, local, and structural characteristics of knowledge production. Data humanism tells us that the challenge of information visualization is to integrate multi-dimensional complex data into a visual display and question the established standards and accept the experience and fuzziness of knowledge.

4.2 Design Aesthetics Drive Information Technology

Embrace Emotional Experiences. "Concept speculation" encourages information visualization design to ask questions through individual experience and invites the audience to intervene in thinking rather than explaining and preaching great propositions. It requires people's participation, sneaking into the information situation, and embracing emotional experience. The emotional experience emphasized here includes two dimensions: (1) the emotional experience dimension of data and information (2) the visualized emotional expression dimension.

The emotional experience dimension of data and information refer to humanistic qualitative information, not just empirical quantitative information. For example, medical data focus on quantitative parameters such as patients' gender, age, onset time, and symptoms. While "conceptual speculation" will actively collect humanized qualitative data - emotional experience, such as patients' psychological changes and nursing feelings. The emotional expression dimension challenges the neutral display principle of "empirical induction", encourages the juxtaposition of rationality and emotion, and explores the coexistence path of visual minimalism and emotional design. It advocates stimulating the emotional resonance of the audience through the aesthetic form of design to trigger the thinking of the problem.

Bruises-The Data We Don't See created by Georgia Lupi and Kaki King (Fig. 2), This work focuses on the impact of children's disease care on individual families, trying to present the emotional experience of children's medical care, which is difficult to capture by relying on the data of clinical medical records alone. The original intention of the creation is that King's daughter was diagnosed with a rare autoimmune disease - idiopathic thrombocytopenic purpura (ITP), which is called a "visual disease", manifested as systemic bruises and vascular rupture. Therefore, Lupi and Kim began to collect humanized data to observe and record King's daughter's skin lesions and the associated emotional dimension data. The relevant data include the quantitative data of golden daughter's blood test, such as platelet count, degree of the bruise, drug treatment, etc.; It also consists of the qualitative data of Kim's emotional dimensions such as hope, stress, and fear. In terms of visual presentation, she hopes to emphasize the particularity of individual families with experiential, emotional, and exploratory visual aesthetics. She uses a flowing timeline to represent the time experience of nursing patients, and each leaf represents the daily data set evenly distributed on this timeline. Lupi's goal is to arouse compassion and help her audience feel part of the story of human life. In this way, the characteristics of information change from self-evident facts to structured interpretations driven by the human agenda.

Fig. 2. Bruises - The Data We Don't See (available at http://giorgialupi.com/bruises-the-data-we-dont-see)

Visual Metaphorical Rhetoric. In visual metaphor rhetoric, the similarity between the visual metaphor and information subject realizes the metonymy process, accompanied by the generation of interpretation and views. Therefore, the symbolic rhetorical power of information visualization design is a significant field of "conceptual speculation". Simulated dendrochronology of U.S. immigration (1830–2015) (Fig. 3), using the metaphorical visual rhetoric of tree rings, presents the racial identity of the American immigrant population. In science, the technology of studying the change of ecological climate over time through tree rings is called tree chronology. According to the tree rings, researchers can trace back to specific environmental conditions thousands of years ago, just like the history of American Immigration. Under the influence of different historical processes, cells leave marks on the tree rings, just as diversified immigrants are natural contributors to the growth of tree trunks in the United States. Here, the growth ring metaphors the United States. According to this metaphorical logic, the wave of immigration makes it denser and denser. Each colored "cell" on the ring represents 100 immigrants in this design. Over time, each ring represents a decade. Color and growth direction show the origin of immigrants. This visual metaphor indicates that the United States is a living organism that takes a long time to grow. It can be seen that visual metaphorical rhetoric helps to embed the author's point of view, reveal the way of thinking information, and produce the meaning and aesthetic influence that the neutrality principle cannot express.

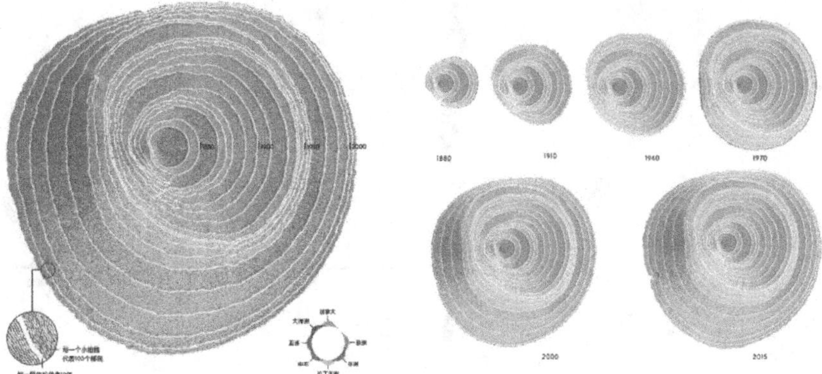

Fig. 3. Simulated dendrochronology of U.S. immigration (1830–2015) (available at https://web.northeastern.edu/naturalizing-immigration-dataviz/) (Color figure online)

Speculative Design Catalyzes Social Dreams. In such an era of media technology, pragmatism is reflected in information visualization design. Designers use confirmatory design solutions to solve human survival and development problems, such as environmental pollution, resource scarcity, and social injustice. Still, human values are the crux of these problems. Therefore, "empirical induction" does not jump out of the limitation of a single thinking mechanism to challenge narrow presupposition. The purpose of introducing "concept speculation" into each process of information visualization design is to arouse people's thinking about dreams and values. And then trigger an action turn: information visualization design is a technically aesthetic tool for practical information and can inspire thinking and change behavior. As a speculative visual expression medium, design links the ideal and reality. Its most crucial significance is to stimulate the reflection on the current mechanism and explore a variety of possibilities of the parallel world to catalyze people's social dreams.

Georgia Lupi's personalization project Dear data (Fig. 4) initiated a challenge to the information thinking mechanism. She believes that the information visualization design can allow people not to be driven by information, advocate the actual integration of data into life, and even become a medium for communication. She had a one-year visual information communication with information designer Stephanie Posavic, two people living in New York and London. This program focuses on 52 common topics, such as complaints, the frequency of laughter, etc. After collecting personalized data, 52 symbolic and poetic visual information models were manually drawn on postcards and finally mailed to each other across the Atlantic. It is a slow, detailed, personalized simulation transmission process that does not rely on automatic processing algorithms but also eliminates computer visualization technology. Lupi is committed to looking at data in different ways and interpreting these data with personal stories, behaviors, and daily life to generate humanized visual information coding and transform the data into a communication medium.

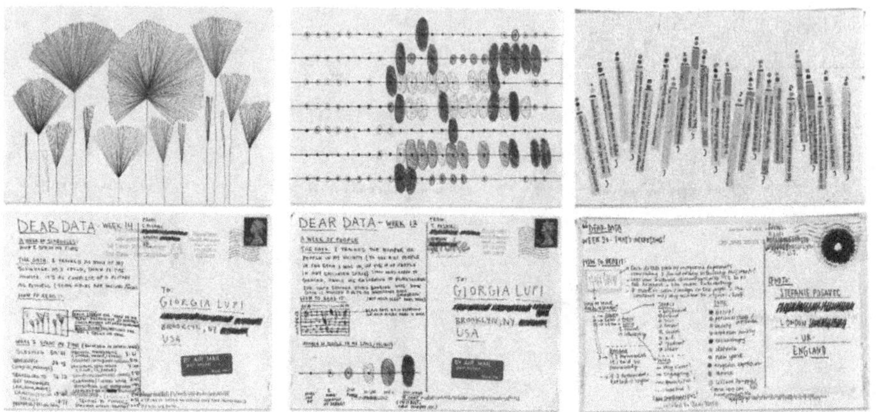

Fig. 4. Dear data (available at http://www.dear-data.com/theproject)

Dear data is a very personal experimental project. Although it does not have universal reference significance, it breaks through the paradigm of information design. It suggests that the goal of visualization in humanistic vision is to hide data, face individuals, and perceive and generate emotional links through visual coding. As Luke stark, a media theorist, said, "data is what we see, hear, feel, breathe and even swallow." [9].

5 Conclusion

This paper initiates a challenge calling for the participation of imagination and intelligence, encourages the creation of knowledge generator from the perspective of humanization, and reconstructs the information visualization design dominated by "empirical induction" with "conceptual speculation." Currently, domestic research on information visualization design is dominated by empirical induction technology. However, engaging in information visualization research in the humanities background needs to embrace technology across the discipline boundary and give play to its discipline advantages and actively reflect on the functionalist shackles of information visualization design. The most outstanding value of speculative lies in putting forward "propose": challenge the single mechanism in the right to information and accept differentiated belief systems, values, and technical methods. While rigorous empirical analysis integrates human initiative into CAPTA, embraces emotion and imagination, asks questions and inspires thinking through the aesthetic differences of design, and explores various possibilities of information to catalyze social dreams and promote people and information relationship development.

References

1. Gitelman, L.:"Raw Data" is an Oxymoron. The MIT Press, London (2013)
2. Harari, Y.N.: A Brief History of Tomorrow. China Citic Press, Beijing (2017)
3. Goldberg, N.: Women Are Not Small Men: Life-Saving Strategies for Preventing and Healing Heart Disease in Women. Ballantine Books, New York (2002)
4. D'Ignazio, C., Klein, L.F.: Data Feminism. The MIT Press, London (2020)
5. Cairo, A.: The Truthful Art. New Riders, London (2016)
6. Amare, N.: A Unified Theory of Information Design: Visuals. Text and Ethics. Routledge, New York (2016)
7. Lupi, G.: Data Humanism, The Revolution will be Visualized. http://giorgialupi.com/data-humanism-my-manifesto-for-a-new-data-wold
8. Drucker, J.: Humanities Approaches to Graphical Display. Digital Humanities Quarterly (2011). http://www.digitalhumanities.org/dhq/vol/5/1/000091/000091.html
9. Luke Stark, "Come on Feel the Data (and Smell It)," Atlantic, May 19, 2014. https://www.theatlantic.com/technology/archive/2014/05/data-visceralization/370899/

Cross-Cultural Differences and HCI

Effects of Field Dependency and Map Type on Wayfinding Strategies

Chieh Cheng[1], Pei-Luen Patrick Rau[1(✉)], and Zhi Guo[1,2]

[1] Tsinghua University, Beijing, China
rpl@mail.tsinghua.edu.cn

[2] State University of New York at Buffalo, Buffalo, NY, USA

Abstract. To upgrade tourism experience, gender and sociocultural differences of wayfinding strategy are critical topics in tourism planning and management. However, the navigation system in real world does not differentiate the gender and regional difference during giving voice navigation. Therefore, in order to provide the future based navigation with more specific foundation, this paper investigates the mediation effect of field dependency on the gender influence and the moderating effect of map type on the regional differences in the wayfinding strategy. The former one was studied by the survey with the embedded figures test and the wayfinding strategy scale. The latter one was examined by the model town experiment simulating a grid-like/askew structure city environment and an askew structure community map. The results show (1) females used more route strategies than males did because females have higher field dependency; (2) participants from Shanghai (an askew-structure city) preferred route strategy in the grid-like/askew structure city maps; (3) mixed strategy was used by participants from Beijing (a grid-structure city) and all participants in askew structure community map. In summary, route wayfinding strategy is the common one most people used, but oriented wayfinding strategy should also be provided for personalized setting (i.e., for males, and for residents from region with grid-like city structure). The results have important implications for the design of sign and route guidance system of tourism and the improvement of public transit and pedestrian mobility. Developers of navigation systems can design the presetting of speech instructions based on city structures and map scales.

Keywords: Field dependency · Map-type · Wayfinding strategy · Gender · Regional culture

1 Introduction

To upgrade tourism experience, the gender and sociocultural differences of wayfinding strategy are critical topics in tourism planning and management as they are the basic elements to guide tourism facilities in providing barrier-free environments for independence and convenience. Tourists almost finish the wayfinding task by themselves with different navigation aids and by asking the local for help and support. In all navigation aid methods, like GPS navigation systems, paper-based travel maps, internet-based

P.-L. P. Rau (Ed.): HCII 2022, LNCS 13311, pp. 315–329, 2022.
https://doi.org/10.1007/978-3-031-06038-0_23

map/route-planning services and the local signage system, voice or language navigation guide is inevitable. Most of wayfinding studies in tourism are mainly focus on the ways of these aids (Chang 2015; Ishikawa 2016) or visual layout design (Leib et al. 2012), but pay little attention to the language or voice content of navigation or wayfinding which is about how to design an easier and more intuitive wayfinding map design. That is to say, although tourism studies pay attention to wayfinding, previous studies focus on wayfinding tools in the hand but not on maps in the head.

Tourists often report difficulties in understanding the context and location of sign and wayfinding within an unfamiliar environment, which was even resulting in traffic jams in most famous tourism sites (Lee et al. 2017). Furthermore, although GPS-based navigation system in wayfinding was widely used, the efficiency was not better or even worse than paper maps (Chang 2015). These findings might be related to the differences in the user-mental and local-logic models (Chang 2017; Lee et al. 2017). Mental mapping is a useful method for revealing how visitors spatially perceive tourism destinations.

Although gender and cultural differences in the wayfinding strategy have been studied by some researchers (Abdul Khanan and Xia 2010; Findlay and Southwell 2004; Lawton and Kallai 2002; Hund et al. 2012; Symonds et al. 2017; Xia et al. 2009; Zhang et al. 2010), navigation systems of tourism in the real world do not consider the gender and regional differences. Due to the diversity of tourist with different cultures and regions, the need to balance the multiple needs and a good tourism experience (O'Connor et al. 2005) is a critical issue in tourism management. In addition, wayfinding is not only a cognitive concept but also a social cultural experience (Symonds et al. 2017). It is necessary to explore the mechanism of wayfinding strategies for the improvement of tourism management and the better application of wayfinding studies. Therefore, the present study aims to investigate the factors influencing gender and regional differences in the wayfinding strategy to get insights into the application of these differences.

1.1 Wayfinding Strategy

Lawton (1994) first suggested two wayfinding strategies: the orientation and route strategies. The orientation strategy indicates that people mainly use cardinal terms and distances for tracking themselves within an environment; the route strategy states that people use left-right terms and landmarks more to clarify the spatial relationship between the destination and themselves. Hund and Minarik (2006) simulated a town environment using a town-scaled map, which contained paths and landmarks. The result showed that people could be more efficient in wayfinding tasks, when corresponding instructions were provided based on their wayfinding strategy. In addition, when the preference for the orientation strategy increased, the efficiency improved. The authors explained that this could be caused by a metaphor of map-like material. When participants could overview the town, orientation-related information became beneficial.

Gender and cultural differences in the wayfinding strategy between the Americans and Hungarians were reported by Lawton and Kallai (2002). Men in both Hungary and America exhibited greater preference for strategies based on absolute reference frames, whereas women reported greater preference for strategies based on route information. Americans used the route strategy more than the Hungarians. Hund et al. (2012) asked

American and Dutch participants to provide directions to a direction-asker, who was driving or walking in town, with maps. He demonstrated that American participants used cardinal descriptions more than the Dutch, in general. The American participants provided street names more frequently, whereas the Dutch participants provided landmark-related information. Levinson (1996) investigated the relationship between Dutch and Tzeltal. In Dutch, front, rear, left, and right are the major terms that describe spatial relationships, whereas east, west, south, and north are the major terms in Tzeltal. The result showed that the Tzeltal tended to use a more absolute frame of reference and the Dutch is more likely to a relative frame of reference. In addition, Liu et al. (2005) found that the spatial-description style varied between North and South in China. Southern college students tended to use more egocentric and intrinsic terms (front, rear, left, right), whereas northern students used more absolute reference frame terms (east, west, south, and north).

Researchers state that males had a higher preference for the orientation strategy, whereas females preferred the route strategy (Chen et al. 2009; Lawton 2010; Lawton and Kallai 2002; Xia et al. 2009). This result is similar to the speculation of the relationship between the field dependency and the frame of reference. Learning strategy is influenced by cognitive style (Boccia et al. 2017). Unfortunately, this has not been researched. Furthermore, previous studies mention that the possible reason for the cultural difference in the wayfinding strategy could be the differences in the city structures. For example, structures in the Netherlands were not similar to those in America, which are not systematic and have an askew structure. But the influences of map type with different scale and structures on region difference in wayfinding is still a question.

1.2 Field Dependency

Field dependency, extensively studied in the education and developmental psychology fields, was first proposed by Witkin et al. (1962). As field dependency is the ability to be aware of the environmental information, it might have an impact on the wayfinding strategy. Li and Zhang (2007) investigated the relationship between field dependency and navigation systems. In this research, it was speculated that field-dependent people mainly use environment-centered frames of reference because they notice more environmental information and that field-independent people use absolute frames of reference more because they notice less environmental information. People who tend to use environment-centered frames of reference and notice environmental information may use mainly cardinal terms, whereas those who tend to use absolute frames of reference and notice less environmental information may use mainly left-right terms. However, the article was only speculative, and did not contain experimental evidence to prove the speculations.

1.3 Cognitive Map, Landmark, and City Structure

City structures are powerful tools for organizing the frequencies of the elements in cognitive maps. People may be aware of different environmental cues cognitively, based on the city structures. Previous researchers had organized the cognitive maps of Beijing residents and the results showed that the path, node, and landmark frequencies were higher than those in districts and borders (Feng 2005; Gu and Song 2001). However, the frequencies of these five elements were nearly equal in Lanzhou. Unlike Beijing, Lanzhou does not have a grid-like structure and is a valley city that developed along the natural boundary, with an askew structure (Zhang et al. 2010). Furthermore, Shanghai is an askew structure and the only city that has an established house numbering system in China. Among the five elements, landmarks and paths are the most frequent (Wu and Wang 2012).

Based on the aforementioned research, typically, people are cognitively aware of the landmarks. It was proven that landmarks can assist people in identifying directions and locations (Xia et al. 2008). Landmarks that feature on cognitive maps can be more powerful as they assist people not only in real time but also cognitively. They are defined as "orientation-landmarks," in this paper. On the other hand, those that do not appear on cognitive maps are defined as "route-landmarks." For example, Tiananmen is a typical orientation landmark in Beijing because all the residents of Beijing know its position and can help people identify other places, based on the geographical relationship with Tiananmen.

1.4 Map Scale

Previous research investigated the wayfinding strategy using several factors (Kato and Takeuchi 2003; Prestopnik and Roskoswoldsen 2000). Although these papers grouped participants based on cognitive or environmental factors, most of them were in a small-scale environment. Malinowski and Gillespie (2001) investigated the impact of individual differences on the wayfinding performance in a large-scale environment. This experiment recruited 978 military college students to test the effects of gender, wayfinding experience, math abilities, and map-using skills on the wayfinding ability, in a large-scale woodland. The result was similar to that of small-scale research. Males were better than females, the experienced ones were better than the in-experienced, those with good math abilities were better than those without, and skilled map-using individuals were better than those who lacked these abilities. Bell (2002) investigated the relationship between scales and the frame of reference. The experiment included three groups of participants: 40 first-grade children, third-grade children, and adults. The result showed that age and scale significantly influenced spatial-description terms. Adult participants tended to use more egocentric and intrinsic frames of reference. In a large-scale environment, participants tended to use more object-centered frames of reference, whereas on a small scale, they used more egocentric frames of reference. Similar experiments were conducted in China (Zhang et al. 2008). Array reconstruction tasks were performed with small animal cards in indoor settings and large animal cards in outdoor settings. The result showed that northern students had a greater preference for the absolute frame of reference, whereas southern students preferred the relative frame of reference. In addition, southern students tended to use more absolute frames of reference in a large scale, but more relative frames of reference in a small scale.

Previous studies showed city structure and map scale both influence wayfinding strategy, and the two dimensions are both critical in the map of a region. But it has not been studied together yet, and whether people from different regions have special preference in various maps is still unknown.

Based on the above literature review, this study aims to investigate the mediation effect of field dependency on the gender influence and the moderating effect of the map-type with city structure and map scale on the regional differences in the wayfinding strategy.

2 The Effect of Field Dependency on Gender Difference

2.1 Objective

According to literature review, it was highly possible that field dependency had an impact on wayfinding strategy. Essentially, field dependency was used to test if people will be influenced by environment information while conducting their primary task. The section investigates the mediation effect of field dependency on the gender and wayfinding strategy through a survey.

2.2 Methods

Participants. A total of 177 participants were recruited, including 129 males and 48 females. Only participants who lived in China for over 10 years were recruited. The average age was 31.79 ± 7.12 years. The participants belonged to more than 22 regions in China. Most of the participants had a bachelors' degree (58.1%).

Measurements. Field dependency was measured using the Chinese version of the Embedded Figures Test (EFT, Xie and Zhang 1988). The test is timed paper and pencil performance test and includes 9 simple figures and 29 complex figures with the one of the 9 simple figures embedded within each complex figure. Participants were asked to locate and trace the specified simple figure within each complex figure. The score of the EFT is the number of items correctly traced. The higher the score is, the higher the field-independence is; the lower the score is, the higher the field dependence is.

Based on the way finding strategy scale with 17 items (Lawton 1994), nine items were added in order to appropriate for the wayfinding situation in China, respectively 5 items for orientation strategy and 4 items for route strategy (see Table 1). 16 items measured orientation strategies, and 10 items measured route strategies. All the items were measured by a five-point Likert scale, ranging from "not at all typical for me" to "extremely typical for me". The reliability of the two subscales is respectively 0.842 and 0.710.

Table 1. The added wayfinding-strategy items

Strategy
I kept track of where I was in relation to the historical and political landmark as I went
I asked for directions telling me the relation between destination and landmarks, such as the center of town, lake, river, or mountain
Ring road and direction (north, south, east, or west) help me locate
I would find out the position of landmarks and district in a new city when I just got there
I would connect the unfamiliar area and familiar area and find out the relationship between them
When I walked from A to B, and needed to go back from B to A, I would choose the same road I just passed
When I went, I always choose the most familiar way instead of the shortest way
When I described the destination, I would refer to the left/right side of the building instead of north, south, east, or west
If there was more than one way to get to destination, I would only choose one to remember

2.3 Results

The gender difference in the orientation strategy was significant ($t = 3.308$, $p < .05$), males (55.2) used the orientation strategy more than females (48.8). The gender difference in the route strategy was also significant; ($t = -2.110$, $p < .05$), females (41.3) used the route strategy more than males (39.2). The gender difference of field dependence was also significant ($t = 2.783$, $p < .05$), male (13.6) had higher field independence than female (11.1).

A mediation-effect test was conducted using regression and Sobel tests. Table 2 shows the results. Gender had a significant negative relationship with the orientation strategy, whereas, field dependency did not have a significant relationship with it. Thus, the Sobel test was used to test the mediation effect of field dependency; the Z value was 0.87, $p = 0.38$. Therefore, the mediation effect of field dependency did not occur in the relationship between the gender and the orientation strategy. Gender had a significant positive relationship with the route strategy, whereas, field dependency had a significant negative relationship with it. A higher score on the field dependency scale indicates field independency. When the regression simultaneously contained gender and field dependencies, the gender coefficient was not significant. Therefore, the effect of gender on the route strategy was totally mediated by the field dependency.

Table 2. Mediation effect of field dependency on the gender and wayfinding strategy

	DV1: orientation strategy		DV2: route strategy	
	Step1	Step2	Step1	Step2
IV				
Gender	-0.24^{**}	-0.23^{**}	0.16^{*}	0.13
Mediator				
Field dependency		0.07		-0.16^{*}
ΔR^2	0.06	0.05	0.03	0.05
ΔF	10.94^{**}	5.88^{**}	4.45^{*}	4.46^{*}
Total R^2	0.06	0.06	0.03	0.05
Adjusted R^2	0.05	0.05	0.02	0.04

Note: N = 177, *p < .05, **p < .01

3 The Effect of Map-Type on Region Difference

3.1 Objective

The section investigates the moderating effect of the map-type with the city structure and the map-scale on the region difference in wayfinding strategy through experiments.

The structure of city where people live influences the person's cognitive map. The city structures are mainly grid-like and askew structures, and the previous study found that the spatial-description style varied between North and South in China. Southern college students tended to use more egocentric and intrinsic terms (front, rear, left, right), whereas northern students used more absolute reference frame terms (east, west, south, and north). Therefore, in this sub study, we selected participants from Beijing (north in China and a grid-like structure city) to represent the people from grid-like structure city and participants from Shanghai (south in China and an askew structure city) to represent the people from an askew structure city.

3.2 Methods

Participants. Forty local Beijing residents (north in China and grid-like structure city, average age = 29.38 ± 9.39 years, average living years = 27.10 ± 7.18, males: females = 1:1) and thirty-nine local Shanghai residents (south in China and askew structure city, average age = 27.44 ± 6.50 years, average living years = 26.13 ± 6.86; males: females≈1:1(19/20)) were recruited. All the participants had continuously lived for more than 20 years in Shanghai and Beijing, respectively. The participants of the two groups had similar educational experience.

Materials. In the map-types, with combinations of the city structure and map scale, the independent variable included three levels: the grid-like structure city map, the askew structure city map, and the askew structure community map (see Fig. 1). The elements and basic rules for the city structures and scales were as follows:

Elements:

Orientation landmark: A card (8 cm * 8 cm) with a color photo and nametag.

Route landmarks: A card (5 cm * 5 cm.) with a black-and-white icon and name-tag.

Roads: Lines in dark-blue with nametags beside them.

Rules for the City Structures:

Grid-like: All the roads were in the north-south and west-east directions. The naming rules followed the "orientation-number road." The number and orientation were decided based on Tiananmen; the number increased with the distance from Tiananmen.

Askew: There were no rules for the road layouts and road names.

Rules for the Map Scale:

City: Contains 30 route landmarks and 10 orientation landmarks; the roads had names. The ten orientation-landmarks and the 30 route landmarks are listed in Table 3 and 4, respectively.

Community: Contains 21 route landmarks; the roads do not have names. Nine route landmarks were deleted from Table 4 because they were rarely shown in the real community.

Based on the abovementioned rules, the three maps are shown below:

Grid-like Structure City Map: Grid-like Structure/City Scale.

Askew Structure City Map: Askew Structure/City Scale.

Askew Structure Community Map: Askew Structure/Community Scale.

Table 3. Orientation-landmarks (10)

Ten orientation-landmarks	
Tsinghua University	798
Xizhimen	Tiananmen
Beijing Zoo	Temple of Heaven
Temple of Earth	Wukesong Basketball Court
Beijing West	Nest-type Beijing Olympic
Railway Station	Stadium

Table 4. Route-landmarks (30)

Thirty route-landmarks				
Coffee shop	Post office	Flower shop	Bakery	Supermarket
Park	Bus stop	Fruit stand	Newsstand	Parking lot
Gas station	Cinema	Mall	Print store	Glasses store
Clothes Store	Barber shop	Drink stand	Bar	Book store
Bicycle store	Noodle shop	Pharmacy	Lake	Library
Metro station	Photo gallery	Police station	Fast food restaurant	Elementary School

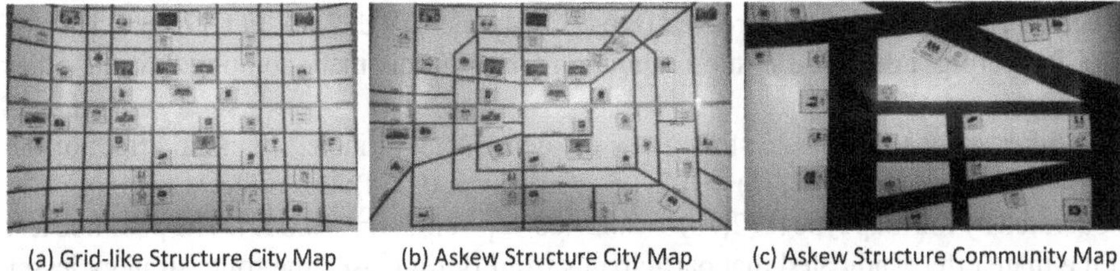

(a) Grid-like Structure City Map (b) Askew Structure City Map (c) Askew Structure Community Map

Fig. 1. The three types of map in the model town experiment

The wayfinding strategy was measured according to Lawton's method, including the orientation and route terms. The cardinal terms and orientation landmarks are referred to as the orientation terms; the left-right, forward-backward, and route terms are referred to as the route terms. All the direction-giving descriptions were analyzed by two researchers and the direction-giving terms were counted, based on the term type.

Procedures. After completing the basic demographic information, the participants were required to complete the orientation-landmark matching questions. After matching the landmarks, they were asked to provide directions with the three maps.

There were four tasks in each map. Task 1 was to describe the position of a land-mark. In Task 2, the participants were asked to close their eyes, while listening to the position descriptions of a landmark and locate the landmark on the map, subsequently. Task 3 was to imagine a direction-asker with a map and low familiarity of the environment (outsider) asking for directions from A to B; participants were required to type the direction-giving descriptions on a laptop. Task 4 was to imagine a direction-asker with high familiarity of the environment (locals), without a map, who was asking for directions from A to B. All the participants were interviewed towards the end of the experiment. Each participant completed the three map tasks. The order of the maps for all the participants followed the Latin square design rule.

3.3 Results

The moderating effects of the map type on the region and orientation or route strategy were firstly examined. After examining the normality, the ANOVA test was used. With respect to the orientation strategy as the dependent variable, the main effect of the region was significant ($F(1,77) = 23.94$, $p < .001$, $\eta^2 = 0.237$); its effect was moderated by the map type ($F(2,76) = 4.29$, $p < .05$, $\eta^2 = 0.101$). The post-hoc test of the main effect indicated that participants from Beijing used the orientation strategy more than those from Shanghai, but it was moderated by the map type. A simple effect test was conducted to determine the influence of the map type on the relationship between the region and the orientation strategy. With the askew and grid-like structure city maps, participants from Beijing used the orientation strategy more than those from Shanghai and the regional differences in using the orientation terms in these two map types were the same (10.85 ± 4.39 vs 6.37 ± 2.80, $F(1,77) = 29.11$, $p < .001$; 10.68 ± 4.23 vs 6.53 ± 3.02, $F(1,77) = 25.13$, $p < .001$). However, the regional differences in the askew structure community map decreased (8.64 ± 5.41 vs 6.49 ± 2.40, $F(1,77) = 5.15$, $p < .05$), indicating a decrease in the orientation terms in this map, compared to the other two maps.

With respect to the route strategy as the dependent variable, the main effect of the region was significant ($F(1,77) = 4.77$, $p < .05$, $\eta^2 = 0.058$); this effect was marginally moderated by the map type ($F(2,76) = 2.82$, $.05 < p < .08$, $\eta^2 = 0.069$). The post-hoc test of the main effect indicated that participants from Beijing used the route strategy lesser than those from Shanghai, but it was moderated by the map type. A simple effect test was conducted to determine the influence of the map type on the relationship between the region and the route strategy. With the askew structure city map, participants from Beijing used the route strategy lesser than those from Shanghai (10.06 ± 2.46 vs 12.13 ± 3.75, $F(1,77) = 8.49$, $p < .05$). However, in the grid-like structure city and askew structure community maps, the regional differences in using the route terms in these two map-types were not significant (11.39 ± 2.16 vs 12.43 ± 3.25, $F(1,77) = 2.85$, $p > .05$; 7.52 ± 3.66 vs 7.77 ± 2.61, $F(1,77) = 0.12$, $p > .05$).

The differences between the orientation and route strategies within the combinations of the region and map types were further tested. The difference was significantly moderated by the region ($F(1,77) = 24.89$, $p < .001$, $\eta^2 = 0.244$) and map type ($F(2,76) = 12.25$, $p < 0.001$, $\eta^2 = 0.220$). The difference was not significant for participants from Beijing (10.06 ± 0.52 vs 9.65 ± 0.36, $F(1,77) = 0.37$, $p > .05$); it statistically existed for participants from Shanghai (6.46 ± 0.52 vs 10.77 ± 0.37, $F(1,77) = 41.11$, $p < .001$) and the route strategy were more likely to be used (see Fig. 2). The wayfinding strategy differences were significant with the askew structure (8.61 ± 0.42 vs 11.09 ± 0.36, $F(1,77) = 15.86$, $p < .001$) and grid-like structure city maps (8.60 ± 0.41 vs 11.91 ± 0.31, $F(1,77) = 36.07$, $p < .001$); the participants in these two maps were more likely to use the route strategy (see Fig. 3). However, this was not significant with the askew structure community map (7.56 ± 0.47 vs 7.64 ± 0.36, $F(1,77) = 0.01$, $p > .05$). The wayfinding strategy differences were moderated by the interaction between the region and map-type (see Fig. 4, $F(2,76) = 4.24$, $p < 0.05$, $\eta^2 = 0.100$). The test of the simple interaction effects indicated the interaction effect of region and wayfinding strategies was significant with the grid-like structure city maps ($F(1, 77) = 22.28$, $p < 0.001$, $\eta^2 = 0.224$) and the askew structure city map ($F(1, 77) = 27.63$, $p < 0.001$, $\eta^2 = 0.264$), but not significant with the askew structure community map ($F(1, 77) = 3.30$, $p > 0.05$, $\eta^2 = 0.041$). In order to get specific results, the simple effect test was conducted and showed that the statistically significant differences in the wayfinding strategy were found only for participants from Shanghai with both the askew structure city ($F(1,77) = 42.15$, $p < .001$) and grid-like structure city maps ($F(1,77) = 56.80$, $p < .001$); these participants were more likely to use the route strategy (6.37 ± 2.80 vs. 12.13 ± 3.75; 6.53 ± 3.01 vs. 12.43 ± 3.25).

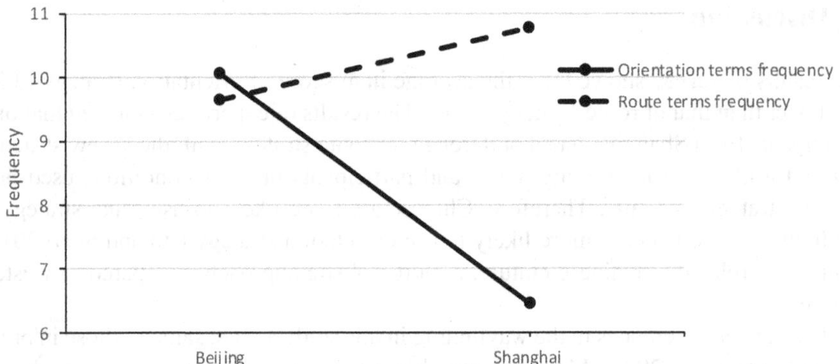

Fig. 2. The difference of wayfinding strategies in Beijing and Shanghai

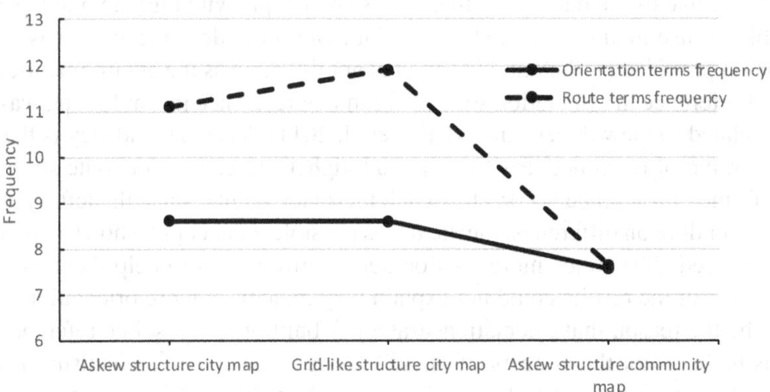

Fig. 3. The difference of wayfinding strategies in each map type

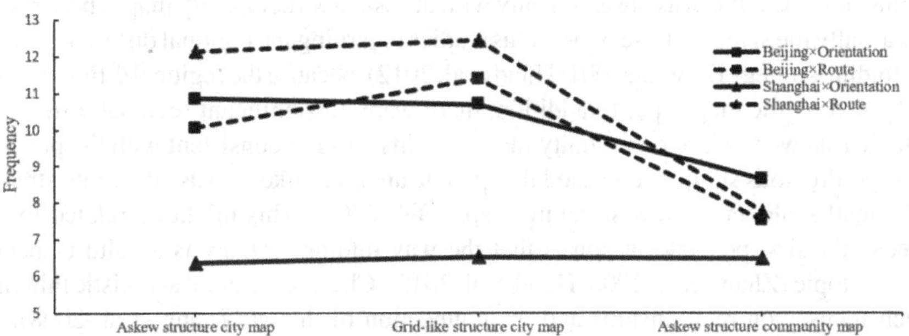

Fig. 4. The difference of wayfinding strategies within combinations of the region and map types

4 Discussion

The results of survey showed that the average item score of orientation strategy (3.23) was lower than that of route strategy (4.44). The results of experiment showed that only participants from Shanghai had a preference for route strategy with the askew structure city and grid-like structure city maps, and participants in other conditions used both the two strategies equally. Therefore, Chinese are more likely to use route strategy in wayfinding. American are more likely to use orientation strategy (Ito and Sano 2011). It might be related to Chinese culture, a more holistic approach, compared to western culture.

The gender differences in the wayfinding in this study are the same as those in previous studies (Lawton 2001). Males are more likely to use the orientation strategy, whereas female are more likely to use the route strategy. Field dependency mediated the effect of gender on the route strategy but not on the orientation strategy. It indicates female used more route strategy because of their high field dependency. It is not consisted with the speculations of Li and Zhang (2007). They speculated people with high field dependency would like to use mainly cardinal terms and people with high field independency would like to use mainly left-right terms. Although field dependency is based on the information provided by the outer world, it is not the same as the environment-centered frames of reference in orientation strategy. Frame of reference in wayfinding was somehow correlated to view dependency (Haun et al. 2011). View dependency is the ability to rotate frame of reference. People who had higher preference for route strategy and relative frame of reference needed to switch their viewpoints, since the left-right would change depending on different subjects. It was possible that people who were more view dependent needed to notice more environmental information to help them rotate their viewpoints. But the results could not explain why male used more orientation strategy. It might be the reason that orientation strategy is built on the absolute reference frame and thus there is not the concept of "field". In the future, the mechanism of the two wayfinding strategies needs to be further explored and studied in order to provide the theoretical foundation for the personalized design of voice navigation.

Participants from Beijing were more likely to use the orientation strategy than those from Shanghai; this difference decreased with the askew structure community map. Participants from Shanghai were more likely to use the route strategy than those from Beijing; however, this was observed only with the askew structure city map. These results are partially the same as those of previous studies regarding the regional differences in the wayfinding strategy (Lawton 2001; Hund et al. 2012), because the regional difference was moderated by the map-type. In addition, there were no significant regional differences with the askew structure community map, and this was not consistent with the previous findings. Previous studies suggested that people are more likely to use the route strategy with small-scale and askew structure maps (Bell 2002). This might be related to two aspects: the first possible reason is that the way-finding strategy is a culture-specific research topic (Zhang et al. 2008; Hund et al. 2012). Chinese are good at holistic thinking, which focuses on relationships and the connection of things (Zhang et al. 2008); the second possible explanation is that the small-scale map in this study is not complicated. Thus, the advantage of the route strategy of people in Shanghai did not work out. All these results imply navigation system should take city structure into account in the future to provide better user experience. In addition, regional difference of orientation wayfinding existed in all three map-types, but regional difference of route wayfinding existed only in the condition of the askew structure community map. It suggests the preference for route wayfinding strategy is more likely to be influenced by map type than orientation wayfinding strategy. The essential reason might be consistent with that of the mediation effects of field dependency only existed in the gender difference of route wayfinding strategy.

There were no differences in the wayfinding strategy for participants from Beijing and this remained stable with different map types. Participants from Shanghai preferred the route strategy to the orientation strategy; however, this was observed only with the grid-like structure city and askew structure city maps. The results suggest that the participants from Beijing used both wayfinding strategies. It might be related two reasons. The first possible reason is that participants from Beijing has better sense of direction. Xu et al. (2010) state that good sense of direction is more likely to use the mixed wayfinding strategy. Lin et al. (2014) also found bike tourists with a better sense of direction promoted successful wayfinding behaviors. The other possible reason is the prevalence of mobile map navigation app. The current map navigation apps use the route strategy to guide users. It leads to the improvement of route strategy as the strategy could be learned. However, Shanghai residents, using relative reference coordinates, they do not have the opportunity to learn the orientation strategy.

5 Conclusion

This paper has investigated the mediation effect of field dependency on the gender influence and the moderating effect of the map type on the regional differences in wayfinding strategy. The results of the two studies show that (1) the mediation effect of field dependency on gender difference of wayfinding strategy occurred only in route strategy: females used more route strategies than males did because females have higher field dependency, but the mediation effect of field dependency on gender difference did not occur in the orientation strategy; (2) participants from Shanghai preferred route strategy to orientation strategy in the grid-like/askew structure city maps; (3) mixed strategy was used in Beijing participants and in askew structure community map; (4) participants from Beijing (a city with grid-like structure) were more likely to use orientation strategy than those from Shanghai (a city with askew structure), and the difference became smaller in askew structure community map; (5) participants from Shanghai were more likely to use route strategy than those in Beijing, but it occurred only in askew structure city map; (6) there is no difference in the wayfinding strategy for participants from Beijing and it remained stable in different map types; (7) participants from shanghai preferred route strategy to orientation strategy and it remained stable only in grid-like structure city map and askew structure community map.

In summary, route wayfinding strategy is the common one most people used, but oriented wayfinding strategy should also be provided for personalized setting (i.e., for males, and for residents from region with grid-like city structure). It indicates that the future navigation system in tourism could continue to mainly use route strategy in direction-giving, but should also provide orientation strategy. Because the mixed strategy is used in many situations, like people from the city with grid-like structure and in the condition of askew structure community map type. In addition, orientation strategy could also train passengers in good sense of direction to help more people (more familiar with route strategy, like female and who lives in the city with askew structure) use mixed strategy and free from of the influence of field, like map type or city structure. Therefore, navigation system developers can present speech or language instructions about wayfinding based on gender, city structures and map scales to im-prove user-experience and user-satisfaction in tourism, as the information about the present study can be used to develop more effective GPS navigation systems, paper-based travel maps, internet-based map/rout-planning services and the local signage system.

References

Abdul Khanan, M., Xia, J.C. Individual differences in the tourist wayfinding decision making process. Int. Arch. Photogrammetry Remote Sens. Spatial Inf. Sci. **28(2)**, 319–324 (2010)

Bell, S.: Spatial cognition and scale: a child's perspective. J. Environ. Psychol. **22**(1), 9–27 (2002)

Boccia, M., Vecchione, F., Piccardi, L., Guariglia, C.: Effect of cognitive style on learning and retrieval of navigational environments. Front. Pharmacol. **8**, 496 (2017)

Chang, H.H.: Which one helps tourists most? perspectives of international tourists using different navigation aids. Tour. Geogr. **17**(3), 350–369 (2015)

Chang, H.H.: Comparison between wayfinding direction descriptors of local and tourist preferences. In: Co-Creation and Well-Being in Tourism, pp. 135–147. Springer, Cham (2017). https://doi.org/10.1007/978-3-319-44108-5_11

Chen, C.H., Chang, W.C., Chang, W.T.: Gender differences in relation to wayfinding strategies, navigational support design, and wayfinding task difficulty. J. Environ. Psychol. **29**(2), 220–226 (2009)

Feng, J.: Spatial cognition and the image space of Beijing's residents. Scientia Geograpgica Sinica **25**(2), 142–154 (2005)

Findlay, C., Southwell, K.: "I just followed my nose": understanding visitor wayfinding and information needs at forest recreation sites. Manag. Leis. **9**(4), 227–240 (2004)

Gu, C.-L., Song, G.-C.: Urban image space and main factors in Beijing. Acta Geogr. Sin. **56**(1), 64–74 (2001)

Haun, D.B., Rapold, C.J., Janzen, G., Levinson, S.C.: Plasticity of human spatial cognition: spatial language and cognition covary across cultures. Cognition **119**(1), 70–80 (2011)

Hund, A.M., Minarik, J.L.: Getting from here to there: spatial anxiety, wayfinding strategies, direction type, and wayfinding efficiency. Spat. Cogn. Comput. **6**(3), 179–201 (2006)

Hund, A.M., Schmettow, M., Noordzij, M.L.: The impact of culture and recipient perspective on direction giving in the service of wayfinding. J. Environ. Psychol. **32**(4), 327–336 (2012)

Ishikawa, T.: Maps in the head and tools in the hand: wayfinding and navigation in a spatially enabled society. In: In: Hunter, R., Anderson, L., Belza, B. (eds.) Community Wayfinding: Pathways to Understanding, pp. 115–136. Springer, Cham (2016). https://doi.org/10.1007/978-3-319-31072-5_7

Ito, K., Sano, Y. Cultural differences in the use of spatial information in wayfinding behavior. In: Proceedings of the 25th International Cartographic Conference (2011)

Kato, Y., Takeuchi, Y.: Individual differences in wayfinding strategies. J. Environ. Psychol. **23**(2), 171–188 (2003)

Lawton, C.A.: Gender differences in way-finding strategies: relationship to spatial ability and spatial anxiety. Sex Roles **30**(11–12), 765–779 (1994)

Lawton, C.A.: Gender, spatial abilities, and wayfinding. In: Handbook of Gender Research in Psychology, pp. 317–341. Springer, New York (2010). https://doi.org/10.1007/978-1-4419-1465-1_16s

Lawton, C.A., Kallai, J.: Gender differences in wayfinding strategies and anxiety about wayfinding: a cross-cultural comparison. Sex Roles **47**(9–10), 389–401 (2002)

Lawton, C.A.: Gender and regional differences in spatial referents used in direction giving. Sex Roles **44**, 321–338 (2001)

Lee, M.Y., Hitchcock, M., Lei, J.W. Mental mapping and heritage visitors' spatial perceptions. J. Heritage Tourism, 1–15 (2017)

Leib, S., Dillman, B., Petrin, D., Young, J.P.: A comparison of the effect of variations to US airport terminal signage on the successful wayfinding of Chinese and American cultural groups. J. Aviation Technol. Eng. **1**(2), 6 (2012)

Levinson, S.C.: Frames of reference and Molyneux's question: Crosslinguistic evidence. Language and space, 109–169 (1996)

Li, J., Zhang, K.: The impact of cognitive style on navigation (In Chinese). Chinese J. Ergon. **13**(1), 46–47 (2007)

Lin, J.-H., Ho, C.-H., Ngan, K.-L., Tu, J.-H., Weerapaiboon, W.: The effects of senses of direction on wayfinding behaviors: evidence from biking Tourists. In: SHS Web of Conferences. EDP Sciences, France (2014)

Liu, L., Zhang, J., Wang, H.: The effect of spatial language habits on people's spatial cognition. Acta Psychol. Sin. **37**(4), 469–475 (2005)

Malinowski, J.C., Gillespie, W.T.: Individual differences in performance on a large-scale, real-world wayfinding task. J. Environ. Psychol. **21**(1), 73–82 (2001)

O'Connor, A., Zerger, A., Itami, B.: Geo-temporal tracking and analysis of tourist movement. Math. Comput. Simul. **69**(1–2), 135–150 (2005)

Prestopnik, J.L., Roskoswoldsen, B.: The relations among wayfinding strategy use, sense of direction, sex, familiarity, and wayfinding ability. J. Environ. Psychol. **20**(2), 177–191 (2000)

Symonds, P., Brown, D.H., Iacono, V.L.: Exploring an absent presence: wayfinding as an embodied sociocultural experience. Sociol. Res. Online **22**(1), 1–20 (2017)

Witkin, H.A., Dyk, R.B., Fattuson, H., Goodenough, D.R., Karp, S.A. Psychological differentiation: Studies of development (1962)

Wu, C.-Z., Wang, J.: The study on tourism destination image of the metropolitan space of Shanghai. Tourism **27**(2), 82–87 (2012)

Xia, J.C., Arrowsmith, C., Jackson, M., Cartwright, W.: The wayfinding process relationships between decision-making and landmark utility. Tour. Manage. **29**(3), 445–457 (2008)

Xia, J., Packer, D. Dong, C. Individual differences and tourist wayfinding behaviours. In: 18th World IMACS/MODSIM Congress. Australia, (2009)

Xie, J., Zhang, H.: Cognitive style: experimental study on a personality dimension. Beijing Normal University Press (1988)

Xu, Q., Luo, Y., Liu, J.: The mechanism of sense of direction and its modulating factors. Adv. Psychol. Sci. **18**(08), 1208 (2010)

Zhang, J., Liu, L., Shi, Y.: The effects of the factors of circumstances and tasks on the choice of reference frame in spatial cognition. Psychol. Explor. **28**(1), 49–54 (2008)

Zhang, X.-H., Su, J.-N., Wei, S.-W.: Image space and its structure of urban residents in Lanzhou City. Hum. Geogr. **25**(4), 54–60 (2010)

Reliability and Validity Assessment of the Chinese Version of Flow Ergonomics

Wen-Ko Chiou[1(✉)], Chao Liu[2(✉)], Hao Chen[2(✉)], and Szu-Erh Hsu[1(✉)]

[1] Department of Industrial Design, Chang Gung University, Taoyuan City, Taiwan
wkchiu@mail.cgu.edu.tw, h410@hotmail.com

[2] Business Analytics Research Center, Chang Gung University, Taoyuan City, Taiwan
174673015@qq.com, victory666666@126.com

Abstract. This study constructs the Chinese version of Flow Ergonomics scale based on Flow Ergonomics theory, and conducts reliability and validity analysis. This study proposes a more generalized theory of Flow Ergonomics based on the integration of mindfulness and flow theory with human factors. In order to evaluate a specific psychological trait and mental state, a Flow Ergonomics scale was developed to test the structural model and serve as the basis for subsequent research. The researchers translated and tested the reliability and validity of the Chinese version of Flow Ergonomics for 100 faculty members. The questionnaire was translated from English to Chinese and then back to English to confirm the consistency of the Chinese and English questionnaires. Flow factor scale consists of seven dimensions with a total of 80 items. In order to ensure its effectiveness, the Chinese version of Flow Ergonomics was used to understand the degree of flow ergonomics of staff. Internal consistency and retest reliability were used to confirm whether the questionnaire could be used effectively in future experiments. The Flow Ergonomics scale was composed of seven dimensions with a total of 80 items, all of which had good reliability and validity. These seven factors are significantly different, and the alpha coefficient shows a high degree of internal consistency for all seven factors. The results of this study confirmed the reliability and validity of Flow Ergonomics scale as an evaluation tool for specific psychological traits and mental states.

Keywords: Flow ergonomics · Mindfulness · Reliability · Validity

1 Introduction

In recent years, the concept of flow proposed by western positive psychologists has also attracted the attention of human factors scholars. Flow provides the spiritual source for people to seek positive psychology and is the ultimate ability of inner happiness. This study first introduces the proposed process and concept definition of flow ergonomics, and summarizes the existing research results abroad, so as to discuss the research direction of flow ergonomics. Secondly, based on grounded theory and qualitative research, the model of flow ergonomics is obtained. The theoretical framework is based on the core categories of flow ergonomics, including oneness transcendence, mindfulness and

P.-L. P. Rau (Ed.): HCII 2022, LNCS 13311, pp. 330–341, 2022.
https://doi.org/10.1007/978-3-031-06038-0_24

flow, positive emotion and meaning, negative emotion, pleasant life, environmental connection and acceptance. In the process of building the model, this study also explains the relationship between the categories. In order to further verify the validity of the model, the flow ergonomics scale was developed in this study, and SPSS22.0 and AMOS22.0 were used to analyze the data. 100 valid questionnaires were collected and tested for reliability and validity. Exploratory and confirmatory factor analyses were carried out to verify the reliability of grounded theory results by structural equation model. The research suggests that the model of flow ergonomics is reasonable.

2 Literature Review

2.1 Human Factors

Human factors is an important engineering and technical discipline. It is a science that studies the interaction and reasonable combination of human, machine and environment, and makes the designed machine and environment system suitable for human's physiological and psychological characteristics, so as to improve efficiency, safety, health and comfort in production. It is called cognitive Human factors that focuses on the study of people's mental cognition to the environment, while it is called entity Human factor that focuses on the study of the physical influence of the environment on people. As a comprehensive science, its research and application range is very wide, so people try to name and define it from various angles. Waterson and Sell (2006) Selected papers published in the Journal of Ergonomics between 1958 and 1999, analyzing trends in article topics. They observed that topics based on human characteristics predominated, and in this group, topics on physiology increased over time, while the frequency of articles on psychology decreased. Topics based on performance-related factors such as age, gender, individual differences, and task-related factors are the next most common category. Articles published on these two topics account for more than 50% of the total. Zavod and Hitt (2000) analysed 511 articles published in the journal of Human Factors between 1988 and 1997. The results showed that subjects related to visual performance (111 articles) dominated, accounting for 22% of the total, followed by industrial human factors and cognitive human factors (10%) and training (9%). Waterson et al. (2012) investigated 987 articles published in 16 IEA conferences and conference, and found that based on ergonomic methods and methods, workload, Topics in physiology and product design declined during this period, while articles on topics such as cognitive ergonomics, human-computer interaction (HCI), organizational design and management, and work and health became mainstream. Over the same period, papers based on topics such as aging, international standards, education and training remained stable. Lee (2010) analyzed 649 articles published in the Korean Journal of Ergonomics between 1982 and 2009. The results showed that between 1982 and 1989, biomechanics, anthropometry and work physiology were the dominant research topics (41%), followed by display and control and work systems and workload analysis (12%). In the 1990s, biomechanics, anthropometry and work physiology, and display control remained the most popular topics, but accident safety became the new hot spot. From 2000 to 2009, biomechanics, anthropometry, and work physiology continued to dominate the publication as the most popular topic category by number of articles, but the second and third topics changed to consumer products and tools, and health and medical systems, respectively. Hwang et al. (1993) showed that man-machine system and industrial safety were the two main research fields of Human factor in Taiwan at that time. Lee and Wang (2000) suggests that academia regard occupational health, the man-machine system and product design as three main areas in the development of Taiwanese for human factor, but now there are few research on the effect of flow ergonomics to human mind, this study from the perspective of flow ergonomics to discuss the development promotion of human mind.

2.2 Maslow's Highest Hierarchy of Needs – Mindfulness, Spirituality, Flow and Happiness

Maslow (1943) first proposed the hierarchy of human needs. A person needs to meet basic physiological needs, including food, warmth and rest, followed by personal safety. Next comes the psychological need for belonging and love. People need intimate relationships and friendship. All humans want warm and harmonious interpersonal relationships. These, along with the need to be respected, are achievements, fame, status, and opportunities for advancement, which represent external approval of one's talents. His early hierarchy consisted of only five layers, with the human need for self-actualization – that is, the fulfillment of life's full potential, including spiritual intelligence and creativity – at the top. Thinking that the needs at the bottom have been satisfied, the person will pay attention to the pursuits at the higher level. Tay and Diener (2011) conducted a cross-cultural research on the relationship between need satisfaction and happiness in 122 countries. They found that the order from the bottom to the top is not an essential condition for happiness. Even if people in economically underdeveloped areas are not fully satisfied with their physiological needs, they can also be happy in the satisfaction of higher needs through interpersonal relationships. Maslow (1969) proposed that the complete expression of the hierarchy of needs model should be divided into six levels, namely physiological needs, safety needs, belongingness and love needs, respect needs, self-actualization needs and transcendental needs. Transcendental needs can also be called spiritual needs or transcendental self-actualization needs. On one hand, he uses the concept of transcendental motivation in the sense of transcending missing motivation, on the other hand, he makes an important supplement to this concept. The "self" in the concept of self-realization is not limited to the individual existence as "ego", but the "enlarged self" that has expanded to include all aspects of the world and has transcended the distinction between self and non-self. Transcendence refers to the highest and most extensive or holistic level of human consciousness. Transcendence functions as an end rather than as a means and has a relationship with one's self, with others of importance, with people in general, with nature, and with the universe. Koltko-Rivera (2006) believed that Maslow expanded the hierarchy of needs from five layers to six layers. Besides physiological, security, belonging and love, respect and self-realization, there were also transcendental needs. Among them, the needs of self-realization and transcendence are all about the transformation of consciousness. Romeu and Albert (2010) believes that people can maximize self-transcendence, such as altruism or spiritual enhancement.

Mindfulness

Mindfulness therapy was founded by Kabat-Zinn, an honorary professor at the University of Massachusetts. Mindfulness is a fully open self-awareness that focuses on the present moment and welcomes every thought in the heart and mind with curiosity and acceptance instead of self-criticism. In other words, it emphasizes facing the present moment and awareness (Kabat-Zinn 1994). Mindfulness practitioners live very clearly in the present moment, but are not involved in it (Bishop et al. 2004). Mindfulness techniques are effective in treating a range of mental health difficulties (Baer 2003) and promoting well-being (Brown and Ryan 2003). As a result, mindfulness is increasingly used as a form of psychological intervention derived from eastern Buddhist meditation practices that utilize concepts related to all things (Baer 2003) and are considered to be related to spirituality (Kornfield 2009). Mindfulness is effective in promoting happiness (Brown and Ryan 2003). Carmody and Baer (2008) found that regular meditation cultivates mindful skills in daily life, thus improving mental functioning and increasing happiness. Similarly, Brown and Ryan (2003) reported that mindfulness was negatively correlated with negative emotions such as anxiety, depression and anger, and positively correlated with happiness.

Flow

Flow is a feeling that one's mental energy is fully invested in a certain activity. When flow is generated, there will be a high degree of excitement and sense of fulfillment. The conceptualization of flow originates from the field of peak experience. In 1968, Maslow began studying peak experiences, the peaks of all experiences that are self-fulfilling. The conclusion is that the peak experiences are available to all (Fritz and Avsec 2007), even though very little is known about these experiences. For example, you don't know what it takes to have peak experience. Maslow's study established that these experiences do exist, may be available to all, and benefit human development. The concept of flow stems from research on the optimal human state (Seligman 2002). Flow is the state of mind in which a person is completely immersed in a current activity, such as reading or running (Csikszentmihaly and Nakmura 2010). Csikszentmuhalyi (1991) describes the conditions required to achieve flow: activities with clear goals, a balance between challenge and skill, and clear and real-time feedback on effectiveness and progress. Flow is described as an intense state in positive psychology, people consider the feeling of enjoyment and the experience of flow to be an optimal state of happiness and have been shown to increase human happiness (Fritz and Avsec 2007). The concept of goals is important for both goal-centered hope and flow. Csikszentmihalyi and Nakmura (2010) described it as a state of high attention to the current task and at the same time self-dynamic. They described the subjective elements of the experience as including enjoyment, reduced self-awareness, and altered sense of time. In his phenomenological analysis of flow, Elkington (2010) defined it as the empirical dynamic nature of flow following the optimal function of consciousness. Elkington (2010) describes the main components needed to experience flow: focus, concentration, clear goals and real-time feedback in the face of an achievable task. It can be controlled because you are fully absorbed in the task, forget about your troubles and achieve a state of oblivion.

Spirituality

Spirituality is spiritual intelligence, or inspiration intelligence, which is the ability of inspiration, insight and intuitive thinking about the nature of things. Yang (2006) believes that spirituality is the ability to connect meaning by seeing the connection between life experience and inner world. Vaughan (2002) believes that spirituality is the ability to create meaning by understanding practical problems, and the ability to solve problems with different levels of consciousness. King et al. (2012) and Sid-Diqui (2013) put forward in their spiritual model that the core of spirituality is "critical existential thinking" and "the ability to deeply understand existential problems", and the core of spirituality is the ability to find meaning in life. King et al. (2012) believes that the core of spirituality is personal meaning production, which refers to the ability to construct personal meaning and purpose in all physical and mental experiences, including the ability to create and master life goals. Emmoms (2000) believes that spirituality is the ability to use spiritual resources to facilitate daily problem solving and goal realization. Spirituality has five characteristics: (a) the ability to transcend the material world; (b) The ability to experience a heightened mental state of consciousness; (c) The ability to connect everyday life experiences; (d) The spiritual capacity to solve problems; (e) The ability to consistently practice high moral behavior. Amram (2007) identifies five core characteristics of spirituality, which include: (a) the ability to develop self-awareness and self-understanding; (b) Love and trust in oneself and others; (c) To derive purpose from all experiences of daily life, including desperate and painful experiences; (d) Transcending the individual self as an interconnected whole; (e) Become open, curious and kind to everything in the world.

Happiness

Happiness is the satisfaction of the mind that lasts for a long time. Happiness is used in psychological or emotional states, including positive or pleasant emotions, ranging from contentment to intense happiness. Broadly defined happiness is a label for a family of happy emotional states such as joy, entertainment, contentment, euphoria and triumph. Happiness is broadly defined as a person's cognitive and emotional assessment of their life (Diener et al. 2002). Happiness appears to be a broad structure that includes emotional responses and cognitive assessments of life satisfaction (Diener et al. 1999). Rather than trying to use a single or composite measure, this is to ensure that all aspects of happiness are captured. There is growing evidence of the importance of happiness (Sheldon and Lyubomirsky 2004). Happiness is a protective factor for the elderly against disability (Ostir et al. 2000). Conversely, low happiness is associated with increased depression (Keyes and Magyar-Moe 2003). A growing number of interventions are aimed at enhancing well-being while reducing symptoms of pain and emotional distress (Diener et al. 2002). The importance of happiness means that we must understand the cognitive and emotional processes and experiences that may sustain and enhance it.

3 Methods

We posted a subject recruitment poster at Chang Gung University and recruited 100 teaching staff subjects from the school. The research assistant explained the content of the consent form and they agreed to participate in the study. Participants will conduct individual questionnaires (100 participants) in the human factors laboratory. The research assistant will explain the content of the consent form at this stage and then begin to answer the questionnaire.

In order to measure the degree of flow ergonomics of practitioners, the flow ergonomics Scale (FES) is proposed in this study. The construction of the scale is based on the flow scale, mindfulness scale and spirituality scale. The questionnaire consists of nine flow questions, 15 mindfulness questions, 26 spirit quotient questions and 25 subjective happiness questions. A scale of 5 point was adopted, with 1 to 5 representing strongly disagree to strongly agree. The final score is FES, and the higher the score is, the better the degree of flow ergonomics is.

The mindfulness scale was used to measure participants' state mindfulness. The State Mindfulness Scale (SMS) developed by Tanay and Bernstein (2013) was adopted. The scale consists of two dimensions: state mindfulness reflecting physical feelings and state mindfulness stating mental events. There are 15 questions about physical mindfulness and 6 questions about mental mindfulness, 21 questions in total. The answer format was Likert five-point scale, with "1" indicating complete disagreement and "5" indicating complete agreement. The sum of the subscales is the sum of the subscales, and the sum of the two subscales is the sum of the total subscales. Previous studies have shown that it has fairly good validity (Botrel and Kubler 2019; Schindler et al. 2019). Cronbach's alpha was 0.95 in this study.

The flow meter is used to measure the flow status of the subject. The flow theory proposed by Csikszentmihalyi (1997) was adopted (Csikszentmihalyi 1997). Liu (2012) proposed a tool for the validation of Flow (The Short Dispositional Flow Scale 2, SDFS-2), which contains 9 dimensions: a total of 9 questions. The format of the answer is likert five-point scale, "1" shows complete disagreement, and "5" indicates complete agreement; The subscale summation score is the subscale score, and the subscale summation is the total scale score. Dfs-2, whose Cronbach's coefficient alpha is between 0.74 and 0.81, is considered as a tool scale for measuring flow.

The psychic table was used to measure the subjects' spirituality. Adopt the Spiritual Attitude and Involvement List (SAIL) developed by Meezenbroek et al. (2012). The scale contains seven dimensions: meaning, trust, acceptance, caring for others, connection with nature, transcendental experience and spiritual activities, with a total of 26 questions. The answer format is Likert six-point scale, "1" means completely inconsistent, "6" means completely consistent; The sum of the subscales is the sum of the subscales, and the sum of the seven subscales is the sum of the total subscales. Previous studies have shown that it has good validity (Thauvoye et al. 2018). Cronbach's alpha was 0.95 in this study.

SWB is composed of two parts, emotional balance and life satisfaction (Diener et al. 2002). Therefore, the positive and negative emotion scale was used to measure the subjects' positive and negative emotional experience, and the life satisfaction scale was used to measure the subjects' life satisfaction (Diener et al. 1999). The positive and negative emotion scale was used to measure the subjects' positive and negative emotional experience. Positive and Negative Affect Scale (PANAS) developed by Watson et al. (1988) was adopted. This scale includes two dimensions: positive emotional experience and negative emotional experience, with 10 questions in each dimension and 20 questions in total. The answer format was Likert five-point scale, with "1" indicating complete disagreement and "5" indicating complete agreement. The sum score of each subscale is the sum score of each subscale, and the sum score of two subscales is the sum score of the total subscale. Previous studies have shown that it has good validity (Chen et al. 2019; Horwood and Anglim 2019) measured Cronbach's alpha of 0.95 in this study. The life satisfaction scale was used to measure the life satisfaction of the subjects. The Satisfaction With Life Scale (SWLS) developed by Diener et al. (1999) was adopted. There are 5 questions in this scale. The answer format is Likert seven-point scale, "1" means completely inconsistent, "7" means completely consistent; The aggregate score is the scale score. Previous studies have shown that it has good validity (Gigantesco et al. 2019; Munoz-rodriguez et al. 2019). Cronbach's alpha measured in this study was 0.95.

4 Results

The flow ergonomics Scale was integrated by the trait Mindfulness Scale (MAAS), flow Scale (SDFS), spirituality Scale (SAIL), Oneness consciousness Scale (PANAS) and life satisfaction Scale (SWLS). This research needs to test and evaluate the reliability and validity of flow ergonomics scale. Exploratory factor analysis (EFA) and confirmatory factor analysis (CFA) were performed on the sample to test the validity of the flow ergonomics scale. The following Pointers were used to determine the goodness of fit of EFA models: root mean square error approximation (RMSEA) less than 0.08, comparison coincidence index (CFI) and non-norming fit index (NNFI) greater than 0.90, chi-square ratio of its degree of freedom (χ^2/ df) less than 3.0. Exploratory factor analysis was used to determine the factor structure of the flow ergonomics scale of flow using the maximum variation rotation method. The kaiser-Meyer-Olkin (KMO) test validated the sampling adequacy of the analysis, and Barlett's spherical test assessed the degree of correlation between variables. Factor extraction was determined by Kaiser criterion (eigenvalue $\geq$ 1). A factor load greater than 0.5 is considered the threshold at which the item makes a sufficient contribution to the factor. Cronbach's alpha coefficient was calculated to determine the internal consistency of the entire scale and each factor, and a value of $\geq$0.70 was considered sufficient. All statistical analyses were performed by SPSS 21.0 and LISREL 8.80, and the statistical significance was $P < 0.05$.

In order to determine the optimal factor structure of the flow ergonomics scale, EFA analysis was performed. The KMO result was 0.746, and the spherical test result was significant, indicating that the flow ergonomics scale is suitable for factor analysis. The eigenvalues of all factors were greater than 1, accounting for 68.3% of the total variance. Among them, the spirituality scale and the Flow scale contain many dimensions, and some dimensions express themes similar to other scales. The results of factor analysis also show the unity between them. According to the results of EFA, the flow ergonomics scale of flow includes seven dimensions: (1) the "transcendence" dimension of the oneness consciousness scale and the "transcendence" dimension of the spirituality scale are merged into the "transcendence and oneness consciousness" dimension; (2) "present", "clear target", "master task", "disappearance of self-consciousness" and "forgetting time" in mindfulness scale and flow scale were combined into "present attention" dimension; (3) The "meaning" of positive emotion and spirituality scale was combined into the "positive emotion and meaning" dimension; (4) The original negative emotion dimension remained unchanged; (5) Life satisfaction and the "pleasure experience dimension" of the cardiac flow scale were combined into the "pleasant life" dimension; (6) The dimensions of "love nature", "care for others" and "believe" were combined into the dimensions of "compassion". (7) The "acceptance" aspect of the spiritual scale becomes the "compassion" aspect of the new scale. A few items not included in any dimension were deleted.

As for the reliability of the flow ergonomics scale, the overall scale showed high internal consistency, which was determined by Cronbach's alpha value ($\alpha = 0.945$). If any item is deleted from the scale, no higher alpha value is found, the CR, AVE and Cronbach alpha values of each subscale are shown in Table 1, and the correlation between each dimension is shown in Table 2. Based on the theoretical basis of literature review and combined with the integration results of all scales of flow ergonomics, we modified the architectural model of the relationship between all dimensions of flow ergonomics scale, and calculated the path coefficient of the model based on the above factor model fitting through CFA examination of samples, as shown in Fig. 1. The model fits well with the data (RMSEA = 0.04; CFI = 0.97; NFI = 0.96; NNFI = 0.99; $\chi^2/df = 0.75$, $p < 0.001$).

Table 1. Structural validity and reliability

	CR	AVE	Alpha
Transcendence and oneness	0.96	0.67	0.97
Present attention	0.93	0.53	0.94
Positive emotion and meaning	0.89	0.55	0.92
Negative emotion	0.94	0.61	0.92
Pleasure life	0.87	0.57	0.92
Compassion	0.83	0.56	0.76
Acceptance	0.83	0.62	0.79

Table 2. Correlation between dimensions and mean and standard deviation

	1	2	3	4	5	6	7
1. Transcendence and oneness	0.82[a]						
2. Present attention	0.38**	0.73[a]					
3. Positive emotion and meaning	0.34**	0.47**	0.74[a]				

(continued)

Table 2. (*continued*)

	1	2	3	4	5	6	7
4. Negative emotion	−0.36*	−0.16	−0.15	0.78[a]			
5. Pleasure life	0.29**	0.40**	0.57**	−0.19	0.75[a]		
6. Compassion	0.45**	0.49**	0.42**	−0.08	0.49**	0.75[a]	
7. Acceptance	0.19	0.22*	0.12	−0.04	0.16	0.12	0.79[a]
Mean	5.50	3.73	3.07	2.05	3.09	3.55	3.89
SD	1.28	0.58	0.78	0.72	0.79	0.74	0.78

**: $p < 0.05$; **: $p < 0.01$

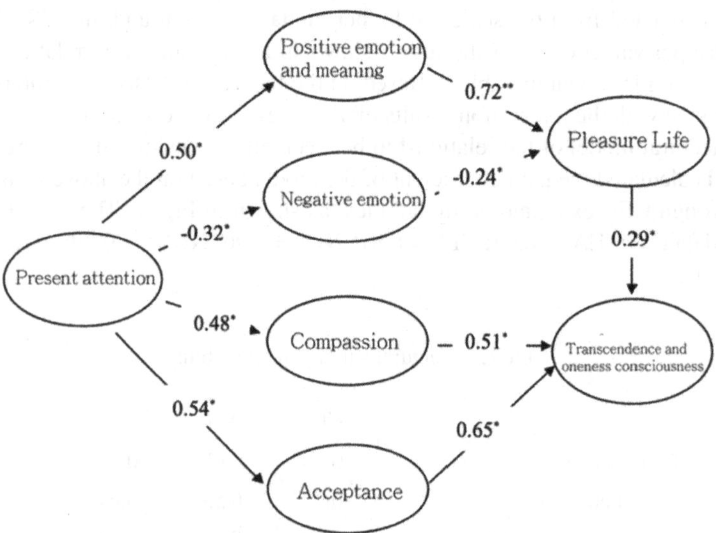

Fig. 1. An architecture model of the relationship between dimensions with path coefficients

5 Research Limitations and Future Studies

One of the main limitations of this paper is that future research would be very effective if it could replicate current research using alternative methods. It must also be pointed out that the correlations between the flow human factors and social expectation scales are not necessarily stronger than those between flow human factors and the other correlational constructs, but they are still quite strong. This can indicate a bias in the general approach that has to be taken into account if these findings are to be interpreted.

Firstly, this paper helps to study individual difference factors at the personality level by developing a reliable and effective measurement tool to identify flow factors. As flow is always an individual difference factor, it has an important impact on individuals' lives and has a significant influence on their life satisfaction. Future research can explore in more depth the interrelationships of the correlational structures discussed in this study. Because flow is a precondition for empathy and connection? What is important is that there is an origin Also, this study relies on self-reported survey data. Future research could combine surveys with field and laboratory experiments to investigate whether individual differences in flow can predict differences in real-life adaptation.

Another starting point for future research is to gain a better understanding of the psychological processes that link flow factors to life satisfaction. Many studies investigate the influence of coping strategies on life satisfaction, especially in religious responses. It would be interesting to examine the ways in which people in the flow have coped with life events, depending on who scores higher. More specifically, a serious life crisis might be seen as an opportunity for spiritual growth. Flow people may have very different coping mechanisms, responsibilities and blame depending on who scores higher. For example, flow can reduce the intensity of dichotomous cognitions needed to blame others. This results in the individual taking more responsibility for their own fate. Given the interrelationship between these coping processes and mindfulness, this is an area of research that has recently attracted a great deal of attention in many academic circles.

6 Conclusions

The purpose of this study was to evaluate the reliability and validity of flow ergonomics scale. Both the overall reliability and the reliability of each subscale show that the alpha value of this study is at a high level. From the validity results, the fit excellence index values of CFA model in this study are all higher than the ideal threshold, and the total variability explanation rate of EFA in this study is high. Flow ergonomics scale was composed of seven dimensions with a total of 80 items, which had good reliability and validity. These seven factors are distinct; In fact, none of the items had more than one factor, and the alpha coefficient showed high internal consistency for all seven factors. On the whole, the results of this study confirmed the reliability and validity of the flow ergonomics scale as an evaluation tool for specific psychological traits and mental states. The flow ergonomics Scale was the first tool to measure mental and spiritual states of transcendence. This study conducted an empirical study on the validity and reliability of flow ergonomics Scale in Taiwan. The measurement results show that the scale has good internal consistency and validity, which is worth further testing and application.

Flow ergonomics can provide new ideas and methods for self-health education and clinical treatment. Traditional cognitive action therapy focuses on helping clients identify "irrational cognitive beliefs" and "repair" their cognitive systems, The concept of flow ergonomics emphasizes that individuals are encouraged to "examine" – actively deconstruct and reconstruct an individual's self-concept system – from a broader perspective of non-judgmental awareness, human factors observer and self-care. The pilot study of this study also preliminatively indicated that flow ergonomics play a significant mediating or moderating role in the relationship between mindfulness, mental health of different personalities and psychological symptoms.

References

Baer, R.A.: Mindfulness training as a clinical intervention: a conceptual and empirical review. Clin. Psychol. Sci. Pract. **10**(2), 125–143 (2003)

Bishop, et al.: Mindfulness: a proposed operational definition. Clin. Psychol. Sci. Pract. **11**(3), 230–241 (2004)

Botrel, L., Kübler, A.: Week-long visuomotor coordination and relaxation trainings do not increase sensorimotor rhythms (SMR) based brain–computer interface performance. Behav. Brain Res. **372**, 111993 (2019)

Brown, K.W., Ryan, R.M.: The benefits of being present: mindfulness and its role in psychological well-being. J. Pers. Soc. Psychol. **84**(4), 822 (2003)

Carmody, J., Baer, R.A.: Relationships between mindfulness practice and levels of mindfulness, medical and psychological symptoms and well-being in a mindfulness-based stress reduction program. J. Behav. Med. **31**(1), 23–33 (2008)

Csikszentmihalyi, M.: Flow and education. NAMTA J. **22**(2), 2–35 (1997)

Csikszentmihalyi, M., Nakamura, J.: Effortless attention in everyday life: a systematic phenomenology. Effortless Atten.: New Perspect. Cogn. Sci. Atten. Action, 179–189 (2010)

Csikszentmihalyi, M.: Design and order in everyday life. Des. Issues **8**(1), 26–34 (1991)

de Jager Meezenbroek, E., et al.: Measuring spirituality as a universal human experience: development of the Spiritual Attitude and Involvement List (SAIL). J. Psychosoc. Oncol. **30**(2), 141–167 (2012)

Diener, E., Lucas, R.E., Oishi, S.: Subjective well-being: the science of happiness and life satisfaction. Handb. Positive Psychol. **2**, 63–73 (2002)

Diener, E., Suh, E.M., Lucas, R.E., Smith, H.L.: Subjective well-being: three decades of progress. Psychol. Bull. **125**(2), 276 (1999)

Emmons, R.A.: Is spirituality an intelligence? Motivation, cognition, and the psychology of ultimate concern. Int. J. Psychol. Relig. **10**(1), 3–26 (2000)

Fritz, B.S., Avsec, A.: The experience of flow and subjective well-being of music students. Horiz. Psychol. **16**(2), 5–17 (2007)

Garcia-Romeu, A.: Self-transcendence as a measurable transpersonal construct. J. Transpers. Psychol. **42**(1), 26 (2010)

Gigantesco, A., et al.: The relationship between satisfaction with life and depression symptoms by gender. Front. Psychiatry **10**, 419 (2019)

Horwood, S., Anglim, J.: Problematic smartphone usage and subjective and psychological well-being. Comput. Hum. Behav. **97**, 44–50 (2019)

Kabat-Zinn, J.: Catalyzing movement towards a more contemplative/sacred-appreciating/non-dualistic society. Paper presented at the Meeting of the Working Group (1994)

Keyes, C.L., Magyar-Moe, J.L.: The measurement and utility of adult subjective well-being (2003)

King, D.B., Mara, C.A., DeCicco, T.L.: Connecting the spiritual and emotional intelligences: confirming an intelligence criterion and assessing the role of empathy. Int. J. Transpers. Stud. **31**(1), 11–20 (2012)

Koltko-Rivera, M.E.: Rediscovering the later version of Maslow's hierarchy of needs: self-transcendence and opportunities for theory, research, and unification. Rev. Gen. Psychol. **10**(4), 302–317 (2006)

Kornfield, J.: A path with heart: a guide through the perils and promises of spiritual life. Bantam (2009)

Maslow, A.H.: Preface to motivation theory. Psychosom. Med. (1943)

Maslow, A.H.: The farther reaches of human nature. J. Transpers. Psychol. **1**(1), 1 (1969)

Muñoz-Rodríguez, J.M., Serrate-González, S., Navarro, A.B.: Generativity and life satisfaction of active older people: advances (keys) in educational perspective. Aust. J. Adult Learn. **59**(1), 94–114 (2019)

Ostir, G.V., Markides, K.S., Black, S.A., Goodwin, J.S.: Emotional well-being predicts subsequent functional independence and survival. J. Am. Geriatr. Soc. **48**(5), 473–478 (2000)

Schindler, S., Pfattheicher, S., Reinhard, M.A.: Potential negative consequences of mindfulness in the moral domain. Eur. J. Soc. Psychol. **49**(5), 1055–1069 (2019)

Seligman, M.E.: Positive psychology, positive prevention, and positive therapy. Handb. Positive Psychol. **2**(2002), 3–12 (2002)

Sheldon, K.M., Lyubomirsky, S.: Achieving sustainable new happiness: prospects, practices, and prescriptions. Positive Psychol. Pract. 127–145 (2004)

Tanay, G., Bernstein, A.: State Mindfulness Scale (SMS): development and initial validation. Psychol. Assess. **25**(4), 1286 (2013)

Tay, L., Diener, E.: Needs and subjective well-being around the world. J. Pers. Soc. Psychol. **101**(2), 354 (2011)

Thauvoye, E., Vanhooren, S., Vandenhoeck, A., Dezutter, J.: Spirituality and well-being in old age: exploring the dimensions of spirituality in relation to late-life functioning. J. Relig. Health **57**(6), 2167–2181 (2018)

Vaughan, F.: What is spiritual intelligence? J. Humanist. Psychol. **42**(2), 16–33 (2002)

Waterson, P., Sell, R.: Recurrent themes and developments in the history of the ergonomics society. Ergonomics **49**(8), 743–799 (2006)

Zavod, M., Hitt, J.M.: Summary of the publishing trends of the Journal of Human Factors from 1988–1997. In: Proceedings of the Human Factors and Ergonomics Society Annual Meeting (2000)

The Integrated Study of Cross-cultural Differences in Visual Merchandising Design and Consumer's Visual Perception on E-Commerce Platform

Tseng-Ping Chiu(✉)

Industrial Design Department, National Cheng Kung University, Tainan 701, Taiwan R.O.C.
mattchiu@gs.ncku.edu.tw

Abstract. E-commerce and merchandise globalization has rapidly developed in recent years. Consequently, the demand for cross-border consumption increases continuously. When a product sells and displays on the online platform, people in different cultural backgrounds might perceive this product differently. In addition, those cultural differences might cause variations of visual perception preference and visual merchandising display on e-commerce websites. Past research has shown the two distinct patterns of visual perception between East and West. East Asians are "context-dependent" by attending to the relationship between the product and contextual information. In contrast, Westerners are described as "context-independent" because they focus on the product itself rather than its context. However, little is known about how cultural differences in consumers' visual perception are related to online merchandise visual design.

In this research, we investigated the consumers' visual perception on E-commerce websites, including Western (e.g., the United States and the United Kingdom) and Eastern countries (e.g., Taiwan and Japan). Study 1 examined the cultural difference of visual merchandising presentation on various cross-border E-commerce websites by using pixel calculation of product in the context. Study 2 investigated various combinations of merchandising visual display, including context-independent and context-dependent visual presentation, to simulate the actual merchandise visual scene on the website. This research contributes to the fields of online merchandise visual presentation and cultural visual perception.

Keywords: Cross-border E-commerce · Cross-cultural differences · Cultural cognition · Visual perception · Online merchandise visual presentation · Consumer behavior

1 Introduction

E-commerce and merchandise globalization has rapidly developed in recent years. Consequently, the demand for cross-border consumption increases continuously [1]. Nowadays, the integrated research of cross-cultural online consumer behavior has been one of the most critical developments in the industrial, governmental, and academic fields.

P.-L. P. Rau (Ed.): HCII 2022, LNCS 13311, pp. 342–356, 2022.
https://doi.org/10.1007/978-3-031-06038-0_25

When a product sells and displays on the online platform, people in different cultural backgrounds might perceive this product differently. As a result, it may cause diverse responses to visual presentation of the product in the marketplace. Does cultural experience influence people's visual perception and shape the way to evaluate the product? And how do these differences result in the behavior of consumption and merchandising visual preference? However, little is known about how cultural differences in people's visual perception relate to online merchandise visual design.

Past research has shown visual perception differs based on cultural background. Westerners tend to be more analytic in their thinking, while East Asians tend to be holistic by attending to the entire field [2, 3]. Consequently, Westerners are described as "Context-independent" because they focus on a focal object rather than its context, whereas East Asians are "Context-dependent" by attending to the relationship between the focal object and its context. In perception tasks, the research has shown East Asians were easily affected by contextual information compared to Westerners [4, 5]. Although the cross-cultural difference in visual perception theory is established in the cross-cultural psychology domain, there is a lack of research to integrate consumer behavior and cognition science research fields into the marketing strategic design domain. In this research, we tend to investigate the consumers' visual perception between Western (e.g., the United States, United Kingdom, and France) and Eastern countries (e.g., Taiwan, Japan, and China) by analyzing the difference of visual merchandising presentation on the online platform of cross-border e-commerce. We examine various combinations of merchandising visual display, including context-independent and context-dependent visual presentation, to simulate the actual merchandise visual scene on the website.

There are two studies of this research. Study 1 investigates the cultural difference in visual merchandising display on E-commerce websites, including Western and Eastern, the most popular Business to Consumer (B2C) websites. Study 2 introduces cognition theory and practice to develop the cross-cultural merchandising visual presentation and consumers' physiological responses. To understand the consumers' visual perception preference, we applied the quantitative methods, including semantic differential technique and aesthetic preference to understand Western (e.g., Americans) and East Asian (e.g., Taiwanese) consumers' visual preferences and how to respond to the visual scenes on different e-commerce platforms between East and West. This research applies both qualitative and quantitative methods to analyze consumers' visual perception and cognition cross-culturally. We expect to organize and establish precise online merchandise visual presentation and marketing strategy design in the future.

2 Literature Review

2.1 Cultural Difference in Cognitive Styles: Analytical vs. Holistic Perception

Prior work in cultural psychology has shown that cultures vary in the extent of attention paid to contextual information [2, 3, 6, 7]. Visual perception has been shown to differ based on cultural background (Nisbett 2003). Westerners tend to be more analytic in their thinking, while East Asians tend to be holistic, attending to the entire field [2, 3]. In perceptual tasks, Westerners are described as "context-independent" because they focus on a salient object rather than its context, whereas East Asians attend to the relationship between an object and its context [4, 5]. Americans prefer context-exclusive images more than Japanese, consistent with analytic vs. holistic patterns of attention [3, 4, 7]. As compared to people engaged in European American cultures (European Americans in short), those engaged in East Asian cultures (East Asians in short) are described as more holistic in cognitive style and thus context-dependent. This finding of cultural cognition has been extended in various ways in subsequent studies, such as the aesthetic appeal of portraits with variations in the size of the model and background [8], the amount of information on the website homepage [9], and artistic expressions of visual artwork [10, 11]. Based on the evidence of cultural variation in attentional pattern, we may expect that the context effect on the aesthetic judgment would be pronounced for East Asians than for European Americans. To test these possibilities, we recruited three cultural groups—European Americans, Asian Americans, and Taiwanese—to investigate the cultural variation in the attentional pattern of visual scenes and its aesthetic judgment.

2.2 Cultural Difference in Visual Merchandising Display

Our additional goal is to explore the potential cultural difference in the effect of matched vs. mismatched context on the aesthetic judgment of a focal object. Cultural products can be conceptualized as a tangible public representation of culture [11, 12]. The visual representations such as drawing, photography, advertisement, media, and web design are some of the dominant cultural products people maintain and consume in everyday life [10]. While the visual representation of marketplace is composed of a focal object and its contextual information (e.g., a design chair is placed in a cozy studio in a product catalog), people in different cultural backgrounds might perceive an object differently. Consequently, they may respond differently to representations of the object in diverse marketplaces. For example, when a product is sold through the Amazon platform, the identical product is displayed differently depending on countries. On the American site, the displays tend to focus on product features and exclude any contextual information; in contrast, the Japanese Amazon site draws attention to the use of the product in the context as opposed to the American site (see Fig. 1). Do these apparent differences of object

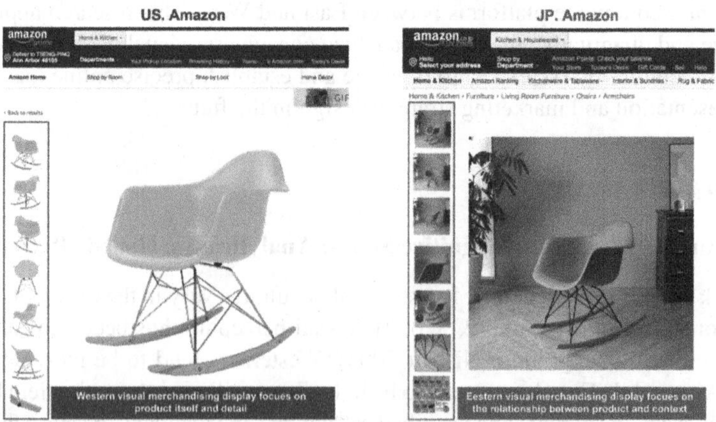

Fig. 1. An example of a best-selling product (armrest chair) is shown on company websites in two countries (left is the American Amazon, right is the Japanese Amazon).

representation within contextual information originate from cultural differences? And how do these differences reflect its aesthetic judgments? In this study, we further explore the differences in people's aesthetic judgments on the visual representation composed of the focal object and contextual information cross-culturally.

3 Study 1

In study 1, we would like to investigate the visual merchandising display on cross-cultural E-commerce websites, including the most popular Western and Eastern platforms, to understand the current merchandising presentations between East and West. This research focuses on Business to Consumer E-commerce websites such as Amazon in the United States, Argos in United Kingdoms, Rakuten in Japan, and Momo in Taiwan. The purpose of study 1 is to examine the relationship between the visual presentation of merchandising (e.g., the product) and cultural cognition of analytical (e.g., a product with less contextual information) or holistic (e.g., a product with much contextual information) styles. Based on the previous research on cultural visual perception, we expect the Western visual merchandising display to focus on the product itself, whereas the Eastern visual merchandising display pays more attention to the product and the relevant context.

3.1 Method

Materials

E-commerce Selection

In this research, we focus on B2C E-commerce based on the United Nations Conference on Trade and Development (UNCTAD, 2020). B2C is a substantial increase in retail sales around the world. The standard of cross-cultural E-commerce was based on the originality of its country, and it is the most popular in the country. We selected the cultural representative E-commerce platforms such as Amazon for the United States; Agros for the United Kingdom; Rakuten for Japan; and Momo for Taiwan. Those E-commerce websites are the most successful Business-to-Consumer website cross-culturally.

Product Selection

A collection of home products, including furniture (e.g., chairs), kitchen products (e.g., kettles, air flyers), lighting (e.g., floor lamps, desk lamps), home appliances (e.g., air-purifier, vacuums), and consumer electronic product (e.g., mouses, keyboards,) was used in the study. The first product selection criterion is the product could fit into the revenant contextual information (e.g., the kettle could be placed on the dining table). The second product selection criterion is that all the products were best-seller or high customer reviews on each E-commerce platform (e.g., the best-seller air flyer on Amazon and Rakuten). We avoided the strong brand image and identity for the product selection to make the product as neutral as possible. Each product was shown in perspective containing its outline, shape, color, material, and detail. There were six product categories, including 240 product stimuli in total. Each product category includes 40 product stimuli: dining chair, floor lamp, kettle, air flyer, dinner plate set, and air purifier, respectively.

In addition, those 40 product stimuli were the top 10 sellers on each of four cultural E-commerce websites, which means 10 product stimuli from Amazon in the U.S., 10 from Agros in the U.K., 10 from Rakuten in Japan, and the rest from Momo in Taiwan (See Fig. 2). There were 240 product stimuli as the final experimental stimuli for Study 1 pixel calculation.

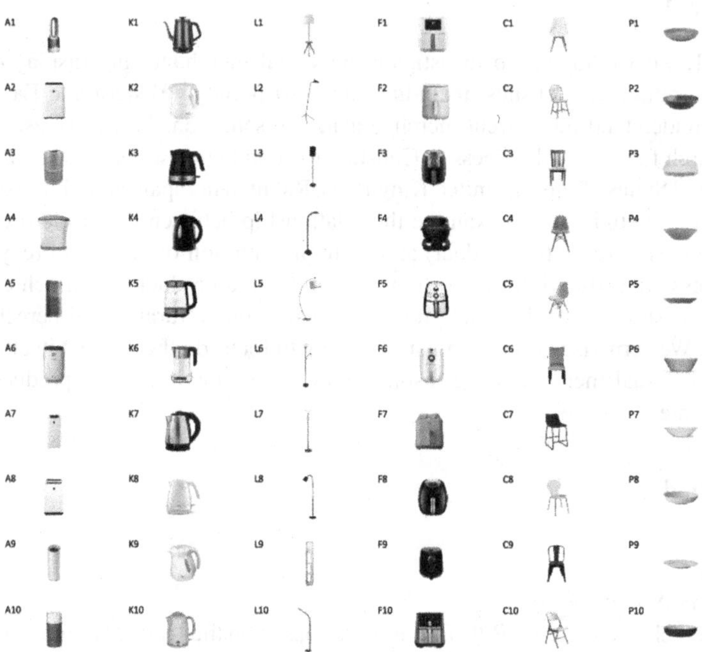

Fig. 2. Study 1 product stimuli overview

Procedure

We collected 240 visual stimuli from the screenshot of the E-commerce websites, including the product and context information. There were 60 visual stimuli from each cultural E-commerce website, respectively. The goal of Study 1 is to investigate the proportion of product and context visual presentation cross-culturally by pixels calculation in the 2D software.

Step 1: Visual stimuli collection and standardization

240 visual stimuli were collected from previous product stimuli selection by screenshot the whole frame of the website on the 27 inches monitor screen. We set the canvas as one grid point equals one pixel on Adobe Photoshop. The purpose is to standardize each visual stimulus in different cultures and countries.

Step 2: Product visual pixels calculation

Each visual stimulus was inserted into Adobe Photoshop CC graphic program to view the total pixel of visual stimulus. Firstly, we drew the product profile according to the edge of the product. Secondly, the product visual pixel calculation proceeded via its silhouette of the product.

Step 3: Context visual pixels calculation
The next step is to set up the visual context frame by applying the originality of the product visual stimuli wireframe. It was the rectangle wireframe encompassing the complete product profile and silhouette. Then, we calculate the pixels of the context visual presentation.

Step 4: The ratio of product and context visual presentation
In the last step, we calculated the ratio of each visual stimuli, which divided the pixels of the product by the pixels of context. The ratio represents the proportion of product in the contextual information. The higher ratio means the visual stimuli take more percentage of product visual presentation. In contrast, the lower ratio indicates the visual stimuli showing more contextual information as opposed to the product (Fig. 3).

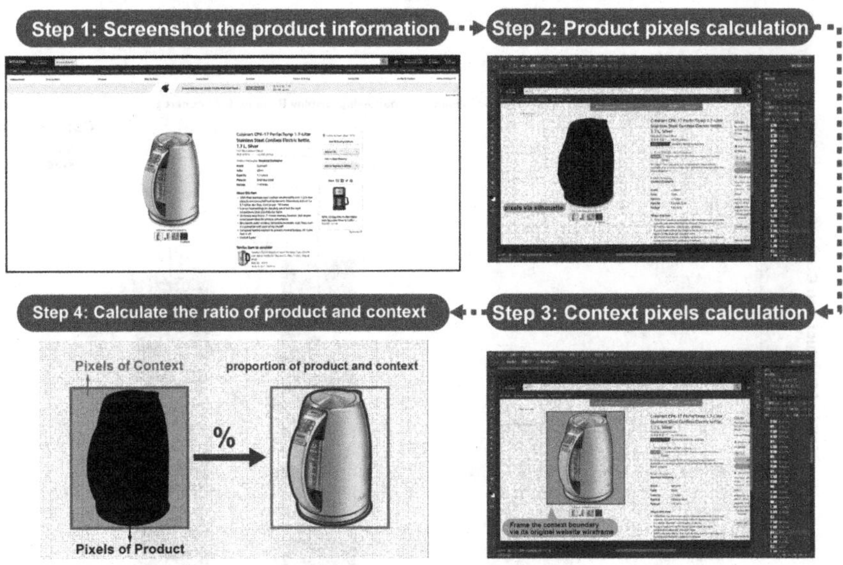

Fig. 3. Each experimental procedure of Study 1

3.2 Results

One-way (Country, between-subject) ANOVA was conducted to compare the ratio of product and context for 4 different cultural E-commerce websites on the visual presentation. An analysis of variance showed that the ratio of product visual presentation on the contextual information layout was significant, F (3, 236) = 29.593. p < .001. Post hoc comparisons using the Tukey HSD test indicated that the mean score of products on context visual presentation for the Taiwanese E-commerce ($M = 21.2\%$, $SD = 0.17$)

and Japanese E-commerce ($M = 28.4\%$, $SD = 0.19$) were significantly lower than the United State E-commerce ($M = 54.5\%$, $SD = 0.30$) and the United Kingdom ($M = 52.1\%$, $SD = 0.39$). As expected, there were no significant differences between Eastern countries (e.g., Taiwan vs. Japan) and Western countries (e.g., the United States vs. the United Kingdoms). Table 1 showed the proportion of product on context visual merchandising display for each country. Figure 4 represents the cultural difference in Eastern and Western visual merchandising display on E-commerce websites.

Table 1. The ratio of product and context visual presentation between East and West

	Eastern e-commerce				Western e-commerce			
	Taiwan		Japan		United States		United Kingdom	
	M	*SD*	*M*	*SD*	*M*	*SD*	*M*	*SD*
The ratio of product and context	21.2%	0.17	28.4%	0.19	54.5%	0.30	52.1%	0.39

Note: N = 240 in total. 60 visual stimuli for every 4 countries equally

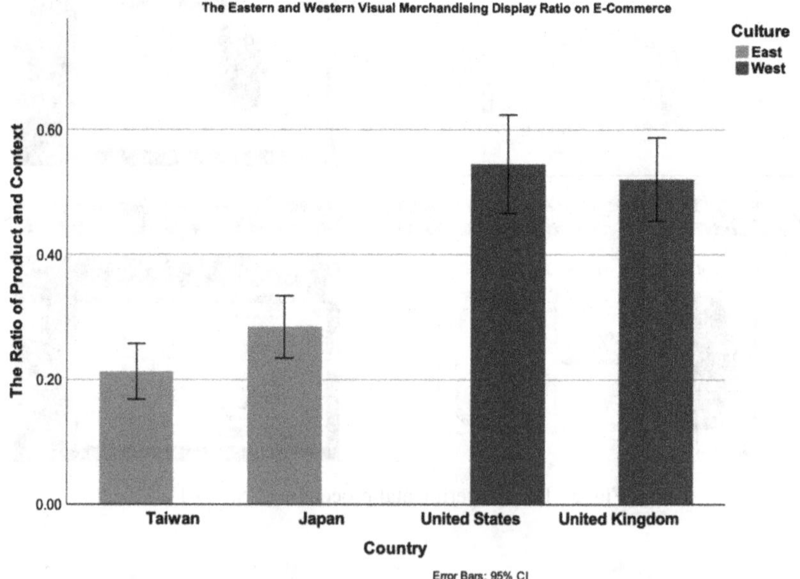

Fig. 4. The cultural difference in product on context visual presentation

3.3 Discussion

The results of Study 1 indicated the product visual presentation plays a vital role by a focus on the product itself and detail on Western visual merchandising display. In contrast, the proportion of product on contextual visual presentation on Eastern websites was significantly less than Western countries. It showed a high possibility that instead of focusing on the product itself, Eastern visual merchandising display draws more attention to product and context together. Therefore, the scale of the product in the context was relatively smaller because contextual information matters. Past research on the cultural difference in visual perception showed Easterners pay more attention in the holistic way, which validated our finding that product visual presentation might fit in the context to compromise the relationship between product and context.

4 Study 2

The purpose of Study 2 is to investigate the possibilities of product visual presentation by the contextual variations. In addition, we examined the Eastern and Western consumer aesthetic preferences whether on product or product on contextual information. In study 2, we presented design products with no context background, in a matched context, or in a mismatched context, and examined whether the attractiveness of the target object would be affected by the context. Subjects were asked to rate the beauty of each product (target attractiveness) and the beauty of the whole visual scene (holistic attractiveness). We tested European American and Taiwanese participants. We anticipated that object attractiveness would be higher in the matched context than in the no-context control and, further, that it would be lower in the mismatched context than in the no-context control). Further, we examined whether these context effects would be more pronounced for Taiwanese than for Americans.

4.1 Method

Participants

We recruited 158 European Americans at a business school in the large midwestern university in the United States ($M_{age} = 19.2$, 45.6% male, 54.4% female) and 57 Taiwanese at the large southern university in Taiwan ($M_{age} = 20.72$, 47.4% male, 52.6% female). Whereas European Americans received course credit, Taiwanese received the equivalent of $USD 5.

Materials

A collection of home products, including furniture (e.g., coffee tables, chairs), kitchen products (e.g., dining table, cabinets), and lighting (e.g., floor lamps, desk lamps), was used in the study. All the products were designed as target objects that fit specific functions and were not portable in use (e.g., an armchair set in a living room). We avoided electronic products such as T.V.s or computers. Each object was shown in perspective containing its outline, shape, color, material, and detail (see Fig. 5). Three distinct variations of each object image were created: set in a matched context, in a mismatched context, and with no context. See Fig. 5 for an example (the desk chair in three versions). In total, three sets of 81 trails were produced, including 27 target objects. Each of the three sets included three contexts. Participants were randomly presented to one of the sets.

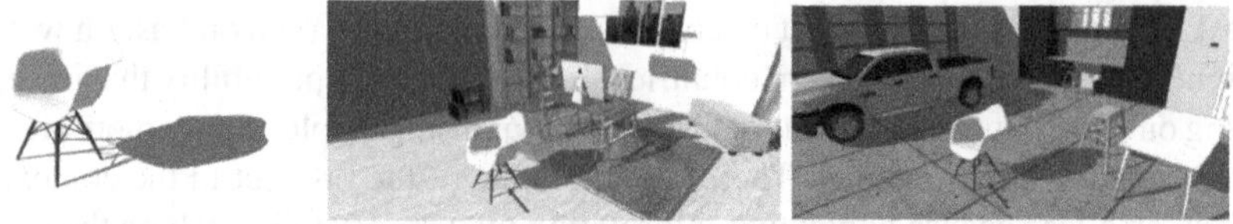

Fig. 5. The target object is presented in three different contexts (left is product without context; medium is context matched to target product; right is context mismatched to target product)

Procedure

Upon arrival in the lab, participants were informed that they would be shown a series of objects one at a time and asked to focus on the target object only. The object was marked by a red arrow (see Fig. 5). Participants were first asked two questions about object attractiveness: "*Do you think the product is beautiful?*" and "*Do you like the product itself?*" The third question was a measure used to check the effectiveness of the context manipulation, "*How well do you think the product fits into this context?*" They were then given two additional questions on the attractiveness of the entire scene: "*Do you like the product in this context?*" and "*Overall, do you like the whole picture?*" Participants responded using a 7-point scale). At the end of the study, participants completed a demographic questionnaire, reporting age, education, occupation, race, parents' race, citizenship, duration of living in the U.S., location of birth, and English language ability.

4.2 Results

Manipulation Check

There was a highly significant main effect of Context on the perceived fit of the context, F (2, 426) = 251.646, $p < .001$. Overall, the manipulation was successful. The fit was rated to be much better in the matched context condition than in the mismatched context condition, with the mean in the no-context control condition falling in-between. However, the interaction between Culture and Context was also significant, F (2, 426) = 42.04, $p < .001$. There was no culture effect either in the matched context or in the control condition. However, in the mismatched context condition, the fit was perceived to be much lower by Americans than by Taiwanese (M = 2.11, SD = 0.81) than for Taiwanese (M = 3.19, SD = 1.01). The simple interaction between Culture and the Mismatch vs. No context contrast was highly significant, F (1, 213) = 57.67, $p < .001$.

Object Attractiveness

We collapsed the first ("*Do you think the product is beautiful?*") and second ("*Do you like the product itself?*") dependent variables (r = .981, n = 215, $p < .001$) to yield our measurement of object attractiveness. A 2 (Culture, between-subject) × 3 (Context, within-subject) Mixed ANOVA performed on the perceived attractiveness index showed a main effect of condition F (2, 426) = 41.88, $p < .001$ (e.g., Table 2), no main effect of culture F (1, 213) = 3.26, p = .072, ns. There was no interaction between culture and condition, F (2, 426) = 2.18, ns. As expected, focal objects were rated significantly more attractive in the Matched Context condition than in the No Context condition, t(428) = 2.32, $p < .05$. Further, as also expected, the objects were rated significantly less attractive in the Mismatched Context condition than in the No Context condition, $t(428) = 3.88, p < .001$.

Table 2. Means and standard deviations for object attractiveness in Study 2 (n = 215)

	No context		Matched context		Mismatched context	
	M	*SD*	*M*	*SD*	*M*	*SD*
Object attractiveness	4.24	1.05	4.47	0.94	3.86	1.04

Note: N = 215 in total. 158 European Americans and 57 East Asians

Holistic Attractiveness

Further, in order to investigate the holistic attractiveness of the whole visual scenes, we collapsed the fourth ("*Do you like the product in this context?*") and fifth ("*Overall, do you like the whole picture?*") dependent variables as our measurement of holistic attractiveness. It also showed a main effect of condition $F\ (2, 426) = 225{,}72, p < .001$. The mean was significantly higher in the Matched Context condition ($M = 4.62$, $SD = 0.89$) than in the No Context condition ($M = 4.25$, $SD = 1.18$), $F\ (1, 213) = 21.36, p < .001$, whereas the mean was lower in the Mismatched Context condition ($M = 2.71$, $SD = 0.91$) than in the No Context condition ($M = 4.25$, $SD = 1.18$), $F(1, 213) = 196.14$, $p < .001$. There is no main effect of culture $F\ (1, 213) = .774, p = .38$, ns. Remember, however, that our manipulation check showed that in the Mismatched context condition, Taiwanese did not perceive as much misfit as Americans did. Thus, if the attractiveness of the whole scene was due to the perceived misfit of the object in the context, the lowering of the attractiveness in the Mismatched (vs. Control) condition should be more pronounced for Americans than for Taiwanese. The interaction between Condition and Culture was significant, $F\ (2, 426) = 23.54, p < .001$. In both the Matched context condition and the

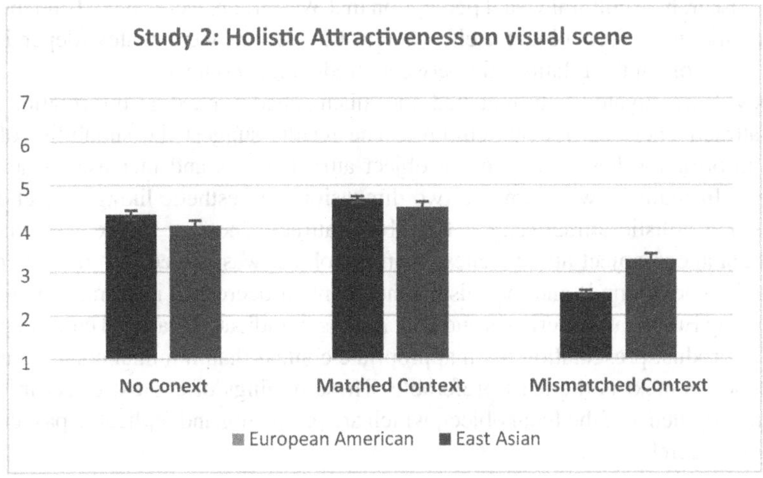

Fig. 6. The holistic attractiveness of visual scenes in Study 2

Control condition, there was no cultural difference in the holistic attractiveness rating, but this rating was significantly less for Taiwanese than for Americans in the Mismatched context condition (as Fig. 6).

4.3 Discussion

In Study 2, we tested whether the attractiveness of design objects could be enhanced when they are placed in matched (vs. mismatched) contexts. Moreover, we explored whether Asians might show this effect more strongly than Americans. We first found that the predicted context effect does exist. Design objects were rated to be more attractive when placed in compatible contexts than in a white background and, conversely, to be less attractive when placed in incompatible contexts than in a white background. Interestingly, Taiwanese reported a relatively attenuated extent of misfit for objects placed in mismatched contexts (e.g., living room sofa in a garage). We suspect that this is because historically functional separation of housing space is less common in Asia, including Taiwan than in the Western world, including the United States. Once this cultural difference is statistically adjusted, there was no evidence that the context effect above varies in magnitude between the two cultures.

5 Conclusion and General Discussion

Two studies demonstrated the cultural difference in visual merchandising display on the E-commerce website. Study 1 showed the significant cultural differences in product visual presentation between East and West, which the product visual display focus on the product itself on Western E-commerce website presentation. Consequently, the proportion of products in the context is relatively larger than in East Asian countries. In contrast, the ratio of product on the context visual presentation on East Asian E-commerce website is much smaller than in Western countries because the whole visual presentation includes both product and contextual information simultaneously. This research finding validates the past research on cultural visual perception that Westerners were context-independent by attending on the focal object itself, whereas East Asians were context-dependent by paying attention on the relationship between product and context.

Study 2 investigated both matched and mismatched contextual information affect object attractiveness across two cultures. The results suggest the suitability of contextual information has an impact on object attractiveness and increase its aesthetic judgment. In Study 2, we examined two dimensions of aesthetic liking: object attractiveness and holistic attractiveness. For object attractiveness, it showed the matched context enhanced object attractiveness than the object was placed in minimal context (e.g., white background) and the mismatched context decreased its attractiveness vice versa among European Americans and East Asians. It indicated that both cultural groups all prefer product presentation in an appropriate context than minimal context, and the mismatched context is the least preferable. These findings of context effect influence aesthetic judgments of the focal object, which are promising and replicated past cultural cognition research.

Furthermore, we tested the holistic attractiveness in Study 2, which intended to investigate the aesthetic judgment of the whole visual scene compared to the object attractiveness. Based on previous evidence of cultural variations in attention [2, 4, 7], East Asians applied the holistic thinking to pay attention on the context more. We predicted the aesthetic judgment of the whole visual scene among East Asians would be more affected by contextual information than European Americans. However, the results of holistic attractiveness showed that context effect, particularly in mismatched settings, was stronger to influence aesthetic liking among European Americans than among East Asians. It indicates that those with holistic attention to East Asians were more tolerant of mismatched information in aesthetic judgments than European Americans.

Overall, this present study identified that visual merchandising display and visual representation on E-commerce could be influenced by the suitability of contextual information cross-culturally. The context moderates the cultural variations in the aesthetic judgment of the design object. Study 1 demonstrated that the Western visual merchandising display draws more attention to the product itself by enlarging its visual presentation than the contextual information. In contrast, East Asian visual merchandising displays encompass the contextual information and set the context as the priority in the visual layout. Therefore, the proportion of product visual presentation is relatively smaller than Western did. Study 2 indicated both European Americans and East Asians preferred the matched context enhancing the object attractiveness, whereas the mismatched context has an adverse effect of decreasing the aesthetic judgment of the object. However, the cultural differences moderate the aesthetic judgment of the mismatched context-setting particularly. Presumably, the mismatched contexts pretended to confuse people. For example, the unusual image of a dining chair set in a bathroom was viewed as "out of order" or unfamiliar to participants. Surprisingly, East Asians showed higher perceptual tolerance for products shown in inappropriate contexts as compared to European Americans. In other words, those with holistic attention to East Asians accepted mismatching visual presentations and indicated greater aesthetic liking even they were acknowledged to a mismatched setting. In contrast, European Americans are sensitive to the logical role of contextual suitability—to draw a line and define what contextual information matches or mismatches to the product itself. This logical role in discriminating the contextual information particularly influences the aesthetic appreciation among European Americans compared to East Asians. We admit that our attempts outlined in these studies focused on some specific product presentations and visual scenes. However, we assert that current findings are generalizable and identify several important implications for the research field of cultural visual perception and marketing application. The implications and limitations are discussed below.

5.1 Implications

Appreciation of Cultural Products

The first implication of this present study is to understand the cultural product, such as the visual scenes in our daily lives. Previous research investigated cultural products created by people who maintain and consume cultural meaning systems in a given cultural setting [12]. People internalize the cultural meaning systems such as values, beliefs, and ideas. Furthermore, they transmitted and produced cultural products, including a variety of public, shared, and tangible representations. Therefore, cultural products are regarded as one of the visual representations such as artwork, advertising, media, and design [10, 11]. The aesthetic appreciation for these kinds of cultural products, such as the product-to-context representation on the website, was not fully addressed. In addition, cultural sensitivity of product-to-context representation may be another evidence of cultural products in current use, which is designed within a single dominant culture. For example, Amazon's U.S. site lists products individually with minimal context, while the Japanese's Amazon site shows products with relevant scenarios or contexts. This present study appears to be the first to establish the aesthetic preference of cultural differences in product representation with contextual information. Our results demonstrated that the aesthetic judgment of products and appreciation of the whole visual scenes are affected by cultural influences. It is important to examine the underlying psychological mechanisms to explain how these cultural variations in aesthetic appreciation arise. Cultural patterns may reveal how aesthetic sense develops as people deal with the demands of surroundings, attention, logical role, and aesthetic gratification and may account for the strong association between an object and the context.

Cultural Variations in Marketing Applications

Secondly, this present study showed that as compared to European Americans, Taiwanese perceive a less misfit between design household objects (e.g., chair) and their context (living room vs. garage). There are some important practical implications for the fields of marketing and design teams since the globalization of E-commerce extends the sale of products to different cultural areas. This study provides guidelines for designers and marketers to consider how to accommodate product representation within the appropriate contextual information for advertisements on the website. While all cultural groups preferred products presented in matched contexts, East Asians were more tolerant of a mismatched setting. For example, Western shoppers would prefer a lounge chair displayed in the living room or without any scene-setting, whereas East Asian shoppers would not only prefer the same lounge chair displayed in the living room but also accept the chair displayed in the mismatching scene such as a garage. People are exposed to visual representations of products within and outside of their context of use when making purchases. For example, a row of coffeepots displayed in a store may highlight the focal product within a mismatching setting, such as on the bookshelf, compared to a display kitchen with a single coffeepot. This difference of product representation in the context may appear in physical settings, catalogs, online listings, and product advertisements. Another potential paradox is that although we found Western advertisements or websites (i.e., U.S. Amazon site) do not present a context as much as Asian advertisements (i.e., Japanese Amazon site), European Americans still responded to the context as strongly as East Asian did. One possibility is that the contextual information in our present study is quite elaborate and vivid. Consequently, European Americans may simply be ignorant of the context effect. Another possibility is that there may be a hidden effect of context, especially when the context given is elaborate; many Western consumers may be distracted by the context and look at certain contextual elements as the focal object. As a result, Western marketers might avoid this hidden context effect and make an advertisement include less contextual information, only highlighting the focal object for consumers. Overall, the present study examines cultural differences in product preference, and it illuminates why current retailers have developed their cultural styles. Understanding the roots of cultural variations in aesthetic preference for the product can help marketers and practitioners to investigate the diverse marketplace.

5.2 Future Research and Limitation

We wish to acknowledge a few limitations of the current work. First, the current finding was based on some household commodities categories. It is crucial to expand the present findings to other domains and product categories. In particular, the objects we used are relatively high-end products that feature unique styles and aesthetics. Future work should explore whether the context effect might be moderated by the product category. Second, our work did not test functionality or pragmatic aspects of design objects. For example, some espresso machines could be stylish and aesthetically appealing, but they may be no different from or even less effective in terms of functions of brewing coffee compared to less expensive and less stylish counterparts. Future work should explore whether the functionality of objects might influence the extent of the context effect. Lastly, we will expand more Eastern and Western E-commerce platforms in the future to investigate the cross-cultural variations in visual merchandising display globally. In sum, it is worth investigating multiple dimensions of contextual effect in cultural variations in the future.

References

1. UNCTAD: Global E-Commerce Jumps to $26.7 Trillion, Covid-19 Boosts Online Retail Sales. UNCTAD, United States (2021)
2. Nisbett, R., et al.: Culture and systems of thought: holistic versus analytic cognition. Psychol. Rev. **108**(2), 291–310 (2001)
3. Masuda, T., Nisbett, R.: Attending holistically versus analytically: comparing the context sensitivity of Japanese and Americans. J. Pers. Soc. Psychol. **81**(5), 922–934 (2001)
4. Nisbett, R., Miyamoto, Y.: The influence of culture: holistic versus analytic perception. TRENDS Cogn. Sci. **9**(10), 467–473 (2005)
5. Chua, H.F., Boland, J.E., Nisbett, R.: Cultural variation in eye movements during scene perception. Proc. Natl. Acad. Sci. U.S.A. **102**(35), 12629–12633 (2005)
6. Markus, H.R., Kitayama, S.: Culture and self: implications for cognition, emotions, and motivation. Psychol. Rev. **98**(2), 224–253 (1991)
7. Nisbett, R.: The Geography of Thought: How Asians and Westerns Think Differently...and Why. Living Together vs. Going It Alone. Simon and Schuster, New York (2003)
8. Masuda, T., et al.: Culture and aesthetic preference: comparing the attention to context of East Asians and Americans. Pers. Soc. Psychol. Bull. **34**(9), 1260–1275 (2008)
9. Wang, H., et al.: How much information? East Asian and North American cultural products and information search performance. Pers. Soc. Psychol. Bull. **38**(12), 1539–1551 (2012)
10. Masuda, T., et al.: Culture and cognition: implications for art, design, and advertisement. In: Okazaki, S. (ed.) Handbook of Research on International Advertising, pp. 109–132. Edward Elgar: Cheltenham (2012)

11. Senzaki, S., Masuda, T., Nand, K.: Holistic versus analytic expressions in artworks: cross-cultural differences and similarities in drawings and collages by Canadian and Japanese school-age children. J. Cross Cult. Psychol. **45**(8), 1297–1316 (2014)
12. Morling, B., Lamoreaux, M.: Measuring culture outside the head: a meta-analysis of individualism-collectivism in cultural products. Pers. Soc. Psychol. Rev. **12**(3), 199–221 (2008)

Evaluation Dataset for Cultural Difference Detection Task

Ikkyu Nishimura(✉), Yohei Murakami, and Mondheera Pituxcoosuvarn

Faculty of Information Science and Engineering, Ritsumeikan University, Kusatsu, Shiga, Japan
is0368xk@ed.ritsumei.ac.jp

Abstract. In recent years, with the improvement of machine translation, conversations across languages have become easier. However, misunderstandings due to cultural differences still exist. In order to detect such cultural differences, a method based on the similarity of feature vectors of images, was proposed. However, there was no available reference with which the accuracy of the detection method could be checked. With the aim of filling this gap, we create an evaluation dataset for cultural difference detection. Specifically, we selected one thousand concepts in different categories. Then, we asked native Japanese speakers and an English speaker to evaluate whether they could relate the images with description and word(s) in their languages. The result is that we were able to create 71 evaluation datasets with exclusive relation cultural differences, 186 evaluation datasets with inclusive relation cultural differences, and 565 evaluation datasets without cultural differences.

Keywords: Intercultural collaboration · Multilingual communication · Machine translation

1 Introduction

In order to tackle international problems, it is necessary to go beyond linguistic and cultural differences and to consider the diversity of society in developing solutions. For this purpose, collaboration among those with different cultures is important. The realization of global citizenship education that fosters such abilities is specified as one of the SDGs (Sustainable Development Goals). For example, a non-profit organization (NPO), called Pangaea, holds a summer school called KISSY[1] that brings together children from various countries with different languages and cultures under the theme of realizing education for global citizenship, and jointly design solutions to the world's problems.

However, differences in language and culture make collaboration difficult. With the steady improvement in the quality of machine translation, language differences are being eliminated, but misunderstandings still occur due to cultural differences. For example, in KISSY, conversations are carried out using a

[1] https://www.pangaean.org/web/english/general/generaltop_en.html.

P.-L. P. Rau (Ed.): HCII 2022, LNCS 13311, pp. 357–369, 2022.
https://doi.org/10.1007/978-3-031-06038-0_26

Fig. 1. Example of cultural differences

unique machine translation tool. Although the translation results are correct, different things are recalled by each participant depending on the culture, and conversations sometimes do not go well.

To detect such cultural differences, a method to detect cultural differences based on the similarity of feature vectors obtained from images on the web was proposed. However, no dataset that could evaluate the method was available. Hence, there was a need for an evaluation dataset for accurately determining cultural differences manually and automatically.

2 Cultural Differences in Multilingual Communication

2.1 Cultural Difference

With the improved accuracy of machine translation, multilingual communication is becoming possible, but there are cases when conversations experience difficulties. One reason for this is cultural differences. People imagine and think differently depending on their cultural background. This causes a gap in communication between the speaker and the listener due to the different images that they recall [1].

For example, "Go-bou (Burdock)" or burdock is a common food in Japan. When "Go-bou" is processed by machine translation, the result is "burdock". When most Japanese people hear the word "Go-bou", they tend think of food with the appearance of a root vegetable (left side of Fig. 1). However, in many other countries, "burdock" is often associated with plants and trees as shown in the right side of Fig. 1. Neither of these images is wrong. They are both the same kind of plant, and the Japanese word "burdock" is the root part of "burdock". In Japan, we have a culture of eating burdock, so the appearance of the root on the left side reminds us of burdock, and it is recognized as a food. Some countries, however, have no experience of eating burdock, so the image on the right is more likely to be associated with burdock.

There are various cases of cultural differences, and the magnitude of the cultural differences varies. The problems that arise in multilingual communication differ according to the degree of cultural differences. Therefore, using a range of

Fig. 2. No culture difference

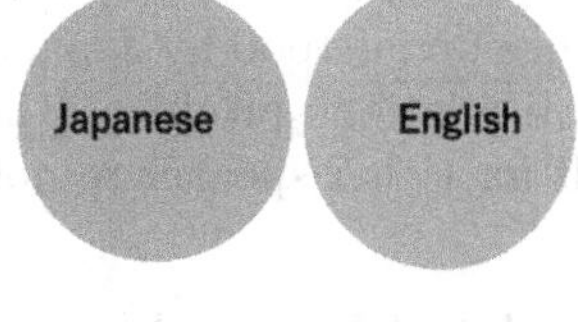

Fig. 3. Cultural difference exists (exclusive relationship)

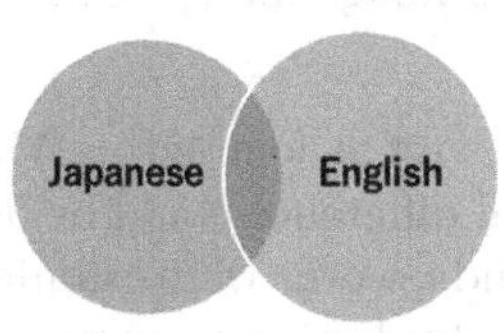

Fig. 4. Cultural difference exists (partial common relationship)

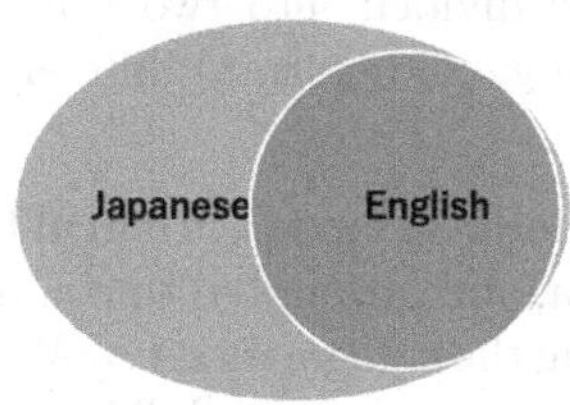

Fig. 5. Cultural difference exists (inclusion relationship)

concepts, we divided cultural differences into four major patterns and introduced examples of problems and cultural differences that occur in each pattern. First, the images evoked by the words in each language are represented by circles in Figs. 2, 3, 4 and 5. When the conceptual ranges of Japanese and English are the same as shown in Fig. 2, we can say that there is no cultural difference between the two languages, because both speakers recall the same things. On the other hand, when the conceptual range of each language is different, we can say that there is a cultural difference.

As shown in Fig. 3, when the range of a concept is not completely identical, such a cultural difference is considered to be an exclusive relation. An example of such a cultural difference is "burdock". While Japanese people recall "burdock" (Fig. 1, left), Americans recall a completely different "burdock" (Fig. 1, right). Since there are so many cultural differences in the exclusive relation, it is highly likely that speakers will notice the misunderstanding, and the danger possible in multilingual communication is low.

Figure 4 shows the partial common relation. An example of such a cultural difference is "dumpling". Steamed dumplings are common in both Japan and China. However, each has its own unique culture of being eaten, particularly on celebratory occasions in China. In Japan, beside steamed dumplings, there is the type of dumpling called "gyoza" which is usually fried before being eaten. Partially common cultural differences are likely to cause misunderstandings between speakers in conversation without being noticed, because the conceptual range is partially the same.

Figure 5 displays the inclusive relation, where one conceptual range is encompassed by the other conceptual range. For example, both Japanese and Americans usually have the same connotation of "whale" in their minds. However, because the Japanese have a food culture in which whales are eaten, the conceptual range understood by Japanese is slightly larger than the English equivalent. Inclusive relations produce a high chance for misunderstanding because it is difficult for either speaker to notice the existence of cultural differences.

2.2 Related Research

Existing research on cultural differences in multilingual communication can be broadly divided into two types: cultural difference analysis based on written knowledge and cultural difference analysis based on image interpretation.

Knowledge-Based Cultural Differences: Yoshino et al. focused on Wikipedia [2] data, and attempted to confirm whether cultural difference could be detected by using the categories set by Wikipedia. In their study, words were examined and the existence of cultural differences was manually judged using a questionnaire.

Then, they calculated the degree of importance to improve the accuracy of detecting cultural differences. Similar work by Ulrike et al. [3] also used Wikipedia but the goal was to examine the cultural diversity of France, Germany, Japan, and the Netherlands. They investigated the relationship between national culture and computer-mediated communication by assessing the Wikipedia editing operations in the different countries. Their research yielded results that well matched the four dimensions of cultural impact presented by Hofstede et al. [4]

With regard to cultural difference in children's communication, one study analyzed KISSY in the field. According to this paper, a Japanese child talked about "An-ko (red bean paste)", however some children from different country could not understand what it looked like because of cultural difference [5].

Images-Based Cultural Differences: Heeryon Cho et al. [6] studied cultural difference in pictograms. Their research focused on pictograms as a communication tool that did not use words to help people from different cultures communicating via a network. Their results showed that pictograms are interpreted differently according to the culture.

Research by Koda et al. [7] focused on cultural differences in avatars, which are often used in online communication in recent years, and determined whether there were cultural differences in the interpretation of avatars' facial expressions. They compared and analyzed the interpretation contents of the avatar's facial expressions between Asia and eight Western countries, and found that there was no cultural difference in the interpretation of negative expressions, unlike the interpretation of positive expressions.

3 Motivation

We have already conducted a preliminary evaluation of a cultural difference detection method. Since there were some problems with the data used in the preliminary evaluation, and there was no problem dataset that could accurately reveal cultural differences, we manually assessed cultural differences and created an appropriate evaluation dataset.

Problems with published studies include:

- English speaker's viewpoint was not considered
- Because it is difficult to obtain evaluations for each image, the judgment of cultural differences was ambiguous
- Homonyms were not considered
- There was bias in the types of concepts

In the data used in the preliminary evaluation, only Japanese speakers made cultural difference judgments based on images acquired from Japanese material using English words. Therefore, the data does not include elements such as English speakers' viewpoints and words. In the questionnaire for the preliminary evaluation, two groups of Japanese words and images (English and Japanese) were shown, and the participants were asked which image differed from the image conjured by the word.

In the questionnaire of the preliminary evaluation, we showed the Japanese word and two groups of images (English and Japanese). This approach makes it possible to predict the concepts that Japanese and English have in common. Words in Japanese were also given, making it possible that the evaluators could recall the word based on that, so it is difficult to know whether the image alone can be recalled from the word. In addition, since only words and images were given, homonyms were not considered. For example, in the case of word "track", where there are two types of tracks, one is a track for vehicle and the other is an athletic track, the word alone suggests both. Therefore, it is necessary to create an evaluation dataset that judges the cultural difference of the target concept from both Japanese and English viewpoints based on multiple elements such as words and descriptions as well as images. In order to create such an evaluation dataset, the cultural differences between concepts should be judged from the viewpoints of both Japanese and English speakers based on elements such as images and words representing the concepts.

4 Dataset Evaluation Design

4.1 Overview

For each concept, Japanese and English words, descriptions of the concept, and images retrieved by word search were shown to speakers of Japanese and English languages. Each speaker was asked to rate on a 5-point scale whether each image could be imagined from the words and descriptions based on information in their native language. First, we selected 1000 synsets (concepts) based on the concepts in the top three layers of WordNet. At that time, the 1000 synsets were selected so that they include various types of concepts based on the concept hierarchy. In WordNet, each synset (concept) is associated with a set of words and a description in each language. Image retrieval was performed for each language using each of those words in Japanese and English as keywords. In the case of multiple words, the images representing the synset were retrieved by using AND search. Among the retrieved images, the top 10 images were used. A question for the questionnaire was created for each synset using the Japanese and English words, the images obtained from those words, and the description of the synset. Then, we ask the speakers of each language how much they could recall each image given the description and keywords. Then, we aggregated the answers for each language, averaged the values, and summarized the results for Japanese and English speakers. Based on the results, we determined whether the Japanese and English images could be recalled or not. Based on the results of whether Japanese or English images can be recalled by Japanese and English speakers, the synset that showed differences in judgments between languages was judged as having cultural differences. On the other hand, synsets that showed no difference in judgment between languages were judged as having no cultural difference. When the image retrieval results are poor, the synset was removed from the dataset.

4.2 Questionnaire Design

The questionnaire used five main types of questions.

A Do the images refer to the same thing (1–5 scale)
B How well do the descriptions match the images (1–5 scale)
C How well the keywords match the image (1–5 scale)
D How well the description matches the keywords (1–5 scale)
E Looking at the keywords and description, how familiar are you with this concept (Yes or No)?

The five-point rating scale is shown below.

1. Completely different
2. Mostly different
3. Fairy correct
4. Mostly correct
5. Completely correct

Among the questions, D (how well the explanation and the keywords matched) and E (whether the concept was known or not, based on the keywords and the explanation) were asked only once per Synset. On the other hand, questions A (whether the objects in the image referred to the same thing), B (how well the description matched the image), and C (how well the keywords matched the image) needed to be answered for each image set. This approach allowed us to evaluate the degree to which each group of images can be recalled from its own keywords and descriptions.

Table 1 shows an example of the questions used in this study. First, the images, descriptions, and keywords acquired in each language were given to the respondents as information. In order to hide from the respondents which language was

Table 1. Questionnaire

Image	Question A	Question B	Question C	Question D	Question E
		Description	Keywords		
Image1	*(1)	*(2)	*(4)	*(6)	*(7)
Image2		*(3)	*(5)		

used to acquire the images, the order in which the images were presented was changed for each synset. For the descriptions and keywords, we used the synset descriptions and word clouds extracted from the WordNet of each survey respondent according to their native language. Based on these, the respondents were asked to answer the questions marked with an asterisk (*) in Table 1.

For each question, (1) in Table 1 asks to what extent image group 1 and image group 2 refer to the same thing. In (2) and (3), question B is asked based on the description and each image group. In parts (4) and (5), question C is asked based on the keywords and the images. (6) and (7) ask about questions D and E based on the descriptions and keywords, respectively.

4.3 Cultural Difference Criteria

Next, we compiled the evaluation data set based on these questionnaires. First, we summarize the results of the questionnaire for each language speaker. In this study, we asked four Japanese speakers and one English speaker to answer the questionnaire. We averaged the values of (1) in Table 1 among the four Japanese speakers. The results of the questionnaire for the respondents whose answer to (7) is "No" were not included. By calculating the average of (1) to (6), we can uniquely determine the results of the questionnaire for this Synset for Japanese. In this way, the questionnaire results were uniquely determined for each language speaker. In the Japanese-English case, information was extracted from the questionnaires for images acquired in Japanese and English, and the questionnaire results for Japanese and English speakers were compared to determine the existence of cultural differences. The upper image group 1 is the group of images acquired with Japanese keywords, and the lower image group 2 is the group of images acquired with English keywords (Tables 2 and 3).

Table 2. Result with no cultural difference

	Evaluator (jpn)	Evaluator (eng)
Image (jpn)	Recallable	Recallable
Image (eng)	Recallable	Recallable

Table 3. Result with culture difference

	Evaluator (jpn)	Evaluator (eng)
Image (jpn)	Recallable	Recallable
Image (eng)	Not recallable	Recallable

First, we checked whether the results of (2) and (4) were both "1" in the case of Japanese questionnaire results. Since image group 1 is a set of images retrieved using Japanese keywords, the fact that Japanese cannot recall these images from both keywords and descriptions indicates that the image retrieval results were poor. Therefore, if the result of (2) and (4) was “1”, we removed the corresponding Synset from the dataset as “not applicable”. If either of the two results was not “1”, the Japanese image was judged to be “recallable”. Next, (3) and (5) are the images retrieved using the English keywords. When both results were “1”, we judged that English images were “not recallable” for Japanese speakers. If either of the results was not “1”, the English image was judged to be “recallable”. Thus, for Japanese speakers, the questionnaire results of the Japanese images and the English images are judged as “recallable” or “not recallable” respectively.

Similarly, for English speakers, when the values of (3) and (5) were both “1”, the synset was removed from the dataset as “not applicable”. Next, if the results of (2) and (4) were both “1”, the synset was judged as “not recallable”, and if either of them was not “1”, the synset is judged as “recallable”. The results of the Japanese and English images are determined. It would be judged as “no cultural difference” when the two results of the Japanese and English speakers. On the other hand, as shown in Table 1, when Japanese speakers could “recall” both Japanese and English images, while English speakers could not “recall” Japanese images, this synset was judged to have a cultural difference. In this case, Japanese speakers could recall both images, but English speakers could only recall one of them, so the range of the concept is wider than that of the image perceived by Japanese speakers. Therefore, this yielded the judgement of “cultural difference exists (inclusive relation)” because it corresponds to the “inclusive relation” explained in chapter? In the case that neither Japanese nor English speakers could “recall” images acquired in the other’s language, there is a conceptual range that is not common to both, which yielded the judgement of “exclusive relation” as described in ? Thus “cultural difference exists (exclusive relationship)”.

Thus, from the questionnaire, each synset is judged as “no cultural difference”, “with cultural difference (inclusive relation)”, “with cultural difference (exclusive relation)”, or “not applicable, and “not applicable”. We removed the “not applicable” synsets and labelled the remaining synsets with the judgment results.

5 Experiment

5.1 Experiment Environment

Four Japanese and one American answered the questionnaires. The target concepts were the subconcepts of the 11 concepts located in the top three layers of the WordNet concept hierarchy. The concepts were selected so that the number of these 11 subconcepts were as equal as possible. Specifically, we selected the concepts from “psychological feature” to “thing” in Fig. 6.

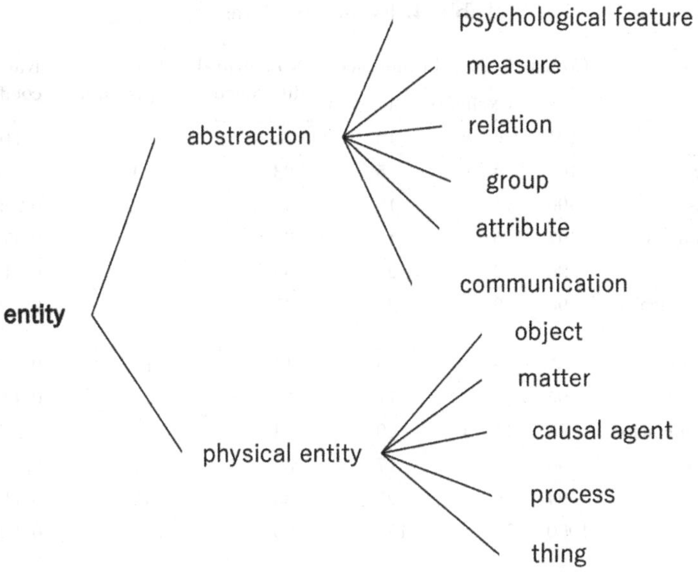

Fig. 6. WordNet concept hierarchy

5.2 Results

First, we removed 178 out of scope concepts from the 1000 concepts, resulting in a total of 822 concepts. There were 257 concepts with cultural differences, 71 of which were exclusive cultural differences, and the remaining 186 were inclusive cultural differences. The number of concepts with "no cultural difference" was 565. The synsets were selected so that the subconcepts of the third layer were evenly distributed, but only 35 subconcepts of "attribute" were associated with Japanese. Therefore, the number of subconcepts for "attribute" is small.

6 Evaluation

6.1 Reliability

Using the Kappa coefficient, we will investigate the degree of agreement between the respondents and verify the reliability of the data. Since the survey respondents were 4 Japanese and 1 American, we investigated Kappa coefficient for the responses of the four Japanese people. As a result, the kappa coefficient was 0.361. On the other hand, in the "object" category, the Kappa coefficient is 0.416, so the questionnaire results of this conceptual group are reliable.

6.2 Recall Level Distribution

The questionnaire used a 5-point scale to answer six of the questions. This section investigates how often the "completely correct" rating was selected (Table 4).

Table 4. Evaluation dataset

Synset	Count	Cultural difference		No cultural difference	Not applicable	Kappa coefficient
		Exclusive	Inclusion			
Object	101	6	10	74	11	0.416
Matter	102	4	5	93	0	0.381
Process	90	11	16	46	17	0.289
Causal agent	97	5	17	66	9	0.353
Thing	96	2	23	59	12	0.348
Psychological feature	98	9	22	47	20	0.356
Attribute	35	5	5	14	11	0.317
Group	95	6	17	52	20	0.324
Communication	96	11	29	44	12	0.282
Measure	96	6	17	37	36	0.332
Relation	94	6	25	33	58	0.332
Total	1000	71	186	565	178	0.361

Table 5. Distribution

Synset	Percentage of propotion (%)				
	1	2	3	4	5
Total	22.3 (6692/30000)	14.6 (4379/30000)	14.9 (4470/30000)	19.9 (5961/30000)	28.2 (8472/30000)
Object	9.9 (242/2448)	6.5 (160/2448)	11.6 (283/2448)	23.8 (583/2448)	48.2 (1180/2448)
Matter	5.5 (134/2424)	3.2 (77/2424)	9.7 (236/2424)	26.8 (650/2424)	54.7 (1327/2424)

As shown in Table 5, "5" was the most frequent answer. On the other hand, "2" was the least frequent response. In the "object" and "matter" categories, where the agreement was high, the majority of responses were "5", indicating that cultural differences were determined by stronger recall.

6.3 Disagreement in Recall Levels

Among the responses to the questionnaire, the target concepts that showed the most variation in the 5-point evaluation were the concepts such as "communication" and "process" category (in Fig. 6). In the case of a concept that actually has a shape, the image shows the target concept, so it is less dependent on the sensitivity of the respondent. On the other hand, "communication" and "process" concepts are abstract concepts, so they depend more on the sensitivity of the respondent. Therefore, there is a strong tendency for these concepts to be evaluated differently.

7 Discussion

7.1 Acquired Cultural Differences

We listed examples of cultural differences we found for each type. An example of a cultural difference (exclusive relationship) is "pudding". In the images obtained from "pudding", there were many images of what we in Japan call "muffins". For the images retrieved from "Pu-rin" or pudding in Japanese language were mostly Japanese pudding and chocolate pudding. It can be said that the Japanese word "Pu-rin" is a Japanese-English word that Japanese derived from somewhere else. On the other hand, "Pu-rin" in Japan is a generic term for soft food made by mixing rice, meat, flour, etc. with milk or eggs, and then hardening it by boiling or steaming. Therefore, the image of this food was obtained from "Pu-rin" (Table 6).

Table 6. Example

Keyword	Image
pudding ()	
pudding	
rinse ()	
rinse	

Next, "rinse" is an example of a cultural difference (inclusive relation). For "Rin-se", images of Japanese hair conditioner were obtained, and for "rinse", many images of rinsing with water were obtained. In fact, the explanation in the questionnaire was "to wash lightly without using soap". Therefore, the images obtained from English were consistent with the description, and Japanese people could associate the word with both images. On the other hand, the American participant could not recall the Japanese images of "rinse" either from the description or from the keyword, so they recalled only the English images. These results suggest that there was a cultural difference (inclusive relation).

7.2 False Detection

A concept with no cultural difference that was detected incorrectly was "Ohm". For this concept, images of the German physicist named Georg Ohm were retrieved in both languages. In addition, the Japanese images were obtained as Japanese anime characters, while the English images obtained were illustrations of the Omega symbol. For this formless concept, there is no object that can be represented well as an image, so the answer depends largely on the perception of the survey respondent. In this case, Ohm was judged as a cultural difference even though it is a common concept (the unit of electric resistance) in both cultures.

8 Conclusion

Since there was no dataset available for judging the performance achieved by using automated cultural difference detection systems, we created an evaluation dataset from the viewpoints of both Japanese and English speakers. As a result, we were able to create 71 evaluation datasets with exclusive relation cultural difference, 186 evaluation datasets with inclusive relation cultural differences, and 565 evaluation datasets without cultural differences. In addition, we successfully detected cultural differences such as "pudding". In the future, we plan to devise and evaluate variants of cultural difference detection methods using these evaluation data sets.

Acknowledgements. This research was partially supported by a Grant-in-Aid for Scientific Research (B) (21H03561, 2021–2024, 21H03556, 2021–2023) and a Grant-in-Aid for Early-Career Scientists (21K17794, 2021–2024) from the Japan Society for the Promotion of Sciences (JSPS).

References

1. Deutscher, G.: Through the Language Glass: Why the World Looks Different in Other Languages. Metropolitan Books (2010)
2. Takashi, Y., Mai, M., Tomohiro, S.: A proposed cultural difference detection method using data from Japanese and Chinese Wikipedia. In: Proceeding of 2015 International Conference on Culture and Computing (Culture Computing), pp. 159–166. IEEE (2015)
3. Pfeil, U., Zaphiris, P., Ang, C.S.: Cultural differences in collaborative authoring of Wikipedia. J. Comput.-Mediated Commun. **12**(1), 88–113 (2006)

4. Hofstede, G.H., Hofstede, G.J., Minkov, M.: Cultures and Organizations: Software of the Mind, vol. 2. McGraw-Hill, New York (2005)
5. Pituxcoosuvarn, M., Ishida, T., Yamashita, N., Takasaki, T., Mori, Y.: Machine translation usage in a children's workshop. In: Egi, H., Yuizono, T., Baloian, N., Yoshino, T., Ichimura, S., Rodrigues, A. (eds.) CollabTech 2018. LNCS, vol. 11000, pp. 59–73. Springer, Cham (2018). https://doi.org/10.1007/978-3-319-98743-9_5
6. Cho, H., Ishida, T., Yamashita, N., Inaba, R., Mori, Y., Koda, T.: Culturally-situated pictogram retrieval. In: Ishida, T., Fussell, S.R., Vossen, P.T.J.M. (eds.) IWIC 2007. LNCS, vol. 4568, pp. 221–235. Springer, Heidelberg (2007). https://doi.org/10.1007/978-3-540-74000-1_17
7. Koda, T.: Cross-cultural comparison of interpretation of avatars' facial expressions. In: Proceedings of the IEEE/IPSJ Symposium on Applications and the Internet (SAINT-2006) (2006)

"Trauma" and Delicate Balance: The Analysis of Salvoj Žižek's Ontology and New Ecological Philosophy

Chao Pan(✉)

Tsinghua University, Beijing, China
panc20@mails.tsinghua.edu.cn

Abstract. Slavoj Žižek reflected on nature centrism from the basic concept of "trauma" in psychoanalysis, and demonstrated that "the Real is a trauma" and "man is the wound of nature." He believed that when facing the natural environment, people should understand and accept the disaster inherently contained. With the emergence of human beings, the original natural balance has been lost, and disasters brought about by human beings to nature are inevitable, meaning that human beings have ruined the original nature. Dealing with the relationship between human beings and natural environment, it is necessary to establish a view of time facing the future and viewing the present and to imagine and project the occurrence of future disasters through human collective fantasy. According to this, human beings are supposed to actively respond to disasters and establish a view beyond the present and themselves. As human beings, we should have the consciousness of tragedy and crisis, reset it to the subject's fantasy world, and establish a delicate balance between human beings and nature.

Keywords: Trauma · Delicate balance · Slavoj Žižek · Fantasy · Nature centrism

1 Nature-centered Ecological View and Utopian Ideal

One of the mainstreams of ecological philosophy is nature centrism, whose basic concept is to emphasize the respect for nature and restore the natural balance of the original ecology. The ecological view of natural centralism is not only a theoretical response to global ecological problems, but also a reflection on Anthropocentrism under modern subjective rationality.[1] For a long time, in the study of western ecological ethics, the most fundamental debate is natural centralism or anthropocentrism,[2] however, both are often reproached a logic of absolutism and essentialism.[3] Taking anthropocentrism as

1 Shi Fengge: Critique of Nature-Centrism Ecological View and Construction of New Ecological Philosophy. Social Sciences Abroad (02), 57 (2021).

2 Liu Fusen: Western "Ecological Ethics" and "Metaphysical Dilemma". Philosophical Research (01), 101(2017).

3 Liu Fusen: Western "Ecological Ethics" and "Metaphysical Dilemma". Philosophical Research (01), 101(2017).

P.-L. P. Rau (Ed.): HCII 2022, LNCS 13311, pp. 370–377, 2022.
https://doi.org/10.1007/978-3-031-06038-0_27

an example, its ideological source can be traced to the view that "Man is the measure of all things" put forward by Protagoras, a Greek philosopher of the 5th century BCE, which is the humanistic metaphysics of western traditional philosophy.[4] Until the 17th century, the French philosopher Descartes took "I think, therefore I am" as the basis of epistemological philosophy to further strengthen the people-centered understanding.[5] From the above point of views, it can be seen that an anthropocentric worldview has dominated for a long time. Until the second half of the 20th century, ecological ethics began to turn from anthropocentrism to natural centrism, and attributed the current causes of ecological crisis to mankind.[6]

For example, as the representative of the animal liberation theory in nature centrism, P. Singer believes that all beings should be equal. The ethical principle of equality should be extended to animals and the interests of each being also should be equally cared about.[7] Anthropocentrism is the "humanistic" metaphysics of western traditional philosophy,[8] while "natural centrism," which opposes the traditional humanistic metaphysics but falls into another metaphysics, that is the naturalistic "materialistic" metaphysics. As a matter of fact, neither of the two approaches goes beyond metaphysical logic, the logic behind absolutism and essentialism. In natural centralism, the right of nature is an "objective right" unrelated to human beings, which has naturalness and natural will. Any life has the right to exist, which belongs to the "natural principle," therefore naturalistic ecological ethics is established on the basis of natural principle. Because materialism denies humanism, it actually moves from one pole to another, which cannot effectively solve the problem between human beings and nature.

The perfect original nature pursued by nature centrism comes from the presupposition of natural ontology with the color of Utopia. From the perspective of temporal logic, it is impossible to realize the original nature, because it belongs to the retrospective construction of thinking. For the word Utopia, people often denounce it as "fantasy" from the point of view of common sense and science.[9] In *Utopia* published in 1516, Thomas Moore invented an equal, happy and perfect island country and named it Utopia. The term Utopia has a two-sided meaning from the beginning. The perfect ideal component coexists with the unrealistic and unrealistic fantasy. In China, the "Peach Blossom Spring" (桃花源) constructed by Tao Qian (陶潜) in the Eastern Jin Dynasty also has the similar meaning of Utopia. At the times when utopianism came into being,

[4] Ancient Greek and Roman Philosophy. Edited and translated by Teaching and Research of Philosophical History Program, the Department of Philosophy, Peking University, p. 138. The Commercial Press, Beijing (1961).

[5] Descartes, René: Discourse on the Method of Rightly Conducting One's Reason and of Seeking Truth in the Sciences. Translated by Guan Zhenhu, p. 36. The Commercial Press, Beijing (1991).

[6] Nie Zhenzhao: From Anthropocentrism to Human Subjectivity: A Possible Solution to Ecological Crises. Foreign Literature Studies 42 (01), 22 (2020). https://doi.org/10.19915/j.cnki.fls.2020.01.003.

[7] P. Singer: Animal Liberation: A New Ethics for our Treatment of Animals. Random House, New York (1975).

[8] Descartes, René: Discourse on the Method of Rightly Conducting One's Reason and of Seeking Truth in the Sciences. Translated by Guan Zhenhu, p. 36. The Commercial Press, Beijing (1991).

[9] He Lai: Utopian spirit and justification of philosophical legitimacy. Social Sciences in China (07), 41 (2013).

the voice against utopianism also arose and formed a critical voice. Therefore, returning to the original natural balance pursued by naturalism is a utopian ideal which cannot be realized in theory and practice.

2 The Concept of "Trauma" and Natural Ecological Environment

In the 1960s and 1970s, Lacan gradually transferred the real to the field of trauma, which is reflected in his definition of "trauma" as "the real" in his seminar report. In this regard, Lacan inherited a lot from Freud. Trauma plays an extremely significant role in Freud's psychoanalytic theory. Since ancient Greece, trauma had always referred to external injury in the sense of surgery and did not have acquired psychological meanings until the period of psychoanalysis. In Lacan's perspective, trauma mainly refers to psychological trauma which refers to events beyond ordinary people's experience in psychiatry. Moreover, the characteristics of trauma are sudden and difficult to resist, causing difficult psychological wounds to the parties. This accidental feature causes people to feel powerless. The sudden and irresistible nature of trauma is inevitable for everyone. Lacan's classic view of psychoanalysis is "How real is Reality." In his view, reality and the real are strictly distinguished. What is "reality"? Lacan believes that people's "sense of reality" is not "endogenous," but given by the external cultural symbolic order. In this regard, Žižek's view is that the symbolic dimension is the invisible order that structures our experience of reality.[10]

The reason why the natural ecological crisis has become a global problem is not only because the crisis itself has destructive power, but also because it contains a variety of symbolic meanings.[11] It is dominated by the discourse of various ideologies. In the current ecological discourse, "ecological crisis" is symbolized as "punishment for human overexploitation of nature" and "nature" is symbolized as "balanced nature." With regard to this ecological discourse, the natural environment has been presupposed that human beings are guilty and nature is balanced and harmonious—a beautiful image. Nature is a harmonious, orderly, organic and balanced process of reproduction. This balance is disturbed by the emergence of human beings, so we must let nature come back to when there were no human beings, which means the recovery of the original balance of nature.

However, since human beings are also a part of nature, it is a utopian ideal to restore the original nature without human beings. Each time when a natural ecological crisis occurs, people realize the broken state of the balance between human beings and nature.[12] In psychoanalysis, people are regarded as natural wounds, while in the pre-linguistic period, the balance between human beings and nature is the same as that between fetus and mother. With the establishment of cultural symbols, human beings began to enter the actual world from the original real world, and human beings began to split and confront with the natural environment. Therefore, human beings became the wounds of nature.[13]

---

[10] Slavoj Žižek: Event: Philosophy in Transit. p.119. Penguin, London (2014).

[11] Hu Shun: On Ecological Crisis from the Perspective of Žižek's Psychoanalytic Philosophy. Theory Horizon (03), 49(2020). https://doi.org/10.13221/j.cnki.lljj.2020.03.008

[12] Slavoj Žižek: Demanding the Impossible. p.11. Polity Press, Cambridge (2013).

[13] Slavoj Žižek: The Sublime Object of Ideology.2nd edn. Xxviii. Verso, London/New York (2008).

However, starting from the human's crisis consciousness, human beings would like to restore the original balance between human beings and nature, but it is impossible for human beings to return to the original real state, just as the baby cannot return to the mother's womb, which is an irreversible process. As for the ecological crisis, we must learn to regard the real ecological crisis as a meaningless fact rather than giving it meaning, Žižek said.[14] For instance, meteorites hitting the earth, volcanic eruptions, tsunamis and mass extinction are all natural features.

The ecological crisis encountered by the natural environment is a traumatic event. In the ecological crisis, we are facing the ultimate form of response of the real. Ecological crisis is accidental, but human beings practical activities are organized by symbolic order. Therefore, human beings disasters caused by ecological crisis urge human beings to think and try to explain the causes. Therefore, the concept of trauma became closely related to the natural environment. The ecological crisis is interpreted retroactively as the imbalance and rupture of the relationship between human beings and nature. The ecological crisis broke out in the form of this "traumatic return," disrupting the balance between human beings and nature, and also maintaining this balance at the same time.

3 Žižek's Anti-utopian New Ecological Philosophy

In the *Sublime Object of Ideology*, Žižek adopted the ontological presupposition of the perfect balance of natural centralism. Starting from the concept of "trauma" in psychoanalysis, Žižek pointed out that human beings are the wound of nature and that the balance of nature can no longer be restored.[15] If human beings would like to live in harmony with the environment, the only thing they can do is to fully accept the gaps and cracks and repair them as much as possible afterwards.[16] In other words, a perfectly balanced Utopia does not exist. Nature is always broken and unbalanced. The inherent attribute of nature is full of disaster and imbalance.

Žižek's analysis of ecological crisis and ecology draws on the theoretical resources of Lacan, Marx and Lenin, and mainly draws on Lacan's later theoretical explorations centered on the real.[17] He believes that the balance of nature is just people's retrospective meaning projection. The reason why people would like to imagine a state of natural "balance" is obviously because the ecological disaster destroys the "objective certainty" of people's real life and the "self-evident certitudes."[18]

---

[14] Slavoj Žižek: Looking Awry: An Introduction to Jacques Lacan through Popular Culture. p.35 Mass: The MIT Press, Cambridge (1991).

[15] Zhang Jian: the Interpretation of Žižek's Thought of Ecological Crisis. Philosophical Trends (01), 43 (2011).

[16] Li Yangquan: Žižek's Ecological View and its Significance. Foreign Literature (02), 128 (2014). https://doi.org/10.16430/j.cnki.fl.2014.02.001

[17] Li Yangquan: Žižek's Ecological View and its Significance. Foreign Literature (02), 129 (2014). https://doi.org/10.16430/j.cnki.fl.2014.02.001

[18] Salvoj Žižek: Looking Awry: an Introducing to Jacques Lacan through Popular Culture. Translated by Ji Guangmao, p.59. Zhejiang University Press, Hangzhou (2011).

From the perspective of Marx, since the birth of mankind nature has always been second nature and humanized nature. Žižek emphasized that nature does not exist. The idea that human beings' intervention disrupts the balance of nature is just a fantasy of human beings themselves; with the development of biogenic technology, nature will no longer exist. Since nature is already "second nature," its balance has always been subordinate and secondary.[19]

From the point of view that man is the wound of nature, Žižek believed that the birth of mankind has long drawn a deep wound to nature, and the balance of nature can no longer be restored. Nature on earth has adapted to human beings' existence, and human beings activities have been completely included in the natural environment. Therefore, one of the viewpoints of new ecological philosophy is to face the natural truth.

The primary feature of new ecological philosophy is its concept of time which is a "future tense" concept of time. It means a concept of time that looks at the present from the future. It determines our current actions retrospectively through the presupposition of the future. The future is generated by our actions in the past, and our past behavior is determined by our expectations for the future and our response to them. The way to deal with ecological problems with the "future tense" concept of time is: we should regard ecological disaster as an inevitable fate, and actively project ourselves into this fate by accepting the perspective of ecological disaster. It is through the projection of the dimension of ecological disaster in the future that people take the initiative to avoid ecological disaster.

Žižek borrowed Rumsfeld's term and called it "unknown non knowledge." For science, "non-knowledge" may be far more than the sum of "known," "unknown" and "ignorance."[20] For Lacan, the symptom of psychoanalysis is a kind of "non-knowledge" in a special sense. The subject shows this image with his own behavior, and this image constantly reappears in his behavior, but he doesn't know this image.[21] In Lacan's view, no matter what form of identity, it cannot bridge the internal division of self itself and the division between individuals and others. The real is not an empirical "reality." It cannot be visualized in imagination or represented in the symbolic world. Therefore, the real is impossible to achieve.[22]

Žižek analyzed current popular views of ecology, such as trying to restore the "natural balance" and so on, and believed that the essence of these views was to escape and deceive oneself and others to avoid meeting the real of disaster. For the ecological crisis, we do not know where the critical point is, and we do not know what disaster we will face. Therefore, when we really realize the ecological crisis, it is always too late, because the emergence of ecological disaster will bring about a subversive impact on the existing symbolic order.

---

19 Salvoj Žižek: In Defence of Lost Causes. p. 445. Verso, London/New York (2008).

20 Li Xingmin: Cultural Implication of Science. p.297. Higher Education Press, Beijing (2007).

21 Jacques Lacan: Selected works of Lacan. Translated by Chu Xiaoquan, p.79. SDX Joint Publishing Company, Shanghai (2019).

22 Jacques Lacan: "The Seminar," Book XI: The Four Foundamantal Concepts of Psychoanalysis. p.167, Penguin, London (1979).

4 Žižek's Critique and Attitude of Confronting

Facing the imbalance of natural environment and the occurrence of ecological crisis, what should human beings do? Žižek criticized three common attitudes towards ecological crisis. The first is the split reaction between knowledge and belief, which is also known as fetishistic effect. In the face of the impending crisis, human beings trend to claim that "I know the authenticity of the ecological crisis," but "I don't believe the disaster will actually happen." The second is a neurotic transformation, which refers to human beings taking a forced and fanatical action to avoid disaster. We know that we are powerless to deal with the crisis, but it is difficult to accept the disaster psychologically, so we can't wait to make some preparations, such as hoarding a lot of food and so on. The third is to take the ecological crisis as an answer to the real, also known as psychotic projection, which is regarded as the punishment of nature to human beings. In Žižek's perspective, these three attitudes are all a kind of escape in essence. In fact, it seems that there is such kind of contradiction in today's ecology insisting that disasters will happen on the one hand and hoping disasters will never happen on the other.[23]

Facing the outbreak of ecological crisis in the natural environment, what kind of attitude did Žižek choose to take? Human beings should turn from fear and worry to an ecology without nature, which requires human beings to learn to accept the reality of ecological crisis and the cruel status quo without giving any information or significance to the reality of ecological crisis.[24] This fear should be pushed to the extreme and reach the level of terror. His view is also in line with Jean Pierre Dupuy's view that disasters must be engraved into the future in a more thorough way and must be regarded as inevitable.[25] Crisis and ecological imbalance both part of natural history, because in the past countless moments, life can move in one direction.

In addition, Žižek also pointed out that in the era of ecological crisis, capitalism will make full use of every opportunity to promote its own development. For example, in the domain of organic food, capitalism spares no effort to transform organic food into the main components of agricultural market and production. Consumers try to prove that they are concerned about ecological problems through buying organic food and gain a sense of psychological sublimity. This consumption behavior offsets the guilt brought by capitalist consumption, thus covering up the most essential problem.

Žižek's critical attitude is to oppose the idealization and sublimation of nature. The supporters of nature centrism have a romantic tendency to try to separate man from nature and hope to return to the pure original nature. Since the 18th century, under the guidance of the spirit of enlightenment with its instrumental rationality as the core, scientific discourse has dominated the world and nature has been calculated by mathematics and formulas. However, due to the occurrence of disasters, human beings cannot bear the crisis brought by rationality. Therefore, human beings began to think about the

[23] Salvoj Žižek: In Defence of Lost Causes. p. 439. Verso, London/New York (2008).

[24] Salvoj Žižek: Looking Awry: an Introduction to Jacques Lacan through Popular Culture. Translated by Ji Guangmao, p 61. Zhejiang University Press, Hangzhou (2011).

[25] Salvoj Žižek. The Grimaces of Real. Translated by Ji Guangmao, p 9, Central Compilation & Translation Press, Beijing (2004).

relationship between human beings and nature and highlight the role of human beings in nature.

5 Seeking a Delicate Balance in Tragic Consciousness

With regard to the relationship between human beings and nature, Engels believed that human beings are the product of nature, developed in their environment and with this environment.[26] The disaster of COVID-19 makes us rethink the relationship between the ecological environment and human beings and how to find the fragile balance between human beings and nature becomes the common problem faced by all mankind. The germination of the concept of balanced nature can be traced back to the sages' thinking on the relationship between human beings and nature. Zhuangzi once said that "Heaven and earth are born with me, and all things are the same with me."[27] With great oriental ecological wisdom, this expression holds that the whole natural world is harmonious and in a dynamic balance and human beings can coexist with nature harmoniously. In Žižek's view, whenever a crisis occurs, people will spontaneously seek some kind of lost balance.[28]

The reason why human beings would like to try to repair the unbalanced nature is that human beings presuppose that nature was a balanced, harmonious and orderly organic whole. Its implicit premise is that the existing world may be the best. No matter what human beings do, they are forbidden to disturb the existing natural balance, because any fundamental change may lead to ecological disasters and unexpected consequences. Actually, it reflects a deep distrust of any change and progress. However, nature itself is crazy and fundamentally unbalanced, which means nature has no harmonious cyclic rhythm.[29] With the rapid development of technology, the original nature has come to an end, and this nature is just the "second nature." It is supposed not to expect to restore the harmony between human beings and nature but to strive to maintain the traumatic "fragile balance" between human beings and nature.

Žižek's view of collective action is closely related to the practice from the perspective of Marx's historical materialism. Marx regarded the practice as the intermediary of objectified activities between human beings and nature. It is based on practice that the ecological view we construct has practical significance. Zizek's criticism of the concept of balanced nature is essentially a radical deconstruction of the current popular ecological discourse. It is safe to say that Žižek's criticism of the balanced view of nature also led to the turn of the eco-philosophical tendencies in Lacan's psychoanalytic theory.[30] After acknowledging the inevitability of natural disasters, how can human beings determine the occurrence of disasters through the "fantasy" collective imagination of the subject

---

[26] Engels, Friedrich: Anti-Dühring. Translated by Central Compilation & Translation Bureau, p.32. People's Publishing House, Beijing (1971).

[27] Zhuangzi:Essay on the Uniformity of All Things. (庄周： 《庄子·齐物论》).

[28] Slavoj Žižek: Demanding the Impossible, p.11. Polity Press, Cambridge (2013).

[29] Taylor Astra: Examined Life: Excursions with Contemporary Thinkers. p. 159. New Press, New York (2009).

[30] Hu Shun: On Žižek Criticism of Balance View of Nature. World Philosophy (05), 55(2020).

in advance, and how can they arrange their behaviors to deal with future disasters under the condition of suffering consciousness?

When dealing with the relationship between human beings and natural ecological environment, it is necessary for human beings to establish a view of time facing the future and viewing the present and to imagine and project the occurrence of future disasters through human collective fantasy. According to this assumption, human beings should actively respond to disasters and establish a view beyond the present and themselves. As human beings, they need to have the consciousness of tragedy and hardship, to reset the disaster consciousness to the subject's fantasy world, and to establish a fragile balance between human beings and nature.

Differences in Color Representations of Tastes: Cross-cultural Study Among Japanese, Russian and Taiwanese

Alexander Raevskiy[1,2], Ivan Bubnov[2], Yi-Chuan Chen[3], and Nobuyuki Sakai[4(✉)]

[1] Japan Society for Promotion of Science (Host organization: Tohoku University), Sendai, Japan
[2] Lomonosov Moscow State University, Moscow, Russia
[3] Mackay Medical College, New Taipei City, Taiwan
[4] Tohoku University, Sendai, Japan
nob_sakai@tohoku.ac.jp

Abstract. The current study explores cultural differences in cross-modal color-taste associations among Japanese, Taiwanese, and Russian respondents. The participants were asked to choose a color from a 35-color palette that corresponds to a particular item including three voices (male, female, and child), five basic tastes, five types of oral chemesthesis (hot, sharp, spicy, fatty, and astringent), and eight functional foods. The results demonstrate that in the cases of voices, three basic tastes (sweet, salty, and sour), and hot and fatty tastes, cross-modal associations were mostly similar among the participants and consistent with previous studies. However, for some specific tastes such as umami, several types of oral chemesthesis, and functional foods, more cultural differences were observed. We also measured the level of consistency/diversity of opinions among the participants of a single nation by calculating the Selected Colors (SC)-80 parameter, which represents the number of colors selected by 80% of the respondents. The results have shown that it is connected with the level of familiarity of certain tastes and foods; however, specific cultural features were also observed.

Keywords: Color representation · Taste · Cross-modal correspondence

1 Introduction

In everyday life we acquire information from different sensory sources, helping with our understanding and perception of the world around us. Although each sense has traditionally been thought to be independent and separate from the others, recent studies have shown that they influence one another during the early processing stage, and such interactions contribute to the phenomena of cross-modal correspondences. Cross-modal correspondences are defined as a tendency for a sensory feature, or attribute, in one modality, either physically present or merely imagined to be matched (or associated) with a sensory feature in another modality [1].

A large body of research has described the existence of cross-modal associations between different sensory modalities, such as speech sounds and shapes [2, 3], colors

The original version of this chapter was revised: an error in the caption for Table 2 in the paper was corrected. The correction to this chapter is available at
https://doi.org/10.1007/978-3-031-06038-0_41

P.-L. P. Rau (Ed.): HCII 2022, LNCS 13311, pp. 378–395, 2022.
https://doi.org/10.1007/978-3-031-06038-0_28

and odors [4], and sounds and tastes [5]. Although the nature of such interactions remains unclear, it is certain that people often map stimulus properties from different sensory modalities onto each other in a consistent manner.

Eating is another good example in which these cross-modal interactions are common and are thus interesting to analyze. Our perception of food commonly emerges from the combination of various information from multiple sensory modalities; for example, olfactory, gustatory, visual, and other information strongly affects our eating experience. It has been proved that the appearance [6], temperature [7], texture and smell [8], and even chewing sounds [9] of food influence the perceived taste.

Still, according to a growing body of scientific research, vision is the main clue used by the brain to help identify sources of food, as well as their expected taste and flavor. It has been suggested that color is a particularly important product-intrinsic cue that supports our psychological expectation of different types of food and drink [6]. Color often helps the brain make predictions regarding edibility, taste, and flavor. Thus, color is often used in marketing to provide necessary information regarding a product, and influences consumer opinions and choices in an extremely delicate manner.

Basic tastes, by contrast, are suggested to be associated with other non-gustatory stimuli. Evidence of consistent mappings between particular tastes and colors has been found in previous studies [10, 11]. The linking of colors with basic tastes has been a source of inspiration for artists and scientists and has been used not only as a basis in scientific research, but also in marketing campaigns and food label production.

It has also been suggested that cultural background plays a profound role in such cross-modal interactions owing to various food preferences and consumption behaviors in different countries [12]. Given these cross-cultural differences, we can expect that associations between gustatory and non-gustatory information in some cases will show significant diversity, which has been proved by studies exploring color–odor [13], color–flavor [14, 15] and shape–flavor [16] associations. Although the results have shown that cross-modal associations between vision and taste/flavor differ among Western and non-Western participants [16, 17], some cross-cultural similarities have also been documented [18, 19]. The above-mentioned studies clearly highlight the role of cultural background in cross-modal associations; however, further research is needed to better understand this impact.

The current study is aimed at comparing cross-modal interactions between colors and audial/gustatory stimuli among Taiwanese, Japanese and Russian participants to determine the impact of cultural background and food preferences on cross-modal correspondence. As another important feature of this study, in addition to matching colors to certain items, a free association method is also applied: The participants were asked to write down the name of a food associated with a particular item. Thus, through a data analysis, we can better understand the roots of such a correspondence.

2 Materials and Methods

In this study, 136 Japanese, 100 Taiwanese, and 102 Russian university students participated online using a Google form. Additional 27 Taiwanese data were repeatedly recorded owing to a technical mistake and were therefore excluded in the final analysis.

The participants were presented with a panel with a round color patch consisting of 30 colors and a 5-color grayscale ranging from white to black. A color patch is presented in Fig. 1.

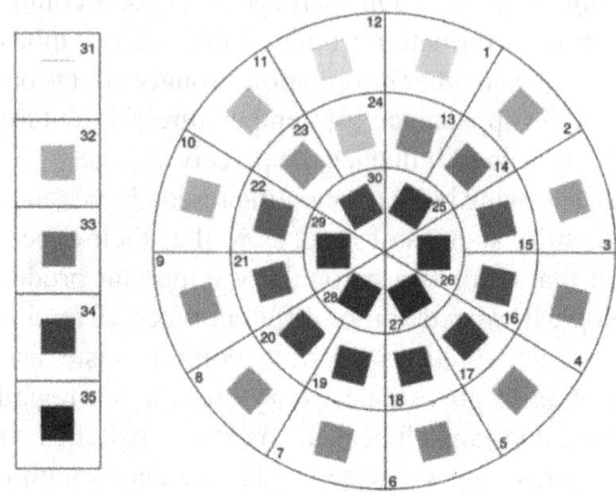

Fig. 1. Color panel used in the current study. (Color figure online)

The participants were asked to select a color that corresponds the most to a given item. The items included three voices (female, male, and child), five basic tastes (sweet, sour, salty, bitter, and umami), five types of oral chemesthesis (hot, spicy, sharp, fatty, and astringent) and eight kinds of functional foods. Functional foods (a term coined in Japan during the 1980s) are specially processed foods that include additional nutrients, such as vitamins, fiber, protein, and minerals, and thus can have beneficial effects on one's physiological state. Because they can have a positive effect on health beyond basic nutrition, the popularity of such foods has recently increased.

In the case of each taste, chemesthesis, and functional food, participants were also asked to write down the imagined food/product when they selected the color.

The results were analyzed in two ways. First, we compared the most commonly selected colors across different nations to understand cultural differences in cross-modal associations. Second, we compared the consistency/diversity of the answers by considering the Selected Colors (SC)-80 parameter, which was used in our study as an index of variability.

The idea behind SC-80 is to calculate the number of colors selected by 80% of the respondents, thus indicating the level of consistency of opinions among representatives of a single nation. For example, in Fig. 2, the horizontal axis represents the number of selected colors, and the vertical axis represents the percentage of respondents. A bold line shows the number of answers selected by 80% of the respondents. Thus, a low SC-80 means higher consistency of opinions among the participants.

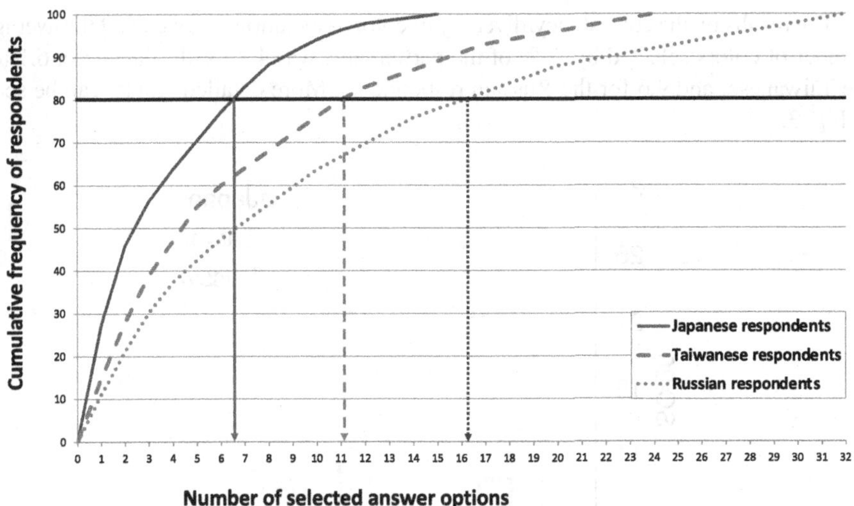

Fig. 2. Example of SC-80 calculation for *umami*. As can be seen by the graph, the Japanese participants demonstrate the highest consistency of opinions, and the Russian participants show the greatest amount of diversity. (Color figure online)

3 Results

3.1 Voices

Color–voice associations showed similarities among the participants, irrespective of the countries (Table 1). Female voices were mostly associated with the pink spectrum; male voices, with the blue spectrum; and child voices, with the yellow spectrum. However, some of the nuances of the selected tones were different, probably resulting from cultural differences, which are discussed below.

Table 1. Results of color-voice associations. (Color figure online)

	Japan	Taiwan	Russia
Female voice	light pink (33%) light coral (18%) light salmon (9%) moccasin (9%)	light pink (32%) light coral (29%) plum (11%)	plum (17%) light salmon (14%) light coral (11%)
Male voice	deep sky blue (43%) dark slate blue (17%) steel blue (7%) dark slate blue (7%)	deep sky blue (28%) steel blue (17%) dark slate blue (8%)	deep sky blue (17%) dark slate blue (13%) fire brick (10%)
Child voice	gold (49%) moccasin (19%) orange (13%)	moccasin (35%) gold (27%) ivory (7%)	moccasin (29%) gold (22%) green yellow (7%)

The results on the consistency/diversity of color associations showed that the average number of colors selected by 80% of the participants was 4.8 for the Japanese, 6.1 for the Taiwanese, and 9.6 for the Russian respondents. More detailed results can be seen in Fig. 3.

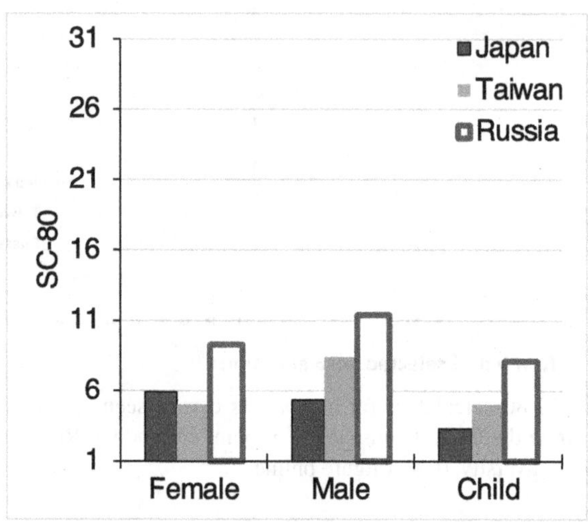

Fig. 3. SC-80 results for color–voice associations. (Color figure online)

3.2 Basic Tastes

Color-taste associations for sweet, salty, and sour were quite similar among the participants from different countries, with little variety, which is thought to have been caused by eating habits and/or individual tastes. However, the results of bitterness and umami showed greater diversity. The results are shown in Table 2.

Table 2. Results of color-tastes associations. (Color figure online)

	Japan	Taiwan	Russia
Sweet	light pink (46%) light coral (18%) light salmon (10%)	light pink (30%) light coral (28%) gold (10%)	light pink (30%) light coral (10%) light salmon (9%)
Salty	ivory (43%) steel blue (21%) cadet blue (7%)	ivory (24%) steel blue (20%) cadet blue (9%)	ivory (18%) steel blue (16%) cadet blue (13%)
Sour	gold (44%) moccasin (42%) green yellow (4%)	gold (27%) green yellow (17%) orange (13%)	gold (27%) moccasin (16%) yellow green (11%)
Bitter	dark sea green (25%) dark olive green (20%) fire brick (11%)	dark olive green (28%) fire brick (16%) yellow green (14%)	dark olive green (22%) dark slate blue (13%) fire brick (13%) black (10%)
Umami	peach puff (27%) orange (18%) moccasin (10%)	peach puff (15%) light salmon (13%) ivory (11%)	fire brick (11%) ivory (10%) light salmon (9%)

Considering the consistency/diversity of the answers, the above-mentioned tendencies among the countries could be observed: The Japanese participants showed a higher average consistency (i.e., lower SC-80 scores) of associations (5) than the Taiwanese (7.7) and Russian (9.8) participants. More detailed results can be seen from the SC-80 data in Fig. 4:

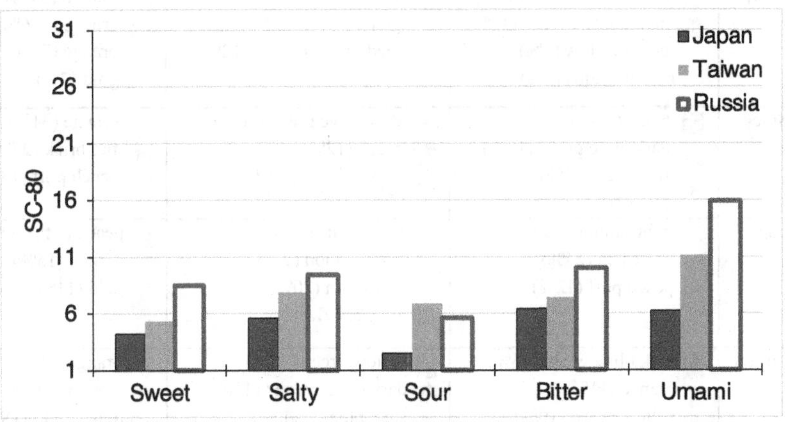

Fig. 4. SC-80 results for color–taste associations. (Color figure online)

3.3 Oral Chemesthesis

The results based on oral chemesthesis showed a high diversity in associations, which can be illustrated by different selected colors, particularly between Asian and Russian participants (see Table 3). The most similar results were found for hot (associated with the red spectrum) and fatty (associated with the yellow spectrum) tastes, whereas other items resulted in greater diversity.

The SC-80 results of associations between color and oral chemesthesis demonstrate a strong association between a hot taste and red among all participants, which is confirmed by the lowest SC-80 scores in the current study (see Fig. 5). Other items showed more diversity (which was the highest in the case of astringent taste); however, the Japanese participants in general showed higher consistency in their associations (5.2) than the Taiwanese (5.8) and Russian (6.4) participants.

Table 3. Results of associations between color and oral chemesthesis. (Color figure online)

	Japan	Taiwan	Russia
Hot	crimson (72%) tomato (25%)	crimson (55%) tomato (39%) fire brick (3%)	tomato (45%) crimson (32%) orange (5%)
Sharp	yellow green (45%) medium sea green (13%) green yellow (8%) medium aqua (8%)	yellow green (48%) green yellow (14%) medium sea green (12%)	tomato (37%) crimson (26%) orange (7%) gold (7%)
Spicy	black (21%) dark olive green (19%) fire brick (14%)	dark olive green (26%) black (12%) (10%)	orange (31%) fire brick (27%) peach puff (13%)
Fatty	light salmon (32%) moccasin (24%) peach puff (12%)	peach puff (21%) light salmon (21%) moccasin (20%) orange (9%)	peach puff (26%) orange (15%) gold (11%)
Astringent	dark olive green (26%) orange (11%) yellow green (10%)	yellow green (13%) dark olive green (11%) steel blue (9%)	orange (28%) tomato (13%) light salmon (8%)

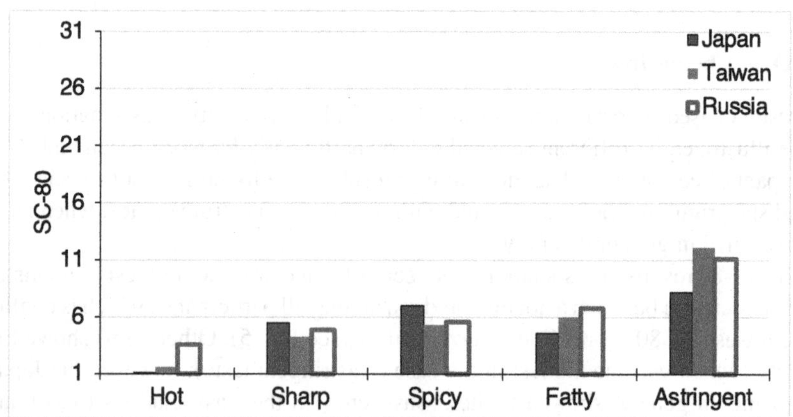

Fig. 5. SC-80 results for associations between color and oral chemesthesis. (Color figure online)

3.4 Functional Foods

The last part of questionnaire was focused on eight functional foods, i.e., functional foods for better sleep, functional foods that inhibit the absorption of dietary fat, functional foods that adjust one's gastrointestinal condition, functional foods that maintain skin moisture, functional foods decreasing blood pressure, salt-reduced foods, high-calorie foods, and comfort foods. The results showed significant diversity of associations in most cases, as described in Table 4.

Table 4. Results of associations between color and functional foods. (Color figure online)

	Japan	Taiwan	Russia
Functional foods for good sleep	steel blue (21%) light steel blue (9%) deep sky blue (8%)	ivory (53%) light steel blue (10%) light salmon (5%)	ivory (12%) steel blue (11%) l.s. blue (10%)
Functional foods that inhibit absorption of dietary fat	m. s. green (26%) yellow green (12%) green yellow (8%)	yellow green (25%) m.s. green (16%) green yellow (9%)	yellow green (22%) green yellow (10%) m.s. green (8%)
Functional foods that adjust gastrointestinal condition	ivory (25%) m. s. green (13%) peach puff (8%)	m. s. green (18%) yellow green (15%) moccasin (10%)	yellow green (17%) m. s. green (15%) ivory (9%)
Functional foods that maintain skin moistness	steel blue (14%) light salmon (12%) cadet blue (12%) light pink (7%)	ivory (22%) cadet blue (15%) steel blue (14%)	steel blue (20%) cadet blue (9%) med. turquoise (9%) m.s. green (8%)
Functional foods decreasing blood pressure	m.s. green (12%) cadet blue (10%) steel blue (7%)	ivory (14%) m.s. green (11%) sea green (8%)	crimson (12%) yellow green (9%) dark slate blue (7%) fire brick (7%)
Salt reduced foods	green yellow (12%) (8%) (7%)	ivory (20%) light salmon (13%) steel blue (10%)	ivory (21%) light salmon (13%) yellow green (11%)
High calorie foods	gold (18%) orange (17%) tomato (13%)	orange (27%) gold (27%) crimson (13%) tomato (11%)	orange (17%) gold (14%) tomato (13%)
Comfort foods	light salmon (13%) peach puff (10%) orange (8%) fire brick (8%)	light coral (12%) moccasin (10%) light pink (9%)	light salmon (11%) peach puff (11%) yellow green (10%) moccasin (9%)

According to the results on the consistency/diversity of color associations, we can also suggest a lower level of familiarity of functional foods compared to the previously discussed items. The mean SC-80 score was the lowest among the Taiwanese respondents (9.4) in comparison to the Japanese (10.9) and Russian (11.7) participants. The difference was particularly significant for functional foods for better sleep and high-calorie foods. More detailed results are presented in Fig. 6.

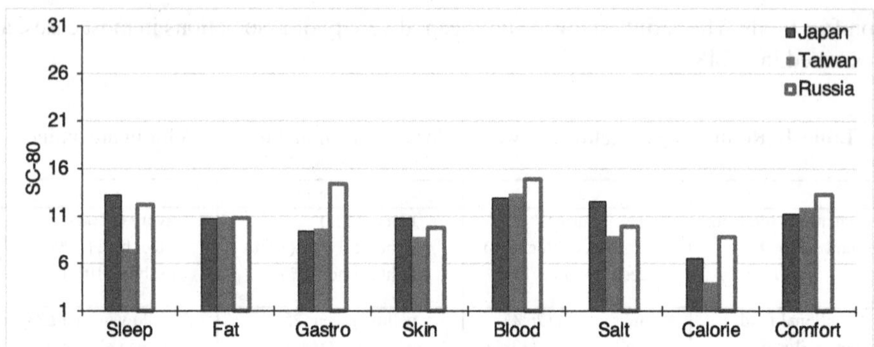

Fig. 6. SC-80 results for associations between color and functional foods. (Color figure online)

4 Discussion

4.1 Voices

A *female voice* was mostly associated with the pink spectrum in all three countries, but with certain differences. Over 30% of Taiwanese and Japanese respondents selected a light pink color, which differs from Russian data, where the most selected color was a darker variant of the pink spectrum, that is, plum. Furthermore, among the Japanese participants, the opposite tendency could be clearly observed: female voice was associated with the yellow spectrum by 25% of the respondents.

Previous experimental studies have demonstrated that a lower pitch is usually associated with darker colors [20, 21], and a high pitch is associated with brighter colors [22, 23]. Thus, the above results may have a correlation with the pitch of the voice, with European voices having a lower pitch compared to Japanese voices on average [24]. Moreover, it has been found that Japanese women tend to speak to strangers in a higher voice than American women because it is considered socially more attractive to do so [25].

Following the above-mentioned common cross-modal correspondence between high pitch and light colors, a *child voice* was associated mainly with the yellow spectrum among a majority of the respondents. Other selected colors were also predominantly close to yellow. Consistently, the *male voice* was lower in pitch and associated mostly with the blue spectrum, which also corresponds with the previous findings on this subject [26].

4.2 Tastes

Sweet taste was mainly associated with pink, which corresponds with previous studies [11, 19]. In some preceding studies [27, 28] sweetness was associated with red; however, the red spectrum was not frequently selected by the respondents of the current study.

Specific food associations with sweet taste differed owing to various eating habits. Nearly 20% of Japanese participants listed fruits (mostly strawberries and peaches, or other sweets with a fruit taste), although this association was practically absent in

Taiwanese and Russian data. The most popular answer among Taiwanese respondents was "candy," which was chosen by 37% of the respondents. Russian participants showed diversity in their associations, with the most frequently mentioned sweet foods being sugar and lollipops.

Salty taste provided a strong association with ivory color (closest to white among the demonstrated color patches) for a majority of the respondents, which corresponds with the previous studies [11, 27, 29]. Another strong color association was the blue spectrum (cadet and steel blues were second and third selected colors among the three countries).

This selection of colors (dominantly white and blue) can be explained by the specific associations with salty taste. The most popular association was salt (41% of all respondents), and the second most popular answer was sea or ocean water (25% of all respondents). Among other food associations, salty snacks (potato chips and popcorn) were also mentioned; however, the total number of such answers was relatively low.

Sour taste demonstrated a similarity in the cross-modal correspondence among the respondents, being mostly associated with the yellow spectrum. Although the most commonly selected color was gold, other responses demonstrated several differences, which can be presumed to be related to the eating habits in the participating countries. The most common association among all respondents was with lemon and other citrus fruits (mentioned by 63% of the participants). However, the Taiwanese respondents mentioned other fruits, such as plums, tangerines, or passion fruit, and the Japanese respondents mentioned vinegar, a frequently used food in Japan.

Cross-modal associations between sour and yellow are consistent with the results of previous studies [27]; however, in some studies, this taste was also associated with green [11, 19, 29]. In the current study, the green spectrum was not popular among the respondents: green-yellow was rarely chosen among the Japanese data (4%) and was selected by 7% of the Taiwanese respondents and 11% of Russian respondents.

The color representation of *bitter taste* showed more diversity among the three countries, though the majority of the selected colors was in a dark spectrum. The most frequently selected color, chosen by 23% of all respondents in the study, was dark olive green, which was the most popular among Russian and Taiwanese respondents, and the second most popular in Japan.

Most of the Japanese respondents showed strong associations of bitter taste with vegetables, herbs, matcha, and green tea, which can explain the tendency for selecting green. The most popular association in Taiwan (nearly 50% of the answers) was bitter melon, which was also mentioned by some Japanese respondents. In Russia this vegetable is unfamiliar, and the most popular answers were bitter chocolate and coffee, with beer also being mentioned. Both the Taiwanese (18%) and Russian (17.6%) respondents mentioned medicine or pills, although this answer is absent in the data from the Japanese respondents.

These results regarding taste–color correspondence are inconsistent with those of previous studies, where bitter taste was associated with black [11, 19] and purple [30], but are consistent with the results from a study by O'Mahony [27], where the participants responded with a green color. This can likely be explained by the cultural differences between the respondents of this and previous studies, or by the more limited variety of color stimuli in other studies. Still, we can observe the common tendency to associate bitter taste with the dark spectrum in all related studies.

The *umami* data showed the most obvious difference in the cross-modal associations among Asian and Russian respondents, which can probably be explained by the lack of knowledge and familiarity with this taste. In both the Japanese and Taiwanese subjects, umami was associated with the pleasant yellow spectrum, and the most popular color was peach puff. Among the Japanese participants the strongest associations were dashi and related products (*konbu* and *katsuobushi*, i.e., fermented skipjack tuna), consommé and miso. Ajinomoto, a product containing glutamic acid, was also frequently mentioned. Taiwanese respondents predominantly (47%) mentioned fish, shrimp, sashimi, and other types of seafood, and 8% answered the ocean itself. The second strong association (21%) was with Ajinomoto and all-purpose seasoning containing glutamic acid. Thus, a high level of familiarity of this taste is suggested for the respondents in Asian countries.

However, these results were completely different from the Russian data, where SC-80 was 15.9 (the highest SC-80 score in the current study), which indicates a considerable diversity of opinions. The most popular color (selected by only 11% of participants) was fire brick, which can likely be connected with the most common association with umami, that is soy sauce (probably one of the most familiar images of Japanese food in Russia). Among the Russian respondents, 17% answered that they did not have any associations with the word. The other answers were different and included meat, chicken, Japanese sweets, sushi, and cheese, among others, which illustrated unfamiliarity with the taste and was reflected in the variety of selected colors.

Previous studies also confirm a tendency toward a lack of strong associations and taste confusion when considering umami [19]. Because umami quite recently became a part of international gastronomic vocabulary, many people still have difficulties in recognizing and distinguishing umami from other taste sensations. Thus, further experimental research is needed to explore the understanding of this taste among different nations.

4.3 Oral Chemesthesis

Hot taste was strongly associated with the red spectrum among all three countries. The two most popular colors were crimson and tomato. The overwhelming majority of respondents mentioned red hot pepper, with other answers including fire, tabasco, kimchi, and different types of spicy foods. The SC-80 score for hot taste was the lowest of all items, which illustrates the consistency of this cross-modal correspondence among representatives of different cultures. The possible reason for such association with red color is its connection to hot temperature. Such cross-modal association with thermal stimuli have been discussed and confirmed in a range of studies [31, 32].

Opinions regarding *sharp taste* showed correspondence among Japanese and Taiwanese respondents, who associated it with yellow-green. This color is close to the color of wasabi, which has an extremely popular association with sharp taste. The most popular association with this taste in both Japan and Taiwan was wasabi itself (81% and 64%, respectively).

However, Russian respondents associated a sharp similarly to hot taste, mostly with the red color. The most possible reason lies in the nuances of the translation, that is, in the Japanese and Taiwanese versions of the online form, the question as about the "taste of wasabi" (thus, providing a direct association), whereas the Russian version used the word "sharp," with a more vague and abstract meaning that can be associated with "hot." Still, another important factor we should not underestimate is the fact that wasabi is less popular in Russia, than in Asian countries, and people are less familiar with its sharp taste.

A similar situation can be seen in the case of *spicy taste*. The dominant association, often mentioned by Asian participants, was black pepper, and the selected colors were mostly within the dark spectrum. However, the most selected color among Russian participants was orange, and the strongest associations were with curry and different spices, such as cinnamon or ginger. The difference can be once again explained by the linguistic nuances. In the Japanese and Taiwanese questionnaires, the term "black pepper" was used, whereas the question in the Russian version contained the word "spicy," which is probably associated more with curry and spices than with black pepper (thus, explaining the orange color).

Fatty taste in all responding countries was mostly associated with the yellow spectrum. However, particular associations with this taste demonstrated certain cultural differences. The most popular answers among the majority of respondents were meat fat and oil, although several specific foods were also mentioned. For example, Taiwanese participants frequently mentioned fried chicken and pork stew, Japanese participants recalled deep fried foods such as tempura, and in Russia, popular answers were butter, lard, and burgers. The average SC-80 for fatty taste was relatively low (4.6 for the Japanese, 6 for the Taiwanese, and 6.8 for the Russia participants), which is confirmed by the selection of yellow spectrum independent of the country and eating habits.

The results for *astringent taste* showed a discrepancy in the answers between the Taiwanese, Japanese, and Russian data. The most popularly selected colors in Japan were olive green, orange, and yellow-green. This color selection can be explained by the common association with this taste sensation, with the most popular answers among the Japanese participants being tea (31%) and matcha (7%). Still, some of them (23%) recalled persimmon, which resulted in the selection of an orange color. In Taiwan, among the most popular associations (25%) were different types of fruits, including unripe fruit, lemon, and guava. The Russian respondents demonstrated the highest consistency in their answers, with 66% associating this taste with persimmon, which was reflected in the color selection as well.

The average SC-80 for astringent taste was the highest among the results for oral chemesthesis (8.2 for the Japanese, 12.1 for the Taiwanese, and 11.1 for the Russian participants), which means that cross-modal associations considering this sensation are extremely individualized and likely dependent on the specific associations with food products.

4.4 Functional Foods

The results regarding *functional foods for better sleep* showed considerable differences in the cross-modal associations. The Taiwanese participants showed a consistency in their answers and mostly associated it with milk and other milk products; consequently, more than one half (53%) selected ivory (white) color. In the Russian participants, the most selected color was also ivory; however, the proportion was much lower (12%). The strongest associations among the Russian participants were connected with tea, including different types of herbal tea (mentioning lavender, chamomile, other herbs, and honey, which is often added to both milk and tea).

The colors selected by the Japanese respondents were of the blue spectrum. The associations were mostly abstract, with the strongest (26.4%) being connected with relaxation, comfort, and sleep. Among the specific foods mentioned, the most popular were supplements for good sleep, products containing GABA, and milk products.

It can be seen that the commonly selected color among all responding nations was light steel blue, which is associated with different kinds of foods and ideas. Thus, we can conclude that this color is associated with the concept of sleep in general. We can also see a tendency of this kind of food (as well as relaxing images in general) being associated with a blue spectrum.

Functional foods that inhibit absorption of dietary fat were dominantly associated with the green and yellow spectrum. The three major colors were the same among the responding nations, differing in ratio. The associations were also quite similar, that is, predominantly different kinds of vegetables (Japanese at 45.2%, Taiwanese at 41%, and Russians at 41%).

However, some specific associations were also mentioned. For example, 23% of Russian respondents recalled various fruits; this answer was rare in Taiwan (7%) and absent in Japan. Among the Taiwanese respondents, 24% answered green tea, which can perhaps be attributed to some successful products and their advertisements. This association was rare in Japan (less than 2%) and absent in Russia. The Japanese respondents often mentioned supplements and foods for specified health use, which were absent in the Russian and Taiwanese data.

The results of the data on *functional foods that adjust one's gastrointestinal condition* showed correspondence between Russian and Taiwanese participants (and a similarity with the previous association): The most selected colors were yellow and medium sea green. Correlated with these results, 41% of the Taiwanese and 31% of the Russian respondents mentioned vegetables in their answers.

In Japan, the most commonly selected color was white, and the strongest association was with yogurt, milk products, and lactic acid bacteria (35.2%). The second popular color was medium sea green. For this, 14% of Japanese respondents mentioned vegetables, and 8.4% mentioned dietary fiber. The SC-80 results showed considerable differences in opinions between the Asian (Japanese at 9.4 and Taiwanese at 9.7) and Russian respondents (14.4).

Functional foods that maintain skin moisture showed a tendency to be associated with the blue spectrum, though with some differences across countries. The most commonly selected color in the Japanese and Russian data was steel blue, but among Taiwanese respondents was ivory (as in the case of functional foods for better sleep).

The most popular associations in Japan were water (29.6%) and collagen (23.5%). These two associations were also mentioned in the Taiwanese data (22% and 8%, respectively). In addition, 24.5% of the Taiwanese participants mentioned various types of fruits; however, owing to their different colors, none of them played a significant role in Taiwanese data. The most popular answer among the Russian respondents was water (35.8%), and the second strongest association was cucumbers (13.2%). Both the Russian and Taiwanese participants mentioned aloe, which was absent among the Japanese responses.

A large diversity could be seen in the results for *functional foods decreasing blood pressure.* None of the colors were chosen by more than 14% of the respondents, and the major chosen colors are also different.

The most popular association among the Taiwanese participants was with various types of vegetables and plants (38.3%); which resulted in a dominance of the green spectrum. However, the major color chosen was white, which is associated with pills, water, and oatmeal.

Vegetables were often mentioned by the Japanese respondents (24.2%), and the most commonly selected color was medium sea green. Other popular associations included healthy and salt-reduced foods, supplements, and some abstract concepts such as "relaxing" and "pleasant" which can be illustrated by the large diversity of the selected colors.

Paradoxically, the major color associated with low blood pressure among the Russian participants was bright red, or crimson. Among the strongest associations with this color were pomegranate and blood itself. Vegetables and tea were also mentioned by the respondents, which resulted in the second major color, yellow-green. In general, the color spectrum associated with those foods in the Russian data is closer to dark red and purple.

In the case of *salt-reduced foods*, we can also see a diversity in the answers and similarities among the Russian and Taiwanese responses in comparison to the Japanese. In both the Taiwanese and Russian responses, the most commonly selected color was ivory, and the second was light salmon. The major associations among the Taiwanese respondents were with boiled foods (dominantly chicken) (28.5%) and vegetables (25%). Among the Russian respondents, this color was associated with rice, cottage cheese, bread, water, and plain food. The major association in the Russian data is greens and vegetables (mentioned by 29.4% of the respondents), with yellow-green being only the third most common color selected.

The Japanese respondents showed a greater diversity of opinions, and the associations were dominantly abstract, including light taste (23%) and healthy and natural (11%). Among the specific products frequently mentioned were vegetables (12.5%) and salt-reduced products, such as miso soup and soy sauce (13.2%). Associated colors are close to the yellow spectrum, and even the most widely selected color was chosen by only 12.5% of the respondents.

Results regarding *high-calorie foods* demonstrated a higher similarity. The yellow spectrum was dominant in all three countries, and the associations were also quite similar among the respondents, with some national differences in several products, e.g., fried chicken in Taiwan (29%), *agemono* (fried foods) in Japan (17%), and burgers and fast food in Russia (38%).

For *comfort foods*, the diversity of the answers and chosen colors was high. As in the case of foods decreasing blood pressure, none of the colors was selected by more than 14% of the participants.

Taiwanese respondents had strong associations with sweet foods (cakes, candies, and chocolate, 58.5%), which resulted in light pink and light coral colors being dominant in the data of sweet taste. The Japanese respondents mentioned home food, food cooked by their mother (16%), and a nostalgic feeling connected with the food eaten as a child (6%). Traditional Japanese food products were also often mentioned (17%). Thus, this suggests that comfort food for the Japanese respondents is connected with their memories of the past. The mostly associated color spectrum was yellow.

The yellow spectrum was dominant in the Russian data as well. The most common associations were with sweets (19%) and vegetables (17%), both of which were insignificant in the Japanese data.

5 General Discussion

The results of this study show several interesting points worthy of discussion. First, we confirmed the hypothesis regarding the critical impact of cultural background and eating habits on the cross-modal associations, which in the current study were more remarkable for specific items such as functional foods, than for voices and three basic tastes (sweet, salty, and sour). Nevertheless, bitter taste and umami showed a significant discrepancy in the selected colors and associations between the participants from the three countries. Such a discrepancy, as indicated by the particular answers and foods mentioned, can be explained by both individual preference (as in the case of bitter taste) and by the familiarity with the taste (as in the case of umami).

The results regarding oral chemesthesis demonstrated more differences between the participants from Asia and Russia. Some (including sharp and spicy taste) were caused by linguistic nuances, and others (astringent taste) by different eating behaviors. Although, both hot and fatty taste showed considerable similarities in their color representations, which makes them similar to the basic tastes, as demonstrated by the familiarity and consistency of commonly selected colors.

The most significant diversities could be observed in the cases of functional foods. Among them, certain similarities of the responses were demonstrated for foods that inhibit the absorption of dietary fat (associated with the yellow-green spectrum), and for high-calorie foods (associated with the yellow and red spectra). However, other types of functional foods showed a high discrepancy in their answers (sometimes with similarities between only two, but not three, of the countries). Thus, we can conclude that these types of foods are not equally familiar to all respondents, evoking more diverse associations.

Second, the SC-80 results showed several tendencies: 1) The Japanese respondents showed a more significant consistency in their cross-modal associations in comparison with the participants from Taiwan and Russia. 2) Consistency of the selected colors is the lowest for functional foods, which means a lack of strong common associations. The same tendency could be seen in the umami results among the Russian data.

A comparative graph of the SC-80 parameters throughout all items of the study is presented in Fig. 7.

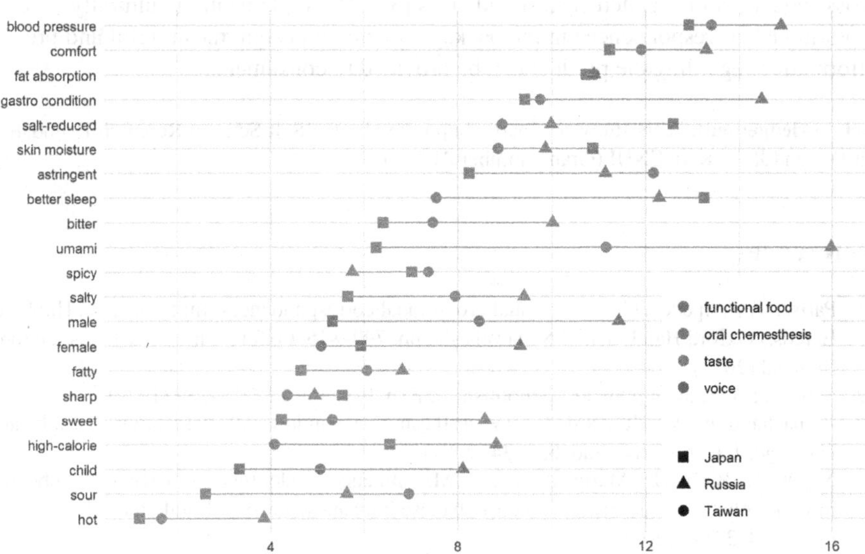

Fig. 7. Comparative SC-80 results for all items. (Color figure online)

The possible reasons for cross-modal mappings between colors and tastes has been discussed for many decades, and related studies have demonstrated that people tend to connect such distant properties in a seemingly consistent manner [33]. Because food colors are often correlated with the properties of taste and help set our gustatory expectations [34], a fundamental affinity among the dimensions of these two stimuli is suggested.

The process of selecting a color associated with a particular item can be underpinned by the semantic network in which different percepts are linked with each other [35, 36]. People typically match pairs of color and taste when they denote similar properties, and such connections are developed based on accumulated knowledge and daily experiences, giving rise to the cultural differences observed in the current study.

In semantic networks, two different representations (such as sweet taste or female voice) can be both related to a single color, which can play an interfering role between two dimensions. As shown in the current study, certain colors likely evoke multiple associated representations, whereas the latter are not connected directly with each other. Moreover, the same color may be associated with different taste representations, depending on the context in which it is presented. Thus, the implicated meaning of a color can be constrained by the presentation format, eliciting quite different expectations [37].

For example, the yellow spectrum is typically associated with a child's voice, sour taste, fatty taste, and high calorie foods. It can be suggested that this multiple cross-modal association with yellow derives from the fact that children need those foods and tastes for their growing. By contrast, pink is associated with both a female voice and sweet taste. This connection is possibly the reason we have the metaphor of a "sweetie".

Knowledge of such color triggers that can evoke specific associations in a particular culture can be used in marketing and food production. For example, consumers may expect a specific taste of a product based on the color of the packaging in line with cross-modal feature-related correspondences [38]. By implementing culturally specific cross-modal correspondences in the packaging or food design, meaningful and precise information regarding the product can be provided to consumers.

Acknowledgement. This study was partly supported by the Salt Science Research Foundation (20D3) and JSPS KAKENHI (Grant Number 21F21013).

References

1. Parise, C.V., Spence, C.: Audiovisual crossmodal correspondences. In: Simner, J., Hubbard, E. (eds.) Oxford Handbook of Synaesthesia, pp. 790–815. Oxford University Press, Oxford, England (2013)
2. Sapir, E.: A study in phonetic symbolism. J. Exp. Psychol. **12**, 225–239 (1929)
3. Ramachandran, V., Hubbard, E.: Synaesthesia – a window into perception, thought and language. J. Conscious. Stud. **8**, 3–34 (2001)
4. Nehme, L., Barbar, R., Maric, Y., Jacquot, M.: Influence of odor function and color symbolism in odor-color associations: a French-Lebanese-Taiwanese cross-cultural study. Food Qual. Prefer. **49**, 33–41 (2016)
5. Knöferle, K., Spence, C.: Crossmodal correspondences between sounds and tastes. Psychon. Bull. Rev. **19**(6), 992–1006 (2012). https://doi.org/10.3758/s13423-012-0321-z
6. Spence, C.: On the psychological impact of food colour. Flavour **4**, 21 (2015)
7. Cruz, A., Green, B.G.: Thermal stimulation of taste. Nature **403**, 889–892 (2000)
8. Bult, J.H.F., De Wijk, R.A., Hummel, T.: Investigations on multimodal sensory integration: Texture, taste, and ortho- and retronasal olfactory stimuli in concert. Neurosci. Lett. **411**, 6–10 (2007)
9. Zampini, M., Spence, C.: Assessing the role of sound in the perception of food and drink. Chemosens. Percept. **3**, 57–67 (2010)
10. Spence, C.: On the relationship (s) between color and taste/flavor. Exp. Psychol. **66**(2), 99–111 (2019)
11. Woods, A.T., Spence, C. Using single colors and color pairs to communicate basic tastes. i-Perception **7**(4), 1–15 (2016)
12. Kittler, P.G., Sucher, K.P.: Food and Culture, 5th edn. Wadsworth, Belmont, CA (2007)
13. Levitan, C.A., Ren, J., Woods, A.T., Boesveldt, S., Chan, J.S., McKenzie, K.J., et al.: Cross-cultural color-odor associations. PLoS ONE **9**, e101651 (2014). https://doi.org/10.1371/journal.pone.0101651
14. Shankar, M.U., Levitan, C., Spence, C.: Grape expectations: the role of cognitive influences in color-flavor interactions. Conscious. Cogn. **19**, 380–390 (2010)
15. Velasco, C., Michel, C., Youssef, J., Gamez, X., Cheok, A.D., Spence, C.: Colour–taste correspondences: designing food experiences to meet expectations or to surprise. Int. J. Food Des. **1**(2), 83–102 (2016)
16. Bremner, A.J., Caparos, S., Davidoff, J., de Fockert, J., Linnell, K.J., Spence, C.: Bouba and Kiki in Namibia? a remote culture make similar shape-sound matches, but different shape-taste matches to Westerners. Cognition **126**, 165–172 (2013)
17. Ngo, M.K., Velasco, C., Salgado, A., Boehm, E., O'Neill, D., Spence, C.: Assessing cross-modal correspondences in exotic fruit juices: the case of shape and sound symbolism. Food Qual. Prefer. **28**, 361–369 (2013)

18. Piqueras-Fiszman, B., Velasco, C., Spence, C.: Exploring implicit and explicit crossmodal colour-flavour correspondences in product packaging. Food Qual. Prefer. **25**, 148–155 (2012)
19. Wan, X., Woods, A.T., van den Bosch, J.J.F., McKenzie, K.J., Velasco, C., Spence, C.: Cross-cultural differences in crossmodal correspondences between basic tastes and visual features. Front. Psychol. Cogn. **5**, 1365 (2014)
20. Ward, J., Huckstepp, B., Tsakanikos, A.: Sound-colour synaesthesia: to what extent does it use cross-modal mechánisms common to us all? Cortex **42**, 264–280 (2006)
21. Miller, C.B., Boteler, E.H., Larcombe, G.K.: Seeing things in my head: a synesthete's images for music and notes. Perception **32**, 1359–1376 (2003)
22. Anikin, A., Johansson, N.: Implicit associations between individual properties of color and sound. Atten. Percept. Psychophys. **81**(3), 764–777 (2018). https://doi.org/10.3758/s13414-018-01639-7
23. Fernay, L., Reby, D., Ward, J.: Visualized voices: a case study of audio-visual synesthesia. Neurocase **18**, 50–56 (2012)
24. Bezooijen, V.R.: Sociocultural aspects of pitch differences between Japanese and Dutch women. Lang. Speech **38**(3), 253–265 (1995)
25. Yamazawa, H., Hollien, H.: Speaking fundamental frequency patterns of Japanese women. Phonetica **49**, 128–140 (1992)
26. Miyahara, T., Koda, A., Sekiguchi, R., Amemiya, T.: A psychological experiment on the correspondence between colors and voiced vowels in non-synesthetes. Kansei Eng. Int. J. **11**, 27–34 (2012)
27. O'Mahony, M.: Gustatory responses to non-gustatory stimuli. Perception **12**, 627–633 (1983)
28. Tomasik-Krotki, J., Strojny, J.: Scaling of sensory impressions. J. Sens. Stud. **23**, 251–266 (2008)
29. Koch, C., Koch, E.C.: Preconceptions of taste based on color. J. Psychol. **137**(3), 233–242 (2003)
30. Fateminia, M., Ghotbabadi, T.D., Azad, K.M.: Perceptions of the taste of colors in children and adults. Color. Res. Appl. **45**(6), 743–753 (2020)
31. Spence, C.: Crossmodal correspondences: a tutorial review. Atten. Percept. Psychophys. **73**(4), 971–995 (2011)
32. Spence, C.: Temperature based cross-modal correspondences: causes and consequences. Multisens. Res. **33**, 645–682 (2020)
33. Spence, C., Levitan, C.A.: Explaining crossmodal correspondences between colours and tastes. i-Perception **12**(3), 1–28 (2021)
34. Piqueras-Fiszman, B., Spence, C.: Senspory expectations based on product-extrinsic food cues: an interdisciplinary review of the empirical evidence and theoretical accounts. Food Qual. Prefer. **40**, 165–179 (2015)
35. Martino, G., Marks, L.E.: Perceptual and linguistic interactions in speeded classification: tests of the semantic coding hypothesis. Perception **28**, 903–924 (1999)
36. Martino, G., Marks, L.E. Syneshtesia. strong and weak. Curr. Direct. Psychol. Sci. **10**, 61–65 (2001)
37. Spence, C., Levitan, C.A. Exploring the links between colours and tastes/flavours. J. Percept. Imaging **5**, 000408-1 – 000408-16 (2022)
38. Velasco, C., Woods, A.T., Petit, O., Cheok, A.D., Spence, C.: Crossmodal correspondences between taste and shape, and their implications for product packaging: a review. Food Qual. Prefer. **52**, 17–26 (2016)

Cultural Differences Between Iranian and Chinese in Visual Search Repetition Effect

Pei-Luen Patrick Rau(✉), Hengameh Akbbrian, and Jian Zheng

Department of Industrial Engineering, Tsinghua University, Beijing, China
rpl@mail.tsinghua.edu.cn

Abstract. People in cultures of a short-term orientation rely more on experience than those in cultures of a long-term orientation do. In visual search tasks, attention is guided by experience and will be directed to the target sooner if the layout is similar to the immediately former task trial. We hypothesize that individuals in countries of a short-term orientation, e.g., Iran, will demonstrate a larger repetition effect while perform visual search tasks than those in countries of a long-term orientation, e.g., China, do. Thirty Iranian and 30 Chinese participants searched for a letter O among reversed Qs, for a vertical line among tilted lines, and vice versa. The layout of each trial could be similar (of the same pattern but with shorter distances among items) or different with the former trial. Iranian participants outperformed the Chinese only in trials similar with former ones. The long-term orientation affects repetition effect in visual search. Cultural differences in visual search repetition effect should be considered in designing for global users and international communications.

Keywords: Cultural difference · Long-term orientation · Repetition effect · Visual attention · Visual search

1 Introduction

Visual search is a common activity that people perform, perhaps unconsciously, every day. Each morning we open our eyes and scan the visual environment, e.g., a bedroom, for a certain object, e.g., an alarm clock [1]. Experience, knowledge, or memory about where the target tends to appear guided attention in visual search [2, 3]. We will probably begin the search for the alarm clock from the desk, rather than the ceiling or floor, because our experience tells us the clock should be on the desk. Experience directs our visual attention to a certain location (the desk) to find the target (the clock) efficiently.

One type of the knowledge is contextual cueing, which refers to the finding that (implicitly) learned associations between targets and the spatial configurations can facilitate visual search [4]: Targets that appear in the same spatial configuration of distractors over repeated trials are detected faster than targets that appear in a new configuration. This repetition effect is most salient between two adjacent trials [5], and the contextual cueing still works in re-scaled display, i.e., the distance between items in the "repeated" trials increases or decreases [6]. For example, in the expanded display, the distance

P.-L. P. Rau (Ed.): HCII 2022, LNCS 13311, pp. 396–404, 2022.
https://doi.org/10.1007/978-3-031-06038-0_29

between items was amplified (e.g., by a factor of 1.25), but the configuration or the relative location among items stayed the same. In this study, we focused on the re-scaled repetition effect.

Two relevant phenomena are the inter-trial priming effect and the visual marking effect. Inter-trial priming indicates that repeated defining feature of the target between successive trials facilitate visual search, compared with changed defining feature of the target [7]. Different from inter-trial priming, in contextual cueing the feature of the target and distractors stay constant throughout a whole block. Visual marking indicates using positional memory to guide visual attention to ignore pre-cued position of distractors and thus facilitate visual search [8]. Visual marking contributes to the contextual cueing effect if trials are exactly repeated, but if trials are rescaled, it is not the location but the spatial association among items that facilitates searching.

According to the model of Guided Search 4.0 [9], the guiding activation of visual attention is a weighted sum of bottom-up and top-down activation. Researchers often use the response time (RT) $\times$ set size function to isolate different processing stages in visual search [10]. If some factors provide guidance for attention in visual search, the searching will become more efficient and the slope will become flatter; otherwise, if the non-search portion of the task, e.g., response priming, is changed, only the intercept but not the slope will be affected [11]. In most contextual cueing studies, only the intercept was affected, indicating that the contextual cueing effect works as a response prime more than attentional guidance [12], although it can provide guidance after some exposure time [13]. In other words, the weight of the contextual cueing in the activation map is only significant under certain circumstances.

The weight associated with the contextual cueing activation in visual search is how much people rely on the implicitly learnt knowledge to find the target. Some people may rely on this knowledge more than others do. The long-term orientation (LTO) refers to the extent of individuals in a culture focusing on the future rather than the present or the past [14]. Countries with higher LTO look forward to the future, whereas countries with low LTO value experience and traditions to a higher extent. Compared with people from a high LTO culture, people in a country with low LTO are more likely to rely on experience of handling similar problems to solve the problem at hand. China is a country with high LTO (87), and Iran is a country with low LTO (14, https://www.hofstede-insights.com/country-comparison/china,iran/). According to the difference in LTO, Iranian would rely more on experience to solve problems than Chinese do. We hypothesize that in a visual search task, although both Chinese and Iranian will respond faster if the current trial is similar to the former one, the Iranian will perform the task more efficiently than the Chinese do in those repeated trials.

Visual attention is affected by cultural factors [e.g., 15, 16]. East Asians attend to the whole field, whereas Americans focus on salient objects [16]. For example, when looking at a picture depicting a tiger in the forest, Americans began to look at the tiger sooner, and fixated more on it, than the Chinese did; whereas, the Chinese made more saccades to the forest than the Americans did [15]. Previous work about the effect of cultural differences on visual search have almost exclusively focused on comparing East Asian and western cultures. For example, Americans are better at searching for long among short lines than searching for short among long lines; there is no significant difference in performing these two tasks by Japanese participants [17]; In a color change detection task, East Asians performed better than Americans did when items were spaced more widely apart, but performed worse than the Americans did when items were spaced close together, and responded slower than Americans did when the changes happened in the screen center [18]. Only a few studies have compared west Asian and western cultures: Saudi participants had more fixations and longer search times than British participants did in a visual search task [19]. The comparison between west and east Asian cultures and the relevant influence on visual search has not been conducted. This study would add to our knowledge about how cultural differences (within Asia) affect top-down processing in visual search.

Because the effect of culture differences on visual search might depend on particular stimuli [17], we used both letters and lines and swapped the roles of target and distractors between blocks. Relevantly, we expected to observe the search asymmetry, i.e., search efficiency changes when targets and distractors switch roles [20].

2 Method

2.1 Participants

Thirty Iranian (15 women, mean age = 22.5 years) were recruited from a university in Iran, and thirty Chinese (14 women, mean age = 25.2 years) were recruited from a university in China. All had normal or corrected to normal vision. Participants received either 30 CNY (equal to 4.6 USD at that time) or gifts of equal worth.

Sample size is calculated on the basis of a previous study [17], with an F to η_p^2 transformation [21], using G* Power [22]. Given that the effect size is very large, i.e., $\eta_p^2 = .70$, having six participants is enough to achieve a power of .95. However, because we planned to use fewer trials than the previous study, we still recruited 30 participants in each group, resulting in a power over .99.

2.2 Apparatus and Stimuli

Stimuli were white letters or lines located within 20 × 20 pixel squares on a black background and presented on a 13.3-inch LCD monitor (resolution 1366 × 768, refresh rate 60 Hz). Letters could be horizontally reversed Q or O [as in 23]; lines could be vertical or tilted [as in 24]. The angle of the intersecting line in the reversed Q stimuli was 45° clockwise from the bottom. The tilted lines (/) were formed by rotating the vertical lines (|) 15° clockwise. Searching for reversed Q among Os and for tilted line among vertical lines should be more efficient than vice versa [20]. Trials could be of normal or contracted display. In the normal display, the distance between items was 90 pixels; in the contracted display, the distance between items was 50 pixels. The distance between the screen and the participants' eyes was about 40 cm. The experiment program was developed using C# in Visual Studio. Figure 1 presents example stimuli.

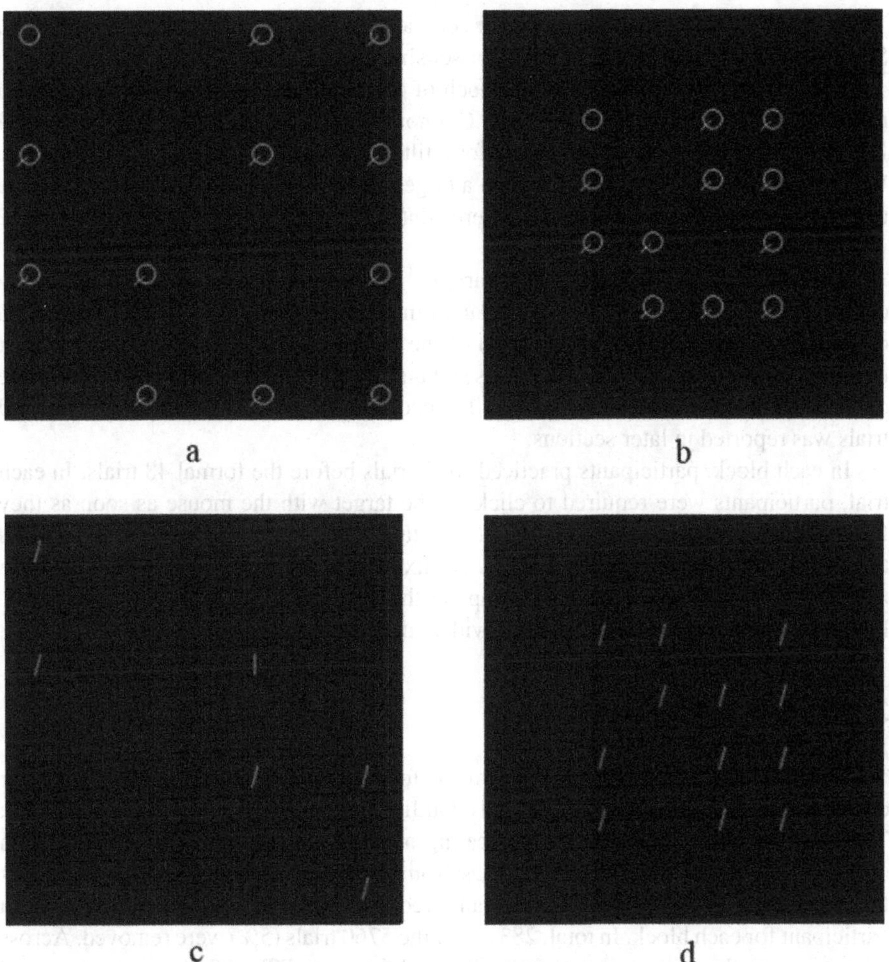

Fig. 1. Stimulus examples trials. A contracted display (b) following a *similar* normal trial (a) in Block 2 (target present). A contracted display (d, target absent) following a *different* normal trial (c, target present) in Block 3.

2.3 Procedure and Design

The independent variables included culture, target couple, density, relation, and set size. The dependent variables were accuracy and RT. Culture was the between-subjects factor of interest. Target couple referred to the combination of target and distractor, and had two levels, i.e., letters and lines, which were later analyzed separately. Density could be normal or contracted, and relation applied only to the contracted trials and referred to whether the current (contracted) trial was similar or different with the former (normal) trial. Later analysis only included the contracted trials. Set size referred to the number of elements, including both the target and distractors, and could be 3, 6, or 12 [as in 17].

The number of the target could be one or zero, and all the other elements are distractors. Set size was varied to calculate the RT × set size function [11].

The experiment included 4 blocks each of 48 trials. The tasks were to search for a reversed Q among Os in Block 1, for an O among reversed Qs in Block 2, for a vertical line among tilted lines in Block 3, and for a tilted line among vertical lines in Block 4. Within each block, half of the trials had a target, and the other half did not. Half of the trials were normal, and the other half were contracted. The set size could be 3, 6, or 12 with equal probability.

The most important independent variable was inter-trial relation. Forty-nine percent of the contracted trials were similar to the former trials: the distribution pattern of distractors and the target (if present) of the current trial remained the same as, but the distance between elements was closer than, the former trial; The other 51% were different from the former trials, see Fig. 1. Accordingly, only analysis on the contracted trials was reported in later sections.

In each block, participants practiced for 7 trials before the formal 48 trials. In each trial, participants were required to click on the target with the mouse as soon as they found it or right click on the background if no target was found. Participants were asked to be as quick and accurate as possible. No fixation or interval was provided between trials; thus, participants needed to complete the 48 trials in each block continuously. Feedback on accuracy and RTs was provided after each block.

3 Results and Discussion

To explore the effect of relation, the analysis focused on contracted trials (96 trials for each participant, and 5760 trials in total). Outliers in data were detected and excluded: Trials with RT less than 100 ms, indicating arbitrary response; Trials of block with an average accuracy less than three SDs from the mean accuracy of all participants for each block; Trials with RT larger than three SDs from the individual mean of each participant for each block. In total, 283 out of the 5760 trials (5%) were removed. Across all conditions, the mean accuracy is 98.7%, and the mean RT is 794.9 ms.

Accuracies of all conditions were above .98, and no significant effect of target, relation, or culture on accuracy were found by repeated-measures ANOVA. Incorrect responses (66 trials) were excluded from the analysis of RT. The mean RT of remaining 5411 correct trials is 789.7 ms. Figures 2 and 3 present the mean RTs with 95% CI as a function of set size within each combination of culture, target, and relation for letters and lines separately.

We calculated the search slope and intercept separately for each combination of participant, target, and relation. We conducted four repeated-measures ANOVA separately on the slope and intercept of searching for letters and lines, with the factors of relation (similar or different), culture (Chinese or Iranian), and target (reversed Q or O for letters, vertical or tilted lines).

$$\text{Slope} = (\text{RT Set size} = 12 - \text{RT Set size} = 3)/(12 - 3) \tag{1}$$

$$\text{Intercept} = \text{RT Set size} = 3 - 3 * \text{Slope} \tag{2}$$

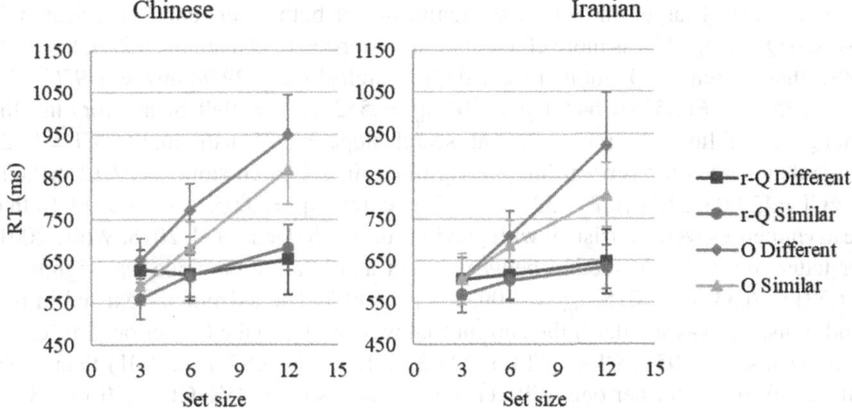

Fig. 2. RT × set size in searching for letters. Error bars represent CI 95%.

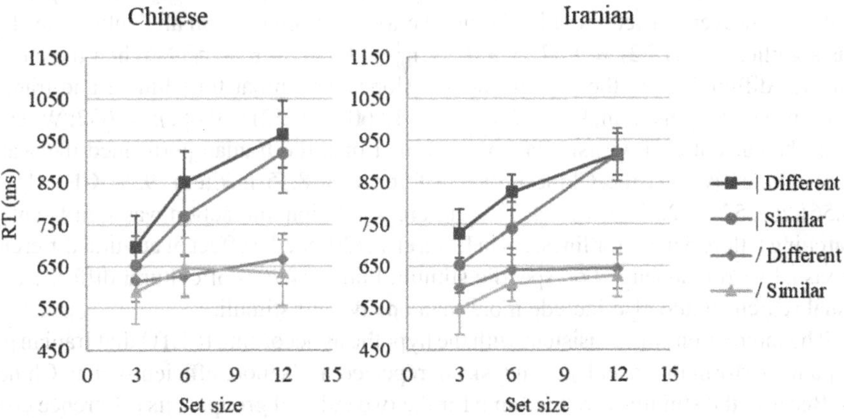

Fig. 3. RT × set size in searching for lines. Error bars represent CI 95%.

The effect of relation on slope was insignificant for either type of targets (p values $\geq .326$). The effect of relation on intercept was significant for both types of targets: For letters, intercept was larger when the pattern of the current trial was different from the former one ($M = 570.73$, 95% CI = [536.27, 605.18]) than it was similar to the former one ($M = 522.84$, 95% CI = [493.81, 551.86]), $F(1,52) = 4.67$, $p = .035$, $\eta_p^2 = .082$, $1 - \beta = .564$; Similarly, for lines, intercept was larger when the pattern of the current trial was different from the former one ($M = 617.91$, 95% CI = [580,04, 655.77]) than it was similar to the former one ($M = 553.92$, 95% CI = [517.26, 590.59]), $F(1,52) = 8.80$, $p = .004$, $\eta_p^2 = .134$, $1 - \beta = .830$. The search was faster when the pattern of the current trial was similar to the former one. The repetition did not change the searching efficiency, i.e., slope, but the "non-search portion" of the tasks [11]. This is consistent with previous studies [5 (experiment 4), 12]. One possible explanation of the result is that the repetition reduces the target threshold and distractor threshold in the asynchronous diffusion model [9], reducing the time needed to make decision [12].

The effect of target on slope was significant for both letters and lines. Search for reversed Q among Os was more efficient (search slope = 6.99 ms/item, 95% CI = [4.08, 9.89]) than search for O among reversed Qs (search slope = 29.98 ms/item, 95% CI = [24.32, 35.64]), $F(1,52) = 64.04, p < .001, \eta_p^2 = .552, 1 - \beta > .999$. Search for tilted line among vertical lines was more efficient (search slope = 5.75 ms/item, 95%CI = [3.24, 8.26]) than search for vertical line among tilted lines (search slope = 27.12 ms/item, 95%CI = [23.03, 31.20]), $F(1,52) = 87.17, p < .001, \eta_p^2 = .605, 1 - \beta > .999$. Both of the asymmetries were consistent with previous research (Ueda et al. 2018; Wolfe 2001). For letters only, the interaction between target and relation on slope was significant, $F(1,52) = 6.33, p = .015, \eta_p^2 = .109, 1 - \beta > .695$. The asymmetry existed in both conditions, but was smaller if the current trial was similar to the former one (difference = 16.84 ms/item, 95% CI = [11.06, 22.62], $t(1, 52) = 5.85, p < .001$) than it was different from the former one (difference = 29.14 ms/item, 95% CI = [20.13, 38.16], $t(1, 52) = 6.49, p < .001$). The effect of target on intercept was insignificant for both letters and lines, p values $\geq .076$.

None of the main effects of culture on slopes or intercepts were significant, p values $\geq .411$. However, for letters only, the interaction between relation and culture on slope was significant, $F(1,52) = 4.62, p = .036, \eta_p^2 = .082, 1 - \beta > .559$. When the current trial was different from the former one, the slope was similar for Chinese and Iranian, difference = 2.44 ms/item, 95% CI = [-7.72, 12.60], $t(1, 52) = 0.48, p = .632$; Whereas when the current trial was similar to the former one, the Iranian performed the search more efficiently than the Chinese did, difference = 8.15 ms/item, 95% CI = [1.74, 14.56], $t(1, 52) = 2.55, p = .014$. This culture × relation interaction was significant for searching letters but not for lines. As in Ueda et al. (2018), the effect of cultural difference on visual search depended on specific stimuli. Future studies of cultural differences in visual search should also include more than one type of stimuli.

The interaction was consistent with the hypothesis according to LTO that Iranian participants perform the visual search tasks in repeated trials more efficiently than Chinese do. Because the stimuli were the same for the two cultural groups, this difference could only be caused by top-down guidance [9]. LTO describes *how each country maintains some links with its past while dealing with present and future challenges.* Countries with a short-term orientation prefer to maintain time-honored traditions; Countries with a long-term orientation take a more pragmatic approach and devote more to the future. Iran has a very strong short-term orientation, so Iranians rely much on their experience. In this study, the Iranian participants allocated more weight to their memory of the former trial to direct their attention in searching for letters than the Chinese did, and they could find the target earlier than the Chinese did if the current trial is similar to the former one and thus performed the searching more efficiently. Furthermore, according to the theory of visual attention [25], information from short them visual memory increased the pertinence of the target location and thus weight associated with the target, resulting in faster processing velocity of the target in Iranian participants.

The findings from this study may shed light on designing for international users. For example, some repeating elements in webpage may facilitate users to find the target information they are looking for, and this repetition effect may be more salient for users from a short-term orientated culture. Similar considerations should also be taken in international communications. While presenting information, some visual strategy may works differently for audiences from different culture backgrounds.

4 Conclusion

In a visual search task, if the current trial is similar to the former one, individuals in countries of a short-term orientation, e.g., Iran, perform the task more efficiently than individuals in countries of a long-term orientation, e.g., China, do. Both groups' responses to trials of repeated configuration are faster than their responses to trials of new configuration. Cultural differences within Asian countries can affect fundamental cognitive processes, e.g., top-down activation of attentional guidance in visual search.

Acknowledgement. This study was funded by a National Key Research and Development Plan 2016YFB1001200.

References

1. Treisman, A.M., Gelade, G.: A feature-integration theory of attention. Cogn. Psychol. **12**, 97–136 (1980). https://doi.org/10.1016/0010-0285(80)90005-5
2. Wolfe, J.M.: Guided search 2.0 a revised model of visual search. Psychon. Bull. Rev. **1**, 202–238 (1994). https://doi.org/10.3758/BF03200774
3. Wolfe, J.M., Horowitz, T.S.: Five factors that guide attention in visual search. Nat. Hum. Behav. **1**, 0058 (2017). https://doi.org/10.1038/s41562-017-0058
4. Chun, M.M., Jiang, Y.: Contextual cueing: implicit learning and memory of visual context guides spatial attention. Cogn. Psychol. **36**, 28–71 (1998). https://doi.org/10.1006/cogp.1998.0681
5. Hillstrom, A.P.: Repetition effects in visual search. Percept. Psychophys. **62**, 800–817 (2000). https://doi.org/10.3758/BF03206924
6. Jiang, Y., Wagner, L.C.: What is learned in spatial contextual cuing—configuration or individual locations? Percept. Psychophys. **66**, 454–463 (2004). https://doi.org/10.3758/BF03194893
7. Maljkovic, V., Nakayama, K.: Priming of pop-out: I. Role of features. Mem. Cogn. **22**, 657–672 (1994). https://doi.org/10.3758/BF03209251
8. Watson, D.G., Humphreys, G.W.: Visual marking: prioritizing selection for new objects by top-down attentional inhibition of old objects. Psychol. Rev. **104**, 90–122 (1997)
9. Wolfe, J.M.: Guided search 4.0: current progress with a model of visual search. In: Integrated Models of Cognitive Systems, pp. 99–119. Oxford University Press, New York (2007)
10. Wolfe, J.M.: "I am not dead yet!" – the Item responds to Hulleman & Olivers. Behav. Brain Sci. **40**, e161 (2017). https://doi.org/10.1017/S0140525X16000303
11. Wolfe, J.M.: Visual search revived: the slopes are not that slippery: a reply to kristjansson (2015). iperception **7**, 1–6 (2016). https://doi.org/10.1177/2041669516643244
12. Kunar, M.A., Flusberg, S., Horowitz, T.S., Wolfe, J.M.: Does contextual cueing guide the deployment of attention? J. Exp. Psychol. Hum. Percept. Perform. **33**, 816–828 (2007). https://doi.org/10.1037/0096-1523.33.4.816
13. Kunar, M.A., Flusberg, S.J., Wolfe, J.M.: Time to guide: evidence for delayed attentional guidance in contextual cueing. Vis. Cogn. **16**, 804–825 (2008). https://doi.org/10.1080/13506280701751224

14. Hofstede, G.: Dimensionalizing cultures: the Hofstede model in context. Online Read. Psychol. Cult. **2**, 8 (2011)
15. Chua, H.F., Boland, J.E., Nisbett, R.E.: Cultural variation in eye movements during scene perception. PNAS **102**, 12629–12633 (2005). https://doi.org/10.1073/pnas.0506162102
16. Nisbett, R.E., Peng, K., Choi, I., Norenzayan, A.: Culture and systems of thought: holistic versus analytic cognition. Psychol. Rev. **108**, 291 (2001)
17. Ueda, Y., Chen, L., Kopecky, J., et al.: Cultural differences in visual search for geometric figures. Cogn. Sci. **42**, 286–310 (2018). https://doi.org/10.1111/cogs.12490
18. Boduroglu, A., Shah, P., Nisbett, R.E.: Cultural differences in allocation of attention in visual information processing. J. Cross Cult. Psychol. **40**, 349–360 (2009). https://doi.org/10.1177/0022022108331005
19. Alotaibi, A., Underwood, G., Smith, A.D.: Cultural differences in attention: eye movement evidence from a comparative visual search task. Conscious. Cogn. **55**, 254–265 (2017). https://doi.org/10.1016/j.concog.2017.09.002
20. Wolfe, J.M.: Asymmetries in visual search: an introduction. Percept. Psychophys. **63**, 381–389 (2001)
21. Lakens, D.: Calculating and reporting effect sizes to facilitate cumulative science: a practical primer for t-tests and ANOVAs. Front. Psychol. **4**, 1–12 (2013). https://doi.org/10.3389/fpsyg.2013.00863
22. Faul, F., Erdfelder, E., Lang, A.-G., Buchner, A.: G* Power 3: a flexible statistical power analysis program for the social, behavioral, and biomedical sciences. Behav. Res. Methods **39**, 175–191 (2007)
23. Treisman, A.M., Souther, J.: Search asymmetry: a diagnostic for preattentive processing of separable features. J. Exp. Psychol. Gen. **114**, 285–310 (1985)
24. Treisman, A.M., Gormican, S.: Feature analysis in early vision: evidence from search asymmetries. Psychol. Rev. **95**, 15 (1988)
25. Bundesen, C.: A theory of visual attention. Psychol. Rev. **97**, 523–547 (1990). https://doi.org/10.1037/0033-295x.97.4.523

Where is Your Product Hiding Inside Navigation? the Study of Differences E-commerce Website Navigation and Product Category Layer Between U.S., France, Japan, and Taiwan

Ya-Chun Yang and Tseng-Ping Chiu(✉)

Department of Industrial Design, National Cheng Kung University, Tainan, Taiwan
{p36094161,mattchiu}@gs.ncku.edu.tw

Abstract. The COVID-19 pandemic caused changes in our living styles severely after 2019 and has accelerated the shift towards a more cyber world. The recent online consumer survey showed that changes in online shopping behaviors are likely to have lasting effects. This study examined the different cultural comparisons of the navigation of website menu and product category layers on e-commerce websites. Our findings indicated that the menu of the Western e-commerce website is more layers than the East Asian website did (H1) through usability testing. In addition, participants spent more time on Western e-commerce websites than on East Asian e-commerce websites did (H2). This research provided a prospective insight for cross-border e-commerce that customized the website menu presentation when worldwide consumers visited them cross-culturally.

Keywords: e-commerce website · Cross-cultural cognition · Usability · Navigation · Hamburger menu · Mega menu

1 Introduction

Since technological development improved, the way of shopping behavior had been changed radically. Unlike traditional catalog shopping, online shopping was viewed as the most accessible and most convenient method for consumers. As a consequence, e-commerce website design has been regarded prospective research filed in the future [1, 2].

Although the COVID-19 outbreak is continuing to damage the economics worldwide since 2020, it showed that e-commerce around the world is still growing significantly than previous years did (Fig. 1). Recent research has shown that in countries such as America, Taiwan, and Japan, e-commerce increased significantly in 2020 [2–5]. In addition, the number of e-commerce goes up, which means that COVID-19 facilitated online shopping and activated consumers' motivation to purchase through e-commerce websites. Hence, how to create a user-friendly website design for worldwide consumers is a crucial issue that all physical retailers transfer to e-commerce.

P.-L. P. Rau (Ed.): HCII 2022, LNCS 13311, pp. 405–416, 2022.
https://doi.org/10.1007/978-3-031-06038-0_30

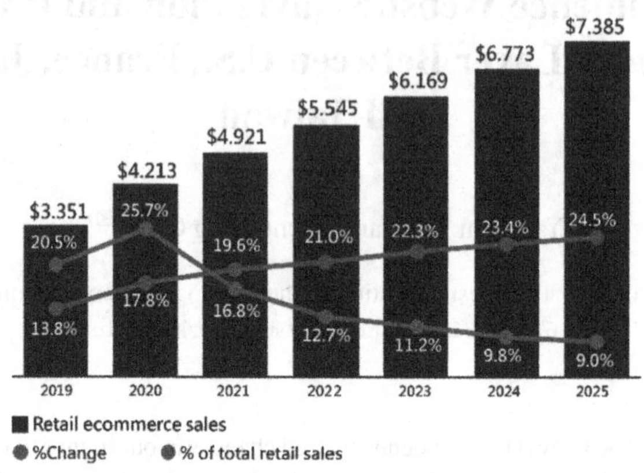

Fig. 1. eMarketer showed the retail ecommerce sales trends (Source: eMarketer).

According to development trends of the global internet and market, more scholars through cultural dimensions to explore website performance. At the same time, the menu of navigation is an important role on the website when people want to locate the target of the website. Under different thinking styles, the performance of form is also the disparity between the Western e-commerce website and the East Asian e-commerce website. The navigation system provides the context of the application and flexibility for users' browsing [6, 7]. Menu of information architecture like an index of wide map let assist consumer what result they want to attain.

The past studies of cultural cognition have indicated Westerner adept at rule-based categorization, whereas East Asians attend to family resemblance-based categorization [5, 8]. In recent years, there were studies oriented towards understanding the role of the culture of e-commerce websites [9–13]. Even more, studies researched that investigating the relationship between navigation and culture on e-commerce websites [14].

The interactivity of a website can be explored from many aspects. For example, the web considered information architecture (IA) and culture. There are three dimensions of 'Context', 'Navigation' and 'Content' of IA [15]. The navigation system in many studies indicated that it was closely related to culture, satisfaction, and usability principles. Even literature showed that the navigation system on the website is also related to usability [11, 16]. Accordingly, this research aimed to investigate the menu of navigation on e-commerce websites in different cultures by applying the principle of usability testing. We supposed that there is a significant difference of layers on the hamburger menu or mega menu between Western and East Asian e-commerce websites.

2 Literature Review

In the past decade, the website has become complex and even large. There are two main ways to seek information on the website: searching and navigation [7]. Searching caused more attention, but navigation is relatively opposite less. The research of navigation and culture is studied much less. Thus, more researchers began start studying the impact of navigation on the culture dimension.

Some studies demonstrated the adapted IA prescription to Islamic culture dimensions through Hofstede's six culture dimensions and other cultural research to analyze the performance of the websites from different countries [10, 11, 17–19]. Wan Abdul Rahim et al. proved the culture related to the menu of navigation by experiment and supply us an estimated standard to estimate the navigation of culture [18]. Even some studies indicated holistic and analytic were related to consumer behavior on the ecommerce [12]. The different thinking styles would perform different user interfaces and even different user experiences. Hence, the purpose of this study is to discuss the menu of the navigation system of information architecture (IA) on e-commerce through different cultural dimensions.

It begins by the hamburger menu. A hamburger menu like vertical drop-down menu is the one of navigation tools and completely provides the hierarchical structure with mouse click actions. It does not show all information at the same time or access sub-level sections directly [20]. It is usually in the upper right or upper left on the website. The form is similar to the normal drop-down menu, but the icon performance like hamburger and could be clicked at the same time. However, the traditional drop-down usually presents the word of the button (for instance, home). Then, what is the mega menu? It is like a horizontal drop-down menu [7], but it can show more content of different levels in the same window with a mouse-over. It needs to mouse-over or mouse click to show more structures; it will hide structures when not used as it takes a part of the webpage. The structure of the mega menu often shows the form of multiple columns [21–23].

With the popularity of network in recent years, the menu of navigation system on website became myriad forms. Through menu iteration in the past, they showed interesting transformation and also had a crucial role to play in driving the website. The scholar ever said the menu like a small IA on the website because it includes many sites page links. In the future, the menu may become breadth and even depth to provide users the direction on the website. [21] Although the existence of menus is small, but the devil is in the details, the menu maybe will importantly function on the website; as a result, Table 1 summarizes the description and some features of common menus of navigation system on the website in this study.

Table 1. Some features of common menus on navigation system

Navigation System	Description of the menu	Example
Drop-down Menu (Scroll Down Menu)	It provides hierarchical structure with mouse click (or mouse-over) completely.	HOME ▾
Hamburger Menu (Hidden Menu)	It like vertical drop-down menu completely provides the hierarchical structure with mouse click actions. Its icon like hamburger; the main links were placed under an icon or button and required the mouse click action to be displayed.	
Mega Menu	It like horizontal drop-down menu shows more content of different levels in the same window with a mouse-over. It needs to mouse-over or mouse click to show more multiple columns of structures. Some mega menus will display all section links by mouse-over at the same time.	HOME ▾
Tab Bars (menu)	It is more applied on mobile app and quickly provides to switch between top-level sections.	HOME | NEW | PRODUCT |

(*continued*)

Table 1. *(continued)*

Navigation System	Description of the menu	Example
Flyout Menu	It is a horizontal version of the drop-down menu, where the submenus 'flyout' from the side when you mouse-over or mouse click the item.	HOME
Dropline Menus	When you mouse-over or mouse click the main menu item, it appears below the main menu with additional choices.	HOME Category Product TEXT01 | TEXT02 | TEXT03 |
Accordion Menus	It is the vertical menu where clicking the main item expands the section below it and provides two levels of structure.	HOME TEXT 01 TEXT 02 TEXT 03 TEXT 04 TEXT 01 TEXT 02 TEXT 03 TEXT 04

In this study, we found that the hamburger menu more prefers to be used on the Western website. Then, the past research that Western consumer behavior has to do with analytic and inferential-categorical cognitive style. Whereas the mega menu normally trends to be used on East Asian websites. It appears that East Asian consumer behavior is relative to holistic and tends to find the object with its relational-contextual cognitive style. Some studies have shown that Westerners is a relatively analytic thinking style, value object-centered, tying object to category. They have a way of using rules and formal logic to decipher. However, East Asians are adept at seeking the whole environment than the object and tend to holistic thinking style to bind the object with its relationship between object and field [16, 24, 25]. Even the research had shown that Westerners and East Asians have different cognitive styles between the different culture dimensions on e-commerce websites [12, 14, 15, 26, 27]. Hence, through next section to understand the disparity between Western e-commerce website and East Asian e-commerce websites.

2.1 Hypotheses

Above all, this part follows on from the past literature review, which laid out the relationship between menu and culture. Through empirical research, the hamburger menu hides most sub-level sections with complete classification. Furthermore, Westerners tend to be analytic thinking and tie the object to the category or use rules and formal logic to decipher. In contrast, the mega menu showed all sections and the relationship between the level and sub-level of multiple columns. Moreover, East Asians were accustomed look at the whole environment to understand the connection between the object and the whole field. Besides, we investigated that the connection between menu and culture with the cultural theories of Hofstede [10, 11]. It seems that Westerners used the hamburger menu because of Low Uncertainty Avoidance. They could take risks and not be afraid of making mistakes. Whereas, because the mega menu could show more information at the same time and decline to get lost on the website. It conformed to avoid taking risks of High Uncertainty Avoidance. Thus, the mega menu was mostly used on the e-commerce website.

In this study, we hypothesized that there is a significant difference in the layers of the home page menu between the Western e-commerce website and the East Asian e-commerce website. In addition, it shall influence the time on looking for the target product on the website and usability test. As a consequence, there are two hypotheses we provided as below:

H1: The menu layers of the Western website home page are more than the East Asian website because the popularity of the hamburger menu for the Western website is higher than the East Asian website.

Besides, past research indicated that East Asians are more inclined to explain events situationally than Westerners [16, 24, 27]. It also showed East Asians were better information-seeking ability when they dealt with the complexity of website information as opposed to Westerners did [28, 29]. Those differences originated from the way of cultural cognition of thinking styles in which Westerners apply analytical thinking to construct objects by their categorization, whereas East Asians used holistic thinking to make the relationship between objects to objects. As a consequence, the second hypothesis we assumed as follows:

H2: People spend more time on Western e-commerce websites rather than East Asian e-commerce websites, because of seeking the goal through the relationship between objects and objects?

3 Method

3.1 Pre-test

In this study, the hamburger menu was defined vertical menu, it like varied dropdown menu. Even some e-commerce website did not show hamburger icon, but they still showed the same form. Usually provides complete hierarchical structure when user mouse clicks, but not easy to see all deep levels at the same time. Then, the mega menu in this study was defined horizontal menu. When user mouse-over on menu item, the mega menu would display all items in the window at the same time.

Through qualitative research to explore the disparity between Western e-commerce website and East Asian e-commerce websites; the hamburger menu trend to be used on most of the Western e-commerce website (e.g., Amazon, Best Buy, Etsy, Walmart, Rakuten, Real.de, bol.com, Cdiscount, Asos), whereas the mega menu trend to be used on most of the East Asian e-commerce website (e.g., Taobao, TMALL, JD JOYBUY, Yahoo! shopping mall, Rakuten, PChome, Momo).

Table 2. Explore the form of menu was used on Western e-commerce website and East Asian e-commerce websites

		Hamburger (drop-down) menu (Vertical menu)		Mega menu (Horizontal menu)	
	Total	Amount	Proportion	Amount	Proportion
Eastern website	11	1	9%	10	91%
Western website	11	8	73%	3	27%

3.2 Official Experiment

Human-Computer Interaction (HCI) is a very important factor of the website. Usability usually has a great relationship with user satisfaction. Even affect the user's emotions, behaviors, etc. In past studies proposed that some guidelines of web usability and avoid getting lost, overload to design website navigation systems [30–33]. Therefore, this experiment is conducted through time records, simple interviews afterward, and questionnaires to discuss usability, time, and culture.

Before the official experiment, three people were invited to do the simple experiment. Qualitative research has found that participants apparently spend less time on the Eastern Asian e-commerce websites and count more layers on the Western e-commerce websites. Through simple experiment improve the official experimental operation process.

1. PARTICIPANTS
   In the experiment, 51 people participated the official experiment (22 females and 29 males). The average age of participants was 23 (Fig. 2).

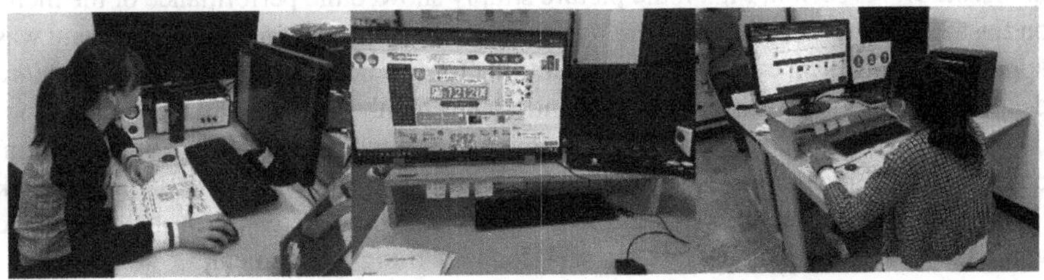

Fig. 2. The test environment and the status of people doing experiment.

2. MATERIALS
Website. Four e-commerce websites selected were B2C (Business to Consumer) and more popular as experiment stimulus: each country corresponds to the individual website is the United State (U.S)-Amazon, France (FR)-Cdiscount, Japan (JP)-Rakuten, Taiwan (TW)-Momo (Fig. 3).
Target product. The robot vacuum cleaners selected were similar appearance in four countries.

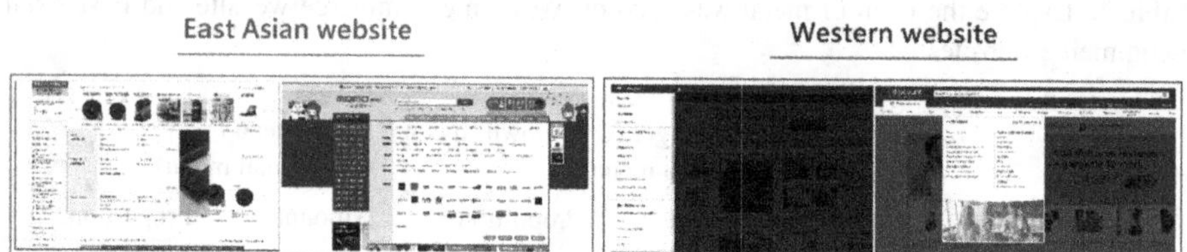

Fig. 3. The e-commerce websites in Taiwan, Japan, U.S., and France.

3. PROCEDURE
The experiment into six steps of three-part. In the first part, participants browsed on the four e-commerce B2C websites randomly and were notified of the rule of this experiment. Second, after browsing the four B2C e-commerce websites, participants got the target product of this task. They would start to seek the goal and simultaneously used screen recording to record time and mouse actions. After finishing seeking the target product on one of all e-commerce B2C websites, the participant would count the number of layers of the homepage to the product page in their mind. Then, they sought the next target product on the other designated e-commerce B2C websites. Finally, the participants were informed to fill out the questionnaire and provided feedback appropriately.

4 Result

As explained earlier, the horizontal menu (mega menu) was more used on Eastern e-commerce websites, and accounts for 91% of all. In contrast, the vertical menu (hamburger menu or drop-down menu) was more used on Western e-commerce websites, and about the proportion of the vertical menu is 73% in all Western e-commerce websites in this study. As seen in Fig. 4, the picture simply showed the performance of the menu on East Asian and Western e-commerce websites. Briefly speaking, the mega menu was applied on East Asian e-commerce websites. Its form is horizontal and usually see more deep levels with 'mouse-over'. On the contrary, the hamburger menu like complex drop-down menu was applied on Western e-commerce websites. The user seeks for detail item on menu with 'mouse click'. Especially, most participants said that 'To their, mouse click is open the new the window(page).' and 'They think they were still in the same page while they were using mouse-over to seek for something on the menu.'.

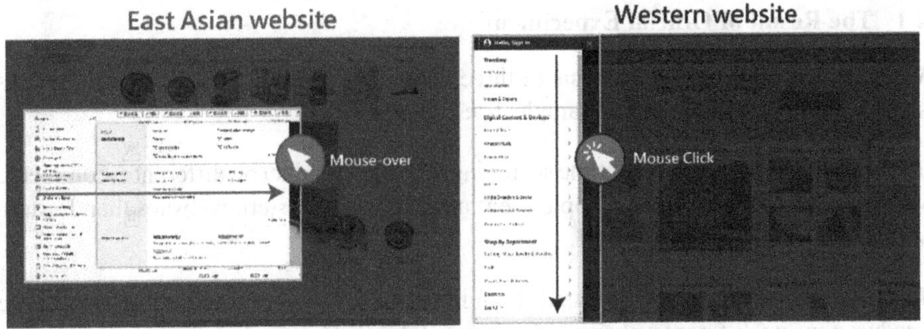

Fig. 4. The form of East Asian and Western e-commerce websites.

As seen in Table 2, the finding of the pre-test through independent sample t-test was found different cultural e-commerce websites have the relation between hamburger menu (or drop-down menu) and mega menu. Turning now to the hamburger menu (or drop-down menu) on culture factor, $p = .029 < .05$. In the other hand, the mega menu on culture factor, also $p = .029 < .05$.

Table 3. The Independent Sample T-test results comparing hamburger menu (or drop-down menu) and mega menu on East Asian and Western culture.

	Western Website (U.S. &France)			East Asian Website (Japan &Taiwan)		
	n	M	*SD*	n	M	*SD*
Hamburger menu (Or drop-down menu)	11	.73	.467	11	.09	.302
Mega menu	11	.27	.467	11	.91	.302

Table 4. Average Ratio in Percentage of spending time, calculating the number of layers and usability on operating e-commerce websites.

	Western Website (U.S. & France)		Eastern Website (Japan &Taiwan)	
	M	*SD*	M	*SD*
People spent time on sites	169.72	130.56	105.15	49.88
People calculated the number of layers	4.16	1.10	3.69	.86
Usability on ecommerce websites	2.31	.52	2.68	.52

4.1 The Result of Official Experiment

We presented in detail the analysis of three variables: Time, Layers, and Usability. As seen in Table 2, through paired sample T-test to analysis.

Times. The participants spent time searching the target product on different e-commerce websites. As seen in Table 3, People spent more time on Western websites than Eastern websites, t (50) = 3.50, p < .001.

Layers. The participants calculated the number of layers (from the homepage to the product page on different websites). As seen in Table 3, The number of layers on Western website is more than the Eastern Asian website, t (50) = 3.15, p = .003.

Usability After finishing the experiment, the participants answer usability of the e-commerce websites and order to sequence with four websites. As seen in Table 3, In usability, Eastern Asian websites are higher than Western websites, t (50) = –.51, p = .015 (Table 4).

5 Conclusion and Discussion

To build a website that lets your customers search successfully, you must look at the process from the user's perspective and try to understand their requirements [34]. Although this experiment is only to explore the usability of the menu, the usability of the website is not only related to navigation but also consumers' emotions and purchase intentions [13, 35–38].

There is limitation and fault imposed by the factor of color, brand, time. The risk is involved as the interval between the website and next website experiment process when participant sought for target may cause be impatient and even influence their deviant impression of the other e-commerce B2C websites. Furthermore, the color and the brand image probably led to the participants' different attitudes during their operation process.

In sum, Through the past studies have shown that Westerners tend to tie the object to the category, and they are belonging low uncertainty avoidance [10, 11, 17] even be classified to more analytic thinking. On the contrary, East Asians were classified as holistic thinking [16, 17, 24, 25, 27] and great at establishing the relationship between object and object. They are high uncertainty avoidance and afraid to lose on the website [10, 11, 17]. Thus, the mega menu was used to show all sections on the most East Asian e-commerce website. Through the experiment, results showed that there were more layers on Western e-commerce websites than on East Asian e-commerce websites, which supported our first hypothesis (H1). Secondly, because East Asians have a holistic and relational contextual thinking style [25], they spent time on Western e-commerce websites longer than on East Asian e-commerce websites as we expected for the second hypothesis (H2).Besides e-commerce shopping has clearly come to be one of the most recent trends. This research provides some perspective insight for cross-border e-commerce that how to customize the website menu presentation when worldwide consumers visiting them cross-culturally.

During this research, many different forms of menu design of navigation did not more studies in the past, even studies about hamburger or mega menu of navigation systems were insufficient in the past two decades. However, it is imperative to dedicate to this study of the relationship among the menu of navigation, dimensions of culture, and satisfaction of the usability as the rise of the e-commerce website.

References

1. Chauhan, T.: Review on factors affecting quality of B2C website. IOSR J. Eng. **4**(1), 22–25 (2014)
2. The Economist, Shopping around the web, in the Economist (2000)
3. The Economist, During the pandemic a digital crimewave has flooded the internet, in the Economist (2020)
4. MIC, 2020 Double 11 online shopping budget averages RMB 10,350 per person for free shipping promotion attractiveness increased by 11.2%, in MIC. 2020, MIC
5. Du, L.: Outbreak Pushes Japan Shoppers to Finally Buy Things Online, in Bloomberg (2020)
6. Zimmermann, G., Strobbe, C., Ziegler, D.: Inclusive responsiveness – why responsive web design is not enough and what we can do about this. In: Di Bucchianico, G. (ed.) AHFE 2018. AISC, vol. 776, pp. 203–215. Springer, Cham (2019). https://doi.org/10.1007/978-3-319-94622-1_20
7. Zheng, J.: Web Navigation Systems for Information Seeking (2015)
8. Fang, X., Holsapple, C.W.: Impacts of navigation structure, task complexity, and users' domain knowledge on web site usability—an empirical study. Inf. Syst. Front. **13**(4), 453–469 (2011)
9. Fleming, J., Koman, R.: Web Navigation: Designing the User Experience. O'reilly Sebastopol, CA (1998)
10. Hofstede, G.: Cultures and Organizations : Software of the Mind. McGraw-Hill, New York (2005)
11. Geert Hofstede, P.D., Gert Van Hofstede, P.D., Michael Minkov, P.D.: Cultures and Organizations: Software of the Mind, ed. third. McGraw-Hill Education (2010)
12. Liao, H., Proctor, R.W., Salvendy, G.: Chinese and US online consumers' preferences for content of e-commerce websites: a survey. Theor. Issues Ergon. Sci. **10**(1), 19–42 (2009)
13. Huang, Y.-F., Chen, W.-T., Kuo, F.-Y.: Investigating the interaction between positive emotion and decoy effect on consumer decision making. Sun Yat-Sen Manag. Rev. **21**(4), 743–767 (2013)
14. Lodge, C.: The impact of culture on usability: designing usable products for the international user. In: Aykin, N. (ed.) UI-HCII 2007. LNCS, vol. 4559, pp. 365–368. Springer, Heidelberg (2007). https://doi.org/10.1007/978-3-540-73287-7_44
15. Marcos, M.-C., et al.: Cultural differences on seeking information: an eye tracking study (2013)
16. Masuda, T., Nisbett, R.E.: Attending holistically versus analytically: comparing the context sensitivity of Japanese and Americans. J. Pers. Soc. Psychol. **81**(5), 922–934 (2001)
17. Wan Mohd Isa, W.A.R., Md Noor, N.L., Mehad, S.: Incorporating the cultural dimensions into the theoretical framework of website information architecture. In: Aykin, N. (ed.) UI-HCII 2007. LNCS, vol. 4559, pp. 212–221. Springer, Heidelberg (2007). https://doi.org/10.1007/978-3-540-73287-7_27
18. Wan Mohd. Isa, W.A.R., Md. Noor, N.L., Mehad, S.: Culture design of information architecture for B2C E-commerce websites. In: Kurosu, M. (ed.) HCD 2009. LNCS, vol. 5619, pp. 805–814. Springer, Heidelberg (2009). https://doi.org/10.1007/978-3-642-02806-9_93

19. Wan Mohd, W.A.R., Md Noor, N.L., Mehad, S.: The information architecture of E-commerce: an experimental study on user performance and preference. Information Systems Development, pp. 723-731 (2010)
20. Pinandito, A., et al. Analysis of web content delivery effectiveness and efficiency in responsive web design using material design guidelines and User centered design. In: 2017 International Conference on Sustainable Information Engineering and Technology (SIET), pp. 435–441. IEEE (2017)
21. Naylor, S.: Breadth and depth: A comparison of search performance in hierarchical and mega menus, pp. 1–64 (2016)
22. Comeaux, D.J.: Web design trends in academic libraries—a longitudinal study. J. Web Librariansh **11**(1), 1–15 (2017)
23. Ouyang, X., Zhou, J.: Smart TV for older adults: a comparative study of the mega menu and tiled menu. In: Zhou, J., Salvendy, G. (eds.) ITAP 2018. LNCS, vol. 10927, pp. 362–376. Springer, Cham (2018). https://doi.org/10.1007/978-3-319-92037-5_27
24. Nisbett, R.E., et al.: Culture and systems of thought: holistic versus analytic cognition. Psychol. Rev. **108**(2), 291–310 (2001)
25. Nisbett, R.: The Geography of Thought: How Asians and Westerners Think Differently--and Why (2003)
26. Bin, Q., Chen, S.-J., Sun, S.Q.: Cultural differences in e-commerce: a comparison between the US and China. J. Glob. Inf. Manag. (JGIM) **11**(2), 48–55 (2003)
27. Miyamoto, Y., Nisbett, R.E., Masuda, T.: Culture and the physical environment holistic versus analytic perceptual affordances. Res. Article **17**(2), 113–119 (2006)
28. Cho, C.-H., Cheon, H.J.: cross-cultural comparisons of interactivity on corporate web sites the United States, the United Kingdom, Japan, and South Korea. J. Citation Rep. **34**(2), 99–115 (2005)
29. Masuda, T., et al.: Culture and cognition-Implications for art, design and advertisement. In: Handbook of Research on International Advertising, pp. 109–133 (2012)
30. Danielson, D.R.: Web navigation and the behavioral effects of constantly visible site maps. Interact. Comput. **14**(5), 601–618 (2002)
31. Palmer, J.W.: Web site usability, design, and performance metrics. Inf. Syst. Res. **13**(2), 151–167 (2002)
32. Loranger, H., Nielsen, J.: Prioritizing Web Usability. New Riders (2006)
33. Tsai, J.Y., et al.: The effect of online privacy information on purchasing behavior: an experimental study. Inf. Syst. Res. **22**(2), 254–268 (2011)
34. Nielsen, J., et al.: E-commerce User Experience. Nielsen Norman Group, pp. 1–51 (2000)
35. Tang, Y.-Y.: A Study on Usability of Shopping Website Interface Design, pp. 1–87 (2007)
36. Lee, Y.F.: Research on User's Expectation and Gratification for Interactive Function of Social Shopping Website, pp. 1–141 (2009)
37. Wang, M.-H., Yeh, Q.-J.: The relationships among consumer attributes, users' satisfactions on web and www purchase intention. J. Bus. Adm. **48**, 121–137 (2000)
38. Lee, S.-H.: The Effect of Website Design Factors and Attitude Toward the Website on Purchase Intention–An Investigation in Taiwan. Executive Master of Business Administration, pp. 1–89 (2007)

Aspects of Intercultural Design

Displacement of Relationship and Boundary: Thoughts on Design Research for Future Society

Renfei Bai[1,2](✉)

[1] Tsinghua University, 30 Shuangqing Road, Haidian District, Beijing, China
bairenfei@163.com

[2] Tianjin University of Science and Technology, 1038 Dagu Nanlu, Hexi District, Tianjin, China

Abstract. Based on Thomas Kuhn's paradigm shift theory, this paper aims to think about how design research can show its value in the topics facing the future society, ask about the scientificity of design research, and put forward the topic of "design research facing the future society". The speculative attribute of design thinking determines that designers can make up future scenes through imagination and graphical language. On the premise of the superposition of "complexity problem" and futurology, this paper takes social network theory as the perspective and speculative design as the method, turns the topic to "speculative research facing the weak relationship of future social network", and deduces the hypothesis that design research will change from "people centered" to "relationship centered". In the evaluation part, this paper advocates asking questions rather than answering questions. Based on the emphasis on uncertainty, the evaluation criteria evolve from "possible certainty" to "possible uncertainty". At the same time, the scope of the subject continues to expand, and multi subjects give full play to the self-organization advantages of the subject through cooperation, so as to realize order in disorder.

Keywords: Future society · Design research · Social network · Speculative design

1 Realistic Dilemma: Questioning the "scientificity" of Design Research

In 1962, Thomas Kuhn, an American philosopher of science, first put forward the concept of "paradigm" in his book *The Structure of Scientific Revolutions,* that is, the inherent model of scientific research advocated and adhered to by the scientific community in a specific period of time, which is a collection of epistemology, world outlook and practice recognized by the members of the community [1]. Thomas Kuhn's theory has triggered the change of epistemology in the field of philosophy of science and has influenced so far. However, its significance is not limited to the field of natural sciences, but also has a far-reaching impact on the development of many disciplines such as humanities and social sciences. The "design science" has the characteristics of natural science and humanities, and is bound to be affected by the "paradigm" theory. Since the design

P.-L. P. Rau (Ed.): HCII 2022, LNCS 13311, pp. 419–428, 2022.
https://doi.org/10.1007/978-3-031-06038-0_31

method movement in the 1960s, the research of many design scholars has effectively promoted the process of design science becoming a "normal science". For example, Herbert Simon, an American interdisciplinary research scholar, put forward the idea of "limited rationality" for artificial science, which is different from the research method of "infinite rationality" for natural science, and provides a methodological basis for design research; The book D*esignerly Ways of Knowing* by Nigel cross, a British design theorist, interprets the essence of design cognition from different angles such as design research, design education and design practice, and analyzes the cognitive and thinking mode of designers [2], which promotes the development of research in the field of design science; Bruce Archer believes that design research is a process of systematically exploring design knowledge, emphasizing the role of artifacts in the system structure. From the perspective of "paradigm shift", the practicality and exploration of "design science" make it show its unique paradigm characteristics, that is, a high degree of integration in the face of the complex world. Specifically, the design research method can not only ensure the normative answer to deterministic problems, but also ensure the exploratory expression of possible problems. It can achieve a good balance in the efficiency and flexibility of solving problems, especially in the aspect of trend insight and meaning mining for the future society. At the same time, although the transformation of design paradigm from agricultural economy and industrial economy to experience economy and knowledge economy at this stage has always followed the change law of industrial economy (see Fig. 1), the continuous integration of design science, natural science and social science also enables the design law to continuously break through the circle of business logic and extend to the level of social logic [3]. In fact, the inquiry about the "scientificity" of design research has never stopped. This is an obstacle for all design researchers.

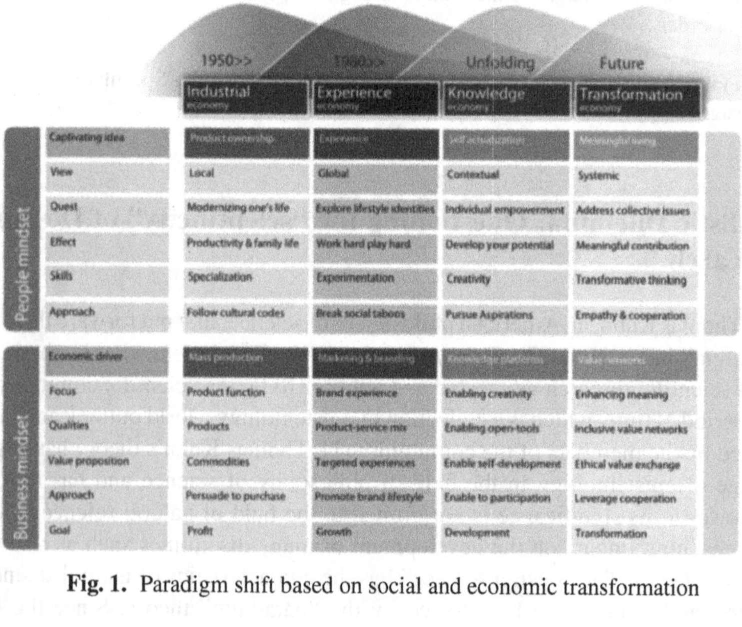

		1950>> Industrial economy	1960>> Experience economy	Unfolding Knowledge economy	Future Transformation economy
People mindset	Captivating idea	Product ownership	Experience	Self actualization	Meaningful living
	View	Local	Global	Contextual	Systemic
	Quest	Modernizing one's life	Explore lifestyle identities	Individual empowerment	Address collective issues
	Effect	Productivity & family life	Work hard play hard	Develop your potential	Meaningful contribution
	Skills	Specialization	Experimentation	Creativity	Transformative thinking
	Approach	Follow cultural codes	Break social taboos	Pursue Aspirations	Empathy & cooperation
Business mindset	Economic driver	Mass production	Marketing & branding	Knowledge platforms	Value networks
	Focus	Product function	Brand experience	Enabling creativity	Enhancing meaning
	Qualities	Products	Product-service mix	Enabling open-tools	Inclusive value networks
	Value proposition	Commodities	Targeted experiences	Enable self-development	Ethical value exchange
	Approach	Persuade to purchase	Promote brand lifestyle	Enable to participation	Leverage cooperation
	Goal	Profit	Growth	Development	Transformation

Fig. 1. Paradigm shift based on social and economic transformation

2 Facing Complex Problems: The Speculative Attribute of Design Research

Richard Buchanan, former dean of CMU School of design, divided design issues into four areas: communication/construction/interaction/integration [4]. Among them, whether it is the communication with graphics, words and other symbols as the media, the construction with tangible artifacts as the carrier, or the behavior interaction connected by activities, as well as the integration idea based on the system environment, all represent the perspective of looking at design problems in different periods of design development, and also reflect the change and iterative process of design problems. Communication, creation, interaction and systematic thinking are interrelated, which together constitute the overall design concept of dynamic development. At present and in the future, symbols, things, behaviors and ideas can still be considered as a whole, but with the addition of more uncertain factors, such as the conflict of value propositions between different design subjects from the perspective of globalization, and the "invasion" of artificial intelligence as a "new species" in the creation process to the existing system, Will make the design problem more and more complex. In fact, since Horst willhelm Jakob rittel and Melvin M. Weber first proposed the wicked problems in the design field in 1973, the discussion on the "complexity" of design problems has never stopped. All disordered, unsolvable and uncertain problems, and even almost all public policy problems, can be regarded as wicked problems. This not only greatly expands the boundary of design problems, but also puts forward new challenges to design research strategies and methods. In addition to the design discipline, complexity research has also attracted extensive attention in traditional disciplines. The exposition of "complexity methods" can be traced back to Edgar Morin, a French thinker. He broke the mechanical determinism and put forward the conceptual model of "unity of diversity", which advanced the classical discipline from reductionism and system theory to complexity theory, and built a new interdisciplinary methodological infrastructure [5]. In the past two decades when complexity research has become a hot spot, the paradigm transformation of design research is also carried out simultaneously. Ezio Manzini believes that future design is mainly reflected in social innovation and sustainability. In order to realize the design turn, we should constantly expand the boundary of design and generate new design knowledge under the future economic model [6]. If we want to better design and study the "complexity", we need to study the mechanism of complexity formation. That is to analyze the underlying logic of complexity from the level of "meta theory". In short, the emergence of "complex" phenomenon stems from the weak order caused by the multi dynamic contradiction between the whole and the part. The lack of order makes human cognition unable to understand the whole through the part, and also unable to judge the dynamic trend through the static phenomenon. Therefore, the nonlinear relationship between the local and the whole and the weak correlation between the local and the local cause the sense of cognitive chaos, which leads to complexity.

In fact, to deal with complex problems, design thinking has unique advantages. From the etymology of "design", it means "giving meaning to things" [7]. It is worth mentioning that the "meaning" here does not occur in the present, but depends on the user's perception in a specific scene and time state. Here, the only thing that can help users explain "meaning" is the symbols used in the design process and the arrangement of symbol order. Therefore, design can be understood as the activity of expressing a certain meaning of things with specific symbols. Because the communication of symbols requires the participation of space and time variables, the design has a certain degree of "future" and "fiction". Finally, the "meaning" of design is conveyed through the process of symbol coding and translation, which reflects the result of the joint coordination of designers, users and all stakeholders. This intermediate loss of symbolic information leads to the uncertainty of design results. If there are great differences between designers and users at the cognitive level, this uncertainty will be infinitely amplified. When the designer's design object changes from tangible material design to intangible non-material design (such as service design), and then to more disorderly complex system design (such as social innovation design), the fictional instinct of design thinking can be released to the greatest extent. Its speculative attribute makes it possible for designers to design and fabricate complexity, and build virtual scenes through imagination driven and graphical symbolic language. Compared with other language methods, graphical design symbols are the media most conducive to the realization of "intellectual equality" between designers and users. It can be seen that it is an appropriate solution to deal with and describe the "complexity" problem with design thinking.

3 Perspective on the Future: A "relationship" Perspective of Social Network

As mentioned above, design thinking itself has a certain degree of "future" and "fiction", which leads to a natural "cognitive difference" between designers and users. Therefore, the French scholar Jacques Lacan put forward the theory of "intersubjectivity", which holds that "the subject is defined by the 'otherness' in its own existence structure, and the otherness in the subject is intersubjectivity". When designed to solve problems about the "future", this "alienation" between subjects will be enhanced. If the disorder and uncertainty caused by "complexity" lead to human cognitive chaos, the admission of "futurism" will enhance the sense of chaos in human cognition in the time dimension. It can be seen that the research on the "future" has typical characteristics of "complexity". If facing the short-term future, it can still make scientific prediction through the regular information in politics, economy, society, science and technology. When facing the long-term future, the upgrading of the complex relationship between subjects greatly enhances the disorder and dynamics of the transformation between different behavior patterns. It is against this background that Ossip K. Flechtheim put forward the concept of "futurology" in the 1940s and it has developed into an independent discipline. When futurology superimposes the complexity of society, it'll create greater obstacles for the research of future society.

Although the speculative nature of design determines that design thinking can fictionalize the future scene through imagination and graphical language, how to enable users to mobilize their imagination to understand and interpret this fictional future is still a great challenge. The crux of the problem lies in the object-oriented fuzziness of the design, in addition to the accompanying "inter subjectivity" problem. Looking at the development process of design theory, in the controllable present and short-term future, design has experienced "material" centered design and "human" centered design, which are respectively used to solve the contradiction between user needs and product functions, as well as the contradiction between organizational vision and user experience. So, facing the future, what should design focus on? This is the first question that should be answered in design speculation.

Therefore, it is necessary to focus on the research problems in order to put forward a practical research scheme within a controllable range. To some extent, the "complexity" of both wicked problem and future problem points to common characteristics, such as chaos, disorder, nonlinearity and so on. The prominence of these characteristics stems from the researchers' excessive attention to the subject boundary attribute and order attribute. Once this boundary and order are lost, there will be a certain degree of "out of control". This is not conducive to the smooth progress of design research. The solution is to change the perspective, restore from the opposite of "complexity", and grasp the more essential "origin". The social network perspective of German sociologist Georg Simmel is introduced here. That is, the complexity is reduced to a relationship based on the interconnection between network nodes. Design researchers can focus on the connection between different subjects, and use the strength of the relationship to analyze the information conversion ability of actors in social networks. Among them, the explicit stipulation reflected by strong relationship can explain the current situation and short-term future, while the trend reflected by weak relationship can be used to predict the long-term future (see Fig. 2).

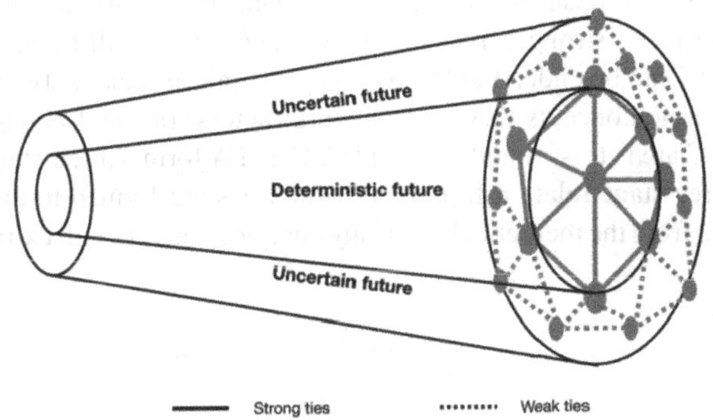

Fig. 2. The cone of relations

In short, the research problem of this paper has changed from "Research on design strategy for future society" to "speculative research on weak relationship of future social network", which makes the research more targeted, purposeful and operable. The object of design is also refocused, from "human" as the center to "relationship" as the center.

4 Social Network Analysis: Inspiration from SFI

The Santa Fe Institute (SFI), founded in 1984, raised the complexity research to a new level. From its research object "complex adaptive system", they attributed the complexity development to the evolution process of a system with adaptive ability from simple to complex. This is reflected in different types of systems such as artificial objects and social organizations, such as artificial intelligence and social self-organization systems with deep learning ability. Their common feature is that they can continuously obtain new experience based on the feedback of the objective world, and complete the renewal of cognitive ability and the improvement of behavior. The management mode of the Institute is of methodological significance. For example, in order to maintain openness and vitality, they encourage interdisciplinary cooperation among scholars and commit to cross research in order to seek new disciplinary directions; At the same time, after the Institute provides a platform, researchers conduct self-management in a "self-organization" way to give full play to the subjective initiative of all participants. It can be seen that complexity is different from systematicness. The latter emphasizes a process of realizing integrity and unity under the strong intervention of the central organization; The former emphasizes the positive role of the constituent elements of the system, which is a process based on "decentralization" and relying on the active "competition and cooperation" of a large number of individuals in the system to realize the overall and orderly development. Therefore, complex system is a mixed state of order and disorder. To study it, we need to find an intermediate state to ensure the smooth operation of complex system [8].

There is a concept of "triadic closure" in Georg Simmel's "social network" theory, that is, it is assumed that there is a ternary structure composed of three subjects A, B and C. There are three kinds of connection relationships in the ternary structure, i.e. A and B, B and C, C and A. Any two groups of connection relationships will affect the third group of relationships, such as strong connection between A and B, B and C, then the probability of strong connection between A and C will be greatly improved. "Ternary closure" can be understood as the simplest unit in social network, but this unit contains three basic concepts in social network: actors, ties and boundaries. Among them, A, B and C are actors. A and B, B and C, C and A form a three-stage relationship. Through the three-stage relationship, three boundaries are formed to distinguish other units. Therefore, from the theoretical level, any complex network will extract the "ternary

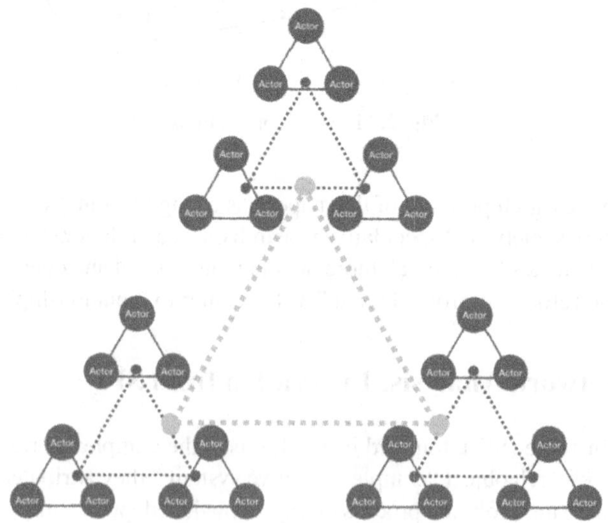

Fig. 3. Complex networks composed of triadic closures

closure" units with the same attributes and make a specific analysis from the perspective of actors, ties and boundaries (see Fig. 3).

In the case of SFI, interdisciplinary scholars constitute active actors. They connect through self-organization and form boundaries at the same time. The existence of boundary forms order in disorder in complex network. The achievement of order can provide a certain degree of "certainty" for design research. This is where the "scientificity" of using design thinking to "make up the future" lies. During the operation of SFI, the organizational structure of the network has been changing dynamically. The main motivation comes from the change of the importance of actors in the network. For example, in the process of interdisciplinary cooperation and cross research, the role and position of members can be divided into primary and secondary, and the results brought by different members in the core position are different. These can be studied and judged from the perspective of "Core-Periphery" structural analysis. In short, in different temporal and spatial ranges, the relative position of actors determines the attribute of the "ternary closure" unit and the position of the unit in the whole social network. There is a similar "Core-Periphery" relationship between units, which determines the evolution process and trend of complex systems. This is in line with the "decentralization" emphasized by SFI and the process of realizing system order through the "competition and cooperation" of individual actors. The "intermediate state" mentioned by Murray Gell Mann is the change trend of "relationship" and "boundary" caused by actors' continuous exploration between "Core-Periphery". This trend can be further understood as that in the context of futurology, the virtual scene is described by evaluating the position change of actors in the "Core-Periphery" structure from the perspective of social network and the "ternary closure" unit formed by actors, ties and boundaries, and finally realize future value (see Fig. 4).

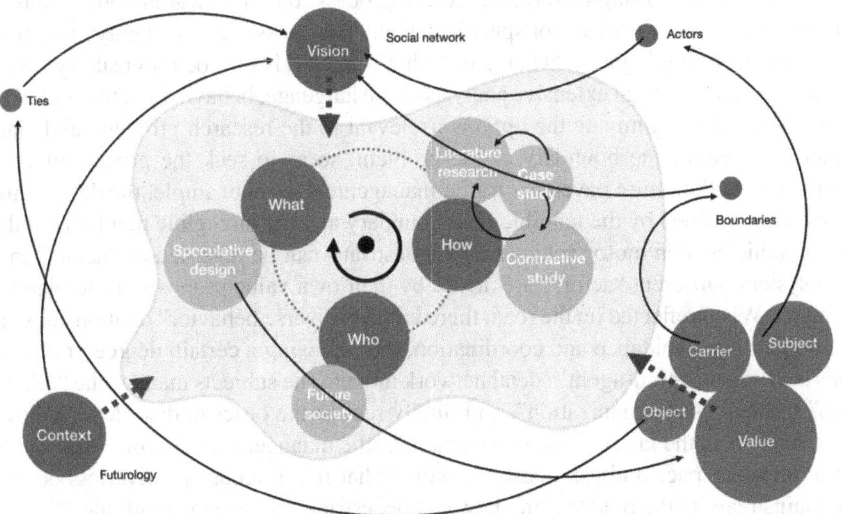

Fig. 4. Thoughts on Design Research for future society

5 Breaking the Infatuation of "result": From "possible Certainty" to "possible Uncertainty"

In fact, when thinking about the future society, it means giving up the pursuit of deterministic "results", because the purpose of speculative design is to ask questions, not to provide explanations. Different from the traditional design that takes a product or a service as the result of the design process, the end of speculative design is open. Because there are no explanatory results, it is impossible to build an accurate evaluation model. Therefore, whether "Braun's ten design principles", "Nielsen's ten principles of interaction design", or "Larry Keeley's ten types of innovation", they are all strengthening the interpretation of some answers and the evaluation method to be avoided by speculative design. In other words, in the process of replacing real design with virtual scene, speculative design also removes the thinking inertia of the real world and realizes the "intellectual equality" between design subjects [9]. Under this situation presupposition, actors are liberated. They are not only the practitioners of design behavior, but also the evaluators of design process, and continue to create value in the social network according to their own understanding.

In other words, due to the influence of the dialectical relationship between "order" and "disorder" in the complex system, the evaluation standard of speculative design evolves from "possible certainty" to "possible uncertainty". "Possible certainty" focuses on the questioning logic of "what is what", and tends to "scientific" reductive thinking, that is, the process of constantly narrowing the problem boundary through hypothesis and analysis in order to seek certainty. In design research, this corresponds to the "research for design" of the three paths of Design Research (research about design / research for design / research through design), which is also the research path held by many design strategy companies (such as IDEO company). They use design thinking tools to encode design knowledge through structured design process, output research conclusions and directions, and provide ideas for specific design; The "possible uncertainty" focuses on the question setting logic of "what is not what", and tends to "sociological" systematic thinking, that is, through extensive analysis of the language, behavior and thought of various stakeholders, eliminate the options irrelevant to the research problem, and clarify rather than reduce the boundary of the problem, so as to seek the process of uncertainty. Taking the future pavement traffic management as an example, the deterministic boundary is defined by the tangible road boundary and the intangible regular boundary. Motor vehicles, non motor vehicles and pedestrians can be regarded as "actors" in the road system. Different "actors" are driven by their own value propositions to plan their behavior. When reflected on the road, there will be "diverse behavior" relationships such as competition, avoidance and coordination, thus showing a certain degree of disorder. This is a typical "multi-agent" social network model. The subjects manage the "relationship" through "self-organization", and finally realize the order in disorder. So, how to ask questions in the face of "future pavement traffic management system"? You can first set a question space and ask questions with "what if". Such as "if driverless occupies the mainstream in the road system, how can pedestrians change the road rules?" "If low flying vehicles participate in the traffic management system, how can the traffic rules be updated to adapt to the participation of new actors?" "If vehicles have deep learning ability, how to reconstruct the actor network based on road traffic?". In such a fictitious scene, a variety of uncertainties will appear at the same time, which requires researchers to infer the possible uncertainties through reflection.

According to Ezio Manzini, the whole society can be regarded as a huge laboratory. Individuals, organizations, communities and other subjects participate in the "laboratory" through different practical behaviors, and carry out value creation activities in the two dimensions of problem-solving and meaning construction. This is an open and collaborative process with research nature [6]. Its open nature is reflected in the continuity and "non closure" of the collaborative process, that is, in the face of complex problems, actors will never be able to put forward definitive answers, but will be replaced by a "social dialogue", which will arouse the interest of different partners and inspire them to look at the problem from a new perspective; Its research nature is reflected in the new "design knowledge" constantly generated in the open process. Especially when facing the unpredictable future social practice, the renewal of knowledge is very important for the improvement of actors' behavior and expression ability. Fundamentally speaking, the complexity of design issues and the openness of design process (open design and collaborative innovation) have become the internal driving force for the continuous change of the concept and scope of design and design research. It is also the key to the transformation of the principle of design evaluation from infatuation with the "certainty" of results to the "uncertainty" of process.

6 Conclusion: Speculative Value

The significance of speculation lies in raising questions, not answering questions, and also in paying attention to uncertainty and confrontation with certainty. In this process, design research has changed from "people centered" to "relationship centered", and actors can realize real "intellectual equality" in relationship. This is an important premise of speculation. Based on the social network, "actors" have produced a new value network in the process of constantly exploring between "Core-Periphery". The object of relational connection also exceeds the limit of "person" and expands the scope of subject. Multi-agent collaboration can give full play to the self-organization advantages among agents and realize order in disorder. Finally, the speculative way broke the infatuation with deterministic results and changed the evaluation criterion from "possible certainty" to "possible uncertainty".

References

1. Thomas, K.: The Structure of Scientific Revolutions. Peking University Press, Beijing (2012)
2. Nigel, C.: Designerly Ways of Knowing. Huazhong University of science and Technology Press, Wuhan (2013)
3. Den, O.: Innovation Design: Creating Value for People, Organizations and Society. Springer, London (2012). https://doi.org/10.1007/978-1-4471-2268-5
4. Richard, B.: Wicked Problem in Design Thingking. Des. Issues **8**(2), 5–21 (1992)
5. Edgar, M.: Lost Paradigm: Human Nature. Peking University Press, Beijing (1999)
6. Ezio, M.: Design. When Everybody Designs. Publishing House of Electronics Industry, Beijing (2015)

7. Roberto, V.: Overcrowded. Designing Meaningful Products in a World Awash with Ideas. Posts & Telecom Press, Beijing (2018)
8. Murray, G.: The Quark and the Jaguar. Holtzbrinck Publishers, LLC, Stuttgart (1994)
9. Li, Z.: The value of fiction: the aesthetic politics and future poetics of speculative design. Theor. Stud. Lit. Art **39**(6), 152–160 (2019)

Future Convergences: Time Matters

Anna Barbara(✉)

Design Department, Politecnico di Milano, Milan, Italy
anna.barbara@polimi.it

Abstract. While in the history of design, spatial qualities have been central to the search for techniques and tools, temporal qualities have come to take part in design, with the advent of the digital revolution, as qualities capable of deforming, compressing, reconfiguring spaces, and supporting new ways of living.

The essay investigates various time-based approaches, developed by scholars and designers from different disciplines, to build tools that can identify convergences capable of generating various forms of future.

The time-based design approach will allow future studies to explore:

Spaces: Digital algorithmic design/production technologies will make spaces and components adaptable and able to govern kinetic and sensory performance.

Experiences: Time-based technologies will make perception and emotions more adaptable, through a continuous dialogue between humans and inhabited spaces and by employing machines and computer systems capable of formulating personalized proposals.

Behaviors: Media technologies, have changed people's behaviors and their interaction with spaces, with people, with objects. Through temporal analysis we could understand parameters such as presence, speed, proximity, to redesign spaces and services.

The essay explores the directions taken by design that can be considered time-based, to identify the temporal and convergence tools that can prefigure future spaces and ensure coherent and congruent visions based on collaboration rather than competition, presence rather than absence, optimization of space rather than unsustainable waste of resources.

The essay aims to demonstrate the relevance of temporal dimensions, which offer increasingly reliable tools, called chronotopes, available to Future Studies to identify trajectories and possible configurations of the world in which future generations will live.

Keywords: Time-based design · Chronotopes · Futures · convergences · Spatial design

1 Temporal Geometries

Time has always been a parameter in the design of spaces and all cultures have tried to represent it, both in a symbolic way to explain it, and in a semantic way to be able to use it.

P.-L. P. Rau (Ed.): HCII 2022, LNCS 13311, pp. 429–438, 2022.
https://doi.org/10.1007/978-3-031-06038-0_32

Exploring the different forms of time, we will find different geometries, each serving to represent, but sometimes also as a design tool:

- *linear* which is often how the story is treated, as a single line of sequences
- *circular* which is linked to seasonality and the cyclical nature of small recurring events
- *parametric* that draws the deformation of space over time
- *layered* that allows a simultaneous reading of distant events
- *overlapped* that represents multifunctionality
- *porous* that represents the unused spaces able to absorb small growths and compressions without collapsing the system.

2 To Design Form of Time

What is increasingly evident is that, in recent years, we are engaged in designing forms of time, much more than forms of space. This has become evident with the digital revolution, but even more so because of the current pandemic.

Designing with time has been happening forever, even the technologies of the 20th century were technologies of speed, of acceleration, but digitization has led to other dizzying movements, to a compression of spaces due to co-presence, ubiquity, overlapping, increasing congestion of spaces and peak stresses on infrastructure and spaces.

Those who study the future must think that managing the forms of time, and coordinating them, is a necessary step toward sustainability. The spaces that the 20th century has left us, are spaces designed on an analog world, where the coordinates to be measured were all internal to the same space. Today, our experiences are simultaneously analog and digital, spaces need to be reconfigured because they are oversized or stressed because they are designed with outdated logic.

Research into the potential, that the digital revolution has brought to architecture, began in the early 1990s and the explorations, both in design, theory, and construction, have been visionary and promising of spatial experiences. In contrast, today there is a sense of inadequacy related to the real estate market and the actual spaces in which we live. Static built spaces, insensitive to the new forms of living that the revolution of digital technologies has introduced (Carpo 2013).

Today we live in a multi-temporal connection in a continuous and 'liquid' flow. When the concept of 'liquid modernity' was introduced (Bauman 2007), a deep reflection on the spatio-temporal morphology of places, relationships and technologies was initiated and is still ongoing.

From that moment on, interior design could no longer be the same as before, because the fluidity of time would also reshape space. Spaces were no longer the frame, the reference set, of human actions but became one of the possible media, able to allow adaptability and flexibility, in a continuous flow of changes characterized by an endemic uncertainty.

The concept of liquid space was adopted by many scholars, architects and designers who adapted it to different contexts. Among them Marcos Novak, who argued "A liquid architecture" is an architecture whose form is contingent on the interests of the beholder; it is an architecture that opens to welcome and closes to defend; it is an architecture without doors and corridors, where the next room is always where it should be and what it should be.

Novak introduced the concept of "liquid architecture" as an expression of the "fourth dimension," incorporating time alongside space, among its primary elements. Novak's liquid architecture would bend, rotate, and change in interaction with the person inhabiting it (Panahi 2017) (Fig. 1).

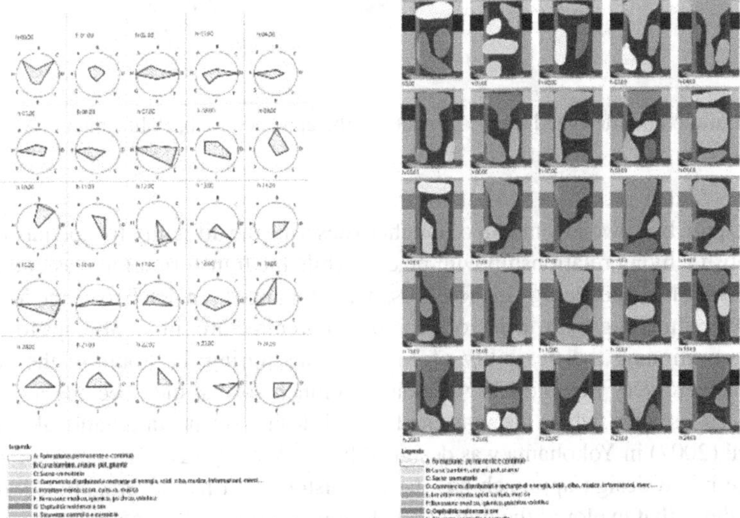

Fig. 1. ON-OFF Chronotopes. Cronos and Kairos project, exhibited at the Venice architecture Biennial in 2010, Designed by the author

3 Time-Based Design

The definition of time-based design comes from Leupen, Heijine, and van Zwol (Leupen, Heijine and Van Zwol 2005) since they began to investigate how the design of spaces should involve time. Leupen recognized that "the speed of modernization, and the unpredictability inherent in the process, makes it very difficult to establish reality for a medium that moves as slowly as buildings (Fig. 2)."

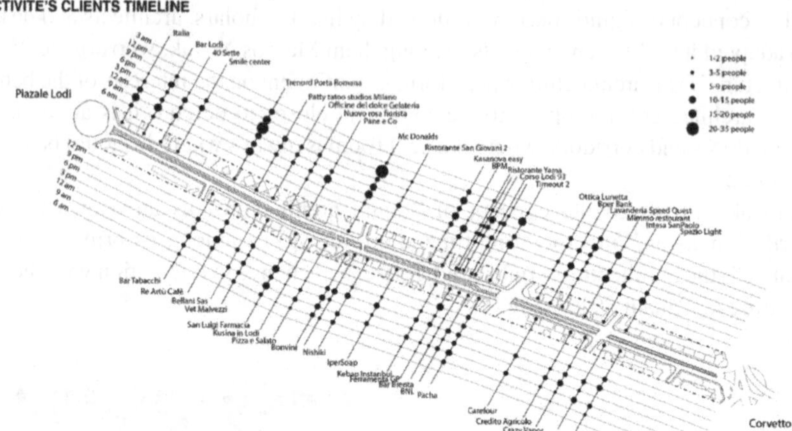

Fig. 2. Chronotopes designed by the students of the ephemeral lab, Politecnico di Milano, a.a. 2021–2022

The term, borrowed from video, sought to describe the difficulty for spatial designers to establish a living relationship with places, while the transformation was underway.

The issue has a genealogy in the 1930s, when Johannes van den Broek and Mart Stam began experimenting with forms of time-based architecture, in an attempt to enhance spaces, questioning the flexibility of environments during the hours of the day. The solutions were very flexible and visionary, so much so that they became a reference, many decades later, when the master plan and design of the International Passenger Terminal (2002) in Yokohama was designed by FOA (Carpo 2013).

Time-based design approach has its own history, that has several strands in space design: those that explored the digital revolution as a possibility to modify spaces over time, such as Eisenman, Lynn, Oosterhuis, and Novak; those that rooted transformations within physical space, as a bottom-up requirement.

The utopian strands of radical architecture also touched on the time-based approach, considering that the temporal dimension would transform buildings into living machines, vehicles on a building scale, adaptable to inhabitants and contexts in a dynamic relationship with people and places (i.e. Walking City by Archigram, Generator Project by Cedric Price and John Frazer).

Others sought to make humans, and their spaces, interact through computers and robots capable of accommodating time spent in spaces.

Finally, the revolution introduced by smart technologies has led to a further possible scenario in time-based design, related to the mediation, between humans and spaces, that these devices play in acceleration, compression, temporal overlap. They can accommodate ever-changing temporal and functional instances within real spaces (Hassanein 2017) (Fig. 3).

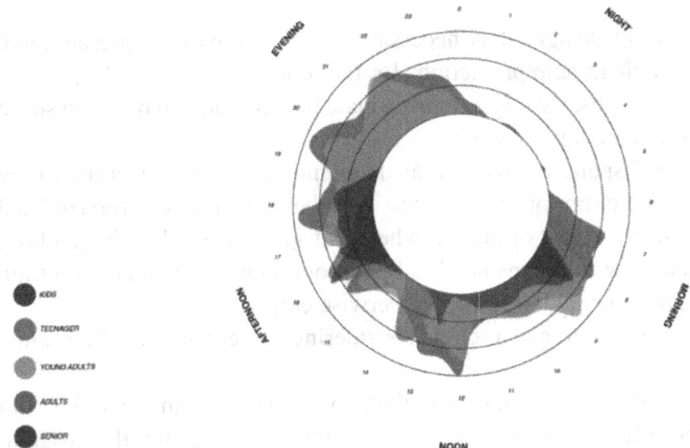

Fig. 3. Chronotopes designed by the students of the ephemeral lab, Politecnico di Milano, a.a. 2021–2022

4 Time Design in the Media Era

Indeed, the most significant implication is related to the advent of smart technologies, which reshape spaces, interiors, architecture, buildings, and infrastructure according to needs, desires, and environmental conditions, as well as personalize the experience (Carpo 2017).

The impact of digital technologies on time-based design concerns not only the production and construction of spaces and their performance, but also the possibility that space "can be controlled, enacted, and animated by digital means" (Bier 2018).

Temporal space, as configured by new media, replaces, or adds new possibilities, but more importantly intensifies social presence. Mobile media have increased spatiotemporal flexibility in social interactions. Time and space have amplified degrees of freedom requiring more flexibility, negotiation, and reconstruction of roles and rules, both in private and in public (Barbara 2020).

Communication makes many activities shareable. When we are connected, we experience co-presence because, in Heideggerian terms, the physical space we are in is juxtaposed with the phenomenological space.

This is a negotiation based on a subjective sense of space and time that, to ensure the process of interaction, requires maximum involvement and identification. The greater the inclusion and involvement, the better the interaction. Context, the space in which the body is physically present, becomes the background and not the scene of the action (Light 2006).

Not only does this give us extra space, but it makes us open, in real time, to monitoring, control, and most importantly, availability. Places and times of disconnection are increasingly rare: everything that can be done online is open 24/7 (Barbara 2012).

5 Chronotopes

If time becomes strategic to design, it is necessary to find forms of representation, measurement, semantics able to help projections for the future.

By constructing chronotopes, we begin to investigate the relationship between space and use, between mobility and digitalization.

Chronotopes can be indispensable tools to analyze, monitor, and project the future of spaces, communities, and entire pieces of cities. Whether it's a house, oversized and inflexible, with respect to the advent of digital; whether it's an existing building, whose function has expired, and new functions need to be reprogrammed; whether it's a train station crowded, for a few hours a day and left otherwise empty.

What should be the correct sizing of a school considering spaces based on their actual use?

One interesting suggestion that emerges is that, for example, many spaces could accommodate many more functions than they have, simply by staggering the program of activities. But this should be given to designers as a starting brief, that is, to think about all the possible lives of the spaces they design.

Chronos et Kairos, in fact, was a project exhibited at the 2010 Venice Architecture Biennial, which tried to host, within the Pirelli skyscraper in Milan, a program of functions that kept changing according to the hours of the day and night. It was filled with commuter-based amenities and spaces to be open 24/7. A way to reuse a building with new lives.

Similar situations could be found in parking lots, or stadiums or stations… and the list could be long.

Does anyone who designs a stadium think about the fact that it only works on Sunday afternoons, maybe even Saturdays, and empty or closed for the rest of the week? What happens on other days? Is an empty stadium a sustainable cost to the owner, to the communities, to the land? (Fig. 4)

It follows that the city is filled of spatial voids, that are temporary, sometimes because they may have fulfilled their function, so they are momentarily empty.

These spaces are not those kinds of voids, the large disused areas, but to the emptied spaces, like the huge subway stations sized only during rush hour, the rooms we don't use because we are in offices…. the spaces during their off- time.

The buildings we will design in the future, will increasingly be "time clocks", which we will ask to synchronize the timing of activities and communities. We can no longer afford monofunctional spaces.

Buildings must be designed to be adaptable over time… because even when they are closed, they use energy, and have social and economic costs.

An empty school at night, or a train station deserted 90% of the time, are unsustainable forms of waste (Barbara 2012).

Using chronotopes, for example, we can measure the on-off activities expected in spaces. This analysis is very interesting because it allows us, for example, to understand how much there are oversized spaces compared to their use and how to downsize them. And if you think about post-pandemic offices you can see how important this assessment is. (Ling and Campbell 2010).

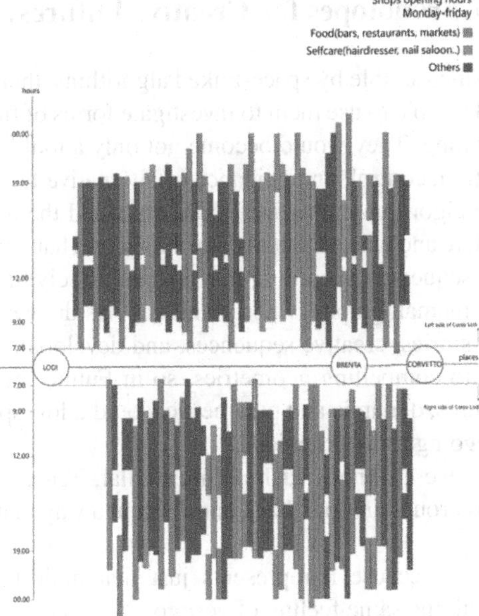

Fig. 4. Chronotopes designed by the students of the ephemeral lab, Politecnico di Milano, a.a. 2021–2022

Therefore, chronotopes have developed over the years, which are forms of analyzing, representing, and writing about the world in motion, the temporal aspects of space (Devron and Gwiadzdzinski 2017) (Fig. 5).

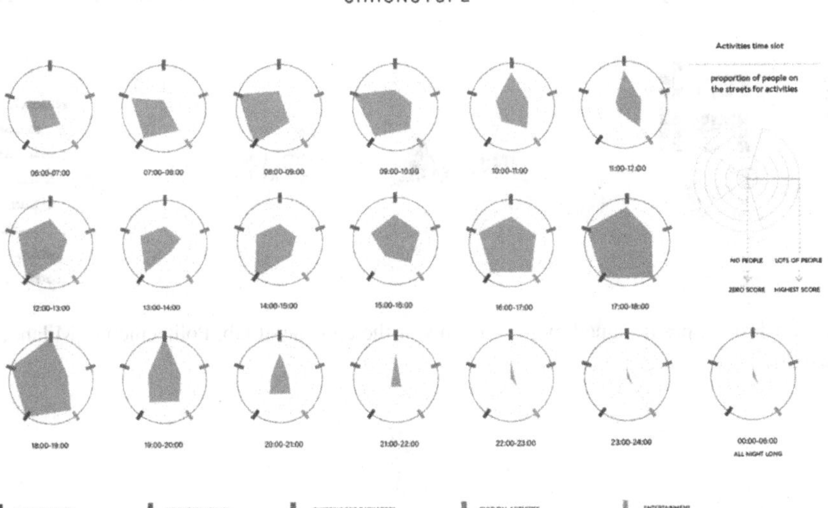

Fig. 5. Chronotopes designed by the students of the ephemeral lab, Politecnico di Milano, a.a. 2021–2022

6 Can We Use Chronotopes for Creative Futures?

If time then becomes measurable by space-linked algorithms, then it is conceivable that Future Studies would be able to use them to investigate forms of futures in space design, architecture, and planning. They would become not only a tool for projection, but also a tool for transformation, control, and guidance of alternative futures.

In addition to the algorithmic dimension, we must add the narrative one, which is able not only to simulate and narrate, but also to connect, as happens in cinematography, temporal, and spatial sequences according to a not exclusively linear logic.

As it happens in cinematography, where some movies draw a multi-chronemic narrative, moving along stories, creative sequences, and developments, able to bend time and space according to compelling geometries, so in Future Studies the construction of temporal architectures, dynamic and parametric, could allow spatial reconfigurations more suited to the ongoing transformations.

There are movies, we all know, such as Interstellar, Tenet, Inception, and others, where the story jumps around in time, back and forth in a way that is sometimes almost impossible to follow.

But it's interesting, because it represents just that multi-temporality that we're experiencing, even with the same feeling of vertigo.

Chronotopes also help us understand that there is not just a unique present and a single future.

It is evident that we can no longer speak of a single time, but of temporalities that move at different speeds and on different planes. The alternative present, as well as the possible, desirable, probable futures, etc., are the same (Raby and Dunne 2013) of a community, or an economy, or a country do not move in sync with each other. The future of one area of the planet may coincide with the near past of another, or our present coincide with desirable futures of some other country.

Our future may yet happen or perhaps somewhere it has already happened (Fig. 6).

Fig. 6. Chronotopes designed by the students of the ephemeral lab, Politecnico di Milano, a.a. 2021–2022

7 Conclusion

The liquidity that Bauman wrote about, adopted by Novak and designers inspired by the digital revolution, is therefore mixed with the temporal revolution introduced by the media in our daily lives. These are all the elements to start a time-based design exploration in the Future Studies about the spaces we live in.

It is therefore necessary for Future Studies to adopt new paradigms, make a synthesis of existing approaches and define criteria for the measurability of the results achieved.

Above all, it is necessary to graft the know-how and the results of these experiments into the profession, even in the most ordinary design, and into the spaces where we will live.

Chronotopes should be the tools of analysis and representation to understand the new relationships between time and real and virtual spaces; to introduce in architecture and in architectural education methodologies and software able to model spaces through time. Regarding the production and construction of time-based forms of space, robotics will continue to intervene in the customization of possible shapes, sizes, interactions. Finally, for experience design, an interactive dimension will be able to manage spaces adaptively according to the demands of an increasingly diverse society.

These conclusions are not the goal, they are the result of exercises carried out in my Laboratory of Spatial Design at the Politecnico di Milano, where we are designing a process of systematization of the existing spaces for educating designers capable of developing Future Studies including time-based qualities in future projects and spaces.

Designing the forms of TIME must not mean designing speed, but it will also have to mean designing rhythm (Lynch 1960) or designing slowness (Sennett 2018). It will not have to mean designing only the future of a small, wealthy elite. The competitive time we have experienced so far has created a divergent future that we can no longer sustain.

We will have to design times that are conciliatory (Bonfiglioli 1990), that slow down, if necessary (Sennett 2018), that decrease eventually (Latouche 2021), that are collaborative with neighboring communities (Manzini 2021), and inclusive of futures, able to bring together innovation and sustainable development accessible to most people.

References

Barbara, A.: Sensi, tempo e architettura. Spazi possibili per umani e non. Postmedia Books, Milano (2012)

Barbara, A.: Timescapes. New forms of time in the mediation between machines, humans and space, in SPOOL, Actuated and Performative Architecture: Merging Forms of Human-Machine Integration, Cyber-physical Architecture #3, pp. 5–15. TU Delft Open (2020)

Bauman, Z.: Liquid Times: Living in an Age of Uncertainty. Polity Press, Cambridge (2007)

Bier, H.H. (ed): Robotic Building, Adaptive Environments Springer (2018)

Bonfiglioli, S.: Architettura del Tempo. Liguori, Napoli (1990)

Carpo, M. (ed): The Digital Turn in Architecture 1992–2012. Wiley, West Sussex (2013)

Carpo, M.: The Second Digital Turn. Design Beyond Intelligence. The MIT Press, Cambridge (2017)

Drevron, G., Gwiazdzinski, L., Klein, O.: Chronotopics. Readings and Writings on a world in Movement, ELya Editions, Grenoble (2017)

Hassanein, H.: Utilization of 'Multiple Kinetic Technology KT' in Interior Architecture Design as Concept of Futuristic Innovation, ARChive, Forthcoming (2017)
Latouche, S.: Breve storia della decrescita. Origine, obiettivi, malintesi e futuro, Bollati Boringhieri (2021)
Leupen, B., Heijne, R., van Zwol, J.: Time-based Architecture. 010 Publishers, Rotterdam (2005)
Light, A.: Adding method to meaning: technique for exploring peoples' experience with technology. Behav. Inf. Technol. **25**(2), 175–187 (2006)
Ling, R., Campbell, S.W.: The Reconstruction of Space and Time. Transaction Publisher (2010)
Lynch, K.: The Image of the City. Harvard-MIT Press (1960)
Manzini, E.: Abitare la prossimità. Egea, Milano (2021)
Panahi, S., Kia, A., Samani, N.B.: Analysis of the liquid architecture ideology based on Marco Novak's theories. Int. J. Archit. Urban Dev. **7**, 63–72 (2017)
Raby, F., Dunne, A.: Speculative Everything: Design, Fiction and Social Dreaming. MIT Press (2013)
Sennett, R.: Costruire e abitare. Etica per la città. Feltrinelli, Milano (2018)

Selecting Criteria of Design of the Year Award

Chun-Yuan Chen(✉), Po-Hsien Lin, and Rungtai Lin

Graduate School of Creative Industry Design, National Taiwan University of Arts, New Taipei City 22058, Taiwan
ccytony1219@gmail.com, {t0131,rtlin}@mail.ntua.edu.tw

Abstract. The definition of "Good Design" is a constant topic that has been discussed in generations. Design awards express the praise of "Good Design" by awarding them, and at the same time try to give the term a more distinct position. Design awards have become the certification standard for design works in the contemporary era, and they also serve as a market operation tool for commercial brands, attracting many design companies or manufacturers to participate.

However, how are design awards selected? Is there a way to predict? Relevant research is rare, which also casts a layer of mystery on this process. This research attempts to use literature analysis, questionnaires and other methods to understand the screening trend of Design of the Year (hereinafter referred to as BDOTY) curated by the Design Museum, UK.

This study found that "Zeitgeist", "Access", "Change" could be used as the evaluation criteria for explaining how BDOTY's made their choices of works for shortlist. This research provide an academic basis for reference and evaluation for prediction of BDOTY or other design awards. It also provides more perspectives for understanding the spirits and operation concepts of BDOTY. The results also served as a reference for nominators or designers who are interested in participating in future BDOTY, for selecting or designing works more suitable for this award. In addition, it helps to found out where Taiwanese designs positioned in BDOTY, and possible reasons why they are in shortlist or got rejected.

Keywords: Design of the year · Design award · Prediction · Good design definition

1 Introduction

The research background of this study is based on the researchers' own experience in nominating for BDOTY. BDOTY is launched every year, and selects the most exciting and critical projects initiated or completed in the past 12 months in the world. BDOTY awards, exhibits and publish catalogue for the selected works. There are six categories of awards in BDOTY: Architecture, Digital, Graphic, Fashion, Product, and Transport.

BDOTY is different from the other design awards, it does not accept self-registration, instead only nominations from design experts invited by the Design Museum could participate.

The nominated projects will be screened by the curators and assistant curators, and they make the "Shortlist". Later, the shortlisted projects data will be collected and a

P.-L. P. Rau (Ed.): HCII 2022, LNCS 13311, pp. 439–450, 2022.
https://doi.org/10.1007/978-3-031-06038-0_33

catalogue will be published. Then the curatorial team will contact the designers and invite their works to be exhibited in the Design Museum. After the exhibition opens, there will be a jury of six with a chair will select the winner for each category, as well as the overall Design of the year.

The vast majority of nominators will more or less have the following questions in their minds: Will the project I nominate be shortlisted (or even win the final grand prize)? Does my nomination match this year's trend or reviewer's favor? After the awards were announced, some nominators may have thought: I don't know why the award I nominated was selected/ rejected? Are there any regrets? Does it seem like that nominating a certain type(s) of project(s) is more likely to be selected? Questions such as these are worth savoring in themselves, but related issues have not been discussed rationally, which triggered the motivation for this study.

2 Literature Review

2.1 The Definition of "Good Design"

How is "Good Design" defined? This topic has been of great interest to design research scholars for a long time, but it is expressed individually, full of various arguments, viewpoints, and guidelines. For example, the "Form Follows Function" proposed by Bauhaus school architect Louis Sulliva, who laid the foundation for modern design, is still the guiding principle that many designers hold as the standard.

In the late 1970s, design guru Dieter Rams proposed the famous "10 Principles of Good Design", which defines "Good Design" must be "Innovative", "Useful", "Aesthetic", " Understandable", "Unobtrusive", "Honest", "Long-lasting", "Thorough down to the last detail", "Environmentally-friendly", "As little design as possible". These principles have become iconic and keep inspiring designers around the world (Walls 2018).

However, there are still different arguments for the definition of "Good Design". Steve Jobs also tried to give his opinion on this: "Design isn't just what it looks like and feels like—design is how it works." (Walker 2003) His views on good design tend to be more pragmatic.

2.2 Design Awards

The definition of "Good Design" is still a vague area of debate and expression. However, there are still continues efforts trying to clinch the most appropriate definition of the term. Design organizations also affirm, promote and try to define "Good Design" through the distribution of awards. Since the 1950s, several design awards have been born, namely iF Design Award (1953, hereinafter referred to as iF), Reddot Design Award (1955, hereinafter referred to as Reddot), and Good Design Award (1957, hereinafter referred to as G-Mark). These design awards later became international design awards.

BDOTY was initiated by the Design Museum in London, UK. The earliest record of the award visible on the official website was in 2008. Compared with the above awards, it is a very young and late design award.

2.3 Criteria for Design Awards

Criteria for iF: In 2021, iF updated and made public its scoring system for the first time. There are five criteria: "Idea", "Form", "Function", "Differentiation", and "Impact" (Yun 2021).

Criteria for Reddot: Reddot has different scoring criteria for each category. Judging criteria for "Product Design" include: "Degree of innovation", "Ergonomics", "Product periphery", "Functionality", "Durability", "Self-explanatory quality", "Formal quality", "Ecological compatibility", "Symbolic and emotional content".

Criteria of "Brands & Communication Design" divides into "Brands", and "Communication Design". Assessment criteria in the "Communication Design" include: "Idea: originality and creativity", "Form: design quality and innovation", "Impact: comprehensibility and emotional significance".

Assessment criteria in the "Brands" include: "Idea: vision and brand values", "Form: design and brand communication", "Impact: brand identity and differentiation". Criteria for "Design Concept" include: "Degree of innovation", "Aesthetic quality", "Realisation possibility", "Functionality", "Emotional content", "Impact" (Reddot 2022).

Criteria for G-Mark: Criteria for G-Mark are: "Good Design", "Design Innovation", "Design Impact". As for the definition of "Good Design", category-specific Evaluation Criteria are listed individually (Good Design Award 2022).

2.4 Prediction of Design Awards

Few studies have been done to understand the trends of design awards. Some scholars have developed a model for the prediction of design awards based on visual elements (Wu et al. 2020). However, this method is based on the "visual" orientation of design awards, and the model does not work if the main criteria of the award is not relevant. Therefore, this study try to put focus back on the criteria of the design awards, hoping to find some clues from them.

3 Methods

3.1 Categorize

To understand the key to BDOTY's shortlist trends, the most direct way might be to obtain the scoring criteria for this award. However, BDOTY does not publicly announce its scoring system nor Judging Criteria during 2014–2019. Therefore, to understand the selection criteria for shortlist of BDOTY, we must look somewhere else. In the nomination invitations that nominators received, we found that the criteria are not mentioned in the first few years until 2017. Even with criteria, it changes every year from 2017–2019. It is quite unusual compare to other design awards, which makes it difficult to speculate on the common standards. Through analysis, some criteria with similar words or meanings can be classified and grouped, which provide a basis for further analysis (Fig. 1 and Table 1).

Table 1. Assortment of BDOTY nomination relevant data, 2014–2019.

Year	2014	2016	2017	2018	2019
Title	Designs of the Year 2014	Designs of the Year 9	Designs of the Year 10	Designs of the Year 11	Designs of the Year 12
Curator	Pete Collard	Gemma Curtin	Glenn Adamson(Guest)	Aric Chen(Guest) Eleanor Watson	Beatrice Galilee(Guest) Maria McLintock
Criteria 1			Design that promotes or delivers change (from using new materials or processes to enabling new ways of living).	Advance change or innovation whether through the use of new materials and technologies, or ways of making and doing.	Designs that inspire you
Criteria 2			Design that captures the spirit of the time (from designs such as the London 2012 Olympic Torch, to a garment that embodies a current trend).	Shift paradigms by questioning Hypothesiss and opening up new ways of seeing and thinking.	Designs that represent change in their field
Criteria 3			Design that enables access (from a website with excellent user experience to design that will improve lives).	Promote access and inclusiveness by improving ease of use and/or addressing the needs of underserved communities.	Designs that capture this moment in time
Criteria 4			Projects that have extended design practice (examples of best practice, work that seem to 'stand out' or signal the future for design).	Expand design practice in ways that push the possibilities of design and/or signal new directions for the discipline	Designs that advance access for minority groups
Criteria 5				Capture the spirit of the times.	Designs that represent intellectual leadership in society

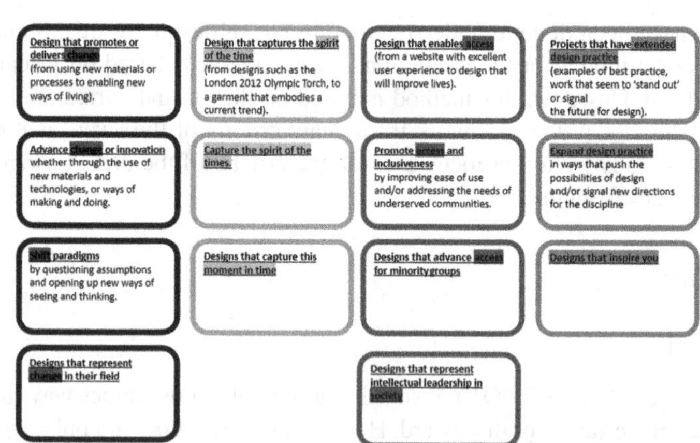

Fig. 1. The criteria (2014–2019) summarized, sorted, and grouped by color.

After several inductions and reorganizations, the original 4 to 5 recommended criteria each year (2014–2019), a total of 14 different criteria can be reduced to 4: "change", "the spirit of the times", "caring", and "Extended Design Practice". After further inspection, "extended design practice" mainly represents whether the work can contribute to the "future" of design, which is the representative attribute of "Time", similar to the attributes of "Spirit of the Time". Thus further combined the two into a single criteria of "Zeitgeist". 3 final criteria are: "Zeitgeist", "Access", "Change" (Figs. 2 and 3).

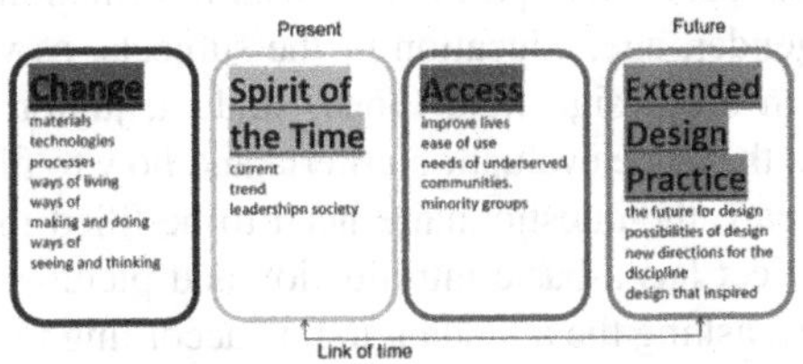

Fig. 2. 14 nomination criteria grouped into 4 categories

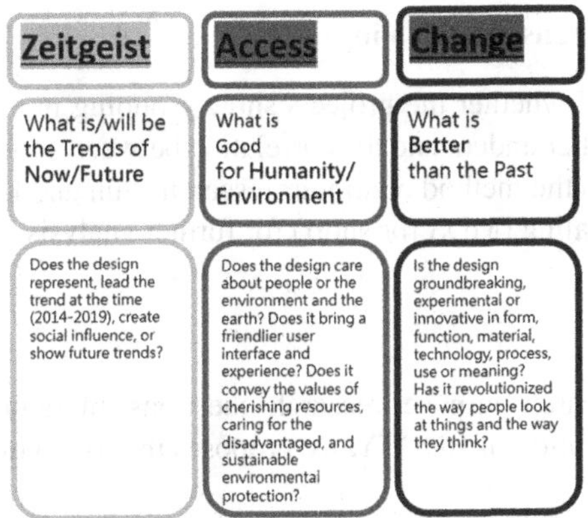

Fig. 3. The 3 criteria of BDOTY are summarized

3.2 Case Selection

This study selected a total of 22 projects from categories of "Graphic", "Transport" and "Product", mostly from 2014 to 2019, for evaluation. Including 9 projects nominated by the authors. 4 of them are in the "Graphic" category, 2 are "Transport", and 2 are "Product". We also select 4 other projects from "Graphic", 4 from "Transport", and 6 from "Product" for evaluation. Among the total 22 projects, there are 3 "Graphic", 1 "Transport", and 2 "Product" projects that have been nominated without being shortlisted, and the others are all shortlisted projects. Originally, we hoped that the number of works in each category would be the same, but there is only one project in "Transport" not in shortlist, it is not meaningful to select too many shortlisted projects in this category to compare with each other. In addition, the answering time of the subjects is also considered. If there are too many questions, the answering fatigue may increase in the second half of the questionnaire and affect the reliability of the answering.

3.3 Survey

The first part of the questionnaire, the first part give a general description of the objectives. In order not to affect the judgment results, the award of the research is not disclosed as BDOTY. Afterwards, the second part is the basic information, which collects basic information such as gender, age, education of the subjects, as well as understand the degree of abstinence in the design field (none, student, junior, experienced, senior); The third part explains the three evaluation criteria and how to fill in the questionnaire. Finally, in the fourth part, the questionnaire need to be filled in scores of criteria for each project. Each project has a basic introduction and pictures. The three evaluation criteria are listed below, asking the attendant to rate according to their understanding of the project in order to facilitate the operation and sending out questionnaires, Google Sheet is used.

3.4 MDS (Multi-dimensional Scaling)

In order to understand whether the projects show grouping in each evaluation criteria dimension, and to further understand the correlation between shortlisting and evaluation criteria, we referred to the method of similar research (Sun and Lin 2020), and adopted Multi-dimensional Scaling (MDS for short) for further analysis.

3.5 Hypothesis

According to the research purpose, research questions, literature discussion, and the experience and observation of BDOTY, we proposes the following hypotheses: □

Hypothesis 1. There should be no significant difference between the evaluation results of the experts and the Design Museum in accordance with the common criteria.

Hypothesis 2. Projects with outstanding scores in individual criteria may have a better chance of being shortlisted than the ones that have higher overall scores but rather average in each criteria.

4 Findings and Discussion

4.1 Subject Profile

A total of 31 valid questionnaires were obtained in this study, and 20 of the subjects (64.5%) were senior design professionals (Fig. 4).

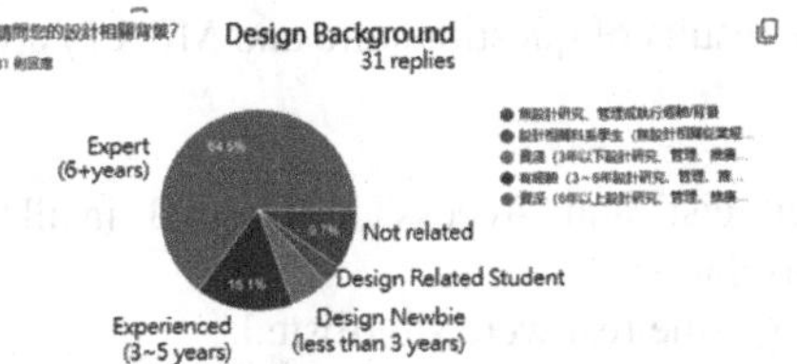

Fig. 4. Subject's design experience distribution map

4.2 Graphic Category

After analysis of scores and MDS model, the results are as follows (Fig. 5 and Table 2):

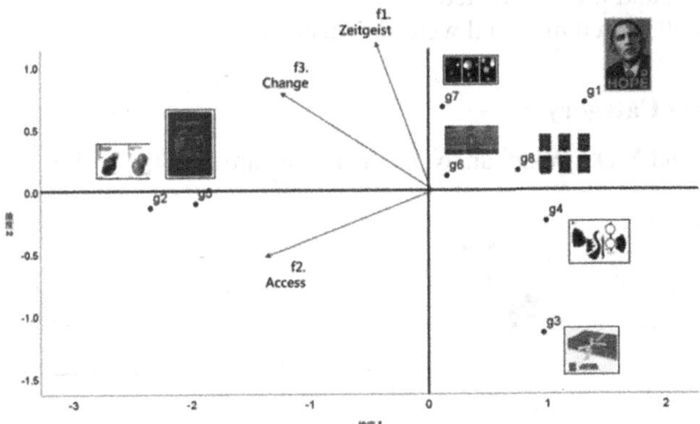

Fig. 5. MDS model of graphic category

Table 2. Average score for each criteria in the graphics category

	g1	g2	g3	g4	g5	g6	g7	g8
F1 Zeitgeist	3.89	4.11	2.71	3.29	4.07	3.68	3.82	3.57
F2 Access	2.36	4.75	2.89	2.57	4.50	3.00	2.86	2.61
F3 Change	2.75	3.93	3.00	3.29	3.79	3.57	3.89	3.46

After analyzing the results of questionnaire and MDS figure, the following findings were obtained:

1. The axis of the "Zeitgeist" and "Access" is about 90° in all three categories; the two criteria are zero correlation.
2. Except g3, g4, and g8, the rest were shortlisted.
3. g3, g4, and g8 have low scores in all criteria ("Zeitgeist", "Access", and "Change"), and they are exactly three projects not in the shortlist.
4. g1 has low scores in "Access" and "Change" but high scores in "Zeitgeist". The overall scores are low, and it only had one score outstanding, but it is shortlisted.
5. Although the "Access" score of g7 is low, but the "Zeitgeist" and "Change" scores high and it is shortlisted.
6. All criteria of g6 score roughly above the average, but no single criteria is particularly outstanding, and it is shortlisted.
7. g2 and g5 all scored high and were shortlisted.

4.3 Transport Category

After scoring and MDS model analysis, the results are as follows (Fig. 6 and Table 3):

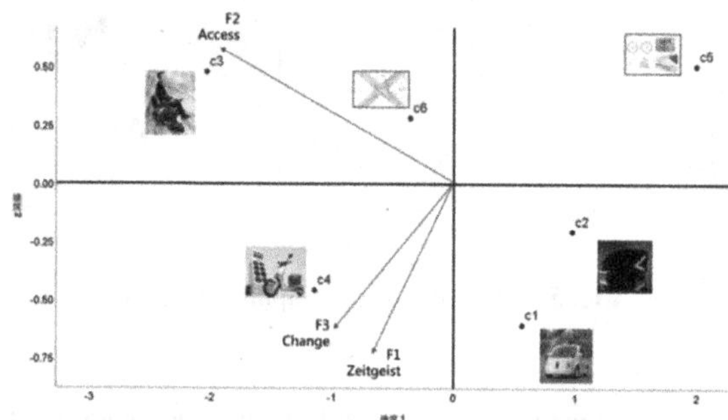

Fig. 6. MDS model of transport category

Table 3. Average score for each criteria in the Transport category

	c1	c2	c3	c4	c5	c6
F1. Zeigeist	4.32	4.00	4.32	4.54	3.82	4.14
F2. Access	3.57	3.50	4.71	4.21	3.29	4.07
F3. Change	4.07	4.11	4.32	4.29	3.61	4.11

After analyzing the results of questionnaire and MDS figure, the following findings were obtained:

1. The axis of the "Zeitgeist" and "Access" is about 90° in all three categories; the two criteria are zero correlation.
2. The "Zeitgeist" and "Change" are close to each other, and the correlation is high. Maybe it's because the transport projects are closely related to the development of science and technology, and the innovation of transport project mostly adopt the "latest" technology, thus it have similar scores in both the "Zeitgeist" and "Change".
3. Scores c5 are average, but no single criteria has outstanding scores. It is the only one not in the shortlist.
4. Except c5, the other project got at least one criteria of 4.00 or higher scores.
5. Both c5 and c2 are wearable devices for cyclists. C2 was shortlisted and c5 was not.
6. The shortlist of Transport category have higher scores than the Graphics category, which may be related to the development of science and technology and the industry's emphasis on environmental protection and carbon reduction. Thus the entry threshold score is increased in Transport category.

4.4 Product Category

After scoring and MDS model analysis, the results are as follows (Fig. 7 and Table 4):

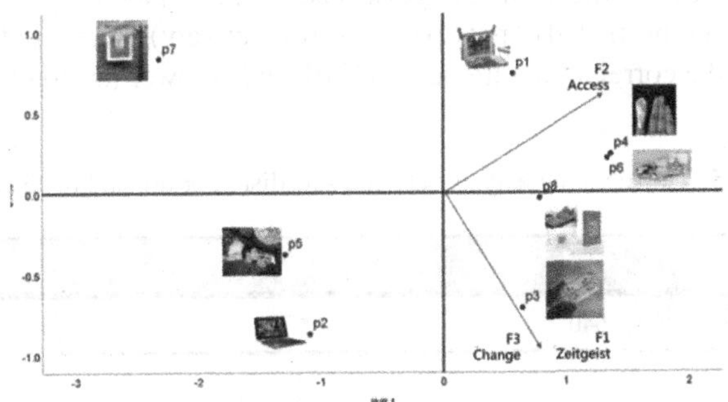

Fig. 7. MDS model of product category

Table 4. Average score for each criteria in the Product category

	p1	p2	p3	p4	p5	p6	p7	p8
F1 Zeitgeist	3.64	3.71	3.93	3.82	3.46	3.64	2.89	3.68
F2 Access	4.00	3.00	3.71	4.21	3.04	4.18	2.93	3.93
F3 Change	3.50	3.71	4.00	3.82	3.64	4.04	3.21	3.93

After analyzing the results of questionnaire and MDS figure, the following findings were obtained:

1. The axis of the "Zeitgeist" and "Access" is about 90° in all three categories; the two criteria are zero correlation.
2. The axes of "Zeitgeist" and "Change" overlap and are completely related. It may be because there are many competitions in the product category, works that can be called "Innovative (Change)" must go through many comparison with similar products with the ones in the present or in the past. Thus, "Change" and "Zeitgeist" are almost regarded as the same dimension among the subjects, and the scores of the two are highly related.
3. Except p2 and p7, the others were in the shortlist.
4. p7 scored low in all criteria.
5. Compared with other projects, p2 and p5 are far away in MDS, and their scores are more moderate. However, p5 is shortlisted and p2 is not. Maybe the Gravity Cup (p5) which is designed for the astronauts, is unfamiliar to the general subjects and thus difficult for them to give a fair score for it.

4.5 Correlation Analysis Between Shortlisted or Not and the 3 Criteria

According to the correlation analysis between being shortlisted and the three criteria of design projects, the two criteria of "Zeitgeist" and "Access" have a significant correlation with whether being shortlisted or not (.640, .568 respectively). Compared with the former two, "Change", the correlation with being shortlisted is lower (.536) (Table 5).

Table 5. Correlation analysis between shortlisted or not and the 3 criteria

	"Zeitgeist"	"Access"	Change
Shortlisted or not	.640**	.568**	.536*

*p<.05, **p<.01

We have the following findings:

a) The two criteria of "Zeitgeist" and "Access" are significantly related to the results of being shortlisted or not for BDOTY.
b) Although the correlation between "Change" and shortlisting is not as significant as the other two, but it could still affect the results to some degree.
c) "Zeitgeist"/"Access" or "Change"/"Access" are independent criteria that have nothing to do with each other.
d) There is no significant correlation between the two criteria of "Zeigeist" and "Change" in the Graphics category, but there is a high degree of consistency in the two categories of Transport and Products. The inference is probably due to the different attributes of the categories.
e) Whether there is a similar situation in other categories of awards (eg: architecture, digital, fashion) deserves further research and exploration.

4.6 Overall Score vs Single Criteria Score

It is mentioned in Hypothesis 2: "Designs with outstanding scores in individual criteria may have a better chance of being shortlisted than the designs that have higher overall scores but rather average in each criteria". After the questionnaire and MDS analysis, it can be seen that this Hypothesis is generally close to the results, and the projects that are not shortlisted are also not outstanding in the score of any single criteria.

The projects that were not shortlisted are: g3, g4, g8 in Graphics category, c5 in Transport category, and p2, p7 in Product category. These projects proved the hypothesis.

Taking the Graphics category as an example, compared with g1 (shortlisted), the average total scores of the three criteria are 9, 8.6, 9.15, and 9.64 for g3, g4, and g8 respectively. The average total score of g1 only beats g3. In the "Access" and "Change" criteria, g1 scores fewer than the other projects that are not in the shortlist, but g1 scores high in "Zeitgeist" criteria (3.89, the third highest score in the category). With only high score in one criteria, g1 was shortlisted.

A similar situation can also be observed in Product category. Compared p2 with p1 their average total score are 11.14 and 10.42 respectively. The total score of the two is not far that much different. p2 even scores slightly more in "Zeitgeist", "Change" than p1. However, p1 with the third highest score of 4.00 in this category, far outperformed p2's 3.00 in "Access" criteria, with no outstanding score in any of the 3 criteria, p2 was not in the shortlist while p1 was. It once again proves that those with outstanding scores in a single criteria have a higher chance of being shortlisted for BDOTY.

5 Conclusions, Implications, and Limitations

5.1 Conclusions

This research tried to find out the factors that determine which project to be shortlisted for BDOTY. The following conclusions are obtained:

1. There is no criteria before 2017 for BDOTY, and even with it (2017–2019), the criteria changed every year. It seems to be obscure how BDOTY made its selection of the shortlist. However, through the three common evaluation criteria summarized in this research – "Zeitgeist", "Access", and "Change", it is still possible to see why a project is shortlisted while others are not.
2. As long as the project is outstanding in any one of the criteria, there is a rather high chance to be shortlisted for BDOTY.
3. A project with a high score in any single criteria have a better chance of being shortlisted than a project with higher total score but average in any criteria.
4. The criteria of BDOTY is quite different from other international awards. BDOTY does not pursue "mass production" or "commercial value", and does not include "aesthetic" in its criteria. The shortlist of BDOTY contain more conceptual and experimental projects.

5.2 Implications

Academically, this study found a way to predict and analyze the results of a design award, and contributes to the relevant research content.

In terms of practical meaning, nominators can use this as a benchmark in the future to evaluate whether the nominated projects have a better chance of being shortlisted. Designers who are interested in being shortlisted or even winning awards in BDOTY could also refer to these three criteria to refine their projects.

5.3 Limitations

This study is limited by factors such as time, scale, manpower, and funding. Thus it has the following limitations, which further discussion and improvement are possible:

1. The number of projects nominated but not in the shortlist are very limited here. Future research might require more projects as samples for further research.
2. Considering factors such as the number of answers to the questionnaire, the time for answering, and the limited number of samples available for research, works in the categories of “Digital”, “Architecture”, and “Fashion” were not included in the questionnaire. Could the same conclusions be drawn for the three evaluation criteria derived from the study?

References

Walls, A.J.: Dieter Rams 10 Principles of Good Design. HackerNoon (2018). https://hackernoon.com/dieter-rams-10-principles-of-good-design-e7790cc983e9

Moriarty, J.: Defining Good Design. Medium (2021). https://medium.com/design-voices/defining-good-design-72062c95de60

Walker, R.: The guts of a new machine. The New York Times (2003). https://www.nytimes.com

Loew, I.: The 13 Principles of Design (And How to Apply Them) (2021). https://paperform.co/blog/principles-of-design/

Wu, J., et al.: Product design award prediction modeling: design visual aesthetic quality assessment via DCNNs. IEEE Access (2020). www.ieeexplore.ieee.org

Sun, Y., Lin, R.: Product design evaluation criteria: in the case of two "100 best-designed products of the modern era. J. Des. **25**, 45–68 (2020)

Yun: The new reform of the 2021 IF competition system, the shortlist is open for the first time! Taiwan Selected Finalists (2021). https://www.designwant.com/article/7103

WDO: iF DESIGN AWARD 2021: The winners have been selected! (2021). https://wdo.org/if-design-award-2021-the-winners-have-been-selected/

IF Design Award: iF Design Award Official Website (2022). http://www.ifdesignasia.com/pages/if-design-award

Able, C.: The 2018 Red Dot Award has come to an end, and many Chinese domestic products have won awards. Does it have any gold content? (2018).https://kknews.cc/zh-tw/design/vykzlyl.html

Good Design Award: Good Design Award Official Website (2022). https://www.g-mark.org/

Reddot Design Award: Reddot Design Award Official Website (2022). https://www.red-dot.org

Digital Thinking: A Methodology to Explore the Design of Body Artifacts

Zhilu Cheng and Jie Hao(✉)

Beijing Institute of Fashion Technology, Beijing 100029, China
jhaohj@126.com

Abstract. In recent years, the wide utilization of digital technology has made a profound impact on people's lifestyles. Designers, assisted by powerful technology, are capable of continuously developing various application virtualization tools which satisfy needs and wants of the public. Built upon digital thinking, this study makes an endeavor to combine technology and design to focus on the body itself. The construction of an innovative path model on design examines the possibility of inspiring design with the experiments on the human body in a digital environment. The methodology model, exhibiting the essential design procedure, is composed of three modules to explain the framework, which are "Perception-Data", "Technology-Verification" and "Realization-Communication". Then the validation system and iteration mechanism are established upon this framework, and the capability of this design method is evaluated by looking into actual cases and the results. This design methodology empowers designers to jump out of the traditional logic on creation and to give a brand-new definition on the body through digital means, thus offering new ideas for the integrative innovation of design.

Keywords: Digital thinking · Future creation · Design methodology · Body

1 Background and Purpose

Recent years have witnessed the significant impact of digital technology on people's lifestyles. New technologies and their utilization are spurring one after another, blurring the line between the physical world and the digital world. As digital life stands for the integration of digital technologies and human life, advanced technologies encourage designers to continuously produce diverse application virtualization software which meets the demand of humans. The mixing of virtual and real-life scenes hence comes in. Nevertheless, as the virtual lifestyle shifts living habits, it makes people pay too much attention to the virtual world, with the disregard for the real life and even for the body itself as a potential consequence. The philosopher Hubert Dreyfus, one of the initial critics of artificial intelligence, asserted, "Human embodiment in the real world is being disrupted by the virtual world, so that it is difficult for human beings to experience really meaningful life in the presence of computers and the Internet." [1] Today, overwhelmed by digital technology and virtual applications, our physical body and real life are increasingly reliant upon the convenience brought by technology, the Internet, as well as the media.

P.-L. P. Rau (Ed.): HCII 2022, LNCS 13311, pp. 451–467, 2022.
https://doi.org/10.1007/978-3-031-06038-0_34

They, with a lack of abundant real experiences in the physical world, are showcasing the tendency of being gradually constrained by technology, and are becoming progressively more homogeneous and inactive. With the increasingly blurring boundary between the digital world and the physical world as well as the deeper integration of real scenes with virtual scenes, it is likely to see the gradual rise of people's concentration on the physical world and the desire for real experiences. "The digital design has differentiated itself from conventional design through various components. Digital technologies affect the basic elements of design such as presentation, generation, evolution and production while transforming the design process." [2] Hence, designers, by means of reexamining and recognizing the human body, are expected to bring more attention to the human body and redefine the body, so that a careful consideration over the future, which may embrace the great integration of the human body and technology, can be brought about.

"Body" is perceived as a significant subject in present design studies, proved to be interdisciplinary and practical. While the past manual manufacturing is characterized by the direct contact between the body and the materials, the present manufacturing allows designers, upon the completion of the design scheme, to ditch human labour and employ machines to do the manufacturing. Moreover, in regard to digital technology, the traditional design process manifests the feature of allowing designers to construct the design form via 3D modelling after they have conceived the form. During this process, the technology is just a means of completing the design, instead of making any impact on the process of creating. However, digital technology not only helps demonstrate designers' concepts, but more importantly plays a significant role in the process of creating or even expanding ideas to conceive design forms, instead of just being a way to finish the design form. The uncertainty and logic existing in digital technology assume a vital part in assisting with devising the design form. On the one hand, as diverse mediums, software, and program languages may display blind spots in operation and lead to randomness, the uncertainty may occur in such a context. On the other hand, the logic of the technology is reflected in the way that the ideas on algorithm, straightened up in the initial stage, can be expressed in such a rigorous language as numbers or codes, and the transformation from numbers into visual forms can be achieved by the technology. As hybrid intelligence and data-driven design have obtained much more significance in design methods, the interdisciplinary feature of design has gradually shifted from helping generate ideas in a multi-disciplinary context to providing interdisciplinary practices for the design process.

Therefore, an ever-increasing number of schools and research institutions start to attach importance to the human body, revolving around the "Body" to carry out teaching and scientific research. They endeavor to apply the body as a tool and a material for exploration, as a way of motivating design innovation. However, as various subjects are established upon different foundations and exhibit diverse subject attributes, there are certain limitations even with the "Body" as the focus or the clue of these studies. Although the human body, considered by multiple disciplines from different perspectives, has not been proven with a systematic process to manifest the forces of physical elements, it is becoming progressively important in the stages of creation, investigation and research. It hence requires to conduct urgent systematic research on the body as a significant component. Are there other innovative approaches inspired by the body? What kind of information is being conveyed from them?

This study considers the body as an underlying instrument for exploration, and on the basis of digital thinking, explores the combination of technology and design to focus on the body itself. By means of constructing an innovative design path and utilizing the relative tools and methods, it investigates the possibility of creating design by obtaining inspiration from the body in a digital environment. This design method empowers designers to think outside the traditional logic of creation. Although it seems that the bodies, as carriers of human physical appearance, look the same, they showcase enormous differences. Habits of physical activity differ from individuals; limitations of the bones are diverse; and plasticity of limb muscles is also different. Hence, all this unique information can serve as research data in the early phase of creation, which enables to build a new definition of the body and helps the body, as a tool, to provide creative insight for innovative design which features integration.

On the basis of digital thinking, this study endeavors to establish the design process and fulfill the following objectives:

1. To expand the understanding of design exploration via applying the body as a tool and a specific material
2. To construct the design model of body creation and conduct the relative case analysis
3. To establish iteration in the design process and analyze the transformation from basic exploration in workshops to mature design

2 Body as an Exploration Tool

Marshall McLuhan proposed that, "Media is the extension of man" [3]. He holds that media is the extension of feelings and senses owned by human beings. The "media" that he raised in fact refers to a broad term. For instance, the vehicle is an extension of legs, the telescope an extension of sight, the telephone an extension of ears and mouth, and multimedia equipment such as television and computer an extension of sight, hearing and touch combined. It can be concluded from his theory that the design research conducted by designers around the body is actually nothing other than a functional "tool" or an aesthetic "decorative object" extended from people's senses. Therefore, it is of crucial significance to secure a more mature understanding of the senses and sensory organs so as to obtain better body experience through "media".

How do researchers make better use of the vast volume of data brought about by the body? "The difference between the general and the professional approach to design thinking is reflected in the current focus in design thinking studies on how designers and practitioners of design thinking think and act in processes" [4]. With the various approaches to exploring the body, the phase of collecting data is in fact to observe the body. In an effort of understanding the body and discerning behaviors, this study, employing the body as an exploration tool and a specific material, carries out a host of "Accessible Workshops", including "Body Perception Workshop", "body Measurement Workshop", "Body Writing Workshop". All these workshops make an endeavor to motivate the desire and curiosity to explore the extensions of the body as well as cognitive boundaries, as a way of challenging the welcomed truth in day by day conduct. They also intend to seek the possibility of expansion, deconstruction, connection, and reconstruction of the body through exploring the body movement, so as to motivate participants to delve into the interaction and association among the inner body, the external environment and multiple dimensions.

"Perception is a dynamic process" [5]. The Experimental path "Body - Low-tech - Multisensory - Media", shown in Fig. 1, is employed in a series of workshops to document the experience of the mixed perception on the senses of the body, including sight, hearing, touch, movement, smell, and taste. "Reaching beyond design's traditional focus on vision, multisensory incorporates the full range of bodily experience. We experience the world with all our senses, using data about the environment to move around, avoid danger, and communicate with others" [5]. According to this, the paper follows a detailed description of the methods and procedures to conduct experiment on body exploration in accessible workshops at the initial phase of experimentation.

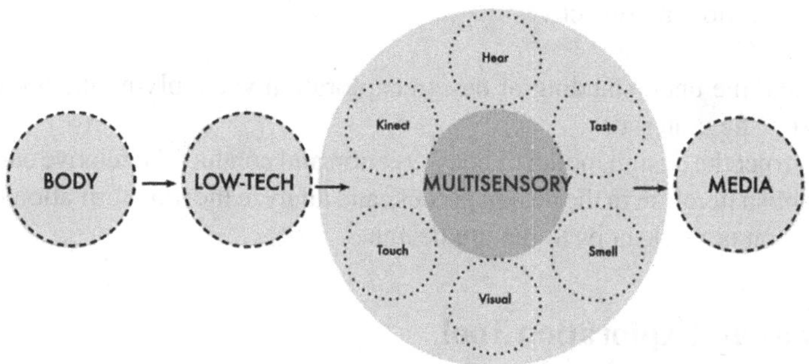

Fig. 1. Experimental path for the accessible workshops

2.1 Accessible Workshop 1: Body Perception

Tools: Body senses and limbs.

Means: Sight, Hearing, Touch, Movement.

Materials: Pens, A4 paper.

Content: Figure 2 indicates that body perception workshops, based on body training techniques frequently applied in theater, are to promote the exploration and creation of designers. The mixed body perception system encourages participants to perceive and observe the body as well as the surrounding space, which entails the sight with the eyes, the hearing with the ears, the temperature of the skin, the smell with the nose, and the touch by the hands, and meanwhile these information is documented on paper by dots and lines.

Method: Perceive the existence of body through different postures and motions, and record the trajectories of static postures and dynamic motion by means of sketches, photographs and videos (see ① in Fig. 2). In addition, the easily available materials and low-tech body movement tools are applied to record the information conveyed by the postures (see ② in Fig. 2). In the end, the recorded postures presented by different body parts are taken as informational support so as to inspire the development of design.

Development: With the body taking initiative to observe and the personalized exploration path, the mixed perception system is stimulated by the own experience of participants to inspect the surrounding space and the known world.

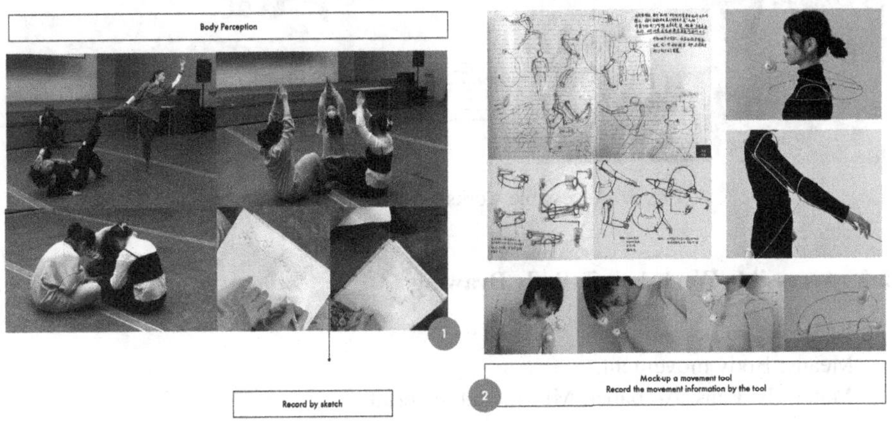

Fig. 2. Accessible workshop 1: body perception

2.2 Accessible Workshop 2: Body Measurement

Tool: Partial body.

Means: Measurement.

Materials: Ropes, Wood strips, Pens, A4 paper.

Content: As shown in Fig. 2, a limited range of materials, including ropes, wood strips, and paper, are utilized to measure a specific part of the body, such as head circumference, eye distance, eyebrow distance, face length and hand length. Then, the obtained anthropometric data are documented by means of rapid sketching in the proportion of 1:1, and the measurement data are utilized to assist in the design exploration.

Method: Measure and analyze various body parts, especially the head and hands. Next, use the easily accessible materials to produce the tools of head and hand measurement for data collection. For instance, a headgear with a simplified scale is produced with wire on the head (as shown on the left side of Fig. 3) to measure various parts of the head, while a tool that can be worn on hands is made using a rope to measure the length of hands and distance, as shown on the right of Fig. 3. Finally, the recorded data on body part measurement can be used to inspire the further development of digital thinking design.

Development: The endeavors are manifested in disassembling the body structure, meticulously measuring parts of the body, and working out the attributes of body parts. The differences in outward appearance of each body part request to expand the various methods to measure the participants in an optimal way.

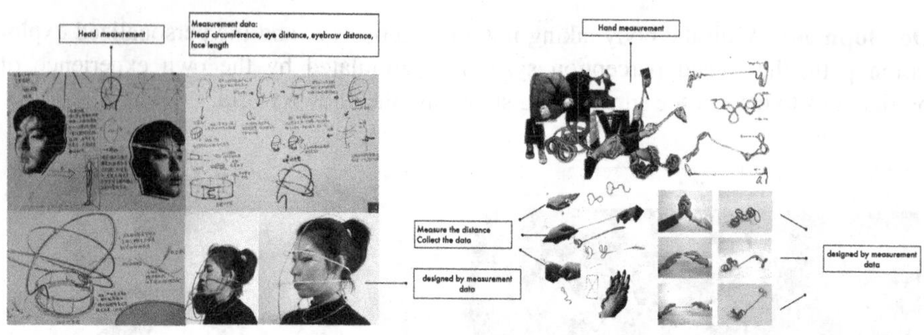

Fig. 3. Accessible workshop 2: body measurement

2.3 Accessible Workshop 3: Body Drawing

Tools: Body limbs.

Means: Body movement.

Materials: Pens, A4 paper, Mix-media materials.

Content: Figure 4 reveals that divergent thinking can be performed in body drawing to consider such questions as how to draw with the body and what are the results. The workshop encourages participants to explore the forms of body movement, in an effort to examine the drawing tools extended from the body as well as the corresponding work.

Method: Conduct research on the forms taken by body movement, and apply simple materials to complete the production of low-tech wearable tools. When these simple drawing tools are worn, drawing can be achieved on paper through dynamic movements. That is to say, the dynamic information on the body can be presented through the medium, which inspires the development of digital thinking design.

Development: The dynamics of the body will update the data linkage of the medium carriers, leading to the consequence that a vast pool of data on the shape is generated by the real-time condition that may shift all the time. However, "Drawing", a visual form to demonstrate the information, enables to investigate the parameters of the changing body which are interpreted by various medium carriers.

A series of accessible workshops allow participants from a variety of disciplines to create together by centering on the body, and to obtain a deeper exploration and understanding of the body in an appealing way. During the exploration process, the limbs, body parts, gestures, and senses are used as tools for creation. The data and information about various bodies are obtained with the assistance of such low-tech means as measurement, sight, hearing, touch, and movement, as well as simple materials including paper, pens, ropes, and sticks. The obtained information may differ from workshops, as they are collected by a range of activities, including the active observation of the body, the dismantling of the body structure, and the examination of dynamic forms of the body. The series of workshops give rise to the vast amounts of data, but a part of the data needs to be selected to conduct in-depth study in a timely manner. The measurement method which is mainly conducted manually lacks variety, presenting sensitive, fuzzy

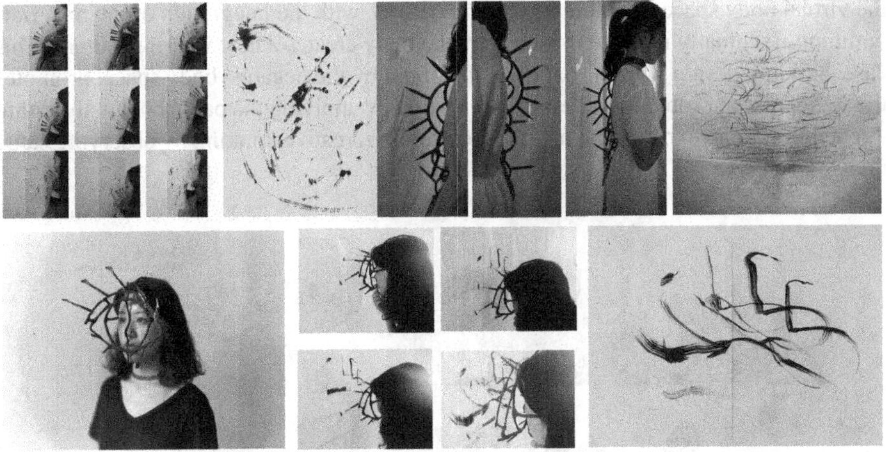

Fig. 4. Accessible workshop 3: body drawing

features for the body cognition and leading to, to some extent, certain expectations for the design results. Hence, the enhancement technology on digital thinking is demanded to offer more possibilities which can be unknown but desirable.

3 Digital Thinking is Engaged in Exploring the Design of Body Artifacts

3.1 Project 1: Virtual Field of the Body

Taking into account the Body Perception in Accessible Workshop 1, this case intends to actively investigate the virtual linkage between the body and the space, and to look into the multiple interaction between the human body and digital materials. Record the information about static posture of the body based on the different postures and motions recorded in the work camp. As shown in Figure x, the record of body shapes presented by different body parts in the daily movements of human body (see ① in Fig. 5) can be used to visualize the negative space created by various postures, and to record the shapes presented by different body parts such as neck, shoulder, chin-hand, finger-hand, shoulder-finger, shoulder-hand, etc. (see ② in Fig. 5), materialize these shapes through digital technology (see ③ in Fig. 5), and make the finalized presentation through the production of wearable objects (see ④ in Fig. 5) and show display (see ⑤ in Fig. 5).This project demonstrates diverse postures of the body and the negative space occupied by the body is also visualized to secure accurate measurement data, so that the virtual space for the audience can be built with plastic manifold materials. In this visual space, 3D scanning offers the visual expression of the negative space which cannot be visually presented before. "Particles" are placed by designers in the body space, and these "particles" together with the restrained human postures compose of a spontaneous endogenous system. This system keeps twisting, refracting, splitting, and extending in the virtual body space, building a "flowing nature" with the integration of the materials within it. Eventually its combination with the body creates a new wearing pattern. This case, building design with the data brought about by the negative body space, promotes the settlement of problems in design exploration by applying the path "body - algorithm - generation", and expands the methods to provoke creative thinking by observing static body postures.

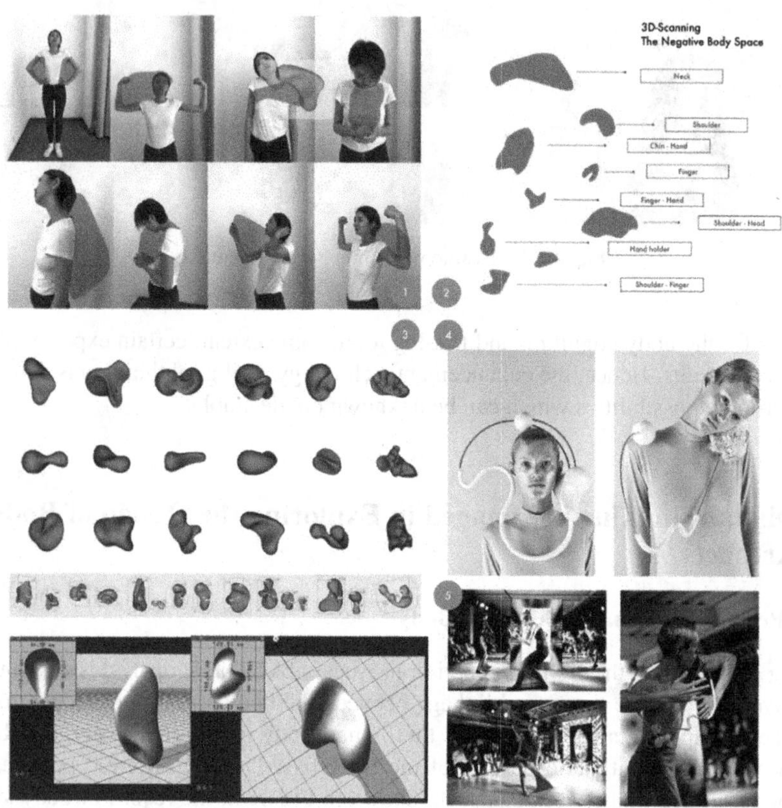

Fig. 5. Design process for virtual field of the body

3.2 Project 2: Parametric Modelling of Human Body Shape

This case, a form of "generative design for the body", continues the body measurement conducted in Accessible Workshop 2. Based on the dimensions of different body parts as recorded using the body measurement tools that are made in the workshop, the development of design is facilitated with the assistance of digital software. The measurements of the body are employed to build the shape of body parts, which helps construct a virtual model. Figure 6 demonstrates the whole procedure of building the forms of "body wearing". Firstly, the initial spatial models of modules are established. Then the variable object forms are developed by employing the parameterized data with the computer, with a basis on the measurement of the length, width, height, and volume of the body parts. Next the functional patterns of "body wearing" which completely satisfy the uniqueness of the anatomical structure of the human body are built by utilizing 3D scanning to establish the virtual mapping of each body part, such as ears, mouth, nose, and chest, as well as by adjusting the density with algorithms. Eventually, the entities are capable of being generated by 3D printing technology. The case helps resolve the problems that disturb the body extension of design by employing the path "algorithm - generation - mapping", which is to say that the body is placed in virtual space to perform digital subtraction and generate a new wearable form.

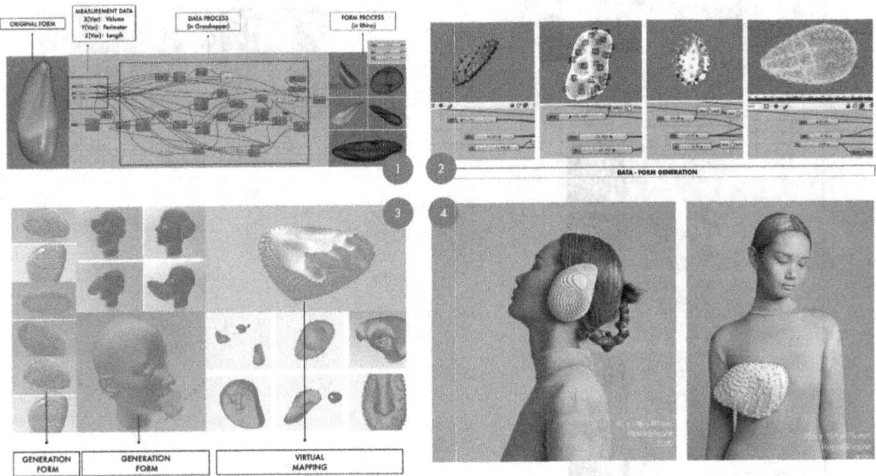

Fig. 6. Design process for parametric modelling of human body shape

3.3 Project 3: Utilizing Human-Computer Interaction to Generate Forms

In regard to the concept of body writing explained in Workshop 3, the body, as the focus of the research, does not need to be constrained to merely drawing, as it owns the diversity of its visual carrier. Instead, various expression forms of its media can be investigated. For instance, a brand-new approach of employing human-computer interaction to design jewelry is shown in Fig. 7. With real-time data of human-computer interaction helping generate design forms, a variable design form is able to be transformed and obtained from the body shape, postures, and movement. The new approach thus plays a part in expanding innovative design ideas and application scenarios. In this case, the "three-dimensional form of design" is shifted by "changing body shape" to achieve a spontaneous design closed loop. The experimental process is as follows: Kinect is connected to the computer by writing Grasshopper Python Code; Rhino-Grasshopper-Firely tool is used to detect the real-time body movement data, which are dismantled, in the space, into 25 real-time dynamic points corresponding to each body part; the corresponding dynamic points are joined to form the human skeleton space, and a three-dimensional visual expression is thus produced. The path "virtual mapping-form generation-aesthetics and functions" aims at improving design; i.e., it assesses the new form after finishing virtual mapping, uses the real-time data to generate infinite design forms, and establishes a great number of evaluation methods, promoting the production of brand new design.

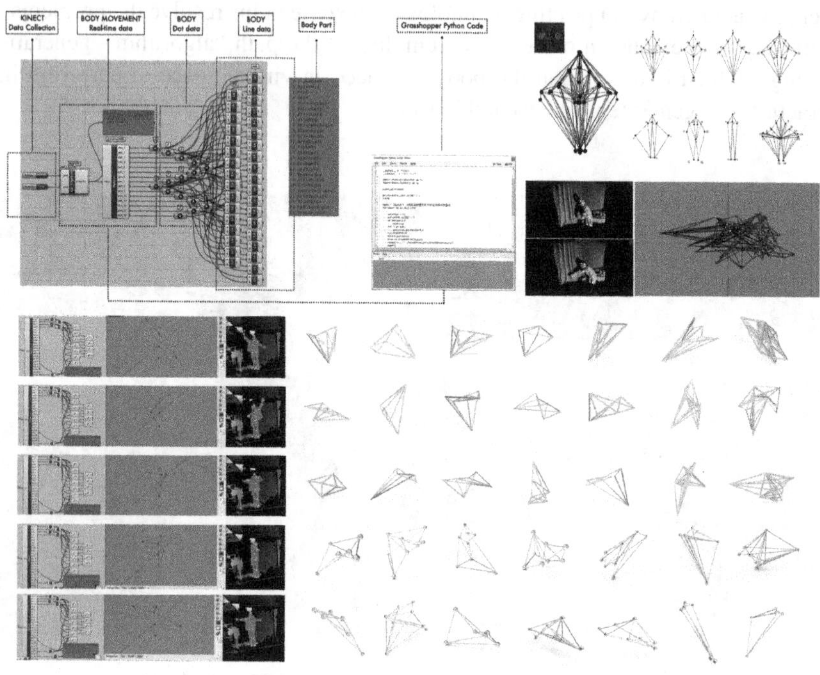

Fig. 7. Design process of utilizing human-computer interaction to generate forms

The exploration of body perception provides enlightenment for all the cases mentioned above. "The detachment from making within contemporary design for manufacturing is not developing the haptic and tacit knowledge within designers that are the traditions of craft and material making and can inform further material opportunities within the digital design development process" [6]. Thus, the design projects of body artifacts built upon the digital world is exhibited at length in body data analysis, algorithm construction, form generation, virtual mapping, as well as aesthetics and functions. The first step is to collect body data, which entails both the traditional measurement methods to collect body data and the digital technology to obtain real-time dynamic body data. Based on the collected data, the second step, Algorithm Construction, aims at constructing algorithm and programming to build the body database. The third step, Form Generation, is expected to generate diverse variable forms and objects through computer parameters and programming. The fourth step, Virtual Mapping, utilizes 3D scanning to check body parts, such as neck and wrist, and digital subtraction is carried out to generate functional jewelry consistent with the uniqueness of human anatomical structure or wearable apparel products. The fifth step, Aesthetics and Functions, endeavors to select the design that brings new aesthetic experience and embraces more potential application with the assistance of specific selection approaches and verification.

4 Digital Thinking Methodology

According to "synesthesia" [7] proposed by Maurice Merleau-Ponty in his theory "body schema" [7], the multisensory system of the human body may showcase multiple senses as a way of perceiving the changes in the environment as well as in the surrounding messages through sight, hearing, smell, touch, taste, movement, and feelings. Since this system of perception is capable of performing independently and completely demonstrating the virtual expression of the outside world in a holistic way, a large amount of information can be accumulated in this sensory system over a time period, a short time or even in real time. Therefore, it requires a methodological path to logically dismantle massive information so as to build databases for creation.

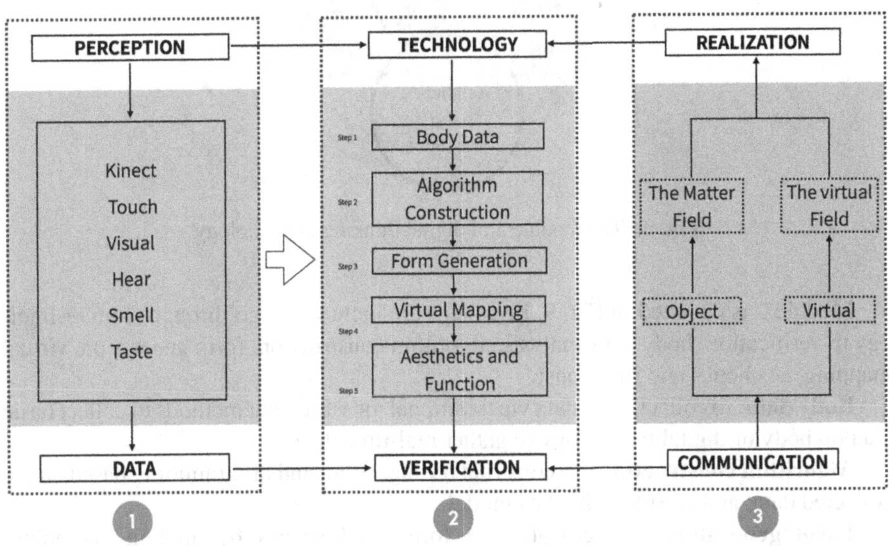

Fig. 8. The construction model of digital thinking methodology

With the intention of expanding design ideas and the channels built upon the framework of digital thinking, the methodology is divided into three modules, as shown in Fig. 8. Module 1 refers to "Perception-Data", Module 2 "Technology-Verification", and Module 3 "Realization-Communication".

The combination of the above three modules establishes the digital thinking methodology. The essential procedure of Module 1 is exhibited in collecting data via the mixed body perception which entails sight, hearing, touch, movement, smell, and taste, with the low-tech approach, high-tech technique and the two combined to conduct the collecting. This module aims at exploring various perceptual experiences which occur between bodies, between body parts, and between the body and the environment.

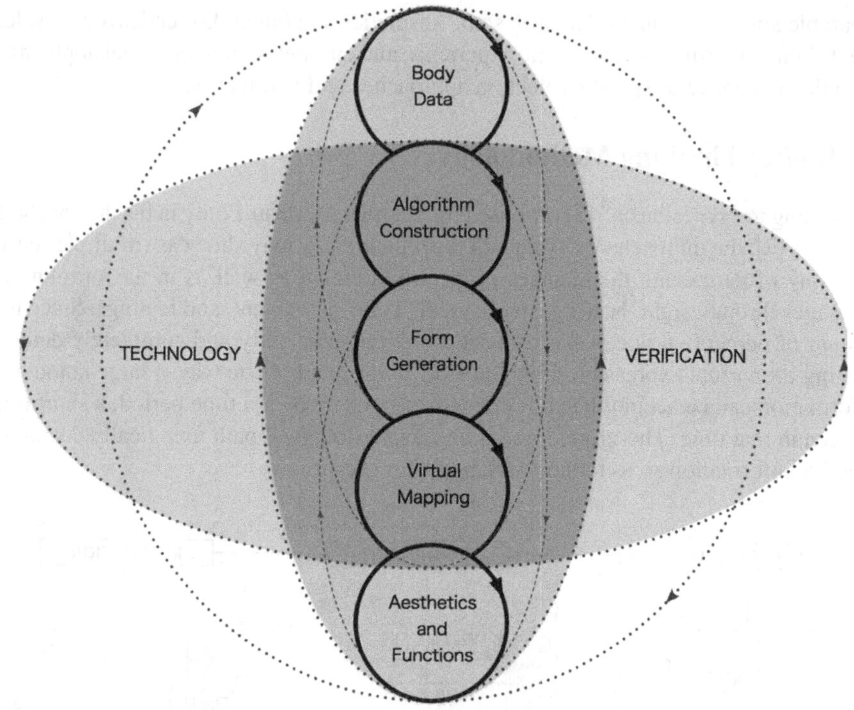

Fig. 9. The module 2 of digital thinking methodology

Module 2 is depicted in Fig. 9. Five steps are included to go through from technology to verification: body data analysis, algorithm construction, form generation, virtual mapping, aesthetics and functions;

Body data: to collect body data via traditional measurement methods to collect basic data on body or digital technology to gather real-time data.

Algorithm construction: to construct the algorithm and programming based on the collected data, and establish the data model.

Form generation: to generate free forms and shapes by applying computer parameters and programming.

Virtual mapping: to develop negative wear patterns through 3D scanning and digital subtraction.

Aesthetics and functions: to bring about innovative aesthetic experience as well as potential application of wearable devices.

The processes reflect a circular procedure of design from technology to verification. Different from the traditional linear procedure of design, this whole procedure proves to be a cyclic path, with three distinct clues and each clue showcasing the possibility of generating a variety of designs. The first clue (the black line in the figure) presents a small design cycle having independent steps. Every step in it, if assisted with different tools and means, enables the construction of an innovative exploration way which exhibits the personal features of designers. The second clue (the red line in the figure) is a medium-size design cycle which including various steps in series. The three cases examined in this paper exemplify the clue. Project 1 conducts the design exploration on the negative space of the body by applying the creation approach "Body data - Form generation". Project 2, based on the data from body parts, utilizes the path "Body data - Algorithm construction - Form generation -Virtual mapping" to extend and develop design. Project 3, employing the path "Body data - Algorithm Construction - Form generation - Aesthetics and functions", aims at using the real-time dynamic data to generate infinite three-dimensional shapes, so that more new design ideas may be motivated. The above three cases exemplify merely three paths, but in fact more design exploration can be promoted by the varied combination of paths. The third clue (the blue line in the figure) is the grand design circle characterized by the procedure "Technology - Verification - Technology". This clue, regarding design as a whole, goes through from importing technology to verification and then returns to the path for the iteration of technology.

Eventually, the application of the design has to experience Module 3 through the functional verification process. In module 3, "The Matter Field", indicating the physical world, and "The Virtual Field", referring to the virtual, world return the design results to the corresponding real and virtual space in a respectively physical and virtual manner. It manifests that the advancement of digital technology allows the diversity of the final design work. "The Matter Field" attempts to construct an entity by matter and data in the physical space, while "The Virtual Field" is expected to build the virtual form by algorithms in the virtual space. The interaction of "The Matter Field" and "The Virtual Field" helps construct the main object of creation. The focus of designers' work is progressively moving away from the research on and application of the "known form" to the exploration and innovation of the "unknown form", while digital thinking proves to be the essential methodology to promote this shift.

5 Evaluation and Verification

5.1 Progress Implementation

Built upon the digital thinking framework, three projects are utilized as testing models to assess the evolution from design exploration to the output of design results, and to evaluate the design schemes brought about by the massive information and data on the body, so that an in-depth re-examination on the relations among different bodies, body parts, and the outside of the body can be secured. In this study, a total of 48 designers and artists have been invited to verify and analyze three design cases. These highly experienced designers, aged from 26 to 45, specialize in different fields of design and research, of whom 12 people are engaged in clothing design, 20 people are dedicated to accessory design, 10 people focus on product design, and 6 people are committed to interaction design. Besides, 20 of them are male and the remaining 28 are female.

The validation framework is essentially composed of Visualization [8], Independence [9], and Mobility. Visualization transfers non-visual information into a visual model as the final output; Independence refers to the depth to which the body data can be obtained by dismantling intricacy relationships, including the separate information on body parts, the complete information after the body parts are connected, as well as the distinctive information on different bodies; Mobility indicates the flow intensity of the dynamic body in both physical space and virtual space, which, on one side, is expressed in such physical forms as body proportions, postures, walking, as well as movement, and, on the other side, is revealed in virtual space where the dynamic performance of body shape in space coordinate axes is conducted.

5.2 Verification Analysis

The above three points consist of the evaluation standards of the digital thinking framework, which empowers to verify the possibility of stretching out body creation with diverse body dimensions. These 48 designers voted on the three projects by considering three factors of evaluation, which are visualization, independence and mobility. On the one hand, this evaluation is intended to reflect the views of cross-disciplinary designers on the outcomes of implementing the digital thinking method. On the other hand, it is expected to verify whether a satisfactory design effect can be achieved.

NAME	N	VISUALIZATION	INDEPENDENCE	MOBILITY
PROJECT 1	48	33	6	9
PROJECT 2	48	16	20	12
PROJECT 3	48	7	12	29

Fig. 10. 48 Designers voted on the three projects

As shown in Figs. 10 and 11, in Project 1, 33 designers considered the case to perform best in visualization. Besides, this case won 6 and 9 votes for independence and mobility, respectively. Given the general feedback from these designers, it can be judged tha the project applies the path "Body data - Form generation" to achieve design transformation. It reveals that the non-visual negative space, a result of static postures, is capable of being converted into a visual design prototype, if the postures are captured by technology, and can eventually obtain an entity as its output. With regard to visualization, since the case is engaged in exploring how to transform the non-visual space in the body into a visual expression, its visual pattern is proved to be the most distinct. Concerning independence, a large amount of information about body parts is involved in this case, including "neck", "shoulder", "finger - palm", "hand - shoulder", "chin - forehead" and other static postures, all of which are separate data, so its independence is moderate. Nevertheless, in regard with mobility, as this case concentrates on static postures with the entity a major output form, it lacks certain mobility.

Relatively speaking, the ratings of Project 2 are relatively balanced and concentrated, with 16 out of 48 votes won for visualization, 20 out of 48 votes won for independence, and 12 out of 48 votes won for mobility, respectively. This project performs the design exploration with the path "Body data - Algorithm construction - Form generation - Virtual

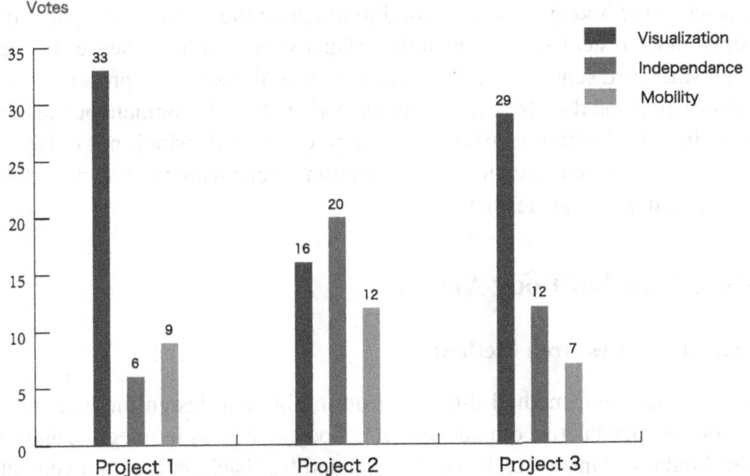

Fig. 11. Visual bar chart of votes for the 3 projects by digital thinking methodology

mapping". Its data are generated by measuring various body parts, including ears, mouth, nose, and chest, and such data on them as the length, width, height and volume are thus obtained. Based on this database, various design forms are then developed with the parameterized method. Due to the differences in individuals, even though the identical parts of different bodies are measured in the same way, the obtained data information can be totally different. Hence, this project demonstrates the greatest distance among its participants, which implies that the case displays the relatively substantial independence.

As for Project 3, 29 designers vote for best mobility, whereas the independence gains 12 votes and visualization gains 7 votes. This project engages in the design technique of employing human-computer interaction to generate design forms, and its transformation path is "Body Data - Algorithm Construction - Form Generation - Aesthetics and Functions". This case puts a focus on the real-time dynamic data of the body, and endeavors to, by "changing body postures", generate an infinite number of "3D design forms". The case shows the biggest pattern of mobility, since the shape changes in real space can be generated in virtual space with 3D technology in real time, and each change is thus capable of gaining a new design; as this project also involves the process of converting non-visual data, i.e. real-time dynamic data, into visual data, it occupies a second place with regard to mobility; since the case has only developed the data on each individual so far, it presents relatively less independence.

The performance of the digital thinking framework motivates designers, in an optimal way, to jump out of the traditional logic on creation, and also examines the visualization, independence, and mobility of design schemes with digital techniques. Hence, it plays a significant part in defining the body in a new way, thus providing fresh ideas for integrated innovation on design. In the future, it is necessary to increase the cases of design practice based on this loop approach, which is crucial to the in-depth verification as to the outcome of its implementation. Through the work camp, body design is inspired, while body data, the non-visual information in the body and the environment are applied to build a set of method systems purposed to integrate individual body parts, postures, movements and physical senses, including visual sense, auditory sense, tactile sense, movement, smell and sense of taste. Through the visual design and presentation of non-visual information and data collected from the body to the environment outside the body, more body-based explorations of design can be conducted, which not only facilitates the formulation of design selection and evaluation mechanism but also materializes the abstract standard of design aesthetics.

6 Future Trend of Body Artifacts

6.1 Broaden the Research Method

To construct a research method different from traditional design methods requires to analyze from the perspective of understanding body as well as to integrate and calculate multimodal data. For instance, data collection and feedback on body movement, sight, touch, smell and taste can be obtained by such techniques as body dynamics, visual images, tactile induction, sound perception, and odor recognition. "Digital media can be "embedded" in a deeper way in different parts and contents of the subject, which may also imply that the fundamental nature of the subject will change." [10] This methodology and path empowers diverse disciplines to expand the knowledge of the body, and explores a new and interesting creation method of developing three-dimensional design, which is generated by the interaction between different human bodies and computers. In this way, a research system which expects to inspire design with the human body is capable of being established. This research path gives priority to integrating the body's unknown features, uncertainty, and mobility into the design process, so as to build a circulation system that spontaneously gives rise to design.

6.2 Re-empower Future Creation

It is very likely that human beings live in a "dematerialized" world in the future, where the interaction between the human body and the outside world might be achieved through "a cyborg", which is to combine the body with machines to conduct interactive "communication" about senses and body feelings. Established upon the digital thinking framework, the hybrid manufacturing entailing both low-tech methods and high-tech techniques promotes to output the work holding physical and virtual attributes, which gives rise to more possibilities of future creation on design. A variety of design proposals which range from the inside to the outside of the body, from part to the whole, and from single-body to multi-body, are expected to empower future design on creation.

7 Conclusion

This paper builds a digital thinking framework and, by combining technology and design through digital thinking, revolves around the body. This methodology is built by conducting research on a couple of actual cases as well as assessing the results of these cases, and after the completion of the methodology, it is ameliorated and perfected by the repeated experiments on a host of design cases. In this way, the verification system is established upon the digital thinking methodology, which endeavors to draw a new definition of the body through digital means and to investigate the possibility of body creation in the digital context. This study, based on the digital thinking framework, aims at building a design system which considers the body as inspiration. A series of accessible workshops with the body as the exploration form are performed, in which the concept of body is expanded and perceived as the tools and materials. The design models on body creation are thus built with the case analysis followed. A design iteration mechanism is then established, implying the transformation from design exploration to mature design.

References

1. Dreyfus, H.: On the Internet (Thinking in Action). Routledge, London (2001)
2. Çakmakçıoğlu, B.: Effect of digital age on the transmission of cultural values in product design, S3824-S3836 (2017). https://doi.org/10.1080/14606925.2017.1352886
3. McLuhan, M.: Understanding Media: The Extensions of Man. The MIT Press, Reprint edition, Massachusetts (1994)
4. Ida, E.: Quick Guide to Design Thinking. Thames Hudson, London (2021)
5. Lupton, E.; Design is Story Telling. Cooper Hewitt, Smithsonian Design Museum, New York (2017)
6. Grimshaw, D.: Crafting the Digital: Developing expression and materiality within digital design and manufacture. (2017). https://doi.org/10.1080/14606925.2017.1352878
7. Merleau-Ponty, M., Cobb, W.: (translator): The Primacy of Perception. Northwestern University Press, Illinois (1964)
8. Scientific Computing and Imaging Institute. https://www.sci.utah.edu/research/visualization.html. Accessed 07 Dec 2021
9. Cambridge Dictionary. https://dictionary.cambridge.org/dictionary/english/independence. Accessed 18 Dec 2021
10. Marner, A., Örtegren, H.: Four approaches to implementing digital media in art education (2013). https://doi.org/10.3402/edui.v4i4.23217

Empathy Design: Poster Design for Animal Protection

Yifan Ding(✉) and Jun Chen

Graduate School of Creative Industry Design, National Taiwan University of Arts, New Taipei City 220307, Taiwan
2929904428@qq.com

Abstract. Empathy is the ability to think differently and understand the content of other people's thoughts, and this ability was used in design creation. This study first examines the relationship between empathy design, animal protection poster design and symbolic communication models. This is followed by a self-analysis of the participants posters, the development of a model of the "designer encode" to "viewer decode" framework, and the improvement of the design of the self-artwork. Finally, the reliability of the proposed model was examined through questionnaire testing of 11 groups of posters on animal protection issues. This study finally establishes a "designer encode" to "viewer decode" architectural model for the implementation of animal protection posters, which is in line with the principles of empathy design. This will be a useful reference for subsequent researchers and designers.

Keywords: Empathy design · Animal protection · Poster design · Symbolic communication

1 Introduction

As society develops, more social topics were exposed, such as the destruction of the natural environment by human and the harm done to animals, all of which are undermining the model of harmonious coexistence between human and nature. In terms of visual communication, posters on social topics usually provide the viewer with a sense of tension and shock and cause a certain amount of introspection. In the design of social topic posters, the visual communication skills are used to transform the content that author want to express in a reasonable way, so that the poster have a better visual performance and promote positive content and ideas.

In recent years, the issue of animal protection has been gaining attention and we can find information about it in news, books, and magazines. In the field of visual communication, poster design for animal protection theme is also occurs frequently in international competitions, but the large number of entries and the similarity in subject matter has led to a variety of visual symbols appearing in poster design, making it possible to begin to follow a pattern in the design of animal protection posters. Researchers have found that posters on animal protection issues can be explored in relation to the theory

P.-L. P. Rau (Ed.): HCII 2022, LNCS 13311, pp. 468–479, 2022.
https://doi.org/10.1007/978-3-031-06038-0_35

of empathy, and there are competitions that use empathy as a theme for their events. Empathy design has been mentioned more often in product design in the past and has been used in poster design for public service. However, the link between empathy and animal poster design has been less explored, so this study will focus on this part.

The objectives of this study are: (1) To explore how the connotation of empathy can be appropriately translated into the design of posters on animal protection issues. (2) To establish a model for the implementation of a "designer encode" to "viewer decode" architecture for animal protection posters, so that they are consistent with the principles of empathy design.

2 Literature Review

2.1 Animal Protection and Empathy Design

Animal Rights, which came into common use in the 18th century, is somewhat philosophical. All animals are equal, whether they are moral agents or moral patients, and should be treated with respect [1]. Animal rights issues are basically companion animals, wild animals, economic animals and zoo and performance animals [2]. Zoos are defined as any enclosed location where wild animals are kept. The functions of zoos are usually divided into five categories: to show off power and wealth, to watch animals fight, to serve as a hunting playground and source of meat, to satisfy the desire to collect and to provide scientific research. Performing animals are groups that specialize in circuses and animals as their main act and are mainly managed to lead groups of animals [3].

Empathy, from the Greek term empatheia meaning em- or 'in' and pathos or 'feeling', describes the ability to understand and share the feelings of another [4]. Empathy is the ability to think differently and understand the content of another person's thoughts [5]. The main components of empathy can be divided into three parts: firstly, the ability to see the world through another person's point of view on a cognitive level; secondly, the ability to engage with the other person's emotions on an emotional level; and thirdly, the ability to convey cognitive and emotional understanding to the other person in verbal and non-verbal ways on a behavioral level [6].

The psychological processes of empathy are mainly applied in the field of psychology, but some researchers in the field of design also acknowledge their existence. Designers should imagine themselves in the user's context or imagine the user in the user's context [7]. Emotional-cognitive interactions emphasize the importance of feeling the emotions of others and understanding them in a purposeful apostolic way [8]. Empathy design in public service posters can be used in ways that express emotion in graphics, convey emotion in color and render emotion through contextual ambience. The methods of expressing emotions in graphics are narrating emotions, highlighting emotions, expressing emotions, setting off emotions and triggering emotions [9]. To sum up, the most important thing to achieve is to think from the viewer's or user's point of view, and a poster design that meets the connotation of empathy should have the effect of making people resonate and empathies with it.

2.2 Poster Design and Symbolic Communication Theory

As "art of the moment", posters can accurately and artistically present various things, express human emotions and embody tangible social values and meanings [10]. The constituent elements of posters can be summarized as textual elements, illustrative elements, color elements and choreographic elements [11]. The creation of posters is created by using a combination of four elements: text, color, graphic and choreography [12]. There are five directions for the creation of posters on animal rights issues, namely pictorial representation, realistic image restructuring, irony, image restructuring and minimalist style [2].

Semiotics is the transformation of social phenomena into signs, and then explores the "meaning" hidden behind them, as well as the relationship between the "form" expressed on the surface of the sign and the "meaning" hidden behind it [13]. Roland Barthes extended Saussure's signifier and signified, breaking away from the traditional linguistic use to turn to textual research and analysis to discuss the duality of symbolic meaning: the original first level of meaning, which expresses "extended meaning", is the more obvious symbolic meaning. To build out the connotation in which it is located is to construct the second level of "connotative meaning" of the myth [14, 15]. From the point of view of the symbolic mode of communication, where artistic creation takes place with the encode of the artist and the decode of the listener, a good communication must have three levels: the first is the technical level, so that the recipient can see and understand how the creator, through his creation, precisely conveys the message he wants to send. The second is the semantic level, so that the recipient of the message understands what he or she wants to say. The third is the effect level, which allows the recipient to act on the original meaning of the message if he or she understands it [16, 17]. In the cognitive ergonomics layer corresponds to do you see it. The semantic layer corresponds to do you understand it. The effect layer corresponds to are you impressed [18]. Based on the above-mentioned literature on poster design elements, this study concludes that a poster work should have four major elements: graphics, color, text and layout, and the designer should integrate their rational configuration and use. This research study is about poster design, which will be based on the three layers of technical layer, semantic layer, and effect layer. After the summary of poster composition elements and the combing of semiotic content, the three levels of communication will be modified into technical use, symbolic expression, and effect expression.

3 Methodology

This study is divided into three research steps. The first step is to collect the finalists and winners of the Red Dot Design Award and Taiwan International Student Design Competition for the five-year period 2016–2020 on the topic of animal protection and analysis them for self-analysis. The reason for choosing these two competitions is that they have numerous amounts of posters on animal protection issues. Five groups of posters (one for each year) were selected as the most relevant to the issue of animal protection, and then the design elements of the posters were analyzed, and the meaningful symbols of the posters were extracted.

The second step was to construct a rubric for the animal poster design, a model of the "designer encode" to "viewer decode" translation architecture and to refine the researcher's original poster work. As can be seen in Fig. 1. The three-stage cognitive schema measure was used as the basis, combined with empathy-related theories and semiotic and cognitive communication theories. The three levels of poster design communication, "technique application", "symbolic performance" and "effect expression", are used to construct a deeper assessment attribute, which corresponds to the three stages of cognition and forms a model of the designer's coding to the viewer's decoding architecture. The researcher's original work, "Tragedy of Life", was then modified and designed into 6 groups. The original work is a TISDC 2019 poster selected with the theme of protecting persecuted animals in circuses and evoking empathy in the viewer.

The third step in the quantitative study was to conduct a questionnaire survey and then analysis the results of the questionnaire. In the questionnaire design, 5 groups of selected poster competition entries and 6 groups of posters designed by the researcher were used for the questionnaire, as shown in Table 1. The questionnaire was administered on a five-point Likert scale, the questions were compiled base on six items: "theme accuracy, visual effects, context creation, expressions, emotion resonance, sympathetic", to ask the participants about their preference for the posters, as shown in Table 2. Based on the analysis of the results, the reliability of the proposed "designer encode" to "viewer decode" model was verified and conclusions were drawn.

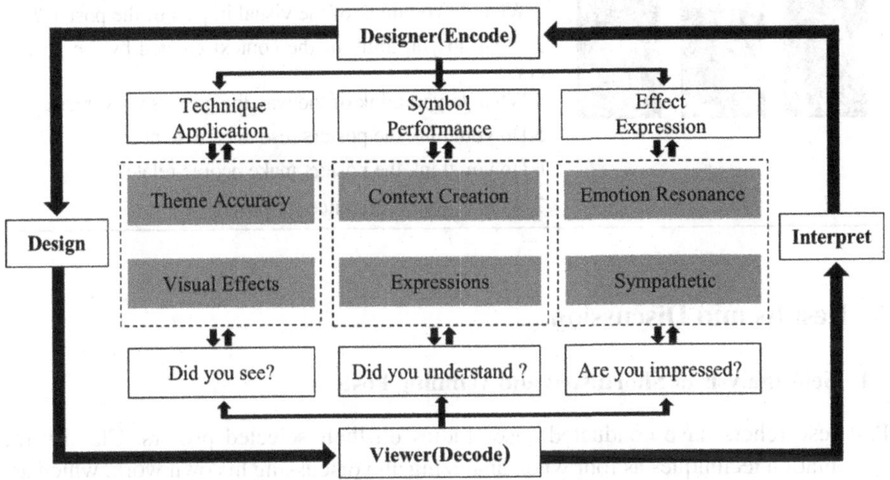

Fig. 1. An architectural model of the "designer encode" to "viewer decode" process.

Table 1. 11 groups of subject posters.

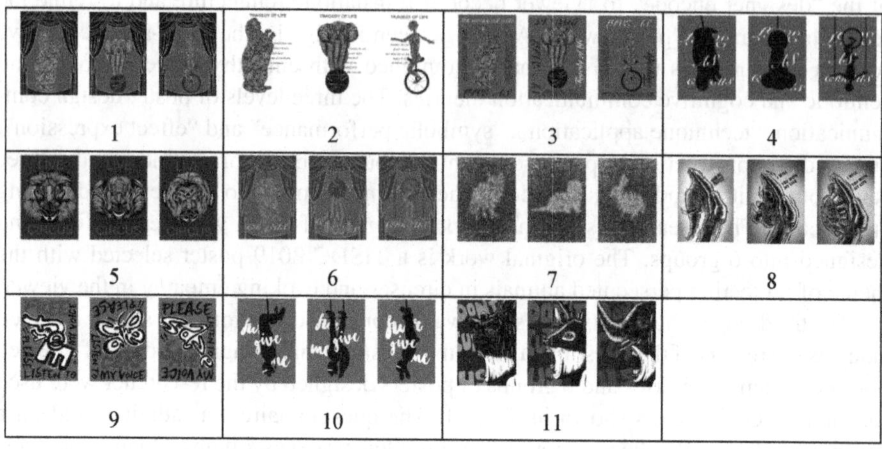

Table 2. Questionnaire about poster preference and the six rating attributes.

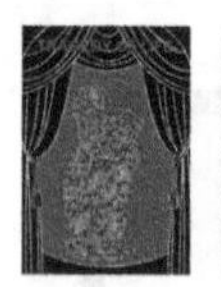 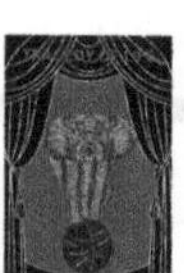 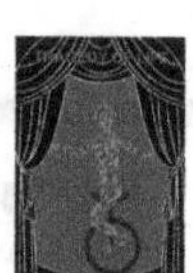	1.Do you think the posters conveys the theme accurately? 2.What do you think of the visual impact of the posters? 3.What do you think of the context created by the posters? 4.What do you think of the way the posters is expressed? 5.Do you think the posters resonates with people? 6.Do you think the posters make people relate? 7.What is your preference for posters?

4 Results and Discussion

4.1 Self-analysis of Shortlisted and Winning Posters

Past researchers have conducted case studies on their selected posters. Classify the presentation techniques as four when analyzing and discussing his own work, which are stylistic features, presentation, color application and textual arrangement [2]. Analyzed and measured the selected poster samples in terms of image symbols and expressions in the posters [10]. In this study, five selected finalist and award-winning posters on the topic of animal protection will be analyzed, using graphics, color and text, and the interpretation of surface and hidden meanings in pictorial symbols as content analysis (Table 3).

Table 3. Competition poster entries and self-analysis.

Poster artwork	Poster content analysis
2016 Eroded by Fashion 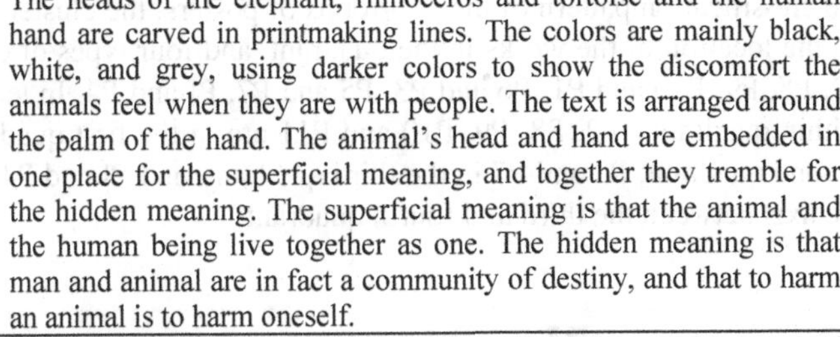	The fox, mink and rabbit are drawn in the picture with lines of fur clothing. The colors are mainly black, white, and grey, using darker colors to show the misery of the fur-taken animals. The text is arranged in a horizontal linear fashion. The animal figures are superficial, while the texture of the fur in the background is implicit. The superficial meaning is the fear presented by the animal in its shrunken state. The implicit meaning is that humans obtain the fur by hurting the animal for sale and use, an act that is incredibly painful for the animal.
2017 Open Hand to Protect	The heads of the elephant, rhinoceros and tortoise and the human hand are carved in printmaking lines. The colors are mainly black, white, and grey, using darker colors to show the discomfort the animals feel when they are with people. The text is arranged around the palm of the hand. The animal's head and hand are embedded in one place for the superficial meaning, and together they tremble for the hidden meaning. The superficial meaning is that the animal and the human being live together as one. The hidden meaning is that man and animal are in fact a community of destiny, and that to harm an animal is to harm oneself.
2018 The Voice of Life 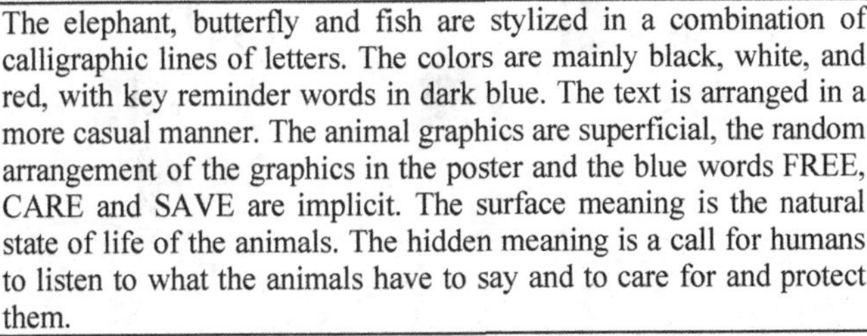	The elephant, butterfly and fish are stylized in a combination of calligraphic lines of letters. The colors are mainly black, white, and red, with key reminder words in dark blue. The text is arranged in a more casual manner. The animal graphics are superficial, the random arrangement of the graphics in the poster and the blue words FREE, CARE and SAVE are implicit. The surface meaning is the natural state of life of the animals. The hidden meaning is a call for humans to listen to what the animals have to say and to care for and protect them.
2019 Furgive Me 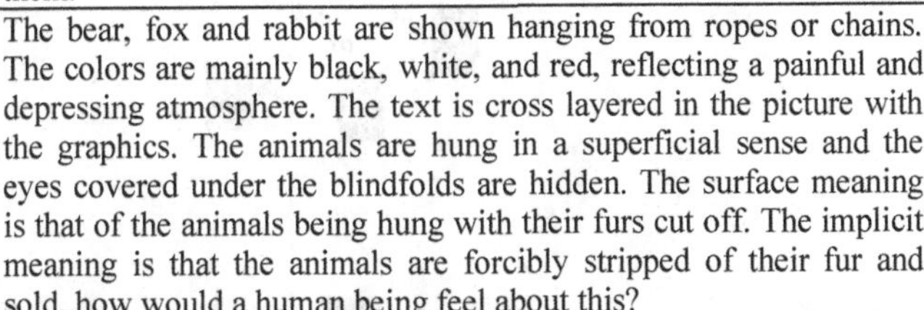	The bear, fox and rabbit are shown hanging from ropes or chains. The colors are mainly black, white, and red, reflecting a painful and depressing atmosphere. The text is cross layered in the picture with the graphics. The animals are hung in a superficial sense and the eyes covered under the blindfolds are hidden. The surface meaning is that of the animals being hung with their furs cut off. The implicit meaning is that the animals are forcibly stripped of their fur and sold, how would a human being feel about this?
2020 Symbiosis 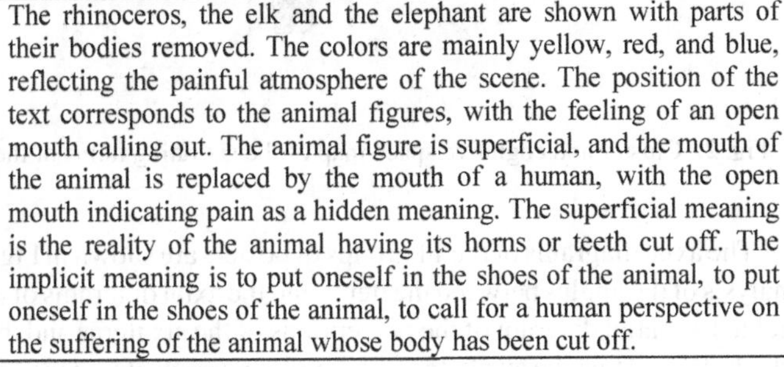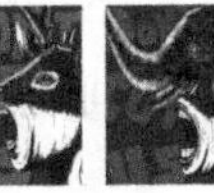	The rhinoceros, the elk and the elephant are shown with parts of their bodies removed. The colors are mainly yellow, red, and blue, reflecting the painful atmosphere of the scene. The position of the text corresponds to the animal figures, with the feeling of an open mouth calling out. The animal figure is superficial, and the mouth of the animal is replaced by the mouth of a human, with the open mouth indicating pain as a hidden meaning. The superficial meaning is the reality of the animal having its horns or teeth cut off. The implicit meaning is to put oneself in the shoes of the animal, to put oneself in the shoes of the animal, to call for a human perspective on the suffering of the animal whose body has been cut off.

4.2 Analysis of Questionnaire Results

A total of 82 valid questionnaires were collected to assess the participants' preference for the 11 groups of posters according to six items. The analysis methods used were Multidimensional Scaling (MDS) and Multiple Regression Analysis. 11 groups of posters were analyzed in categorical clusters and cognitive space with six items. The stress coefficients were well matched and the RSQ was close to 1, indicating that the spatial relationship between the 11 groups of posters and the six items was appropriate for this study. As can be seen in Fig. 2, p9 and P10 are more clustered, with very similar levels of preference between the two, while the rest of the samples are slightly scattered, indicating that the animal posters sampled in this study have a wide range of styles. To find the classification pattern of the 11 groups of posters, the cluster distribution was based on the location of the works in the quadrant, and four types of clusters were explored: P2, P8, P9, P10 and P1, P6 and P3, P5 and P7, PI and P4. In terms of works scattered within quadrants, P2, P8, P9, P10 and P11 are in the first quadrant, P6 and P3 in the second quadrant, P5 and P7 in the third quadrant, and PI and P4 close to the middle of the axis between the third and fourth quadrant.

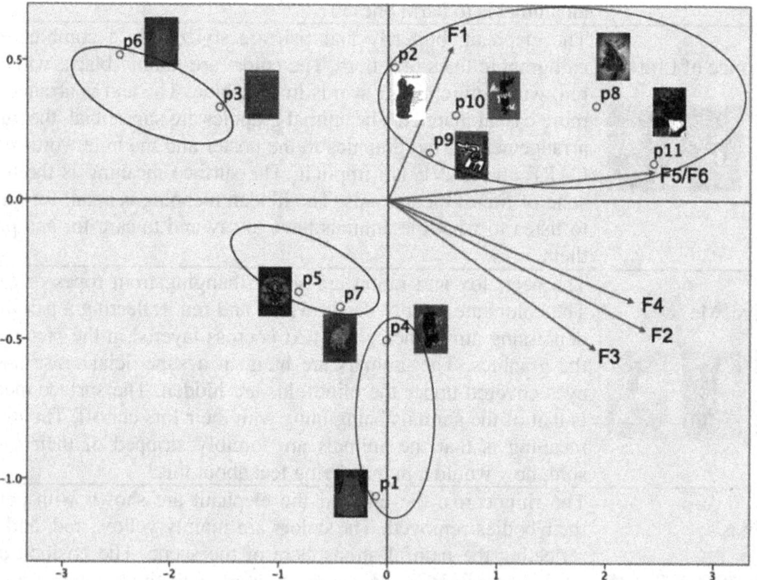

Fig. 2. Cluster and cognitive space map of the six rating items of the 11 groups of posters.

The axial diagrams of the 11 groups of posters are shown in Fig. 2. Multiple regression analysis of the angles between the items and the axial diagrams of the 11 groups of posters yielded a spatial diagram of the perceptions of the six items and the 11 groups of posters, which showed that the attributes and samples were clustered in space: F1 theme accuracy, F5 emotion resonance and F6 sympathetic were concentrated in the first quadrant, while F2 visual effects, F3 context creation and F4 expressions were concentrated in the fourth quadrant. The main factors influencing the participants' ratings can be identified as: F1 thematic accuracy, F5 emotion resonance and F6 sympathetic. F1, F2 and F3 show an angle close to 90°, indicating that thematic accuracy is related to visual effect and contextualization.

In the regression analysis of the factors influencing the preference of the posters, all three groups used preference as a dependent variable and six attributes of the posters (theme accuracy, visual effects, context creation, expressions, emotion resonance, sympathetic) as predictive variables to examine their correlation with preference.

Table 4. Multiple regression results for group 11 posters.

Independent variable	Predictor variable	B	r	β	t
Preference level	F1 Theme accuracy	.040	.702***	.043	.512
	F2 Visual effects	.132	.740***	.116	1.488
	F3 Context creation	.403	.876***	.392	3.219**
	F4 Expressions	−.040	.756***	-.038	.709
	F5 Emotion resonance	.244	.838***	.237	2.298*
	F6 Sympathetic	.245	.847***	.233	2.198*
	R = .909		R^2 = .813	F = 59.652***	

* $p < 0.05$ ** $p < 0.01$ *** $p < 0.001$

As shown in Table 4, the Pearson product difference correlation revealed that the preference of group 11 posters was positively correlated with six of the poster items (theme accuracy, visual effects, context creation, expressions, emotion resonance, sympathetic). In terms of t-values, F3, F5 and F6 had the highest β-values, with significant predictive power, indicating that context creation, emotion resonance and sympathetic were the most important factors influencing respondents' preference for this group of posters.

As shown in Table 5, the Pearson product difference correlation test showed that the preference of group 8 posters was positively correlated with six items of the posters (theme accuracy, visual effects, context creation, expressions, emotion resonance, sympathetic). In terms of t-values, F2 had the highest β-values and a significant level of predictive power, indicating that visual effects was an important factor influencing respondents' preference for this group of posters.

Table 5. Multiple regression results for group 8 posters.

Independent variable	Predictor variable	B	r	β	t
Preference level	F1 Theme accuracy	−.043	.538***	−.040	−.466
	F2 Visual effects	.640	.799***	.575	6.235***
	F3 Context creation	−.252	.667***	−.230	−1.777
	F4 Expressions	.059	.693***	.053	.441
	F5 Emotion resonance	.373	.763***	.378	2.411
	F6 Sympathetic	.192	.723***	.183	1.396
	R = .861		R^2 = .742	F = 35.874***	

* p < 0.05 ** p < 0.01 *** p < 0.001

Table 6. Multiple regression results for group 2 posters.

Independent variable	Predictor variable	B	r	β	t
Preference level	F1 Theme accuracy	.056	.632***	.053	.688
	F2 Visual effects	.211	.790***	.188	1.811
	F3 Context creation	−.017	.708***	−.015	−.168
	F4 Expressions	.415	.824***	.381	3.455**
	F5 Emotion resonance	.122	.761***	.119	1.258
	F6 Sympathetic	.290	.763***	.272	2.947**
	R = .885		R^2 = .783	F = 45.224***	

* p < 0.05 ** p < 0.01 *** p < 0.001

As shown in Table 6, the Pearson product difference correlation shows that the preference of group 2 posters is positively correlated with the six special measures of posters (theme accuracy, visual effects, context creation, expressions, emotion resonance, sympathetic). In terms of t-values, F4 and F6 had the highest β-values, with significant predictive power, indicating that expressions and sympathetic were the most important factors influencing respondents' preference for this group of posters.

In terms of the above results, the Pearson product difference correlation between the groups showed that respondents' preference was positively correlated with all six items of the posters. In terms of t-values, visual effect, context creation, expressions, emotion resonance, sympathetic were the factors that influenced respondents' preference for the sample posters. The emotion resonance and sympathetic is particularly important.

4.3 Discussion

This study analyzed the poster entries from previous competitions and found that there were common qualities between the winning and finalist posters. These common characteristics are mainly in the three elements of graphics, colors, and text. The entries used clear graphics to draw animal figures and used them as the main body of the image. The graphics allow the viewer to clearly recognize and understand the hidden content behind the message. The colors used are black, grey, and white, or black and red to reflect the miserable environment in which the animals are being persecuted. The text is written to match the theme and is designed to match the graphics, which can be used to illustrate the graphics and colors. Finally, the three elements of graphic, color and text are arranged in a logical way to create a good animal protection theme.

This study uses a three dimensions and cognitive model of communication to measure viewers' preferences for animal protection posters. The assessment focused on six items in the process of coding from the "designer encode" to "viewer decode" translation. The results show that these six items can be used effectively to measure animal protection posters and can provide ideas for designers. The results are as follows: (1) The six items show a positive correlation, with theme accuracy, visual effects, context creation, expressions, emotion resonance, sympathetic being interrelated. This demonstrates the reliability of the "designer encode" to "viewer decode" architecture model proposed in this study for the implementation of animal protection posters, which can be seen in Fig. 1. (2) The results of this study show that it is particularly important for posters to resonate with the viewer and to be empathetic, which can be achieved through visual effect, expressions, and context creation. The real meaning of empathy is emotion resonance and sympathetic, suggesting that the design of posters on animal issues can be combined with the meaning of empathy. It also demonstrates that the architectural model proposed in this study is in line with the principles of empathy design.

5 Conclusion

In refining the design for themselves, the researcher drew on the experience of the best entries in the competition on the topic of animal protection posters and considered how such posters could be favored by the judges. In terms of cognitive communication, the first step is to attract the judges by communicating the theme precisely and with strong visuals, is "did you see?". The second step is to help the judges understand the content of the poster symbols through good Context creation and expression, is "did you understand?". The third step is to make the judges emotion resonance and feel the same way, is "are you impressed?". If you have completed all three steps, you will have done a great job at the event.

The contribution of this research is the development of a model for the implementation of a "designer encode" to "viewer decode" architecture for posters on animal protection issues, and its compliance with the concept of empathetic design. How to present a heart-warming animal poster design to the viewer? Designers need to consider the technique application, symbolic performance, and effect expression to make their works communicate with the viewer. In the process of improving the posters, the researcher found that the visual effects is the most important and necessary condition to determine the attractiveness of the work. In designing posters on animal issues, designers should first put themselves in the shoes of the viewer and consider whether the work will resonate with them and make them feel the same way. The next step is to convey the mood you want to create through the visuals and present your ideas in a way that is acceptable to the viewer. In terms of future recommendations, the researcher believes that subsequent researchers could collect more samples for analysis when analyzing posters on animal protection issues to increase the diversity of the sample. The "designer encode" to "viewer decode" proposed in this study could also be further optimization.

References

1. Regan, T.: The Case for Animal Rights. University of California Press, California (1983)
2. Chen, Y.W.: The "Animal Rights" Characteristics on Poster Design (Unpublished master's thesis). National Taichung University of Education, Taichung (2012)
3. Eric, B., Elisabeth, H.: Zoo: A History of Zoological Gardens in the West. Reaktion Books, London (2003)
4. Cynthia, L.B., Daniela, K.R.: The promise of empathy: design, disability, and knowing tee "Other". In: Proceedings of the 2019 CHI Conference on Human Factors in Computing in Computing Systems, pp. 1–13(2019)
5. Kajonius, P.J., Björkman, T.: Individuals with dark traits have the ability but not the disposition to empathize. Personality Individ. Differ. **155**, 1–5 (2020)
6. Bouton, B.: Empathy research and teacher preparation: benefits and obstacles. Southeast. Reg. Assoc. Teacher Educ. **25**(2), 16–25 (2016)
7. Kouprie, M., Visser, F.S.: A framework for empathy in design: stepping into and out of the user's life. J. Eng. Des. **20**(5), 437–448 (2009)
8. Chang-Arana, A.M., Piispanen, M., Himberg, T., Surma-Aho, A., Alho, J., Sams, M., et al.: Empathic accuracy in design: exploring design outcomes through empathic performance and physiology. Des. Sci. **6** 1–34 (2020)
9. Zhu, S.S.: Research on the Empathic Design in Public Class Poster (Unpublished master's thesis). Zhe Jiang Sci-Tech University, Zhejiang (2016)
10. Ding, J.J.: Creation and Study of Environmental Issue Poster Design (Unpublished master's thesis). Asia University, Taichung (2021)
11. Lin, P.C.: Commercial Design, 1st edn. Artistes Press, Taipei (1986)
12. Zhu, Q.Y.: Poster Design, 1st edn. China Construction Industry Press, Beijing (2005)
13. Chen, J.H., Yang, T.M.: Introduction to Visual Communication Design, 3rd edn. Chun Hwa Press, Taipei (2014)
14. Barthes, R.: Elements of Semiology, 1st edn. Hill and wang, New York (1967)
15. Su, P.H.: A semiotic study of appropriating ancient cultural texts in creative design to enhance digital innovation. Taiwan J. Arts **98**, 171–198 (2016)

16. Fiske, J.: Introduction to Communication Studies, 3rd edn. Routledge, London (2010)
17. Lin, R.: An application of the semantic differential to icon design. In: Proceedings of the Human Factors Society Annual Meeting, pp. 336–340 (1992)
18. Lin, R., Lee, S.: Turning "poetry" into "painting": The sharing of creative experience, 1st edn. National Taiwan University of Arts, New Taipei City (2015)

Development and Validation of a Model for Estimation of the Effects of Ritual Design on Audiences' Satisfaction with Fashion Show

Yu-Ju Lin[1](✉), Jun-Liang Chen[2], I.-Hsiu Huang[3], and Mo-Li Yeh[4]

[1] Department of Commercial Design and Management, National Taipei University of Business, Taoyuan 324022, Taiwan
naralin@ntub.edu.tw

[2] Department of Crafts and Design, National Taiwan University of Arts, New Taipei 220307, Taiwan

[3] Freeimage Design, Taipei 106092, Taiwan

[4] College of Humanities and Design, Lunghwa University of Science and Technology, Taoyuan 333326, Taiwan

Abstract. The modern economic era is experience-oriented, with pleasure generated through perceptual experiences to create an enjoyable process and more sales. Under the influence of the coronavirus-19 (COVID-19) pandemic, people have begun to pursue a sense of ritual and to focus on their emotion, which has enhanced the connection between brands and consumers. The new emphasis on enhancing consumer experiences illustrates how incorporation of ritual and cultural imagery have become a means through which fashion brands can distinguish themselves from global competitors. Although international fashion weeks are now being hosted through virtual catwalks, these shows lack face-to-face interactions and a sense of on-site ritual. Therefore, many have proposed that the COVID-19 era fashion industry should be redesigned to ensure shows maintain a strong sense of ritual that enables audiences to transform their perceptions through a cultivated atmosphere to experience pleasure and satisfaction. In the present study, we explored the incorporation of cultural experiences into fashion curation to identify modern design focuses for fashion curation. We also analyzed the shows of different brands participating in the fashion weeks and discussed whether incorporation of ritual in the design of the shows affected their experiential value and audience satisfaction. Our conclusions were as follows: 1. use of ritual in designing fashion shows was effective, 2. ritual in the design of fashion shows increased participants' satisfaction with the show and its experiential value. Future studies should integrate design practice into our proposed research framework to provide a reference for fashion curation and instruction to develop curators that meet the needs of the fashion industry.

Keywords: Ritual design · Experiential value · Satisfaction · Fashion show

P.-L. P. Rau (Ed.): HCII 2022, LNCS 13311, pp. 480–496, 2022.
https://doi.org/10.1007/978-3-031-06038-0_36

1 Introduction

Fashion shows are a channel through which brands communicate with their audience and sell products. Brands with a unique aesthetic can quickly establish themselves in the market. Fashion is a communication tool [1]. That fashion is fashion because the cultural texture that supports clothing design can reflect a culture's current social atmosphere through creation of pleasing visuals or a fantasy. When brands seek to produce quality designs, their core focus is creating an atmosphere and their audience' projections [2]. Fashion shows are a form of multisensory stimulation. In addition to providing aesthetically pleasing visual stimulation, fashion shows with a sense of ritual serve as a channel through which designers present the culture of their brand to their audience. The focus of fashion shows is communication with the audience. Participating in fashion weeks strengthens brands' perceived cultural uniqueness and rarity. Furthermore, because the atmospheric experience is a key factor affecting the audience's perceptions of the shows, designers spend heavily on show decorations to cultivate discussion of the sensory experience created through the show. As a fashion week convention, catwalks have the strongest sense of ritual in fashion shows. However, runway designs have changed from a conventional T-shaped catwalk to more diverse shapes. For example, in the 2017 fall–winter Chanel fashion show, the Grand Pala is was decorated to resemble a NASA space station, with models walking out of a space capsule and the hash tag "Chanel Ground Control" being displayed. The audience witnessed the "launch" of the double C rocket, and the show concluded with the rocket ascending at curtain call. In the 2020 fall–winter Gucci show, named Gucci the Ritual by Alessandro Michele, the guests were incorporated into the ritual. Guests entered the show from backstage. The show started with dimmed lights, and a voice-over from Federico Fellini, an Italian film director, was played. A metronome swaying back and forth was hung above the stage, and the models stood at fixed points on the edge of a round turntable to display the clothing. At the end of the show, the models walked out from the round turntable, and the show's dressers took the models' vacated spots. Spotlights were shone on the dressers, bringing the focus to the behind-the-scenes dressers at that moment in the show.

The theme of the first Taipei Fashion Week in 2018 was "culture style," emphasizing that each designer should develop a unique aesthetic and culture to cultivate brand appeal. This theme of culture instilled the shows with a perceived sense of ritual, which emphasizes that, in the modern marketing environment, consumers' perception of a brand having "warmth" and "attitude" is essential. When consumers are familiar with and emotionally connect with a product or experience, they are more likely to experience pleasure and satisfaction. Rituals can influence emotions. Although the forms rituals take are ever-changing, they can enhance consumers' feelings, guide them toward understanding the meaning of an event, and provide them with a profound emotional or sentimental experience [3, 4].

Fashion shows are dynamic; they can elicit joy and energy in society and the general public. The conventional fashion weeks of the fashion industry were suspended due only to the pandemic, although the rapid development of digital technology and online social communities had already led to debate on the necessity of physical fashion shows. Ralph Toledano, the president of the French Fashion Federation, stated that fashion weeks are a time of enthusiasm, excitement, and celebration for brands; audiences of shows can see, understand, smell, and physically feel the results of months of labor. This in-person experience provided by physical fashion shows is unobtainable through a screen [5]. Natacha Ramsay Levi, the creative director of Chloé, emphasized the value of physical fashion shows, indicating that they create conversations, convey targeted meanings, and provide a real, irreplaceable experience [6]. The perspectives of medial value and online participation, the influence of online fashion weeks is far weaker than that of physical fashion weeks [7]. Although the pandemic has increased use of online transactions and entertainment, it has also led consumers to more eagerly seek out physical, emotional exchanges. According to the United States Federal Reserve System, with recent relaxations of intermittent lockdowns, consumers who were previously bored at home have rushed to visit physical stores; the amount of revenge consumption has been considerable [8], and physical experiences have been increasingly considered unique and irreplaceable. An increasing number of people have begun to view the distinct experience of physical activities as important [9]. Therefore, the experience of on-site fashion shows has become essential. Brands now strive to create an immersive experience and strengthen their audience's sensory impressions. Furthermore, a sense of ritual is established in the preparation of the fashion show.

Fashion has a long history as the embodiment of social phenomena. Fashion shows in fashion weeks can create immense commercial value generated by brand images. In Taiwan, brands have responded to the new generation's demand for entertaining experiences by providing audiences with unforgettable fashion experiences, thereby enhancing the Taiwanese fashion industry's connection with the world and clearly presenting their brand image and concept. This improves their fame and their audience's impressions, which affects consumers' behavior. Runway shows as contemporary rituals in which people who view fashion as a form of religion gather and celebrate beauty [10]. However, these conventional events create connections and encourage people to feel the connections, which, in itself, in stills fashion shows with deep meaning. Fashion is a complex mechanism. Fashion shows are conducted as rituals that resemble religious ceremonies. A fashion show requires effort from many people, and its core value lies in its very existence [11]. A Vox News report indicated that fashion weeks have decoupled from past retail purposes and have instead become a marketing strategy for brand image building. Brands often create fashion week themes because fashion weeks provide them with an excellent platform for self-expression. Through fashion shows, brands present their unique brand images, personalities, and cultures through the senses. Regarding the literature discussing the effects of ritual in fashion show designs on audiences, we discovered that ritual has been widely discussed in the fields of religion, anthropology, psychology, and social and behavioral sciences. Research into design and marketing has also investigated experiential value and audience satisfaction through ritual, which is revealing of how the fashion industry has developed, with brands being encouraged to incorporate surprise, pleasure, and reality into their fashion curation. Through their design concepts, brands can deliver messages and perpetuate their stories and value to gain a competitive advantage in the market. Accordingly, in this study, we discussed the effects of ritual in fashion show design on experiential value and audience satisfaction to explore the effectiveness of fashion shows that incorporate cultural experiences as well as the meaning and characteristics of fashion shows. We expected this study to provide two contributions. First, Taiwan has recently consciously promote edits fashion industry through implementation of unique local elements and through vertical, horizontal, and cross-border cooperation between industries. To increase the global visibility of Taiwan's fashion industry and to establish its brand image, we developed a design model intended to add value to fashion shows through incorporating ritual design. Second, our discussion of ritual design in fashion shows may serve as a reference for fashion curation and the cultivation of curators that meet the needs of the fashion industry.

2 Literature Review

2.1 Fashion Curation in the Era of the User Experience

As a social psychological phenomenon, fashion reflects the material and immaterial aspects of public pursuit and imitation. Fashion has always been a key commercial element driving consumption and creating commercial value in the general market. Historically, catwalk shows during fashion weeks have been exclusively open to the media, buyers, and fashion industry personnel. However, to increase their direct interaction with consumers, brands have begun selling fashion show tickets to the public. Moreover, contemporary fashion shows have included more direct creative experiences for consumers [12]. In fashion shows, fashion designers can introduce new products on the runway and advertise through the media attention to establish their brand image [13]. During fashion curation, interpreting the context of the season and pairing the new clothing is essential. That consumers no longer evaluate a brand's value on the basis of its fame and price; instead, they buy products from a brand because they like and even understand it [14]. Fashion experiences have become increasingly common, and the new generation's understanding of fashion is changing. Educating the public on continuing a cultural identity and cultural confidence can increase their awareness of local brands. Fashion shows are a convention in fashion weeks and, therefore, have a high sense of ritual; audiences deeply value the 20-min presentation. That a sense of ritual can be created through external factors (e.g., scenery, arrangements, language, and music), although internal perceptions are most influential during performance of the ritual [15]. A feeling of ritual can be elicited by a particular time and place or through performing particular behaviors, indicating the perceived content of activities must be related to corresponding and valuable emotional experiences. In addition to the cultural context and narrative atmosphere of the experience, fashion curators should consider how they can combine multiple factors with ritual design to elicit consumer emotions and to enhance the show's experiential value. When a group of people engage in ritual behavior, they feel an affinity or comradery with each other due to their shared goals or values. Therefore, cultivating a sense of ritual is essential to establishing strong connections and high levels of empathy with the industry [16–20].

2.2 Models of Ritual Design

Singer off stated that a life of ritual provides people with a sense of existence. Ritual behaviors are not performed to impress others but to perceive life authentically and enthusiastically. A sense of ritual cultivates symbolic meaning (deepening awareness of self), develops sustained emotional states, and strengthens the utility of relationships [21]. That the communication and maintenance of collective memory occur through commemorative ceremonies and bodily practices [22]. The collective memory of a group includes those memories that are commonly elicited and stored; such memories shape the group's behaviors and thinking. That rituals have transcended religious boundaries; they have become a universal human tendency and a social practice that presents a localized vignette of a given culture. Researchers have developed models to measure ritual design in various fields; all of these models have included measurement of ritual experience [23]. Investigated peak experience through behavioral design and discussed through elevation, insight, pride, and connection [24]. Maslow's Hierarchy of Needs and proposed that ritual design satisfy users 'need for self-esteem and self-actualization and indicated that a sense of authority, respect for existence, expectations, and honor can add value [25]. When a sense of ritual is incorporated into experiential design, brands create a consumer experience, establish their brand identity, engage users, and convey their brand concepts, thereby enabling consumers to form a deeper impression of and emotional connection to them. Accordingly, ritual in fashion show designs is the main influencer of audience satisfaction and experiential value. In the present study, we proposed a ritual design model and conducted analysis of elevation, insight, pride, connection, authoritativeness, presence, and anticipation in behavioral design.

2.3 Association Between Ritual Design and Satisfaction and Experiential Value

That rituals enable practitioners to experience true pleasure. Ritual is distinct from the ordinary life and elicits surprise and emotion through experiences; perceived experiential value is the final step of consumers' mental evaluation of satisfaction after an experience [26]. Ritual is regulatory psychosocial functions into three categories—regulating social connections, emotions, and performance goal states, that the same core psychological mechanisms, bottom-up and top-down cognitive processes, underlie all three functions [27]. Ritual behavior is a channel for rapid understanding of a core concept that is not restrained by language and knowledge barriers and that connects the thoughts of two individuals, creating mutuality between them. Ritual design can effectively improve participants' experiences and increase the intensity of these experiences [28]. That ritual behavior is one of the highest forms of experience; ritual design is spiritual. Providers of ritual-based experiential services ensure consumers have high expectations and unforgettable experiences by improving the ritual process as consumers use or experience the product. In doing so, they increase consumers' engagement with products and encourage more consumption as they satisfy consumers' experiential needs. Rituals can establish meaning through communication and connection. External stimulation from experiences elicits a feeling of ritual, which further influences perceived experiential value. The purpose of a fashion show is to provide an audience with a fashion experience; such an experience can be enriched through ritual because ritual adds a depth of connection based on the ritual's meaning, form, and conditioning. According to the experiential value scale developed by Holbrook, consumer return on investment, service excellence, aesthetic, and playfulness can not only be used to predict price and quality but can also serve as criteria for measuring emotions [29].

3 Research Methods

We explored designs of fashion shows and discussed the core elements of these designs. Referring to the framework presented in the literature, we divided the research process into five stages. The first was a literature review. The second involved design of a questionnaire; the scale constructs and items were developed through theoretical construction and analysis. The third was participant selection and survey administration, in which the design elements of ritual design for fashion curation were analyzed. We used the five fashion shows SILZENCE men participated in during the 2019–2021 Taipei Fashion Weeks as research samples and conducted a questionnaire survey. The final stage involved presenting the research findings and discussion. We conducted a validation analysis, a structural model analysis, and hypothesis validation of the valid questionnaires retrieved from the third stage and presented analyses and recommendations.

3.1 Conceptual Framework and Research Hypothesis

This is a confirmatory study. We developed the research framework according to relevant theories. Satisfaction was defined as a mediator to enable discussion of whether ritual design affects experiential value. Ritual design, comprising elevation, insight, pride, and connection constructs, were defined as the independent variable; satisfaction, as perceived by the audience, was defined as the mediator; experiential value was defined as the dependent variable. Each variable was measured through multiple items. According to the relevant theories and literature, we proposed the following hypotheses. H1: Ritual design in fashion shows are essential factors. H1a: Ritual design in fashion shows significantly affects experiential value (with the audience's overall enjoyment increasing the experiential value). H1b: Ritual design of fashion shows significantly affect satisfaction. H1c1: Elevation significantly affects experiential value. H1c2: Elevation significantly affects satisfaction. Furthermore. H1d1: Insight significantly affects experiential value. H1d2: Insight significantly affects satisfaction. H1e1: Pride significantly affects experiential value. H1e2: Pride significantly affects satisfaction. H1f1: Connection significantly affects experiential value. H1f2: Connection significantly affects satisfaction. H1g1: Authoritativeness significantly affects experiential value. H1g2: Authoritativeness significantly affects satisfaction. H1h1: Expected significantly affects experiential value. H1h2: Expected significantly affects satisfaction. H1i1: Presence significantly affects experiential value. H1i2: Presence significantly affects satisfaction. Furthermore, we proposed H2: Satisfaction significantly affects experiential value. To discuss the correlation between ritual design of fashion shows, satisfaction, and experiential value with satisfaction as the mediator of ritual design of fashion shows and experiential value, we proposed H3a: Satisfaction is a mediator between ritual design of fashion shows and experiential value, H3a: Satisfaction is a mediator between ritual design of fashion shows and experiential value, and H3b: ritual design of fashion shows can affect satisfaction and increase experiential value. These hypotheses were proposed to enable exploration of the aforementioned aspects of fashion shows. The research framework and hypothetical model are presented in Fig. 1.

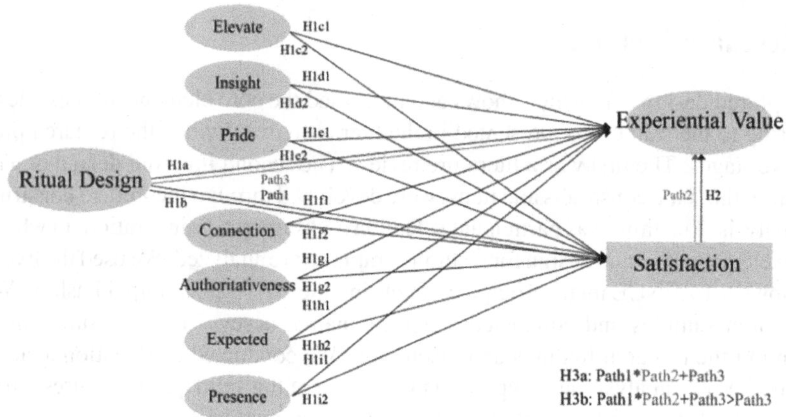

Fig. 1. The research framework and hypothetical model.

3.2 Participant Selection and Testing

The Taiwanese government has promoted Taipei Fashion Week to encourage innovation and development in Taiwan's fashion industry and to increase its global visibility and reputation. This has boosted the positive development of Taiwan's fashion industry. The local textile industry and functional textile companies must connect through the annual selection of domestic designer brands to participate in the fashion show. The integration of upstream, midstream, and downstream companies demonstrates the development of the fashion industry in the country. Furthermore, the introduction of cultural elements into the designs of commodities and the use of unique local elements has promoted the development of the local fashion industry. This has enabled audiences to develop a sense of familiarity with local designs, which has bolstered the fashion industry and increased its business and influence in the global market. To satisfy our research purpose, we selected SILZENCE men as our research subject based on the following three selection criteria: first, the selected brand should curate fashion shows using East Asian aesthetic inspiration; second, the selected brand should have been selected for participation in Taipei Fashion Week for 5 consecutive years; third, the designer of the selected brand should be the fashion curator. The samples we gathered are the five fashion shows curated by SILZENCE men during Taipei Fashion Week (Table 1).

Table 1. Case study the five fashion shows SILZENCE men participated in during the 2018–2021 Taipei fashion weeks as research samples.

Type	Photo
2018Taipei Fashion Week SS19 - In Between Black and White	To imitate the visuals of Chinese calligraphy and blank-leaving in paintings, long scrolls were placed in the room. A panoramic projection of virtual and real images, with light and dark shades and layers of ink paintings, was displayed. When the models walked on the runway, they appeared to be the subjects of a poetic ink painting.
2019Taipei Fashion Week SS20- Permeate	Because fashion shapes attitudes toward life,the room was decorated with furniture to create a juxtaposition of the ancient and the modern. Forty statements on the contemplation of life were displayed to enable the audience to experience life with the designer and to pass down classic Eastern phrasesof restraint and elegance.
2020Taipei Fashion Week SS21- Signature	As the sounds of wind, water, and birdsong faded away, several dancers started the show and established the concept of the life of a flower. The fan-shaped exhibition space cultivated a sense of humanistic appeal and spatial depth.
2021Taipei Fashion Week AW21- Void Color	The background of the stage was decorated based on the color scheme of relics in the National Palace Museum to showcase East Asian colors and aesthetics.
2021Taipei Fashion Week SS22- Dust and Light	  The space was interspersed with panoramic projections of landscapes, symbolizing the conflict between Chinese culture and the locality. Images of wind and scenery were used in displays of magnificent landscapes.

3.3 Research Instruments

A questionnaire was designed based on a literature review and data analysis. For ritual design, we discussed the effects of the fashion shows on experiential value and audience satisfaction. We compiled and defined secondary elements, such as the measurement constructs and items, and developed a measurement scale for investigation of the effects of ritual design on experiential value and satisfaction. The constructs of the scale and the basis for measurement were the elevation, insight, pride, connection, authoritativeness, expected and presence produced by the ritual design and the measurement items for experiential value and satisfaction. The questionnaire comprised eight constructs, with 21 items in total. To ensure the feasibility of the questionnaire, we conducted a confirmatory factor analysis. The assessment scale in Table 2.

Table 2. Ritual Design/Experiential Value/Satisfaction and Assessment Scale.

Facets	Variable	
Ritual design	Elevation	**E1.** The fashion show surprised and delighted me
		E2. The fashion show experience was beyond ordinary
		E3. I enjoyed the fashion show
	Insight	**I1.** The fashion show offered the appeal of an instant contrast with daily life
		I2. The experience was visually striking
		I3. The show gave me a deep cultural understanding
	Pride	**P1.** I am willing to try clothing with Chinese cultural elements
		P2. I am proud of Chinese culture
	Connection	**C1.** The fashion show was memorable
		C2. The fashion show caused me to feelan unforgettable sense of commonality
	Authoritativeness	**A1.** The brand fully presented cultural confidence
		A2. I felt the power of conveyance of East Asian fashion
	Expected	**EX1.** I am willing to follow the long-term development of the brand
		EX2. I look forward to attending future fashion shows from this brand

(*continued*)

Table 2. (*continued*)

Facets	Variable	
	Presence	**PR1.** My taste in fashion has improved
		PR2. I feel as though I am part of the world of fashion
Experiential value	**EV1.** Customer Retum on Investment: I think the fashion shows were worth watching	
	EV2. Service Excellence: The fashion show met my expectations	
	EV3. Aesthetics: The overall atmosphere was pleasing	
	EV4. Playfulness: I was completely immersed in the fashion show	
Satisfaction	**S1.** I was satisfied with the fashion show	

Source: [24, 30–35]

3.4 Experiment Design

Participants were selected through purposive sampling. In total, 118 participants were recruited, with 52 men and 66 women. Participants were aged between 25 and 65 and were audience members of the five fashion shows; they generally followed brands, fashion, and trends. The questionnaire was distributed online. We invited the audience to participate in the survey in advance and requested consent. The items were measured using a 7-point Likert-type scale, For items, 1 point means "very disagree", 2 points means "disagree", and 3 points means "Slightly disagree", 4 for "average", 5 for "slightly agree", 6 for "meet", and 7 for "very agree", and the questionnaire consisted of 21 items. We retrieved 113 valid questionnaires, with the number of participants five times the number of questionnaire items, which met the requirement for the sample size. The statistics were analyzed through structural equation modeling using SPSS22.0 and Amos 22.0. Because the scale items were developed based on theoretical framework proposed by researchers in different fields, we omitted the exploratory factor analysis that would otherwise be conducted in the pretest and did not include new items. A more rigorous statistical procedure was then adopted, and a confirmatory factor analysis was conducted to verify the reliability of the questionnaire. Furthermore, we performed a multivariate test for normality to ensure the data had multivariate normality. Finally, structural equation modeling and hypothesis verification was used to establish a path diagram of our developed model and to verify our proposed hypotheses.

4 Research Results and Discussion

4.1 Confirmatory Factor Analysis

The standardized factor loadings (SFLs) for the elevation, insight, pride, connection, authoritativeness, expected and presence of ritual design were 0.72–0.76, 0.72–0.73, 0.74–0.84, 0.79–0.85, 0.85–0.86, 0.76–0.88 and 0.72–0.78, respectively; the SFL for experiential value was 0.82–0.87. The estimated SFLs of all the items were > 0.7, indicating that the scale satisfied the requisite standards. Furthermore, the convergent reliability and average variance extracted (AVE) of the scale were 0.72–0.91 and 0.53–0.71. This indicated that the research model had acceptable internal consistency. According to the diagonal values, the square roots of the AVEs of the dimensions ranged between 0.73 and 0.85, larger than the correlation coefficient of each dimension and constituting ≥ 75% of the overall comparative values. Therefore, the discriminant validity of the research model was satisfactory (Tables 3 and 4).

Table 3. Analysis of CFA results for the research model. ($n = 113$)

Facets	Variable	M	SD	SK	KU	SFL	SMC	EV	C.R	AVE
Ritual design	**E.** Elevation	**5.82**							**0.78**	**0.54**
	E1	5.83	1.07	−1.26	1.74	0.72	0.52	0.55		
	E2	5.76	1.07	−0.42	−0.49	0.76	0.57	0.48		
	E3	5.86	0.97	−0.35	−0.93	0.73	0.53	0.45		
	I. Insight	**5.90**							**0.77**	**0.53**
	I1	5.83	0.97	−0.43	−0.39	0.72	0.52	0.45		
	I2	5.87	0.93	−0.64	0.34	0.73	0.53	0.41		
	I3	6.00	0.95	−0.75	0.09	0.73	0.54	0.42		
	P. Pride	**5.95**							**0.77**	**0.63**
	P1	5.92	1.15	−1.19	1.09	0.84	0.70	0.40		
	P2	5.98	0.97	−0.73	0.07	0.74	0.55	0.43		
	C. Connection	**5.95**							**0.81**	**0.67**
	C1	5.93	1.02	−0.93	0.56	0.85	0.72	0.30		
	C2	5.96	1.00	−0.77	0.06	0.79	0.63	0.37		
	A. Authoritativeness	**5.99**							**0.85**	**0.73**
	A1	5.95	1.10	−1.11	1.07	0.85	0.72	0.34		
	A2	6.02	1.07	−1.05	0.48	0.86	0.75	0.29		
	EX. Expected	**5.99**							**0.81**	**0.68**
	EX1	5.93	1.11	−1.01	0.31	0.88	0.78	0.27		
	EX2	6.05	0.98	−1.08	0.99	0.76	0.58	0.40		
	PR. Presence	**5.72**							**0.72**	**0.56**
	PR1	6.01	1.01	−0.94	0.47	0.72	0.52	0.49		
	PR2	5.42	1.18	−0.61	0.19	0.78	0.62	0.54		
	Mardia	**76.999**					**$p(p + 2) = 16 \times 18 = 288$**			

(continued)

Table 3. (*continued*)

Facets	Variable	M	SD	SK	KU	SFL	SMC	EV	C.R	AVE
Experiential value	**EV. Experiential Value**	**5.93**							**0.91**	**0.71**
	EV1	5.94	0.98	−1.04	1.05	0.82	0.67	0.32		
	EV2	5.95	1.06	−0.81	0.12	0.82	0.67	0.37		
	EV3	5.92	1.16	−0.94	0.08	0.86	0.74	0.35		
	EV4	5.92	1.02	−0.82	0.18	0.87	0.76	0.25		
	Mardia	**5.93**						**$p(p+2) = 4 \times 6 = 24$**		
Satisfaction	S1	6.16	0.86	−1.10	1.21	0.93	0.97	0.69		

*Note 1: * α = 0.05, indicating the level of statistical significance*
Note 2: M = mean; SD = standard deviation; SK = skewness; KU = kurtosis; SFL = standardized factor loading; SMC = square multiple correlation; EV = error variance; CR = convergent reliability; AVE = average variance extracted.
Note 3: p = the number of observed variables.

Table 4. Analysis of discriminant validity.

Code	Facets	Amount	Correlation coefficient							
			E	I	P	C	A	EX	PR	EV
E	Elevation	3	**0.74**							
I	Insight	3	0.16**	**0.73**						
P	Pride	2	0.55**	0.46**	**0.79**					
C	Connection	2	0.28**	0.28**	0.42**	**0.82**				
A	Authoritativeness	2	0.28**	0.28**	0.39**	0.64**	**0.85**			
EX	Expected	2	0.33**	0.28**	0.43**	0.57**	0.64**	**0.82**		
PR	Presence	2	0.54**	0.48**	0.52**	0.30**	0.32**	0.34**	**0.75**	
EV	Experiential value	4	0.18**	0.55**	0.59**	0.33**	0.37**	0.36**	0.61**	**0.84**

Note 1: The variable mean indicates the aggregate mean of all the items
Note 2: The diagonal value indicates the square root of the AVE of the latent variable, which should be larger than the nondiagonal value.
*Note 3: *α = 0.05 indicates a significant correlation between the variables.*

4.2 Structural Model Analysis and Research Hypothesis Verification

Nearly all the indices in the model attained or were close to the level of acceptance, indicating a satisfactory fit between the structural model and the theoretical framework with the empirical data. According to the model path analysis results, the factors related to the ritual design of the fashion show were critical; ritual design, experiential value, and satisfaction mutually influenced each other. H1a: Ritual design in fashion shows significantly affect experiential value and H1b: Ritual design of fashion shows significantly affect satisfaction. The above two assumptions are effective. As revealed in the structural equation model, in this structural model, it is assumed that H1c1, H1c2, H1d1, H1d2, H1e1, H1e2, H1f1, H1f2, H1g1, H1g2, H1h1, H1h2, H1i1 and H1i2, and H2: Satisfaction affects the experience value significantly, and the above hypotheses are effective. The 95% confidence interval of the direct effect path of the ritual design of the fashion show curation on the experience value does not contain zero (0.069, 0.256), $p < 0.05$, indicating significant, indicating that the mediating effect exists, all of the above can prove the research hypothesis H3a: Satisfaction is a mediator between ritual design of fashion shows and experiential value, so the hypothesis is effective. Through the model path parameters, it can be known that the influence path coefficient (direct effect) of the ritual sense design of the fashion show curation on the experience value is 0.74, and the path coefficient (indirect effect) of the ritual sense design of the fashion show curation on the experience value through satisfaction is: 0.422 (0.62 * 0.68), the total effect is $0.62 * 0.68 + 0.74 = 1.16 > 0.74$ (total effect > direct effect), which can prove the research hypothesis H3b: Ritual design of fashion shows can affect satisfaction and increase experiential value, the hypothesis is effective. The factors of elevate, insight, pride, connection, authoritativeness, expected, and presence for existence in the ritual design of fashion show curation have a significantly on satisfaction. It can be seen that the ceremony of fashion show curation the sense design must have these factors in order to achieve the audience's satisfaction and experience value. Through the structural model diagram, as shown in Fig. 2, this research observes the standardized regression coefficients (factor loadings) of each factor dimension and its measurement variables in the ritual design of fashion show curatorial design. The expected and presence are the highest, and the elevate is second. Then, according to the analysis of the topics in each dimension, it can be found that each topic has a high factor load. Among them, the P1 of the pride (I am willing to try clothing with Chinese cultural elements) is 0.84; C1 of the connection (The fashion show was memorable) of the sense of connection dimension is 0.85; A1 of the authoritativeness (The brand fully presented cultural confidence) is 0.85;

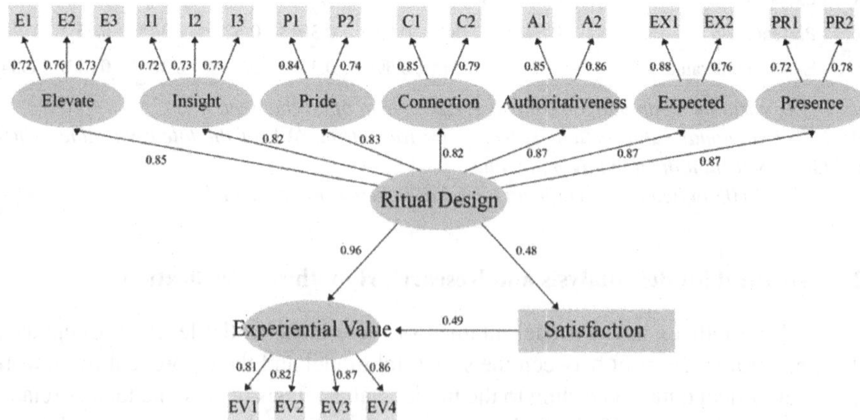

Fig. 2. Analysis of mediation using SEM the path diagram.

A2 (I felt the power of conveyance of East Asian fashion) is 0.86; EX1 of the expected (I am willing to follow the long-term development of the brand) is 0.88. The above are all topics with the highest load of dimension factors, that is, influential variables, and the ritual design of fashion show curation should improve the satisfaction and experience of the audience. The value affects factors that can be considered more.

Table 5. SEM-analysis results.

	Variable	SFL	C.R	*p*	Hypothetical test
H1a	Ritual Design → Experiential Value	0.96	22.14	***	Effective
H1b	Ritual Design → Satisfaction	0.48	3.33	***	Effective
H1c1	Elevation → Experiential Value	0.89	46.81	***	Effective
H1c2	Elevation → Satisfaction	3.13	21.46	***	Effective
H1d1	Insight → Experiential Value	0.91	49.44	***	Effective
H1d2	Insight → Satisfaction	3.10	20.94	***	Effective
H1e1	Pride → Experiential Value	0.88	42.53	***	Effective
H1e2	Pride → Satisfaction	3.10	20.85	***	Effective
H1f1	Connection → Experiential Value	0.84	39.27	***	Effective
H1f2	Connection → Satisfaction	3.08	21.07	***	Effective
H1g1	Authoritativeness → Experiential Value	0.91	59.82	***	Effective
H1g2	Authoritativeness → Satisfaction	3.24	23.42	***	Effective
H1h1	Expected → Experiential Value	0.93	58.67	***	Effective
H1h2	Expected → Satisfaction	3.29	23.58	***	Effective
H1i1	Presence → Experiential Value	1.04	59.60	***	Effective
H1i2	Presence → Satisfaction	3.41	23.41	***	Effective
H2	Satisfaction → Experiential Value	0.49	3.38	***	Effective

Note: $*p < 0.05$, $**p < 0.01$, $***p < 0.001$

5 Conclusion

An increasing number of Taiwanese fashion brands have emerged in the global market, and their outstanding performance has led to higher consumption. With the rise of a new generation of consumers, fashion shows have expended effort to present different fashion show aesthetics and runways, which has successfully strengthened their image. In this changing environment, brands must develop a distinctive and communicative concept that accounts for audience thoughts and demands. These thoughts and demands must be analyzed through research to enable establishment of an effective model that can be applied within the fashion industry. Using a literature review, relevant theories, and analysis, we investigated an audience's thoughts on fashion shows a brand hosted over several years from the perspective of ritual-based design by using scales developed based on the literature review. The findings may serve as a reference for future fashion shows intending to incorporate ritual design. Our conclusions are as follows:

1. We conducted a questionnaire survey on ritual design of fashion shows. The goodness-of-fit of the overall theoretical mode was in accordance with the standard, indicating that the questionnaire had a high degree of internal consistency. On the basis of this framework, we measured the effects of ritual design of fashion shows on satisfaction and experiential value. The findings may serve as a reference for the fashion industry to enable value to be added to fashion shows through ritual-based show designs.
2. Through structural equation modeling, we discovered that ritual design of fashion shows affected experiential value and that a correlation between ritual design, satisfaction, and experiential value was present, with the three influencing each other. Participants' perceptions of ritual design directly affected their satisfaction. Although the other factors did not directly affect satisfaction and experiential value, they were necessary conditions of ritual design, requiring interaction with variables to affect satisfaction. When creating ritual design, curators are advised to consider factors, such as having a deep understanding of culture or pride in Chinese culture, to satisfy audiences' psychological needs. The findings demonstrated that satisfaction had a mediating effect on ritual-based design and experiential value, and ritual design in fashion shows affected audiences' satisfaction with the show and increased experiential value.

Our study provided two contributions to the literature. First, Taiwan's fashion industry was developed relatively late. Therefore, brands should seek to establish their own identity and style through vertical cooperation between industries, horizontal cooperation, and cross-border cooperation. We established a model to add value to fashion shows through implementation of ritual design to increase the global visibility of Taiwan's fashion industry through the enhancement of Taiwanese brand images. Second, our findings on the effects of ritual design of fashion shows could serve a reference for future fashion show designs and the cultivation of curators that suit the needs of the fashion industry. However, we only explored offline fashion shows. In the post-pandemic era, physical and virtual experience events may coexist, with the purpose of both types of events creating immersive experiences. Future studies should investigate the influence of both online and offline fashions shows and conduct further analysis on consumers' recognition of brands with virtual designs and their acceptance and purchase intention of such brands.

References

1. DemnaGvasalia: Fashion's Warhol. https://www.businessoffashion.com/reviews/fashion-week/balenciaga-spring-summer-2018. Accessed 5 Oct 2021
2. Fashion as a Projection of Dreams: New York Fashion Week Feature Shows. https://www.wazaiii.com/articles?id=RunwayShowNewYorkSS2021. Accessed 5 Oct 2021

3. Norton, M.I., Gino, F.: Rituals alleviate grieving for loved ones, lovers, and lotteries. J. Exp. Psychol. Gen. **143**(1), 266–272 (2014)
4. Fei, X.Z., Huang, Y.J.: Research on scale development of perceived ritualization in consumption. J. Mark. Sci. **14**(3–4), 69–96 (2018)
5. [Technology. Future] Open unlimited creative digital fashion shows a trend, https://www.hk01.com. Accessed 5 Oct 2021
6. What is the carbon footprint of conscious/digital fashion week. https://www.vogue.com.tw/fashion/article/fashion-show-carbon-footprint. Accessed 5 Oct 2021
7. Dive into the digital fashion week, will we usher in a better future. https://www.yicai.com/news/100795833.html. Accessed 5 Oct 2021
8. After the unblocking of "Science and Technology", physical consumption will return to Cyberbiz to provide 3 keys to e-commerce. https://www.chinatimes.com/realtimenews/20210721004531-260410?chdtv. Accessed 5 Oct 2021
9. Why fashion shows have become an 'arms race' for luxury brands. https://www.beautimode.com/article/content/85767. Accessed 5 Oct 2021
10. Maverick-RICK OWENS: https://www.prestigeonline.com/tw/style. Accessed 5 Oct 2021
11. Selling 21st Century Clothes Using 19th Century Logic: What Is the Meaning of Fashion Week: https://www.cw.com.tw/article/5102743?template=fashion. Accessed 5 Oct 2021
12. Bringing Fashion Week to the general public: London Fashion Week Festival, Anya Hind march brand special exhibition will be open to consumers: https://luxe.co/post/88246. Accessed 5 Oct 2021
13. Chen, P.L.: Curatorial and spatial design studies of the fashion show (2012)
14. Confidence in wearing: Guochao clothing interprets oriental fashion: https://www.fashionexpress.org.tw/focus/paper/5111732518. Accessed 5 Oct 2021
15. From ritual to ritual sense, re-imagining the sense of ritual in the era of mobile Internet. https://twgreatdaily.com/xyXlPnUBeElxlkkaS4Pt.html. Accessed 5 Oct 2021
16. Li, W.T.: A Study on the Design of Ritual Image of Products (2019)
17. Thomas, J., Coleman, I., Jonathan, J., Valerie, V.M.: Contemporary pragmatism. Introduction Spec. Issue: What Religious Beliefs **15**(3), 279–283 (2018)
18. Chen, X.Y.: Model of Ritual Sense Design Under Experiential Marketing and Service (2018)
19. Regional Revitalization Combining Ritual, Design and Customer Service Management: https://www.thenewslens.com/article/120637. Accessed 21 Oct 2021
20. Five senses experience marketing can also be digitized! See how Japan's "Ito Garden" uses ZOOM to promote the ritual sense of tea drinking: https://www.foodnext.net/column/columnist/paper/5975550639. Accessed 5 Oct 2021
21. Lorelies, S.: Why Do We Need Rituals. 1nd edn. China Renmin University Press, Beijing (2009)
22. Connerton, P.: How Society Remembers, 1st edn. Shanghai People's Publishing House, Shanghai (1989)
23. Holly, N.B., Kimberly, S.: Recapturing the power of ritual to enhance community in aging. J. Relig. Spiritual. Aging **31**(2), 1–15 (2018)
24. Chip, H., Dan, H.: The Power of Moments: Why Certain Experiences Have Extraordinary Impact. 1nd edn. The New York Times (2017)
25. Ceremony experience design: let users feel different values in the product experience. https://kknews.cc/zh-tw/news/vk4jnpa.html. Accessed 5 Oct 2021
26. Kao, R.F.: A sense of ritual: to live the life into an exquisite life. 1nd edn. China Times Publishing Co., Taipei (2018)
27. Nicholas, M., Hobson, J., Schroeder, J.L., Risen, D.X., Michael, I.: The psychology of rituals: An integrative review and process-based framework. Pers. Soc. Psychol. Rev. **22**(3), 260–284 (2017)

28. Wu, H.W.: Aesthetics of Ritual design: A Case Analysis of Ask This of Rikyu and Jiro Dreams of Sushi (2016)
29. Mathwick, C., Malhotra, N., Rigdon, E.: Experiential value: conceptualization, measurement and application in the catalog and internet shopping environment. J. Retail. **77**, 39–56 (2001)
30. Kahneman, D.: Evaluation by moments, past and future. In: Kahneman, D., Tversky, A. (eds.) Choices, Values and Frames. Cambridge University Press, 693 (2000)
31. Wang, C.C., Zhu, H.B.: The Power of Moments: Insight into hidden and unknown needs, and grasp the critical moment to influence customer decision-making. 1nd edn. CommonWealth Magazine, Taipei (2021)
32. Maslow, A.H.: Motivation and Personality, Prabhat Prakashan (1954)
33. Lee, E.J., Overby, J.W.: Creating Value for Online Shoppers: Implication for Satisfaction and Loyalty. J. Consum. Satisfaction Dissatisfaction Complain. Behav. **17**, 54–67 (2004)
34. Holbrook, M.B.: Consumption experience, customer value, and subjective personal introspection: an illustrative photographic essay. J. Bus. Res. **59**(6), 714–725 (2006)
35. Mathwick, C., Malhotra, N., Rigdon, E.: Experiential value: conceptualization, measurement and application in the catalog and internet shopping environment. J. Retail. **77**(1), 39–56 (2001)

How Discursive Design Therapy is Possible: Theory and Strategy

Yujia Liu and Li Zhang(✉)

School of Art and Design, Guangdong University of Technology, Guangzhou 510090, China
lizhang116@gdut.edu.cn

Abstract. Emerging technology represented by NBIC is gradually becoming the dominant prolificacy of social development. However, ordinary people who are most affected by it cannot participate in its application decision-making because they do not understand the technology and its social risks, thus gradually marginalizing and infecting many contemporary mental diseases, such as social fear. Helping ordinary people understand the risks of technology and acquiring a social discourse on technology has become an important challenge for contemporary design practice. A new concept of "discursive design therapy" is proposed and its possibilities in terms of both theory and strategies are demonstrated in this study. Discursive design therapy is both as an effective way of social therapy and an iterative version based on the concept of art therapy. Its strategies include four steps: identification, materialization, interaction, and feedback, involving interdisciplinary knowledge and skills, such as psychoanalysis, behavioral interaction, object construction, and discoursing design. Compared to psychotherapy and art therapy, the advantages of discursive design therapy are embodied mainly in experience and awareness: on the one hand, it is achieved through tangible training based on the everyday use of objects; on the other hand, it achieves intellectual healing by reflective imagination and critical speculation to obtain the therapeutic effect of physical and mental co-construction.

Keywords: Discursive design · Design therapy · Critical speculation · Reflective imagination

1 Introduction

With rapid changes due to the digital revolution, the development and iteration of new and emerging technologies represented by NBIC (Nanotechnology, Biotechnology, Information technology and Cognitive science) is overwhelming to the general public. However, it is these ordinary people who are most affected by technology. Not being part of the system of power and technology, they lack a voice in the truth and development of technology, or do not even know how to speak due to a lack of understanding. In this techno-social context, coupled with the semantic turn in design (Klaus 2005), *Discursive Design: Critical, Speculative, and Alternative Things* (Bruce and Tharp 2018) introduces the concept of discursive design, linking discourse to design.

P.-L. P. Rau (Ed.): HCII 2022, LNCS 13311, pp. 497–507, 2022.
https://doi.org/10.1007/978-3-031-06038-0_37

Discursive design, with discourse as the design goal and object aiming to provoke discourse, activates the meaning of the designed objects through the production of discourse. The communicative ethical value of design is thus emphasized (Li 2021). Communication ethics is not only a concern for public attention and participation in social issues but is also the principle behind individual psychotherapy.

Expression is one of the most common, even essential, aspects of psychotherapy. However, it needs to be activated. It is the methodology of discursive design to materialize discourse into objects using design and to activate discourse with objects. As a type of emerging design practice, discursive design differs from traditional design in that objects have an alternative aesthetic, whose artistic form is partly in line with the artistic experience of art therapy. Therefore, this study aims to explore the concept of discursive design therapy, proposing it as an iterative concept of art therapy.

2 What is Design Therapy?

Designing therapy involves using discourse design to realize psychotherapy. From the perspective of designers, combined with discursive design and the theory and methods of psychology, specific design activities are carried out for the target users so that the results of the design activities can convey the discourse of the treater and stimulate the discourse of the treated, leading to the psychological healing of the treated. Treatment in design therapy does not refer to professional and medical treatment but to a kind of psychotherapy.

"Psychotherapy is the informed and intentional application of clinical methods and interpersonal stances derived from established psychological principles for the purpose of assisting people to modify their behaviors, cognitions, emotions, and/or other personal characteristics in directions that the participants deem desirable" (Norcross Norcross and Lambert 2011).

2.1 General Psychotherapy

Psychotherapy is also called psychological therapy or talking therapy. Talking therapy is most commonly used in psychotherapy. Talking psychotherapy is referred to in this paper as general psychotherapy, which is an interactive process that takes place between the treater and the treated through verbal communication alone (see Fig. 1). Its advantage lies in guidance, and the treater can integrate the treatment strategy and method into the treatment process to form a targeted treatment plan. However, talking therapy also has some drawbacks.

First, it offers a single guidance result without a whitespace of discourse. The treatment is mainly in a state of receiving external discourse during the session. Although there is a process of expression, the values received by the treated are inspired and guided in a single way, and the whole process is controlled by the treater. The second is the limitations of the treatment groups. Talking psychotherapy would not proceed successfully in situations in which the patient has speech impairment, whether it be an inability or an unwillingness to speak for physical or psychological reasons. Third, there is limited effectiveness in dealing with emotional distress. According to research on the division of brain functions, language is mainly controlled by the left hemisphere, while emotion is mainly controlled by the right hemisphere (Sperry 1981). Therefore, talking therapy is effective in correcting patients' diseases caused by wrong cognition or thinking, while it is ineffective in dealing with patients' emotional disorders, traumatic experiences, and other psychological problems, with emotional distress as the main symptoms.

Fig. 1. General psychotherapy process. This is an interactive process that takes place between the treater and the treated through discourse alone with the guiding strategies of the treater.

2.2 Art Therapy

The above deficiencies of talking psychotherapy can be complemented by art therapy. Modern art therapy, which began in the 1950s, is an emerging discipline that combines psychology, art, and medicine. It uses art as a method and means of diagnosing, treating, or rehabilitating certain illnesses in an artistic interaction with the patient under the guidance of a professional. Art therapy is defined as "an integrative mental health and human services profession that enriches the lives of individuals, families, and communities through active art-making, creative process, applied psychological theory, and human experience within a psychotherapeutic relationship" (AATA 2017). During the whole process of art therapy, the treater may be absent, and the treated gains an intellectual feeling by interacting with the artistic experience (see Fig. 2).

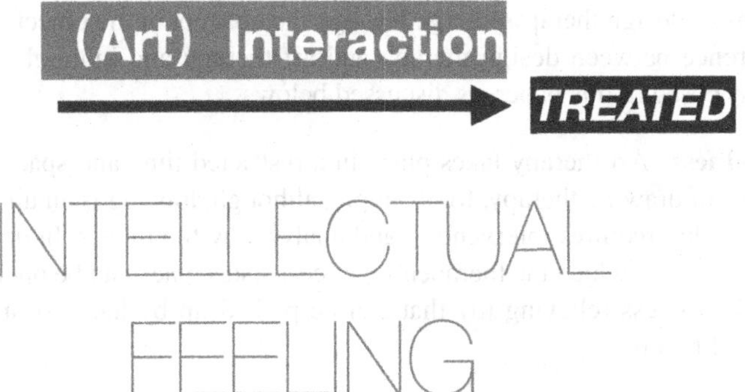

Fig. 2. Art therapy process. During the whole process of art therapy, the treater may be absent, and the treated gains an intellectual feeling by interacting with the artistic experience.

2.3 Design Therapy

Design therapy transforms the direct verbal expressions that the treater wants to convey in general psychotherapy into the form of metaphorical objects. The treated person then interacts with the object to stimulate their feelings, thus achieving a psychological healing effect. The object of design is the discourse of the treater, and the result of the design is the existence of the object containing the discourse and the behavior of intellectual interaction between the treated and the object. Design therapy inserts an object into the human–human aspect of general psychotherapy, delivering the discourse of the treater to the treated in an object-mediated way, which forms a human (discourse)–object–human process. Correspondingly, design therapy replaces the artistic experience in art therapy with an absent stand-in for the treater, forming a state of human–object unity in which the therapeutic process is an interactive process between human and object (see Figs. 3 and 4).

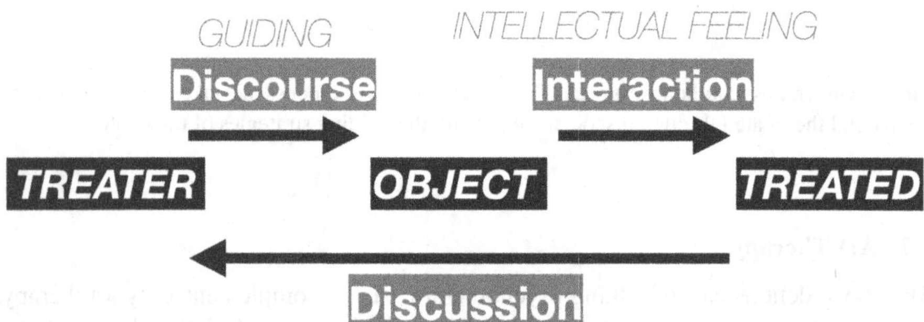

Fig. 3. Design therapy process. Design therapy inserts an object into the human–human aspect of general psychotherapy, incorporating the guidance of general psychotherapy and the artistic experience of art therapy.

The concept of the object is central to design therapy. In contrast to general psychotherapy, the object is the wrapping of the treater's discourse and the catalyst of the discourse of the treated. In contrast to art therapy, the object is the physical embodiment of the absent treater's alternative integrated into the artistic experience. In discursive design, the object is the vehicle and stimulus of discourse with an alternative aesthetic. The strengths of design therapy emerge through the concept of the object, which stands as the difference between design therapy and art therapy and highlights why design therapy is proposed in this paper, as discussed below.

Unrestrictedness. Art therapy takes place in a restricted time and space. In the most common case of drawing therapy, for example, although drawing is an unrestricted act, it is a process that requires intervention and analysis by the treater. In design therapy, the time and space in which the therapeutic process takes place can be open-ended. The object can be a stress-relieving toy that can be picked up by hand, or a headset that facilitates meditation.

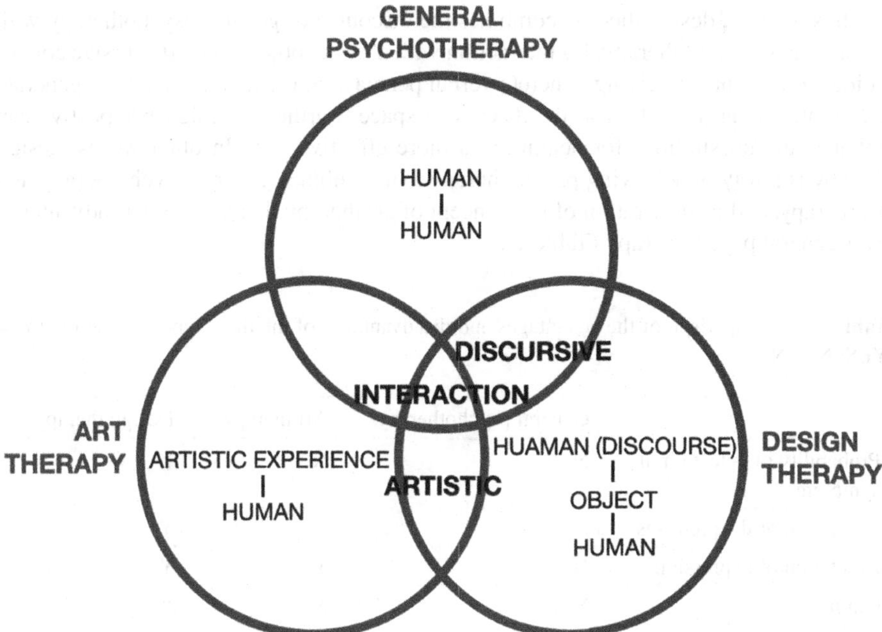

Fig. 4. A diagram of the interaction process among general psychotherapy, art therapy, and design therapy.

Physicality. In art therapy, interaction with a person is often a non-physical art experience, whereas design therapy materializes the art experience as a designed object with an alternative aesthetic. People interact with the object, and in addition to mobilizing the sense of hearing and sight, the process of ownership and use provides a more profound experience. We refer to objects in design therapy as 'wrapping paper'. There are two reasons for this designation. First, objects with an alternative aesthetic are different from usual objects with a certain function in everyday life. Through defamiliarization, they bring a sense of ritual to the user's experience of life. This is similar to Halloween teaching people to face their fears by dressing up in different costumes. Given that gifts are one of the sources of a sense of ritual in life, the object is formalized through the concept of gift wrapping paper. Second, the object itself in design therapy is the wrapping of the treater's words. To peel back the wrapping paper is to lift the aesthetic surface of the discourse, the essence of which is the transmission of discourse.

Universality. Design therapy is unique to both general psychotherapy and art therapy in that it can provide spiritual relief for potential patients who do not proactively seek treatment. while both general psychotherapy and art therapy require the person to actively seek treatment and are often expensive, design therapy is a more universal way of providing moment-to-moment emotional relief through stuff that can be incorporated into a person's life.

In summary, design therapy combines the discourse of general psychotherapy with the interaction of art therapy. By interacting with abstract objects with discursive connotations, rather than receiving concrete verbal persuasion, the treated is able to generate more intellectual reflection in the discursive space. Further, a design perspective can enhance the possibilities for healing in a more effective way. In other words, design therapy is a way of achieving psychotherapy that combines general psychotherapy and art therapy, and is an iteration of the concept of art therapy that already has advantages over general psychotherapy (Table 1).

Table 1. A comparison of the advantages and disadvantages of the three types of therapy (Y = YES; N = NO).

	General psychotherapy	Art therapy	Design therapy
Probability of detection of symptoms	N	N	Y
Limitation of the premises	N	N	Y
Limitation of expression	N	Y	Y
Guiding	Y	N	Y
Whitespace in discourse	N	Y	Y

3 Is Design Therapy Possible?

There are four links in the process of design therapy: the delivery of the treater's discourse, the design of the object as a wrapping of the discourse, the interaction of the object with the treated, and the discussion of the treated stimulated by the object—the production of the discourse. Of these, the interaction between the object and the treated is a familiar aspect, so there are three key segments of design therapy. Therefore, when we allude to why design therapy is possible, we ask, "What is design therapy?" "Why is therapy by discursive design possible" How achieve therapy by discursive design". The next section will focus on why therapy by discursive design is possible.

By analogy with the distinction between design and research, the relationship between discourse and design can be divided into three categories: About, For, and Through, with discursive design primarily concerned with "discourse through design" (*Discursive Design* 2018, p. 80). Discourse through design regards design as a medium that ultimately ends up as a designed object that embodies or articulates discourse. "Discourse is gradually expanding from a verbal phenomenon in the field of linguistics to a social practice in an interdisciplinary context" (Zhang 2021). The design activity we are familiar with is situational interaction and social practice. When discourse becomes a situational interaction and social practice—that is, when discourse can become a design activity—discursive design becomes possible.

Regarding discourse, the two concepts that must necessarily be identified are langue and parole (de Saussure 2011). Parole is the activity of human speaking, langue is the rule and tool that determines speaking, and discourse is the product of speaking. In psychotherapy, the most common approach is talking, and even "talking" is part of the definitions of psychotherapy. Further, *talking cure* is a specialized form of cognitive therapy (Bankart 1997). The legitimacy of verbal communication in psychotherapy is unquestionable. Similarly, the validity of the product of the speaking activity, the discourse, for psychotherapy is a given. The validity of "discourse through design" for psychotherapy is then also inevitable (see Fig. 5).

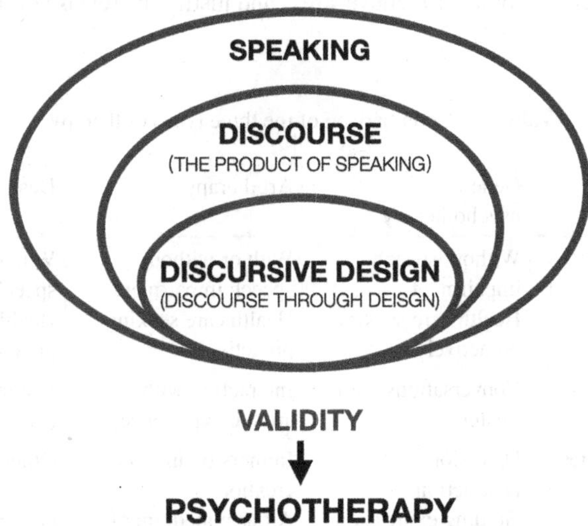

Fig. 5. The process of argumentation for the validity of discourse design therapy.

4 How Discursive Design Therapy is Possible

The cover work of *Discursive Design* is Umbrellas for the Civil but Discontent Man (Fig. 6), a typical case of discursive design that can also be used as an explanation of the concept and strategy of design therapy.

Fig. 6. Umbrellas for the civil but discontent man. The handle of this set of umbrellas was designed in the style of a sword hilt.

In this design case, the most targeted groups to be treated are those with psychiatric disorders with superficial violent tendencies, such as schizophrenia, mania, depression, and personality disorders. However, it is also suitable for people who are not aware of their violent tendencies, or even just ordinary people with stressful lives. In general psychotherapy, the treater often adopts the strategy of talking to the treated with the right values. In art therapy, the most common method is painting. Both verbal and artistic expressions are cathartic ways of releasing the violent emotions within. However, an ordinary person with underlying signs does not actively seek treatment. Design therapy, by contrast, takes the form of objects, where the designer can be seen as the treater, and the design treater infuses the object with therapeutic strategies so that the umbrella can be used as an everyday object to relieve stress and justify the release of inner aggression (Table 2).

Table 2. A comparison of the three types of therapy.

	General psychotherapy	Art therapy	Design therapy
Target groups	Without speech impairment Health care seeking proactively	With or without speech impairment Health care seeking proactively	With or without speech impairment Health care seeking proactively or not
Treatment methods	Conversations with treater	Interaction with artistic experience	Playing with everyday objects;
Treatment strategies	Diversion Distraction Guiding expression	Immersion in artistic creation Art as a medium of communication and expression	Object as a catalyst of expression Object as a companion Object as a discursive scenario

The production of the discourse of a design work requires the following six steps: encounter, inspect, recognize, decipher, interpret and reflect (*Discursive Design* 2018, p. 111). Take Fig. 6 for example. It looks like both an umbrella and a sword. The audience may see it inadvertently while browsing the web, meet it on the shelf of a store, or encounter someone using it on the street; then they inspect it with curiosity; they recognize it through website descriptions, labels, and conversations with others; they decipher the designer's intentions and the message he wants to convey; they interpret it in the light of their own experience and understanding; and finally, this attractive and novel object brings the audience into a profound reflection on the repressive nature of civilized society. In this process, the audience's psychology changes: fascinated, curious, puzzled, enlightened, and reflective. It is through the attraction of alternative objects that discursive design begins to lead the audience to think and reflect on themselves, to understand the discourse that the designer is conveying, and to produce their own discourse.

Based on the discourse production steps of discursive design, and taking into account the definitional model of design therapy, this study proposes a possible methodology of design therapy for the four components of design therapy: identification, materialization, interaction, and feedback. This is a systematic process that integrates psychoanalysis, object design, and interaction design, involving human, object, and discourse. The four steps are the recognition of the treater's discourse, the materialization of the discourse, the interaction process between the treated and the object, and the feedback from the treated to the treater (see Fig. 7).

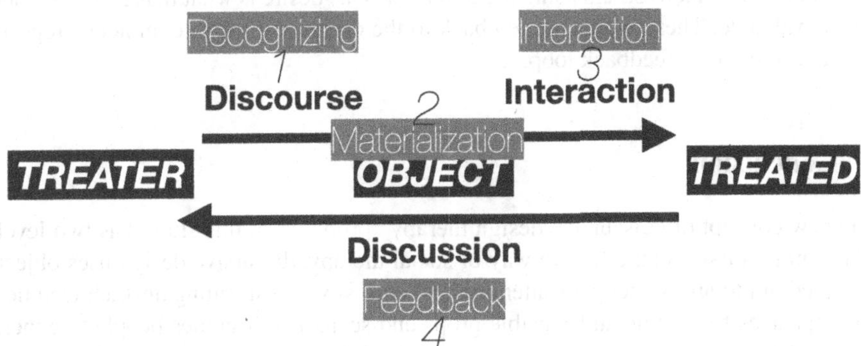

Fig. 7. Design therapy strategy, including four steps: the recognition of the treater's discourse, the materialization of the discourse, the interaction process between the treated and the object, and the feedback from the treated to the treater.

Step 1: Discourse Recognition. The discourse is generated by the target group, similar to the user research process in traditional design. In this case, the discourse that needs to be conveyed to the targeted group is permission for a justified public expression of personal aggression, which echoes Freud's statement that "civilized society is a repression of human nature" (Freud 2015).

Step 2: Objectification of the Discourse. The best materialization option for aggressive expression is weapons. Considering the public context in which it is designed, an umbrella can be used as the vehicle, given the same way it is used, and the sword can be carried on the back. The handle of the object in Fig. 6 is designed in the form of a sword hilt, thus creating a dissonant but perfect pairing of two opposing images: the full black umbrella, representing the elegant gentleman, and the sword, representing violence; and a mishmash of two scenarios: the melancholy rainy day of civilized society and the savage battlefield, full of freedom and wildness. There are subtle differences between this umbrella and other umbrellas. This defamiliarization gives the umbrella an alternative aesthetic. Initially, the users are attracted by this aesthetic feeling outside of its actual function, and then stimulated by the sense of ambiguity. An unusual umbrella brings a sense of ritual to daily life. At the same time, it is a presence that can accompany us at all times, without the restrictive presence of art therapy scenarios, such as art galleries and therapy rooms.

Step 3: The Interaction Between the Treated Object. In the course of everyday life, one can wield an umbrella, draw it like a sword, or throw it to the back like a swordsman. In the process, the civilized modern man holding the handle enters the world of the tyrannical warrior, the medieval barbarian, or the triumphant cavalryman.

Step 4: Feedback from the Treated. Through this interaction, a bond is created between the human and the umbrella. This silent interaction is, in fact, a dialogue between the repression and rebellion of the user's inner instability and the designer's desire to release the aggressive discourse of human nature. The treated have a desire to express themselves and talk to others using the umbrella. This desire is what makes design therapy so valuable. These words are fed back to the designer through comments, reports, etc., thus creating a feedback loop.

5 Conclusion

The new concept of "discursive design therapy" proposed in this study has two levels of meaning. First, as an effective way of social therapy, discursive design uses objects as a medium to arouse people's attention and curiosity, transforming abstract technical consequences for visible and sensible props and scenarios. It guides people to experience technical consequences in a concrete and subtle way, thus activating the intrinsic motivation of individual communication and achieving the psychological healing effect, as "being able to talk is to remove pain". Second, design therapy, as an iterative version based on the concept of art therapy, integrates the pragmatic nature of psychotherapy and the retreat nature of art therapy by using props as "discourse catalysts," allowing people to "physically" engage with the technology and its outcomes in the context of everyday use, and to critically imagine and speculate the social risk of technology in a reflective situation. The strategies of discursive design therapy include four steps: identification, materialization, interaction, and feedback, involving interdisciplinary knowledge and skills, behavioral interaction, object construction, and discoursing design.

The constant development of technology has not only brought about more convenient living conditions but also negative effects, such as the constant squeezing of living space and the increasing pressure of life. Mental stress is a social concern that cannot be ignored, especially by ordinary people who are constantly striving to make the world better. The concept of design therapy and the practice of its strategies can not only complement art therapy theoretically but also represent a broader social concern.

Acknowledgements. This work was supported by the Key Program of Social Science Plan of Beijing Municipal Commission of Education under Grant No. SZ202011232025 and Beijing Municipal Social Science Foundation under Grant No. 19YTB052.

References

Bankart, C.P.: Talking Cures: A History of Western and Eastern Psychotherapies, 2nd edn. Thomson Brooks/Cole Publishing Co, Salt Lake City (1997)

De Saussure, F.: Course in General Linguistics. Columbia University Press, New York City (2011)
Definition of Profession. https://www.arttherapy.org/upload/2017_DefinitionofProfession.pdf
Dunne, A., Raby, F.: Speculative Everything: Design, Fiction, and Social Dreaming. MIT Press, Cambridge (2013)
Educational Design—What is Art Therapy?. https://www.joshkale.com/apps/photos/photo?photoid=205098755
Freud, S.: Civilization and Its Discontents. Broadview Press, Peterborough (2015)
Krippendorff, K.: The Semantic Turn: A New Foundation for Design, 1st edn. CRC Press, Boca Raton (2005)
Li, Z.: How to design discourse: Alternative things and ethics of communication. Art Des. Res. **05**, 58–64 (2021)
Materious umbrellas for the civil but discontent man. https://www.materious.com/copy-of-5-ghost-still. Accessed 27 Dec 2021
Norcross, J.C., Lambert, M.J.: Psychotherapy Relationships that Work II, vol. 48, no. 1, p. 4. Educational Publishing Foundation (2011)
Pei-xin, M.: Artistic assessment of painting and therapeutic intervention of painting for schizophrenic patients. Doctoral dissertation, Normal University, Beijing (2004)
Tharp, B.M., Tharp, S.M.: Discursive Design: Critical, Speculative, and Alternative Things. MIT Press, Cambridge (2019)
Xiao-guang, Y., Yue-ji, S., Jun, W., et al.: The concept, development and education of art therapy. Dalian Med. Univ. (03), 57–58+64 (2005)
Xin-wang, L.: Physiological Psychology. Science Press, Beijing (2001)
Yang-ning, X., XIiao-yang, D.: Psychotherapy. China Medical Science and Technology Press, Beijing (2006)

DesignEva: A Design-Supported Tool with Multi-faceted Perceptual Evaluation

Yun Lou[1], Weiyue Gao[1], Pei Chen[1], Xuanhui Liu[1(✉)], Changyuan Yang[1,3], and Lingyun Sun[1,2]

[1] Alibaba-Zhejiang University Joint Institute of Frontier Technologies, Zhejiang University, Hangzhou 310027, China
{inlab_ly,chenpei,liuxuanhui,sunly}@zju.edu.cn
[2] State Key Laboratory of CAD&CG, Zhejiang University, 310027 Hangzhou, China
[3] Alibaba Group, Hangzhou 311121, China
changyuan.yangcy@alibaba-inc.com

Abstract. Perceptual design evaluation helps designers recognize how others perceive their work and iterate their design process. Organizing user studies to gather human perceptual evaluation is time-consuming. Thus, computational evaluation methods are proposed to provide rapid and reliable feedback for designers. In recent years, the development of deep neural networks has enabled Artificial Intelligence (AI) to conduct perceptual quality evaluation as human beings. This article proposes to utilize AI to provide designers with real-time evaluations of their designs and to facilitate the iterative design. To achieve this, we developed a prototype, DesignEva, a design-supported tool to offer multi-faceted perceptual evaluation on design works, including aesthetics, visual importance, memorability, and sentiment. In addition, based on designers' current works, DesignEva also searches for similar examples from the material library as references to inspire designers. We conducted a user study to verify the effectiveness of our proposed prototype. The experimental results showed that DesignEva could help designers reflect on their designs from different perspectives in a timely way.

Keywords: Design evaluation · Perceptual evaluation · Design-supported tool

1 Introduction

Design evaluation helps designers recognize how their works are perceived by others, and thus promotes their self-reflection [1] and design iterations [2]. Perceptual aspects of design are essential to the ultimate usability of the design [3]. Conventionally, designers evaluate their works by conducting user studies to receive reviews from domain experts or target users. These feedback is valuable but require extensive time and effort [4]. For example, when needing to know users' attention to the current work, traditional methods use eye-tracking techniques [5] or cursor-based attention tracking techniques [6] to measure individuals' eye movements. The process of collecting data is cumbersome and time-consuming, which cannot support fast iteration. This issue motivates researchers to develop computational evaluation tools.

P.-L. P. Rau (Ed.): HCII 2022, LNCS 13311, pp. 508–519, 2022.
https://doi.org/10.1007/978-3-031-06038-0_38

Methods for computational design evaluation allow designers to understand possible performances of design works timely, without actually conducting user studies [7, 8]. Traditional rule-based methods evaluate the quality of works by judging whether they conform to specific design rules. However, these methods cannot perform the perceptual evaluation. Methods based on machine learning try to model user perceptions with hand-crafted features (e.g., nonsemantic object statistics, semantic object statistics, scene category) [9–12]. However, only using limited low-level features is hard to construct a powerful prediction model with high accuracy.

The recent development of deep learning enables Artificial Intelligence (AI) to extract high-level features from datasets automatically, which has shown promising progress in tasks such as image classification [13] and object recognition [14]. These studies demonstrate the unprecedented predictive ability of AI by more closely replicating the mechanism underlying human visual recognition [15], which also benefits the research on perceptual quality evaluation [16, 17] and similarity judgement [15]. Specifically, by learning large quantities of data with perceptual annotations, AI automatically learns to understand latent patterns in images that affect users' perceptions. The perceptual evaluation ability of AI can be used to produce evaluation that is highly coincided with humans' perceptions, thereby helping designers understand their works more conveniently.

In this work, we developed a design-supported prototype DesignEva. It can offer multi-dimensional perceptual evaluations on poster designs, including aesthetics, visual importance, memorability, and sentiment, which offers multiple perspectives for designers to understand their works. We also utilized the ability of AI to compare image perception similarity to achieve similar recommendations. To verify the effectiveness of DesignEva, we conducted a user study, in which we asked participants to design posters with DesignEva. The experimental results showed that participants' opinions on DesignEva were positive. By providing participants with timely multi-faceted feedback during the design process, DesignEva can inspire participants to reflect and help them achieve design goals. In addition, based on the participants' opinions on our prototype, we discuss the design implications for AI-driven design evaluation systems.

2 Related Work

2.1 Perceptual Evaluation of Design

Perceptual evaluation of design reflects an audience's subjective feeling when viewing the design works. It can reveal gaps between what is intended by the designer and how an audience interprets the design [18]. Existing research has shown that designers with feedback during the iteration process can produce designs with higher quality than those without feedback [19, 20]. The design evaluation connects designers with the audience and helps designers iterate in-process solutions [21, 22] and compare alternatives [23]. However, conducting real user studies with target users to gather perceptual evaluation requires much effort and time. For example, professional equipment is required to capture user feedback [5]. The long period required for user studies makes it difficult to support fast iteration [4]. Therefore, computational design evaluation methods are proposed to help designers acquire evaluation quickly and easily.

2.2 Computational Evaluation of Design

Computational evaluation of design facilitates designers to get timely feedback at a minimal cost. Computational evaluation methods can be divided into rule-based and data-driven methods. The rule-based methods encode and apply design knowledge in rules to produce feedback on designs [24, 25]. The limitation of rule-based methods is that they are domain-specific and only consider fundamental design principles, which cannot be used to depict users' perceptions toward designs. The data-driven methods first construct image datasets with detailed human ratings. Then they compute features of images and model the relationship between features and user perceptions. The relationship models can be used as prediction models to evaluate unseen design works perceptually. Traditional machine learning models rely on hand-curated features to model user perceptions [26]. However, manually selected features may not portray all the aspects of designs, and models fitted with these features are hard to achieve exact prediction. The recent development of Artificial Intelligence (AI) such as deep convolutional neural networks (CNNs) enables computers to extract high-level characteristics from images automatically. Researchers found that the internal activations of networks trained for classification did indeed correspond to human perceptual judgement [15, 27]. Therefore, research on perceptual quality evaluation uses the classification models trained on large-scale image datasets as initialization, and then fine-tune the models on new datasets with human annotations. These researches produce quantitative models of human perceptions and enable AI to offer precisely perceptual prediction by replicating human visual cognition [15]. AI-driven methods have been widely applied into design evaluation systems. For example, Wu *et al.* [4] developed a system to assist designers in examining user engagement with their animation designs. Swearngin *et al.* [28] proposed TapShoe to predict the tappability of mobile interfaces perceived by human users. In our work, we develop a prototype to offer multi-faceted perceptual evaluation to designers to help them understand current works from various perspectives.

3 System Design and Implementation

3.1 Evaluation Indicators

Before developing our system, we invited three design experts to discuss how to measure the quality of graphic designs. The experts pointed out that a high-quality design needs to meet the basic aesthetic standards and be able to highlight the design subject. In addition, it should stand out among various design works and leave a deep impression on the audience. Finally, appropriate emotions should be conveyed. Based on expert suggestions, we evaluate designs from the following dimensions in our system.

Aesthetics. Aesthetic assessment quantifies semantic characteristics associated with beauty in images [17]. To design a beautiful work is an essential requirement for a designer.

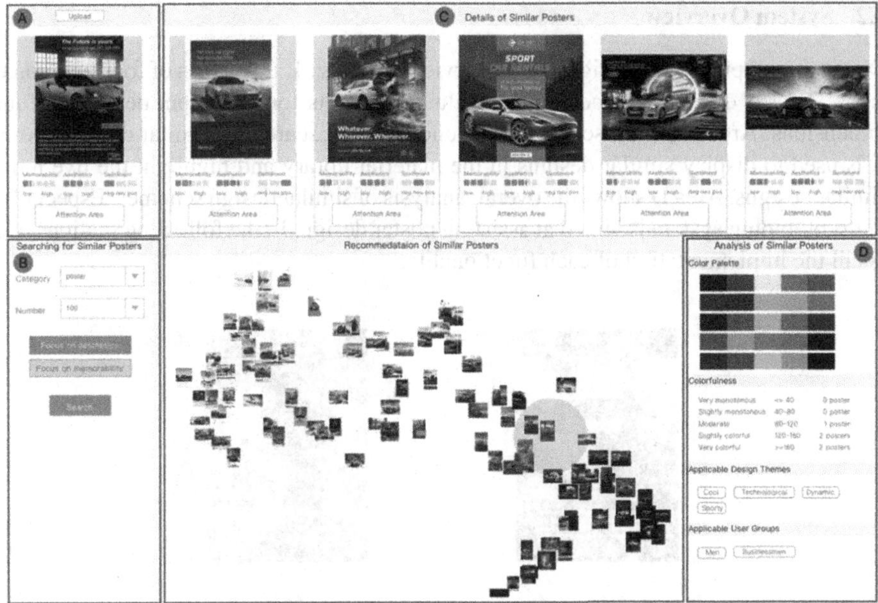

Fig. 1. The overview of DesignEva. It contains four functional areas: Area A displays evaluation results; Area B is for users to input searching conditions; Area C displays similar design recommendations; Area D displays the analysis results for similar designs.

Memorability. Image memorability refers to how easy it is for a person to remember the visual content of a particular image. It has been studied by psychologists for a long time [29]. They verified that image memorability has a stable property and can be quantitatively measured. Individuals tend to remember the same images with the same probability. Isola et al. [30] designed a Visual Memory Game to aggregate quantified memorability scores of images.

Visual Importance. The graphic design contains several elements, such as main objects, background, titles and text descriptions. Design works should provide effective management of attention to avoid secondary elements distracting [31]. The visual importance of the design work describes the perceived relative weighting of design elements and reflects the eye movements of viewers.

Sentiment. Understanding the sentiments evoked by designs is crucial in helping designers to utilize appropriate design elements. For example, when we design a poster with the theme of celebrating Christmas, we want to convey joy. But if we adopt a black and white color scheme, it may be hard to evoke viewers' pleasure. Design works with appropriate sentiments can strengthen the opinions conveyed in the content and effectively influence the viewers [32].

3.2 System Overview

Our proposed prototype DesignEva is overviewed in Fig. 1. It consists of four functional areas. Area A displays the perceptual evaluation results for user input designs in four dimensions. Area B is for users to fill in conditions for searching similar designs. Area C is used to display similar designs in the material library and highlight the five most similar designs. Area D shows the overall analysis of similar design schemes. Especially, our prototyping system is aimed at assisting poster design. In the following sections, we detail the implementation of each functionality.

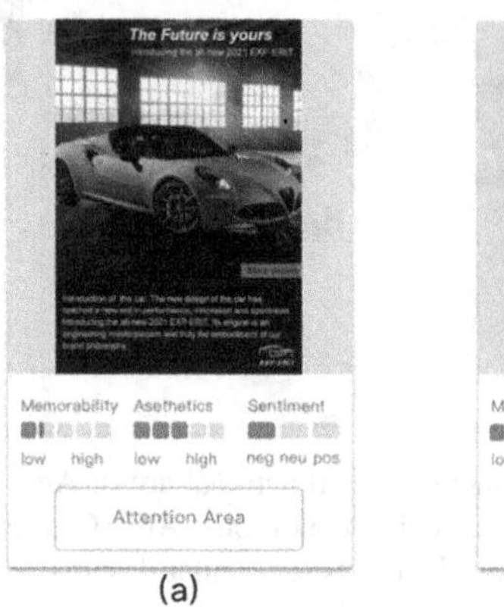

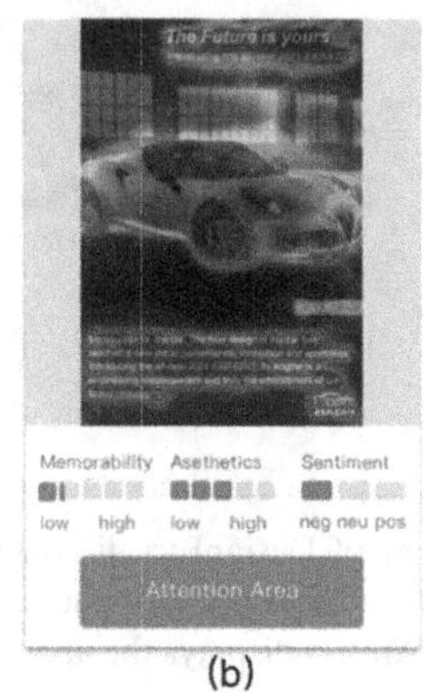

Fig. 2. The display of evaluation results. Our prototype defaults to display the results of memorability, aesthetics and sentiment in the form shown in (a). When the user clicks the button "Attention Area", the prototype will display the importance prediction result, as shown in (b).

3.3 Display of Evaluation

Users can upload their poster designs to DesignEva at any stage of the design process to get feedback. When they upload a poster, DesignEva will automatically output the evaluation results of memorability, aesthetics, sentiment and visual importance that correlate well with human perceptions.

We adopt NIMA [17] to evaluate aesthetics in our system, which fine-tunes MobileNet [33] on the AVA dataset [34]. The AVA dataset contains about 255K images. These images are obtained from DPChallenge.com and labelled by amateur photographers. Specifically, each image receives 78–549 ratings. After training, input an arbitrary image, NIMA predicts its aesthetic scores range from 1 to 10, with 10 being the highest aesthetic score.

Our system employs the AMNet [16] model to predict memorability scores. The AMNet starts with ResNet50 [13] pre-trained on ImageNet [35], and then conducts transfer learning on the LaMem dataset [36], which contains 60K images. The output memorability score ranges from 0 to 1, and being closer to 1 means the image is more memorable. The evaluation results of memorability and aesthetics are both scores, but they are different magnitudes. Displaying different score results will confuse users. Therefore, we present the results of memorability and aesthetics in segmented forms, which allows users to clearly understand the rating of the design is low, medium or high.

We use the FCN-16 model [37] to predict important areas of designs. It is a neural network pre-trained for semantic segmentation and is fine-tuned on a graphics design importance dataset [38]. Given a design, the model produces a pixel-wise heatmap to show the importance of each region of the design, as shown in Fig. 2(b).

The sentiment prediction is given by the VGG-T4SA model [39], which is a VGG-19 model [40] pre-trained on ImageNet [35] for image classification and then is fine-tuned on the T4SA (Twitter for Sentiment Analysis) dataset. The T4SA dataset contains 1.4M images, and each image has a sentiment label (positive, neutral, negative). The result of sentiment prediction is the category of sentiment that an image belongs to.

3.4 Searching for Similar Examples

We crawled posters from the web to construct a material library. We perform perceptual evaluations on these posters in advance and store the evaluation results. After users receive the evaluation results of their designs, they can search for similar designs from our material library to inspire their work. Especially, the above evaluation indicators are not all positively correlated. It has been found that the memorability and aesthetics of images have little to no correlation [36]. Images containing strange objects tend to have high memorability scores, but this often leads to low aesthetic scores. Therefore, in the design process, designers need to adjust works according to practical requirements. They need to clarify the keys of current design requirements and balance the relationships among various perceptual dimensions. When searching for similar examples, users are required to choose a dimension that is more concerned with the current design. For example, if the user clicks the button "Focus on aesthetics", then the aesthetic scores of all recommended similar designs will be higher than the average aesthetic score of designs in the material library. In addition, users can choose the number of similar designs to be recommended.

3.5 Recommendation of Similar Examples

We construct an autoencoder to extract the high dimensional features of posters to determine their similarities. First, we use the poster dataset (the material library) to train the autoencoder. After training, given a poster, the autoencoder outputs a 2048-dimensional latent vector for it. We compute the cosine distance between the feature of the input image and the features of images in the material library separately to measure their similarities. Thus, we obtain 100 posters (the number is set by the user) in the material library that are most similar to the user input poster. We use the TSNE algorithm [41] to reduce and visualize all vectors. The TSNE algorithm visualizes high-dimensional data by giving each datapoint a location in a two-dimensional map while maintains the relationship between data. As can be seen, in the visualized area, the user input poster is highlighted by the red rectangle. The positions of similar posters depend on their similarities to the user input poster. Overall, posters with closer distances have more similar color schemes. Hovering the mouse over the thumbnail of a poster can get its evaluation results, as shown in Fig. 3.

3.6 Analyses of Similar Examples

We further analyze the five most similar designs to provide users with more reference information. Specifically, we extract the main color palette of the five most similar posters. We also analyze the colorfulness [42] of these designs. We divide colorfulness into five levels: very monotonous, slightly monotonous, moderate, slightly colorful, and very colorful. In addition, we put together the labels of these five posters in the material library for display. These labels are divided into two parts, one part represents the applicable theme of posters, such as "technical" and "dynamic". The other part indicates that the targeting users of the posters, such as "businessmen".

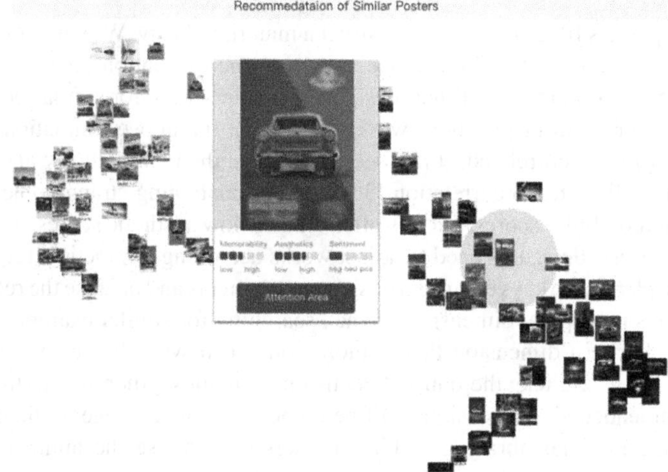

Fig. 3. The display of the recommendation of similar designs. The user input design is highlighted by the red rectangle, the positions of recommended designs are determined by their similarity distances from the user input design. The user can hover the mouse on the thumbnail of a design to see its detailed information. (Color figure online)

4 User Study

To evaluate DesignEva, we conducted a user study to observe whether DesignEva could play a positive role in users' design process.

4.1 Procedure

We recruited 20 students from a university (age: 19–25, 12 females, 8 males) to participate in our experiment. All participants were majors in design, including undergraduates and postgraduates. The task of the participants was to refine a car-themed advertising poster. First, we introduced the functions of our system to participants. Then, each participant was shown evaluation results of one poster. The task of each participant is to improve the poster using DesignEva. Finally, at the end of the task, the participants were asked to complete a System Usability Scale (SUS) questionnaire [43]. We also conducted semi-structured interviews to gain a deep understanding of the participants' experiences with DesignEva.

4.2 Results

Overall, the opinions of participants on DesignEva were positive, with most participants agreeing that DesignEva is beneficial for iteration in the design process. The average SUS score is 81.1 (i.e., significantly above the average SUS score, 68). Participants stated that they found DesignEva was easy and straightforward to learn and use.

First, most participants agreed with the accuracy of the evaluation results given by DesignEva, as P5 said: "AI's predictions are close to my expectations." When we introduced the system's functions, many of the participants expressed surprise and asked how AI can achieve predictions. P2 noted: "When I didn't know how it works, I felt very confused. But when I know that AI has gained the evaluation ability from big data, I am willing to believe its evaluation results." Most participants said that they would reflect on their works after getting the evaluation of AI. When asked whether DesignEva interfered with their original design trajectory in the design process, P12 mentioned: "I think this tool may enhance my self-confidence." P14 noted: "I will use AI's evaluation results as references, but I will stick to my own ideas and will not solely rely on AI's judgement."

Among four perceptual evaluations, most participants thought that the display of importance areas was the most useful feedback for them, as P16 noted: "The attention map of visual importance enables me to know which areas need to be adjusted, but how to achieve high memorability and aesthetics is not specific." In addition, participants also appreciated the function of searching for similar designs. P11 noted: "Similar recommendations are in line with my usual habit of searching for materials extensively in the design process." P4 said: "This is the advanced version of the image search function, which can save much time when searching for materials." Similarly, P14 noted: "I will observe other cases displayed in the system to think about the reasons why these works get high scores, and then I can optimize my works." While two participants thought the analyses of similar design schemes are most useful to them, as P4 said: "If the target user groups of similar posters are consistent with my expected goals, I will be encouraged." Interestingly, four participants mentioned that DesignEva not only can be used to help designers improve their designs, but also can be used to assist companies in making advertising decisions."

As for the limitations, more than ten participants mentioned that they wanted to know AI depended on what factors to make evaluations. P1 said: "I hope the system can give me specific suggestions on how to modify the poster to achieve high scores, such as which font and layout should be used." Four participants noted that AI failed to understand design creativity, which disappointed them, as P7 noted: "AI seems to be unable to understand some creative expressions. Some posters containing metaphors have not received high ratings, but humans will appreciate the creativity in them." In addition, three participants suggested that we can use AI to analyze the design trend, as

P2 noted: "I hope the system can recommend similar designs based on the latest trends in design, such as current popular layouts and colors." Similarly, P15 said: "I think AI can be used to predict the direction of future design trends and help designers choose better design solutions."

Finally, one participant said he disagreed to use AI to evaluate design works. He mentioned: "Design creativity cannot be quantitatively evaluated. AI may have learned some patterns from big data, but it cannot understand the unique ideas of designers. What's more, everyone has their design preference, and it is difficult to have a general evaluation criterion." But he also said that he viewed it from the perspective of a mature designer pursuing artistic expression. He thought that our tool still made sense for novice designers or commercial poster design.

5 Discussion

5.1 Providing Feedback in Design Language

Designers are accustomed to using design skills they have learned and accumulated to complete design works. Therefore, the feedback should be shown to them in design language. However, the neural networks are trained with images and their score labels. If we want neural networks to learn the relationship between design elements (such as layout and color) and perceptual scores, we need to annotate training images. Labelling design elements in images requires professional knowledge. The finely annotated training data is the key for AI to understand human perceptions.

5.2 Understanding Creativity Rather Than Regular Pattern

Deep learning techniques use large-scale datasets to train neural networks to learn which images are beautiful or memorable in human perceptions. Therefore, when new images arrive, AI is able to predict how humans perceive when they see these images. The essence of the learning of neural networks is to capture the data distribution of a specific dataset, that is, to learn the regular pattern of data. However, design is one of the tasks that best reflects human creativity. Excellent designers pursue the originality and uniqueness of their design works. It is important to enable AI to have the capability to understand and detect the unique pattern in each design.

5.3 Following the Design Trend

People's preference for design works are not constant, and design trends are coming and going. AI needs to continuously learn the latest works to be aware of changes in design trends. However, before training AI, we need to obtain human ratings on the new data, which is time-consuming. Therefore, how to ensure AI can continuously learn new data is the key to enabling AI to advance with the times.

6 Limitations and Future Work

Due to the difficulty of constructing datasets, we did not construct a unified dataset with multi-dimensional human annotations. Neural network models used for prediction in our prototype were trained on different datasets, respectively. In the future, we hope to train a single model to learn multi-dimensional perceptual ratings, which enables the model to better capture the correlations across various perceptual dimensions.

7 Conclusion

In this work, we propose DesignEva, a design-supported tool to offer multi-faceted perceptual evaluation of design works. We use deep neural networks trained on large-scale human-annotated datasets to predict memorability, aesthetics, sentiment and visual importance for posters. We also utilize a neural network to extract features from designs and use these features to calculate their similarities. Thus, we can recommend perceptual similar examples for the user input design. The user study experiment results indicate that participants' opinions on DesignEva were generally positive. DesignEva effectively promotes designers' reflection in the design process. However, using artificial intelligence to perform the perceptual evaluation of designs is still unfamiliar to the participants. They hope DesignEva can give perceptual evaluation combined with the modification suggestions of specific design elements.

References

1. Krause, M., Garncarz, T., Song, J., Gerber, E.M., Bailey, B.P., Dow, S.P.: Critique style guide: improving crowdsourced design feedback with a natural language model. In: Proceedings of the 2017 CHI Conference on Human Factors in Computing Systems, pp. 4627–4639 (2017)
2. Xu, A., Rao, H., Dow, S.P., Bailey, B.P.: A classroom study of using crowd feedback in the iterative design process. In: Proceedings of the 18th ACM Conference on Computer Supported Cooperative Work and Social Computing, pp. 1637–1648 (2015)
3. Rosenholtz, R., Dorai, A., Freeman, R.: Do predictions of visual perception aid design? ACM Trans. Appl. Percept. (TAP) **8**, 1–20 (2011)
4. Wu, Z., Jiang, Y., Liu, Y., Ma, X.: Predicting and diagnosing user engagement with mobile UI animation via a data-driven approach. In: Proceedings of the 2020 CHI Conference on Human Factors in Computing Systems, pp. 1–13 (2020)
5. AlRahayfeh, A., Faezipour, M.: Eye tracking and head movement detection: a state-of-art survey. IEEE J. Transl. Eng. Health Med. **1**, 2100212 (2013)
6. Kim, N.W., et al.: BubbleView: an interface for crowdsourcing image importance maps and tracking visual attention. ACM Trans. Comput.-Hum. Interact. **24** (2017). https://doi.org/10.1145/3131275
7. Fraser, C.A., Ngoon, T.J., Weingarten, A.S., Dontcheva, M., Klemmer, S.: CritiqueKit: a mixed-initiative, real-time interface for improving feedback. In: Adjunct Publication of the 30th Annual ACM Symposium on User Interface Software and Technology, pp. 7–9 (2017)
8. Miniukovich, A., De Angeli, A.: Computation of interface aesthetics. In: Proceedings of the 33rd Annual ACM Conference on Human Factors in Computing Systems, pp. 1163–1172 (2015)

9. Gygli, M., Grabner, H., Riemenschneider, H., Nater, F., Van Gool, L.: The interestingness of images. In: Proceedings of the IEEE International Conference on Computer Vision, pp. 1633–1640 (2013)
10. Khosla, A., Das Sarma, A., Hamid, R.: What makes an image popular? In: Proceedings of the 23rd International Conference on World Wide Web, pp. 867–876 (2014)
11. Pang, X., Cao, Y., Lau, R.W., Chan, A.B.: Directing user attention via visual flow on web designs. ACM Trans. Graph. (TOG) **35**, 1–11 (2016)
12. Yang, J., Sun, Y., Liang, J., Yang, Y.-L., Cheng, M.-M.: Understanding image impressiveness inspired by instantaneous human perceptual cues. In: Thirty-Second AAAI Conference on Artificial Intelligence (2018)
13. He, K., Zhang, X., Ren, S., Sun, J.: Deep residual learning for image recognition. In: Proceedings of the IEEE Conference on Computer Vision and Pattern Recognition, pp. 770–778 (2016)
14. Girshick, R.: Fast R-CNN. In: Proceedings of the IEEE International Conference on Computer Vision, pp. 1440–1448 (2015)
15. Zhang, R., Isola, P., Efros, A.A., Shechtman, E., Wang, O.: The unreasonable effectiveness of deep features as a perceptual metric. In: Proceedings of the IEEE Conference on Computer Vision and Pattern Recognition, pp. 586–595 (2018)
16. Fajtl, J., Argyriou, V., Monekosso, D., Remagnino, P.: AmNet: memorability estimation with attention. In: Proceedings of the IEEE Conference on Computer Vision and Pattern Recognition, pp. 6363–6372 (2018)
17. Talebi, H., Milanfar, P.: NIMA: neural image assessment. IEEE Trans. Image Process. **27**, 3998–4011 (2018)
18. Fitch, S.: Art critiques: a guide. Stud. Art Educ. **57**, 185–187 (2016)
19. Dow, S.P., Glassco, A., Kass, J., Schwarz, M., Schwartz, D.L., Klemmer, S.R.: Parallel prototyping leads to better design results, more divergence, and increased self-efficacy. ACM Trans. Comput.-Hum. Interact. (TOCHI) **17**, 1–24 (2010)
20. Dutton, T.A.: Design and studio pedagogy. J. Arch. Educ. **41**, 16–25 (1987)
21. Dow, S.P., Heddleston, K., Klemmer, S.R.: The efficacy of prototyping under time constraints. In: Proceedings of the Seventh ACM Conference on Creativity and Cognition, pp. 165–174 (2009)
22. Vredenburg, K., Mao, J.-Y., Smith, P.W., Carey, T.: A survey of user-centered design practice. In: Proceedings of the SIGCHI Conference on Human Factors in Computing Systems, pp. 471–478 (2002)
23. Dow, S., Fortuna, J., Schwartz, D., Altringer, B., Schwartz, D., Klemmer, S.: Prototyping dynamics: sharing multiple designs improves exploration, group rapport, and results. In: Proceedings of the SIGCHI Conference on Human Factors in Computing Systems, pp. 2807–2816 (2011)
24. Lok, S., Feiner, S., Ngai, G.: Evaluation of visual balance for automated layout. In: Proceedings of the 9th International Conference on Intelligent User Interfaces, pp. 101–108 (2004)
25. Wang, Z., Bovik, A.C., Sheikh, H.R., Simoncelli, E.P.: Image quality assessment: from error visibility to structural similarity. IEEE Trans. Image Process. **13**, 600–612 (2004)
26. Reinecke, K., et al.: Predicting users' first impressions of website aesthetics with a quantification of perceived visual complexity and colorfulness. In: Proceedings of the SIGCHI Conference on Human Factors in Computing Systems, pp. 2049–2058 (2013)
27. Tariq, T., Tursun, O.T., Kim, M., Didyk, P.: Why are deep representations good perceptual quality features? In: European Conference on Computer Vision, pp. 445–461. Springer (2020)

28. Swearngin, A., Li, Y.: Modeling mobile interface tappability using crowdsourcing and deep learning. In: Li, Y., Hilliges, O. (eds.) Artificial Intelligence for Human Computer Interaction: A Modern Approach. HIS, pp. 73–96. Springer, Cham (2021). https://doi.org/10.1007/978-3-030-82681-9_3
29. Rock, I., Engelstein, P.: A study of memory for visual form. Am. J. Psychol. **72**, 221–229 (1959)
30. Isola, P., Xiao, J., Torralba, A., Oliva, A.: What makes an image memorable? In: CVPR 2011, pp. 145–152. IEEE (2011)
31. Rensink, R.A.: The Management of Visual Attention in Graphic Displays. Cambridge University Press, Cambridge (2011)
32. Pilli, S., Patwardhan, M., Pedanekar, N., Karande, S.: Predicting sentiments in image advertisements using semantic relations among sentiment labels. In: Proceedings of the IEEE/CVF Conference on Computer Vision and Pattern Recognition Workshops, pp. 408–409 (2020)
33. Howard, A.G., et al.: MobileNets: efficient convolutional neural networks for mobile vision applications. arXiv preprint arXiv:1704.04861 (2017)
34. Murray, N., Marchesotti, L., Perronnin, F.: AVA: A large-scale database for aesthetic visual analysis. In: 2012 IEEE Conference on Computer Vision and Pattern Recognition, pp. 2408–2415. IEEE (2012)
35. Russakovsky, O., et al.: ImageNet large scale visual recognition challenge. Int. J. Comput. Vis. **115**, 211–252 (2015)
36. Khosla, A., Raju, A.S., Torralba, A., Oliva, A.: Understanding and predicting image memorability at a large scale. In: Proceedings of the IEEE International Conference on Computer Vision, pp. 2390–2398 (2015)
37. Bylinskii, Z., et al.: Learning visual importance for graphic designs and data visualizations. In: Proceedings of the 30th Annual ACM Symposium on User Interface Software and Technology, pp. 57–69 (2017)
38. O'Donovan, P., Agarwala, A., Hertzmann, A.: Learning layouts for single-pagegraphic designs. IEEE Trans. Vis. Comput. Graph. **20**, 1200–1213 (2014)
39. Vadicamo, L., et al.: Cross-media learning for image sentiment analysis in the wild. In: Proceedings of the IEEE International Conference on Computer Vision Workshops, pp. 308–317 (2017)
40. Simonyan, K., Zisserman, A.: Very deep convolutional networks for large-scale image recognition. arXiv preprint arXiv:1409.1556 (2014)
41. Van der Maaten, L., Hinton, G.: Visualizing data using t-SNE. J. Mach. Learn. Res. **9** (2008)
42. Hasler, D., Suesstrunk, S.E.: Measuring colorfulness in natural images. In: Human Vision and Electronic Imaging VIII, pp. 87–95. International Society for Optics and Photonics (2003)
43. Brooke, J., et al.: SUS-A quick and dirty usability scale. Usabil. Eval. Ind. **189**, 4–7 (1996)

The *Zhou Li* Paradigm of Active Design

Na Tian(✉)

Tongji University, Shanghai 200092, People's Republic of China
727099128@qq.com

Abstract. The article mainly discusses three issues. First of all, through the rethinking of design boundary and positioning, it points out the active design proposal rationality and possibility of existence. Secondly, consider the research category and core issues of active design from the perspective of design. According to research, active design is not a new thing. Looking back on history, 'Specify the system of clothes, ruling the world with courtesy' in China's pre-Qin period is a model of active design under the Chinese agricultural civilized lifestyle. Finally, taking the political order system of "setting up officials and dividing duties" in the Tian Guan system of Zhou Li as an example, this paper verifies the logic and ultimate purpose of active design. The Zhou Li is an important document in the Confucian classics, and it is also a traceable text for research in various disciplines. It is no exception to the study of design, and it also provides a comprehensive description of active design.

Keywords: *Zhou Li* · Kaogongology · Design governance · Design order

1 About Active Design

The proposal of the concept of active design has sublimated the thinking of the academic circles on the boundary and positioning of design. Taking a look at the problems first problems related to the current design boundary and design positioning.

The industrial revolution is recognized as an extremely important critical point in the process of human history. Since then, design research has gradually changed from a marginal research object to a main research object, although design has been quietly creating the second artificial world since the birth of mankind. As far as the historical development of design research is concerned, the boundary problem of design has also extended from the superficial level of 'objects' to the deep level of 'problems'. From the broad definition of design, design is still related to the creation, including the form of the object, the function of the object and the way of using the object, etc., which also makes the design process show an obvious feature, that is, the focus of design must always be around the end product. That's why the design object mainly focuses on the substance rather than others. However, with the passage of time, various problems in human social life continue to emerge, and even some wicked problems, just like contemporary beauty Richard Buchanan, an America design theorist, put forward the "wicked problems in design thinking" [1]. 'problems' have suddenly become an important content of design, and new terms such as experience design, service design, and social innovation design

P.-L. P. Rau (Ed.): HCII 2022, LNCS 13311, pp. 520–529, 2022.
https://doi.org/10.1007/978-3-031-06038-0_39

have emerged. Thus, the boundary of design once again arouses the thinking of design researchers.

The positioning of the design is reflected by the value of the design, and the value of the design is often reversed through the end product or result of the design. Usually, design starts after the client puts forward requirements. Compared with the proposer of the problem, the design is in a passive vassal position, that is to say, the design lags behind the problem. Obviously, in this situation in human society the design lacks vitality and innovation. When people found this, some scholars proposed that we should turn the design from the passive to the objective to stimulate the innovation driving force of design, such as Xiaofeng Fang [2] of Tsinghua University and Yongqi Lou [3] of Tongji University And other scholars. So, how to turn passive design into active design? Regarding this issue, we need to find an entry point that makes active design possible. We can try to change the positioning of the design. In the past, the design appeared after the problem, that is, the problem and the design have a sequence. Is there a possibility that the design itself is the problem, that is to say, the design and the problem are an organic whole. If this hypothesis holds, "design is the problem" means that the problem is the ontology of the existence and development of design, and there is no design if there is no problem. Design is not only an important means of creating an artificial world, but also a way of human survival and development. It constantly solves all kinds of problems that arise in the process of human development. The inherent driving force of design makes human beings have the essence of 'God' (the creator). From this perspective, the positioning of design has a new definition, so it is possible to change the passive role of design into an active one.

2 Thinking Perspective of Active Design

Design research is different from designology, just as business is different from economics. Examining active design from the perspective of designology is undoubtedly a novel and necessary subject. As far as the basic fields of design are concerned, the basic fields of contemporary design are divided into three major sections, namely meta-designology, applied-designology and social-designology [4]. The main research content of meta-designology is the problem between ontology and method, that is, the problem of design creation in the life landscape; the main research content of applied-designology is the relationship between technology and the world problems, that is, problems in the design of world construction; The main research content of social-designology is the problem between capital and governance, that is, the design behavior in the social environment. The core issue of social design is design governance, which is a kind of design behavior problems. Design has been in the continuous historical flow from encountering problems, exploring ways to solve problems, and then realizing certain goals, and constantly plays its innovation driving force. Obviously, in relation to the repositioning of design and the core content of social design, the study of active design should belong to the research category of social-designology. To some extent, design governance is active design. In terms of design historical development, the concept of active design is new and contemporary. Has active design already existed in the historical stream of design? According to research, active design is not a new thing. Looking back on history, *'Specify the system of clothes, ruling the world with courtesy'* in China's pre-Qin period is a model of active design under the Chinese agricultural civilized lifestyle. It is not only the beginning of human beings walking out of nature and building an artificial world order, but also the beginning of design governance to create an artificial world, improve the human world, serve the human society, and build a beautiful community with a shared future for mankind. This is also the core content of active design, that is, to realize the order of existence. This is also the core content of active design, that is, to realize the order of existence.

3 The *Zhou Li* Paradigm of Active Design

If *'Specify the system of clothes, ruling the world with courtesy'* is a model of active design, then *Zhou Li* [5] is an important paradigm of active design in the form of Kaogongology[1] [6]. The *Zhou Li* is an important document in the Confucian classics, and it is also a traceable text for research in various disciplines. It is no exception to the study of design, and it also provides a comprehensive description of active design.

The beginning of *Zhou Li* is *'create a nation.'*, 'create' is innovative design, and 'nation' is an artificial world created by human beings, a comprehensive 'design order' system, a model of a "political order" system and a universal "existence order". Through the logic of active design, through *'distinguishing orientation'* (the design thought of Yin, Yang and Five elements), *'planning urban and rural areas'* (spatial order), *'division of labor'* (political order), to achieve a *'better world'*, which is a universal order of existence. Due to the limited research progress, the active design thinking is discussed by taking the political order system design of *'division of labor'* as an example.

In *Zhou Li*, people (Gongjiang)[2] are divided into the Wang (king), Six Guan (six official systems ——Tian Guan, Di Guan, Chun Guan, Xia Guan, Qiu Guan, Dong Guan——) and Nine Zhi (nine posts of the people). In order to present the political order in China's farming and civilized society, people are divided into three levels,

[1] Professor Zou Qichang of Tongji University believes that there are two basic forms of Chinese design theory system at present. One is the system form of "design" in modern China. The other is the traditional Chinese design theory system, that is, the design theory form of "examination of engineering and learning" with "Yi" and "Li" as the ideological source. Chinese tradition The design theory system has roughly experienced three periods. The first stage is the Pre-Qin and Han Dynasties. This period is when the design thought was founded and the system was formed period; The second stage is from the Eastern Han Dynasty to the song and Yuan Dynasties, that is, the mature period of Chinese traditional design thought; The third stage is the Ming and Qing Dynasties. This period presents the summary characteristics of Chinese traditional design thought, and it is also the transformation period of Chinese traditional design thought. This study focuses on the traditional Chinese design theory. The first historical stage in the system, that is, the design thought from the Pre-Qin Dynasty to the Han Dynasty, is selected to present the Chinese biography. Based on the classics of the design thought system of "examination of engineering and learning", this paper analyzes its design thought and design method.

[2] The meaning of Gongjiang can be divided into broad sense and narrow sense. The broad sense of Gongjiang refers to all people with certain skills, and its meaning is equal to that of human beings. Gongjiang = designer + maker + doer + Practice... In a narrow sense, Gongjiang refers to craftsman. This study adopts the broad meaning of Gongjiang.

namely Wang (the most senior management Gongjiang), Guan (second-high management Gongjiang), and Min (general Gongjiang). Although the full text rarely mentions the Wang, who always occupies an important position, and all behaviors and activities are carried out around the Wang with the purpose of creating a nation. As the head of state, the Wang also has corresponding duties, such as attending major court meetings with the participation of the common people; participating in national sacrificial activities, regularly inspecting federal countries, and signing and issuing various documents issued by the Six Guan. The role of the Wang is to lead or rule the country, so it can be seen as the most senior management Gongjiang. The second-level Gongjiang are called Guan and are divided into six major structural systems. The "six" here does not mean that there are only six types of functions. The number of functions is designed based on the thinking of Yin, Yang and Five elements, and each function is responsible and handled. The six officials make the nation achieve the goals of equalization, security, peace, peace, criticism, and wealth through measures such as governance, education, ritual, administration, punishment, and affairs. Therefore, it can be considered as the next-level management Gongjiang. The Gongjiang at the third level are called Min. This is an innovative design of the political order of nation, which can be seen from the Tian Guan system.

3.1 The Governance Gongjiang

Tian Guan system is divided into sixty genera, all of which are called governance Gongjiang. Among them, Tai Zai is the head of the Six Guan, who leading other Gongjiang to perform management functions. Therefore, the political order in which division of labor can be seen best in the Tian Guan system, which are divided into five types according to their duties that a total of 63 governance Gongjiang in the Tian Guan system.

In the system of Tian Guan, the head of Tian Guan is the commander of the heavenly officials, that is, the great ruler. The sixty heavenly officials are subordinate officials, collectively known as "governance officials", which are under the leadership of the emperor of the tomb under the guidance of the "government" to assist the "King" to achieve the goal of "equalizing" the state. The most important thing about the power of the big slaughter is "control" "Six codes, governing the country", which covers 360 official positions in the six official systems, so Dazai is also known as zuozai, which means president, therefore, although Tianguan and other five senses are the six official systems, Tianguan commands other five senses. Therefore, in heaven, you can see it best the institutional structure of the Gongjiang industry. Tianguanzhong slaughter system has 63 "governance" craftsmen, which are divided into five types according to their duties.

Gongjiang in Charge of Court Affairs. Tai Zai is the Gongjiang responsible for assisting the monarch in governing the nation. Xiao Zai is the Gongjiang in charge of criminal law decrees within the court. Zai Fu is the Gongjiang who is responsible for arranging the ministers' duties according to their superiors and inferiors to deal with the guests and the officials. Gong Zheng is the Gongjiang in charge of prohibition in the court. Gong Bo is When there is a big event in charge of the palace, the Gongjiang of the sages are called together. Nei Zai is the Gongjiang in charge of teaching the harem's concubines in accordance with the rules. Nei Xiaochen is the Gongjiang who is responsible for informing the queen of the etiquette when offering sacrifices, receiving guests or holding funerals. Hun Ren is the Gongjiang responsible for inspecting the entry and exit of people and guests in the palace. Si Ren is the Gongjiang responsible for the commandments of female officials and female slaves in the palace. Nei shu is the Gongjiang responsible for conveying the instructions of all small matters inside and outside the palace and clearing the way for the insiders. Jiu pin is the female Gongjiang, who are also concubines of the monarch, are responsible for educating women and assisting the queen in offering sacrifices. Shi fu is the female Gongjiang, also concubines and concubines of monarchs, officials responsible for mourning for ministers. Nv yu is the female Gongjiang, the royal wife of the king, are responsible for offering women's merits on time. Nv zhu is the female Gongjiang, who responsible for holding sacrifices to remove disease and misfortune. Nv shi is the female Gongjiang, who responsible for checking the expenditures of the harem and recording the queen's orders.

Gongjiang in Charge of Food. Shan Fu is the Gongjiang in charge of the king's diet. Pao ren is the Gongjiang responsible for providing the livestock required for the sacrifice. Nei Yong is the Gongjiang responsible for slaughtering and offering sacrifices for the king. Wai Yong is the Gongjiang responsible for entertaining the elderly and orphans with gifts and cooking food for them. Heng Ren is the Gongjiang who is responsible for providing cooking utensils for cooking meat and controlling the amount of water and heat. Dian Shi is the Gongjiang responsible for planting the king's borrowed fields and providing grain. Shou Ren is the Gongjiang responsible for contributing to the beast. Yu Ren is the Gongjiang responsible for providing fish for sacrifice and guests. Bie Ren is the Gongjiang responsible for providing clams, snails and ant eggs for sacrifice. La Ren is the Gongjiang responsible for supplying dry meat for sacrifice. Jiu Zheng is the Gongjiang responsible for providing the monarch with wine according to a certain system. Wine Ren is the Gongjiang responsible for providing wine for the banquet of the emperor. Jiang Ren is the Gongjiang responsible for providing drinks required by guests during their stay. Ling Ren is the Gongjiang responsible for the decrees related to ice storage and ice production. Bian Ren is the Gongjiang in charge of sacrificing food in the ancestral temple. Hai Ren is the Gongjiang responsible for offering food filled with beans for sacrifice and banquet. Xi Ren is the Gongjiang who offer sacrifices, recommend the beans of shame. Yan Ren is the Gongjiang responsible for supplying salt for sacrifice. Mi Ren is the Gongjiang responsible for providing cloth towels for covering eating utensils.

Gongjiang in Charge of Medicine. Yi Shi is the Gongjiang responsible for medical decrees and providing drugs. Shi Yi is the Gongjiang responsible for preparing meals for the monarch according to the climate. Ji Yi is the Gongjiang responsible for treating people's diseases, recording the cause of death of patients and reporting it to doctors. Yang Yi is the Gongjiang responsible for drug treatment of patients with carbuncle and ulcer. Shou Yi is the Gongjiang responsible for treating livestock diseases and counting the number of dead animals.

Gongjiang in Charge of Residence and Clothing. Zhang She is the Gongjiang responsible for the affairs of the palace house when the monarch goes out. Zhang Ci is the Gongjiang responsible for making beds and setting screens for the monarch during the grand brigade Festival. Mu Ren is the Gongjiang responsible for managing and providing curtain strategies and ribbons needed by the monarch when he goes out. Si Qiu is the Gongjiang duty of Qiu is to serve the needs of the emperor. Zhang Pi is the Gongjiang who is responsible for providing animal hair for making felt for state affairs. Dian Fugong is the Gongjiang responsible for checking and collecting the sewing work assigned to concubines in autumn. Dian Si is the Gongjiang responsible for collecting and identifying silk fabrics offered by female workers for use. Dian Xi is the Gongjiang responsible for collecting linen fabrics offered by female workers for use. Nei Sifu is the Gongjiang responsible for managing and supplying the clothes worn by the queen and internal and external life women. Feng Ren is the Gongjiang in charge of sewing in the palace. Ran Ren is the Gongjiang responsible for dyeing affairs. Zhui Shi is the Gongjiang responsible for making the headdress of concubines for sacrifice and entertaining guests. Lv Ren is the Gongjiang responsible for distinguishing the shoes worn by the husband and wife. Xia Cai is the Gongjiang in charge of summoning the soul of the monarch during the great funeral.

Gongjiang in Charge of Collection and Examination. Da Fu is the Gongjiang responsible for collecting and issuing property. Yu Fu is the Gongjiang responsible for collecting jade ornaments, weapons and other treasures for the use of the monarch. Nei Fu is the Gongjiang responsible for collecting valuable goods contributed by the vassal states. Wai Fu is the Gongjiang responsible for providing sacrifices and entertaining guests. Si Hui is according to the nine tribute laws, the Gongjiang who collect the finance and taxes of the vassal states. Si Shu is the Gongjiang responsible for managing the copy of tax collection. Zhi Nei is the Gongjiang responsible for recording the copy of the order of the person receiving the property for year-end assessment. Zhi Sui is the Gongjiang responsible for the relevant provisions of the state's property expenditure. Zhi Bi is the Gongjiang responsible for assisting the company to assess the remaining financial expenditure.

3.2 The General Gongjiang

A general Gongjiang is someone who has a certain skill to survive. There is a rule that '*set nine posts serve all the people*' in *Zhou Li*. The so-called nine posts: "*First, farmers are engaged in agriculture. Second, landscape workers manage mountain forests and gardens. Third, the person in charge of mountains and rivers. The fourth is herdsmen to raise Tibetan birds and animals. Fifth, craftsmen can make utensils and appreciate all kinds of materials. Sixth, businessmen are engaged in capital exchange activities. Seventh, female craftsmen are engaged in the textile and silk industry. Eighth, slaves engaged in civil engineering. Ninth, there are no fixed workers and often change jobs.*"

In the Tian Guan system, people's occupations are divided into nine categories (the nine types of occupations here are not really nine. In the traditional Chinese cultural concept, nine represents a very large number), including agriculture, sideline, fishery, animal husbandry, handicraft industry, commerce and service industry. Even those who do not have jobs will be provided with vocational training so that they can get a job, or serve as labor in government organs, etc.

After understanding the types of Gongjiang in the Tian Guan system, how are these Gongjiang organized? What is its organizational structure like? What are his design principles and structural patterns? First of all, we should to know how these Gongjiang are organized. The principle of organizational design is the principle of responsibility, that is, the setting of Guan Zhi, Guan Chang and Guan Shu.

The so-called responsibility principle was originally the legalist thought of governing the country. Legalists took the principle of responsibility as a basic principle and extended it to all aspects in order to establish a stable social order. For example, in Shang Yang's book *Shang Jun Shu* [7]: "If the responsibility is fixed, the people will cheat their integrity, the people will be the original courtiers, and each will have autonomy. Therefore, if the responsibility is fixed, the way of potential governance is benefiting people; if the responsibility is uncertain, the way of potential chaos is chaotic."

Responsibilities define the scope of people's rights, and the treacherous people can be exploited seamlessly. In addition, *Han Feizi* [8] mentions: '*The ministers keep their duties, and all officials are regular*.' The most basic point is to clearly define the duties of officials at all levels and to make quantitative and qualitative regulations. Then, whether the entire national administrative agency can operate effectively depends to some extent on the degree of due diligence of officials, and only a certain score can evaluate the work of officials in terms of quality and quantity.

Guan Zhi. Guan Zhi refers to naming each Gongjiang. The name of Gongjiang is to determine the title of each craftsman, such as Tai Zai, Xiao Zai, Zai Fu, and so on. From a macro perspective, there are six categories of administrative positions, teaching positions, ritual positions, political positions, criminal positions, and ministerial positions, which are managed by the chiefs of the six officials. There are one hundred and sixty positions, which are generally called off Gongjiang positions." For example, in the entire Tian Guan system, the names of Gongjiang mentioned are all positions. Well, once the Gongjiang name is determined, it is necessary to stipulate the duties. This is the official routine.

Guan Chang. Guan Chang refers to the content that Gongjiang often engage in. The function of Gongjiang means that each Gongjiang has a clear work content, and it is not easy to change. For example, in the Tian Guan system, the position of Tai Zai is in charge of the six codes of state construction, in order to assist the king to equalize the state; the position of the Xiao Zai is in charge of the palace type of the state construction to govern the decree of the royal palace. The position of Zai Fu, in charge of the law of ruling the dynasty, the position of the king. The division of labor of Gongjiang is extremely fine, specific and subtle, and each performs its own duties without surpassing each other.

The name and function of Gongjiang has been set, so how to organize these Gongjiang? Then it needs to be structured through the Guan Shu system.

Guan Shu. Guan Shu refers to the organizational structure among Gongjiang. In Tian Guan systenm, the organizational structure of Gongjiang is usually a vertical hierarchical and segmented organizational system, which is mainly common through the design of Guan Shu. According to the rank of nobility and inferiority, Guan Shu can be divided into four levels from top to bottom.

Zong Shu. All governance Gongjiang are divided into Six Guan—Tian Guan, Di Guan, Chun Guan, Xia Guan, Qiu Guan, Dong Guan—and each Guan has sixty subordinate management Gongjiang.

Fen Shu. Each Guan has its vertical structure. The chief of the Six Guan in the rank is Qing, and the rest of the ranks are below it. For example, the order of rank in Zhou Li, Qing – Zhong Da Fu – Xia Da Fu – Shang Shi – Zhong Shi-Xia Shi. Such as, the Zheng refers to Tai Zai, that is, the leader of Tian Guan; the Er refers to the deputy second of Tai Zai, named Xiao Zai, which rank is the Zhong Da Fu. This is a macro ownership relationship.

Dang Guan Zhi Shu. The subordinate of each Guan is the subordinate relationship of another level, which refers to the relationship between an official and his subordinates. Such as Gong Zheng, the rank of nobility is Shang Shi. Among its subordinates are four Zhong Shi, eight Xia Shi, two Fu, four Shi, four Xu, and four Tu.

Rong San Zhi Shu. Redundant and scattered people refer to the subordinate relationship of redundant and scattered people outside the establishment of government officials. For example, those who look after dogs and lead dogs are subordinate to dog people, and the brave people of the country are subordinate to Siyou. Redundant personnel have no rank and fixed number.

Through the above organizational structure of Gongjiang, we found, in the Tian Guan system the entire craftsman industry organization presents a vertical structure of segmentation and inlaid layers. The position of each Gongjiang in the hierarchy, their duties and authority are also clearly defined. The superiority and inferiority do not surpass each other, and the responsibilities do not surpass each other. The above organizational structure can also be regarded as the division of labor mode of Gongjiang, where there is division of labor, there is cooperation. So what is the collaboration model of the Gongjiang industry? The main cooperation mode of the Gongjiang industry is the Guan Lian system.

The division of labor has advantages and disadvantages. The advantage is to clarify the responsibilities of all officials, but the disadvantages are also quite obvious. For example, the positions of various departments are not connected and separated from each other. Therefore, in order to avoid this phenomenon, *Zhou Li* put forward the concept of Guan Lian. The official cooperation recorded in *Zhou Li* mainly includes six categories: politics, military and economy, including the cooperation between production, construction, taxation, meeting ceremony and alliance oath. But in fact, the cooperation among Six Guan is not these six categories, but all things have cooperation. Take urban construction as an example, first of all, the magistrate should measure and delimit the area and plot. The second step is to make a master plan by Xia Guan. In the third step, the Dong Guan shall carry out the engineering design and determine the construction body planning according to the data and data provided by the local official and summer official. The fourth step is the implementation of the project. First, Di Guan concentrate their labor to the designated place. Then, the people from all localities who came to service were transferred to the military justice department under the jurisdiction of Xia Guan. Next, the constructors in charge of technology are dispatched by the Dong Guan to construct according to the design and progress. When the project is completed or comes to an end, the construction party (local official), the supervisor (Di Guan) and the technical responsible party (Dong Guan) shall sign the project acceptance contract for assessment. Other campaigns to build cities and canals, as well as field hunting and military training activities, are generally completed by various cooperation as described above.

Guan Lian is a special requirement of the state for the organizational structure of the Gongjiang industry. It is not only important to cooperation, but also everything. In other words, all matters of the government are handled jointly by the officials of each department according to law. Therefore, the Guan Lian in *Zhou Li* presents a complex phenomenon.

The role of the Guan Lian has two aspects. One is to supplement the Guan Chang, that is, one person is difficult to defeat the power of hundreds of people, and the Guan Chang is always in charge of division, Official liaison and cooperation. Another one, it can check and balance all officials to prevent fraud and arbitrariness.

The whole organizational structure of Gongjiang is a complete system with clear division of labor and cooperation, which effectively realizes the ruling order of the country.

Above, we found that the division of Gongjiang duties in *Zhou Li* is a way of life and state created in line with the law of beauty. It is a state of high unity of material civilization and spiritual civilization. The active design here is more about changing human life from disorder to orderly high-quality life.

4 Conclusion

The conclusion is that *Zhou Li* is an important paradigm of active design in the initial stage of Chinese traditional design thought. As we all know, the operation and development of things has its own law. The law is the inevitable, essential and stable connection between the nature and various phenomena in society. It is rhythmic and not messy. This law is actually an order. When this order (Law) is broken and things change from an orderly state to a mixed state, problems arise. If the problem needs to be solved, it is necessary to restore or give order to the mixed state (or problem) of things, and the process of restoring or giving order is design, which is also the standard goal of design. What is the ultimate goal of design, that is, to achieve the stability of the operation order of things, make its sustainable development, and try to avoid the breaking of the order through the design. In other words, the ultimate purpose of design is not only to solve the problem, but also to minimize the possibility of the occurrence of the problem (or breaking of the order).The stable political, social and ecological (overall trend) order of Chinese traditional society (before the 1920s) for thousands of years is a very convincing case if design can be seen as the driving force to realize the logical and sustainable development of society. Such a stable political, social and ecological order must be enabled by a design paradigm, which is the *Zhou Li* paradigm. As an important model in the initial stage of Chinese traditional design theory system, *Zhou Li* systematically constructed a typical paradigm of design serving national governance for the first time.

References

1. Buchanan, R.: Wicked problems in design thinking. Des. Issues **08**(02), 5–21 (1992)
2. Xiaofeng, F.: On design activism. Zhuangshi **07**, 12–16 (2015)
3. Yongqi, L.: Design activism in an era of transformation. Chin. J. Des. **07**, 17–19 (2015)
4. Qichang, Z.: Design governance: concept, system and strategy – an outline of the research on the basic problems of social-designology. Cult. Art Res. **05**, 53–62 (2021)
5. Yirang, S.: Zhou Li. Zhonghua Publishing House, Shanghai (1987)
6. Qichang, Z.: Kaogongji. People's Publishing House, Beijing (2020)
7. Yiranng, S., Lei, S.: Shangjunshu. Zhonghua Publishing House, Shanghai (2009)
8. Huaping, G.: Hanfeizi. Zhonghua Publishing House, Shanghai (2015)

The Effect of Involvement and Place Attachment on Travel Motivation and Behavioral Intentions for Festival Activity

Hui-Yun Yen[1(✉)] and Xin Yue Hu[2]

[1] Department of Advertising, Chinese Culture University, Taipei 11114, Taiwan
pccu.yhy@gmail.com

[2] Graduate School of Business, Kyung Hee University, Seoul 02447, Republic of Korea

Abstract. Festivals are events that can bring people joy and that involve shared planning. They involve the marketization of local traditions or cultures as well as activities to promote certain products, services, thoughts, information, and groups. Festivals can attract tourists and are the most direct and concrete channel to promote local culture to outsiders. This study researched the Xitang Hanfu Cultural Festival. Literature review and data analysis were conducted to integrate related studies and design a questionnaire using involvement, place attachment, travel motivation, and behavioral intention as the evaluation dimensions. The results were as follows: First, the proposed questionnaire was feasible and can serve as a reference for other academic institutions or industries. Second, the factor loading of most of the observed variables of each dimension exceeded 0.8. These variables had strong influences and should be considered in future studies. Third, peoples' place dependence or place identity had a positive effect on their travel motivation, and their involvement had a positive effect on their behavioral intention. Therefore, festivals should be promoted to the public when they are hosted in the future, and they should be advertised differently to different target audiences such as travelers, tourists, residents, and people interested in local culture. The results of this study can provide a reference for future studies investigating how the involvement and place attachment of tourists in festivals affected their travel motivation and behavioral intention.

Keywords: Involvement · Place attachment · Travel motivation · Behavioral intentions · Festival activity

1 Introduction

As the economies of various countries become prosperous, there is a wave of tourism that combines celebrations with featured scenic spots. Festival activity is a prevailing social and humanistic phenomenon worldwide, also has played a crucial role in politics, economy, and society throughout human history. Festival activity is able experienced, enthusiastic participation from tourists interested in featured scenic spots. Moreover, many countries have a rich cultural heritage that can support the cultural connotation of

P.-L. P. Rau (Ed.): HCII 2022, LNCS 13311, pp. 530–542, 2022.
https://doi.org/10.1007/978-3-031-06038-0_40

festival activity, and these activities have a personal style and attitude toward life that can affect people's emotions. The holding of festival activity helps to strengthen the creativity and self-confidence of the local cultural and creative industries; it can also shape the image of the city to achieve sustainable development of cultural and social harmony and interaction. Festival activities integrate the features of products, services, ideas, information, groups, etc., not only can attract tourists, but also the most direct and specific publicity channel for local culture.

2 Conceptual Background

Travelers experience the perception and sensory stage during emotional transference. They form travel motivations based on their experiences and preferences, then they implement their travel plans. The behavioral intentions of travelers progress from perception (emotion) to demand (motivation) to behavior. Therefore, travel perception (emotion) affects travel behavioral intention and travel motivation [1–4]. Studies related to festivals have explored the relationship between emotional and psychological variables and future behavior and have used involvement and place attachment as variables [5, 6]. The aforementioned future behavior refers to behavioral intention and travel motivation. Behavioral intention is the intention and willingness of an individual to perform a behavior [7]. Travel motivation is the driving force of travel activities and is the inner driving force of actual travel behavior [8]. Chang and Chia [9] investigated the development process of travel perceived was motivation (unsatisfied demand), behavior (on-site experiences), and perceived value (level of satisfaction of traveler demands). Additionally, the study revealed the internal connections between consumer demand, travel motivation, participatory behavior, and perceived value and explained how travel motivation is an antecedent of behavioral intention. The present study further discusses involvement, place attachment, travel motivation, and behavioral intention.

2.1 Involvement

Involvement is a mental state and serves as the core concept of self-involvement. Involvement is a state of motivation, encouragement, or interest; it is broadly defined as an individual's demand for a target and their interest and valuation of that target. When individuals have a higher level of involvement in a situation, they become more unwilling to accept opposing views and have stronger opinions. Additionally, they are prone to agreeing with opinions similar to theirs and to elaborate on such opinions. Involvement is used in the study of consumer behavior to explain the different choices of consumers due to their different emotional involvement [10–12]. Specific stimulation or scenarios can arouse involvement. Such arousal can take the form of mental states such as emotional engagement, participatory motivation, curiosity, and anticipation towards leisure activities, recreational environments, related recreational facilities, or products. Involvement is also the level of participation of an individual in an activity. When individuals are highly involved, they place the center of their life in the activity. Stronger personal involvement increases individual's level of involvement, which in turn prompts individuals to behave and respond to engage in the activity [5, 13].

Attraction, centrality, and self-expression are the three main factors that have been used to evaluate the level of involvement of tourists. Attraction refers to the importance and joy of the activity, centrality refers to the lifestyle choices and personal investments made by an individual to support their continued association in the activity, and self-expression refers to the expression of personal identity after participating in the activity [14, 15].

2.2 Place Attachment

Place attachment can reflect personal emotions and how an individual evaluates a site. Satisfying the demands of residents can increase their place attachment. Place familiarity creates place identity, which then transforms into place attachment. People form emotional connections with places, and strong emotions drive people to engage in concrete supportive actions [16]. Williams et al. [17] divided place attachment into place dependence and place identity. Place dependence refers to how individuals maintain an intimate sense of belonging with a place; acknowledge the importance or multiple unique functions of a place; and uses the place to satisfy their demands or goals. Place identity refers to the feelings of individuals; place identity refers to the emotional connections of individuals with places after a specific period and after having certain experiences. Place identity is the emotional identity of individuals with natural environments. Moore and Grafe [18] discovered that functional place dependence forms in a short time if the resources of an environment are beneficial and convenient for people. Contrarily, place identity, which involves emotional aspects, takes longer to form.

2.3 Travel Motivation and Behavioral Intention

As an internal driver of behavior and decision-making, motivation dictates how people behave. Iso-Ahola [19] posited that the motivation to travel stems from social and psychological forces that urge participation in tourism activities and that tourism motivation is composed of seeking and escaping. Here, seeking refers to individuals searching for environments different from those in their daily lives to obtain psychological compensation, whereas escape refers to the individual's desire to escape from their daily environment. Seeking and escaping serve as drivers for individuals to form travel motivation, which then acts as the internal driver to urge individual to participate in activities, initiate travel activities, and pursue their goals [20].

Maslow's hierarchy of needs [21] is the motivational theory most used by researchers. The theory indicates that the five human needs classified from bottom to top are physiological needs, safety needs, love and belonging needs, esteem needs, and self-actualization needs. Scholars such as Nickerson and Ellis [22], Goeldner and Ritchie [23] and Pearce [24] have all used the hierarchy of needs to develop evaluation dimensions for travel motivation. They argued that higher levels of motivation include lower levels of motivation, and individuals only pursue higher levels of motivation after their lower levels of motivation are satisfied.

Behavioral intention refers to the possibility or attitude of an individual to engage in a specific behavior after undergoing personal subjective judgments and is a psychological precedent to an action [25, 26]. In other words, behavioral intention is the attitude of individuals during behavioral decision-making. Behavioral intention can be used to make effective predictions about the likelihood of a specific behavior occurring in the future; measuring the behavioral intention of individuals can generate data similar to each individual's actual behavior. Therefore, behavioral intention is a reliable antecedent variable used to predict actual behavior [27].

Jones and Sasser [28] indicated that consumers exhibit three forms of behavioral intentions, namely repurchase intention, repeated behavior, and suggestive behavior. Behavioral intention can be classified as positive or negative. Positive behavioral intentions include consumers' willingness to talk about the excellent performance of a company with others, recommend a company to others, stay loyal to a company, make more purchases, and purchase a product at a higher price. Negative behavioral intentions include consumers leaving a company or lowering their purchases from a company.

3 Methods

3.1 Research Hypotheses

This study applies the cultural emotion model of festival activities to discover people's participation, motivation and behavioral intentions and other related issues. The aim of this study was to solve problems related to local cultural through the implementation of culture emotion and value-added aesthetic economy, and to explore the influence of travel motivation and behavioral Intentions in terms of the degree of people's emotion of travel by constructing a cultural emotion on travel motivation and behavioral intentions model. The researchers take the XiTang Han-Fu Culture Festival as a case study, which is a successful combination of traditional Chinese clothing and tourism products, they are reflected in the main activities of the festival. The revival of Hanfu has moved from the Internet to reality. Wearing Hanfu in daily life has gradually formed a social boom. Many organizations and companies have also participated in this Hanfu innovation, and they have also organized activities related to Hanfu culture. The purpose of this study is to investigate the following research questions:

(a) What are the cultural emotion of festival activity features?
(b) What is the relationship between cultural emotion and travel motivation?
(c) What is the relationship between cultural emotion and behavioral intentions?

According to the studies in related fields, the following seven related research hypotheses are generated: hypothesis 1: There is a significant effect of involvement on travel motivation; hypothesis 2: There is a significant effect of place attachment on travel motivation; hypothesis 3: There is a significant effect of involvement on behavioral intentions; hypothesis 4: There is a significant effect of place attachment on behavioral intentions; hypothesis 5: There is a significant effect of travel motivation on behavioral intentions; hypothesis 6: Tourism motivation plays a significant intermediary role in the relationship between involvement and behavioral intentions; hypothesis 7: Tourism motivation plays a significant intermediary role in the relationship between place attachment and behavioral intentions. The research hypothesis is presented in Fig. 1.

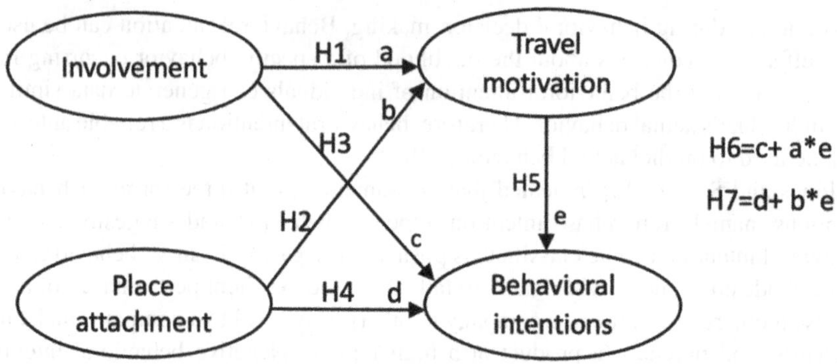

Fig. 1. Research hypothesis

3.2 Research Case

The study case was the Xitang Hanfu Cultural Festival. The old township of Xitang is situated in Jiashan County, Jiaxing City, Zhejiang Province, China, and borders Shanghai Municipality and Jiangsu Province. Xitang has a long history and was the birthplace of the ancient Wuyue culture. Xitang was a town in the Tang and Song dynasties and developed into a renowned city, as well as a commercial center and famous tourism destination, in the Ming and Qing dynasties. Xitang was among the first batch of famous historical and cultural cities in China, and its excellent location in the Jiangnan region, rich historical heritage, and beautiful atmosphere converted it into a gathering place for hanfu (i.e., traditional Chinese clothing) enthusiasts (Chu 2014).

The Xitang Hanfu Cultural Festival is a hanfu cultural event initiated by the renowned Taiwanese lyricist Vincent Fang. The festival aims to promote traditional Chinese clothing and rituals and organizes large-scale presentations of traditional Chinese clothing, rituals, and culture. The Xitang Hanfu Cultural Festival attracts hanfu enthusiasts nationwide and includes other activities such as calligraphy, traditional dancing, and activities that incorporate elements of traditional culture with hanfu. Since 2013, the Xitang Hanfu Cultural Festival has been celebrated annually for 8 consecutive years. The festival has become a cultural brand for Xitang and has established the crucial status of Xitang for hanfu enthusiasts (Wang 2015; Hsu 2013). The images of Xitang Hanfu Cultural Festival are presented in Fig. 2.

Fig. 2. 2020 Xitang Hanfu Cultural Festival [29]

3.3 Research Tool

This study conducted a literature review and data analysis and integrated related studies to design the research tools. The evaluation dimensions of this study were involvement, place attachment, travel motivation, and behavioral intention. Involvement consisted of three observed variables, namely attraction, centrality, and self-expression. Place attachment had two observed variables, namely place dependence and place identity. Travel motivation comprised five observed variables, namely physiological needs, safety needs, love and belonging needs, esteem needs, and self-actualization needs. Behavioral intention had three observed variables, namely intention to participate, repeated behavior, and suggestive behavior. The questionnaire of this study consisted of 4 dimensions, 13 variables; 39 items were used to reflect the latent variables of each dimension. The definitions of the items were taken from the theoretical analysis of the literature review. All the items were constructed on a theoretical basis. The questionnaire is presented in Table 1.

Table 1. The questionnaire

	Dimension	Code	Item
Involvement	Attraction	Att1	I am interested in participating in this festival activity
		Att2	This festival activity makes me happy
		Att3	It is very important to me to be part of this festival activity
	Centrality	Cen1	I found that my life is closely related to this festival activity
		Cen2	I like to discuss this festival activity with my friends
		Cen3	My friends and I like to go to this festival activity often
	Self-expression	Exp1	I can provide other people the information about this festival activity
		Exp2	Through this festival activity, I can express my own style
		Exp3	When I participated in this festival activity, I was happy for others to see me
Place attachment	Place dependence	Rel1	Compared with other tourist attractions, I prefer to go to this place
		Rel2	Compared with other festivals, this festival activity makes me satisfied
		Rel3	Other festival tourism cannot replace this festival tourism

(continued)

Table 1. (*continued*)

	Dimension	Code	Item
	Place identity	Ide1	This festival activity means a lot to me
		Ide2	I have a strong sense of identity with this festival activity
		Ide3	This festival activity gives me a sense of belonging
Travel motivation	Physiological	Phy1	This festival activity gave me a novel experience and satisfied my curiosity
		Phy2	This festival activity showed me historical costumes
		Phy3	This festival activity allows me to know and experience traditional culture
	Safety	Safe1	The safety of this festive activity will affect my willingness to travel
		Safe2	This festive activity allows me to travel in a relaxed way
		Safe3	Participating in this festival activity makes me feel safe
	Love and belonging	Soc1	This festival activity allows me to interact with people and meet new friends
		Soc2	This festival activity allows me to express my ideas or expertise to others
		Soc3	This festival activity allows me to gain respect from others
	Esteem	Res1	This festival activity can satisfy my pursuit of aesthetics and the learning of new knowledge
		Res2	This festival activity made me know myself better
		Res3	This festival activity allows me to achieve personal achievement and prestige
	Self-actualization	Self1	This festive activity soothes, settles or liberates the emotional level of the individual
		Self2	This festive activity enhances personal abilities and vision
		Self3	This festival activity allows me to reduce mental stress, tension or frustration

(*continued*)

Table 1. *(continued)*

	Dimension	Code	Item
Behavioral intentions	Intention to participate	Int1	I participated in this festival because I like the culture
		Int2	I will buy this festival activity related products
		Int3	I will search for information about this festival activity
	Repeated behavior	Rep1	I will participate in this festival activity again
		Rep2	I will buy this festival activity related products again
		Rep3	I am willing to pay more for this festival activity
	Suggestive behavior	Rec1	I would recommend this festival activity to others
		Rec2	I would like to let others know that I participated in this festival activity
		Rec3	I will encourage my friends to go to this festival activity

4 Findings and Analysis

The researchers test the proposed research model, a cultural emotion assessment scale for festival activity based on the literature review was used to measure a person's travel motivation and behavioral intentions. A total of 256 questionnaires was collected in this study, and 220 valid questionnaires were obtained after deleting invalid or randomly filling in questionnaires.

4.1 Convergent Validity and Discriminant Validity

This study collected 220 valid responses and used confirmatory factor analysis (CFA) to measure the covariance between the observed variables and the latent variables. Therefore, this study first used CFA to measure the convergent validity and discriminant validity of the questionnaire.

The standardized factor loadings (SFLs) of CFA demonstrated that the factor loading of the involvement dimension was 0.777–0.901, the factor loading of the place attachment dimension was 0.843–0.888, the factor loading of the travel motivation dimension was 0.613–0.840, and the factor loading of the behavioral intention dimension was 0.878–0.913. The SFL of each item was >0.6; therefore, the questionnaire was deemed acceptable. In addition, the composite reliability of each dimension was 0.818–0.887, and the average variance extracted (AVE) was 0.561–0.724. Bagozzi and Yi [30] recommended that composite reliability and AVE should be greater than 0.60 and 0.50, respectively. Since both outcome values were separately equal to or greater than both recommended values, the questionnaire had acceptable internal consistency.

Discriminant validity measures two different constructs. If correlation analysis reveals two constructs to have a low correlation, then the two constructs have discriminant validity [2]. This study defines discriminant validity as dimensions where over 75% of the square roots of the AVE were greater than the correlation coefficient of the dimension [31]. The values presented diagonally reveals that the square root of AVE of each dimension was 0.749–0.851, and 75% of the square roots of the AVE were greater than the correlation coefficient of each dimension. The analysis results determined that the questionnaire had discriminant validity.

4.2 Multivariate Normality Testing

The structural equation model of this study adopted multivariate normality testing to explore the normality of the observed variables and the multivariate normality of the observed variables after they are integrated. The normality of the observed variables is determined by the coefficient of skewness and the coefficient of kurtosis. If the absolute value of the skewness and kurtosis of the observed variables is smaller than 2, then the observed variables exhibit a normal distribution [32]. Given that the absolute values of the skewness and kurtosis of all the observed variables (items) in each dimension of the structural equation model of this study were smaller than 2, the observed variables had a normal distribution. The multivariate normality test used Mardia's coefficient to find the multivariate kurtosis. Mardia's coefficient is often used as a multivariate kurtosis index to determine multivariate normality. If the coefficient is smaller than $p\ (p + 2)$, with p being the number of observed variables, then the data has multivariate normality [33]. Mardia's coefficient of this study was 45.043, and $p\ (p + 2)$ was 195 and was greater than Mardia's coefficient. Therefore, the data of this study had a multivariate normal distribution.

4.3 Structural Model Analysis and Research Hypotheses Verification

To demonstrate the measured effects between the latent variables and observed variables and to determine the causal relationships between latent variables, this study used structural equation models to verify the model and research hypotheses. After derivation, the final model of this study had 4 dimensions and 13 observed variables. The independent variables were involvement and place attachment, and the dependent variables were travel motivation and behavioral intention.

This study tested the goodness of fit of the model. The results indicated that the specific value of the chi-square and the degree of freedom was between 1 and 5 ($\chi^2 \div df = 1.45$), both conforming to the testing standards. The goodness-of-fit index of 0.946 was >0.9, the adjusted goodness-of-fit index of 0.915 was >0.9, and the root-mean-square error of approximation of 0.045 was between 0.05 and 1. Other indices also conformed to the testing standards (root-mean-square residual = 0.029, <0.08; parsimony goodness-of-fit index = 0.593, >0.5; normed fit index = 0.966, >0.9; relative fit index = 0.954, >0.9; incremental fit index = 0.989, >0.9; nonnormed fit index (Tucker–Lewis index) = 0.985, >0.9; comparative fit index = 0.989, >0.9; relationship of parsimony = 0.731, >0.5; parsimony normed fit index = 0.706, >0.5; and parsimony comparative fit index = 0.723, >0.5). The structural model testing standards used the definitions proposed by

Hair et al. [34], and Blunch [35]. All the indices conformed to the testing standards after model adjustments.

The path diagram and analysis of the structural model are illustrated in Table 2, respectively. The results are as follows: H1 hypothesized that involvement had a positive and significant effect on travel motivation, and H1 was not supported. H2 hypothesized that place attachment had a positive and significant effect on travel motivation, and H2 was supported. H3 hypothesized that involvement had a positive and significant effect on behavioral intention, and H3 was supported. H4 hypothesized that place attachment had a positive and significant effect on behavioral intention, and H4 was not supported. H5 hypothesized that travel motivation had a positive and significant effect on behavioral intention, and H5 was not supported. The path coefficients of the model demonstrated that the path coefficient of involvement on behavioral intention, which represented the direct effect, was 0.765; the path coefficient of involvement on behavioral intention through travel motivation, which represented the indirect effect, was −0.002 (−0.032 × 0.076). The overall effect was 0.765 + (−0.032 × 0.076) = 0.765 − 0.002 = 0.763, which is <0.765. The overall effect was smaller than the direct effect and the path coefficient was not significant. Therefore, H6, which hypothesized that travel motivation had a mediating effect between involvement and behavioral intention, was not supported. The path coefficient of place attachment on behavioral intention, which represented the direct effect, was 0.123; the path coefficient of place attachment on behavioral intention through travel motivation, which represented the indirect effect, was 0.192 (0.947 × 0.076). The overall effect was 0.123 + (0.947 × 0.076) = 0.192, which was >0.123. Although the overall effect was larger than the direct effect, the path coefficient was not significant. Therefore, H7, which hypothesized that travel motivation had a mediating effect between place attachment and behavioral intention, was not supported.

Using the structural equation model of this study to observe each dimension and the factor loading of the observed variables revealed that the factor loading of three observed variables were smaller than 0.8, namely attraction under the involvement dimension (0.777), physiological needs under the travel motivation dimension (0.613), and safety needs under the travel motivation dimension (0.673). The factor loadings of all the other observed variables were greater than 0.8. Such variables had strong influences and should be considered in future studies.

Table 2. The analysis of the structural model

	variable	path coefficient	*CR*	*P*	hypotheses verification
H1	Involvement → Travel motivation	**−0.032**	**−0.282**	**0.778**	**Not supported**
H2	Place attachment → Travel motivation	**0.947**	**6.778**	***	**Supported**
H3	Involvement → Behavioral intentions	**0.765**	**8.614**	***	**Supported**
H4	Place attachment → Behavioral intentions	**0.123**	**0.640**	**0.522**	**Not supported**

(continued)

Table 2. (*continued*)

	variable	path coefficient	*CR*	*P*	hypotheses verification
H5	Travel motivation → Behavioral intentions	**0.076**	**0.478**	**0.633**	**Not supported**
H6	Involvement → Travel motivation → Behavioral intentions	**0.765 + (−0.032 x 0.076) = 0.765 – 0.002 = 0.763 < 0.765**			**Not supported**
H7	Place attachment → Travel motivation → Behavioral intentions	0.123 + (0.947 × 0.076) = 0.192 > 0.123			**Not supported**

5 Conclusions

Hanfu has reappeared on the streets of China since 2003, and its revival is increasing in momentum. Of all the activities related to hanfu, the Xitang Hanfu Cultural Festival has the most participants, the longest history, and the largest scale. The festival is crucial for the development and inheritance of Chinese culture, and boasts a unique cultural status. The results of this study can serve as a reference for future studies investigating how the involvement and place attachment of tourists in festivals affected their travel motivation and behavioral intention. The conclusions are listed as follows:

1. This study used a questionnaire to investigate the effect of involvement and place attachment on travel motivation and behavioral intention. The analyses demonstrated that the goodness of fit of the structural equation model conformed to the testing standards. Therefore, the questionnaire is feasible and can serve as a reference for academic institutions or industries.
2. The structural equation model of this study revealed the standard regression coefficient (factor loading) of each dimension and the observed variables. Three observed variables had a factor loading smaller than 0.8, namely attractiveness under the involvement dimension (0.777), physiological needs under the travel motivation dimension (0.613), and safety needs under the travel motivation dimension (0.673). The factor loadings of all other observed variables were greater than 0.8; these variables have strong influences and should be considered in future studies.
3. The results indicated that, in terms of participation in festivals, the place dependence or place identity of people, such as their preference, sense of identity, or sense of belonging for a place, had a positive effect on their travel motivation. Aspects of involvement, such as attractiveness, centrality, and self-expression, had a positive effect on behavioral intention if the aspects included factors such as interest in participation, joyful feelings, opportunity to express oneself, life experiences, and making new friends. Therefore, festivals should be promoted to the public when they are hosted in the future, and they should be advertised differently to different target audiences such as travelers, tourists, residents, and people interested in local culture.

Acknowledgements. The author gratefully acknowledge the support for this research provided by the Ministry of Science and Technology of Taiwan under grant No. MOST-110-2221-E-034-012.

References

1. Oliver, R.L.: Whence Consumer Loyalty? J. Mark. **63**(4), 33–44 (1999)
2. Anderson, J.C., Gerbing, D.W.: Structural equation modeling in practice: a review and recommended two-step approach. Psychol. Bull. **103**(3), 411–423 (1988)
3. Baker, D.A., Crompton, J.L.: Quality, satisfaction and behavioral intentions. Ann. Tour. Res. **27**(3), 785–804 (2000)
4. Li, Y., Liu, K.W.: An analysis on the differences of domestic tourist expenditure at tourist destination-a case study of Xi' an in golden week. Hum. Geogr. **23**(1), 115–118 (2008). (in Chinese, semantic translation)
5. Pan, S.L., Wu, H.C., Chou, J.: Research on the relationships among volunteer interpreters' activity involvement, place attachment and satisfaction: a case study from the national museum of natural science. J. Outdoor Recreat. Study **21**(3), 23–47 (2008). (in Chinese, semantic translation)
6. Kao, C.L., Lin, Y.H.: Relation among attendees' emotion, satisfaction, and behavioral intention in traditional cultural festival. Bull. Geograph. Soc. China **63**, 55–76 (2019). (in Chinese, semantic translation)
7. Fishbein, M., Ajzen, I.: Belief, attitude, intention, and behavior: an introduction to theory and research. Philos. Rhetor. **10**(2), 177–189 (1977)
8. Xie, Y.: Tourism Experience Research. Nankai University Press, Tianjin (2005). (in Chinese, semantic translation)
9. Zhang, T., Jia H.S.: Research on the dimension of festival consumers' perceived value and its mechanism of action. Tour. Trib. **5**(23), 74–79 (2008). (in Chinese, semantic translation)
10. Rothschild, M.L.: Perspectives on Involvement: Current Problems and Future Directions. ACR North American Advances (1984)
11. Zaichkowsky, J.L.: Measuring the involvement construct. J. Consum. Res. **12**(3), 341–352 (1985)
12. Dimanche, F., Havitz, M.E., Howard, D.R.: Testing the involvement profile (IP) scale in the context of selected recreational and touristic activities. J. Leis. Res. **23**(1), 51–66 (1991)
13. Lee, T.H., Chang, Y.S.: The influence of experiential marketing and activity involvement on the loyalty intentions of wine tourists in Taiwan. Leis. Stud. **31**(1), 103–121 (2012)
14. Havitz, M.E., Dimanche, F.: Leisure involvement revisited: drive properties and paradoxes. J. Leis. Res. **31**(2), 122–149 (1999)
15. Kyle, G., Bricker, K., Graefe, A., Wickham, T.: An examination of recreationists' relationships with activities and settings. Leis. Sci. **26**(2), 123–142 (2004)
16. Tuan, Y.F.: Space and Place: The Perspective of Experience. U of Minnesota Press, Minneapolis (1977)
17. Williams, D.R., Patterson, M.E., Roggenbuck, J.W., Watson, A.E.: Beyond the commodity metaphor: examining emotional and symbolic attachment to place. Leis. Sci. **14**(1), 29–46 (1992)
18. Moore, R.L., Graefe, A.R.: Attachments to recreation settings: the case of rail-trail users. Leis. Sci. **16**(1), 17–31 (1994)
19. Iso-Ahola, S.E.: Toward a social psychological theory of tourism motivation: a rejoinder. Ann. Tour. Res. **9**(2), 256–262 (1982)
20. Zhang, H.M., Lu, L.: A review of foreign tourism motivation research in the past 10 years. Reg. Res. Dev. **24**(2), 60–64 (2005). (in Chinese, semantic translation)

21. Maslow, A.H.: A theory of human motivation. Psychol. Rev. **50**(4), 370–396 (1943)
22. Nickerson, N.P., Elli, G.D.: Traveler types and activation theory: a comparison of two models. J. Travel Res. **29**(3), 26–31 (1991)
23. Goeldner, C., Ritchie, J.: Tourism: Principles, Practices, Philosophies. Wiley, Hoboken (2003)
24. Pearce, P.: The Ulysses Factor: Evaluating Visitors in Tourist Settings. Springer, Heidelberg (2012). https://doi.org/10.1007/978-1-4612-3924-6
25. Gollwitzer, P.M., Bargh, J.A. (eds.): The Psychology of Action: Linking Cognition and Motivation to Behavior. Guilford Press, New York (1996)
26. Zeithaml, V.A., Berry, L.L., Parasuraman, A.: The behavioral consequences of service quality. J. Mark. **60**(2), 31–46 (1996)
27. Folkes, V.S.: Recent attribution research in consumer behavior: a review and new directions. J. Consum. Res. **14**(4), 548–565 (1988)
28. Jones, T.O., Sasser, W.E.: Why satisfied customers defect. Harv. Bus. Rev. **73**(6), 88 (1995)
29. Gu, Y. https://zj.zjol.com.cn/news/1554051.html. Accessed 30 Sep 2021. (in Chinese, semantic translation)
30. Bagozzi, R.P., Yi, Y.: On the evaluation of structural equation models. J. Acad. Mark. Sci. **16**(1), 74–94 (1988)
31. Hair, J.F., Anderson, R.E., Tatham, R.L., Black, W.C.: Multivariate Data Analysis. Prentice Hall, Upper Saddle River (1998)
32. Bollen, K.A., Long, J.S. (eds.): Testing Structural Equation Models. Sage, Thousand Oaks (1993)
33. Bollen, K.A.: Structural Equation Models. Wiley, Hoboken (1998)
34. Hair, J.F., Black, W.C., Babin, B.J., Anderson, R.E., Tatham, R.L.: Multivariate data analysis, 7th edn. Prentice Hall, Upper Saddle River (2010)
35. Blunch, N.J.: Introduction to Structural Equation Modelling using SPSS and AMOS. Sage, London (2008)

Correction to: Differences in Color Representations of Tastes: Cross-cultural Study Among Japanese, Russian and Taiwanese

Alexander Raevskiy, Ivan Bubnov, Yi-Chuan Chen, and Nobuyuki Sakai

Correction to: Chapter "Differences in Color Representations of Tastes: Cross-cultural Study Among Japanese, Russian and Taiwanese" in: P.-L. P. Rau (Ed.): *Cross-Cultural Design. Interaction Design Across Cultures*, LNCS 13311, https://doi.org/10.1007/978-3-031-06038-0_28

In an older version of this paper, there was an error in the caption for Table 2. The caption reads 'color-voice associations', instead of 'color-tastes associations'. This has been corrected.

The updated version of this chapter can be found at https://doi.org/10.1007/978-3-031-06038-0_28

P.-L. P. Rau (Ed.): HCII 2022, LNCS 13311, p. C1, 2022.
https://doi.org/10.1007/978-3-031-06038-0_41

Author Index

Printed in the United States
by Baker & Taylor Publisher Services